Journeyman Electrician Exam
Based on 2017 National Electrical Code

(also Electrician, Master Electrician, Electrical Licensing)
Suitable for Electrical Certification Study

QuickPass™ Study Tools

Builder's Book, Inc.

BOOKSTORE / PUBLISHER

Contractor's Book Center

8001 Canoga Avenue / Canoga Park, CA 91304

1-800-273-7375 / www.buildersbook.com

ISBN: 978-1-62270-258-9

© 2020 Builder's Book, Inc. All rights reserved. No part of this book may be reproduced or utilized in any form or by any means, electronic or mechanical, including photocopying, recording, or by any information storage and retrieval systems, without advance written permission of the publisher.

Journeyman Electrician Exam
Based on 2017 National Electrical Code

Practice Exams for the Electrical Licensing Exams Including Journeyman Electrician, Electrician, Master Electrician, and Electrical Certification
QuickPassTM Study Tools

Study guide for the Journeyman Electrician Exam.
Based on the 2017 NFPA® National Electrical Code®

NOTICE TO THE READER

This book and CD-ROM are designed to provide study material for the purpose of preparation for Journeyman and related electrical licensing exams. This book and CD-ROM shall not be used for any other purpose. For code related needs see the appropriate NFPA® codes. The publisher has made every effort to provide complete and accurate information, but does not guarantee the accuracy or completeness of any information published herein, nor shall the publisher have any liability or responsibility to any person or entity for any errors, omissions, or damages arising out of the use of this information. This book is provided with the understanding that the publisher is not attempting to render legal, business or any other advice or professional service. If such services are required, the assistance of an appropriate professional should be sought.

For future updates, errata, amendments and other changes,
please contact Builder's Book, Inc., 1-800-273-7375.

The information in this book is subject to change without notice.

© 2020 Builder's Book, Inc. All rights reserved.

ALL RIGHTS RESERVED

NFPA®, NEC®, National Electrical Code® and National Fire Protection Association® are all registered trademarks and property of the National Fire Protection Association®.

QuickPass™ is a registered trademark and property of Builder's Book, Inc.
©2020 Builder's Book, Inc.

Journeyman Electrician Exam
Based on 2017 National Electrical Code

TABLE OF CONTENTS

Exam 1 – General Trade Knowledge 1

Exam 2 – Article 90 Introduction 10

Exam 3 – Chapter 1: General 15

Exam 4 – Chapter 2: Wiring and Protection 01 67

Exam 5 – Chapter 2: Wiring and Protection 02 133

Exam 6 – Chapter 2: Wiring and Protection 03 201

Exam 7 – Chapter 3: Wiring Methods and Materials 264

Exam 8 – Chapter 4: Equipment for General Use 393

Exam 9 – Chapter 5: Special Occupancies 465

Exam 10 – Chapter 6: Special Equipment 503

Exam 11 – Chapter 7: Special Conditions 592

Exam 12 – Chapter 8: Communications Systems 629

Exam 13 – Chapter 9: Tables 646

Exam 14 – Annexes 653

Exam 15 – Blueprint Reading 667

AC/DC Formulas 719

EXAM 1

General Trade Knowledge

1. What relationship does Ohm's Law represent?

    A. voltage, current and power

    B. voltage, current and power factor

    C. voltage, current and resistance

    D. voltage, current and wattage

    Reference: Builder's Comprehensive Dictionary, 3rd Ed.

2. What is one kVA equal to?

    A. One hundred watts

    B. One hundred kilo-watts

    C. One hundred volt-amps

    D. One thousand watts

    Reference: Builder's Comprehensive Dictionary, 3rd Ed.

3. Of the following, which measures a unit of electrical power?

    A. conductance

    B. resistance

    C. voltage

    D. watt

    Reference: Builder's Comprehensive Dictionary, 3rd Ed.

4. What might be the reason for an indication of positive continuity when checking for continuity between the neutral bar of a panelboard and a circuit breaker, using a continuity tester?

    A. conductor grounded

    B. luminaire or an appliance may be turned on

    C. either A or B

    D. neither A nor B

    Reference: Builder's Comprehensive Dictionary, 3rd Ed.

General Trade Knowledge

EXAM 1

General Trade Knowledge

5. Which of the following might be the result, if a branch circuit's voltage drop is too great?

   A. overheating of a motor or unsatisfactory motor speed

   B. unsatisfactory illumination of luminaires

   C. both A and B

   D. neither A nor B

   Reference: Builder's Comprehensive Dictionary, 3rd Ed.

6. Which of the following would be true of a grounding conductor, under normal circumstances?

   A. carry current.

   B. improve current flow.

   C. not carry current.

   D. reduce circuit resistance.

   Reference: Builder's Comprehensive Dictionary, 3rd Ed.

7. What does a megger measure?

   A. current

   B. insulation resistance

   C. reactance

   D. specific gravity

   Reference: Builder's Comprehensive Dictionary, 3rd Ed.

8. What kind of motor is an ac motor with nine (9) leads coming out of it?

   A. dual voltage motor

   B. multi-speed motor

   C. two-phase motor

   D. two speed motor

   Reference: Builder's Comprehensive Dictionary, 3rd Ed.

EXAM 1

General Trade Knowledge

9. What is used to increase or decrease ac voltages?

    A. motor

    B. overload device

    C. rectifier

    D. transformer

    Reference: Builder's Comprehensive Dictionary, 3rd Ed.

10. What is the full-load current rating of a 240-volt, single-phase 10 kW commercial dishwasher?

    A. 21 amperes

    B. 24 amperes

    C. 30 amperes

    D. 42 amperes

    Reference: Builder's Comprehensive Dictionary, 3rd Ed.

11. What current would be in a 120-volt, single-phase branch circuit meant to supply fifteen (15), 150-watt incandescent luminaries?

    A. 9.37 amperes

    B. 14.1 amperes

    C. 18.75 amperes

    D. 36.50 amperes

    Reference: Builder's Comprehensive Dictionary, 3rd Ed.

12. What is the full-load current rating of a 15 kW, 208-volt, single-phase heat pump?

    A. 33 amperes

    B. 46 amperes

    C. 66 amperes

    D. 72 amperes

    Reference: Builder's Comprehensive Dictionary, 3rd Ed

EXAM 1

General Trade Knowledge

13. The current draw of a 9 kW, 208-volt, 3-phase electric steamer installed in a commercial establishment would be:

    A. 4.3 amperes

    B. 25 amperes

    C. 43 amperes

    D. 75 amperes

    Reference: Builder's Comprehensive Dictionary, 3rd Ed

14. What is the total measured current in the home run supplying the load for a 120-volt branch circuit that is only meant to have six (6) 100-watt incandescent lighting fixtures connected to it?

    A. 5 amperes

    B. 12 amperes

    C. 20 amperes

    D. 30 amperes

    Reference: Builder's Comprehensive Dictionary, 3rd Ed

15. If a dwelling unit has a connected lighting load of 9,600 VA, what is the minimum number of 120-volt, 15-ampere, general lighting branch circuits required?

    A. three

    B. four

    C. five

    D. six

    Reference: Builder's Comprehensive Dictionary, 3rd Ed

16. What is the maximum load per line for a single-phase, 240-volt, 15 kVA standby generator?

    A. 31.25 amperes

    B. 41.66 amperes

    C. 52.50 amperes

    D. 62.50 amperes

    Reference: Builder's Comprehensive Dictionary, 3rd Ed.

EXAM 1

General Trade Knowledge

17. What is the current each ungrounded (phase) conductor of an office building that has a 208Y/120-volt, 3-phase service with a balanced net computed load of 90 kVA will carry at full load?

    A. 188 amperes

    C. 433 amperes

    B. 250 amperes

    D. 750 amperes

    Reference: Builder's Comprehensive Dictionary, 3rd Ed

18. If a transformer is installed to supply a 243 ampere, 208-volt, 3-phase load, the kVA rating of the transformer must be a minimum of:

    A. 350 kVA

    C. 150 kVA

    B. 112-1/2 kVA

    D. 300 kVA

    Reference: Builder's Comprehensive Dictionary, 3rd Ed

19. What is the full-load current rating of a single-phase, 120/240-volt, 18 kW rated home standby generator?

    A. 75 amperes

    C. 100 amperes

    B. 87 amperes

    D. 150 amperes

    Reference: Builder's Comprehensive Dictionary, 3rd Ed

20. What is the full-load current rating of a 15kW, 208-volt, single-phase heat pump?

    A. 42 amperes

    C. 72 amperes

    B. 65 amperes

    D. 125 amperes

    Reference: Builder's Comprehensive Dictionary, 3rd Ed

General Trade Knowledge

EXAM 1

General Trade Knowledge

21. When each length of a heating cable has a blue lead wire, it indicates that the requirement for that element is _____ volts.

    A. 120

    B. 208

    C. 240

    D. 277

    Reference: *Builder's Comprehensive Dictionary, 3rd Ed.*

EXAM 1

EXAM 1 ANSWERS

1. **Answer C.** Voltage, current and resistance

   Electrical resistance in a circuit. The symbol for ohm is the Greek capital letter omega (Ω).

   ohms = volts ÷ amperes

   Relationship of electrical units of amperes, volts, and ohms as a function of each other:

   amperes = volts ÷ ohms

   ohms = volts ÷ amperes

   volts = amperes × ohms

   Reference: Builder's Comprehensive Dictionary, 3rd Ed. Ohm's law

2. **Answer D.** One thousand watts

   A kilovolt-ampere, commonly referred to as a kVA, is commonly used as a unit of power in obtaining the electrical capacity of circuit breakers, uninterrupted power supplies and wirings. A kVA is equivalent to 1,000 volt-amperes.

   Reference: reference.com

3. **Answer D.** Watt

   Unit of electrical power. Volts and amperes together give the total electrical power or wattage. When one volt causes one ampere of current to flow, one watt of power is used. Electrical appliances and light bulbs are rated in watts (for example, a 60-watt bulb). Equipment or light bulbs normally state what wattage they use. The wattage is a function of the amps (rate of flow) times the 120 volt current supplied. A 100-watt light bulb draws approximately 0.83 amp (0.83 × 120V = 100 watts).

   Reference: Builder's Comprehensive Dictionary, 3rd Ed. watt (W)

4. **Answer C.** Either A or B

   Reference: Builder's Comprehensive Dictionary, 3rd Ed.

5. **Answer C.** Both A and B

   Reference: Builder's Comprehensive Dictionary, 3rd Ed.

6. **Answer C.** Not carry current.

   In an electrical wiring system, a conductor used to make ground to a conducting body or to earth. The bond or connection is made by a pressure connector clip, clamp, screw, metal strap, lug, or bushing. (Solder is not used.) conductors used for grounding an electrical system are normally white or gray colored. Outside grounding is made using a copper ground rod or an underground metallic water pipe system. Reference: Builder's Comprehensive Dictionary, 3rd Ed.

7. **Answer B.** Insulation resistance

   The insulation resistance (IR) test (also commonly known as a Megger) is a spot insulation test which uses an applied DC voltage (typically either 250Vdc, 500Vdc or 1,000Vdc for low voltage equipment <600V and 2,500Vdc and 5,000Vdc for high voltage equipment) to measure insulation resistance in either kΩ, MΩ or GΩ. The measured resistance is intended to indicate the condition of the insulation or dielectric between two conductive parts, where the higher the resistance, the better the condition of the insulation. Ideally, the insulation resistance would be infinite, but as no insulators are perfect, leakage currents through the dielectric will ensure that a finite (though high) resistance value is measured.

   Reference: Builder's Comprehensive Dictionary, 3rd Ed.

8. **Answer A.** Dual voltage motor

   A type of three-phase motor that operates on two voltage levels. Dual voltage motors allow the same motor to be used with two different power line voltages. The motor has the ability to operate on two different voltages and still maintain the motor characteristics of the nameplate specifications.

   Reference: Builder's Comprehensive Dictionary, 3rd Ed.

9. **Answer D.** Transformer

   Electrical device used to decrease or increase voltage. A transformer is used to decrease voltage from power lines so it can be used in the home. A transformer that decreases voltage is called a step-down transformer. (One that increases voltage is called as step-up transformer.) In arc welding, a power supply that steps the available AC voltage down for welding. The voltage is stepped down to a low voltage and a high amperage, as required.

   Reference: Builder's Comprehensive Dictionary, 3rd Ed.

EXAM 1

EXAM 1 ANSWERS

10. Answer D. 42 amperes

Single Phase Current Formula

$I = P \div E$

$I = \dfrac{10kW \times 1000}{240 \text{ volts}} = \dfrac{10,000}{240} = 41.6 \text{ amperes}$

Reference: Builder's Comprehensive Dictionary, 3rd Ed.

11. Answer C. 18.75 amperes

Single-Phase Current Formula

$I = P \div E$

$I = \dfrac{150 \text{ watts} \times 15}{120 \text{ volts}} = \dfrac{2250}{120} = 18.75 \text{ amperes}$

Reference: Builder's Comprehensive Dictionary, 3rd Ed.

12. Answer D. 72 amperes

Single-Phase Current Formula

$I = P \div E$

$I = \dfrac{15 \text{ kW} \times 1,000}{208 \text{ volts}} = \dfrac{15,000}{208} = 72 \text{ amperes}$

Reference: Builder's Comprehensive Dictionary, 3rd Ed.

13. Answer B. 25 amperes

Three-Phase Current Formula

$I = P \div E \times 1.732$

$I = \dfrac{9 \text{ kW} \times 1,000}{208 \times 1.732} = \dfrac{9,000}{360.25} = 24.9 \text{ amperes}$

Reference: Builder's Comprehensive Dictionary, 3rd Ed.

14. Answer A. 5 amperes

Single-Phase Current Formula

100 watts × 6 luminaires = 600 watts total

$I = P \div E$ I = 600 watts ÷ 120 volts = 5 amperes

Reference: Builder's Comprehensive Dictionary, 3rd Ed.

15. Answer D. six

120 volts × 15 amperes = 1,800 VA (one circuit)

9,600 VA (load) ÷ 1,800 VA (one circuit) = 5.3 = 6 circuits

Reference: Builder's Comprehensive Dictionary, 3rd Ed.

16. Answer D. 62.50 amperes

Single-Phase Current Formula

$I = P \div E$

$\dfrac{15 \text{ kVA} \times 1,000}{240 \text{ volts}} = \dfrac{15,000}{240} = 62.50 \text{ amperes}$

Reference: Builder's Comprehensive Dictionary, 3rd Ed.

17. Answer B. 250 amperes

3-Phase Current Formula

$I = \dfrac{KVA \times 1,000}{E \times 1.732}$

$I = \dfrac{90 \times 1,000}{208 \times 1.732} = \dfrac{90,000}{360.25} = 250 \text{ amperes}$

Reference: Builder's Comprehensive Dictionary, 3rd Ed.

18. Answer A. 90 kVA

3-phase power formula

First find the VA:
208 volts × 1.732 × 243 amperes = 87,542 VA

87,542 divided by 1000 = 87.5 kVA

Reference: Builder's Comprehensive Dictionary, 3rd Ed.

19. Answer B. 87 amperes

Single-Phase Current Formula

$I = \dfrac{power}{volts}$

$I = \dfrac{18 \text{ kw} \times 1,000}{240 \text{ volts}} = \dfrac{18,000}{240} = 75 \text{ amperes}$

Reference: Builder's Comprehensive Dictionary, 3rd Ed.

EXAM 1

EXAM 1 ANSWERS

20. **Answer C.**   72 amperes

    Single-Phase Current Formula

    $$I = \frac{Power}{volts}$$

    $$I = \frac{15 \text{ kW} \times 1{,}000}{240 \text{ volts}} = \frac{15{,}000}{240} = 72.1 \text{ amperes}$$

    Reference: Builder's Comprehensive Dictionary, 3rd Ed.

21. **Answer B.**   208

    Each unit shall be marked with the identifying name or identification symbol, catalog number, and ratings in volts and watts or in volts and amperes.

    The NEC no longer contains a color code for voltage marking. however the industry standard is:

    208/120v (a)black, (B) red, (C) blue and grounded/neutral white

    480/277v (A) brown, (B)Orange, (C) yellow and grounded/neutral gray.

    Reference: Builder's Comprehensive Dictionary, 3rd Ed.

EXAM 2

Article 90 Introduction

1. Who is the NEC not designed to be an instruction manual or design specification for?

    A. electrical engineers

    B. power linemen

    C. untrained persons

    D. none of the above

    Reference: 2017 National Electrical Code, Article 90 Introduction. 90.1 Purpose. 90.1(A) Practical Safeguarding.

2. What is the purpose of the NEC?

    A. For future expansion of electrical use.

    B. The practical safeguarding of persons and property.

    C. To have an installation that is efficient.

    D. To provide an installation that is adequate for good service.

    Reference: 2017 National Electrical Code, Article 90 Introduction. 90.1 Purpose. 90.1(A) Practical Safeguarding

3. What is the purpose of the NEC (National Electrical Code), with regard to the hazards arising from the use of electricity, with regard to persons or property?

    A. Adequate Safety

    B. Economical protection

    C. Practical Safeguarding

    D. Protection

    Reference: 2017 National Electrical Code, Article 90 Introduction. 90.1 Purpose. 90.1(A) Practical Safeguarding.

4. An electrical installation in compliance with the provisions of the NEC will be essentially:

    A. a good electrical system

    B. an efficient system

    C. free from hazard

    D. all of these

    Reference: 2017 National Electrical Code, Article 90 Introduction. 90.1 Purpose. 90.1(B) Adequacy.

EXAM 2

Article 90 Introduction

5. True or False: The NEC does not cover installations in ships, underground mines or transmission lines.

    A. True   B. False

Reference: 2017 National Electrical Code, Article 90 Introduction. 90.2 Scope. 90.2(B) Not Covered

6. Of the following, what areas of construction does the NEC not include in its coverage?

    A. automotive vehicles other than mobile homes and RVs

    B. installations used by the electric utility

    C. parking lots

    D. private premises

Reference: 2017 National Electrical Code, Article 90 Introduction. 90.2 Scope. 90.2(B) Not Covered

7. Where does this code not cover the installation of optical fiber cables and raceways, or conductors, equipment and raceways for electrical, signaling, and communications?

    A. Installations controlled by communications utilities.

    B. Conductors & equipment connected to electricity.

    C. Public & private premises, incl. mobile homes.

    D. Yards, lots, carnivals and industrial substations.

Reference: 2017 National Electrical Code, Article 90 Introduction. 90.2 Scope. 90.2(B) Not Covered.

8. True or False: Specific requirements in the code may be waived or alternate methods may be permitted where assurance of the achievement of equivalent objectives may be done by the Authority Having Jurisdiction.

    A. True   B. False

Reference: 2017 National Electrical Code, Article 90 Introduction. 90.4 Enforcement.

Article 90 Introduction

EXAM 2

Article 90 Introduction

9. True or False: Mandatory rules of this Code are those that identify actions that are specifically required or prohibited and are characterized by the use of the terms shall or shall not.

   A. True   B. False

   Reference: 2017 National Electrical Code, Article 90 Introduction. 90.5 Mandatory Rules, Permissive Rules, and Explanatory Materials. 90.5(A) Mandatory Rules.

10. True or False: Permissive rules of this Code are those that identify actions that are allowed but not required, are normally used to describe options or alternative methods, and are characterized by the use of the terms shall be permitted or shall not be required.

    A. True   B. False

    Reference: 2017 National Electrical Code, Article 90 Introduction. 90.5 Mandatory Rules, Permissive Rules, and Explanatory Materials. 90.5(B) Permissive Rules

11. Because limiting the number of circuits on a single enclosure minimizes the effects from a ground fault or short circuit in one circuit, the NEC provides that the number or circuits and wires in a single enclosure be:

    A. restricted to 1 circuit   C. unrestricted

    B. restricted to 3 circuits   D. varyingly restricted

    Reference: 2017 National Electrical Code, Article 90 Introduction. 90.8 Wiring Planning. 90.8(B) Number of Circuits in Enclosures.

EXAM 2

EXAM 2 ANSWERS

1. **Answer C.** untrained persons

   The purpose of this Code is the practical safeguarding of persons and property from hazards arising from the use of electricity. This Code is not intended as a design specification or an *instruction manual for untrained persons.*

   Reference: 2017 National Electrical Code, Article 90 Introduction. 90.1 Purpose. 90.1(A) Practical Safeguarding.

2. **Answer B.** The practical safeguarding of persons and property.

   The purpose of this Code is the practical safeguarding of persons and property from hazards arising from the use of electricity. This Code is not intended as a design specification or an instruction manual for untrained persons.

   Reference: 2017 National Electrical Code, Article 90 Introduction. 90.1 Purpose. 90.1(A) Practical Safeguarding

3. **Answer C.** Practical Safeguarding

   The purpose of this Code is the practical safeguarding of persons and property from hazards arising from the use of electricity. This Code is not intended as a design specification or an instruction manual for untrained persons.

   Reference: 2017 National Electrical Code, Article 90 Introduction. 90.1 Purpose. 90.1(A) Practical Safeguarding.

4. **Answer C.** free from hazard

   This *Code* contains provisions that are considered necessary for safety. *Compliance there with and proper maintenance result in an installation that is essentially free from hazard but not necessarily efficient,* convenient, or adequate for good service or future expansion of electrical use.

   Informational Note: Hazards often occur because of overloading of wiring systems by methods or usage not in conformity with this Code. This occurs because initial wiring did not provide for increases in the use of electricity. An initial adequate installation and reasonable provisions for system changes provide for future increases in the use of electricity.

   Reference: 2017 National Electrical Code, Article 90 Introduction. 90.1 Purpose. 90.1(B) Adequacy.

5. **Answer A.** True

   This Code does not cover the following:

   (1) Installations in ships, watercraft other than floating buildings, railway rolling stock, aircraft, or automotive vehicles other than mobile homes and recreational vehicles

   Informational Note: Although the scope of this *Code* indicates that the *Code* does not cover installations in ships, portions of this *Code* are incorporated by reference into Title 46, Code of Federal Regulations, Parts 110–113.

   (2) *Installations underground in mines* and self-propelled mobile surface mining machinery and its attendant electrical trailing cable

   (3) Installations of railways for generation, transformation, *transmission, energy storage,* or distribution of power used exclusively for operation of rolling stock or installations used exclusively for signaling and communications purposes

   Review the 4 items in list (A) covered and the 5 items in list (B) not covered.

   Reference: 2017 National Electrical Code, Article 90 Introduction. 90.2 Scope. 90.2(B) Not Covered

6. **Answer A.** automotive vehicles other than mobile homes and RVs

   This Code does not cover the following:

   (1) Installations in ships, watercraft other than floating buildings, railway rolling stock, aircraft, or *automotive vehicles other than mobile homes and recreational vehicles*

   Informational Note: Although the scope of this *Code* indicates that the *Code* does not cover installations in ships, portions of this *Code* are incorporated by reference into Title 46, Code of Federal Regulations, Parts 110–113.

   Review the 4 items in list (A) covered and the 5 items in list (B) not covered.

   Reference: 2017 National Electrical Code, Article 90 Introduction. 90.2 Scope. 90.2(B) Not Covered

EXAM 2

EXAM 2 ANSWERS

7. **Answer A.** Installations controlled by communications utilities.

This Code does not cover the following:

(4) *Installations of communications equipment under the exclusive control of communications utilities located outdoors or in building spaces used exclusively for such installations*

Review the 4 items in list (A) covered and the 5 items in list (B) not covered.

Reference: 2017 National Electrical Code, Article 90 Introduction. 90.2 Scope. 90.2(B) Not Covered.

8. **Answer A.** True

This *Code* is intended to be suitable for mandatory application by governmental bodies that exercise legal jurisdiction over electrical installations, including signaling and communications systems, and for use by insurance inspectors. The authority having jurisdiction for enforcement of the *Code* has the responsibility for making interpretations of the rules, for deciding on the approval of equipment and materials, and for granting the special permission contemplated in a number of the rules.

By special permission, the authority having jurisdiction may waive specific requirements in this Code or permit alternative methods where it is assured that equivalent objectives can be achieved by establishing and maintaining effective safety.

Reference: 2017 National Electrical Code, Article 90 Introduction. 90.4 Enforcement.

9. **Answer A.** True

Mandatory rules of this Code are those that identify actions that are specifically required or prohibited and are characterized by the use of the terms shall or shall not.

Reference: 2017 National Electrical Code, Article 90 Introduction. 90.5 Mandatory Rules, Permissive Rules, and Explanatory Materials. 90.5(A) Mandatory Rules.

10. **Answer A.** True

Permissive rules of this Code are those that identify actions that are allowed but not required, are normally used to describe options or alternative methods, and are characterized by the use of the terms shall be permitted or shall not be required.

Reference: 2017 National Electrical Code, Article 90 Introduction. 90.5 Mandatory Rules, Permissive Rules, and Explanatory Materials. 90.5(B) Permissive Rules

11. **Answer D.** varyingly restricted

It is elsewhere provided in this Code that the number of circuits confined in a single enclosure be varyingly restricted. Limiting the number of circuits in a single enclosure minimizes the effects from a short circuit or ground fault.

Reference: 2017 National Electrical Code, Article 90 Introduction. 90.8 Wiring Planning. 90.8(B) Number of Circuits in Enclosures.

EXAM 3

Chapter 1 General

1. Admitting close approach; not guarded by locked doors, elevation, or other effective means.

     A. Accessible (as applied to equipment).

     B. Approachable

     C. Handy

     D. Open

     Reference: 2017 National Electrical Code – Chapter 1 General, Article 100, Definitions

2. What is defined as not guarded by elevation, locked doors, or other effective means; admitting close approach.

     A. Accessible (as applied to equipment).

     B. Approve

     C. Open

     D. Workable

     Reference: 2017 National Electrical Code – Chapter 1 General, Article 100, Definitions

3. What is defined as Capable of being removed or exposed without damaging the building structure or finish or not permanently closed in by the structure or finish of the building.

     A. Accessible (as applied to wiring methods).

     B. Approachable

     C. Handy

     D. Open

     Reference: 2017 National Electrical Code – Chapter 1 General, Article 100 Definitions.

4. Capable of being reached quickly for operation, renewal, or inspections without requiring those to whom ready access is requisite to climb over or remove obstacles or to resort to portable ladders, and so forth.

     A. Accessible, Readily (Readily Accessible).

     B. Approachable

     C. Handy

     D. Open

     Reference: 2017 National Electrical Code – Chapter 1 General, Article 100 Definitions.

Chapter 1 General   15

EXAM 3

Chapter 1 General

5. In amperes, the maximum current that a conductor can continuously carry under conditions of use, without going over its temperature rating.

    A. Ampacity

    B. Capacitance

    C. Power Factor

    D. Voltage

    Reference: 2017 National Electrical Code – Chapter 1 General, Article 100 Definitions

6. The NEC defines a conductor's ampacity as 'the maximum current, in amperes, that a conductor can carry continuously under the conditions of use without exceeding its:

    A. allowable voltage drop limitations

    B. melting point

    C. rated voltage

    D. temperature rating

    Reference: 2017 National Electrical Code – Chapter 1 General, Article 100 Definitions

7. A device intended to provide protection from the effects of arc faults by recognizing characteristics unique to arcing and by functioning to de-energize the circuit when an arc fault is detected.

    A. Arc-Fault Circuit Interrupter (AFCI)

    B. Circuit Breaker

    C. Ground-Fault circuit Interrupter

    D. none of the above

    Reference: 2017 National Electrical Code – Chapter 1 General, Article 100 Definitions.

8. The definition of combustible dust as dust particles 500 microns or smaller in size includes which of the following conditions when dispersed and ignited in air?

    A. can't be extinguished

    B. present a fire hazard

    C. present an explosion hazard

    D. Either B or C

    Reference: 2017 National Electrical Code – Chapter 1 General, Article 100 Definitions.

EXAM 3

Chapter 1 General

9. What type of equipment does not permit arcs, sparks, or heat inside an enclosure to ignite specified dust outside or in the vicinity, and excludes dust?

    A. Dust-ignitionproof

    B. Dusttight

    C. Both A and B

    D. Either A or B

    Reference: 2017 National Electrical Code – Chapter 1 General, Article 100 Definitions.

10. An organization, office, or individual responsible for enforcing the requirements of a code or standard, or for approving equipment, materials, an installation, or a procedure.

    A. Authority Having Jurisdiction (AHJ)

    B. Building and Safety Department (BSD)

    C. Code Enforcement Agency (CEA)

    D. National Building Authority (NBA)

    Reference: 2017 National Electrical Code – Chapter 1 General, Article 100: Definitions

11. Connected to establish electrical continuity and conductivity.

    A. Bonded (Bonding)

    B. Conducted (Conducting)

    C. Connected (Connecting)

    D. Grounded (Grounding)

    Reference: 2017 National Electrical Code – Chapter 1 General, Article 100 Definitions.

12. What is the definition of a Bonding Conductor or Jumper?

    A. Conductors between overcurrent device & outlet(s).

    B. Performs a function without needing human intervention

    C. reliable conductor for connected parts conductivity.

    D. synthetic chlorinated hydrocarbon used for insulation.

    Reference: 2017 National Electrical Code – Chapter 1 General, Article 100, Definitions

EXAM 3

Chapter 1 General

13. A conductor that is reliable and able to ensure, between metal parts that are required to be electrically connected, the required electrical conductivity.

    A. Bonding Jumper

    B. Connection

    C. Soldering

    D. Welding

    Reference: 2017 National Electrical Code – Chapter 1 General, Article 100, Definitions

14. What is the term for a connector between two or more portions of the equipment grounding conductor.

    A. Aluminum Wire

    B. Branch Circuit

    C. Copper Wire

    D. Equipment Bonding Jumper

    Reference: 2017 National Electrical Code – Chapter 1 General, Article 100, Definitions

15. A branch circuit that supplies two or more receptacles or outlets for lighting and appliances.

    A. Branch Circuit, Appliance

    B. Branch Circuit, General-Purpose

    C. Branch Circuit, Individual

    D. Branch Circuit, Multiwire

    Reference: 2017 National Electrical Code – Chapter 1 General, Article 100 Definitions.

16. An enclosure provided with a trim, mat, or frame in which swinging doors or a door have been or can be hung, design for flush mounting or surface mounting.

    A. Cabinet

    B. Controller

    C. Cutout Box

    D. Panel Board

    Reference: 2017 National Electrical Code – Chapter 1 General, Article 100, Definitions

EXAM 3

Chapter 1 General

17. A device designed to open and close a circuit by nonautomatic means and to open the circuit automatically on a predetermined overcurrent without damage to itself when properly applied within its rating.

    A. Arc-Fault Circuit Interrupter

    B. Circuit Breaker

    C. Ground-Fault Circuit Interrupter

    D. Overcurrent Protective Device

    Reference: 2017 National Electrical Code – Chapter 1 General, Article 100 Definitions.

18. What is a qualifying term signifying that a delay in the tripping action of a circuit breaker is intentional, where the delay decreases as the magnitude of the current increases?

    A. Delayed Trip

    B. Inverse Time

    C. Slow Blow

    D. Time Protected

    Reference: 2017 National Electrical Code – Chapter 1 General, Article 100, Definitions

19. What is the device designed to open a circuit automatically when a predetermined overcurrent occurs, without damage to itself when properly applied to its rating, and to open and close the circuit non-automatically?

    A. Cartridge Fuse

    B. Circuit Breaker

    C. Fuse

    D. Fusible Link

    Reference: 2017 National Electrical Code – Chapter 1 General, Article 100 Definitions.

20. Rendered inaccessible by the structure or finish of the building.

    A. Concealed

    B. Hidden

    C. Masked

    D. Screened

    Reference: 2017 National Electrical Code – Chapter 1 General, Article 100 Definitions.

EXAM 3

Chapter 1 General

21. How does the NEC define 'concealed'?

    A. attached to the surface

    B. made inaccessible by the structure or finish of the building

    C. not readily visible

    D. surrounded by walls

    Reference: 2017 National Electrical Code – Chapter 1 General, Article 100 Definitions.

22. What is an LB an example of?

    A. Conduit Body

    B. Connector

    C. Fitting

    D. Junction Box

    Reference: 2017 National Electrical Code – Chapter 1 General, Article 100, Definitions

23. What is the name of a device for connecting at least two conductors or at least two conductors and a terminal using mechanical pressure, and no solder?

    A. Pressure Connector

    B. Solder Connector

    C. Type P Connector

    D. Wire Splice

    Reference: 2017 National Electrical Code – Chapter 1 General, Article 100, Definitions

24. A load where the maximum current is expected to continue for 3 hours or more.

    A. Coordinated Load

    B. Continuous Load

    C. Demand

    D. Stable Load

    Reference: 2017 National Electrical Code – Chapter 1 General, Article 100 Definitions.

EXAM 3

Chapter 1 General

25. How long is the maximum current expected to last, in hours, for it to be defined a Continuous Load?

    A. 1
    B. 2
    C. 3
    D. 4

    Reference: 2017 National Electrical Code – Chapter 1 General, Article 100, Definitions

26. A continuous load, as defined by the NEC is a load where the maximum current is expect to continue for how many hours or more?

    A. three
    B. four
    C. six
    D. eight

    Reference: 2017 National Electrical Code – Chapter 1 General, Article 100 Definitions

27. What is a group of devices or a single device that governs, in a preset fashion, the amount of electricity delivered to the equipment it is attached to?

    A. Circuit Breaker
    B. Controller
    C. Governor
    D. Remote Relay

    Reference: 2017 National Electrical Code – Chapter 1 General, Article 100, Definitions

28. What is the correct term for the ratio of the maximum demand of a system to the total connected load of the system?

    A. demand factor
    B. full-load amperes
    C. full-load current
    D. ratio factor

    Reference: 2017 National Electrical Code – Chapter 1 General, Article 100 Definitions

EXAM 3

Chapter 1 General

29. A device, or group of devices, or other means by which the conductors of a circuit can be disconnected from their source of supply.

    A. Circuit Breaker
    B. Disconnecting Means
    C. Ground-Fault Circuit Interrupter
    D. Surge-Protective Device(SPD)

    Reference: 2017 National Electrical Code – Chapter 1 General, Article 100 Definitions.

30. What is the term for a group of devices, or a single device, or other method that the conductors of a circuit can be disconnected from their power source?

    A. Closed Circuit Switch
    B. Disconnecting Means
    C. Relay Switch
    D. Switch

    Reference: 2017 National Electrical Code – Chapter 1 General, Article 100, Definitions

31. What is the definition of Continuous Duty?

    A. Operation at a mostly constant load for 2 or more hours.
    B. Operation at a mostly constant load for an indefinite time.
    C. Operation at a mostly constant voltage for an indefinitely long time.
    D. Operation at a mostly constant load for normal device requirements.

    Reference: 2017 National Electrical Code – Chapter 1 General, Article 100, Definitions

32. Electrically connected to, or is, a source of voltage.

    A. Bonded (Bonding)
    B. Connected
    C. Energized
    D. Grounded

    Reference: 2017 National Electrical Code – Chapter 1 General, Article 100 Definitions.

EXAM 3

Chapter 1 General

33. What is the definition of Externally Operable?

    A. Able to be inadvertently touched or approached by a person.

    B. Can be operated without the operator contacting live parts.

    C. Can't be operated without exposing operator to live parts.

    D. Enclosed in a case capable of withstanding specified explosion.

    Reference: 2017 National Electrical Code – Chapter 1 General, Article 100, Definitions

34. All circuit conductors between the service equipment, the source of a separately derived system, or other power supply source and the final branch-circuit overcurrent device.

    A. Branch Circuits

    B. Conductors

    C. Feeder

    D. Premises Wiring

    Reference: 2017 National Electrical Code – Chapter 1 General, Article 100 Definitions.

35. An unintentional, electrically conducting connection between an ungrounded conductor of an electrical circuit and the normally non-current-carrying conductors, metallic enclosures ...

    A. Arc-Fault Circuit Interrupter

    B. Coordination (Selective)

    C. Ground Fault

    D. Ground-Fault Current Path

    Reference: 2017 National Electrical Code – Chapter 1 General, Article 100 Definitions.

Chapter 1 General

EXAM 3

Chapter 1 General

36. What is a Ground Fault?

    A. An unintended conducting connection to metal or earth.

    B. Connected (connecting) to ground or to a ground connection.

    C. Connected to ground without any resistor or impedance device.

    D. The conductors between final overcurrent device and the outlet(s).

    Reference: 2017 National Electrical Code – Chapter 1 General, Article 100, Definitions

37. A device intended for the protection of personnel that functions to de-energize a circuit or portion thereof within an established period of time when a current to ground exceeds the values established for a Class A device.

    A. Arc-Fault Circuit Interrupter (AFCI)

    B. Electronically Activated Fuse

    C. Ground-Fault Circuit Interrupter (GFCI)

    D. Ground-Fault Current Path

    Reference: 2017 National Electrical Code – Chapter 1 General, Article 100 Definitions.

38. What is a Ground-Fault Circuit Interrupter (GFCI)?

    A. A device to protect personnel that de energizes a circuit.

    B. A system or circuit conductor that is intentionally grounded.

    C. All conductors between service equipment, and power supply source.

    D. An unintended conducting connection to metal or earth.

    Reference: 2017 National Electrical Code – Chapter 1 General, Article 100 Definitions.

24　　Chapter 1 General

EXAM 3

Chapter 1 General

39. A Ground Fault Circuit Interrupter intended _____ is required by the NEC for specific utilization equipment, receptacle outlets, and branch-circuits.

    A. for the protection of equipment from overloads

    B. for the protection of personnel

    C. to prevent overloading the circuit breakers

    D. to prevent overloading the conductors

    Reference: 2017 National Electrical Code – Chapter 1 General, Article 100 Definitions.

40. Connected (connecting) to ground or to a conductive body that extends the ground connection.

    A. Bonded (Bonding)

    B. Effective Ground-Fault Current Path

    C. Grounded (Grounding)

    D. Separately Derived System

    Reference: 2017 National Electrical Code – Chapter 1 General, Article 100 Definitions.

41. A system or circuit conductor that is intentionally grounded.

    A. Bonding Jumper, Main

    B. Grounded Conductor

    C. Ground-Fault Circuit Interrupter

    D. Premises Wiring System

    Reference: 2017 National Electrical Code – Chapter 1 General, Article 100 Definitions.

42. What is the term for an electrical system that is comprised of multiple power sources?

    A. emergency system

    B. hybrid system

    C. legally required standby system

    D. optional standby system

    Reference: 2017 National Electrical Code – Chapter 1 General, Article 100 Definitions

EXAM 3

Chapter 1 General

43. True or False: Where this Code specifies that one equipment shall be "in sight from," "within sight from," or "within sight," and so forth, of another equipment, the specified equipment is to be visible and not more than 15 m (50 ft.) distant from the other.

    A. True
    B. False

    Reference: 2017 National Electrical Code – Chapter 1 General, Article 100 Definitions.

44. What is the term for a system for producing electric power, operated parallel with and able to deliver energy to a primary source electric supply system?

    A. Interactive System
    B. Motor Control Center
    C. Multioutlet Assembly
    D. Supplementary Overcurrent Protective Device

    Reference: 2017 National Electrical Code – Chapter 1 General, Article 100, Definitions

45. What is the name of a device that gives a way to connect bonding conductors for communications systems to the grounding electrode system?

    A. Explosionproof Apparatus
    B. Grounding Electrode
    C. Grounding Electrode Conductor
    D. Intersystem Bonding Termination

    Reference: 2017 National Electrical Code – Chapter 1 General, Article 100, Definitions

46. Equipment or materials to which has been attached a label, symbol, or other identifying mark of an organization that is acceptable to the authority having jurisdiction is:

    A. Branded
    B. Labeled
    C. Marked
    D. Tagged

    Reference: 2017 National Electrical Code – Chapter 1 General, Article 100 Definitions.

EXAM 3

Chapter 1 General

47. What kind of condition is it considered when electrical wiring is installed under roofed open porches or canopies?

    A. damp

    B. dry

    C. moist

    D. wet

    Reference: 2017 National Electrical Code – Chapter 1 General, Article 100 Definitions

48. When an installation in concrete slabs or masonry or underground, in direct contact with the earth, is in a location that can be saturated with water or other liquids (vehicle washing areas, for example), or is exposed to weather in an unprotected location, that is known as a:

    A. Damp Location

    B. Dry Location

    C. High Humidity Location

    D. Wet Location

    Reference: 2017 National Electrical Code – Chapter 1 General, Article 100, Definitions

49. A complete lighting unit consisting of a light source such as a lamp or lamps, together with the parts designed to position the light source and connect it to the power supply.

    A. Fixture

    B. Lighting Unit

    C. Luminaire

    D. Radiant Unit

    Reference: 2017 National Electrical Code – Chapter 1 General, Article 100 Definitions.

50. What is the term for a complete lighting unit, possibly including parts to protect the ballast or light source, or to distribute the light, that includes a light source such as a lamp or lamps, along with parts meant to connect the light source to the power supply and position it?

    A. Lamp

    B. Lampholder

    C. Luminaire

    D. Outline Lighting

    Reference: 2017 National Electrical Code – Chapter 1 General, Article 100, Definitions

EXAM 3

Chapter 1 General

51. Which of the following are always true of a neutral conductor?

    A. it is a grounded conductor not intended to carry current

    B. it is an ungrounded conductor

    C. it is connected to the neutral point of a system

    D. it is white in color

    Reference: 2017 National Electrical Code – Chapter 1 General, Article 100 Definitions

52. What do you call the midpoint on a single-phase, 3-wire system, or the common point on a wye-connection in a polyphase system, or a midpoint of a 3-wire, direct-current system, or midpoint of a single-phase portion of a 3-phase delta system?

    A. Neutral Point

    B. Plenum

    C. Service Point

    D. Switching Device

    Reference: 2017 National Electrical Code – Chapter 1 General, Article 100, Definitions

53. Requiring human intervention to perform a function.

    A. Hand-Operated

    B. Manual

    C. Nonautomatic

    D. Physical

    Reference: 2017 National Electrical Code – Chapter 1 General, Article 100 Definitions.

54. The point on a wiring system where current is taken to supply utilization equipment is the:

    A. load center

    B. outlet

    C. panelboard

    D. wall switch

    Reference: 2017 National Electrical Code – Chapter 1 General, Article 100 Definitions

EXAM 3

Chapter 1 General

55. What is the term for a conductor in excess of rated ampacity that, when it persists for a sufficient length of time, would cause damage or dangerous overheating, or of operation of equipment in excess of normal, full-load rating? This does not include a ground fault or a short circuit, or any other kind of fault.

    A. Arc Fault   C. Overload

    B. Ground Fault   D. Short Circuit

    Reference: 2017 National Electrical Code – Chapter 1 General, Article 100, Definitions

56. A single panel or group of panel units designed for assembly in the form of a single panel, including buses and automatic overcurrent devices, and equipped with or without switches for the control of light, heat, or power circuits.

    A. Circuit Panel   C. Panelboard

    B. Enclosure   D. Switchboard

    Reference: 2017 National Electrical Code – Chapter 1 General, Article 100 Definitions.

57. What is the term for a chamber or compartment that forms part of an air distribution system, where one or more air ducts are connected?

    A. Air Vent   C. Heat Exchange

    B. Duct   D. Plenum

    Reference: 2017 National Electrical Code – Chapter 1 General, Article 100, Definitions

58. An enclosed channel of metal or nonmetallic materials designed expressly for holding wires, cables, or busbars, with additional functions as permitted in this *Code*.

    A. Channel   C. Duct

    B. Conduit   D. Raceway

    Reference: 2017 National Electrical Code – Chapter 1 General, Article 100 Definitions.

Chapter 1 General   29

EXAM 3

Chapter 1 General

59. What is defined as being treated, protected, or constructed to prevent rain from interfering with the successful operation of the equipment under specific test conditions?

    A. Rainproof
    B. Raintight
    C. Waterproof
    D. Watertight

    Reference: 2017 National Electrical Code – Chapter 1 General, Article 100, Definitions

60. The conductors and equipment for delivering electric energy from the serving utility to the wiring system of the premises served.

    A. Channel
    B. Conduit
    C. Raceway
    D. Service

    Reference: 2017 National Electrical Code – Chapter 1 General, Article 100 Definitions.

61. The overhead conductors between the utility electric supply system and the service point.

    A. Aerial Wiring
    B. Overhead Wiring
    C. Power Lines
    D. Service Drop

    Reference: 2017 National Electrical Code – Chapter 1 General, Article 100 Definitions.

62. What do you call the conductors overhead between the service point and the electric supply system from the utility?

    A. Power Entrance
    B. Service Drop
    C. Service Entrance
    D. Service Lateral

    Reference: 2017 National Electrical Code – Chapter 1 General, Article 100, Definitions

EXAM 3

Chapter 1 General

63. The underground conductors between the utility electric supply system and the service point.

    A. Buried Conductors C. Service Lateral

    B. Power Lines D. Underground Lines

    Reference: 2017 National Electrical Code – Chapter 1 General, Article 100 Definitions.

64. The connection point between the premises wiring and the serving utility facilities is called the:

    A. Meter Base C. Power Entrance

    B. Meter Socket D. Service Point

    Reference: 2017 National Electrical Code – Chapter 1 General, Article 100, Definitions

65. A device manually operated, used combined with a transfer switch, to give a way to disconnect a transfer switch and directly connect to a power source.

    A. 4 Way Switch C. Double Pole Switch

    B. Bypass Isolation Switch D. Transfer Switch

    Reference: 2017 National Electrical Code – Chapter 1 General, Article 100, Definitions

66. What is the term for a switch meant to be used in branch circuits and general distribution? The rating is in amperes, and it can interrupt the rated current at the rated voltage.

    A. Breaker Switch C. Isolation Switch

    B. General-Use Switch D. Toggle Switch

    Reference: 2017 National Electrical Code – Chapter 1 General, Article 100, Definitions

EXAM 3

Chapter 1 General

67. A large single panel, frame, or assembly of panels on which are mounted on the face, back, or both, switches, overcurrent and other protective devices, buses, and usually instruments.

    A. Cabinet

    B. Enclosure

    C. Panelboard

    D. Switchboard

    Reference: 2017 National Electrical Code – Chapter 1 General, Article 100 Definitions.

68. Of the following, which is defined by the NEC as 'utilization equipment'?

    A. molded circuit breaker

    B. motor controller

    C. thermal overload device

    D. water heater

    Reference: 2017 National Electrical Code – Chapter 1 General, Article 100 Definitions

69. What is the term for the greatest effective root-mean-square (rms) difference of potential on a circuit between any two conductors?

    A. Amperage

    B. Power Factor

    C. Voltage

    D. Wattage

    Reference: 2017 National Electrical Code – Chapter 1 General, Article 100, Definitions

70. A nominal value assigned to a circuit or system for the purpose of conveniently designating its voltage class.

    A. Amperage

    B. Current

    C. Load

    D. Voltage, Nominal

    Reference: 2017 National Electrical Code – Chapter 1 General, Article 100 Definitions.

EXAM 3

Chapter 1 General

71. What is the correct name of assembly made up of at least two single-pole fuses?

    A. Gang Disconnect

    B. Main Disconnect

    C. Multiple Fuse

    D. Parallel Breaker

    Reference: 2017 National Electrical Code – Chapter 1 General, Article 100, Definitions

72. Which of the following statements is true regarding installed listed or labeled equipment, according to the NEC?

    A. It is only required if in an industrial environment.

    B. It may be installed however the contractor determines best.

    C. It may be required acceptable by the contractor.

    D. It shall be installed in accordance with the instructions.

    Reference: 2017 National Electrical Code – Chapter 1 General, Article 110 Requirements for Electrical Installation. 110.3 Examination, Identification, Installation, and Use of Equipment. 110.3(B) Installation and Use.

73. Everywhere in the code, the voltage a circuit operates at is the voltage considered, and electrical equipment voltage rating will be the _____ or more of the connected circuit.

    A. over current protection rating

    B. nominal voltage

    C. stable effective voltage

    D. under current protection rating

    Reference: 2017 National Electrical Code – Chapter 1 General, Article 110 Requirements for Electrical Installation. 110.4 Voltages.

74. Conductors normally used to carry current shall be of _____ unless otherwise provided in this Code.

    A. aluminum

    B. copper

    C. steel

    D. none of the above

    Reference: 2017 National Electrical Code – Chapter 1 General, Article 110 Requirements for Electrical Installation. 110.5 Conductors

Chapter 1 General   33

EXAM 3

Chapter 1 General

75. Normally when conductors are used to carry current, they are made of _____, unless the Code provides otherwise. When material is not specified, then any sizes and material mentioned in the code is considered to apply to copper conductors.

    A. aluminum

    B. copper

    C. copper alloy

    D. copper clad

    Reference: 2017 National Electrical Code – Chapter 1 General, Article 110 Requirements for Electrical Installation. 110.5 Conductors

76. Conductor sizes are expressed in _____ or in circular mils.

    A. American Wire Gauge (AWG)

    B. fractions of an inch

    C. millimeters

    D. none of the above

    Reference: 2017 National Electrical Code – Chapter 1 General, Article 110 Requirements for Electrical Installation. 110.6 Conductor Sizes.

77. The size of conductors can be expressed in AWG (American Wire Gauge), or:

    A. circular mils

    B. sq. inches

    C. standard English system sizes

    D. standard metric sizes

    Reference: 2017 National Electrical Code – Chapter 1 General, Article 110 Requirements for Electrical Installation. 110.6 Conductor Sizes.

78. Conductor sizes in the National Electrical Code are expressed either in American Wire Gauge (AWG) or:

    A. circular centimeters

    B. circular diameter

    C. circular mils

    D. International Standard Gage (ISG)

    Reference: 2017 National Electrical Code – Chapter 1 General, Article 110 Requirements for Electrical Installation. 110.6 Conductor Sizes.

EXAM 3

Chapter 1 General

79. Other than as permitted or required elsewhere in the Code, completed wiring installations must be free from _____, short circuits, or any connections to ground.

    A. fuses

    B. ground faults

    C. switches

    D. terminals

    Reference: 2017 National Electrical Code – Chapter 1 General, Article 110 Requirements for Electrical Installation. 110.7 Wiring Integrity.

80. When equipment is intended to interrupt power at fault levels, it must have an interrupt rating at least the nominal _____ of the circuit, and the current available at the line terminals of the equipment.

    A. power

    B. resistance

    C. size

    D. voltage

    Reference: 2017 National Electrical Code – Chapter 1 General, Article 110 Requirements for Electrical Installation. 110.9 Interrupting Rating.

81. Unused openings, other than those intended for the operation of equipment, those intended for mounting purposes, or those permitted as part of the design for listed equipment, shall be _____ ...

    A. closed

    B. open

    C. perforated

    D. scored

    Reference: 2017 National Electrical Code – Chapter 1 General, Article 110 Requirements for Electrical Installation. 110.12 Mechanical Execution of Work. 110.12(A) Unused Openings.

EXAM 3

Chapter 1 General

82. If a metal box, cabinet, or other such enclosure has unused openings, they:

    A. do not need to be closed, if on the bottom of the enclosure

    B. do not need to be closed if the enclosure is in a dry area

    C. should be effectively closed

    D. should be left open

    Reference: 2017 National Electrical Code – Chapter 1 General, Article 110 Requirements for Electrical Installation. 110.12 Mechanical Execution of Work. 110.12(A) Unused Openings.

83. All electrical equipment must be secured firmly to the surface it is mounted on, and wooden plugs driven into holes in concrete, masonry, plaster, or similar surfaces must:

    A. be a minimum of 3/4" diameter

    B. be oversized to provide a tight fit

    C. insulate the equipment from the mounting surface

    D. not be used

    Reference: 2017 National Electrical Code – Chapter 1 General, Article 110 Requirements for Electrical Installation. 110.13 Mounting and Cooling of Equipment. 110.13(A) Mounting.

84. When electrical equipment depends on _____ and the natural circulation of air to cool exposed surfaces, it must be installed so that the flow of air over the surface is not obstructed by adjacent surfaces, including walls and installed equipment.

    A. convection principles

    B. direct contact of cooling fins

    C. heat sinks

    D. independent fans

    Reference: 2017 National Electrical Code – Chapter 1 General, Article 110 Requirements for Electrical Installation. 110.13 Mounting and Cooling of Equipment. 110.13(B) Cooling.

EXAM 3

Chapter 1 General

85. The _____ must be used to identify devices like pressure splicing connectors, soldering lugs, and pressure terminal connectors, and they must be correctly installed and used.

    A. location of the installation
    C. proper spacing

    B. material of the conductor
    D. size of conductors

    Reference: 2017 National Electrical Code – Chapter 1 General, Article 110 Requirements for Electrical Installation. 110.14 Electrical Connections.

86. Connection by means of wire-binding screws or studs and nuts that have upturned lugs or the equivalent shall be permitted for _____ AWG or smaller conductors.

    A. 4 AWG
    C. 10 AWG

    B. 8 AWG
    D. 14 AWG

    Reference: 2017 National Electrical Code – Chapter 1 General, Article 110 Requirements for Electrical Installation. 110.14 Electrical Connections. 110.14(A) Terminals.

87. The only wire splicing means or connectors installed on conductors must be _____, to be used for direct burial.

    A. encased in concrete
    C. made waterproof

    B. listed for such use
    D. not be used

    Reference: 2017 National Electrical Code – Chapter 1 General, Article 110 Requirements for Electrical Installation. 110.14 Electrical Connections. 110.14(B) Splices.

88. The temperature rating associated with the ampacity of a conductor shall be selected and coordinated so as not to exceed the _____ temperature rating of any connected termination, conductor, or device.

    A. highest
    C. lowest

    B. labeled
    D. none of the above

    Reference: 2017 National Electrical Code – Chapter 1 General, Article 110 Requirements for Electrical Installation. 110.14 Electrical Connections. 110.14(C) Temperature Limitations.

Chapter 1 General

EXAM 3

Chapter 1 General

89. For a size 6 AWG THHN copper conductor connected to a fusible disconnect switch with terminals rated for 75°C, what is the maximum current load, in amperes?

    A. 55 amperes   C. 65 amperes

    B. 60 amperes   D. 75 amperes

Reference: 2017 National Electrical Code – Chapter 1 General, Article 110 Requirements for Electrical Installation. 110.14 Electrical Connections. 110.14(C) Temperature Limitations.

90. Given the following information, what is the allowable ampacity of a size 3 AWG THHN copper conductor?

    A. 81.6 amperes   C. 105.6 amperes

    B. 85 amperes   D. 110 amperes

Reference: 2017 National Electrical Code – Chapter 3 Wiring Methods and Materials, Article 310 Conductors for General Wiring. 310.15 Ampacities for Conductors Rated 0-2000 Volts. 310.15(A) General. 310.15(A)(2) Selection of Ampacity.

91. On a 4-wire, delta-connected system where the midpoint of one phase winding is grounded, only the conductor or busbar having the higher phase voltage to ground shall be durably and permanently marked by an outer finish that is _____ in color.

    A. blue   C. orange

    B. green   D. yellow

Reference: 2017 National Electrical Code – Chapter 1 General, Article 110 Requirements for Electrical Installation. 110.15 High-Leg Marking.

EXAM 3

Chapter 1 General

92. Only the busbar or conductor with the higher phase voltage to ground must be permanently and durably marked by an outer finish colored _____ or by other effective means, on a 4-wire delta-connected system when the midpoint of one phase winding is grounded.

    A. Black or Red   C. Red

    B. Orange   D. Yellow

    Reference: 2017 National Electrical Code – Chapter 1 General, Article 110 Requirements for Electrical Installation. 110.15 High-Leg Marking.

93. The conductor on a 4-wire, delta-connected system, since it has the higher voltage to ground, if the grounded conductor is also present to supply lighting or similar loads, shall be identified by which color?

    A. green   C. red

    B. orange   D. white

    Reference: 2017 National Electrical Code – Chapter 1 General, Article 110 Requirements for Electrical Installation. 110.15 High-Leg Marking.

94. The parts of electric equipment that produce arcs, flames, molten metal, or sparks in ordinary operation must be separated or enclosed, and isolated from all:

    A. combustible material.   C. other electrical components.

    B. metal parts.   D. possible contact with people.

    Reference: 2017 National Electrical Code – Chapter 1 General, Article 110 Requirements for Electrical Installation. 110.18 Arcing Parts.

Chapter 1 General

EXAM 3

Chapter 1 General

95. Each _____ means shall be legibly marked to indicate its purpose unless located and arranged so the purpose is evident.

    A. charging   C. disconnecting

    B. connecting   D. none of the above

    Reference: 2017 National Electrical Code – Chapter 1 General, Article 110 Requirements for Electrical Installation. 110.22 Identification of Disconnecting Means. 110.22(A) General.

96. Access and _____ space shall be provided and maintained about all electric equipment to permit ready and safe operation and maintenance of such equipment.

    A. air-flow   C. ventilation

    B. repair   D. working

    Reference: 2017 National Electrical Code – Chapter 1 General, Article 110 Requirements for Electrical Installation. 110.26 Spaces About Electrical Equipment.

97. When grounded parts are opposite the service, the required minimum working space in front of 120/240 volt, single-phase service equipment is:

    A. 2 feet   C. 3 feet

    B. 2-1/2 feet   D. 4 feet

    Reference: 2017 National Electrical Code – Chapter 1 General, Article 110 Requirements for Electrical Installation. 110.26 Spaces About Electrical Equipment. 110.26(A) Working Space. 110.26(A)(1) Depth of Working Space.

EXAM 3

Chapter 1 General

98. What is the minimum working space required by the NEC in new installations between a 480-volt motor control center and a 480Y/277-volt switchboard facing each other?

    A. 3 feet

    B. 3-1/2 feet

    C. 4 feet

    D. 6 feet

    Reference: 2017 National Electrical Code – Chapter 1 General, Article 110 Requirements for Electrical Installation. 110.26 Spaces About Electrical Equipment. 110.26(A) Working Space. 110.26(A)(1) Depth of Working Space.

99. Where rear access is required to work on nonelectrical parts on the back of enclosed equipment, a minimum horizontal working space of _____ inches shall be provided.

    A. 18 in.

    B. 24 in.

    C. 30 in.

    D. 36 in.

    Reference: 2017 National Electrical Code – Chapter 1 General, Article 110 Requirements for Electrical Installation. 110.26 Spaces About Electrical Equipment. . 110.26(A) Working Space. 110.26(A)(1) Depth of Working Space. 110.26(A)(1)(a) Dead-Front Assemblies.

100. In front of electric equipment, the working space width must be at least _____ in., or the width of the equipment, whichever is greater. Also, the working space must have space for doors or hinged panels to open _____ degrees or more.

    A. 30, 90

    B. 45, 60

    C. 60, 45

    D. 90, 30

    Reference: 2017 National Electrical Code – Chapter 1 General, Article 110 Requirements for Electrical Installation. 110.26 Spaces About Electrical Equipment. . 110.26(A) Working Space. 110.26(A)(2) Width of Working Space.

Chapter 1 General 41

EXAM 3

Chapter 1 General

101. In front of disconnects, motor controllers, panelboards, and switchboards, the required width of the working space must be either the width of the equipment or _____, whichever is more.

    A. 2 feet

    B. 3 feet

    C. 4 feet

    D. 30 inches

    Reference: 2017 National Electrical Code – Chapter 1 General, Article 110 Requirements for Electrical Installation. 110.26 Spaces About Electrical Equipment. 110.26(A) Working Space. 110.26(A)(2) Width of Working Space.

102. The width of the working space in front of the electric equipment shall be the width of the equipment or _____ inches, whichever is greater.

    A. 18 in.

    B. 24 in.

    C. 30 in.

    D. 36 in.

    Reference: 2017 National Electrical Code – Chapter 1 General, Article 110 Requirements for Electrical Installation. 110.26 Spaces About Electrical Equipment. . 110.26(A) Working Space. 110.26(A)(2) Width of Working Space.

103. The width of the working space for the maintenance of electrical equipment such as motor control centers, panelboards, switchboards and switchgear of 600 volts or less shall never be less than:

    A. 24 inches

    B. 30 inches

    C. 36 inches

    D. 48 inches

    Reference: 2017 National Electrical Code – Chapter 1 General, Article 110 Requirements for Electrical Installations. 110.26 Spaces About Electrical Equipment. 110.26(A) Working Space. 110.26(A)(2) Width of Working Space.

EXAM 3

Chapter 1 General

104. For the working space in front of a 120/240-volt, single-phase, 400 ampere rated disconnect switch located in a commercial occupancy, what is the minimum required height?

    A. 6 feet

    B. 6 feet, 3 inches

    C. 6 feet, 6 inches

    D. 8 feet

    Reference: 2017 National Electrical Code – Chapter 1 General, Article 110 Requirements for Electrical Installation. 110.26 Spaces About Electrical Equipment. 110.26(A) Working Space. 110.26(A)(3) Height of Working Space.

105. _____ or more entrances of sufficient area must be provided for access to and egress from working space around electrical equipment.

    A. 1

    B. 2

    C. 3

    D. 4

    Reference: 2017 National Electrical Code – Chapter 1 General, Article 110 Requirements for Electrical Installation. 110.26 Spaces About Electrical Equipment. . 110.26(C) Entrance to and Egress from Working Space. 110.26(C)(1) Minimum Required.

106. For equipment rated 1200 amperes or more and over 6 feet wide that contain overcurrent devices, there shall be one entrance to and egress from the required working space not less than _____ inches wide and _____ feet high at each end of the working space.

    A. 24, 6

    B. 24, 6-1/2

    C. 30, 6-1/2

    D. 36, 8

    Reference: 2017 National Electrical Code – Chapter 1 General, Article 110 Requirements for Electrical Installation. 110.26 Spaces About Electrical Equipment. . 110.26(C) Entrance to and Egress from Working Space. 110.26(C)(2) Large Equipment.

Chapter 1 General   43

EXAM 3

Chapter 1 General

107. Personnel door(s) must open in the direction of egress and have listed panic hardware if they are located less than 25 feet from the nearest edge of the working space of electrical equipment installed in an equipment room, containing overcurrent devices, and rated at _____ or more.

    A. 600 amperes
    B. 800 amperes
    C. 1000 amperes
    D. 2000 amperes

    Reference: 2017 National Electrical Code – Chapter 1 General, Article 110 Requirements for Electrical Installation. 110.26 Spaces About Electrical Equipment. 110.26(C) Entrance to and Egress from Working Space. 110.26(C)(3) Personnel Doors.

108. All switchboards, panelboards, and motor control centers shall be located in dedicated spaces and protected from _____.

    A. damage
    B. handling
    C. sparks
    D. none of the above

    Reference: 2017 National Electrical Code – Chapter 1 General, Article 110 Requirements for Electrical Installation. 110.26 Spaces About Electrical Equipment. . 110.26(E) Dedicated Equipment Space.

109. All distribution boards, motor control centers, panel-boards and switchboards must be protected from damage and located in _____ spaces.

    A. dedicated
    B. dry
    C. exterior
    D. interior

    Reference: 2017 National Electrical Code – Chapter 1 General, Article 110 Requirements for Electrical Installation. 110.26 Spaces About Electrical Equipment. 110.26(E) Dedicated Equipment Space.

EXAM 3

Chapter 1 General

110. The space equal to the width and depth of the equipment and extending from the floor to a height of _____ feet above the equipment or to the structural ceiling, whichever is lower, shall be dedicated to the electrical installation.

    A. 4   C. 6

    B. 5   D. 8

    Reference: 2017 National Electrical Code – Chapter 1 General, Article 110 Requirements for Electrical Installation. 110.26 Spaces About Electrical Equipment. . 110.26(E) Dedicated Equipment Space. 110.26(E)(1) Indoor. 110.26(E)(1)(a) Dedicated Electrical Space.

111. Electrical equipment rooms or enclosures housing electrical apparatus that are controlled by a lock(s) shall be considered accessible to _____ persons.

    A. authorized   C. trained

    B. qualified   D. none of the above

    Reference: 2017 National Electrical Code – Chapter 1 General, Article 110 Requirements for Electrical Installation. 110.26 Spaces About Electrical Equipment. . 110.26(F) Locked Electrical Equipment Rooms or Enclosures.

112. Live parts of electrical equipment operating at _____ volts or more shall be guarded against accidental contact.

    A. 30   C. 75

    B. 50   D. 120

    Reference: 2017 National Electrical Code – Chapter 1 General, Article 110 Requirements for Electrical Installation. 110.27 Guarding of Live Parts. 110.27(A) Live Parts Guarded Against Accidental Contact.

Chapter 1 General   45

EXAM 3

Chapter 1 General

113. Unless allowed or required elsewhere in the Code, any live electrical equipment parts operating at least _____ volts must be guarded by approved enclosures or other means against accident contact.

    A. 35
    B. 50
    C. 80
    D. 100

    Reference: 2017 National Electrical Code – Chapter 1 General, Article 110 Requirements for Electrical Installation. 110.27 Guarding of Live Parts. . 110.27(A) Live Parts Guarded Against Accidental Contact.

114. In places where electric equipment might be physically damaged, _____ or enclosures should be strong enough and arranged to prevent physical damage.

    A. conductors
    B. equipment
    C. guards
    D. insulation

    Reference: 2017 National Electrical Code – Chapter 1 General, Article 110 Requirements for Electrical Installation. 110.27 Guarding of Live Parts. 110.27(B) Prevent Physical Damage.

115. Safe access to working space around electric equipment installed on balconies, mezzanine floors, platforms, or in attic or roof rooms or spaces must be provided by:

    A. collapsible ladders
    B. elevators
    C. permanent ladders or stairways
    D. temporary ladders

    Reference: 2017 National Electrical Code – Chapter 1 General, Article 110 Requirements for Electrical Installation. 110.33 Entrance to Enclosures and Access to Working Space. 110.33(B) Access.

EXAM 3

Chapter 1 General

116. Unless they are under _____, the entrance to any buildings, enclosures, rooms, or vaults with exposed conductors or live parts operating at over 600 volts nominal must be kept locked.

    A. amperage limit of 1200 amperes

    B. protection of a circuit ground fault device

    C. the legal occupancy limit of the building

    D. the observation of a qualified person at all times

Reference: 2017 National Electrical Code – Chapter 1 General, Article 110 Requirements for Electrical Installation. 110.34 Work Space and Guarding. 110.34(C) Locked Rooms or Enclosures.

117. Bare live circuit conductors must _____. Circuit conductors as metal-clad cable, as bare wire, cable, and busbars must be permitted to be installed in raceways or cable trays; or as Type MV cables or conductors as provided in 300.37, 300.39, 300.40, and 300.50.

    A. be installed in PVC RNC

    B. be marked as live

    C. conform with 490.24

    D. not be allowed

Reference: 2017 National Electrical Code – Chapter 1 General, Article 110 Requirements for Electrical Installation. 110.36 Circuit Conductors.

118. Conductors, based on the _____ °C temperature rating and ampacity as given in Table 310.60(C)(67) through Table 310.60(C)(86), may be terminated unless otherwise identified.

    A. 60

    B. 75

    C. 90

    D. 100

Reference: 2017 National Electrical Code – Chapter 1 General, Article 110 Requirements for Electrical Installation. 110.40 Temperature Limitations at Terminations.

EXAM 3

Chapter 1 General

119. In tunnels, cables and conductors must be located _____ and guarded or placed so that they are protected from physical damage.

    A. above the tunnel floor

    B. in RNC

    C. under the tunnel floor

    D. within RNC

    Reference: 2017 National Electrical Code – Chapter 1 General, Article 110 Requirements for Electrical Installation. 110.51 General. 110.51(C) Protection Against Physical Damage.

120. All metal parts of electric equipment and all metal cable sheaths and raceways must be grounded solidly and bonded to metal rails and pipes at the portal and at intervals throughout a tunnel of _____ ft. or less.

    A. 500

    B. 1000

    C. 1500

    D. 2000

    Reference: 2017 National Electrical Code – Chapter 1 General, Article 110 Requirements for Electrical Installation. 110.54 Bonding and Equipment Grounding Conductors. 110.54(A) Grounded and Bonded.

121. What is the minimum diameter for round access opening in a manhole?

    A. 24 inches

    B. 26 inches

    C. 30 inches

    D. 36 inches

    Reference: 2017 National Electrical Code – Chapter 1 General, Article 110 Requirements for Electrical Installations. 110.75 Access to Manholes. 110.75(A) Dimensions.

EXAM 3

EXAM 3 ANSWERS

1. **Answer A.** Accessible (as applied to equipment).

   Admitting close approach; not guarded by locked doors, elevation, or other effective means.

   Reference: 2017 National Electrical Code – Chapter 1 General, Article 100, Definitions. Accessible (as applied to equipment).

2. **Answer A.** Accessible (as applied to equipment).

   Admitting close approach; not guarded by locked doors, elevation, or other effective means.

   Reference: 2017 National Electrical Code – Chapter 1 General, Article 100, Definitions. Accessible (as applied to equipment).

3. **Answer A.** Accessible (as applied to wiring methods).

   Capable of being removed or exposed without damaging the building structure or finish or not permanently closed in by the structure or finish of the building.

   Reference: 2017 National Electrical Code – Chapter 1 General, Article 100 Definitions. Accessible (as applied to wiring methods.)

4. **Answer A.** Accessible, Readily (Readily Accessible).

   Capable of being removed or exposed without damaging the building structure or finish or not permanently closed in by the structure or finish of the building.

   Reference: 2017 National Electrical Code – Chapter 1 General, Article 100 Definitions. Accessible, Readily (Readily Accessible)

5. **Answer A.** Ampacity

   The maximum current, in amperes, that a conductor can carry continuously under the conditions of use without exceeding its temperature rating.

   Reference: 2017 National Electrical Code – Chapter 1 General, Article 100 Definitions. Ampacity.

6. **Answer D.** temperature rating

   The maximum current, in amperes, that a conductor can carry continuously under the conditions of use without exceeding its temperature rating.

   Reference: 2017 National Electrical Code – Chapter 1 General, Article 100 Definitions. Ampacity

EXAM 3

EXAM 3 ANSWERS

7. **Answer A.** Arc-Fault Circuit Interrupter (AFCI)

   A device intended to provide protection from the effects of arc faults by recognizing characteristics unique to arcing and by functioning to de-energize the circuit when an arc fault is detected.

   Reference: 2017 National Electrical Code – Chapter 1 General, Article 100 Definitions. Arc-Fault Circuit Interrupter (AFCI)

8. **Answer D.** Either B or C

   Dust particles that are 500 microns or smaller (i.e., material passing a U.S. No. 35 Standard Sieve as defined in ASTM E11-2015, Standard Specification for Woven Wire Test Sieve Cloth and Test Sieves), and present a fire or explosion hazard when dispersed and ignited in air. (CMP-14)

   Informational Note: See ASTM E1226-2012a, Standard Test

   Method for Explosibility of Dust Clouds, or ISO 6184-1, Explosion protection systems — *Part 1: Determination of explosion indices of combustible dusts in air, for procedures for determining the explosibility of dusts.*

   Reference: 2017 National Electrical Code – Chapter 1 General, Article 100 Definitions. Combustible Dust[as applied to Hazardous (Classified) Locations].

9. **Answer A.** Dust-ignitionproof

   Equipment enclosed in a manner that excludes dusts and does not permit arcs, sparks, or heat otherwise generated or liberated inside of the enclosure to cause ignition of exterior accumulations or atmospheric suspensions of a specified dust on or in the vicinity of the enclosure. (CMP-14)

   Informational Note: For further information on dust ignition proof enclosures, see ANSI/UL 1202-2013, Enclosures for Electrical Equipment, and ANSI/UL 1203-2013, Explosion proof and Dust-Ignition proof Electrical Equipment for Hazardous (Classified) Locations.

   Reference: 2017 National Electrical Code – Chapter 1 General, Article 100 Definitions. Dust-ignition proof [as applied to Hazardous (Classified) Locations].

10. **Answer A.** Authority Having Jurisdiction (AHJ)

    An organization, office, or individual responsible for enforcing the requirements of a code or standard, or for approving equipment, materials, an installation, or a procedure.

    Informational Note: The phrase "authority having jurisdiction," or its acronym AHJ, is used in NFPA documents in a broad manner, since jurisdictions and approval agencies vary, as do their responsibilities. Where public safety is primary, the authority having jurisdiction may be a federal, state, local or other regional department or individual such as a fire chief; fire marshal; chief of a fire prevention bureau, labor department, or health department; building official; electrical inspector; or others having statutory authority. For insurance purposes, an insurance inspection department, rating bureau, or other insurance company representative may be the authority having jurisdiction. In many circumstances, the property owner or his or her designated agent assumes the role of the authority having jurisdiction; at government installations, the commanding officer or departmental official may be the authority having jurisdiction.

    Reference: 2017 National Electrical Code – Chapter 1 General, Article 100: Definitions. Authority Having Jurisdiction (AHJ)

11. **Answer A.** Bonded (Bonding)

    Connected to establish electrical continuity and conductivity.

    Reference: 2017 National Electrical Code – Chapter 1 General, Article 100 Definitions. Bonded (Bonding)

12. **Answer C.** reliable conductor for connected parts conductivity.

    A reliable conductor to ensure the required electrical conductivity between metal parts required to be electrically connected.

    Reference: 2017 National Electrical Code – Chapter 1 General, Article 100, Definitions. Bonding Conductor or Jumper

EXAM 3

EXAM 3 ANSWERS

13. **Answer A.** Bonding Jumper

    A reliable conductor to ensure the required electrical conductivity between metal parts required to be electrically connected.

    Reference: 2017 National Electrical Code – Chapter 1 General, Article 100, Definitions. Bonding Conductor or Jumper

14. **Answer D.** Equipment Bonding Jumper

    The connection between two or more portions of the equipment grounding conductor.

    Reference: 2017 National Electrical Code – Chapter 1 General, Article 100, Definitions. Bonding Jumper, Equipment.

15. **Answer B.** Branch Circuit, General-Purpose

    A branch circuit that supplies two or more receptacles or outlets for lighting and appliances.

    Reference: 2017 National Electrical Code – Chapter 1 General, Article 100 Definitions. Branch Circuit, General-Purpose

16. **Answer A.** Cabinet

    An enclosure that is designed for either surface mounting or flush mounting and is provided with a frame, mat, or trim in which a swinging door or doors are or can be hung.

    Reference: 2017 National Electrical Code – Chapter 1 General, Article 100, Definitions. Cabinet

17. **Answer B.** Circuit Breaker

    A device designed to open and close a circuit by nonautomatic means and to open the circuit automatically on a predetermined overcurrent without damage to itself when properly applied within its rating.

    Informational Note: The automatic opening means can be integral, direct acting with the circuit breaker, or remote from the circuit breaker.

    Adjustable (as applied to circuit breakers). A qualifying term indicating that the circuit breaker can be set to trip at various values of current, time, or both, within a predetermined range.

    Instantaneous Trip (as applied to circuit breakers). A qualifying term indicating that no delay is purposely introduced in the tripping action of the circuit breaker.

    Inverse Time (as applied to circuit breakers). A qualifying term indicating that there is purposely introduced a delay in the tripping action of the circuit breaker, which delay decreases as the magnitude of the current increases.

    Nonadjustable (as applied to circuit breakers). A qualifying term indicating that the circuit breaker does not have any adjustment to alter the value of the current at which it will trip or the time required for its operation.

    Setting (of circuit breakers). The value of current, time, or both, at which an adjustable circuit breaker is set to trip.

    Reference: 2017 National Electrical Code – Chapter 1 General, Article 100 Definitions. Circuit Breaker

EXAM 3

EXAM 3 ANSWERS

18. **Answer B.** Inverse Time

    Inverse Time (as applied to circuit breakers). A qualifying term indicating that there is purposely introduced a delay in the tripping action of the circuit breaker, which delay decreases as the magnitude of the current increases.

    Reference: 2017 National Electrical Code – Chapter 1 General, Article 100, Definitions. Circuit Breaker. *Inverse Time (as applied to circuit breakers).*

19. **Answer B.** Circuit Breaker

    A device designed to open and close a circuit by nonautomatic means and to open the circuit automatically on a predetermined overcurrent without damage to itself when properly applied within its rating.

    Informational Note: The automatic opening means can be integral, direct acting with the circuit breaker, or remote from the circuit breaker.

    Adjustable (as applied to circuit breakers). A qualifying term indicating that the circuit breaker can be set to trip at various values of current, time, or both, within a predetermined range.

    Instantaneous Trip (as applied to circuit breakers). A qualifying term indicating that no delay is purposely introduced in the tripping action of the circuit breaker.

    Inverse Time (as applied to circuit breakers). A qualifying term indicating that there is purposely introduced a delay in the tripping action of the circuit breaker, which delay decreases as the magnitude of the current increases.

    Nonadjustable (as applied to circuit breakers). A qualifying term indicating that the circuit breaker does not have any adjustment to alter the value of the current at which it will trip or the time required for its operation.

    Setting (of circuit breakers). The value of current, time, or both, at which an adjustable circuit breaker is set to trip.

    Reference: 2017 National Electrical Code – Chapter 1 General, Article 100 Definitions. Circuit Breaker

20. **Answer A.** Concealed

    Rendered inaccessible by the structure or finish of the building.

    Informational Note: Wires in concealed raceways are considered concealed, even though they may become accessible by withdrawing them.

    Reference: 2017 National Electrical Code – Chapter 1 General, Article 100 Definitions. Concealed.

21. **Answer B.** made inaccessible by the structure or finish of the building

    Rendered inaccessible by the structure or finish of the building.

    Informational Note: Wires in concealed raceways are considered concealed, even though they may become accessible by withdrawing them.

    Reference: 2017 National Electrical Code – Chapter 1 General, Article 100 Definitions. Concealed.

22. **Answer A.** Conduit Body

    A separate portion of a conduit or tubing system that provides access through a removable cover(s) to the interior of the system at a junction of two or more sections of the system or at a terminal point of the system.

    Boxes such as FS and FD or larger cast or sheet metal boxes are not classified as conduit bodies.

    Reference: 2017 National Electrical Code – Chapter 1 General, Article 100, Definitions. Conduit Body

23. **Answer A.** Pressure Connector

    A device that establishes a connection between two or more conductors or between one or more conductors and a terminal by means of mechanical pressure and without the use of solder.

    Reference: 2017 National Electrical Code – Chapter 1 General, Article 100, Definitions. Connector, Pressure (Solderless)

EXAM 3

EXAM 3 ANSWERS

24. **Answer B.** Continuous Load

    A load where the maximum current is expected to continue for 3 hours or more.

    Reference: 2017 National Electrical Code – Chapter 1 General, Article 100 Definitions. Continuous Load

25. **Answer C.** 3

    A load where the maximum current is expected to continue for 3 hours or more.

    Reference: 2017 National Electrical Code – Chapter 1 General, Article 100, Definitions. Continuous Load

26. **Answer A.** three

    A load where the maximum current is expected to continue for 3 hours or more.

    Reference: 2017 National Electrical Code – Chapter 1 General, Article 100 Definitions. Continuous Load

27. **Answer B.** Controller

    A device or group of devices that serves to govern, in some predetermined manner, the electric power delivered to the apparatus to which it is connected.

    Reference: 2017 National Electrical Code – Chapter 1 General, Article 100, Definitions. Controller

28. **Answer A.** demand factor

    The ratio of the maximum demand of a system, or part of a system, to the total connected load of a system or the part of the system under consideration.

    Reference: 2017 National Electrical Code – Chapter 1 General, Article 100 Definitions. Demand Factor

29. **Answer B.** Disconnecting Means

    A device, or group of devices, or other means by which the conductors of a circuit can be disconnected from their source of supply.

    Reference: 2017 National Electrical Code – Chapter 1 General, Article 100 Definitions. Disconnecting Means

30. **Answer B.** Disconnecting Means

    A device, or group of devices, or other means by which the conductors of a circuit can be disconnected from their source of supply.

    Reference: 2017 National Electrical Code – Chapter 1 General, Article 100, Definitions. Disconnecting Means.

31. **Answer B.** Operation at a mostly constant load for an indefinite time.

    Operation at a substantially constant load for an indefinitely long time.

    Reference: 2017 National Electrical Code – Chapter 1 General, Article 100, Definitions. Duty, Continuous

32. **Answer C.** Energized

    Electrically connected to, or is, a source of voltage.

    Reference: 2017 National Electrical Code – Chapter 1 General, Article 100 Definitions. Energized.

33. **Answer B.** Can be operated without the operator contacting live parts.

    Capable of being operated without exposing the operator to contact with live parts.

    Reference: 2017 National Electrical Code – Chapter 1 General, Article 100, Definitions. Externally Operable

34. **Answer C.** Feeder

    All circuit conductors between the service equipment, the source of a separately derived system, or other power supply source and the final branch-circuit overcurrent device.

    Reference: 2017 National Electrical Code – Chapter 1 General, Article 100 Definitions. Feeder.

EXAM 3

EXAM 3 ANSWERS

35. Answer C. Ground Fault

An unintentional, electrically conductive connection between an ungrounded conductor of an electrical circuit and the normally non-current-carrying conductors, metallic enclosures, metallic raceways, metallic equipment or earth.

Reference: 2017 National Electrical Code – Chapter 1 General, Article 100 Definitions. Ground Fault.

36. Answer A. An unintended conducting connection to metal or earth.

An unintentional, electrically conductive connection between an ungrounded conductor of an electrical circuit and the normally non-current-carrying conductors, metallic enclosures, metallic raceways, metallic equipment or earth.

Reference: 2017 National Electrical Code – Chapter 1 General, Article 100, Definitions. Ground Fault

37. Answer C. Ground-Fault Circuit Interrupter (GFCI)

A device intended for the protection of personnel that functions to deenergize a circuit or portion thereof within an established period of time when a current to ground exceeds the values established for a Class A device.

Informational Note: Class A ground-fault circuit interrupters trip when the current to ground is 6 mA or higher and do not trip when the current to ground is less than 4 mA. For further information, see UL 943, *Standard for Ground Fault Circuit Interrupters*.

Reference: 2017 National Electrical Code – Chapter 1 General, Article 100 Definitions. Ground-Fault Circuit Interrupter (GFCI).

38. Answer A. A device to protect personnel that de energizes a circuit.

A device intended for the protection of personnel that functions to de energize a circuit or portion thereof within an established period of time when a current to ground exceeds the values established for a Class A device.

Informational Note: Class A ground-fault circuit interrupters trip when the current to ground is 6 mA or higher and do not trip when the current to ground is less than 4 mA. For further information, see UL 943, *Standard for Ground Fault Circuit Interrupters*.

Reference: 2017 National Electrical Code – Chapter 1 General, Article 100 Definitions. Ground-Fault Circuit Interrupter (GFCI).

39. Answer B. for the protection of personnel

A device intended for the protection of personnel that functions to deenergize a circuit or portion thereof within an established period of time when a current to ground exceeds the values established for a Class A device.

Informational Note: Class A ground-fault circuit interrupters trip when the current to ground is 6 mA or higher and do not trip when the current to ground is less than 4 mA. For further information, see UL 943, *Standard for Ground Fault Circuit Interrupters*.

Reference: 2017 National Electrical Code – Chapter 1 General, Article 100 Definitions. Ground-Fault Circuit Interrupter (GFCI).

40. Answer C. Grounded (Grounding)

Connected (connecting) to ground or to a conductive body that extends the ground connection.

Review and know the difference between the different meanings of Ground, Grounded and Grounding.

Reference: 2017 National Electrical Code – Chapter 1 General, Article 100 Definitions. Grounded (Grounding).

EXAM 3

EXAM 3 ANSWERS

41. Answer B. Grounded Conductor

A system or circuit conductor that is intentionally grounded.

Reference: 2017 National Electrical Code – Chapter 1 General, Article 100 Definitions. Grounded Conductor

42. Answer B. hybrid system

A system comprised of multiple power sources. These power sources could include photovoltaic, wind, micro-hydro generators, engine-driven generators, and others, but do not include electric power production and distribution network systems. Energy storage systems such as batteries, flywheels, or superconducting magnetic storage equipment do not constitute a power source for the purpose of this definition. The energy regenerated by an overhauling (descending) elevator does not constitute a power source for the purpose of this definition.

Reference: 2017 National Electrical Code – Chapter 1 General, Article 100 Definitions. Hybrid System

43. Answer A. True

Where this Code specifies that one equipment shall be "in sight from," "within sight from," or "within sight of," and so forth, another equipment, the specified equipment is to be visible and not more than 15 m (50 ft.) distant from the other.

Reference: 2017 National Electrical Code – Chapter 1 General, Article 100 Definitions. In Sight From (Within Sight From, Within Sight).

44. Answer A. Interactive System

An electric power production system that is operating in parallel with and capable of delivering energy to an electric primary source supply system.

Reference: 2017 National Electrical Code – Chapter 1 General, Article 100, Definitions. Interactive System

45. Answer D. Intersystem Bonding Termination

A device that provides a means for connecting intersystem bonding conductors for communications systems to the grounding electrode system.

Reference: 2017 National Electrical Code – Chapter 1 General, Article 100, Definitions. Intersystem Bonding Termination

46. Answer B. Labeled

Equipment or materials to which has been attached a label, symbol, or other identifying mark of an organization that is acceptable to the authority having jurisdiction and concerned with product evaluation, that maintains periodic inspection of production of labeled equipment or materials, and by whose labeling the manufacturer indicates compliance with appropriate standards or performance in a specified manner.

Reference: 2017 National Electrical Code – Chapter 1 General, Article 100 Definitions. Labeled.

47. Answer A. damp

Locations protected from weather and not subject to saturation with water or other liquids but subject to moderate degrees of moisture.

Informational Note: Examples of such locations include partially protected locations under canopies, marquees, roofed open porches, and like locations, and interior locations subject to moderate degrees of moisture, such as some basements, some barns, and some cold-storage warehouses

Reference: 2017 National Electrical Code – Chapter 1 General, Article 100 Definitions. Location, Damp

48. Answer D. Wet Location

Installations underground or in concrete slabs or masonry in direct contact with the earth; in locations subject to saturation with water or other liquids, such as vehicle washing areas; and in unprotected locations exposed to weather.

Reference: 2017 National Electrical Code – Chapter 1 General, Article 100, Definitions. Location, Wet.

49. Answer C. Luminaire

A complete lighting unit consisting of a light source such as a lamp or lamps, together with the parts designed to position the light source and connect it to the power supply. It may also include parts to protect the light source or the ballast or to distribute the light. A lampholder itself is not a luminaire.

Reference: 2017 National Electrical Code – Chapter 1 General, Article 100 Definitions. Luminaire.

EXAM 3 ANSWERS   55

EXAM 3

EXAM 3 ANSWERS

50. **Answer C.** Luminaire

A complete lighting unit consisting of a light source such as a lamp or lamps, together with the parts designed to position the light source and connect it to the power supply. It may also include parts to protect the light source or the ballast or to distribute the light. A lampholder itself is not a luminaire.

Reference: 2017 National Electrical Code – Chapter 1 General, Article 100, Definitions. Luminaire.

51. **Answer C.** it is connected to the neutral point of a system

The conductor connected to the neutral point of a system that is intended to carry current under normal conditions.

Reference: 2017 National Electrical Code – Chapter 1 General, Article 100 Definitions. Neutral Conductor

52. **Answer A.** Neutral Point

The common point on a wye-connection in a polyphase system or midpoint on a single-phase, 3-wire system, or midpoint of a single-phase portion of a 3-phase delta system, or a midpoint of a 3-wire, direct-current system.

Informational Note: At the neutral point of the system, the vectorial sum of the nominal voltages from all other phases within the system that utilize the neutral, with respect to the neutral point, is zero potential.

Reference: 2017 National Electrical Code – Chapter 1 General, Article 100, Definitions. Neutral Point.

53. **Answer C.** Nonautomatic

Requiring human intervention to perform a function.

Reference: 2017 National Electrical Code – Chapter 1 General, Article 100 Definitions. Nonautomatic.

54. **Answer B.** outlet

A point on the wiring system at which current is taken to supply utilization equipment.

Reference: 2017 National Electrical Code – Chapter 1 General, Article 100 Definitions. Outlet

55. **Answer C.** Overload

Operation of equipment in excess of normal, full-load rating, or of a conductor in excess of rated ampacity that, when it persists for a sufficient length of time, would cause damage or dangerous overheating. A fault, such as a short circuit or ground fault, is not an overload.

Reference: 2017 National Electrical Code – Chapter 1 General, Article 100, Definitions. Overload.

56. **Answer C.** Panelboard

A single panel or group of panel units designed for assembly in the form of a single panel, including buses and automatic overcurrent devices, and equipped with or without switches for the control of light, heat, or power circuits; designed to be placed in a cabinet or cutout box placed in or against a wall, partition, or other support; and accessible only from the front.

Reference: 2017 National Electrical Code – Chapter 1 General, Article 100 Definitions. Panelboard.

57. **Answer D.** Plenum

A compartment or chamber to which one or more air ducts are connected and that forms part of the air distribution system.

Reference: 2017 National Electrical Code – Chapter 1 General, Article 100, Definitions. Plenum.

58. **Answer D.** Raceway

An enclosed channel of metallic or nonmetallic materials designed expressly for holding wires, cables, or busbars, with additional functions as permitted in this Code.

Informational Note: A raceway is identified within specific article definitions.

Reference: 2017 National Electrical Code – Chapter 1 General, Article 100 Definitions. Raceway.

59. **Answer A.** Rainproof

Constructed, protected, or treated so as to prevent rain from interfering with the successful operation of the apparatus under specified test conditions.

Reference: 2017 National Electrical Code – Chapter 1 General, Article 100, Definitions. Rainproof.

EXAM 3

EXAM 3 ANSWERS

60. **Answer D.** Service

    The conductors and equipment for delivering electric energy from the serving utility to the wiring system of the premises served.

    Reference: 2017 National Electrical Code – Chapter 1 General, Article 100 Definitions. Service.

61. **Answer D.** Service Drop

    The overhead conductors between the utility electric supply system and the service point.

    Reference: 2017 National Electrical Code – Chapter 1 General, Article 100 Definitions. Service Drop.

62. **Answer B.** Service Drop

    The overhead conductors between the utility electric supply system and the service point.

    Reference: 2017 National Electrical Code – Chapter 1 General, Article 100, Definitions. Service Drop.

63. **Answer C.** Service Lateral

    The overhead conductors between the utility electric supply system and the service point.

    Reference: 2017 National Electrical Code – Chapter 1 General, Article 100 Definitions. Service Lateral.

64. **Answer D.** Service Point

    The point of connection between the facilities of the serving utility and the premises wiring.

    Reference: 2017 National Electrical Code – Chapter 1 General, Article 100, Definitions. Service Point.

65. **Answer B.** Bypass Isolation Switch

    A manually operated device used in conjunction with a transfer switch to provide a means of directly connecting load conductors to a power source and of disconnecting the transfer switch.

    Reference: 2017 National Electrical Code – Chapter 1 General, Article 100, Definitions. Switch, Bypass Isolation.

66. **Answer B.** General-Use Switch

    A switch intended for use in general distribution and branch circuits. It is rated in amperes, and it is capable of interrupting its rated current at its rated voltage.

    Reference: 2017 National Electrical Code – Chapter 1 General, Article 100, Definitions. Switch, General-Use.

67. **Answer D.** Switchboard

    A large single panel, frame, or assembly of panels on which are mounted on the face, back, or both, switches, overcurrent and other protective devices, buses, and usually instruments. These assemblies are generally accessible from the rear as well as from the front and are not intended to be installed in cabinets.

    Reference: 2017 National Electrical Code – Chapter 1 General, Article 100 Definitions. Switchboard.

68. **Answer D.** water heater

    Equipment that utilizes electric energy for electronic, electromechanical, chemical, heating, lighting, or similar purposes.

    Reference: 2017 National Electrical Code – Chapter 1 General, Article 100 Definitions. Utilization Equipment

69. **Answer C.** Voltage

    The greatest root-mean-square (rms) (effective) difference of potential between any two conductors of the circuit concerned.

    Reference: 2017 National Electrical Code – Chapter 1 General, Article 100, Definitions. Voltage (of a circuit).

70. **Answer D.** Voltage, Nominal

    A nominal value assigned to a circuit or system for the purpose of conveniently designating its voltage class (e.g., 120/240 volts, 480Y1277 volts, 600 volts).

    Informational Note No. 1: The actual voltage at which a circuit operates can vary from the nominal within a range that permits satisfactory operation of equipment.

    Informational Note No. 2: See ANSI C84.1-2006, *Voltage Ratings for Electric Power Systems and Equipment (60 Hz)*.

    Reference: 2017 National Electrical Code – Chapter 1 General, Article 100 Definitions. Voltage, Nominal.

EXAM 3 ANSWERS

EXAM 3

EXAM 3 ANSWERS

71. Answer C. Multiple Fuse

An assembly of two or more single-pole fuses.

Reference: 2017 National Electrical Code – Chapter 1 General, Article 100, Definitions II. Over 600 Volts, Nominal. Multiple Fuse.

72. Answer D. It shall be installed in accordance with the instructions.

Listed or labeled equipment shall be installed and used in accordance with any instructions included in the listing or labeling.

Reference: 2017 National Electrical Code – Chapter 1 General, Article 110 Requirements for Electrical Installation. 110.3 Examination, Identification, Installation, and Use of Equipment. 110.3(B) Installation and Use.

73. Answer B. nominal voltage

Throughout this Code, the voltage considered shall be that at which the circuit operates. The voltage rating of electrical equipment shall not be less than the nominal voltage of a circuit to which it is connected.

Reference: 2017 National Electrical Code – Chapter 1 General, Article 110 Requirements for Electrical Installation. 110.4 Voltages.

74. Answer B. copper

Conductors normally used to carry current shall be of copper unless otherwise provided in this Code. Where the conductor material is not specified, the material and the sizes given in this Code shall apply to copper conductors. Where other materials are used, the size shall be changed accordingly.

Informational Note: For aluminum and copper-clad aluminum conductors, see 310.15.

Reference: 2017 National Electrical Code – Chapter 1 General, Article 110 Requirements for Electrical Installation. 110.5 Conductors

75. Answer B. copper

Conductors normally used to carry current shall be of copper unless otherwise provided in this Code. Where the conductor material is not specified, the material and the sizes given in this Code shall apply to copper conductors. Where other materials are used, the size shall be changed accordingly.

Informational Note: For aluminum and copper-clad aluminum conductors, see 310.15.

Reference: 2017 National Electrical Code – Chapter 1 General, Article 110 Requirements for Electrical Installation. 110.5 Conductors

76. Answer A. American Wire Gauge (AWG)

Conductor sizes are expressed in American Wire Gauge (AWG) or in circular mils.

Reference: 2017 National Electrical Code – Chapter 1 General, Article 110 Requirements for Electrical Installation. 110.6 Conductor Sizes.

77. Answer A. circular mils

Conductor sizes are expressed in American Wire Gauge (AWG) or in circular mils.

Reference: 2017 National Electrical Code – Chapter 1 General, Article 110 Requirements for Electrical Installation. 110.6 Conductor Sizes.

78. Answer C. circular mils

Conductor sizes are expressed in American Wire Gage (AWG) or in circular mils.

Reference: 2017 National Electrical Code – Chapter 1 General, Article 110 Requirements for Electrical Installation. 110.6 Conductor Sizes.

EXAM 3

EXAM 3 ANSWERS

79. **Answer B.** ground faults

Completed wiring installations shall be free from short circuits, ground faults, or any connections to ground other than as required or permitted elsewhere in this Code.

Reference: 2017 National Electrical Code – Chapter 1 General, Article 110 Requirements for Electrical Installation. 110.7 Wiring Integrity.

80. **Answer D.** voltage

Equipment intended to interrupt current at fault levels shall have an interrupting rating at nominal circuit voltage sufficient for the current that is available at the line terminals of the equipment.

Equipment intended to interrupt current at other than fault levels shall have an interrupting rating at nominal circuit voltage sufficient for the current that must be interrupted.

Reference: 2017 National Electrical Code – Chapter 1 General, Article 110 Requirements for Electrical Installation. 110.9 Interrupting Rating.

81. **Answer A.** closed

Unused openings, other than those intended for the operation of equipment, those intended for mounting purposes, or those permitted as part of the design for listed equipment, shall be closed to afford protection substantially equivalent to the wall of the equipment. Where metallic plugs or plates are used with nonmetallic enclosures, they shall be recessed at least 6 mm (14 in.) from the outer surface of the enclosure.

Reference: 2017 National Electrical Code – Chapter 1 General, Article 110 Requirements for Electrical Installation. 110.12 Mechanical Execution of Work. 110.12(A) Unused Openings.

82. **Answer C.** should be effectively closed

Unused openings, other than those intended for the operation of equipment, those intended for mounting purposes, or those permitted as part of the design for listed equipment, shall be closed to afford protection substantially equivalent to the wall of the equipment. Where metallic plugs or plates are used with nonmetallic enclosures, they shall be recessed at least 6 mm (1/4 in.) from the outer surface of the enclosure.

Reference: 2017 National Electrical Code – Chapter 1 General, Article 110 Requirements for Electrical Installation. 110.12 Mechanical Execution of Work. 110.12(A) Unused Openings.

83. **Answer D.** not be used

Electrical equipment shall be firmly secured to the surface on which it is mounted. Wooden plugs driven into holes in masonry, concrete, plaster, or similar materials shall not be used.

Reference: 2017 National Electrical Code – Chapter 1 General, Article 110 Requirements for Electrical Installation. 110.13 Mounting and Cooling of Equipment. 110.13(A) Mounting.

84. **Answer A.** convection principles

Electrical equipment that depends on the natural circulation of air and convection principles for cooling of exposed surfaces shall be installed so that room airflow over such surfaces is not prevented by walls or by adjacent installed equipment. For equipment designed for floor mounting, clearance between top surfaces and adjacent surfaces shall be provided to dissipate rising warm air.

Electrical equipment provided with ventilating openings shall be installed so that walls or other obstructions do not prevent the free circulation of air through the equipment.

Reference: 2017 National Electrical Code – Chapter 1 General, Article 110 Requirements for Electrical Installation. 110.13 Mounting and Cooling of Equipment. 110.13(B) Cooling.

85. **Answer B.** material of the conductor

Because of different characteristics of dissimilar metals, devices such as pressure terminal or pressure splicing connectors and soldering lugs shall be identified for the material of the conductor and shall be properly installed and used. Conductors of dissimilar metals shall not be intermixed in a terminal or splicing connector where physical contact occurs between dissimilar conductors (such as copper and aluminum, copper and copper-clad aluminum, or aluminum and copper-clad aluminum), unless the device is identified for the purpose and conditions of use. Materials such as solder, fluxes, inhibitors, and compounds, where employed, shall be suitable for the use and shall be of a type that will not adversely affect the conductors, installation, or equipment.

Connectors and terminals for conductors more finely stranded than Class B and Class C stranding as shown in Chapter 9, Table 10, shall be identified for the specific conductor class or classes.

Reference: 2017 National Electrical Code – Chapter 1 General, Article 110 Requirements for Electrical Installation. 110.14 Electrical Connections.

EXAM 3

EXAM 3 ANSWERS

86. **Answer C.** 10 AWG

    Connection of conductors to terminal parts shall ensure a thoroughly good connection without damaging the conductors and shall be made by means of pressure connectors (including set-screw type), solder lugs, or splices to flexible leads. Connection by means of wire-binding screws or studs and nuts that have upturned lugs or the equivalent shall be permitted for 10 AWG or smaller conductors.

    Terminals for more than one conductor and terminals used to connect aluminum shall be so identified.

    Reference: 2017 National Electrical Code – Chapter 1 General, Article 110 Requirements for Electrical Installation. 110.14 Electrical Connections. 110.14(A) Terminals.

87. **Answer B.** listed for such use

    Conductors shall be spliced or joined with splicing devices identified for the use or by brazing, welding, or soldering with a fusible metal or alloy. Soldered splices shall first be spliced or joined so as to be mechanically and electrically secure without solder and then be soldered. All splices and joints and the free ends of conductors shall be covered with an insulation equivalent to that of the conductors or with an identified insulating device.

    Wire connectors or splicing means installed on conductors for direct burial shall be listed for such use.

    Reference: 2017 National Electrical Code – Chapter 1 General, Article 110 Requirements for Electrical Installation. 110.14 Electrical Connections. 110.14(B) Splices.

88. **Answer C.** lowest

    The temperature rating associated with the ampacity of a conductor shall be selected and coordinated so as not to exceed the lowest temperature rating of any connected termination, conductor, or device. Conductors with temperature ratings higher than specified for terminations shall be permitted to be used for ampacity adjustment, correction, or both.

    Reference: 2017 National Electrical Code – Chapter 1 General, Article 110 Requirements for Electrical Installation. 110.14 Electrical Connections. 110.14(C) Temperature Limitations.

89. **Answer C.** 65 amperes

    The temperature rating associated with the ampacity of a conductor shall be selected and coordinated so as not to exceed the lowest temperature rating of any connected termination, conductor, or device. Conductors with temperature ratings higher than specified for terminations shall be permitted to be used for ampacity adjustment, correction, or both.

    Reference: 2017 National Electrical Code – Chapter 1 General, Article 110 Requirements for Electrical Installation. 110.14 Electrical Connections. 110.14(C) Temperature Limitations.

90. **Answer B.** 85 amperes

    Size 3 AWG THHN ampacity before derating – 110 amperes (90°C Column)

    110 amperes x .96 (temperature correction) = 105.6 amperes

    NOTE: Size 3 AWG (60°C Column) with an allowable ampacity of 85 amperes should be selected

    The temperature rating associated with the ampacity of a conductor shall be selected and coordinated so as not to exceed the lowest temperature rating of any connected termination, conductor, or device. Conductors with temperature ratings higher than specified for terminations shall be permitted to be used for ampacity adjustment, correction, or both.

    Reference: 2017 National Electrical Code – Chapter 1 General, Article 110 Requirements for Electrical Installation. 110.14 Electrical Connections. 110.14(C) Temperature Limitations

    Where more than one ampacity applies for a given circuit length, the lowest value shall be used.

    Reference: 2017 National Electrical Code – Chapter 3 Wiring Methods and Materials, Article 310 Conductors for General Wiring. 310.15 Ampacities for Conductors Rated 0-2000 Volts. 310.15(A) General. 310.15(A)(2) Selection of Ampacity.

EXAM 3

EXAM 3 ANSWERS

91. **Answer C.** orange

    On a 4-wire, delta-connected system where the midpoint of one phase winding is grounded, only the conductor or bus bar having the higher phase voltage to ground shall be durably and permanently marked by an outer finish that is orange in color or by other effective means. Such identification shall be placed at each point on the system where a connection is made if the grounded conductor is also present.

    Reference: 2017 National Electrical Code – Chapter 1 General, Article 110 Requirements for Electrical Installation. 110.15 High-Leg Marking.

92. **Answer B.** Orange

    On a 4-wire, delta-connected system where the midpoint of one phase winding is grounded, only the conductor or bus bar having the higher phase voltage to ground shall be durably and permanently marked by an outer finish that is orange in color or by other effective means. Such identification shall be placed at each point on the system where a connection is made if the grounded conductor is also present.

    Reference: 2017 National Electrical Code – Chapter 1 General, Article 110 Requirements for Electrical Installation. 110.15 High-Leg Marking.

93. **Answer B.** orange

    On a 4-wire, delta-connected system where the midpoint of one phase winding is grounded, only the conductor or busbar having the higher phase voltage to ground shall be durably and permanently marked by an outer finish that is orange in color or by other effective means. Such identification shall be placed at each point on the system where a connection is made if the grounded conductor is also present.

    Reference: 2017 National Electrical Code – Chapter 1 General, Article 110 Requirements for Electrical Installation. 110.15 High-Leg Marking.

94. **Answer A.** combustible material.

    Parts of electrical equipment that in ordinary operation produce arcs, sparks, flames, or molten metal shall be enclosed or separated and isolated from all combustible material.

    Informational Note: For hazardous (classified) locations, see Articles 500 through 517. For motors, see 430.14.

    Reference: 2017 National Electrical Code – Chapter 1 General, Article 110 Requirements for Electrical Installation. 110.18 Arcing Parts.

EXAM 3 ANSWERS

EXAM 3

EXAM 3 ANSWERS

95. **Answer C.** disconnecting

    Each disconnecting means shall be legibly marked to indicate its purpose unless located and arranged so the purpose is evident. The marking shall be of sufficient durability to withstand the environment involved.

    Reference: 2017 National Electrical Code – Chapter 1 General, Article 110 Requirements for Electrical Installation. 110.22 Identification of Disconnecting Means. 110.22(A) General.

96. **Answer D.** working

    Review Table 110.26(A)(1) Working Spaces. on page 70-40

    Access and working space shall be provided and maintained about all electrical equipment to permit ready and safe operation and maintenance of such equipment.

    Reference: 2017 National Electrical Code – Chapter 1 General, Article 110 Requirements for Electrical Installation. 110.26 Spaces About Electrical Equipment.

97. **Answer C.** 3 feet

    The depth of the working space in the direction of live parts shall not be less than that specified in Table 110.26(A)(1) unless the requirements of 110.26(A)(1)(a), (A)(1)(b), or (A)(1)(c) are met. Distances shall be measured from the exposed live parts or from the enclosure or opening if the live parts are enclosed.

    Reference: 2017 National Electrical Code – Chapter 1 General, Article 110 Requirements for Electrical Installation. 110.26 Spaces About Electrical Equipment. 110.26(A) Working Space. 110.26(A)(1) Depth of Working Space. Table 110.26(A)(1) Working Spaces (page 70-40)

98. **Answer C.** 4 feet

    The depth of the working space in the direction of live parts shall not be less than that specified in Table 110.26(A)(1) unless the requirements of 110.26(A)(1)(a), (A)(1)(b), or (A)(1)(c) are met. Distances shall be measured from the exposed live parts or from the enclosure or opening if the live parts are enclosed.

    Reference: 2017 National Electrical Code – Chapter 1 General, Article 110 Requirements for Electrical Installation. 110.26 Spaces About Electrical Equipment. 110.26(A) Working Space. 110.26(A)(1) Depth of Working Space. Table 110.26(A)(1) Working Spaces (page 70-40)

99. **Answer C.** 30 in.

    Working space shall not be required in the back or sides of assemblies, such as dead-front switchboards, switchgear, or motor control centers, where all connections and all renewable or adjustable parts, such as fuses or switches, are accessible from locations other than the back or sides. Where rear access is required to work on nonelectrical parts on the back of enclosed equipment, a minimum horizontal working space of 762 mm (30 in.) shall be provided.

    Reference: 2017 National Electrical Code – Chapter 1 General, Article 110 Requirements for Electrical Installation. 110.26 Spaces About Electrical Equipment. . 110.26(A) Working Space. 110.26(A)(1) Depth of Working Space. 110.26(A)(1)(a) Dead-Front Assemblies.

100. **Answer A.** 30, 90

    The width of the working space in front of the electrical equipment shall be the width of the equipment or 762 mm (30 in.), whichever is greater. In all cases, the work space shall permit at least a 90 degree opening of equipment doors or hinged panels.

    Reference: 2017 National Electrical Code – Chapter 1 General, Article 110 Requirements for Electrical Installation. 110.26 Spaces About Electrical Equipment. . 110.26(A) Working Space. 110.26(A)(2) Width of Working Space.

101. **Answer D.** 30 inches

    The width of the working space in front of the electrical equipment shall be the width of the equipment or 762 mm (30 in.), whichever is greater. In all cases, the work space shall permit at least a 90 degree opening of equipment doors or hinged panels.

    Reference: 2017 National Electrical Code – Chapter 1 General, Article 110 Requirements for Electrical Installation. 110.26 Spaces About Electrical Equipment. 110.26(A) Working Space. 110.26(A)(2) Width of Working Space.

102. **Answer C.** 30 in.

    The width of the working space in front of the electrical equipment shall be the width of the equipment or 762 mm (30 in.), whichever is greater. In all cases, the work space shall permit at least a 90 degree opening of equipment doors or hinged panels.

    Reference: 2017 National Electrical Code – Chapter 1 General, Article 110 Requirements for Electrical Installation. 110.26 Spaces About Electrical Equipment. . 110.26(A) Working Space. 110.26(A)(2) Width of Working Space.

EXAM 3

EXAM 3 ANSWERS

103. Answer B.   30 inches

The width of the working space in front of the electrical equipment shall be the width of the equipment or 762 mm (30 in.), whichever is greater. In all cases, the work space shall permit at least a 90 degree opening of equipment doors or hinged panels.

Reference: 2017 National Electrical Code – Chapter 1 General, Article 110 Requirements for Electrical Installations. 110.26 Spaces About Electrical Equipment. 110.26(A) Working Space. 110.26(A)(2) Width of Working Space.

104. Answer C.   6 feet, 6 inches

The work space shall be clear and extend from the grade, floor, or platform to a height of 2.0 m (6-1/2 ft.) or the height of the equipment, whichever is greater. Within the height requirements of this section, other equipment that is associated with the electrical installation and is located above or below the electrical equipment shall be permitted to extend not more than 150 mm (6 in.) beyond the front of the electrical equipment.

Reference: 2017 National Electrical Code – Chapter 1 General, Article 110 Requirements for Electrical Installation. 110.26 Spaces About Electrical Equipment. 110.26(A) Working Space. 110.26(A)(3) Height of Working Space.

105. Answer A.   1

At least one entrance of sufficient area shall be provided to give access to and egress from working space about electrical equipment.

Reference: 2017 National Electrical Code – Chapter 1 General, Article 110 Requirements for Electrical Installation. 110.26 Spaces About Electrical Equipment. . 110.26(C) Entrance to and Egress from Working Space. 110.26(C)(1) Minimum Required.

106. Answer B.   24, 6-1/2

For equipment rated 1200 amperes or more and over 1.8 m (6 ft.) wide that contains overcurrent devices, switching devices, or control devices, there shall be one entrance to and egress from the required working space not less than 610 mm (24 in.) wide and 2.0 m (6-1/2 ft.) high at each end of the working space.

A single entrance to and egress from the required working space shall be permitted where either of the conditions in 110.26(C)(2)(a) or (C)(2)(b) is met.

Reference: 2017 National Electrical Code – Chapter 1 General, Article 110 Requirements for Electrical Installation. 110.26 Spaces About Electrical Equipment. . 110.26(C) Entrance to and Egress from Working Space. 110.26(C)(2) Large Equipment.

107. Answer B.   800 amperes

Where equipment rated 800 A or more that contains overcurrent devices, switching devices, or control devices is installed and there is a personnel door(s) intended for entrance to and egress from the working space less than 7.6 m (25 ft.) from the nearest edge of the working space, the door(s) shall open in the direction of egress and be equipped with listed panic hardware.

Reference: 2017 National Electrical Code – Chapter 1 General, Article 110 Requirements for Electrical Installation. 110.26 Spaces About Electrical Equipment. 110.26(C) Entrance to and Egress from Working Space. 110.26(C)(3) Personnel Doors.

108. Answer A.   damage

All switchboards, switch-gear, panelboards, and motor control centers shall be located in dedicated spaces and protected from damage.

Reference: 2017 National Electrical Code – Chapter 1 General, Article 110 Requirements for Electrical Installation. 110.26 Spaces About Electrical Equipment. . 110.26(E) Dedicated Equipment Space.

EXAM 3

EXAM 3 ANSWERS

109. Answer A.   dedicated

All switchboards, switch-gear, panelboards, and motor control centers shall be located in dedicated spaces and protected from damage.

Reference: 2017 National Electrical Code – Chapter 1 General, Article 110 Requirements for Electrical Installation. 110.26 Spaces About Electrical Equipment. 110.26(E) Dedicated Equipment Space.

110. Answer C.   6

The space equal to the width and depth of the equipment and extending from the floor to a height of 1.8 m (6 ft.) above the equipment or to the structural ceiling, whichever is lower, shall be dedicated to the electrical installation. No piping, ducts, leak protection apparatus, or other equipment foreign to the electrical installation shall be located in this zone.

Reference: 2017 National Electrical Code – Chapter 1 General, Article 110 Requirements for Electrical Installation. 110.26 Spaces About Electrical Equipment. . 110.26(E) Dedicated Equipment Space. 110.26(E)(1) Indoor. 110.26(E)(1)(a) Dedicated Electrical Space.

111. Answer B.   qualified

Electrical equipment rooms or enclosures housing electrical apparatus that are controlled by a lock(s) shall be considered accessible to qualified persons.

Reference: 2017 National Electrical Code – Chapter 1 General, Article 110 Requirements for Electrical Installation. 110.26 Spaces About Electrical Equipment. . 110.26(F) Locked Electrical Equipment Rooms or Enclosures.

112. Answer B.   50

Review the 4 approved ways.

Except as elsewhere required or permitted by this Code, live parts of electrical equipment operating at 50 volts or more shall be guarded against accidental contact by approved enclosures or by any of the following means:

(1) By location in a room, vault, or similar enclosure that is accessible only to qualified persons.

(2) By suitable permanent, substantial partitions or screens arranged so that only qualified persons have access to the space within reach of the live parts. Any openings in such partitions or screens shall be sized and located so that persons are not likely to come into accidental contact with the live parts or to bring conducting objects into contact with them.

(3) By location on a suitable balcony, gallery, or platform elevated and arranged so as to exclude unqualified persons.

(4) By elevation above the floor or other working surface as shown in 110.27(A)(4)(a) or (b) below:

   a. A minimum of 2.5 m (8 ft.) for 50 to 300 volts

   b. A minimum of 2.6 m (8-1/2 ft.) for 301 to 600 volts

Reference: 2017 National Electrical Code – Chapter 1 General, Article 110 Requirements for Electrical Installation. 110.27 Guarding of Live Parts. 110.27(A) Live Parts Guarded Against Accidental Contact.

EXAM 3

EXAM 3 ANSWERS

113. **Answer B.** 50

    Except as elsewhere required or permitted by this Code, live parts of electrical equipment operating at 50 volts or more shall be guarded against accidental contact by approved enclosures or by any of the following means:

    (1) By location in a room, vault, or similar enclosure that is accessible only to qualified persons.

    (2) By suitable permanent, substantial partitions or screens arranged so that only qualified persons have access to the space within reach of the live parts. Any openings in such partitions or screens shall be sized and located so that persons are not likely to come into accidental contact with the live parts or to bring conducting objects into contact with them.

    (3) By location on a suitable balcony, gallery, or platform elevated and arranged so as to exclude unqualified persons.

    (4) By elevation above the floor or other working surface as shown in 110.27(A)(4)(a) or (b) below:

    a. A minimum of 2.5 m (8 ft.) for 50 to 300 volts

    b. A minimum of 2.6 m (8-1/2 ft.) for 301 to 600 volts

    Reference: 2017 National Electrical Code – Chapter 1 General, Article 110 Requirements for Electrical Installation. 110.27 Guarding of Live Parts. . 110.27(A) Live Parts Guarded Against Accidental Contact.

114. **Answer C.** guards

    In locations where electrical equipment is likely to be exposed to physical damage, enclosures or guards shall be so arranged and of such strength as to prevent such damage.

    Reference: 2017 National Electrical Code – Chapter 1 General, Article 110 Requirements for Electrical Installation. 110.27 Guarding of Live Parts. 110.27(B) Prevent Physical Damage.

115. **Answer C.** permanent ladders or stairways

    Permanent ladders or stairways shall be provided to give safe access to the working space around electrical equipment installed on platforms, balconies, or mezzanine floors or in attic or roof rooms or spaces.

    Reference: 2017 National Electrical Code – Chapter 1 General, Article 110 Requirements for Electrical Installation. 110.33 Entrance to Enclosures and Access to Working Space. 110.33(B) Access.

116. **Answer D.** the observation of a qualified person at all times

    The entrance to all buildings, vaults, rooms, or enclosures containing exposed live parts or exposed conductors operating at over 600 volts, nominal, shall be kept locked unless such entrances are under the observation of a qualified person at all times.

    Permanent and conspicuous danger signs shall be provided. The danger sign shall meet the requirements in 110.21(B) and shall read as follows:

    DANGER - HIGH VOLTAGE - KEEP OUT

    Reference: 2017 National Electrical Code – Chapter 1 General, Article 110 Requirements for Electrical Installation. 110.34 Work Space and Guarding. 110.34(C) Locked Rooms or Enclosures.

117. **Answer C.** conform with 490.24

    Circuit conductors shall be permitted to be installed in raceways; in cable trays; as metal-clad cable Type MC; as bare wire, cable, and busbars; or as Type MV cables or conductors as provided in 300.37, 300.39, 300.40, and 300.50. Bare live conductors shall comply with 490.24.

    Insulators, together with their mounting and conductor attachments, where used as supports for wires, single-conductor cables, or busbars, shall be capable of safely withstanding the maximum magnetic forces that would prevail if two or more conductors of a circuit were subjected to short-circuit current.

    Exposed runs of insulated wires and cables that have a bare lead sheath or a braided outer covering shall be supported in a manner designed to prevent physical damage to the braid or sheath. Supports for lead-covered cables shall be designed to prevent electrolysis of the sheath.

    Reference: 2017 National Electrical Code – Chapter 1 General, Article 110 Requirements for Electrical Installation. 110.36 Circuit Conductors.

118. **Answer C.** 90

    Conductors shall be permitted to be terminated based on the 90°C (194°F) temperature rating and ampacity as given in Table 310.60(C)(67) through Table 310.60(C)(86), unless otherwise identified.

    Reference: 2017 National Electrical Code – Chapter 1 General, Article 110 Requirements for Electrical Installation. 110.40 Temperature Limitations at Terminations.

EXAM 3

EXAM 3 ANSWERS

119. **Answer A.** above the tunnel floor

    Conductors and cables in tunnels shall be located above the tunnel floor and so placed or guarded to protect them from physical damage.

    Reference: 2017 National Electrical Code – Chapter 1 General, Article 110 Requirements for Electrical Installation. 110.51 General. 110.51(C) Protection Against Physical Damage.

120. **Answer B.** 1000

    All non-current-carrying metal parts of electrical equipment and all metal raceways and cable sheaths shall be solidly grounded and bonded to all metal pipes and rails at the portal and at intervals not exceeding 300 m (1000 ft.) throughout the tunnel.

    Reference: 2017 National Electrical Code – Chapter 1 General, Article 110 Requirements for Electrical Installation. 110.54 Bonding and Equipment Grounding Conductors. 110.54(A) Grounded and Bonded.

121. **Answer B.** 26 inches

    Rectangular access openings shall not be less than 650 mm x 550 mm (26 in. x 22 in.). Round access openings in a manhole shall be not less than 650 mm (26 in.) in diameter.

    Reference: 2017 National Electrical Code – Chapter 1 General, Article 110 Requirements for Electrical Installations. 110.75 Access to Manholes. 110.75(A) Dimensions.

EXAM 4

Chapter 2 Wiring and Protection 01

1. How should an insulated grounded conductor 6 AWG or smaller be identified?

   A. 3 continuous white stripes on entire length on any but green insulation.

   B. A continuous gray outer finish.

   C. A continuous white outer finish.

   D. Any of the above and more options are available.

   Reference: 2017 National Electrical Code – Chapter 2 Wiring and Protection, Article 200 Use and Identification of Grounded Conductors. 200.6 Means of Identifying Grounded Conductors. 200.6(A) Sizes 6 AWG or Smaller.

2. What is one method of marking an insulated grounded conductor when it is larger than 6 AWG?

   A. by noting which terminal to which it is connected

   B. by using a bare copper conductor

   C. distinctive green marking around terminations when installed

   D. when installed, distinctive white or gray mark around termination

   Reference: 2017 National Electrical Code – Chapter 2 Wiring and Protection, Article 200 Use and Identification of Grounded Conductors. 200.6 Means of Identifying Grounded Conductors. 200.6(B) Sizes 4 AWG or Larger.

3. An insulated grounded conductor larger than _____ AWG shall be permitted to be marked with white tape at the time of installation.

   A. 2

   B. 4

   C. 8

   D. 10

   Reference: 2017 National Electrical Code – Chapter 2 Wiring and Protection, Article 200 Use and Identification of Grounded Conductors. 200.6 Means of Identifying Grounded Conductors. 200.6(B) Sizes 4 AWG or Larger.

Chapter 2 Wiring and Protection 01

EXAM 4

Chapter 2 Wiring and Protection 01

4. Grounded (neutral) conductors larger than size 4 AWG may be identified by the terminations having _____ colored phase tape, at the time of installation.

   A. blue

   B. orange

   C. red

   D. white

   Reference: 2017 National Electrical Code – Chapter 2 Wiring and Protection, Article 200 Use and Identification of Grounded Conductors. 200.6 Means of Identifying Grounded Conductors. 200.6(B) Sizes 4 AWG or Larger. 200.6(B)(4)

5. When an insulated conductor is intended to be used as a grounded conductor and contained inside a flexible cord, it should be identified with an _____ outer finish or other methods allowed by Article 400.22.

   A. bare

   B. green

   C. varnished

   D. white or gray

   Reference: 2017 National Electrical Code – Chapter 2 Wiring and Protection, Article 200 Use and Identification of Grounded Conductors. 200.6 Means of Identifying Grounded Conductors. 200.6(C) Flexible Cords.

6. When you see an insulated black conductor with three (3) continuous white stripes along its entire length, you know it is a:

   A. equipment grounding conductor

   B. grounded conductor

   C. phase of a delta-connected system

   D. ungrounded conductor

   Reference: 2017 National Electrical Code – Chapter 2 Wiring and Protection, Article 200 Use and Identification of Grounded Conductors. 200.7 Use of Insulation of a White or Gray Color or with Three Continuous White or Gray Stripes. 200.7(A) General. 200.7(A)(2)

EXAM 4

Chapter 2 Wiring and Protection 01

7. The identification of terminals to which a *grounded* conductor is to be substantially _____ in color.

   A. blue   C. white

   B. green   D. yellow

   Reference: 2017 National Electrical Code – Chapter 2 Wiring and Protection, Article 200 Use and Identification of Grounded Conductors. 200.9 Means of Identification of Terminals.

8. Terminals that a grounded conductor is to be connected to should be primarily _____, and other terminals should be a color that is easily differentiated.

   A. black   C. green

   B. gold   D. white

   Reference: 2017 National Electrical Code – Chapter 2 Wiring and Protection, Article 200 Use and Identification of Grounded Conductors. 200.9 Means of Identification of Terminals.

9. For devices with screw shells, the terminal for the _____ conductor shall be the one connected to the screw shell.

   A. bare   C. insulated

   B. grounded   D. ungrounded

   Reference: 2017 National Electrical Code – Chapter 2 Wiring and Protection, Article 200 Use and Identification of Grounded Conductors. 200.10 Identification of Terminals. 200.10(C) Screw Shells.

10. The conductor attached to a screw shell device with attached leads must have a _____ finish, and the outer finish of the other conductor must be a solid color that will not be mistaken for the color of the grounded conductor terminal.

    A. black   C. green

    B. gold   D. white or gray

    Reference: 2017 National Electrical Code – Chapter 2 Wiring and Protection, Article 200 Use and Identification of Grounded Conductors. 200.10 Identification of Terminals. 200.10(D) Screw Shell Devices with Leads.

EXAM 4

Chapter 2 Wiring and Protection 01

11. Of the following, as outlined in the code, which is not defined as a special purpose branch circuit?

    A. Circuits and equipment operating at less than 50 volts.

    B. Cranes and hoists

    C. Fixed electric space-heating equipment

    D. High pressure sodium parking lot lighting

    Reference: 2017 National Electrical Code – Chapter 2 Wiring and Protection, Article 210 Branch Circuits. 210.2 Other Articles for Specific-Purpose Branch Circuits.

12. If a branch circuit served by size 12 AWG conductors is protected by a 15-ampere circuit breaker, what kind of rating does it have?

    A. 10 ampere

    B. 15 ampere

    C. 20 ampere

    D. 25 ampere

    Reference: 2017 National Electrical Code – Chapter 2 Wiring and Protection, Article 210 Branch Circuits. 210.3 Rating.

13. All conductors in a multiwire circuit must originate from the same _____ or similar distribution equipment.

    A. junction box

    B. location

    C. meter

    D. panelboard

    Reference: 2017 National Electrical Code – Chapter 2 Wiring and Protection, Article 210 Branch Circuits. 210.4 Multiwire Branch Circuits. 210.4(A) General.

EXAM 4

Chapter 2 Wiring and Protection 01

14. On branch circuits, the nominal voltage must not be more than _____ between conductors in dwelling units, guest rooms or suites of hotels, motels, and other similar occupancies that supply the terminals of lighting fixtures (luminaries) and cord-and-plug-connected loads of up to 1440 volt-amperes, nominal, or up to 1/4hp.

    A. 110   C. 220

    B. 120   D. 400

    Reference: 2017 National Electrical Code – Chapter 2 Wiring and Protection, Article 210 Branch Circuits. 210.6 Branch-Circuit Voltage Limitations. . 210.6(A) Occupancy Limitation.

15. For conductors on a branch circuit that supplies luminaires in a residence, what is the maximum allowable voltage between conductors on a branch circuit supplying luminaires in a residence?

    A. 120 volts   C. 240 volts

    B. 150 volts   D. 250 volts

    Reference: 2017 National Electrical Code – Chapter 2 Wiring and Protection, Article 210 Branch Circuits. 210.6 Branch-Circuit Voltage Limitations. 210.6(A) Occupancy Limitation.

16. Which of the following is allowed to be supplied by circuits not exceeding 120 volts, nominal, between conductors?

    A. Auxiliary equipment of electric-discharge lamps

    B. Cord-and-plug-connected or permanently connected utilization equipment

    C. The terminals of lampholders applied within their voltage ratings

    D. All of the above

    Reference: 2017 National Electrical Code – Chapter 2 Wiring and Protection, Article 210 Branch Circuits. 210.6 Branch-Circuit Voltage Limitations. . 210.6(B) 120 Volts Between Conductors.

EXAM 4

Chapter 2 Wiring and Protection 01

17. A way to _____ ungrounded conductors supplying devices or equipment supplied on the same yoke by two or more branch circuits must be made available where the branch circuits start.

    A. connect

    B. disconnect

    C. energize

    D. simultaneously disconnect

    Reference: 2017 National Electrical Code – Chapter 2 Wiring and Protection, Article 210 Branch Circuits. 210.7 Multiple Branch Circuits.

18. True or False: In dwelling units, all 125-volt, single phase, 15- and 20-ampere receptacles installed in the following locations shall have ground-fault circuit-interrupter (GFCI) protection for personnel; Bathrooms, Unfinished basements, Garages, Kitchen countertops, Outdoors, Crawl spaces, Boathouses; Laundry, utility, and sinks not in a kitchen.

    A. True

    B. False

    Reference: 2017 National Electrical Code – Chapter 2 Wiring and Protection, Article 210 Branch Circuits. 210.8 Ground-Fault Circuit-Interrupter Protection for Personnel. 210.8(A) Dwelling Units.

19. All 125-volt, single-phase, 15- and 20-ampere receptacles in dwelling units that are installed in _____ must have ground-fault circuit-interrupter protection for personnel. Exceptions ignored.

    A. Bathrooms

    B. Bedrooms

    C. Garages, & other accessory buildings with a floor at or below grade

    D. Both A and C

    Reference: 2017 National Electrical Code – Chapter 2 Wiring and Protection, Article 210 Branch Circuits. 210.8 Ground-Fault Circuit-Interrupter Protection for Personnel. . 210.8(A) Dwelling Units.

EXAM 4

Chapter 2 Wiring and Protection 01

20. If 15- and 20-ampere, 125-volt, single-phase receptacles are installed in a residential garage, they must be:

    A. a single receptacle

    B. provided with a metal faceplate

    C. provided with AFCI protection

    D. provided with GFCI protection

    Reference: 2017 National Electrical Code – Chapter 2 Wiring and Protection, Article 210 Branch Circuits. 210.8 Ground-Fault Circuit-Interrupter Protection for Personnel. 210.8(A) Dwelling Units.

21. Where receptacles in kitchens are made available to serve countertop surfaces, what is the distance that the outlets must be GFCI protected?

    A. within 3 ft. of the sink

    B. within 6 ft. of the sink

    C. within 24 ft. of the sink

    D. all of these

    Reference: 2017 National Electrical Code – Chapter 2 Wiring and Protection, Article 210 Branch Circuits. 210.8 Ground-Fault Circuit-Interrupter Protection for Personnel. . 210.8(A) Dwelling Units. . 210.8(A)(6)

22. Which of the following statements is correct regarding GFCI protection for a 125-volt receptacle outlet installed on a residence kitchen island countertop, 8 feet from the kitchen sink?

    A. not required if receptacle is not within 6 feet of the sink.

    B. not required on receptacles on kitchen islands.

    C. required for countertop receptacles in residential kitchen

    D. None of the above.

    Reference: 2017 National Electrical Code – Chapter 2 Wiring and Protection, Article 210 Branch Circuits. 210.8 Ground-Fault Circuit-Interrupter Protection for Personnel. 210.8(A) Dwelling Units. 210.8(A)(6)

Chapter 2 Wiring and Protection 01

EXAM 4

Chapter 2 Wiring and Protection 01

23. GFCI protection must be provided in dwelling units, where 125-volt, single-phase receptacle outlets are installed within what distance from the outer edge of a laundry room sink?

    A. 5 feet

    B. 6 feet

    C. 8 feet

    D. 10 feet

    Reference: 2017 National Electrical Code – Chapter 2 Wiring and Protection, Article 210 Branch Circuits. 210.8 Ground-Fault Circuit-Interrupter Protection for Personnel. 210.8(A) Dwelling Units. 210.8(A)(7) Sinks

24. Sinks located in areas other than kitchens where receptacles are installed within _____ feet of the outside edge of the sink, require GFCI protection.

    A. 2

    B. 5

    C. 6

    D. 10

    Reference: 2017 National Electrical Code – Chapter 2 Wiring and Protection, Article 210 Branch Circuits. 210.8 Ground-Fault Circuit-Interrupter Protection for Personnel. 210.8(A) Dwelling Units. 210.8(A)(7) Sinks

25. GFCI protection must be provided in dwelling units for all 15- and 20-ampere 125-volt receptacles located within what distance from the outer edge of a bathtub or shower stall?

    A. 4 feet

    B. 6 feet

    C. 8 feet

    D. 10 feet

    Reference: 2017 National Electrical Code – Chapter 2 Wiring and Protection, Article 210 Branch Circuits. 210.8 Ground-Fault Circuit-Interrupter Protection for Personnel. 210.8(A) Dwelling Units. 210.8(A)(9)

26. For protection of personnel, all 15- and 20 ampere, 125-volt, single-phase receptacles installed on rooftops other than dwelling units shall have:

    A. AFCI protection

    B. GFCI protection

    C. Both A and B

    D. Neither A nor B

    Reference: 2017 National Electrical Code – Chapter 2 Wiring and Protection, Article 210 Branch Circuits. 210.8 Ground-Fault Circuit-Interrupter Protection for Personnel. 210.8(B) Other Than Dwelling Units. 210.8(B)(3)

EXAM 4

Chapter 2 Wiring and Protection 01

27. Outlets that supply boat hoists installed in dwelling unit locations and supplied by _____ shall have ground-fault circuit-interrupter protection for personnel.

    A. all 125-volt, 15- and 20-ampere or greater branch circuits

    B. all 20-ampere branch circuits

    C. outlets not exceeding 240 volts

    D. three wire branch circuits 125-volt, 15- and 20-ampere

    Reference: 2017 National Electrical Code – Chapter 2 Wiring and Protection, Article 210 Branch Circuits. 210.8 Ground-Fault Circuit-Interrupter Protection for Personnel. 210.8(C) Boat Hoists.

28. If there is a grounded neutral conductor, two-wire DC circuits and AC circuits of two or more _____ may be allowed to be tapped from the _____ conductors of the circuits.

    A. grounded

    B. grounding

    C. hot leg

    D. ungrounded

    Reference: 2017 National Electrical Code – Chapter 2 Wiring and Protection, Article 210 Branch Circuits. 210.10 Ungrounded Conductors Tapped from Grounded Systems.

29. The total _____ load and the rating or size of circuits used will determine the minimum number of branch circuits.

    A. amperage

    B. area of

    C. calculated

    D. voltage

    Reference: 2017 National Electrical Code – Chapter 2 Wiring and Protection, Article 210 Branch Circuits. 210.11 Branch Circuits Required. . 210.11(A) Number of Branch Circuits.

Chapter 2 Wiring and Protection 01   75

EXAM 4

Chapter 2 Wiring and Protection 01

30. If a load calculation is based on volt-amperes per square foot or per square meter, the wiring system up to and including the branch-circuit panelboard(s) must be made available to serve at least the calculated load. The load must be _____ among multioutlet branch circuits inside the panelboard(s). Branch-circuit overcurrent devices and circuits may only be required to be installed to accommodate the connected load.

    A. connected in parallel

    B. concentrated

    C. determined and calculated

    D. evenly proportioned

    Reference: 2017 National Electrical Code – Chapter 2 Wiring and Protection, Article 210 Branch Circuits. 210.11 Branch Circuits Required. . 210.11(B) Load Evenly Proportioned Among Branch Circuits.

31. What total minimum volt-amperes (VA) shall be included when calculating the demand load for small-appliance and laundry circuit loads a one-family dwelling?

    A. 1,500 VA

    B. 3,000 VA

    C. 4,500 VA

    D. 6,000 VA

    Reference: 2017 National Electrical Code – Chapter 2 Wiring and Protection, Article 210 Branch Circuits. 210.11 Branch Circuits Required. 210.11(C) Dwelling Units. 210.11(C)(1)&(2)

    Reference: 2017 National Electrical Code – Chapter 2 Wiring and Protection, Article 220 Branch-Circuit, Feeder, and Service Calculations. 220.52 Small Appliance and Laundry Loads – Dwelling Unit. 220.52(A)&(B)

32. Which of the following outlet(s) are permitted to be connected to the branch-circuit provided to supply the laundry room receptacle outlet(s) in dwelling units?

    A. Luminaires in the laundry room.

    B. One receptacle outlet only in the hallway.

    C. Receptacle outlets in the bathroom.

    D. None of these.

    Reference: 2017 National Electrical Code – Chapter 2 Wiring and Protection, Article 210 Branch Circuits. 210.11 Branch Circuits Required. 210.11(C) Dwelling Units. 210.11(C)(2) Laundry Branch Circuits.

EXAM 4

Chapter 2 Wiring and Protection 01

33. What is the minimum supply for receptacle outlets in a dwelling unit that has more than one bathroom?

    A. one 15-ampere branch circuit which may also serve bathroom lighting

    B. one 15-ampere branch circuit which supplies no other outlets

    C. one 20-ampere branch circuit which may also serve bathroom lighting

    D. one 20-ampere branch circuit which supplies no other outlets

    Reference: 2017 National Electrical Code – Chapter 2 Wiring and Protection, Article 210 Branch Circuits. 210.11 Branch Circuits Required. 210.11(C) Dwelling Units. 210.11(C)(3) Bathroom Branch Circuits.

34. True or False: At least one 20-ampere branch circuit shall be provided to supply the bathroom receptacle(s). Such circuit shall have no other outlets.

    A. True

    B. False

    Reference: 2017 National Electrical Code – Chapter 2 Wiring and Protection, Article 210 Branch Circuits. 210.11 Branch Circuits Required. 210.11(C) Dwelling Units. 210.11(C)(3) Bathroom Branch Circuits.

35. All 120-volt, single phase, 15- and 20-ampere branch circuits supplying outlets installed in dwelling unit _____ shall be protected by a listed arc-fault circuit interrupter, combination type installed to provide protection of the branch circuit.

    A. bathrooms

    B. bedrooms

    C. kitchens

    D. laundry rooms

    Reference: 2017 National Electrical Code – Chapter 2 Wiring and Protection, Article 210 Branch Circuits. 210.12 Arc-Fault Circuit-Interrupter Protection. 210.12(A) Dwelling Unit.

EXAM 4

Chapter 2 Wiring and Protection 01

36. Listed arc-fault circuit interrupters should protect all 120-volt, single-phase, 15- and 20-ampere branch circuits in dwelling units, supplying outlets installed in:

    A. dining rooms

    B. hallways

    C. kitchens

    D. all of these locations

    Reference: 2017 National Electrical Code – Chapter 2 Wiring and Protection, Article 210 Branch Circuits. 210.12 Arc-Fault Circuit-Interrupter Protection. 210.12(A) Dwelling Units.

37. All 120-volt, single-phase, 15- and 20-ampere branch circuits supplying outlets in dwelling unit closets, dining rooms, family rooms, hallways, or similar areas or rooms must be protected by a listed _____ placed to give protection of the branch circuit.

    A. arc-fault circuit interrupter, combination-type

    B. bonded jumper

    C. fuse

    D. ground fault interrupter

    Reference: 2017 National Electrical Code – Chapter 2 Wiring and Protection, Article 210 Branch Circuits. 210.12 Arc-Fault Circuit-Interrupter Protection. . 210.12(A) Dwelling Units.

38. Branch-circuit conductors must have an ampacity of at least the _____ load to be served, for branch circuits of up to 600 volts.

    A. constant

    B. intermittent

    C. maximum

    D. minimum

    Reference: 2017 National Electrical Code – Chapter 2 Wiring and Protection, Article 210 Branch Circuits. 210.19 Conductors - Minimum Ampacity and Size. 210.19(A) Branch Circuits Not More Than 600 Volts. 210.19(A)(1) General.

EXAM 4

Chapter 2 Wiring and Protection 01

39. Where a branch circuit supplies continuous loads or any combination of continuous and noncontinuous loads, the minimum branch-circuit conductor size shall have an allowable ampacity not less than the noncontinuous load plus _____ percent of the continuous load.

    A. 75

    B. 80

    C. 100

    D. 125

    Reference: 2017 National Electrical Code – Chapter 2 Wiring and Protection, Article 210 Branch Circuits. 210.19 Conductors - Minimum Ampacity and Size. 210.19(A) Branch Circuits Not More Than 600 Volts. 210.19(A)(1) General.

40. Generally, what is the minimum required ampacity of branch circuit conductors serving continuous loads, such as fluorescent lighting in a retail shopping mall, office building, or school classroom?

    A. 80%

    B. 115%

    C. 125%

    D. 150%

    Reference: 2017 National Electrical Code – Chapter 2 Wiring and Protection, Article 210 Branch Circuits. 210.19 Conductors – Minimum Ampacity and Size. 210.19(A) Branch Circuits Not More Than 600 Volts. 210.19(A)(1) General.

41. When a branch circuit supplied any combination of noncontinuous and continuous l voads or continuous loads, the minimum branch-circuit conductor size, before the application of correction or adjustment factors, must have an allowable ampacity of at least _____ percent of the continuous load plus the noncontinuous load. Exceptions ignored.

    A. 50

    B. 75

    C. 100

    D. 125

    Reference: 2017 National Electrical Code – Chapter 2 Wiring and Protection, Article 210 Branch Circuits. 210.19 Conductors - Minimum Ampacity and Size. 210.19(A) Branch Circuits Not More Than 600 Volts. 210.19(A)(1) General.

Chapter 2 Wiring and Protection 01

EXAM 4

Chapter 2 Wiring and Protection 01

42. Conductors for branch circuits that supply more than one receptacle for _____ loads must have an ampacity of at least the rating of the branch circuit.

    A. cord-and-plug-connected portable

    B. most

    C. permanent

    D. washing machine

    Reference: 2017 National Electrical Code – Chapter 2 Wiring and Protection, Article 210 Branch Circuits. 210.19 Conductors - Minimum Ampacity and Size. 210.19(A) Branch Circuits Not More Than 600 Volts. 210.19(A)(2) Branch Circuits with More than One Receptacle.

43. For ranges of 8-3/4 kW or more rating, the minimum branch-circuit rating shall be _____ amperes.

    A. 10

    B. 20

    C. 40

    D. 50

    Reference: 2017 National Electrical Code – Chapter 2 Wiring and Protection, Article 210 Branch Circuits. 210.19 Conductors - Minimum Ampacity and Size. 210.19(A) Branch Circuits Not More Than 600 Volts. 210.19(A)(3) Household Ranges and Cooking Appliances.

44. Where a branch circuit supplies continuous loads or any combination of continuous and noncontinuous loads, the rating of the overcurrent device shall not be less than the noncontinuous load plus _____ percent of the continuous load.

    A. 75

    B. 80

    C. 100

    D. 125

    Reference: 2017 National Electrical Code – Chapter 2 Wiring and Protection, Article 210 Branch Circuits. 210.20 Overcurrent Protection. 210.20(A) Continuous and Noncontinuous Loads.

EXAM 4

Chapter 2 Wiring and Protection 01

45. If a branch circuit supplies any combination of noncontinuous and continuous loads, the overcurrent device rating must be at least _____ percent of the continuous load combined with the noncontinuous load.

    A. 80   C. 115

    B. 100   D. 125

    Reference: 2017 National Electrical Code – Chapter 2 Wiring and Protection, Article 210 Branch Circuits. 210.20 Overcurrent Protection. . 210.20(A) Continuous and Noncontinuous Loads.

46. Lampholders, where they are connected to a branch circuit with a rating of more than 20 amperes, must be of _____ and these lampholders must have a rating of at least 660 watts if of the admedium type, and at least 750 watts if of any other kind.

    A. heavy-duty type   C. high voltage

    B. high amperage   D. rough use

    Reference: 2017 National Electrical Code – Chapter 2 Wiring and Protection, Article 210 Branch Circuits. 210.21 Outlet Devices. . 210.21(A) Lampholders.

47. When a 20-ampere branch circuit serves a single receptacle outlet, the rating of the receptacle generally must be at least:

    A. 10 amperes   C. 16 amperes

    B. 15 amperes   D. 20 amperes

    Reference: 2017 National Electrical Code – Chapter 2 Wiring and Protection, Article 210 Branch Circuits. 210.21 Outlet Devices. 210.21(B) Receptacles. 210.21(B)(1) Single Receptacle on an Individual Branch Circuit.

48. If a single receptacle is installed on an individual branch circuit, it must have an ampere rating of not less than _____ of the branch circuit.

    A. 50%   C. 100%

    B. 80%   D. 125%

    Reference: 2017 National Electrical Code – Chapter 2 Wiring and Protection, Article 210 Branch Circuits. 210.21 Outlet Devices. 210.21(B) Receptacles. 210.21(B)(1) Single Receptacle on an Individual Branch Circuit.

EXAM 4

Chapter 2 Wiring and Protection 01

49. The ampere rating of a range receptacle in the 40 amp range circuit must be allowed to be _____ amps

    A. 40

    B. 50

    C. 40 or 50

    D. all of the above

    Reference: 2017 National Electrical Code – Chapter 2 Wiring and Protection, Article 210 Branch Circuits. 210.21 Outlet Devices. 210.21(B) Receptacles. 210.21(B)(3) Receptacle Ratings.

50. What ampere rating are receptacles required to have where two (2) or more general-purpose receptacle outlets are connected to a branch circuit with a rating of 20-amperes?

    A. 15 amperes

    B. 20 amperes

    C. either A or B

    D. neither A nor B

    Reference: 2017 National Electrical Code – Chapter 2 Wiring and Protection, Article 210 Branch Circuits. 210.21 Outlet Devices. 210.21(B) Receptacles.

51. On a 20 amp rated circuit, an outlet shall be rated at _____ amps.

    A. 15

    B. 20

    C. 30

    D. Either A or B

    Reference: 2017 National Electrical Code – Chapter 2 Wiring and Protection, Article 210 Branch Circuits. 210.21 Outlet Devices. 210.21(B) Receptacles. 210.21(B)(3) Receptacle Ratings.

52. True or False: A 15- or 20-ampere branch circuit may be allowed to supply lighting units, other utilization equipment, or a combination of both. Exceptions ignored.

    A. True

    B. False

    Reference: 2017 National Electrical Code – Chapter 2 Wiring and Protection, Article 210 Branch Circuits. 210.23 Permissible Loads, Multiple-Outlet Branch Circuits. 210.23(A) 15- and 20-Ampere Branch Circuits.

EXAM 4

Chapter 2 Wiring and Protection 01

53. What is the maximum rating allowed of any one cord-and-plug-connected appliance connected to a 20-ampere branch circuit?

    A. 10 amperes

    B. 16 amperes

    C. 20 amperes

    D. 25 amperes

    Reference: 2017 National Electrical Code – Chapter 2 Wiring and Protection, Article 210 Branch Circuits. 210.23 Permissible Loads, Multiple-Outlet Branch Circuits. 210.23(A) 15- and 20-Ampere Branch Circuits. 210.23(A)(1) Cord-and-Plug-Connected Equipment Not Fastened in Place.

54. Where a 30-ampere branch circuit is permitted for fixed lighting units with heavy-duty lampholders in anything other than a dwelling unit(s) or utilization equipment in any occupancy, the rating of any one cord-and-plug-connected utilization equipment must not be more than _____ percent of the ampere rating of the branch circuit.

    A. 50

    B. 80

    C. 100

    D. 125

    Reference: 2017 National Electrical Code – Chapter 2 Wiring and Protection, Article 210 Branch Circuits. 210.23 Permissible Loads, Multiple-Outlet Branch Circuits. 210.23(B) 30-Ampere Branch Circuits.

55. What is the maximum ampere rating for any single cord-and-plug-connected appliance connected to a 30-ampere rated branch circuit?

    A. 16 amperes

    B. 24 amperes

    C. 27 amperes

    D. 30 amperes

    Reference: 2017 National Electrical Code – Chapter 2 Wiring and Protection, Article 210 Branch Circuits. 210.23 Permissible Loads, Multiple-Outlet Branch Circuits. 210.23(B) 30-Ampere Branch Circuits.

EXAM 4

Chapter 2 Wiring and Protection 01

56. Branch circuits larger than _____ amperes shall supply only nonlighting outlet loads.

   A. 50
   B. 60
   C. 75
   D. 80

   Reference: 2017 National Electrical Code – Chapter 2 Wiring and Protection, Article 210 Branch Circuits. 210.23 Permissible Loads, Multiple-Outlet Branch Circuits. 210.23(D) Branch Circuits Larger Than 50 Amperes.

57. Only _____ outlet loads may be supplied by branch circuits of over 50 amperes.

   A. cooking equipment
   B. lighting
   C. non-lighting
   D. ranges

   Reference: 2017 National Electrical Code – Chapter 2 Wiring and Protection, Article 210 Branch Circuits. 210.23 Permissible Loads, Multiple-Outlet Branch Circuits. 210.23(D) Branch Circuits Larger Than 50 Amperes.

58. A 15-amp rated circuit requires a branch circuit copper conductor size of: No.:

   A. 10
   B. 12
   C. 14
   D. 18

   Reference: 2017 National Electrical Code – Chapter 2 Wiring and Protection, Article 210 Branch Circuits. 210.24 Branch-Circuit Requirements - Summary.

59. A 40-amp rated circuit requires a branch circuit copper conductor size of No.:

   A. 6
   B. 8
   C. 10
   D. 12

   Reference: 2017 National Electrical Code – Chapter 2 Wiring and Protection, Article 210 Branch Circuits. 210.24 Branch-Circuit Requirements - Summary.

EXAM 4

Chapter 2 Wiring and Protection 01

60. A 30-amp rated circuit requires a branch circuit copper conductor size of No.:

    A. 8   C. 12

    B. 10   D. 14

    Reference: 2017 National Electrical Code – Chapter 2 Wiring and Protection, Article 210 Branch Circuits. 210.24 Branch-Circuit Requirements - Summary.

61. Which of the following statements is true of a size 14 AWG branch-circuit conductor protected by a 15 ampere rated circuit breaker that is supplying three (3) 20 ampere rated duplex receptacles?

    A. 20 ampere rated receptacles do not comply with the NEC

    B. complies with the NEC.

    C. would comply with the NEC if the breaker was rated 20-amperes.

    D. would comply with the NEC if the wire was size 12 AWG.

    Reference: 2017 National Electrical Code – Chapter 2 Wiring and Protection, Article 210 Branch Circuits. 210.24 Branch-Circuit Requirements – Summary

62. Wherever flexible cords with attachment plugs are to be used, a receptacle outlet must be installed, and where such cords may be permanently connected, then receptacles are _____ for the same type of cords.

    A. installed   C. permanently installed

    B. marked   D. permitted to be omitted

    Reference: 2017 National Electrical Code – Chapter 2 Wiring and Protection, Article 210 Branch Circuits. 210.50 General. . 210.50(B) Cord Connections.

Chapter 2 Wiring and Protection 01

EXAM 4

Chapter 2 Wiring and Protection 01

63. What is the minimum distance between the intended location of a washing machine and the receptacle installed for it in a dwelling unit laundry room?

    A. 3 feet

    B. 4 feet

    C. 6 feet

    D. 10 feet

    Reference: 2017 National Electrical Code – Chapter 2 Wiring and Protection, Article 210 Branch Circuits. 210.50 General. 210.50(C) Appliance Receptacle Outlets.

64. Appliance receptacle outlets installed in a dwelling unit for specific appliances, such as laundry equipment, shall be installed within _____ feet of the intended location of the appliance.

    A. 3

    B. 5

    C. 6

    D. 10

    Reference: 2017 National Electrical Code – Chapter 2 Wiring and Protection, Article 210 Branch Circuits. 210.50 General. 210.50(C) Appliance Receptacle Outlets.

65. When appliance receptacle outlets are installed in a dwelling unit for laundry equipment or other specific appliances, they must be no more than _____ ft. of the intended location.

    A. 3

    B. 4

    C. 6

    D. 8

    Reference: 2017 National Electrical Code – Chapter 2 Wiring and Protection, Article 210 Branch Circuits. 210.50 General. . 210.50(C) Appliance Receptacle Outlets.

66. What is the maximum distance that a receptacle outlet installed for a specific appliance can be from the intended location of the appliance?

    A. 4 feet

    B. 5 feet

    C. 6 feet

    D. 8 feet

    Reference: 2017 National Electrical Code – Chapter 2 Wiring and Protection, Article 210 Branch Circuits. 210.50 General. 210.50(C) Appliance Receptacle Outlets.

EXAM 4

Chapter 2 Wiring and Protection 01

67. Required 125-volt, 15- and 20-ampere receptacles in dwelling units shall not be located higher than _____ feet above the floor.

    A. 3

    B. 4

    C. 5-1/2

    D. 6

    Reference: 2017 National Electrical Code – Chapter 2 Wiring and Protection, Article 210 Branch Circuits. 210.52 Dwelling Unit Receptacle Outlets. (4)

68. If a permanently installed electric baseboard heater is equipped with a factory installed receptacle outlet(s), or separate outlet assemblies are provided by the manufacturer, it is allowed for them to be permitted as the required outlet(s) for the wall space that the heaters use. These receptacle outlets must:

    A. be connected to and controlled by the heater circuits.

    B. be installed above the heating elements.

    C. be rated the same as the heater circuits.

    D. not be connected to the heater circuits.

    Reference: 2017 National Electrical Code – Chapter 2 Wiring and Protection, Article 210 Branch Circuits. 210.52 Dwelling Unit Receptacle Outlets.

69. This is the 6/12 rule. 6 feet from every opening and every 12 feet after that.

    A. 2

    B. 3

    C. 5

    D. 6

    Reference: 2017 National Electrical Code – Chapter 2 Wiring and Protection, Article 210 Branch Circuits. 210.52 Dwelling Unit Receptacle Outlets. 210.52(A) General Provisions. 210.52(A)(1) Spacing.

EXAM 4

Chapter 2 Wiring and Protection 01

70. Receptacle outlets in every bedroom, den, dining room, family room, kitchen, library, living room, parlor, recreation room, sunroom, or similar area or room of a dwelling unit must be installed so that any point measured along the floor line in any wall space horizontally is _____ ft. or less from a receptacle outlet.

    A. 2
    B. 3
    C. 6
    D. 12

    Reference: 2017 National Electrical Code – Chapter 2 Wiring and Protection, Article 210 Branch Circuits. 210.52 Dwelling Unit Receptacle Outlets. 210.52(A) General Provisions. 210.52(A)(1) Spacing.

71. A required 125-volt, 15- and 20-ampere receptacle in dwelling units shall be installed in any wall space _____ feet or more in width.

    A. 1
    B. 2
    C. 3
    D. 5

    Reference: 2017 National Electrical Code – Chapter 2 Wiring and Protection, Article 210 Branch Circuits. 210.52 Dwelling Unit Receptacle Outlets. 210.52(A) General Provisions. 210.52(A)(2) Wall Space.

72. For purposes of outlet spacing, any unbroken space _____ ft. or more in width including space measured around corners and unbroken along the floor line by fireplaces, doorways, and other similar openings will be considered a wall space.

    A. 1
    B. 2
    C. 3
    D. 4

    Reference: 2017 National Electrical Code – Chapter 2 Wiring and Protection, Article 210 Branch Circuits. 210.52 Dwelling Unit Receptacle Outlets. . 210.52(A) General Provisions. . 210.52(A)(2) Wall Space.

EXAM 4

Chapter 2 Wiring and Protection 01

73. A general-use receptacle outlet must be provided in any dwelling unit bedroom wall that is at least _____ wide.

    A. 2 feet

    B. 4 feet

    C. 6 feet

    D. 10 feet

    Reference: 2017 National Electrical Code – Chapter 2 Wiring and Protection, Article 210 Branch Circuits. 210.52 Dwelling Receptacle Outlets. 210.52(A) General Provisions. 210.52(A)(2) Wall Space. 210.52(A)(2)(1)

74. For a receptacle outlet that is in or on the floor of a dwelling unit to be counted as part of the required number of receptacle outlets, it must be under _____ from a wall.

    A. 12 inches

    B. 18 inches

    C. 24 inches

    D. 30 inches

    Reference: 2017 National Electrical Code – Chapter 2 Wiring and Protection, Article 210 Branch Circuits. 210.52 Dwelling Receptacle Outlets. 210.52(A) General Provisions. 210.52(A)(3) Floor Receptacles.

75. Unless they are within _____ of the wall, receptacle outlets in floors may not be counted as a part of the minimum required number of receptacle outlets.

    A. 1 ft.

    B. 1.5 ft.

    C. 2 ft.

    D. 8 in

    Reference: 2017 National Electrical Code – Chapter 2 Wiring and Protection, Article 210 Branch Circuits. 210.52 Dwelling Unit Receptacle Outlets. 210.52(A) General Provisions. 210.52(A)(3) Floor Receptacles.

76. Receptacle outlets in floors shall not be counted as part of the required number of receptacle outlets unless located within _____ inches of the wall.

    A. 18

    B. 20

    C. 24

    D. 30

    Reference: 2017 National Electrical Code – Chapter 2 Wiring and Protection, Article 210 Branch Circuits. 210.52 Dwelling Unit Receptacle Outlets. 210.52(A) General Provisions. 210.52(A)(3) Floor Receptacles.

EXAM 4

Chapter 2 Wiring and Protection 01

77. In the kitchen, pantry, breakfast room, dining room, or similar area of a dwelling unit, receptacles shall be _____-ampere.

    A. 10

    B. 20

    C. 30

    D. 40

    Reference: 2017 National Electrical Code – Chapter 2 Wiring and Protection, Article 210 Branch Circuits. 210.52 Dwelling Unit Receptacle Outlets. 210.52(B) Small Appliances. 210.52(B)(1) Receptacle Outlets Served.

78. _____ small-appliance branch circuits will serve all floor and wall receptacle outlets, and all receptacle and countertop outlets for refrigeration units in breakfast rooms, dining rooms, kitchens, pantries, and similar areas of a dwelling unit. Exceptions ignored.

    A. One

    B. Two

    C. Two or more 20-ampere

    D. At least three

    Reference: 2017 National Electrical Code – Chapter 2 Wiring and Protection, Article 210 Branch Circuits. 210.52 Dwelling Unit Receptacle Outlets. . 210.52(B) Small Appliances. 210.52(B)(1) Receptacle Outlets Served.

79. Small-appliance branch circuits shall not:

    A. serve a dining room and a kitchen.

    B. serve more than one dining room.

    C. serve more than one kitchen.

    D. serve more than two kitchens.

    Reference: 2017 National Electrical Code – Chapter 2 Wiring and Protection, Article 210 Branch Circuits. 210.52 Dwelling Unit Receptacle Outlets. . 210.52(B) Small Appliances. 210.52(B)(3) Kitchen Receptacle Requirements.

EXAM 4

Chapter 2 Wiring and Protection 01

80. Receptacles installed in a kitchen to serve countertop surfaces shall be supplied by not fewer than _____ small-appliance branch circuits.

    A. one

    B. two

    C. three

    D. four

    Reference: *2017 National Electrical Code – Chapter 2 Wiring and Protection, Article 210 Branch Circuits. 210.52 Dwelling Unit Receptacle Outlets. 210.52(B) Small Appliances. 210.52(B)(3) Kitchen Receptacle Requirements.*

81. A receptacle outlet shall be installed at each wall countertop space that is _____ inches or wider.

    A. 6

    B. 9

    C. 12

    D. 18

    Reference: *2017 National Electrical Code – Chapter 2 Wiring and Protection, Article 210 Branch Circuits. 210.52 Dwelling Unit Receptacle Outlets. 210.52(C) Countertops. 210.52(C)(1) Wall Countertop Spaces And work surface.*

82. What is the maximum wall line distance allowed for receptacles meant to serve kitchen countertop surfaces in a residence, measured horizontally from the location of the receptacle?

    A. 18 inches

    B. 24 inches

    C. 36 inches

    D. 48 inches

    Reference: *2017 National Electrical Code – Chapter 2 Wiring and Protection, Article 210 Branch Circuits. 210.52 Dwelling Receptacle Outlets. 210.52(C) Countertops. 210.52(C)(1) Wall Countertop Spaces.*

83. True or False: If the back of a non-corner sink is 14" from a wall in a dwelling unit, is it required by the code to have an outlet installed in that area if the nearest countertop outlet is 3 feet away.

    A. True

    B. False

    Reference: *2017 National Electrical Code – Chapter 2 Wiring and Protection, Article 210 Branch Circuits. 210.52 Dwelling Unit Receptacle Outlets. . 210.52(C) Countertops. . 210.52(C)(1) Wall Countertop Spaces.*

EXAM 4

Chapter 2 Wiring and Protection 01

84. Each wall countertop space that is at least _____ must have a receptacle outlet installed, so that any point along the wall line is _____ or less, measured horizontally, from a receptacle outlet in that space. Exceptions ignored.

    A. 2 ft., 4 ft.

    B. 12 in., 24 in.

    C. 18 in., 36 in.

    D. 24 in., 48 in.

    Reference: 2017 National Electrical Code – Chapter 2 Wiring and Protection, Article 210 Branch Circuits. 210.52 Dwelling Unit Receptacle Outlets. . 210.52(C) Countertops. . 210.52(C)(1) Wall Countertop Spaces.

85. What is the minimum wall countertop space that is required to have a receptacle outlet for dwelling unit kitchens?

    A. 10 inches

    B. 12 inches

    C. 18 inches

    D. 24 inches

    Reference: 2017 National Electrical Code – Chapter 2 Wiring and Protection, Article 210 Branch Circuits. 210.52 Dwelling Receptacle Outlets. 210.52(C) Countertops. 210.52(C)(1) Wall Countertop Spaces.

86. At least one receptacle outlet shall be installed at each island countertop space with a long dimension of _____ inches or greater and a short dimension of _____ inches or greater.

    A. 18, 9

    B. 24, 12

    C. 30, 12

    D. 36, 18

    Reference: 2017 National Electrical Code – Chapter 2 Wiring and Protection, Article 210 Branch Circuits. 210.52 Dwelling Unit Receptacle Outlets. 210.52(C) Countertops. 210.52(C)(2) Island Countertop Spaces.

87. At least one receptacle outlet shall be installed at each peninsular countertop space with a long dimension of _____ inches or greater and a short dimension of _____ inches or greater.

    A. 18, 9

    B. 24, 12

    C. 30, 12

    D. 36, 18

    Reference: 2017 National Electrical Code – Chapter 2 Wiring and Protection, Article 210 Branch Circuits. 210.52 Dwelling Unit Receptacle Outlets. 210.52(C) Countertops. 210.52(C)(3) Peninsular Countertop Spaces.

EXAM 4

Chapter 2 Wiring and Protection 01

88. If an island or peninsular counter top has a _____ installed, and the width of the countertop behind the installation is under 300 mm (12 in.), then the countertop space is considered to be divided into two separate countertop spaces by it.

    A. picture

    B. range, counter-mounted cooking unit, or sink

    C. wall outlets

    D. wall switches

    Reference: 2017 National Electrical Code – Chapter 2 Wiring and Protection, Article 210 Branch Circuits. 210.52 Dwelling Unit Receptacle Outlets. . 210.52(C) Countertops. 210.52(C)(4) Separate Spaces.

89. Receptacle outlets serving countertops shall be located above, but not more than _____ inches ABOVE, the countertop.

    A. 6

    B. 12

    C. 18

    D. 20

    Reference: 2017 National Electrical Code – Chapter 2 Wiring and Protection, Article 210 Branch Circuits. 210.52 Dwelling Unit Receptacle Outlets. 210.52(C) Countertops. 210.52(C)(5) Receptacle Outlet Location.

90. Receptacle outlets serving countertops shall be permitted to be mounted not more than _____ inches BELOW, the countertop.

    A. 6

    B. 9

    C. 12

    D. 15

    Reference: 2017 National Electrical Code – Chapter 2 Wiring and Protection, Article 210 Branch Circuits. 210.52 Dwelling Unit Receptacle Outlets. 210.52(C) Countertops. 210.52(C)(5) Receptacle Outlet Location.

91. What is generally the maximum distance above the countertop for receptacle outlets in dwelling unit kitchens?

    A. 12 inches

    B. 18 inches

    C. 20 inches

    D. 24 inches

    Reference: 2017 National Electrical Code – Chapter 2 Wiring and Protection, Article 210 Branch Circuits. 210.52 Dwelling Receptacle Outlets. 210.52(C) Countertops. 210.52(C)(5) Receptacle Outlet Location.

EXAM 4

Chapter 2 Wiring and Protection 01

92. Receptacle outlets serving countertops shall be permitted to be mounted not more than _____ inches below the countertop.

    A. 6

    B. 9

    C. 12

    D. 15

    Reference: 2017 National Electrical Code – Chapter 2 Wiring and Protection, Article 210 Branch Circuits. 210.52 Dwelling Unit Receptacle Outlets. 210.52(C) Countertops. 210.52(C)(5) Receptacle Outlet Location. Exception

93. In a dwelling unit bathroom, there must be a minimum of one receptacle outlet, and it is required to be a minimum of how far from the outside edge of each basin?

    A. 12 inches (1 ft.)

    B. 18 inches (1-1/2 ft.)

    C. 24 inches (2 ft.)

    D. 36 inches (3 ft.)

    Reference: 2017 National Electrical Code – Chapter 2 Wiring and Protection, Article 210 Branch Circuits. 210.52 Dwelling Receptacle Outlets. 210.52(D) Bathrooms.

94. In dwelling units, at least one receptacle outlet shall be installed in bathrooms within _____ feet of the outside edge of each basin.

    A. 1-1/2

    B. 2

    C. 3

    D. 5

    Reference: 2017 National Electrical Code – Chapter 2 Wiring and Protection, Article 210 Branch Circuits. 210.52 Dwelling Unit Receptacle Outlets. 210.52(D) Bathrooms.

EXAM 4

Chapter 2 Wiring and Protection 01

95. In bathrooms in dwelling units, one or more receptacle outlets must be installed _____ or less from the outside edge of each basin, and the receptacle outlet must be located on a partition or wall adjacent to the basin, countertop, or side of the basin cabinet less than 300 mm (12 in.) below the countertop. If the outlet is to be installed in the countertop, the receptacle outlet assembly must be listed for the application.

   A. 3 ft.
   B. 4 ft.
   C. 6 ft.
   D. 18 in.

   Reference: 2017 National Electrical Code – Chapter 2 Wiring and Protection, Article 210 Branch Circuits. 210.52 Dwelling Unit Receptacle Outlets. 210.52(D) Bathrooms.

96. For dwelling units, at least one receptacle outlet accessible at grade level and not more than _____ feet above grade shall be installed at the front and back of each dwelling.

   A. 3
   B. 5
   C. 6
   D. 6-1/2

   Reference: 2017 National Electrical Code – Chapter 2 Wiring and Protection, Article 210 Branch Circuits. 210.52 Dwelling Unit Receptacle Outlets. 210.52(E) Outdoor Outlets. 210.52(E)(1) One-Family and Two-Family Dwellings.

97. In each unit of a two-family dwelling or one-family dwelling that is at grade level, one or more receptacle outlets that is accessible while standing at grade level and located _____ above grade level or less, must be installed at the front and back of the dwelling.

   A. 6.5 feet
   B. 6-1/2 ft.
   C. 78 in
   D. all of the above

   Reference: 2017 National Electrical Code – Chapter 2 Wiring and Protection, Article 210 Branch Circuits. 210.52 Dwelling Unit Receptacle Outlets. . 210.52(E) Outdoor Outlets. . 210.52(E)(1) One-Family and Two-Family Dwellings.

EXAM 4

Chapter 2 Wiring and Protection 01

98. In dwelling units, at least _____ receptacle outlet shall be installed for the laundry.

    A. one

    B. two

    C. three

    D. none

    Reference: 2017 National Electrical Code – Chapter 2 Wiring and Protection, Article 210 Branch Circuits. 210.52 Dwelling Unit Receptacle Outlets. 210.52(F) Laundry Areas.

99. For a one-family dwelling, at least _____ receptacle outlet shall be installed in each basement, attached garage and in detached garages with electric power.

    A. one

    B. two

    C. three

    D. none

    Reference: 2017 National Electrical Code – Chapter 2 Wiring and Protection, Article 210 Branch Circuits. 210.52 Dwelling Unit Receptacle Outlets. 210.52(G) Basements, Garages, and Accessory Buildings

100. At least one receptacle outlet in a one-family dwelling, as well as those from specific equipment, must be installed in each attached garage, in each basement, and in each:

    A. 6' space along the floor line

    B. 12' or wider carport

    C. detached garage or accessory building with electric power

    D. walkway to the garage

    Reference: 2017 National Electrical Code – Chapter 2 Wiring and Protection, Article 210 Branch Circuits. 210.52 Dwelling Unit Receptacle Outlets. 210.52(G) Basements, Garages, and Accessory Buildings. 210.52(G)(1) Garages.

EXAM 4

Chapter 2 Wiring and Protection 01

101. Which of the following statements is true of a residential branch circuit in an attached garage, supplying 125-volt, single-phase receptacle outlets?

    A. It may also supply any receptacles outside of the garage.

    B. It may not supply outlets outside of the garage

    C. It may supply only exterior luminaires when mounted on garage wall

    D. It may supply receptacles in the laundry room

    Reference: 2017 National Electrical Code – Chapter 2 Wiring and Protection, Article 210 Branch Circuits. 210.52 Dwelling Receptacle Outlets. 210.52(G) Basements, Garages, and Accessory Buildings. 210.52(G)(1) Garages.

102. What is the minimum length of a hallway in a dwelling unit she must be supplied with at least one receptacle outlet?

    A. 10 feet

    B. 20 feet

    C. 25 feet

    D. 30 feet

    Reference: 2017 National Electrical Code – Chapter 2 Wiring and Protection, Article 210 Branch Circuits. 210.52 Dwelling Receptacle Outlets. 210.52(H) Hallways.

103. In dwelling units, hallways of _____ feet or more in length shall have at least one receptacle.

    A. 5

    B. 8

    C. 10

    D. 15

    Reference: 2017 National Electrical Code – Chapter 2 Wiring and Protection, Article 210 Branch Circuits. 210.52 Dwelling Unit Receptacle Outlets. 210.52(H) Hallways.

Chapter 2 Wiring and Protection 01

EXAM 4

Chapter 2 Wiring and Protection 01

104. A hallway in a dwelling unit shall be provided with at least one 125-volt, 15- or 20-ampere rated receptacle if it is at least _____ long.

    A. 10 feet

    B. 12 feet

    C. 15 feet

    D. 20 feet

    Reference: 2017 National Electrical Code – Chapter 2 Wiring and Protection, Article 210 Branch Circuits. 210.52 Dwelling Unit Receptacle Outlets. 210.52(H) Hallways.

105. Guest rooms in hotels, motels, and similar occupancies shall have at least _____ receptacle outlets installed that are readily accessible.

    A. one

    B. two

    C. three

    D. four

    Reference: 2017 National Electrical Code – Chapter 2 Wiring and Protection, Article 210 Branch Circuits. 210.60 Guest Rooms, Guest Suites, Dormitories, and Similar Occupancies. 210.60(B) Receptacle Placement.

106. What is the minimum number of general purpose receptacles required to be readily accessible when installed in sleeping rooms of dorms, or guest rooms of hotels and motels?

    A. one

    B. two

    C. three

    D. all

    Reference: 2017 National Electrical Code – Chapter 2 Wiring and Protection, Article 210 Branch Circuits. 210.60 Guest Rooms, Guest Suites, Dormitories, and Similar Occupancies. 210.60(B) Receptacle Placement.

107. What is the minimum number of single-phase, 125-volt, 15- or 20-ampere rated receptacle outlet(s) required to be readily accessible in guest rooms and guest suites of hotels and motels?

    A. One

    B. Two

    C. Three

    D. Four

    Reference: 2017 National Electrical Code – Chapter 2 Wiring and Protection, Article 210 Branch Circuits. 210.60 Guest Rooms, Guest Suites, Dormitories, and Similar Occupancies. 210.60(B) Receptacle Placement.

EXAM 4

Chapter 2 Wiring and Protection 01

108. What is the required minimum of 125-volt, single-phase 15- or 20-ampere rated receptacle outlets to be provided within 18 inches of the top of a retail furniture store with 80 continuous linear feet of display show window, according to the NEC?

   A. six

   B. seven

   C. eight

   D. nine

   Reference: 2017 National Electrical Code – Chapter 2 Wiring and Protection, Article 210 Branch Circuits. 210.62 Show Windows.

109. At least one receptacle outlet shall be installed within 18 inches of the top of a show window for each _____ linear feet.

   A. 8

   B. 10

   C. 12

   D. 15

   Reference: 2017 National Electrical Code – Chapter 2 Wiring and Protection, Article 210 Branch Circuits. 210.62 Show Windows.

110. Each _____ or major fraction thereof of show window area measured horizontally at its maximum width shall have one or more receptacle outlets installed within 450 mm (18 in.) of the top of the show window.

   A. 6 linear ft.

   B. 8 linear ft.

   C. 10 linear ft.

   D. 12 linear ft.

   Reference: 2017 National Electrical Code – Chapter 2 Wiring and Protection, Article 210 Branch Circuits. 210.62 Show Windows.

EXAM 4

Chapter 2 Wiring and Protection 01

111. One receptacle outlet shall be installed at an accessible location for the servicing of heating, air-conditioning, and refrigeration within _____ feet and on the same level as the equipment.

    A. 10   C. 25

    B. 15   D. 50

    Reference: 2017 National Electrical Code – Chapter 2 Wiring and Protection, Article 210 Branch Circuits. 210.63 Heating, Air-Conditioning, and Refrigeration Equipment Outlet.

112. For the servicing of air-conditioning, heating and refrigeration equipment, a 125-volt, single-phase, 15- or 20-ampere-rated receptacle outlet must be installed within _____ of the equipment, at an accessible location.

    A. 6 ft.   C. 15 ft.

    B. 10 ft.   D. 25 ft.

    Reference: 2017 National Electrical Code – Chapter 2 Wiring and Protection, Article 210 Branch Circuits. 210.63 Heating, Air-Conditioning, and Refrigeration Equipment Outlet.

113. Which of the following statements is correct, regarding a 15- or 20-ampere, 125-volt, rated receptacle for heating, air-conditioning or refrigeration equipment installed on the roof of an apartment building?

    A. is not required by the NEC

    B. may connect to line side of disconnect, if outlet is GFCI protected

    C. shall be on roof with equipment and 75 feet or less away

    D. shall be on the same level & 25 feet or less away

    Reference: 2017 National Electrical Code – Chapter 2 Wiring and Protection, Article 210 Branch Circuits. 210.63 Heating, Air-Conditioning, and Refrigeration Equipment Outlet.

EXAM 4

Chapter 2 Wiring and Protection 01

114. At least one 125-volt, single-phase, 15- or 20-ampere rated receptacle outlet is required to be installed within a minimum of what distance from the electrical service equipment, on anything other than one- or two-family dwellings?

    A. 10 feet

    B. 25 feet

    C. 50 feet

    D. 75 feet

    Reference: 2017 National Electrical Code – Chapter 2 Wiring and Protection, Article 210 Branch Circuits. 210.64 Electrical Service Areas.

115. At least one wall switch-controlled lighting outlet shall be installed in every _____ room and bathroom.

    A. dining

    B. finished

    C. habitable

    D. wired

    Reference: 2017 National Electrical Code – Chapter 2 Wiring and Protection, Article 210 Branch Circuits. 210.70 Lighting Outlets Required. 210.70(A) Dwelling Units. 210.70(A)(1) Habitable Rooms.

116. One or more _____ outlet must be installed in every bathroom and habitable room. Exceptions ignored.

    A. 20 amp

    B. appliance

    C. hair dryer

    D. wall switch-controlled lighting

    Reference: 2017 National Electrical Code – Chapter 2 Wiring and Protection, Article 210 Branch Circuits. 210.70 Lighting Outlets Required. . 210.70(1) Habitable Rooms.

Chapter 2 Wiring and Protection 01

EXAM 4

Chapter 2 Wiring and Protection 01

117. For dwelling units, detached garages with electric power, and attached garages, one or more _____ must be installed to give illumination on the exterior of outdoor exits or entrances with access at grade level.

    A. Flood light

    B. Motion detector

    C. Security camera

    D. Wall switch controlled lighting outlet.

    Reference: 2017 National Electrical Code – Chapter 2 Wiring and Protection, Article 210 Branch Circuits. 210.70 Lighting Outlets Required. . 210.70(A) Dwelling Units. . 210.70(A)(2) Additional Locations.

118. For dwelling units and garages, at least one wall switch-controlled lighting outlet shall be installed to provide illumination on the _____ side of outdoor entrances or exits with grade level access.

    A. adjoining

    B. exterior

    C. facing

    D. interior

    Reference: 2017 National Electrical Code – Chapter 2 Wiring and Protection, Article 210 Branch Circuits. 210.70. 210.70(A) Dwelling Units. 210.70(A)(2) Additional Locations. 210.70(A)(2)(b).

119. Interior stairs shall have switches at each end, where the stairway between floor levels has ____ risers or more.

    A. five

    B. six

    C. eight

    D. ten

    Reference: 2017 National Electrical Code – Chapter 2 Wiring and Protection, Article 210 Branch Circuits. 210.70 Lighting Outlets Required. 210.70(A) Dwelling Units. 210.70(A)(2) Additional Locations. 210.70(A)(2)(c)

EXAM 4

Chapter 2 Wiring and Protection 01

120. When residential lighting outlets have been installed on interior stairways, where should a wall switch be provided, disregarding exceptions?

    A. at any convenient location

    B. at each level if more than six (6) steps

    C. every seven (7) steps

    D. near the stairs

    Reference: 2017 National Electrical Code – Chapter 2 Wiring and Protection, Article 210 Branch Circuits. 210.70 Lighting Outlets Required. 210.70(A) Dwelling Units. 210.70(A)(2) Additional Locations. 210.70(A)(2)(c)

121. Attics, underfloor spaces, utility rooms, and basements used for storage or containing equipment that requires servicing shall be provided a lighting outlet located at or _____ the equipment.

    A. above

    B. near

    C. on

    D. under

    Reference: 2017 National Electrical Code – Chapter 2 Wiring and Protection, Article 210 Branch Circuits. 210.70. 210.70(A) Dwelling Units. 210.70(A)(3) Storage or Equipment Spaces.

122. At least one _____ containing a switch or controlled by a walls switch must be installed in attics or underfloor spaces containing equipment requiring servicing, such as heating, air-conditioning, and refrigeration equipment. One or more point of control should be at the normal point of entry for such spaces.

    A. junction box

    B. lighting outlet

    C. panelboard

    D. power control

    Reference: 2017 National Electrical Code – Chapter 2 Wiring and Protection, Article 210 Branch Circuits. 210.70 Lighting Outlets Required. . 210.70(3) Storage or Equipment Spaces.

EXAM 4

Chapter 2 Wiring and Protection 01

123. Before the application of any correction or adjustment factors, the minimum feeder-circuit conductor size must have an allowable ampacity of at least _____ percent of the continuous load plus the noncontinuous load. Exceptions ignored.

    A. 80

    B. 100

    C. 125

    D. 150

    Reference: 2017 National Electrical Code – Chapter 2 Wiring and Protection, Article 215 Feeders. 215.2 Minimum Rating and Size. 215.2(A) Feeders Not More Than 600 Volts. 215.2(A)(1) General.

EXAM 4

EXAM 4 ANSWERS

1. **Answer D.** Any of the above and more options are available.

   An insulated grounded conductor of 6 AWG or smaller shall be identified by one of the following means:

   (1) A continuous white outer finish.

   (2) A continuous gray outer finish.

   (3) Three continuous white or gray stripes along the conductor's entire length on other than green insulation.

   (4) Wires that have their outer covering finished to show a white or gray color but have colored tracer threads in the braid identifying the source of manufacture shall be considered as meeting the provisions of this section.

   (5) The grounded conductor of a mineral-insulated, metal-sheathed cable (Type MI) shall be identified at the time of installation by distinctive marking at its terminations.

   (6) A single-conductor, sunlight-resistant, outdoor-rated cable used as a grounded conductor in photovoltaic power systems, as permitted by 690.31, shall be identified at the time of installation by distinctive white marking at all terminations.

   (7) Fixture wire shall comply with the requirements for grounded conductor identification as specified in 402.8.

   (8) For aerial cable, the identification shall be as above. or by means of a ridge located on the exterior of the cable so as to identify it.

   Reference: 2017 National Electrical Code – Chapter 2 Wiring and Protection, Article 200 Use and Identification of Grounded Conductors. 200.6 Means of Identifying Grounded Conductors. 200.6(A) Sizes 6 AWG or Smaller.

2. **Answer D.** when installed, distinctive white or gray mark around termination

   An insulated grounded conductor 4 AWG or larger shall be identified by one of the following means:

   (1) A continuous white outer finish.

   (2) A continuous gray outer finish.

   (3) Three continuous white or gray stripes along the conductor's entire length on other than green insulation.

   (4) At the time of installation, by a distinctive white or gray marking at its terminations. This marking shall encircle the conductor or insulation.

   Reference: 2017 National Electrical Code – Chapter 2 Wiring and Protection, Article 200 Use and Identification of Grounded Conductors. 200.6 Means of Identifying Grounded Conductors. 200.6(B) Sizes 4 AWG or Larger.

3. **Answer B.** 4

   An insulated grounded conductor 4 AWG or larger shall be identified by one of the following means:

   (1) A continuous white outer finish.

   (2) A continuous gray outer finish.

   (3) Three continuous white or gray stripes along the conductor's entire length on other than green insulation.

   (4) At the time of installation, by a distinctive white or gray marking at its terminations. This marking shall encircle the conductor or insulation.

   Reference: 2017 National Electrical Code – Chapter 2 Wiring and Protection, Article 200 Use and Identification of Grounded Conductors. 200.6 Means of Identifying Grounded Conductors. 200.6(B) Sizes 4 AWG or Larger.

EXAM 4
EXAM 4 ANSWERS

4. **Answer D.** white

   An insulated grounded conductor 4 AWG or larger shall be identified by one of the following means:

   (1) A continuous white outer finish.

   (2) A continuous gray outer finish.

   (3) Three continuous white or gray stripes along the conductor's entire length on other than green insulation.

   (4) At the time of installation, by a distinctive white or gray marking at its terminations. This marking shall encircle the conductor or insulation.

   Reference: 2017 National Electrical Code – Chapter 2 Wiring and Protection, Article 200 Use and Identification of Grounded Conductors. 200.6 Means of Identifying Grounded Conductors. 200.6(B) Sizes 4 AWG or Larger. 200.6(B)(4)

5. **Answer D.** white or gray

   An insulated conductor that is intended for use as a grounded conductor, *where contained within a flexible cord, shall be identified by a white or gray outer finish or by methods permitted by 400.22.*

   Reference: 2017 National Electrical Code – Chapter 2 Wiring and Protection, Article 200 Use and Identification of Grounded Conductors. 200.6 Means of Identifying Grounded Conductors. 200.6(C) Flexible Cords.

6. **Answer B.** grounded conductor

   The following shall be used only for the grounded circuit conductor, unless otherwise permitted in 200.7(B) and (C):

   (1) A conductor with continuous white or gray covering

   (2) A conductor with three continuous white or gray stripes on other than green insulation

   (3) A marking of white or gray color at the termination

   Reference: 2017 National Electrical Code – Chapter 2 Wiring and Protection, Article 200 Use and Identification of Grounded Conductors. 200.7 Use of Insulation of a White or Gray Color or with Three Continuous White or Gray Stripes. 200.7(A) General. 200.7(A)(2)

7. **Answer C.** white

   The identification of terminals to which a grounded conductor is to be connected shall be substantially white in color. The identification of other terminals shall be of a readily distinguishable different color.

   Reference: 2017 National Electrical Code – Chapter 2 Wiring and Protection, Article 200 Use and Identification of Grounded Conductors. 200.9 Means of Identification of Terminals.

8. **Answer D.** white

   The identification of terminals to which a grounded conductor is to be connected shall be substantially white in color. The identification of other terminals shall be of a readily distinguishable different color.

   Reference: 2017 National Electrical Code – Chapter 2 Wiring and Protection, Article 200 Use and Identification of Grounded Conductors. 200.9 Means of Identification of Terminals.

9. **Answer B.** grounded

   For devices with screw shells, *the terminal for the grounded conductor shall be the one connected to the screw shell.*

   Reference: 2017 National Electrical Code – Chapter 2 Wiring and Protection, Article 200 Use and Identification of Grounded Conductors. 200.10 Identification of Terminals. 200.10(C) Screw Shells.

10. **Answer D.** white or gray

    For screw shell devices with attached leads, the conductor attached to the screw shell shall have a white or gray finish. *The outer finish of the other conductor shall be of a solid color that will not be confused with the white or gray finish used to identify the grounded conductor.*

    Informational Note: The color gray may have been used in the past as an ungrounded conductor. Care should be taken when working on existing systems.

    Reference: 2017 National Electrical Code – Chapter 2 Wiring and Protection, Article 200 Use and Identification of Grounded Conductors. 200.10 Identification of Terminals. 200.10(D) Screw Shell Devices with Leads.

EXAM 4

EXAM 4 ANSWERS

11. **Answer D.** High pressure sodium parking lot lighting

    Branch circuits shall comply with this article and also with the applicable provisions of other articles of this Code. *The provisions for branch circuits supplying equipment listed in Table 210.2 amend or supplement* the provisions in this article. *Table on page 70-52.*

    Reference: 2017 National Electrical Code – Chapter 2 Wiring and Protection, Article 210 Branch Circuits. 210.2 Other Articles for Specific-Purpose Branch Circuits.

12. **Answer B.** 15 ampere

    Branch circuits recognized by this article shall be rated in accordance with the maximum permitted ampere rating or setting of the overcurrent device. *The rating for other than individual branch circuits shall be 15, 20, 30, 40, and 50 amperes. Where conductors of higher ampacity are used for any reason, the ampere rating or setting of the specified overcurrent device shall determine the circuit rating.*

    Exception: Multioutlet branch circuits greater than 50 amperes shall be permitted to supply non lighting outlet loads on industrial premises where conditions of maintenance and supervision ensure that only qualified persons service the equipment.

    Reference: 2017 National Electrical Code – Chapter 2 Wiring and Protection, Article 210 Branch Circuits. 210.3 Rating.

13. **Answer D.** panelboard

    Branch circuits recognized by this article shall be permitted as multiwire circuits. A multi wire circuit shall be permitted to be considered as multiple circuits. *All conductors of a multi wire branch circuit shall originate from the same panelboard* or similar distribution equipment.

    Informational Note No. 1: A 3-phase. 4-wire, wye-connected power system used to supply power to nonlinear loads may necessitate that the power system design allow for the possibility of high harmonic currents on the neutral conductor.

    Informational Note No.2: See 300.13(B) for continuity of grounded conductors on multiwire circuits.

    Reference: 2017 National Electrical Code – Chapter 2 Wiring and Protection, Article 210 Branch Circuits. 210.4 Multiwire Branch Circuits. 210.4(A) General.

14. **Answer B.** 120

    In dwelling units and guest rooms or guest suites of hotels, motels, and similar occupancies, the voltage shall not exceed 120 volts, nominal, between conductors that supply the terminals of the following:

    (1) Luminaires

    (2) Cord-and-plug-connected loads 1440 volt-amperes, nominal, or less or less than 1/4 hp

    Reference: 2017 National Electrical Code – Chapter 2 Wiring and Protection, Article 210 Branch Circuits. 210.6 Branch-Circuit Voltage Limitations. . 210.6(A) Occupancy Limitation.

EXAM 4

EXAM 4 ANSWERS

15. Answer A. 120 volts

In dwelling units and guest rooms or guest suites of hotels, motels, and similar occupancies, *the voltage shall not exceed 120 volts, nominal, between conductors that supply the terminals of the following:*

(1) Luminaires

(2) Cord-and-plug-connected loads 1440 volt-amperes, nominal, or less or less than 1/4 hp

Reference: 2017 National Electrical Code – Chapter 2 Wiring and Protection, Article 210 Branch Circuits. 210.6 Branch-Circuit Voltage Limitations. 210.6(A) Occupancy Limitation.

16. Answer D. All of the above

Circuits not exceeding 120 volts, nominal, between conductors shall be permitted to supply the following:

(1) *The terminals of lampholders applied within their voltage ratings*

(2) *Auxiliary equipment of electric-discharge lamps Informational Note: See 410.137 for auxiliary equipment limitations.*

(3) *Cord-and-plug-connected or permanently connected utilization equipment*

Reference: 2017 National Electrical Code – Chapter 2 Wiring and Protection, Article 210 Branch Circuits. 210.6 Branch-Circuit Voltage Limitations. . 210.6(B) 120 Volts Between Conductors.

17. Answer D. simultaneously disconnect

Where two or more branch circuits supply devices or equipment on the same yoke or mounting strap, *a means to simultaneously disconnect the ungrounded supply conductors shall be provided at the point at which the branch circuits originate.*

Reference: 2017 National Electrical Code – Chapter 2 Wiring and Protection, Article 210 Branch Circuits. 210.7 Multiple Branch Circuits.

18. Answer A. True

All 125-volt, single-phase, 15- and 20- ampere receptacles installed in the locations specified in 210.8(A)(1) through (10) shall have ground-fault circuit interrupter protection for personnel.

(1) *Bathrooms*

(2) *Garages, and also accessory buildings that have a floor located at or below grade level not intended as habitable rooms and limited to storage areas, work areas, and areas of similar use*

(3) *Outdoors*

Exception to (3): Receptacles that are not readily accessible and are supplied by a branch circuit dedicated to electric snow-melting, deicing, or pipeline and vessel heating equipment shall be permitted to be installed in accordance with 426.28 or 427.22, as applicable.

(4) *Crawl spaces — at or below grade level*

(5) *Unfinished portions or areas of the basement not intended as habitable rooms Exception to (5): A receptacle supplying only a permanently installed fire alarm or burglar alarm system shall not be required to have ground fault circuit-interrupter protection. Informational Note: See 760.41(B) and 760.121(B) for power supply requirements for fire alarm systems. Receptacles installed under the exception to. 210.8(A)(5) shall not be considered as meeting the requirements of 210.52(G).*

(6) *Kitchens — where the receptacles are installed to serve the countertop surfaces*

(7) *Sinks — where receptacles are installed within 1.8 m (6 ft) from the top inside edge of the bowl of the sink*

(8) *Boathouses*

(9) *Bathtubs or shower stalls — where receptacles are installed within 1.8 m (6 ft) of the outside edge of the bathtub or shower stall*

(10) *Laundry areas*

Reference: 2017 National Electrical Code – Chapter 2 Wiring and Protection, Article 210 Branch Circuits. 210.8 Ground-Fault Circuit-Interrupter Protection for Personnel. 210.8(A) Dwelling Units.

EXAM 4

EXAM 4 ANSWERS

19. **Answer D.** Both A and C

    All 125-volt, single-phase, 15- and 20- ampere receptacles installed in the locations specified in 210.8(A)(1) through (10) shall have ground-fault circuit interrupter protection for personnel.

    (1) Bathrooms

    (2) Garages, and also accessory buildings that have a floor located at or below grade level not intended as habitable rooms and limited to storage areas, work areas, and areas of similar use

    (3) Outdoors

    Exception to (3): Receptacles that are not readily accessible and are supplied by a branch circuit dedicated to electric snow-melting, deicing, or pipeline and vessel heating equipment shall be permitted to be installed in accordance with 426.28 or 427.22, as applicable.

    (4) Crawl spaces — at or below grade level

    (5) Unfinished portions or areas of the basement not intended as habitable rooms

    Exception to (5): A receptacle supplying only a permanently installed fire alarm or burglar alarm system shall not be required to have groundfault circuit-interrupter protection.

    Informational Note: See 760.41(B) and 760.121(B) for power supply requirements for fire alarm systems.

    Receptacles installed under the exception to. 210.8(A)(5) shall not be considered as meeting the requirements of 210.52(G).

    (6) Kitchens — where the receptacles are installed to serve the countertop surfaces

    (7) Sinks — where receptacles are installed within 1.8 m

    (6 ft) from the top inside edge of the bowl of the sink

    (8) Boathouses

    (9) Bathtubs or shower stalls — where receptacles are installed within 1.8 m (6 ft) of the outside edge of the bathtub or shower stall

    (10) Laundry areas

    Reference: 2017 National Electrical Code – Chapter 2 Wiring and Protection, Article 210 Branch Circuits. 210.8 Ground-Fault Circuit-Interrupter Protection for Personnel. . 210.8(A) Dwelling Units.

20. **Answer D.** provided with GFCI protection

    All 125-volt, single-phase, 15- and 20- ampere receptacles installed in the locations specified in 210.8(A)(1) through (10) shall have ground-fault circuit interrupter protection for personnel.

    (2) *Garages*, and also accessory buildings that have a floor located at or below grade level not intended as habitable rooms and limited to storage areas, work areas, and areas of similar use

    Reference: 2017 National Electrical Code – Chapter 2 Wiring and Protection, Article 210 Branch Circuits. 210.8 Ground-Fault Circuit-Interrupter Protection for Personnel. 210.8(A) Dwelling Units.

21. **Answer D.** all of these

    All 125-volt, single-phase, 15- and 20-ampere receptacles installed in the locations specified in 210.5(A)(1) through (10) *shall have ground-fault circuit-interrupter protection for personnel.*

    (6) Kitchens - *where the receptacles are installed to serve the countertop surfaces*

    Reference: 2017 National Electrical Code – Chapter 2 Wiring and Protection, Article 210 Branch Circuits. 210.8 Ground-Fault Circuit-Interrupter Protection for Personnel. . 210.8(A) Dwelling Units. . 210.8(A)(6)

22. **Answer C.** required for countertop receptacles in residential kitchen

    All 125-volt, single-phase, 15- and 20-ampere receptacles installed in the locations specified in 210.8(A)(1) through (10) shall have ground-fault circuit-interrupter protection for personnel.

    (6) Kitchens - *where the receptacles are installed to serve the countertop surfaces.*

    Reference: 2017 National Electrical Code – Chapter 2 Wiring and Protection, Article 210 Branch Circuits. 210.8 Ground-Fault Circuit-Interrupter Protection for Personnel. 210.8(A) Dwelling Units. 210.8(A)(6)

EXAM 4
EXAM 4 ANSWERS

23. **Answer B.** 6 feet

All 125-volt, single-phase, 15- and 20-ampere receptacles installed in the locations specified in 210.8(A)(1) through (10) shall have ground-fault circuit-interrupter protection for personnel.

(7) Sinks — where receptacles are installed within 1.8 m (6 ft) from the top inside edge of the bowl of the sink

Reference: 2017 National Electrical Code – Chapter 2 Wiring and Protection, Article 210 Branch Circuits. 210.8 Ground-Fault Circuit-Interrupter Protection for Personnel. 210.8(A) Dwelling Units. 210.8(A)(7) Sinks

24. **Answer C.** 6

All 125-volt, single-phase, 15- and 20-ampere receptacles installed in the locations specified in 210.8(A)(1) through (10) shall have ground-fault circuit-interrupter protection for personnel.

(7) Sinks - where receptacles are installed within 1.5 m (6 ft.) of the outside edge of the sink

Reference: 2017 National Electrical Code – Chapter 2 Wiring and Protection, Article 210 Branch Circuits. 210.8 Ground-Fault Circuit-Interrupter Protection for Personnel. 210.8(A) Dwelling Units. 210.8(A)(7) Sinks

25. **Answer B.** 6 feet

All 125-volt, single-phase, 15- and 20-ampere receptacles installed in the locations specified in 210.8(A)(1) through (10) shall have ground-fault circuit-interrupter protection for personnel.

(9) Bathtubs or shower stalls - where receptacles are installed within 1.8 m (6 ft.) of the outside edge of the bathtub or shower stall

Reference: 2017 National Electrical Code – Chapter 2 Wiring and Protection, Article 210 Branch Circuits. 210.8 Ground-Fault Circuit-Interrupter Protection for Personnel. 210.8(A) Dwelling Units. 210.8(A)(9)

26. **Answer B.** GFCI protection

All single-phase receptacles rated 150 volts to ground or less, 50 amperes or less and three phase receptacles rated 150 volts to ground or less, 100 amperes or less installed in the following locations shall *have ground-fault circuit-interrupter protection for personnel.*

(3) Rooftops.

Reference: 2017 National Electrical Code – Chapter 2 Wiring and Protection, Article 210 Branch Circuits. 210.8 Ground-Fault Circuit-Interrupter Protection for Personnel. 210.8(B) Other Than Dwelling Units. 210.8(B)(3)

27. **Answer C.** outlets not exceeding 240 volts

GFCI protection shall be provided for outlets not exceeding 240 volts that supply boat hoists installed in dwelling unit locations.

Reference: 2017 National Electrical Code – Chapter 2 Wiring and Protection, Article 210 Branch Circuits. 210.8 Ground-Fault Circuit-Interrupter Protection for Personnel. 210.8(C) Boat Hoists.

28. **Answer D.** ungrounded

Two-wire dc circuits and ac circuits of two or more ungrounded conductors shall be permitted to be tapped from the ungrounded conductors of circuits that have a grounded neutral conductor. Switching devices in each tapped circuit shall have a pole in each ungrounded conductor. All poles of multipole switching devices shall manually switch together where such switching devices also serve as a disconnecting means as required by the following:

(1) 410.93 for double-pole switched lampholders

(2) 410.104(8) for electric-discharge lamp auxiliary equipment switching devices

(3) 422.31 (8) for an appliance

(4) 424.20 for a fixed electric space-heating unit

(5) 426.51 for electric deicing and snow-melting equipment

(6) 430.85 for a motor controller

(7) 430.103 for a motor

Reference: 2017 National Electrical Code – Chapter 2 Wiring and Protection, Article 210 Branch Circuits. 210.10 Ungrounded Conductors Tapped from Grounded Systems.

EXAM 4
EXAM 4 ANSWERS

29. Answer C. calculated

The minimum number of branch circuits shall be determined from the total calculated load and the size or rating of the circuits used. In all installations, the number of circuits shall be sufficient to supply the load served. In no case shall the load on any circuit exceed the maximum specified by 220.18.

Reference: 2017 National Electrical Code – Chapter 2 Wiring and Protection, Article 210 Branch Circuits. 210.11 Branch Circuits Required. . 210.11(A) Number of Branch Circuits.

30. Answer D. evenly proportioned

Where the load is calculated on the basis of volt-amperes per square meter or per square foot, the wiring system up to and including the branch-circuit panelboard(s) shall be provided to serve not less than the calculated load. *This load shall be evenly proportioned among multioutlet branch circuits within the panelboard(s).* Branch-circuit overcurrent devices and circuits shall be required to be installed only to serve the connected load.

Reference: 2017 National Electrical Code – Chapter 2 Wiring and Protection, Article 210 Branch Circuits. 210.11 Branch Circuits Required. . 210.11(B) Load Evenly Proportioned Among Branch Circuits.

31. Answer C. 4,500 VA

(1) Small Appliance Branch Circuits. In addition to the number of branch circuits required by other parts of this section, two or more 20-ampere small-appliance branch circuits shall be provided for all receptacle outlets specified by 210.52(B).

(2) Laundry Branch Circuits. In addition to the number of branch circuits required by other parts of this section, at least one additional 20-ampere branch circuit shall be provided to *supply the laundry receptacle outlet(s) required by 210.52(F). This circuit shall have no other outlets.*

Reference: 2017 National Electrical Code – Chapter 2 Wiring and Protection, Article 210 Branch Circuits. 210.11 Branch Circuits Required. 210.11(C) Dwelling Units. 210.11(C)(1)&(2)

(A) Small-Appliance Circuit Load. In each dwelling unit, the load shall be calculated at 1500 volt-amperes for each *2-wire small-appliance branch circuit as covered by 210.11(C)(1). Where the load is subdivided through two or more feeders, the calculated load for each shall include not less than 1500 volt-amperes for each 2-wire small-appliance branch circuit.* These loads shall be permitted to be included with the general lighting load and subjected to the demand factors provided in Table 220.42.

Exception: The individual branch circuit permitted by 210.52(B)(1), Exception No.2, shall be permitted to be excluded from the calculation required by 220.52.

(B) Laundry Circuit Load. *A load of not less than 1500 volt-amperes shall be included for each 2-wire laundry branch circuit installed as covered by 210.11(C)(2).* This load shall be permitted to be included with the general lighting load and subjected to the demand factors provided in Table 220.42. Table on page 70-70.

Reference: 2017 National Electrical Code – Chapter 2 Wiring and Protection, Article 220 Branch-Circuit, Feeder, and Service Calculations. 220.52 Small Appliance and Laundry Loads – Dwelling Unit. 220.52(A)&(B)

2 – small appliance circuits@ 1,500 VA ea.= 3,000 VA

1 laundry circuit@ 1,500 VA= 1,500 VA

TOTAL= 4,500 VA

32. Answer D. None of these.

In addition to the number of branch circuits required by other parts of this section, *at least one additional 20-ampere branch circuit shall be provided to supply the laundry receptacle outlet(s)* required by 210.52(F). This circuit shall have no other outlets.

Reference: 2017 National Electrical Code – Chapter 2 Wiring and Protection, Article 210 Branch Circuits. 210.11 Branch Circuits Required. 210.11(C) Dwelling Units. 210.11(C)(2) Laundry Branch Circuits.

EXAM 4

EXAM 4 ANSWERS

33. Answer D. one 20-ampere branch circuit which supplies no other outlets

In addition to the number of branch circuits required by other parts of this section, at least one 120-volt, ***20-ampere branch circuit shall be provided to supply the bathroom(s) receptacle outlet(s). Such circuits shall have no other outlets.***

Exception: Where the 20-ampere circuit supplies a single bathroom, outlets for other equipment within the same bathroom shall be permitted to be supplied in accordance with 210.23(A)(1) and (A)(2).

Reference: 2017 National Electrical Code – Chapter 2 Wiring and Protection, Article 210 Branch Circuits. 210.11 Branch Circuits Required. 210.11(C) Dwelling Units. 210.11(C)(3) Bathroom Branch Circuits.

34. Answer A. True

In addition to the number of branch circuits required by other parts of this section, at least one 120-volt, ***20-ampere branch circuit shall be provided to supply the bathroom(s) receptacle outlet(s). Such circuits shall have no other outlets.***

Exception: Where the 20-ampere circuit supplies a single bathroom, outlets for other equipment within the same bathroom shall be permitted to be supplied in accordance with 210.23(A)(1) and (A)(2).

Reference: 2017 National Electrical Code – Chapter 2 Wiring and Protection, Article 210 Branch Circuits. 210.11 Branch Circuits Required. 210.11(C) Dwelling Units. 210.11(C)(3) Bathroom Branch Circuits.

35. Answer B. bedrooms

Arc-fault circuit-interrupter protection shall be provided as required in 210.12(A), (B), and (C). The arc-fault circuit interrupter shall be installed in a readily accessible location.

*All 120-volt, single-phase, 15- and 20- ampere branch circuits supplying outlets or devices installed in dwelling unit kitchens, family rooms, dining rooms, living rooms, parlors, libraries, dens, **bedrooms**, sunrooms, recreation rooms, closets, hallways, laundry areas, or similar rooms or areas shall be protected by any of the means described in 210.12(A)(1) through (6):*

Reference: 2017 National Electrical Code – Chapter 2 Wiring and Protection, Article 210 Branch Circuits. 210.12 Arc-Fault Circuit-Interrupter Protection. 210.12(A) Dwelling Unit.

36. Answer D. all of these locations

A Arc-fault circuit-interrupter protection shall be provided as required in 210.12(A), (B), and (C). The arc-fault circuit interrupter shall be installed in a readily accessible location.

All 120-volt, single-phase, 15- and 20- ampere branch circuits supplying outlets or devices installed in dwelling unit kitchens, family rooms, dining rooms, living rooms, parlors, libraries, dens, bedrooms, sunrooms, recreation rooms, closets, hallways, laundry areas, or similar rooms or areas shall be protected by any of the means described in 210.12(A)(1) through (6):

Reference: 2017 National Electrical Code – Chapter 2 Wiring and Protection, Article 210 Branch Circuits. 210.12 Arc-Fault Circuit-Interrupter Protection. 210.12(A) Dwelling Units.

EXAM 4

EXAM 4 ANSWERS

37. **Answer A.** arc-fault circuit interrupter, combination-type

    A Arc-fault circuit-interrupter protection shall be provided as required in 210.12(A), (B), and (C). The arc-fault circuit interrupter shall be installed in a readily accessible location.

    All 120-volt, single-phase, 15- and 20- ampere branch circuits supplying outlets or devices installed in dwelling unit kitchens, family rooms, dining rooms, living rooms, parlors, libraries, dens, bedrooms, sunrooms, recreation rooms, closets, hallways, laundry areas, or similar rooms or areas shall be protected by any of the means described in 210.12(A)(1) through (6):

    Reference: 2017 National Electrical Code – Chapter 2 Wiring and Protection, Article 210 Branch Circuits. 210.12 Arc-Fault Circuit-Interrupter Protection. . 210.12(A) Dwelling Units.

38. **Answer C.** maximum

    Branch-circuit conductors shall have an ampacity not less than the maximum load to be served. Conductors shall be sized to carry not less than the larger of 210.19(A)(1)(a) or (b).

    (a) Where a branch circuit supplies continuous loads or any combination of continuous and noncontinuous loads, the minimum branch-circuit conductor size shall have an allowable ampacity not less than the noncontinuous load plus 125 percent of the continuous load.

    (b) The minimum branch-circuit conductor size shall have an allowable ampacity not less than the maximum load to be served after the application of any adjustment or correction factors.

    Reference: 2017 National Electrical Code – Chapter 2 Wiring and Protection, Article 210 Branch Circuits. 210.19 Conductors - Minimum Ampacity and Size. 210.19(A) Branch Circuits Not More Than 600 Volts. 210.19(A)(1) General.

39. **Answer D.** 125

    Branch-circuit conductors shall have an ampacity not less than the maximum load to be served. Conductors shall be sized to carry not less than the larger of 210.19(A)(1)(a) or (b).

    (a) Where a branch circuit supplies continuous loads or any combination of continuous and noncontinuous loads, the minimum branch-circuit conductor size *shall have an allowable ampacity not less than the noncontinuous load plus 125 percent of the continuous load.*

    (b) The minimum branch-circuit conductor size shall have an allowable ampacity not less than the maximum load to be served after the application of any adjustment or correction factors.

    Reference: 2017 National Electrical Code – Chapter 2 Wiring and Protection, Article 210 Branch Circuits. 210.19 Conductors - Minimum Ampacity and Size. 210.19(A) Branch Circuits Not More Than 600 Volts. 210.19(A)(1) General.

40. **Answer C.** 125%

    Branch-circuit conductors shall have an ampacity not less than the maximum load to be served. Conductors shall be sized to carry not less than the larger of 210.19(A)(1)(a) or (b).

    (a) Where a branch circuit supplies continuous loads or any combination of continuous and noncontinuous loads, the minimum branch-circuit conductor size shall have an allowable ampacity not less than the *noncontinuous load plus 125 percent of the continuous load.*

    (b) The minimum branch-circuit conductor size shall have an allowable ampacity not less than the maximum load to be served after the application of any adjustment or correction factors.

    Reference: 2017 National Electrical Code – Chapter 2 Wiring and Protection, Article 210 Branch Circuits. 210.19 Conductors – Minimum Ampacity and Size. 210.19(A) Branch Circuits Not More Than 600 Volts. 210.19(A)(1) General.

EXAM 4
EXAM 4 ANSWERS

41. Answer D. 125

Branch-circuit conductors shall have an ampacity not less than the maximum load to be served. Conductors shall be sized to carry not less than the larger of 210.19(A)(1)(a) or (b).

(a) Where a branch circuit supplies continuous loads or any combination of continuous and noncontinuous loads, the minimum branch-circuit conductor size shall have an allowable ampacity not less than the n*oncontinuous load plus 125 percent of the continuous load.*

(b) The minimum branch-circuit conductor size shall have an allowable ampacity not less than the maximum load to be served after the application of any adjustment or correction factors.

Reference: 2017 National Electrical Code – Chapter 2 Wiring and Protection, Article 210 Branch Circuits. 210.19 Conductors - Minimum Ampacity and Size. 210.19(A) Branch Circuits Not More Than 600 Volts. 210.19(A)(1) General.

42. Answer A. cord-and-plug-connected portable

Conductors of branch circuits supplying more than one receptacle for cord-and-plug-connected portable loads shall have an ampacity of not less than the rating of the branch circuit.

Reference: 2017 National Electrical Code – Chapter 2 Wiring and Protection, Article 210 Branch Circuits. 210.19 Conductors - Minimum Ampacity and Size. 210.19(A) Branch Circuits Not More Than 600 Volts. 210.19(A)(2) Branch Circuits with More than One Receptacle.

43. Answer C. 40

Branch circuit conductors supplying household ranges, wall-mounted ovens, counter-mounted cooking units, and other household cooking appliances shall have an ampacity not less than the rating of the branch circuit and not less than the maximum load to be served. **For ranges of 8 3⁄4 kW or more rating, the minimum branch-circuit rating shall be 40 amperes.**

Exception No. 1: Conductors tapped from a 50-ampere branch circuit supplying electric ranges, wall-mounted electric ovens, and counter mounted electric cooking units shall have an ampacity of not less than\ 20 amperes and shall be sufficient for the load to be served. These tap conductors include any conductors that are a part of the leads supplied with the appliance that are smaller than the branch-circuit conductors. The taps shall not be longer than necessary for servicing the appliance.

Exception No. 2: The neutral conductor of a 3-wire branch circuit supplying a household electric range, a wall-mounted oven, or a counter-mounted cooking unit shall be permitted to be smaller than the ungrounded conductors where the maximum demand of a range of 83⁄4-kW or more rating has been calculated according to Column C of Table 220.55, but such conductor shall have an ampacity of not less than 70 percent of the branch-circuit rating and shall not be smaller than 10 AWG.

Reference: 2017 National Electrical Code – Chapter 2 Wiring and Protection, Article 210 Branch Circuits. 210.19 Conductors - Minimum Ampacity and Size. 210.19(A) Branch Circuits Not More Than 600 Volts. 210.19(A)(3) Household Ranges and Cooking Appliances.

EXAM 4

EXAM 4 ANSWERS

44. Answer D.   125

Where a branch circuit supplies continuous loads or any combination of continuous and noncontinuous loads, *the rating of the overcurrent device shall not be less than the noncontinuous load plus 125 percent of the continuous load.*

Reference: 2017 National Electrical Code – Chapter 2 Wiring and Protection, Article 210 Branch Circuits. 210.20 Overcurrent Protection. 210.20(A) Continuous and Noncontinuous Loads.

45. Answer D.   125

Where a branch circuit supplies continuous loads or any combination of continuous and noncontinuous loads, the rating of the overcurrent device shall not be less than the *noncontinuous load plus 125 percent of the continuous load.*

Reference: 2017 National Electrical Code – Chapter 2 Wiring and Protection, Article 210 Branch Circuits. 210.20 Overcurrent Protection. . 210.20(A) Continuous and Noncontinuous Loads.

46. Answer A.   heavy-duty type

Where connected to a branch circuit having a rating in excess of 20 amperes, lampholders shall be of the heavy-duty type. *A heavy-duty lampholder shall have a rating of not less than 660 watts if of the admedium type, or not less than 750 watts if of any other type.*

Reference: 2017 National Electrical Code – Chapter 2 Wiring and Protection, Article 210 Branch Circuits. 210.21 Outlet Devices. . 210.21(A) Lampholders.

47. Answer D.   20 amperes

A single receptacle installed on an individual branch circuit shall have an ampere rating not less than that of the branch circuit. Informational Note: See the definition of receptacle in Article 100

Reference: 2017 National Electrical Code – Chapter 2 Wiring and Protection, Article 210 Branch Circuits. 210.21 Outlet Devices. 210.21(B) Receptacles. 210.21(B)(1) Single Receptacle on an Individual Branch Circuit.

48. Answer C.   100%

A single receptacle installed on an individual branch circuit *shall have an ampere rating not less than that of the branch circuit.*

Informational Note: See the definition of receptacle in Article 100

Reference: 2017 National Electrical Code – Chapter 2 Wiring and Protection, Article 210 Branch Circuits. 210.21 Outlet Devices. 210.21(B) Receptacles. 210.21(B)(1) Single Receptacle on an Individual Branch Circuit.

EXAM 4

EXAM 4 ANSWERS

Table 210.21(B)(3) Receptacle Ratings for Various Size Circuits

Circuit Rating (Amperes)	Receptacle Rating (Amperes)
15	Not over 15
20	15 or 20
30	30
40	40 or 50
50	50

49. **Answer D.** all of the above

Where connected to a branch circuit supplying two or more receptacles or outlets, receptacle ratings shall conform to the values listed in **Table 210.21(B)(3)**, or, *where rated higher than 50 amperes, the receptacle rating shall not be less than the branch-circuit rating.*

Exception No. 1: Receptacles installed exclusively for the use of one or more cord-and-plug-connected arc welders shall be permitted to have ampere ratings not less than the minimum branch-circuit conductor ampacity determined by 630.11(A) or (B) for arc welders.

Exception No. 2: The ampere rating of a receptacle installed for electric discharge lighting shall be permitted to be based on 410.62(C).

Reference: 2017 National Electrical Code – Chapter 2 Wiring and Protection, Article 210 Branch Circuits. 210.21 Outlet Devices. 210.21(B) Receptacles. 210.21(B)(3) Receptacle Ratings.

50. **Answer C.** either A or B

Where connected to a branch circuit supplying two or more receptacles or outlets, receptacle ratings shall conform to the values listed in Table 210.21(B)(3), or, where rated higher than 50 amperes, *the receptacle rating shall not be less than the branch-circuit rating.*

Reference: 2017 National Electrical Code – Chapter 2 Wiring and Protection, Article 210 Branch Circuits. 210.21 Outlet Devices. 210.21(B) Receptacles. Table 210.21(B)(3) Receptacle Ratings for Various Size Circuits (page 70-59)Insert

51. **Answer D.** Either A or B

Where connected to a branch circuit supplying two or more receptacles or outlets, receptacle ratings shall conform to the values listed in Table 210.21(B)(3), or, where rated higher than 50 amperes, the receptacle rating shall not be less than the branch-circuit rating. Table on page 70-59.

Reference: 2017 National Electrical Code – Chapter 2 Wiring and Protection, Article 210 Branch Circuits. 210.21 Outlet Devices. 210.21(B) Receptacles. 210.21(B)(3) Receptacle Ratings.

EXAM 4
EXAM 4 ANSWERS

52. Answer A. True

A 15- or 20-ampere branch circuit shall be permitted to supply lighting units or other utilization equipment, or a combination of both, and shall comply with 210.23(A)(1) and (A)(2).

Reference: 2017 National Electrical Code – Chapter 2 Wiring and Protection, Article 210 Branch Circuits. 210.23 Permissible Loads, Multiple-Outlet Branch Circuits. 210.23(A) 15- and 20-Ampere Branch Circuits.

53. Answer B. 16 amperes

The rating of anyone cord-and-plug-connected utilization equipment not fastened in place shall not exceed 80 percent of the branch-circuit ampere rating.

Reference: 2017 National Electrical Code – Chapter 2 Wiring and Protection, Article 210 Branch Circuits. 210.23 Permissible Loads, Multiple-Outlet Branch Circuits. 210.23(A) 15- and 20-Ampere Branch Circuits. 210.23(A)(1) Cord-and-Plug-Connected Equipment Not Fastened in Place.

20 amps x 80% = 16 amperes

54. Answer B. 80

A 30-ampere branch circuit shall be permitted to supply fixed lighting units with heavy-duty lampholders in other than a dwelling unit(s) or utilization equipment in any occupancy. *A rating of anyone cord-and-plug-connected utilization equipment shall not exceed 80 percent of the branch-circuit ampere rating.*

Reference: 2017 National Electrical Code – Chapter 2 Wiring and Protection, Article 210 Branch Circuits. 210.23 Permissible Loads, Multiple-Outlet Branch Circuits. 210.23(B) 30-Ampere Branch Circuits.

55. Answer B. 24 amperes

A 30-ampere branch circuit shall be permitted to supply fixed lighting units with heavy-duty lampholders in other than a dwelling unit(s) or utilization equipment in any occupancy. *A rating of anyone cord-and-plug-connected utilization equipment shall not exceed 80 percent of the branch-circuit ampere rating.*

30 amperes x 80% = 24 amperes

Reference: 2017 National Electrical Code – Chapter 2 Wiring and Protection, Article 210 Branch Circuits. 210.23 Permissible Loads, Multiple-Outlet Branch Circuits. 210.23(B) 30-Ampere Branch Circuits.

56. Answer A. 50

Branch circuits larger than 50 amperes shall supply only nonlighting outlet loads.

Reference: 2017 National Electrical Code – Chapter 2 Wiring and Protection, Article 210 Branch Circuits. 210.23 Permissible Loads, Multiple-Outlet Branch Circuits. 210.23(D) Branch Circuits Larger Than 50 Amperes.

57. Answer C. non-lighting

Branch circuits larger than 50 amperes shall supply only nonlighting outlet loads.

Reference: 2017 National Electrical Code – Chapter 2 Wiring and Protection, Article 210 Branch Circuits. 210.23 Permissible Loads, Multiple-Outlet Branch Circuits. 210.23(D) Branch Circuits Larger Than 50 Amperes.

EXAM 4

EXAM 4 ANSWERS

Table 210.24 Summary of Branch-Circuit Requirements

Circuit Rating	15 A	20 A	30 A	40 A	50 A
Conductors (min. size):					
Circuit wires[1]	14	12	10	8	6
Taps	14	14	14	12	12
Fixture wires and cords — see 240.5					
Overcurrent Protection	15 A	20 A	30 A	40 A	50 A
Outlet devices:					
Lampholders permitted	Any type	Any type	Heavy duty	Heavy duty	Heavy duty
Receptacle rating[2]	15 max. A	15 or 20 A	30 A	40 or 50 A	50 A
Maximum Load	15 A	20 A	30 A	40 A	50 A
Permissible load	See 210.23(A)	See 210.23(A)	See 210.23(B)	See 210.23(C)	See 210.23(C)

[1]These gauges are for copper conductors.
[2]For receptacle rating of cord-connected electric-discharge luminaires, see 410.62(C).

58. Answer C. 14

The requirements for circuits that have two or more outlets or receptacles, other than the receptacle circuits of 210.11 (C)(1), (C)(2), and (C)(3), are summarized in Table 210.24. This table provides only a summary of minimum requirements. See 210.19, 210.20, and 210.21 for the specific requirements applying to branch circuits.

Reference: 2017 National Electrical Code – Chapter 2 Wiring and Protection, Article 210 Branch Circuits. 210.24 Branch-Circuit Requirements - Summary.

59. Answer B. 8

The requirements for circuits that have two or more outlets or receptacles, other than the receptacle circuits of 210.11 (C)(1), (C)(2), and (C)(3), are summarized in Table 210.24. This table provides only a summary of minimum requirements. See 210.19, 210.20, and 210.21 for the specific requirements applying to branch circuits. .

Reference: 2017 National Electrical Code – Chapter 2 Wiring and Protection, Article 210 Branch Circuits. 210.24 Branch-Circuit Requirements - Summary.

60. Answer D. 14

The requirements for circuits that have two or more outlets or receptacles, other than the receptacle circuits of 210.11 (C)(1), (C)(2), and (C)(3), are summarized in Table 210.24. This table provides only a summary of minimum requirements. See 210.19, 210.20, and 210.21 for the specific requirements applying to branch circuits.

Reference: 2017 National Electrical Code – Chapter 2 Wiring and Protection, Article 210 Branch Circuits. 210.24 Branch-Circuit Requirements - Summary.

61. Answer A. 20 ampere rated receptacles do not comply with the NEC

The requirements for circuits that have two or more outlets or receptacles, other than the receptacle circuits of 210.11(C)(1), (C)(2), and (C)(3), are summarized in Table 210.24. This table provides only a summary of minimum requirements. See 210.19, 210.20, and 210.21 for the specific requirements applying to branch circuits.

Reference: 2017 National Electrical Code – Chapter 2 Wiring and Protection, Article 210 Branch Circuits. 210.24 Branch-Circuit Requirements – Summary. Table 210.24 Summary of Branch-Circuit Requirements (page 70-60)

EXAM 4

EXAM 4 ANSWERS

62. **Answer D.** permitted to be omitted

    A receptacle outlet shall be installed wherever flexible cords with attachment plugs are used. Where flexible cords are permitted to be permanently connected, *receptacles shall be permitted to be omitted for such cords.*

    Reference: 2017 National Electrical Code – Chapter 2 Wiring and Protection, Article 210 Branch Circuits. 210.50 General. . 210.50(B) Cord Connections.

63. **Answer C.** 6 feet

    Appliance receptacle outlets installed in a dwelling unit for specific appliances, *such as laundry equipment, shall be installed within 1.8 m (6 ft.) of the intended location of the appliance.*

    Reference: 2017 National Electrical Code – Chapter 2 Wiring and Protection, Article 210 Branch Circuits. 210.50 General. 210.50(C) Appliance Receptacle Outlets.

64. **Answer C.** 6

    Appliance receptacle outlets installed in a dwelling unit for specific appliances, such as laundry equipment, *shall be installed within 1.8 m (6 ft.) of the intended location of the appliance.*

    III. Required Outlets

    Reference: 2017 National Electrical Code – Chapter 2 Wiring and Protection, Article 210 Branch Circuits. 210.50 General. 210.50(C) Appliance Receptacle Outlets.

65. **Answer C.** 6

    Appliance receptacle outlets installed in a dwelling unit for specific appliances, such as laundry equipment, *shall be installed within 1.8 m (6 ft.) of the intended location of the appliance.*

    Reference: 2017 National Electrical Code – Chapter 2 Wiring and Protection, Article 210 Branch Circuits. 210.50 General. . 210.50(C) Appliance Receptacle Outlets.

66. **Answer C.** 6 feet

    Appliance receptacle outlets installed in a dwelling unit for specific appliances, such as laundry equipment, *shall be installed within 1.8 m (6 ft.) of the intended location of the appliance.*

    Reference: 2017 National Electrical Code – Chapter 2 Wiring and Protection, Article 210 Branch Circuits. 210.50 General. 210.50(C) Appliance Receptacle Outlets.

67. **Answer C.** 5-1/2

    This section provides requirements for 125-volt, 15- and 20-ampere receptacle outlets. The receptacles required by this section shall be in addition to any receptacle that is:

    (1) Part of a luminaire or appliance, or

    (2) Controlled by a wall switch in accordance with 210.70(A)(1), Exception No.1, or

    (3) Located within cabinets or cupboards, or

    (4) Located more than 1.7 m *(5-1/2 ft.) above the floor*

    Permanently installed electric baseboard heaters equipped with factory-installed receptacle outlets or outlets provided as a separate assembly by the manufacturer shall be permitted as the required outlet or outlets for the wall space utilized by such permanently installed heaters. Such receptacle outlets shall not be connected to the heater circuits.

    Reference: 2017 National Electrical Code – Chapter 2 Wiring and Protection, Article 210 Branch Circuits. 210.52 Dwelling Unit Receptacle Outlets. (4)

EXAM 4
EXAM 4 ANSWERS

68. **Answer D.** not be connected to the heater circuits.

This section provides requirements for 125-volt, 15- and 20-ampere receptacle outlets. The receptacles required by this section shall be in addition to any receptacle that is:

(1) Part of a luminaire or appliance, or

(2) Controlled by a wall switch in accordance with 210.70(A)(1), Exception No.1, or

(3) Located within cabinets or cupboards, or

(4) Located more than 1.7 m (5-1/2 ft.) above the floor

Permanently installed electric baseboard heaters equipped with factory-installed receptacle outlets or outlets provided as a separate assembly by the manufacturer shall be permitted as the required outlet or outlets for the wan space utilized by such permanently installed heaters. *Such receptacle outlets shall not be connected to the heater circuits.*

Reference: 2017 National Electrical Code – Chapter 2 Wiring and Protection, Article 210 Branch Circuits. 210.52 Dwelling Unit Receptacle Outlets.

69. **Answer D.** Required.

Receptacles shall be installed such that no point measured horizontally along *the floor line of any wall space is more than 1.8 m (6 ft.) from a receptacle outlet.*

Reference: 2017 National Electrical Code – Chapter 2 Wiring and Protection, Article 210 Branch Circuits. 210.52 Dwelling Unit Receptacle Outlets. 210.52(A) General Provisions. 210.52(A)(1) Spacing.

70. **Answer C.** 6

Receptacles shall be installed such that no point measured *horizontally along the floor line of any wall space is more than 1.8 m (6 ft.) from a receptacle outlet.*

Reference: 2017 National Electrical Code – Chapter 2 Wiring and Protection, Article 210 Branch Circuits. 210.52 Dwelling Unit Receptacle Outlets. 210.52(A) General Provisions. 210.52(A)(1) Spacing.

71. **Answer B.** 2

As used in this section, a wall space shall include the following:

(1) *Any space 600 mm (2 ft) or more in width (including space measured around corners) and unbroken along the floor line by doorways and similar openings*, fireplaces, and fixed cabinets that do not have countertops or similar work surfaces

(2) The space occupied by fixed panels in walls, excluding sliding panels

(3) The space afforded by fixed room dividers, such as freestanding bar-type counters or railings

Reference: 2017 National Electrical Code – Chapter 2 Wiring and Protection, Article 210 Branch Circuits. 210.52 Dwelling Unit Receptacle Outlets. 210.52(A) General Provisions. 210.52(A)(2) Wall Space.

72. **Answer B.** 2

As used in this section, a wall space shall include the following:

(1) *Any space 600 mm (2 ft) or more in width (including space measured around corners) and unbroken along the floor line* by doorways and similar openings, fireplaces, and fixed cabinets

(2) The space occupied by fixed panels in exterior walls, excluding sliding panels

(3) The space afforded by fixed room dividers, such as freestanding bar-type counters or railings

Reference: 2017 National Electrical Code – Chapter 2 Wiring and Protection, Article 210 Branch Circuits. 210.52 Dwelling Unit Receptacle Outlets. . 210.52(A) General Provisions. . 210.52(A)(2) Wall Space.

73. **Answer A.** 2 feet

As used in this section, a wall space shall include the following:

(1) *Any space 600 mm (2 ft.) or more in width (including space measured around corners) and unbroken along the floor line by doorways and similar openings, fireplaces, and fixed cabinets*

Reference: 2017 National Electrical Code – Chapter 2 Wiring and Protection, Article 210 Branch Circuits. 210.52 Dwelling Receptacle Outlets. 210.52(A) General Provisions. 210.52(A)(2) Wall Space. 210.52(A)(2)(1)

EXAM 4

EXAM 4 ANSWERS

74. Answer B. 18 inches

Receptacle outlets in or on floors shall not be counted as part of the required number of receptacle outlets unless located within *450 mm (18 in.) of the wall.*

Reference: 2017 National Electrical Code – Chapter 2 Wiring and Protection, Article 210 Branch Circuits. 210.52 Dwelling Receptacle Outlets. 210.52(A) General Provisions. 210.52(A)(3) Floor Receptacles.

75. Answer B. 1.5 ft.

Receptacle outlets in or on floors shall not be counted as part of the required number of receptacle outlets *unless located within 450 mm (18 in.) of the wall.*

Reference: 2017 National Electrical Code – Chapter 2 Wiring and Protection, Article 210 Branch Circuits. 210.52 Dwelling Unit Receptacle Outlets. 210.52(A) General Provisions. 210.52(A)(3) Floor Receptacles.

76. Answer A. 18

Receptacle outlets in or on floors shall not be counted as part of the required number of receptacle outlets unless located within *450 mm (18 in.) of the wall*.

Reference: 2017 National Electrical Code – Chapter 2 Wiring and Protection, Article 210 Branch Circuits. 210.52 Dwelling Unit Receptacle Outlets. 210.52(A) General Provisions. 210.52(A)(3) Floor Receptacles.

77. Answer B. 20

In the kitchen, pantry, breakfast room, dining room, or similar area of a dwelling unit, the two or more 20-ampere small-appliance branch circuits required by 210.11(C)(1) shall serve all wall and floor receptacle outlets covered by 210.52(A), all countertop outlets covered by 210.52(C), and receptacle outlets for refrigeration equipment.

Reference: 2017 National Electrical Code – Chapter 2 Wiring and Protection, Article 210 Branch Circuits. 210.52 Dwelling Unit Receptacle Outlets. 210.52(B) Small Appliances. 210.52(B)(1) Receptacle Outlets Served.

78. Answer C. Two or more 20-ampere

In the kitchen, pantry, breakfast room, dining room, or similar area of a dwelling unit, the two or more 20-ampere small-appliance branch circuits required by 210.11(C)(1) shall serve all wall and floor receptacle outlets covered by 210.52(A), all countertop outlets covered by 21 0.52(C), and receptacle outlets for refrigeration equipment.

Reference: 2017 National Electrical Code – Chapter 2 Wiring and Protection, Article 210 Branch Circuits. 210.52 Dwelling Unit Receptacle Outlets. . 210.52(B) Small Appliances. 210.52(B)(1) Receptacle Outlets Served.

79. Answer C. serve more than one kitchen.

Receptacles installed in a kitchen to serve countertop surfaces shall be supplied by not fewer than two small-appliance branch circuits, either or both of which shall also be permitted to supply receptacle outlets in the same kitchen and in other rooms specified in 210.52(B)(1). Additional small-appliance branch circuits shall be permitted to supply receptacle outlets in the kitchen and other rooms specified in 210.52(B)(J). *No small-appliance branch circuit shall serve more than one kitchen.*

Reference: 2017 National Electrical Code – Chapter 2 Wiring and Protection, Article 210 Branch Circuits. 210.52 Dwelling Unit Receptacle Outlets. . 210.52(B) Small Appliances. 210.52(B)(3) Kitchen Receptacle Requirements.

80. Answer B. two

Receptacles installed in a kitchen to serve countertop surfaces shall be supplied by not fewer than two small-appliance branch circuits, either or both of which shall also be permitted to supply receptacle outlets in the same kitchen and in other rooms specified in 210.52(B)(1). Additional small-appliance branch circuits shall be permitted to supply receptacle outlets in the kitchen and other rooms specified in 210.52(B)(J). No small-appliance branch circuit shall serve more than one kitchen.

Reference: 2017 National Electrical Code – Chapter 2 Wiring and Protection, Article 210 Branch Circuits. 210.52 Dwelling Unit Receptacle Outlets. 210.52(B) Small Appliances. 210.52(B)(3) Kitchen Receptacle Requirements.

EXAM 4

EXAM 4 ANSWERS

81. **Answer C.** 12

    A receptacle outlet shall be installed at each wall countertop and work surface that is 300 mm (12 in.) or wider. Receptacle outlets shall be installed so that no point along the wall line is more than 600 mm (24 in.) measured horizontally from a receptacle outlet in that space.

    Exception: Receptacle outlets shall not be required on a wall directly behind a range, counter-mounted cooking

    Reference: 2017 National Electrical Code – Chapter 2 Wiring and Protection, Article 210 Branch Circuits. 210.52 Dwelling Unit Receptacle Outlets. 210.52(C) Countertops. 210.52(C)(1) Wall Countertop Spaces And work surface.

82. **Answer B.** 24 inches

    A receptacle outlet shall be installed at each wall countertop and work surface that is 300 mm (12 in.) or wider. Receptacle outlets shall be installed so that *no point along the wall line is more than 600 mm (24 in.) measured horizontally from a receptacle outlet in that space.*

    Exception: Receptacle outlets shall not be required on a wall directly behind a range, counter-mounted cooking

    Reference: 2017 National Electrical Code – Chapter 2 Wiring and Protection, Article 210 Branch Circuits. 210.52 Dwelling Receptacle Outlets. 210.52(C) Countertops. 210.52(C)(1) Wall Countertop Spaces.

83. **Answer A.** True

    A receptacle outlet shall be installed at each wall countertop and work surface that is 300 mm (12 in.) or wider. Receptacle outlets shall be installed so that no point along the wall line is more than 600 mm (24 in.) measured horizontally from a receptacle outlet in that space.

    Exception: Receptacle outlets shall not be required on a wall directly behind a range, counter-mounted cooking

    Reference: 2017 National Electrical Code – Chapter 2 Wiring and Protection, Article 210 Branch Circuits. 210.52 Dwelling Unit Receptacle Outlets. . 210.52(C) Countertops. . 210.52(C)(1) Wall Countertop Spaces.

84. **Answer B.** 12 in., 24 in.

    A receptacle outlet shall be installed at each wall countertop and work surface that is 300 mm (12 in.) or wider. Receptacle outlets shall be installed so that *no point along the wall line is more than 600 mm (24 in.) measured horizontally* from a receptacle outlet in that space.

    Exception: Receptacle outlets shall not be required on a wall directly behind a range, counter-mounted cooking

    Reference: 2017 National Electrical Code – Chapter 2 Wiring and Protection, Article 210 Branch Circuits. 210.52 Dwelling Unit Receptacle Outlets. . 210.52(C) Countertops. . 210.52(C)(1) Wall Countertop Spaces.

85. **Answer B.** 12 inches

    A receptacle outlet shall be installed at each wall countertop and work surface that is 300 mm (12 in.) or wider. Receptacle outlets shall be installed so that no point along the wall line is more than 600 mm (24 in.) measured horizontally from a receptacle outlet in that space.

    Exception: Receptacle outlets shall not be required on a wall directly behind a range, counter-mounted cooking

    Reference: 2017 National Electrical Code – Chapter 2 Wiring and Protection, Article 210 Branch Circuits. 210.52 Dwelling Receptacle Outlets. 210.52(C) Countertops. 210.52(C)(1) Wall Countertop Spaces.

86. **Answer B.** 24, 12

    At least one receptacle shall be installed at each island countertop space with a long dimension of 600 mm (24 in.) or greater and a short dimension of 300 mm (12 in.) or greater.

    Reference: 2017 National Electrical Code – Chapter 2 Wiring and Protection, Article 210 Branch Circuits. 210.52 Dwelling Unit Receptacle Outlets. 210.52(C) Countertops. 210.52(C)(2) Island Countertop Spaces.

EXAM 4

EXAM 4 ANSWERS

87. Answer B. 24, 12

At least one receptacle outlet shall be installed at each peninsular countertop space with a *long dimension of 600 mm (24 in.) or greater* and *a short dimension of 300 mm (12 in.) or greater.* A peninsular countertop is measured from the connecting edge.

Reference: 2017 National Electrical Code – Chapter 2 Wiring and Protection, Article 210 Branch Circuits. 210.52 Dwelling Unit Receptacle Outlets. 210.52(C) Countertops. 210.52(C)(3) Peninsular Countertop Spaces.

88. Answer B. range, counter-mounted cooking unit, or sink

Countertop spaces separated by rangetops, refrigerators, or sinks shall be considered as separate countertop spaces in applying the requirements of 210.52(C)(1). If a range, counter-mounted cooking unit, or sink is installed in an island or peninsular countertop and *the depth of the countertop behind the range, counter-mounted cooking unit*, or sink is less than 300 mm (12 in.), the range, counter-mounted cooking unit, or sink shall be considered to divide the countertop space into two separate countertop spaces. Each separate countertop space shall comply with the applicable requirements in 210.52(C).

Reference: 2017 National Electrical Code – Chapter 2 Wiring and Protection, Article 210 Branch Circuits. 210.52 Dwelling Unit Receptacle Outlets. . 210.52(C) Countertops. 210.52(C)(4) Separate Spaces.

89. Answer D. 20

Receptacle outlets shall be located on or above, but not more than 500 mm (20 in.) above, the countertop or work surface. Receptacle outlet assemblies listed for use in countertops or work surfaces shall be permitted to be installed in countertops or work surfaces. Receptacle outlets rendered not readily accessible by appliances fastened in place, appliance garages, sinks, or range tops as covered in 210.52(C)(1), Exception, or appliances occupying dedicated space shall not be considered as these required outlets.

Informational Note: See 406.5(E) and 406.5(G) for requirements for installation of receptacles in countertops and 406.5(F) and 406.5(G) for requirements for installation of receptacles in work surfaces.

Exception to (5): To comply with the following conditions (1) and (2), receptacle outlets shall be permitted to be mounted not more than 300 mm (12 in.) below the countertop or work surface. Receptacles mounted below a countertop or work surface in accordance with this exception shall not be located where the countertop or work surface extends more than 150 mm (6 in.) beyond its support base.

(1) Construction for the physically impaired

(2) On island and peninsular countertops or work surface where the surface is flat across its entire surface (no backsplashes, dividers, etc.) and there are no means to mount a receptacle within 500 mm (20 in.) above the countertop or work surface, such as an overhead cabinet

Reference: 2017 National Electrical Code – Chapter 2 Wiring and Protection, Article 210 Branch Circuits. 210.52 Dwelling Unit Receptacle Outlets. 210.52(C) Countertops. 210.52(C)(5) Receptacle Outlet Location.

EXAM 4

EXAM 4 ANSWERS

90. Answer C. 12

Receptacle outlets shall be located on or above, but not more than 500 mm (20 in.) above, the countertop or work surface. Receptacle outlet assemblies listed for use in countertops or work surfaces shall be permitted to be installed in countertops or work surfaces. Receptacle outlets rendered not readily accessible by appliances fastened in place, appliance garages, sinks, or range tops as covered in 210.52(C)(1), Exception, or appliances occupying dedicated space shall not be considered as these required outlets.

Informational Note: See 406.5(E) and 406.5(G) for requirements for installation of receptacles in countertops and 406.5(F) and 406.5(G) for requirements for installation of receptacles in work surfaces.

Exception to (5): To comply with the following conditions (1) and (2), receptacle outlets shall be permitted to be mounted not more than 300 mm (12 in.) below the countertop or work surface. Receptacles mounted below a countertop or work surface in accordance with this exception shall not be located where the countertop or work surface extends more than 150 mm (6 in.) beyond its support base.

(1) Construction for the physically impaired

(2) On island and peninsular countertops or work surface where the surface is flat across its entire surface (no backsplashes, dividers, etc.) and there are no means to mount a receptacle within 500 mm (20 in.) above the countertop or work surface, such as an overhead cabinet

Reference: 2017 National Electrical Code – Chapter 2 Wiring and Protection, Article 210 Branch Circuits. 210.52 Dwelling Unit Receptacle Outlets. 210.52(C) Countertops. 210.52(C)(5) Receptacle Outlet Location.

91. Answer C. 20 inches

Receptacle outlets shall be located on or above, but not more than 500 mm (20 in.) above, the countertop or work surface. Receptacle outlet assemblies listed for use in countertops or work surfaces shall be permitted to be installed in countertops or work surfaces. Receptacle outlets rendered not readily accessible by appliances fastened in place, appliance garages, sinks, or range tops as covered in 210.52(C)(1), Exception, or appliances occupying dedicated space shall not be considered as these required outlets.

Informational Note: See 406.5(E) and 406.5(G) for requirements for installation of receptacles in countertops and 406.5(F) and 406.5(G) for requirements for installation of receptacles in work surfaces.

Exception to (5): To comply with the following conditions (1) and (2), receptacle outlets shall be permitted to be mounted not more than 300 mm (12 in.) below the countertop or work surface. Receptacles mounted below a countertop or work surface in accordance with this exception shall not be located where the countertop or work surface extends more than 150 mm (6 in.) beyond its support base.

(1) Construction for the physically impaired

(2) On island and peninsular countertops or work surface where the surface is flat across its entire surface (no backsplashes, dividers, etc.) and there are no means to mount a receptacle within 500 mm (20 in.) above the countertop or work surface, such as an overhead cabinet

Reference: 2017 National Electrical Code – Chapter 2 Wiring and Protection, Article 210 Branch Circuits. 210.52 Dwelling Receptacle Outlets. 210.52(C) Countertops. 210.52(C)(5) Receptacle Outlet Location.

EXAM 4

EXAM 4 ANSWERS

92. **Answer C.**   12

    Receptacle outlets shall be located on or above, but not more than 500 mm (20 in.) above, the countertop or work surface. Receptacle outlet assemblies listed for use in countertops or work surfaces shall be permitted to be installed in countertops or work surfaces. Receptacle outlets rendered not readily accessible by appliances fastened in place, appliance garages, sinks, or range tops as covered in 210.52(C)(1), Exception, or appliances occupying dedicated space shall not be considered as these required outlets.

    Informational Note: See 406.5(E) and 406.5(G) for requirements for installation of receptacles in countertops and 406.5(F) and 406.5(G) for requirements for installation of receptacles in work surfaces.

    Exception to (5): To comply with the following conditions (1) and (2), receptacle outlets shall be permitted to be mounted not more than 300 mm (12 in.) below the countertop or work surface. Receptacles mounted below a countertop or work surface in accordance with this exception shall not be located where the countertop or work surface extends more than 150 mm (6 in.) beyond its support base.

    (1) Construction for the physically impaired

    (2) On island and peninsular countertops or work surface where the surface is flat across its entire surface (no backsplashes, dividers, etc.) and there are no means to mount a receptacle within 500 mm (20 in.) above the countertop or work surface, such as an overhead cabinet

    Reference: 2017 National Electrical Code – Chapter 2 Wiring and Protection, Article 210 Branch Circuits. 210.52 Dwelling Unit Receptacle Outlets. 210.52(C) Countertops. 210.52(C)(5) Receptacle Outlet Location. Exception

93. **Answer D.**   36 inches (3 ft.)

    At least one receptacle outlet shall be installed in bathrooms within 900 mm (3 ft) of the outside edge of each basin. The receptacle outlet shall be located on a wall or partition that is adjacent to the basin or basin countertop, located on the countertop, or installed on the side or face of the basin cabinet. In no case shall the receptacle be located more than 300 mm (12 in.) below the top of the basin or basin countertop. Receptacle outlet assemblies listed for use in countertops shall be permitted to be installed in the countertop.

    Informational Note: See 406.5(E) and 406.5(G) for requirements for installation of receptacles in countertops.

    Reference: 2017 National Electrical Code – Chapter 2 Wiring and Protection, Article 210 Branch Circuits. 210.52 Dwelling Receptacle Outlets. 210.52(D) Bathrooms.

94. **Answer C.**   3

    At least one receptacle outlet shall be installed in bathrooms within 900 mm (3 ft) of the outside edge of each basin. The receptacle outlet shall be located on a wall or partition that is adjacent to the basin or basin countertop, located on the countertop, or installed on the side or face of the basin cabinet. In no case shall the receptacle be located more than 300 mm (12 in.) below the top of the basin or basin countertop. Receptacle outlet assemblies listed for use in countertops shall be permitted to be installed in the countertop.

    Informational Note: See 406.5(E) and 406.5(G) for requirements for installation of receptacles in countertops.

    Reference: 2017 National Electrical Code – Chapter 2 Wiring and Protection, Article 210 Branch Circuits. 210.52 Dwelling Unit Receptacle Outlets. 210.52(D) Bathrooms.

EXAM 4

EXAM 4 ANSWERS

95. **Answer A.** 3 ft.

    At least one receptacle outlet shall be installed in bathrooms within 900 mm (3 ft) of the outside edge of each basin. The receptacle outlet shall be located on a wall or partition that is adjacent to the basin or basin countertop, located on the countertop, or installed on the side or face of the basin cabinet. In no case shall the receptacle be located more than 300 mm (12 in.) below the top of the basin or basin countertop. Receptacle outlet assemblies listed for use in countertops shall be permitted to be installed in the countertop.

    Informational Note: See 406.5(E) and 406.5(G) for requirements for installation of receptacles in countertops.

    Reference: 2017 National Electrical Code – Chapter 2 Wiring and Protection, Article 210 Branch Circuits. 210.52 Dwelling Unit Receptacle Outlets. 210.52(D) Bathrooms.

96. **Answer D.** 6-1/2

    For a one-family dwelling and each unit of a two-family dwelling that is at grade level, *at least one receptacle outlet readily accessible from grade and not more than 2.0 m (6-1/2 ft.) above grade* level shall be installed at the front and back of the dwelling.

    Reference: 2017 National Electrical Code – Chapter 2 Wiring and Protection, Article 210 Branch Circuits. 210.52 Dwelling Unit Receptacle Outlets. 210.52(E) Outdoor Outlets. 210.52(E)(1) One-Family and Two-Family Dwellings.

97. **Answer D.** all of the above

    For a one-family dwelling and each unit of a two-family dwelling that is at grade level, *at least one receptacle outlet readily accessible from grade and not more than 2.0 m (6-1/2 ft.) above grade level* shall be installed at the front and back of the dwelling.

    Reference: 2017 National Electrical Code – Chapter 2 Wiring and Protection, Article 210 Branch Circuits. 210.52 Dwelling Unit Receptacle Outlets. . 210.52(E) Outdoor Outlets. . 210.52(E)(1) One-Family and Two-Family Dwellings.

98. **Answer A.** one

    Review the 2 exceptions in this article.

    In dwelling units, at least one receptacle outlet shall be installed in areas designated for the installation of laundry equipment.

    Exception No.1: A receptacle for laundry equipment shall not be required in a dwelling unit of a multifamily building where laundry facilities are provided on the premises for use by all building occupants.

    Exception No.2: A receptacle for laundry equipment shall not be required in other than one-family dwellings where laundry facilities are not to be installed or permitted.

    Reference: 2017 National Electrical Code – Chapter 2 Wiring and Protection, Article 210 Branch Circuits. 210.52 Dwelling Unit Receptacle Outlets. 210.52(F) Laundry Areas.

99. **Answer A.** one

    For one and two- family dwellings, *at least one receptacle outlet shall be installed in the areas specified in 210.52(G)(1) through (3)*. These receptacles shall be in addition to receptacles required for specific equipment.

    (1) Garages. In each attached garage and in each detached garage with electric power, at least one receptacle outlet shall be installed in each vehicle bay and not more than 1.7 m (5 1⁄2 ft) above the floor.

    (2) Accessory Buildings. In each accessory building with electric power.

    (3) Basements. In each separate unfinished portion of a basement.

    Reference: 2017 National Electrical Code – Chapter 2 Wiring and Protection, Article 210 Branch Circuits. 210.52 Dwelling Unit Receptacle Outlets. 210.52(G) Basements, Garages, and Accessory Buildings

EXAM 4

EXAM 4 ANSWERS

100. **Answer C.** detached garage or accessory building with electric power

For one and two- family dwellings, at least one receptacle outlet shall be installed in the areas specified in 210.52(G)(1) through (3). These receptacles shall be in addition to receptacles required for specific equipment.

(1) *Garages. In each attached garage and in each detached garage with electric power,* at least one receptacle outlet shall be installed in each vehicle bay and not more than 1.7 m (5 1/2 ft) above the floor.

(2) *Accessory Buildings. In each accessory building with electric power.*

(3) **Basements.** In each separate unfinished portion of a basement.

Reference: 2017 National Electrical Code – Chapter 2 Wiring and Protection, Article 210 Branch Circuits. 210.52 Dwelling Unit Receptacle Outlets. 210.52(G) Basements, Garages, and Accessory Buildings. 210.52(G)(1) Garages.

101. **Answer B.** It may not supply outlets outside of the garage

For one and two- family dwellings, at least one receptacle outlet shall be installed in the areas specified in 210.52(G)(1) through (3). These receptacles shall be in addition to receptacles required for specific equipment.

(1) **Garages.** In each attached garage and in each detached garage with electric power, *at least one receptacle outlet shall be installed in each vehicle bay and not more than 1.7 m (5 1/2 ft) above the floor.*

(2) **Accessory Buildings.** In each accessory building with electric power.

(3) **Basements.** In each separate unfinished portion of a basement.

Reference: 2017 National Electrical Code – Chapter 2 Wiring and Protection, Article 210 Branch Circuits. 210.52 Dwelling Receptacle Outlets. 210.52(G) Basements, Garages, and Accessory Buildings. 210.52(G)(1) Garages.

102. **Answer A.** 10 feet

In dwelling units, hallways of 3.0 m (10 ft.) or more in length shall have at least one receptacle outlet.

As used in this subsection, the hallway length shall be considered the length along the centerline of the hallway without passing through a doorway.

Reference: 2017 National Electrical Code – Chapter 2 Wiring and Protection, Article 210 Branch Circuits. 210.52 Dwelling Receptacle Outlets. 210.52(H) Hallways.

103. **Answer C.** 10

In dwelling units, hallways of 3.0 m (10 ft.) or more in length shall have at least one receptacle outlet.

As used in this subsection, the hallway length shall be considered the length along the centerline of the hallway without passing through a doorway.

Reference: 2017 National Electrical Code – Chapter 2 Wiring and Protection, Article 210 Branch Circuits. 210.52 Dwelling Unit Receptacle Outlets. 210.52(H) Hallways.

104. **Answer A.** 10 feet

In dwelling units, hallways of 3.0 m (10 ft.) or more in length shall have at least one receptacle outlet.

As used in this subsection, the hallway length shall be considered the length along the centerline of the hallway without passing through a doorway.

Reference: 2017 National Electrical Code – Chapter 2 Wiring and Protection, Article 210 Branch Circuits. 210.52 Dwelling Unit Receptacle Outlets. 210.52(H) Hallways.

105. **Answer B.** two

In applying the provisions of 210.52(A), the total number of receptacle outlets shall not be less than the minimum number that would comply with the provisions of that section. These receptacle outlets shall be permitted to be located conveniently for permanent furniture layout. *At least two receptacle outlets shall be readily accessible. Where receptacles are installed behind the bed,* the receptacle shall be located to prevent the bed from contacting any attachment plug that may be installed or the receptacle shall be provided with a suitable guard.

Reference: 2017 National Electrical Code – Chapter 2 Wiring and Protection, Article 210 Branch Circuits. 210.60 Guest Rooms, Guest Suites, Dormitories, and Similar Occupancies. 210.60(B) Receptacle Placement.

EXAM 4

EXAM 4 ANSWERS

106. **Answer B.** two

In applying the provisions of 210.52(A), the total number of receptacle outlets shall not be less than the minimum number that would comply with the provisions of that section. These receptacle outlets shall be permitted to be located conveniently for permanent furniture layout. *At least two receptacle outlets shall be readily accessible*. Where receptacles are installed behind the bed, the receptacle shall be located to prevent the bed from contacting any attachment plug that may be installed or the receptacle shall be provided with a suitable guard.

Reference: 2017 National Electrical Code – Chapter 2 Wiring and Protection, Article 210 Branch Circuits. 210.60 Guest Rooms, Guest Suites, Dormitories, and Similar Occupancies. 210.60(B) Receptacle Placement.

107. **Answer B.** Two

In applying the provisions of 210.52(A), the total number of receptacle outlets shall not be less than the minimum number that would comply with the provisions of that section. These receptacle outlets shall be permitted to be located conveniently for permanent furniture layout. *At least two receptacle outlets shall be readily accessible*. Where receptacles are installed behind the bed, the receptacle shall be located to prevent the bed from contacting any attachment plug that may be installed or the receptacle shall be provided with a suitable guard.

Reference: 2017 National Electrical Code – Chapter 2 Wiring and Protection, Article 210 Branch Circuits. 210.60 Guest Rooms, Guest Suites, Dormitories, and Similar Occupancies. 210.60(B) Receptacle Placement.

108. **Answer B.** seven

At least one 125-volt, single-phase, 15- or 20-ampere-rated receptacle outlet shall be installed within 450 mm (18 in.) *of the top of a show window for each 3.7 linear m (12 linear ft.)* or major fraction there of show window area measured horizontally at its maximum width.

Reference: 2017 National Electrical Code – Chapter 2 Wiring and Protection, Article 210 Branch Circuits. 210.62 Show Windows.

80 ft. (show window) = 6.7 = 7 receptacles

12 ft. (per receptacle)

109. **Answer C.** 12

At least one 125-volt, single-phase, 15- or 20-ampere-rated receptacle outlet shall be installed within 450 mm (18 in.) of *the top of a show window for each 3.7 linear m (12 linear ft.)* or major fraction thereof of show window area measured horizontally at its maximum width.

Reference: 2017 National Electrical Code – Chapter 2 Wiring and Protection, Article 210 Branch Circuits. 210.62 Show Windows.

110. **Answer D.** 12 linear ft.

At least one 125-volt, single-phase, 15- or 20-ampere-rated receptacle outlet shall be installed within 450 mm (18 in.) of *the top of a show window for each 3.7 linear m (12 linear ft.) or major fraction thereof of show window area measured horizontally at its maximum width.*

Reference: 2017 National Electrical Code – Chapter 2 Wiring and Protection, Article 210 Branch Circuits. 210.62 Show Windows.

111. **Answer C.** 25

A 125-volt, single-phase, 15- or 20-ampere-rated receptacle outlet shall be installed at an accessible location for the servicing of heating, air-conditioning, and refrigeration equipment. *The receptacle shall be located on the same level and within 7.5 m (25 ft.) of the heating*, air-conditioning, and refrigeration equipment. The receptacle outlet shall not be connected to the load side of the equipment disconnecting means.

Informational Note: See 210.8 for ground-fault circuit-interrupter requirements.

Reference: 2017 National Electrical Code – Chapter 2 Wiring and Protection, Article 210 Branch Circuits. 210.63 Heating, Air-Conditioning, and Refrigeration Equipment Outlet.

EXAM 4

EXAM 4 ANSWERS

112. **Answer D.** 25 ft.

    A 125-volt, single-phase, 15- or 20-ampere-rated receptacle outlet shall be installed at an accessible location for the servicing of heating, air-conditioning, and refrigeration equipment. *The receptacle shall be located on the same level and within 7.5 m (25 ft.) of the heating*, air-conditioning, and refrigeration equipment. The receptacle outlet shall not be connected to the load side of the equipment disconnecting means.

    Informational Note: See 210.8 for ground-fault circuit-interrupter requirements.

    Reference: 2017 National Electrical Code – Chapter 2 Wiring and Protection, Article 210 Branch Circuits. 210.63 Heating, Air-Conditioning, and Refrigeration Equipment Outlet.

113. **Answer D.** shall be on the same level & 25 feet or less away

    A 125-volt, single-phase, 15- or 20-ampere-rated receptacle outlet shall be installed at an accessible location for the servicing of heating, air-conditioning, and refrigeration equipment. *The receptacle shall be located on the same level and within 7.5 m (25 ft.) of the heating, air-conditioning, and refrigeration equipment.* The receptacle outlet shall not be connected to the load side of the equipment disconnecting means.

    Informational Note: See 210.8 for ground-fault circuit-interrupter requirements.

    Reference: 2017 National Electrical Code – Chapter 2 Wiring and Protection, Article 210 Branch Circuits. 210.63 Heating, Air-Conditioning, and Refrigeration Equipment Outlet.

114. **Answer C.**

    At least one 125-volt, single phase, 15- or 20-ampere-rated *receptacle outlet shall be installed in an accessible location within 7.5 m (25 ft) of the indoor electrical service equipment. The required receptacle outlet shall be located within the same room or area as the service equipment.*

    Exception No. 1: The receptacle outlet shall not be required to be installed in one- and two-family dwellings.

    Exception No. 2: Where the service voltage is greater than 120 volts to ground, a receptacle outlet shall not be required for services dedicated to equipment covered in Articles 675 and 682.

    Reference: 2017 National Electrical Code – Chapter 2 Wiring and Protection, Article 210 Branch Circuits. 210.64 Electrical Service Areas.

115. **Answer C.** habitable

    At least one wall switch-controlled lighting outlet shall be installed in every habitable room, kitchen, and bathroom.

    Reference: 2017 National Electrical Code – Chapter 2 Wiring and Protection, Article 210 Branch Circuits. 210.70 Lighting Outlets Required. 210.70(A) Dwelling Units. 210.70(A)(1) Habitable Rooms.

116. **Answer D.** wall switch-controlled lighting

    At least one wall switch-controlled lighting outlet shall be installed in every habitable room, kitchen, and bathroom.

    Reference: 2017 National Electrical Code – Chapter 2 Wiring and Protection, Article 210 Branch Circuits. 210.70 Lighting Outlets Required. . 210.70(1) Habitable Rooms.

EXAM 4

EXAM 4 ANSWERS

117. Answer D. Wall switch controlled lighting outlet.

Additional lighting outlets shall be installed in accordance with the following:

(1) At least one wall switch–controlled lighting outlet shall be installed in hallways, stairways, attached garages, and detached garages with electric power.

(2) *For dwelling units, attached garages, and detached garages with electric power, at least one wall switch controlled lighting outlet shall be installed to provide illumination on the exterior side of outdoor entrances or exits with grade-level access.* A vehicle door in a garage shall not be considered as an outdoor entrance or exit.

(3) Where one or more lighting outlet(s) are installed for interior stairways, there shall be a wall switch at each floor level, and landing level that includes an entryway, to control the lighting outlet(s) where the stairway between floor levels has six risers or more.

Exception to (A)(2)(1), (A)(2)(2), and (A)(2)(3): In hallways, in stairways, and at outdoor entrances, remote, central, or automatic control of lighting shall be permitted.

(4) Lighting outlets controlled in accordance with. 210.70(A)(2)(3) shall not be controlled by use of dimmer switches unless they provide the full range of dimming control at each location.

Reference: 2017 National Electrical Code – Chapter 2 Wiring and Protection, Article 210 Branch Circuits. 210.70 Lighting Outlets Required. . 210.70(A) Dwelling Units. . 210.70(A)(2) Additional Locations.

118. Answer B. exterior

Additional lighting outlets shall be installed in accordance with the following:

(1) At least one wall switch–controlled lighting outlet shall be installed in hallways, stairways, attached garages, and detached garages with electric power.

(2) For dwelling units, attached garages, and detached garages with electric power, at least one wall switch controlled lighting outlet shall be installed to *provide illumination on the exterior side* of outdoor entrances or exits with grade-level access. A vehicle door in a garage shall not be considered as an outdoor entrance or exit.

(3) Where one or more lighting outlet(s) are installed for interior stairways, there shall be a wall switch at each floor level, and landing level that includes an entryway, to control the lighting outlet(s) where the stairway between floor levels has six risers or more.

Exception to (A)(2)(1), (A)(2)(2), and (A)(2)(3): In hallways, in stairways, and at outdoor entrances, remote, central, or automatic control of lighting shall be permitted.

(4) Lighting outlets controlled in accordance with. 210.70(A)(2)(3) shall not be controlled by use of dimmer switches unless they provide the full range of dimming control at each location.

Reference: 2017 National Electrical Code – Chapter 2 Wiring and Protection, Article 210 Branch Circuits. 210.70. 210.70(A) Dwelling Units. 210.70(A)(2) Additional Locations. 210.70(A)(2)(b).

119. Answer B. six

Where one or more lighting outlet(s) are installed for interior stairways, there shall be a wall switch at each floor level, and landing level that includes an entryway, to control the lighting outlet(s) where the stairway between floor levels has six risers or more.

Reference: 2017 National Electrical Code – Chapter 2 Wiring and Protection, Article 210 Branch Circuits. 210.70 Lighting Outlets Required. 210.70(A) Dwelling Units. 210.70(A)(2) Additional Locations. 210.70(A)(2)(c)

EXAM 4

EXAM 4 ANSWERS

120. Answer B. at each level if more than six (6) steps

Additional lighting outlets shall be installed in accordance with the following:

(1) At least one wall switch–controlled lighting outlet shall be installed in hallways, stairways, attached garages, and detached garages with electric power.

(2) For dwelling units, attached garages, and detached garages with electric power, at least one wall switch controlled lighting outlet shall be installed to provide illumination on the exterior side of outdoor entrances or exits with grade-level access. A vehicle door in a garage shall not be considered as an outdoor entrance or exit.

(3) Where one or more lighting outlet(s) are installed for interior stairways, there shall be a wall switch at each floor level, and landing level that includes an entryway, to control the lighting outlet(s) *where the stairway between floor levels has six risers or more.*

Exception to (A)(2)(1), (A)(2)(2), and (A)(2)(3): In hallways, in stairways, and at outdoor entrances, remote, central, or automatic control of lighting shall be permitted.

(4) Lighting outlets controlled in accordance with. 210.70(A)(2)(3) shall not be controlled by use of dimmer switches unless they provide the full range of dimming control at each location.

Reference: 2017 National Electrical Code – Chapter 2 Wiring and Protection, Article 210 Branch Circuits. 210.70 Lighting Outlets Required. 210.70(A) Dwelling Units. 210.70(A)(2) Additional Locations. 210.70(A)(2)(c)

121. Answer B. near

For attics, underfloor spaces, utility rooms, and basements, at least one lighting outlet containing a switch or controlled by a wall switch shall be installed where these spaces are used for storage or contain equipment requiring servicing. At least one point of control shall be at the usual point of entry to these spaces. *The lighting outlet shall be provided at or near the equipment requiring servicing.*

Reference: 2017 National Electrical Code – Chapter 2 Wiring and Protection, Article 210 Branch Circuits. 210.70. 210.70(A) Dwelling Units. 210.70(A)(3) Storage or Equipment Spaces.

122. Answer B. lighting outlet

For attics, underfloor spaces, utility rooms, and basements, at least one lighting outlet containing a switch or controlled by a wall switch shall be installed where these spaces are used for storage or contain equipment requiring servicing. At least one point of control shall be at the usual point of entry to these spaces. *The lighting outlet shall be provided at or near the equipment requiring servicing.*

Reference: 2017 National Electrical Code – Chapter 2 Wiring and Protection, Article 210 Branch Circuits. 210.70 Lighting Outlets Required. . 210.70(3) Storage or Equipment Spaces.

EXAM 4

EXAM 4 ANSWERS

123. Answer C.   125

Feeder conductors shall have an ampacity not less than required to supply the load as calculated in Parts III, IV, and V of Article 220. Conductors shall be sized to carry not less than the larger of 215.2(A)(1)(a) or (b).

(a) Where a feeder supplies continuous loads or any combination of continuous and noncontinuous loads, the minimum feeder conductor size shall have an allowable ampacity *not less than the noncontinuous load plus 125 percent of the continuous load.*

Exception No. 1: If the assembly, including the overcurrent devices protecting the feeder(s), is listed for operation at 100 percent of its rating, the allowable ampacity of the feeder conductors shall be permitted to be not less than the sum of the continuous load plus the noncontinuous load.

Exception No. 2: Where a portion of a feeder is connected at both its supply and load ends to separately installed pressure connections as covered in 110.14(C)(2), it shall be permitted to have an allowable ampacity not less than the sum of the continuous load plus the noncontinuous load. No portion of a feeder installed under the provisions of this exception shall extend into an enclosure containing either the feeder supply or the feeder load terminations, as covered in 110.14(C)(1).

Exception No. 3: Grounded conductors that are not connected to an overcurrent device shall be permitted to be sized at 100 percent of the continuous and noncontinuous load.

(b) The minimum feeder conductor size shall have an allowable ampacity not less than the maximum load to be served after the application of any adjustment or correction factors.

Informational Note No. 1: See Examples D1 through D11 in Informative Annex D.

Informational Note No. 2: Conductors for feeders, as defined in Article 100, sized to prevent a voltage drop exceeding 3 percent at the farthest outlet of power, heating, and lighting loads, or combinations of such loads, and where the maximum total voltage drop on both feeders and branch circuits to the farthest outlet does not exceed 5 percent, will provide reasonable efficiency of operation. Informational Note No. 3: See 210.19(A), Informational Note No. 4, for voltage drop for branch circuits.

Reference: 2017 National Electrical Code – Chapter 2 Wiring and Protection, Article 215 Feeders. 215.2 Minimum Rating and Size. 215.2(A) Feeders Not More Than 600 Volts. 215.2(A)(1) General.

EXAM 5

Chapter 2 Wiring and Protection 02

1. Where the assembly is listed for operation at _____ percent of its rating, including the overcurrent devices protecting the feeder(s), the allowable ampacity of the feeder conductors is not permitted to be less than the sum of the noncontinuous load plus the continuous load.

    A. 80

    B. 100

    C. 125

    D. 150

    Reference: 2017 National Electrical Code – Chapter 2 Wiring and Protection, Article 215 Feeders. 215.2 Minimum Rating and Size. 215.2(A) Feeders Not More Than 600 Volts. 215.2(A)(1) General. Exception No. 1

2. Where the feeder conductors carry the total load supplied by service conductors with an ampacity of 55 amperes or less, the ampacity of a feeder conductor must _____ that of the service conductors. Exceptions ignored.

    A. be equal to

    B. be rated greater than

    C. not be greater than

    D. not be less than

    Reference: 2017 National Electrical Code – Chapter 2 Wiring and Protection, Article 215 Feeders. 215.2 Minimum Rating and Size. 215.2(A) Feeders Not More Than 600 Volts. 215.2(A)(3) Ampacity Relative to Service Conductors.

3. The ampacity of feeders over 600 volts supplying transformers and utilization equipment shall not be less than the sum of the combined nameplate ratings of the transformers and 125 percent of the potential designed load of the utilization equipment that is going to be operated:

    A. continuously

    B. independently

    C. non continuously

    D. simultaneously

    Reference: 2017 National Electrical Code – Chapter 2 Wiring and Protection, Article 215 Feeders. 215.2 Minimum Rating and Size. 215.2(B) Feeders over 600 Volts. . 215.2(B)(2) Feeders Supplying Transformers and Utilization Equipment.

EXAM 5

Chapter 2 Wiring and Protection 02

4. The overcurrent device rating for a feeder that supplies any combination of noncontinuous loads and continuous loads must not be less than _____ percent of the continuous load plus the noncontinuous load. Exceptions ignored.

   A. 80　　　　　　　　　　　　C. 125

   B. 100　　　　　　　　　　　 D. 150

   Reference: 2017 National Electrical Code – Chapter 2 Wiring and Protection, Article 215 Feeders. 215.3 Overcurrent Protection.

5. The overcurrent device's ampere rating where the assembly, including the overcurrent devices protecting the feeder(s), is listed for operation at _____ percent of the rating, is not allowed to be at least the sum of the noncontinuous and continuous loads.

   A. 80　　　　　　　　　　　　C. 125

   B. 100　　　　　　　　　　　 D. 150

   Reference: 2017 National Electrical Code – Chapter 2 Wiring and Protection, Article 215 Feeders. 215.3 Overcurrent Protection.

6. What is the minimum rating required, disregarding exceptions, for an overcurrent protection device on a feeder circuit supplying a continuous load of 240 amperes?

   A. 240 amperes　　　　　　　C. 275 amperes

   B. 250 amperes　　　　　　　D. 300 amperes

   Reference: 2017 National Electrical Code – Chapter 2 Wiring and Protection, Article 215 Feeders. 215.3 Overcurrent Protection.

EXAM 5

Chapter 2 Wiring and Protection 02

7. A common neutral may be utilized by two sets of 4-wire or 5-wire feeders or up to three sets of:

    A. 2-wire feeders

    B. 3-wire feeders

    C. 100 amp feeders

    D. insulated conductors

    Reference: 2017 National Electrical Code – Chapter 2 Wiring and Protection, Article 215 Feeders. 215.4 Feeders with Common Neutral Conductor. 215.4(A) Feeders with Common Neutral.

8. A _____ must be provided prior to the installation of feeders, if required by the authority having jurisdiction.

    A. diagram showing feeder details

    B. feeder conductor meter test

    C. flexible mirror scope inspection device

    D. sample calculation

    Reference: 2017 National Electrical Code – Chapter 2 Wiring and Protection, Article 215 Feeders. 215.5 Diagrams of Feeders.

9. If a feeder supplies branch circuits where equipment grounding conductors are required, the feeder will provide or include a(n) _____, in accordance with the requirements of 250.134, that the equipment grounding conductors of the branch circuits will be connected to.

    A. chase connection

    B. equipment grounding conductor

    C. grounded earth electrode

    D. water pipe

    Reference: 2017 National Electrical Code – Chapter 2 Wiring and Protection, Article 215 Feeders. 215.6 Feeder Equipment Grounding Conductor.

Chapter 2 Wiring and Protection 02

EXAM 5

Chapter 2 Wiring and Protection 02

10. Two-wire AC circuits and DC circuits of at least two _____ will be allowed to be tapped from underground conductors of circuits with a grounded neutral conductor. Switching devices in each tapped circuit must have a pole in each ungrounded conductor.

    A. grounded conductors

    B. grounding conductors

    C. ungrounded conductors

    D. ungrounding conductors

    Reference: 2017 National Electrical Code – Chapter 2 Wiring and Protection, Article 215 Feeders. 215.7 Ungrounded Conductors Tapped from Grounded Systems.

11. For general lighting in restaurant occupancies, a unit load of at least _____ VA per square foot is required.

    A. 1

    B. 2

    C. 3

    D. 4

    Reference: 2017 National Electrical Code – Chapter 2 Wiring and Protection, Article 220 Branch-Circuit, Feeder, and Service Calculations. 220.12 Lighting Load for Specified Occupancies.

12. For a dwelling with 2,600 square feet of habitable space, what is the required minimum number of 15-ampere, 120-volt, general lighting branch circuits?

    A. three

    B. four

    C. five

    D. six

    Reference: 2017 National Electrical Code – Chapter 2 Wiring and Protection, Article 220 Branch-Circuit, Feeder, and Service Calculations

EXAM 5

Chapter 2 Wiring and Protection 02

13. If a dwelling has 70 feet by 30 feet of livable space, what is the minimum number of 120-volt, 15-ampere, general lighting branch circuits required?

    A. two

    B. three

    C. four

    D. five

    Reference: 2017 National Electrical Code – Chapter 2 Wiring and Protection, Article 220 Branch-Circuit, Feeder, and Service Calculations

14. What is the maximum square footage an office building could have with a calculated lighting load of 24,500 VA?

    A. 4500

    B. 5600

    C. 7000

    D. 8300

    Reference: 2017 National Electrical Code – Chapter 2 Wiring and Protection, Article 220 Branch-Circuit, Feeder, and Service Calculations. 220.12 Lighting Load for Specified Occupancies.

15. General lighting in dwelling units is required to have a unit load of at least _____ VA.

    A. 1

    B. 2

    C. 3

    D. 4

    Reference: 2017 National Electrical Code – Chapter 2 Wiring and Protection, Article 220 Branch-Circuit, Feeder, and Service Calculations. 220.12 Lighting Load for Specified Occupancies.

16. If a warehouse area is 10,000 square feet for storage and uses high pressure sodium lighting, what is the maximum lighting load?

    A. 2625

    B. 3510

    C. 5262

    D. 31500

    Reference: 2017 National Electrical Code – Chapter 2 Wiring and Protection, Article 220 Branch-Circuit, Feeder, and Service Calculations. 220.12 Lighting Load for Specified Occupancies.

EXAM 5

Chapter 2 Wiring and Protection 02

17. In church occupancies, the required unit load is at least _____ per square foot for general lighting.

    A. 1 VA

    B. 2 VA

    C. 3 VA

    D. 4 VA

    Reference: 2017 National Electrical Code – Chapter 2 Wiring and Protection, Article 220 Branch-Circuit, Feeder, and Service Calculations. 220.12 Lighting Load for Specified Occupancies.

18. In hospital occupancies, the unit load for general lighting must be at least _____ VA per square foot.

    A. 1

    B. 2

    C. 3

    D. 4

    Reference: 2017 National Electrical Code – Chapter 2 Wiring and Protection, Article 220 Branch-Circuit, Feeder, and Service Calculations. 220.12 Lighting Load for Specified Occupancies.

19. If a warehouse uses mercury vapor lighting in the storage area, and the storage area is 40,500 square feet of space, what is the minimum lighting load?

    A. 5,165 VA

    B. 6,625 VA

    C. 7,875 VA

    D. 10,125 VA

    Reference: 2017 National Electrical Code – Chapter 2 Wiring and Protection, Article 220 Branch-Circuit, Feeder, and Service Calculations. 220.12 Lighting Load for Specified Occupancies.

20. What is the minimum computed branch circuit load, in volt-amps, allowed by the NEC for a branch circuit serving an exterior electric sign, when calculating a building or structure's total load?

    A. 1,200 volt amps

    B. 1,500 volt amps

    C. 1,800 volt amps

    D. 2,000 volt amps

    Reference: 2017 National Electrical Code – Chapter 2 Wiring and Protection, Article 220 Branch-Circuit, Feeder, and Service Calculations. 220.14 Other Loads – All Occupancies. 220.14(F) Sign and Outdoor Lighting.

EXAM 5

Chapter 2 Wiring and Protection 02

21. Show windows must be calculated either at 200 volt-amperes per _____ feet of show window, or the unit load per outlet as required in other provisions of Article 220.14.

    A. 1
    B. 2
    C. 3
    D. 4

    Reference: 2017 National Electrical Code – Chapter 2 Wiring and Protection, Article 220 Branch-Circuit, Feeder, and Service Calculations. 220.14 Other Loads - All Occupancies. . 220.14(G) Show Windows.

22. Show window loads shall be computed at 200 volt-amperes per _____ foot of show window.

    A. 1
    B. 3
    C. 5
    D. 10

    Reference: 2017 National Electrical Code – Chapter 2 Wiring and Protection, Article 220 Branch-Circuit, Feeder, and Service Calculations. 220.14 Other Loads - All Occupancies. 220.14(G) Show Windows. 220.14(G)(2)

23. Loads for convenience receptacle outlets shall be computed at not less than _____ volt-amperes for each single or for each multiple receptacle on one yoke.

    A. 80
    B. 120
    C. 150
    D. 180

    Reference: 2017 National Electrical Code – Chapter 2 Wiring and Protection, Article 220 Branch-Circuit, Feeder, and Service Calculations. 220.14 Other Loads - All Occupancies. 220.14(I) Receptacle Outlets.

24. What is the minimum volt-amps (VA) per outlet for general-purpose receptacle loads, before taking demand factors into consideration for commercial buildings?

    A. 100 VA
    B. 120 VA
    C. 150 VA
    D. 180 VA

    Reference: 2017 National Electrical Code – Chapter 2 Wiring and Protection, Article 220 Branch-Circuit, Feeder, and Service Calculations. 220.14 Other Loads – All Occupancies. 220.14(I) Receptacle Outlets.

Chapter 2 Wiring and Protection 02

EXAM 5

Chapter 2 Wiring and Protection 02

25. What is the minimum volt-amps (VA) to be included for the general-use receptacle outlets, when calculating the total load on a dwelling?

    A. none

    B. one VA

    C. two VA

    D. three VA

    Reference: 2017 National Electrical Code – Chapter 2 Wiring and Protection, Article 220 Branch-Circuit, Feeder, and Service Calculations. 220.14 Other Loads – All Occupancies. 220.14(J)Dwelling Occupancies. 220.14(J)(1)

26. For circuits supplying loads consisting of motor-operated utilization equipment that is fastened in place and has a motor larger than 1/8 hp in combination with other loads, the total computed load shall be based on _____ percent of the largest motor load plus the sum of the other loads.

    A. 75

    B. 80

    C. 100

    D. 125

    Reference: 2017 National Electrical Code – Chapter 2 Wiring and Protection, Article 220 Branch-Circuit, Feeder, and Service Calculations. 220.18 Maximum Loads. 220.18(A) Motor-Operated and Combination Loads.

27. The total calculated load for circuits supplying loads made up of motor-operated utilization equipment fastened in place that has a motor larger than _____ hp in combination with other loads, will be based on _____ percent of the largest motor load and the sum of the other loads.

    A. 1/8, 125

    B. 1/4, 110

    C. 1/2, 150

    D. 3/4, 80

    Reference: 2017 National Electrical Code – Chapter 2 Wiring and Protection, Article 220 Branch-Circuit, Feeder, and Service Calculations. 220.18 Maximum Loads. 220.18(A) Motor-Operated and Combination Loads.

EXAM 5

Chapter 2 Wiring and Protection 02

28. The calculated load for circuits supplying lighting units that have autotransformers, ballasts, or transformers will be based on:

    A. efficiency ratio of the luminaire

    B. number of lamps per unit x the wattage of each lamp

    C. total ampere ratings of units and not total watts of the lamps

    D. total watts for the lamps

    Reference: *2017 National Electrical Code – Chapter 2 Wiring and Protection, Article 220 Branch-Circuit, Feeder, and Service Calculations. 220.18 Maximum Loads. . 220.18(B) Inductive and LED Lighting Loads.*

29. The lighting demand factor of the first 3000 VA or less in dwelling units is _____ percent.

    A. 50

    B. 80

    C. 100

    D. 125

    Reference: *2017 National Electrical Code – Chapter 2 Wiring and Protection, Article 220 Branch-Circuit, Feeder, and Service Calculations. 220.42 General Lighting.*

30. The lighting demand factor in hospitals of the _____ VA is 20 percent.

    A. all lighting

    B. first 3000

    C. remainder over 50,000

    D. VA Load from 3001 to 120,000

    Reference: *2017 National Electrical Code – Chapter 2 Wiring and Protection, Article 220 Branch-Circuit, Feeder, and Service Calculations. 220.42 General Lighting.*

EXAM 5

Chapter 2 Wiring and Protection 02

31. For track lighting in other than dwelling units or guest rooms of hotels or motels, an additional load of _____ volt-amperes shall be included for every 2 feet of lighting track or fraction thereof.

    A. 50
    B. 80
    C. 120
    D. 150

    Reference: 2017 National Electrical Code – Chapter 2 Wiring and Protection, Article 220 Branch-Circuit, Feeder, and Service Calculations. 220.43 Show-Window and Track Lighting. 220.43(B) Track Lighting.

32. In each dwelling unit, the load shall be computed at _____ volt-amperes for each 2-wire small-appliance branch circuit required.

    A. 1000
    B. 1200
    C. 1500
    D. 2000

    Reference: 2017 National Electrical Code – Chapter 2 Wiring and Protection, Article 220 Branch-Circuit, Feeder, and Service Calculations. 220.52 Small-Appliance and Laundry Loads – Dwelling Unit. 220.52(A) Small Appliance Circuit Load.

33. In each dwelling unit, the small appliance circuit load will be calculated at _____ for each 2-wire small appliance branch circuit as determined by 210.11(1). If the load is subdivided between two or more feeders, the calculated load for each will include at least _____ for each 2-wire small appliance branch circuit.

    A. 500 volt-amperes, 1500 volt-amperes
    B. 1000 volt-amperes, 1000 volt-amperes
    C. 1500 volt-amperes, 1500 volt-amperes
    D. 2000 volt-amperes, 1000 volt-amperes

    Reference: 2017 National Electrical Code – Chapter 2 Wiring and Protection, Article 220 Branch-Circuit, Feeder, and Service Calculations. 220.52 Small-Appliance and Laundry Loads – Dwelling Unit. 220.52(A) Small-Appliance Circuit Load.

EXAM 5

Chapter 2 Wiring and Protection 02

34. A load of not less than _____ volt-amperes shall be included for each 2-wire laundry branch circuit installed as required.

    A. 1000

    B. 1200

    C. 1500

    D. 2000

    Reference: 2017 National Electrical Code – Chapter 2 Wiring and Protection, Article 220 Branch-Circuit, Feeder, and Service Calculations. 220.52 Small-Appliance and Laundry Loads – Dwelling Unit. 220.52(B) Laundry Circuit Load.

35. A load for laundry circuits of at least 1500 volt-amperes must be included for each 2-wire laundry branch circuit installed, and this load is allowed to be included with the _____ load and subject to the demand factors designated in Table 220.42.

    A. general lighting

    B. heating

    C. overall appliance

    D. utility circuit

    Reference: 2017 National Electrical Code – Chapter 2 Wiring and Protection, Article 220 Branch-Circuit, Feeder, and Service Calculations. 220.52 Small-Appliance and Laundry Loads – Dwelling Unit. 220.52(B) Laundry Circuit Load.

36. If they are served by the same feeder or service in a one-family, two-family or multifamily dwelling, it is allowable to apply a demand factor of 75 percent to the nameplate rating load of _____ or more appliances fastened in place, other than air-conditioning equipment, clothes dryers, electric ranges, or space-heating equipment.

    A. one

    B. two

    C. three

    D. four

    Reference: 2017 National Electrical Code – Chapter 2 Wiring and Protection, Article 220 Branch-Circuit, Feeder, and Service Calculations. 220.53 Appliance Load - Dwelling Unit(s).

EXAM 5

Chapter 2 Wiring and Protection 02

37. What is the allowed demand factor to be applied to the nameplate-rating load of four (4) or more fastened in place water heaters placed in a multifamily dwelling unit, when apply the standard calculation method for dwellings?

    A. 50%   C. 75%

    B. 60%   D. 80%

    Reference: 2017 National Electrical Code – Chapter 2 Wiring and Protection, Article 220 Branch-Circuit, Feeder, and Service Calculations. 220.53 Appliance Load – Dwelling Unit(s).

38. The load for household electric clothes dryers in a dwelling unit(s) shall be _____ watts (volt-amperes) or the nameplate rating, whichever is larger, for each dryer served.

    A. 1000   C. 5000

    B. 2000   D. 10,000

    Reference: 2017 National Electrical Code – Chapter 2 Wiring and Protection, Article 220 Branch-Circuit, Feeder, and Service Calculations. 220.54 Electric Clothes Dryers – Dwelling Unit(s).

39. In a multi-family dwelling unit, what is the demand factor percentage for 9 household electric clothes dryers?

    A. 55   C. 85

    B. 65   D. 100

    Reference: 2017 National Electrical Code – Chapter 2 Wiring and Protection, Article 220 Branch-Circuit, Feeder, and Service Calculations. 220.54 Electric Clothes Dryers - Dwelling Unit(s).

40. For each dryer service in a dwelling unit(s), the load for household electric clothes dryers is the nameplate rating or _____, whichever is higher.

    A. 4000   C. 7500

    B. 5000   D. 10,000

    Reference: 2017 National Electrical Code – Chapter 2 Wiring and Protection, Article 220 Branch-Circuit, Feeder, and Service Calculations. 220.54 Electric Clothes Dryers - Dwelling Unit(s).

EXAM 5

Chapter 2 Wiring and Protection 02

41. What is the minimum watts (VA), other than nameplate rating (whichever is larger) clothes dryers are to be calculated at when doing residential feeder and service calculations?

    A. 3,000

    B. 4,500

    C. 5,000

    D. 6,000

    Reference: 2017 National Electrical Code – Chapter 2 Wiring and Protection, Article 220 Branch-Circuit, Feeder, and Service Calculations. 220.54 Electric Clothes Dryers – Dwelling Unit(s).

42. When calculating the total load of two or more single-phase ranges supplied by a 3-phase, 4 wire feeder or service, how much must the calculation be on the maximum number connected between any two phases?

    A. one and one half

    B. twice

    C. three times

    D. four times

    Reference: 2017 National Electrical Code – Chapter 2 Wiring and Protection, Article 220 Branch-Circuit, Feeder, and Service Calculations. 220.55 Electric Cooking Appliances in Dwelling Units and Household Cooking Appliances Used in Instructional Programs.

43. When applying the general method of calculation for dwellings, what is the minimum feeder demand on the ungrounded conductors for a one-family dwelling that is to have a cooktop rated 6 kW, three (3) wall-mounted ovens rated at 6, 8, and 3.5 kW, and a broiler rated 3.5 kW?

    A. 12.2 kW

    B. 18.6 kW

    C. 27.3 kW

    D. 30.1 kW

    Reference: 2017 National Electrical Code – Chapter 2 Wiring and Protection, Article 220 Branch-Circuit, Feeder, and Service Calculations

EXAM 5

Chapter 2 Wiring and Protection 02

44. When applying the standard method of calculation for dwelling units, if a branch circuit supplies a 7 kW counter-mounted cooktop and a 5 kW wall-mounted oven in a residence, what will the demand factor be on an ungrounded service-entrance and feeder conductor?

    A. 7.8 kW

    B. 8.0 kW

    C. 9.5 kW

    D. 12.0 kW

    Reference: 2017 National Electrical Code – Chapter 2 Wiring and Protection, Article 220 Branch-Circuit, Feeder, and Service Calculations

45. Where it is unlikely that two or more noncoincident loads will be in use simultaneously, it shall be permissible to use only the _____ load(s) that will be used at one time, in computing the total load of a feeder or service.

    A. average

    B. continuous

    C. largest

    D. smallest

    Reference: 2017 National Electrical Code – Chapter 2 Wiring and Protection, Article 220 Branch-Circuit, Feeder, and Service Calculations. 220.60 Noncoincident Loads.

46. When calculating a general load, it must be at least _____ percent of the first 10 kVA, added to _____ percent of the remaining loads.

    A. 80, 100

    B. 90, 50

    C. 100, 40

    D. 100, 125

    Reference: 2017 National Electrical Code – Chapter 2 Wiring and Protection, Article 220 Branch-Circuit, Feeder, and Service Calculations. 220.82 Dwelling Unit. 220.82(B) General Loads.

EXAM 5

Chapter 2 Wiring and Protection 02

47. Calculating the load of a feeder or service that supplies three or more dwelling units of a multifamily dwelling may be done according to Table 220.84 instead of Part III of Article 220.84, if which conditions are met?

    A. Each dwelling unit has electric cooking equipment.

    B. Each dwelling unit has electric resistance heating systems.

    C. No dwelling unit is supplied by more than one feeder.

    D. A and C

    Reference: 2017 National Electrical Code – Chapter 2 Wiring and Protection, Article 220 Branch-Circuit, Feeder, and Service Calculations. 220.84 Multifamily Dwelling. 220.84(A) Feeder or Service Load.

48. What demand factor must be used to calculate the service load of a multifamily dwelling that has 11 units?

    A. 37

    B. 42

    C. 45

    D. 50

    Reference: 2017 National Electrical Code – Chapter 2 Wiring and Protection, Article 220 Branch-Circuit, Feeder, and Service Calculations. 220.84 Multifamily Dwelling. 220.84(C) Calculated Loads.

49. If each unit in a 12 unit condo had an 8kW electric range, applying the optional method of calculation for multifamily dwellings, what would the calculated demand load be on the ungrounded (line) service entrance conductors for the electric ranges?

    A. 25.9 kW

    B. 30.7 kW

    C. 32.0 kW

    D. 39.4 kW

    Reference: 2017 National Electrical Code – Chapter 2 Wiring and Protection, Article 220 Branch-Circuit, Feeder, and Service Calculations. 220.84 Multifamily Dwelling.

EXAM 5

Chapter 2 Wiring and Protection 02

50. Overhead conductors for festoon lighting shall not be smaller than _____ AWG unless the conductors are supported by messenger wires.

    A. 2

    B. 4

    C. 8

    D. 12

    Reference: 2017 National Electrical Code – Chapter 2 Wiring and Protection, Article 225 Outside Branch Circuits and Feeders. 225.6 Conductor Size and Support. 225.6(B) Festoon Lighting.

51. When overhead conductors for festoon lighting are in spans more than _____ ft., they must be supported by messenger wire. All such conductors may not be less than 12 AWG unless supported by messenger wires.

    A. 40

    B. 50

    C. 60

    D. 100

    Reference: 2017 National Electrical Code – Chapter 2 Wiring and Protection, Article 225 Outside Branch Circuits and Feeders. 225.6 Conductor Size and Support. 225.6(B) Festoon Lighting.

52. Where overhead spans of open conductors and open multiconductor cables of 600 volts or less, nominal, pass over alleys, driveways on other than residential property, parking areas subject to truck traffic, roads, and other land traversed by vehicles such as cultivated, forest, grazing, and orchard, the clearance must be at least _____ ft.

    A. 10

    B. 12

    C. 15

    D. 18

    Reference: 2017 National Electrical Code – Chapter 2 Wiring and Protection, Article 225 Outside Branch Circuits and Feeders. 225.18 Clearance for Overhead Conductors and Cables. 225.18(4)

EXAM 5

Chapter 2 Wiring and Protection 02

53. Overhead spans of open conductors and open multiconductor cables shall be _____ feet over residential property and driveways where the voltage does not exceed 300 volts to ground.

    A. 10   C. 15

    B. 12   D. 20

    Reference: 2017 National Electrical Code – Chapter 2 Wiring and Protection, Article 225 Outside Branch Circuits and Feeders. 225.18 Clearance for Overhead Conductors and Cables. 225.18(3)

54. When overhead spans of open conductors or open multiconductor cables of 600 volts, nominal or less, where the voltage is 300 volts or more to ground, pass over the areas listed in the 12 ft. classification, what must the minimum clearance be in feet?

    A. 10   C. 15

    B. 12   D. 18

    Reference: 2017 National Electrical Code – Chapter 2 Wiring and Protection, Article 225 Outside Branch Circuits and Feeders. 225.18 Clearance for Overhead Conductors and Cables. 225.18(3)

55. When overhead spans of open conductors and open multiconductor cables of 600 volts or less, nominal, with a voltage of 150 volts to ground or less, pass over sidewalks, or come from any platform or projection where someone might reach them, and accessible to pedestrians only, the minimum clearance is _____ ft.

    A. 10   C. 15

    B. 12   D. 18

    Reference: 2017 National Electrical Code – Chapter 2 Wiring and Protection, Article 225 Outside Branch Circuits and Feeders. 225.18 Clearance for Overhead Conductors and Cables. 225.18(1)

EXAM 5

Chapter 2 Wiring and Protection 02

56. What is the minimum clearance in feet for overhead spans of open conductors and open multiconductor cables of 600 volts or less, nominal, over residential property and driveways, and those commercial areas not subject to truck traffic where the voltage does not exceed 300 volts to ground?

    A. 10

    B. 12

    C. 14

    D. 18

    Reference: 2017 National Electrical Code – Chapter 2 Wiring and Protection, Article 225 Outside Branch Circuits and Feeders. 225.18 Clearance for Overhead Conductors and Cables. 225.18(2)

57. What is the minimum clearance over residential driveways of overhead spans of open conductors of up to 300 volts to ground?

    A. 10 feet

    B. 12 feet

    C. 15 feet

    D. 18 feet

    Reference: 2017 National Electrical Code – Chapter 2 Wiring and Protection, Article 225 Outside Branch Circuits and Feeders. 225.18 Clearance for Overhead Conductors and Cables. 225.18(2)

58. What is the minimum clearance above finished grade for conductors of up to 1000 volts passing above a public driveway?

    A. 10 feet

    B. 15 feet

    C. 18 feet

    D. 20 feet

    Reference: 2017 National Electrical Code – Chapter 2 Wiring and Protection, Article 225 Outside Branch Circuits and Feeders. 225.18 Clearance for Overhead Conductors and Cables. 225.18(4)

EXAM 5

Chapter 2 Wiring and Protection 02

59. When overhead spans of open conductors and open multiconductor cables pass over a roof, the vertical clearance must be at least _____ ft. above the surface. This clearance must be maintained for at least _____ ft. in all directions from the edge of the roof. Exceptions ignored.

    A. 8' 6", 3'

    B. 8' 6", 10'

    C. 12' 6", 4'

    D. 12' 6", 6'

    Reference: 2017 National Electrical Code – Chapter 2 Wiring and Protection, Article 225 Outside Branch Circuits and Feeders. 225.19 Clearances from Buildings for Conductors of Not over 1000 Volts, Nominal. 225.19(A) Above Roofs.

60. What is the minimum clearance from chimneys, signs, and TV antennas for outside open conductors of up to 600 volts?

    A. 3 feet

    B. 4 feet

    C. 6 feet

    D. 8 feet

    Reference: 2017 National Electrical Code – Chapter 2 Wiring and Protection, Article 225 Outside Branch Circuits and Feeders. 225.19 Clearances from Buildings for Conductors of Not over 1000 Volts, Nominal. 225.19(B) From Nonbuilding to Nonbridge Structures.

61. Final spans to buildings shall be permitted to be attached to the building, but they shall be kept not less than _____ feet from windows that are designed to be opened.

    A. 1

    B. 3

    C. 5

    D. 10

    Reference: 2017 National Electrical Code – Chapter 2 Wiring and Protection, Article 225 Outside Branch Circuits and Feeders. 225.19 Clearances from Buildings for Conductors of Not over 1000 Volts, Nominal. 225.19(D) Final Spans. 225.19(D)(1) Clearance from Windows.

Chapter 2 Wiring and Protection 02

EXAM 5

Chapter 2 Wiring and Protection 02

62. Conductor installed on buildings, poles, or structures must be _____ as in the guidelines for services in Article 230.50.

    A. hidden

    B. protected

    C. at least 3ft from the ground

    D. Properly spaced

    Reference: 2017 National Electrical Code – Chapter 2 Wiring and Protection, Article 225 Outside Branch Circuits and Feeders. 225.20 Protection Against Physical Damage.

63. Where raceways are on exteriors of buildings or other structures, they must be arranged so they drain, and designated as _____ for wet locations.

    A. rainproof

    B. raintight

    C. listed or approved

    D. waterproof

    Reference: 2017 National Electrical Code – Chapter 2 Wiring and Protection, Article 225 Outside Branch Circuits and Feeders. 225.22 Raceways on Exterior Surfaces of Buildings or Other Structures.

64. Connections to circuit wires for outdoor lampholders attached as pendants must be:

    A. aligned.

    B. sleeved.

    C. staggered.

    D. taped.

    Reference: 2017 National Electrical Code – Chapter 2 Wiring and Protection, Article 225 Outside Branch Circuits and Feeders. 225.24 Outdoor Lampholders.

EXAM 5

Chapter 2 Wiring and Protection 02

65. Outdoor lighting must be located below all electric utilization equipment including energized conductors and transformers, unless the following is applicable:

    A. Clearances or other safeguards provided for relamping operations.

    B. Equipment controlled by disconnecting means lockable in closed position.

    C. Equipment controlled by disconnecting means lockable in open position.

    D. all of the above

    Reference: 2017 National Electrical Code – Chapter 2 Wiring and Protection, Article 225 Outside Branch Circuits and Feeders. 225.25 Location of Outdoor Lamps.

66. Trees and other vegetation must _____ to support overhead conductor spans.

    A. be branches minimum 4 inches in diameter

    B. be pruned clean and used

    C. be used only temporarily

    D. not be used

    Reference: 2017 National Electrical Code – Chapter 2 Wiring and Protection, Article 225 Outside Branch Circuits and Feeders. 225.26 Vegetation as Support.

67. When a raceway enters a building or structure from an underground distribution system, in accordance with 300.5(G), it must be _____, even if it is unused or a spare raceway.

    A. insulated

    B. labeled

    C. listed

    D. sealed

    Reference: 2017 National Electrical Code – Chapter 2 Wiring and Protection, Article 225 Outside Branch Circuits and Feeders. 225.27 Raceway Seal.

EXAM 5

Chapter 2 Wiring and Protection 02

68. What must be done with a raceway enters a building or structure from an underground distribution system?

   A. marked

   B. Provided with a drain hole

   C. Schedule 40 PVC only

   D. sealed

   Reference: 2017 National Electrical Code – Chapter 2 Wiring and Protection, Article 225 Outside Branch Circuits and Feeders/. 225.27 Raceway Seal.

69. When a branch circuit or feeder is serving a building or other structure, disconnecting means on the load side of a service must only be supplied by _____, all special conditions ignored.

   A. a separate service

   B. multiple branch circuit feeders

   C. new service entrance cabling

   D. only one feeder or branch circuit

   Reference: 2017 National Electrical Code – Chapter 2 Wiring and Protection, Article 225 Outside Branch Circuits and Feeders. 225.30 Number of Supplies.

70. Means shall be provided for _____ all ungrounded conductors that supply or pass through a building or structure.

   A. connecting

   B. disconnecting

   C. replacing

   D. servicing

   Reference: 2017 National Electrical Code – Chapter 2 Wiring and Protection, Article 225 Outside Branch Circuits and Feeders. 225.31 Disconnecting Means.

71. All _____ conductors that pass through a building or structure or supply it must have a means supplied for disconnection.

   A. bonding

   B. grounded

   C. grounding

   D. ungrounded

   Reference: 2017 National Electrical Code – Chapter 2 Wiring and Protection, Article 225 Outside Branch Circuits and Feeders. 225.31 Disconnecting Means.

EXAM 5

Chapter 2 Wiring and Protection 02

72. The disconnecting means for a building or structure served, where the conductors pass through the building or structure, must be installed _____, and it must be in a readily accessible location, closest to the point of entrance of the conductors. Exceptions ignored.

    A. either inside or outside
    C. inside and outside
    B. inside
    D. outside

    Reference: 2017 National Electrical Code – Chapter 2 Wiring and Protection, Article 225 Outside Branch Circuits and Feeders. 225.32 Location.

73. The disconnecting means shall be at a _____ accessible location nearest the point of entrance of the conductors.

    A. clearly
    C. openly
    B. easily
    D. readily

    Reference: 2017 National Electrical Code – Chapter 2 Wiring and Protection, Article 225 Outside Branch Circuits and Feeders. 225.32 Location.

74. There shall be no more than _____ disconnects per supply grouped in any one location.

    A. two
    C. six
    B. four
    D. eight

    Reference: 2017 National Electrical Code – Chapter 2 Wiring and Protection, Article 225 Outside Branch Circuits and Feeders. 225.33 Maximum Number of Disconnects.

75. Each supply's disconnecting means must be _____ switches or less, or _____ circuit breakers in a single enclosure, in or on a switchboard, or in a group of separate enclosures.

    A. two, two
    C. six, six
    B. three, three
    D. eight, eight

    Reference: 2017 National Electrical Code – Chapter 2 Wiring and Protection, Article 225 Outside Branch Circuits and Feeders. 225.33 Maximum Number of Disconnects. 225.33(A) General.

EXAM 5

Chapter 2 Wiring and Protection 02

76. On multiwire circuits, two or three single-pole breakers or switches capable of individual operation are allowed as one multipole disconnect, one pole for each ungrounded conductor, as long as they have a master handle to disconnect all ungrounded conductors or identified handle ties with no more than _____ hand operations.

    A. four

    B. six

    C. eight

    D. twelve

    Reference: 2017 National Electrical Code – Chapter 2 Wiring and Protection, Article 225 Outside Branch Circuits and Feeders. 225.33 Maximum Number of Disconnects. 225.33(B) Single-Pole Units.

77. Each disconnect shall be marked to indicate the _____ served.

    A. amperage

    B. area

    C. load

    D. voltage

    Reference: 2017 National Electrical Code – Chapter 2 Wiring and Protection, Article 225 Outside Branch Circuits and Feeders. 225.34 Grouping of Disconnects. 225.34(A) General.

78. In a multiple-occupancy building, each occupant shall have _____ to the occupant's supply disconnecting means.

    A. access

    B. keys

    C. no access

    D. permissions

    Reference: 2017 National Electrical Code – Chapter 2 Wiring and Protection, Article 225 Outside Branch Circuits and Feeders. 225.35 Access to Occupants.

EXAM 5

Chapter 2 Wiring and Protection 02

79. When a building or structure has branch circuits, feeders, services, or any combination thereof supplying it or passing through it, a permanent directory or plaque must be located each place there is a _____, showing all other branch circuits, feeders, or services, and which sections they supply. Exceptions ignored.

    A. conductor terminal

    B. control panel

    C. feeder and branch-circuit disconnect location

    D. wet location

    Reference: 2017 National Electrical Code – Chapter 2 Wiring and Protection, Article 225 Outside Branch Circuits and Feeders. 225.37 Identification.

80. Each building or structure disconnecting means shall _____ disconnect all *ungrounded supply conductors* that it controls from the building or structure wiring system.

    A. never

    B. previously

    C. simultaneously

    D. subsequently

    Reference: 2017 National Electrical Code – Chapter 2 Wiring and Protection, Article 225 Outside Branch Circuits and Feeders. 225.38 Disconnect Construction. 225.38(B) Simultaneous Opening of Poles.

81. Where the disconnecting means for a building or structure does not disconnect _____ conductors from the same type of conductors in the wiring, another method must be provided for this purpose at the same location. A bus or terminal that all _____ conductors can attach with pressure connectors is allowed for this purpose.

    A. grounded, grounded

    B. grounding, grounding

    C. ungrounded, grounding

    D. uninsulated, ungrounded

    Reference: 2017 National Electrical Code – Chapter 2 Wiring and Protection, Article 225 Outside Branch Circuits and Feeders. 225.38 Disconnect Construction. . 225.38(C) Disconnection of Grounded Conductor.

EXAM 5

Chapter 2 Wiring and Protection 02

82. Any disconnecting means for a building or structure must plainly show whether it is:

    A. correct

    B. hot or cold

    C. normal

    D. open or closed

    Reference: 2017 National Electrical Code – Chapter 2 Wiring and Protection, Article 225 Outside Branch Circuits and Feeders. 225.38 Disconnect Construction. . 225.38(D) Indicating.

83. For installations to supply only *limited loads of a single branch circuit*, the branch circuit disconnecting means shall have a rating of not less than _____ amperes.

    A. 15

    B. 20

    C. 40

    D. 50

    Reference: 2017 National Electrical Code – Chapter 2 Wiring and Protection, Article 225 Outside Branch Circuits and Feeders. 225.39 Rating of Disconnect. 225.39(A) One-Circuit Installation.

84. The branch circuit disconnecting means for an installation to supply only limited loads of a single branch circuit shall have a rating of at least _____ amperes.

    A. 10

    B. 15

    C. 20

    D. 30

    Reference: 2017 National Electrical Code – Chapter 2 Wiring and Protection, Article 225 Outside Branch Circuits and Feeders. 225.39 Rating of Disconnect. . 225.39(A) One-Circuit Installation.

85. For installations consisting of *not more than two 2-wire branch circuits*, the feeder or branch-circuit disconnecting means shall have a rating of not less than _____ amperes.

    A. 10

    B. 15

    C. 20

    D. 30

    Reference: 2017 National Electrical Code – Chapter 2 Wiring and Protection, Article 225 Outside Branch Circuits and Feeders. 225.39 Rating of Disconnect. 225.39(B) Two-Circuit Installations.

EXAM 5

Chapter 2 Wiring and Protection 02

86. For a *one-family dwelling*, the feeder disconnecting means shall have a rating of not less than _____ amperes, 3-wire.

    A. 40   C. 100

    B. 50   D. 120

    Reference: 2017 National Electrical Code – Chapter 2 Wiring and Protection, Article 225 Outside Branch Circuits and Feeders. 225.39 Rating of Disconnect. 225.39(C) One-Family Dwelling.

87. The feeder disconnecting means for a one-family dwelling must have a rating of at least _____ amperes, 3-wire.

    A. 60   C. 100

    B. 90   D. 125

    Reference: 2017 National Electrical Code – Chapter 2 Wiring and Protection, Article 225 Outside Branch Circuits and Feeders. 225.39 Rating of Disconnect. . 225.39(C) One-Family Dwelling.

88. Branch-circuit overcurrent devices for a feeder overcurrent device that is not readily accessible must be installed on the load side, and must be mounted in a readily accessible place, and must have _____ rating in amperes than the feeder overcurrent device.

    A. 150 percent of the   C. a lower

    B. a higher   D. the same

    Reference: 2017 National Electrical Code – Chapter 2 Wiring and Protection, Article 225 Outside Branch Circuits and Feeders. 225.40 Access to Overcurrent Protective Devices.

EXAM 5

Chapter 2 Wiring and Protection 02

89. Where a building disconnecting means is made up of air, oil, vacuum, or sulfur hexafluoride or oil switched circuit breakers, an isolating switch with _____ and following the requirements of 230.204(B), (C), and (D) must be installed on the supply side all associated equipment and the disconnecting means.

    A. a hand operated lever
    B. an explosion proof housing
    C. visible break contacts
    D. none of the above

    Reference: 2017 National Electrical Code – Chapter 2 Wiring and Protection, Article 225 Outside Branch Circuits and Feeders. 225.51 Isolating Switches.

90. The electrical disconnecting means for a building or structural may be:

    A. electrically operated by a remote-control device.
    B. located wherever practical.
    C. protected from public tampering by locks or disguises.
    D. all of the above.

    Reference: 2017 National Electrical Code – Chapter 2 Wiring and Protection, Article 225 Outside Branch Circuits and Feeders. 225.52 Disconnecting Means. 225.52(A) Location.

91. All ungrounded supply conductors controlled by a building or structure disconnect must _____ disconnect and must have a fault-closing rating of at least the maximum available short-circuit current available at the supply terminals. Exceptions ignored.

    A. automatically
    B. directly
    C. remotely
    D. simultaneously

    Reference: 2017 National Electrical Code – Chapter 2 Wiring and Protection, Article 225 Outside Branch Circuits and Feeders. 225.52 Disconnecting Means. 225.52(B) Type.

EXAM 5

Chapter 2 Wiring and Protection 02

92. Disconnecting means shall be capable of being _____ in the open position.

    A. latched   C. wedged

    B. locked   D. wired

    Reference: 2017 National Electrical Code – Chapter 2 Wiring and Protection, Article 225 Outside Branch Circuits and Feeders. 225.52 Disconnecting Means. 225.52(C) Locking

93. All means for disconnecting must be capable of being locked _____, and the provisions for locking must be in place whether the lock is installed or not.

    A. from public tampering   C. in the open position

    B. in the closed position   D. A and B

    Reference: 2017 National Electrical Code – Chapter 2 Wiring and Protection, Article 225 Outside Branch Circuits and Feeders. 225.52 Disconnecting Means. 225.52(C) Locking.

94. When there are a combination of branch-circuits, feeders, or services for a building or structure _____, there must be a directory or permanent plaque installed at each branch-circuit disconnection location and feeder, showing other branch-circuits, feeders, and services supplying the building or structure or passing through it, and what area is served by each one.

    A. passing through it   C. supplying it

    B. passing through or supplying it   D. any of the above

    Reference: 2017 National Electrical Code – Chapter 2 Wiring and Protection, Article 225 Outside Branch Circuits and Feeders. 225.52 Disconnecting Means. 225.52(F) Identification.

Chapter 2 Wiring and Protection 02

EXAM 5

Chapter 2 Wiring and Protection 02

95. When an outdoor branch circuit has 600 V conductors and is strung between poles over water that is unsuitable for boating, the conductors are messenger wire supported twisted cable units and 15 ft. above the water, an inspection will conclude that:

    A. installation meets Code requirements.

    B. installation violates Code height requirement.

    C. installation violates Code voltage requirement.

    D. none of the above.

    Reference: 2017 National Electrical Code – Chapter 2 Wiring and Protection, Article 225 Outside Branch Circuits and Feeders. 225.60 Clearances over Roadways, Walkways, Rail, Water, and Open Land. 225.60(A) 22 kV, Nominal, to Ground or Less.

96. A building or other structure served shall be supplied by only _____ service.

    A. one

    B. two

    C. three

    D. four

    Reference: 2017 National Electrical Code – Chapter 2 Wiring and Protection, Article 230 Services. 230.2 Number of Services.

97. How many services are allowed for electrical supply to a building or other structure? Exceptions ignored.

    A. only one

    B. only two

    C. only three

    D. only four

    Reference: 2017 National Electrical Code – Chapter 2 Wiring and Protection, Article 230 Services. 230.2 Number of Services.

EXAM 5

Chapter 2 Wiring and Protection 02

98. When conductors are installed under at least _____ in. of concrete beneath a building or other structure or when they are installed within a building or other structure in a raceway that is encased in concrete or brick at least _____ in thick, they shall be considered outside of a building or other structure.

   A. 2, 2

   B. 3, 3

   C. 4, 4

   D. 6, 6

   Reference: 2017 National Electrical Code – Chapter 2 Wiring and Protection, Article 230 Services. 230.6 Conductors Considered Outside the Building.

99. Conductors other than service conductors shall not be _____ in the same service raceway or service cable.

   A. bundled

   B. installed

   C. placed

   D. spliced

   Reference: 2017 National Electrical Code – Chapter 2 Wiring and Protection, Article 230 Services. 230.7 Other Conductors in Raceway or Cable.

100. Other than _____, conductors must not be installed in the same service cable or service raceway.

   A. copper

   B. SE or USE

   C. service conductors

   D. ungrounded

   Reference: 2017 National Electrical Code – Chapter 2 Wiring and Protection, Article 230 Services. 230.7 Other Conductors in Raceway or Cable.

Chapter 2 Wiring and Protection 02

EXAM 5

Chapter 2 Wiring and Protection 02

101. When service conductors are installed as multiconductor cable or open conductors without an overall outer jacket, they must have a clearance of _____ ft. or more from balconies, doors, fire escapes, ladders, porches, stairs, windows that are meant to be opened, or similar places.

     A. 3   C. 8

     B. 5   D. 10

     Reference: 2017 National Electrical Code – Chapter 2 Wiring and Protection, Article 230 Services. 230.9 Clearances on Buildings. 230.9(A) Clearances.

102. Generally, service conductors installed as open conductors must have a minimum clearance from balconies, doors, porches, and windows that are designed to be opened of:

     A. 3 feet   C. 6 feet

     B. 5 feet   D. 8 feet

     Reference: 2017 National Electrical Code – Chapter 2 Wiring and Protection, Article 230 Services. 230.9 Clearances on Buildings. 230.9(A) Clearances.

103. Individual conductors on overhead service must be covered or insulated, however the _____ conductor on a multiconductor cable is allowed to be bare.

     A. grounded   C. isolated hot leg

     B. grounding   D. ungrounded

     Reference: 2017 National Electrical Code – Chapter 2 Wiring and Protection, Article 230 Services. 230.22 Insulation or Covering.

EXAM 5

Chapter 2 Wiring and Protection 02

104. Overhead service-drop conductors shall not be smaller than _____ AWG copper.

    A. 2   C. 6

    B. 4   D. 8

    Reference: 2017 National Electrical Code – Chapter 2 Wiring and Protection, Article 230 Services. 230.23 Size and Rating. 230.23(B) Minimum Size.

105. Overhead service-drop conductors that are allowed for a dwelling unit must generally have a minimum size of:

    A. 2 AWG copper or 3 AWG aluminum

    B. 4 AWG copper or 1 AWG aluminum

    C. 6 AWG copper or 4 AWG aluminum

    D. 8 AWG copper or 6 AWG aluminum

    Reference: 2017 National Electrical Code – Chapter 2 Wiring and Protection, Article 230 Services. 230.23 Size and Rating. 230.23(B) Minimum Size.

106. Conductors for overhead service drop shall not be smaller than:

    A. 2 AWG aluminum   C. 8 AWG aluminum

    B. 6 AWG copper   D. 8 AWG copper

    Reference: 2017 National Electrical Code – Chapter 2 Wiring and Protection, Article 230 Services. 230.23 Size and Rating. 230.23(B) Minimum Size.

107. Overhead service-drop conductors shall have a vertical clearance of not less than _____ feet above the roof surface.

    A. 6   C. 10

    B. 8   D. 12

    Reference: 2017 National Electrical Code – Chapter 2 Wiring and Protection, Article 230 Services. 230.24 Clearances. 230.24(A) Above Roofs.

Chapter 2 Wiring and Protection 02

EXAM 5

Chapter 2 Wiring and Protection 02

108. When 600 volts or less, nominal, overhead service must follow minimum clearances as measured from:

    A. final grade

    B. the foundation wall

    C. the guy wire anchor

    D. the top of the mast

    Reference: 2017 National Electrical Code – Chapter 2 Wiring and Protection, Article 230 Services. 230.24 Clearances. . 230.24(B) Vertical Clearance for Overhead Service Conductors.

109. What is the minimum clearance from final grade for the overhead service-drop conductors at the electrical service provided for a residence?

    A. 8 feet

    B. 10 feet

    C. 12 feet

    D. 15 feet

    Reference: 2017 National Electrical Code – Chapter 2 Wiring and Protection, Article 230 Services. 230.24 Clearances. 230.24(B) Vertical Clearance for Overhead Service Conductors. 230.24(B)(1)

110. What is the minimum allowed height from the ground of service-drop conductors up to 1000 volts over an apple orchard or orange grove?

    A. 12 feet

    B. 15 feet

    C. 18 feet

    D. 21 feet

    Reference: 2017 National Electrical Code – Chapter 2 Wiring and Protection, Article 230 Services. 230.24 Clearances. 230.24(B) Vertical Clearance for Overhead Service Conductors. 230.24(B)(4)

111. What is the minimum vertical clearance from final grade for open overhead service conductors up to 1000 volts over public driveways?

    A. 10 feet

    B. 12 feet

    C. 15 feet

    D. 18 feet

    Reference: 2017 National Electrical Code – Chapter 2 Wiring and Protection, Article 230 Services. 230.24 Clearances. 230.24(B) Vertical Clearance for Overhead Service Conductors. 230.24(B)(4)

EXAM 5

Chapter 2 Wiring and Protection 02

112. In no case shall the point of attachment for overhead service-drop conductors be less than _____ feet above finished grade.

    A. 10   C. 15

    B. 12   D. 20

    Reference: 2017 National Electrical Code – Chapter 2 Wiring and Protection, Article 230 Services. 230.26 Point of Attachment.

113. Minimum clearance must be provided in point of attachment of service-drop cables on a building or structure, but in no case is the point of attachment to be under _____ ft. above finished grade.

    A. 8   C. 12

    B. 10   D. 14

    Reference: 2017 National Electrical Code – Chapter 2 Wiring and Protection, Article 230 Services. 230.26 Point of Attachment.

114. Attachment to buildings or other structures for multiconductor cables used for overhead service conductors must be by fittings identified for use with service conductors. Open conductors must attach to noncombustible, _____ insulators securely attached to the building or other structure, or to fittings identified for use with service conductors.

    A. glass   C. nonabsorbent

    B. metallic   D. plastic

    Reference: 2017 National Electrical Code – Chapter 2 Wiring and Protection, Article 230 Services. 230.27 Means of Attachment.

EXAM 5

Chapter 2 Wiring and Protection 02

115. When rigid metal conduit (RMC) is used as a service mast for the support of service-drop conductors when installing overhead service, aside from the mast being of adequate strength, which of the following is true?

    A. a minimum of 2 inches in diameter

    B. a minimum of 3 inches in diameter

    C. less than 4 feet in length

    D. supported by braces or guys

    Reference: 2017 National Electrical Code – Chapter 2 Wiring and Protection, Article 230 Services. 230.28 Service Masts as Supports.

116. A service mast that is used for supporting service-drop conductors must be of sufficient strength or be supported by _____ to safely withstand the imposed strain of the service-drop. ***

    A. angle ties

    B. braces or guys

    C. lateral cables

    D. rigid metallic tubing

    Reference: 2017 National Electrical Code – Chapter 2 Wiring and Protection, Article 230 Services. 230.28 Service Masts as Supports. 230.28(a) Attachment.

117. When service conductors pass over a roof, they must be supported securely by substantial structures, and the supports must be _____ where practicable.

    A. coated with a non-conductive coating

    B. independent of the building

    C. part of the building structure

    D. waterproof

    Reference: 2017 National Electrical Code – Chapter 2 Wiring and Protection, Article 230 Services. 230.29 Supports over Buildings.

EXAM 5

Chapter 2 Wiring and Protection 02

118. Insulation for _____ must be provided for underground service conductors.

    A. exposure to the elements

    B. identification purposes

    C. the applied voltage

    D. workers safety

    Reference: 2017 National Electrical Code – Chapter 2 Wiring and Protection, Article 230 Services. 230.30 Installation. 230.30(A) Insulation.

119. Sufficient ampacity to carry current must be in underground service conductors for the load as calculated, and the conductors must be at least _____ aluminum or copper-clad aluminum.

    A. 4 AWG copper or 6 AWG

    B. 6 AWG copper or 6 AWG

    C. 8 AWG copper or 6 AWG

    D. 8 AWG copper or 8 AWG

    Reference: 2017 National Electrical Code – Chapter 2 Wiring and Protection, Article 230 Services. 230.31 Size and Rating. 230.31(B) Minimum Size.

120. What is the minimum size underground installed service-lateral conductors allowed by the NEC, aside from any exceptions?

    A. 2 AWG aluminum

    B. 4 AWG aluminum

    C. 6 AWG copper

    D. 8 AWG copper

    Reference: 2017 National Electrical Code – Chapter 2 Wiring and Protection, Article 230 Services. 230.44 Cable Trays.

121. Of the following methods, which one is not approved for service-entrance conductor installation?

    A. Busways

    B. Electrical metallic tubing

    C. Type MC Cable

    D. Type NM cable

    Reference: 2017 National Electrical Code – Chapter 2 Wiring and Protection, Article 230 Services. 230.43 Wiring Methods for 1000 Volts, Nominal, or Less.

Chapter 2 Wiring and Protection 02   169

EXAM 5

Chapter 2 Wiring and Protection 02

122. When cable tray systems are used to support service-entrance conductors, they may only contain _____. Exceptions ignored.

    A. branch feeder

    B. insulated

    C. service-entrance

    D. Type MC cable

    Reference: 2017 National Electrical Code – Chapter 2 Wiring and Protection, Article 230 Services. 230.44 Cable Trays.

123. Where service cables are subject to physical damage, they must be protected by any of the following methods, except:

    A. Electrical metallic tubing

    B. Rigid metal conduit

    C. Schedule 80 rigid PVC conduit

    D. all are acceptable

    Reference: 2017 National Electrical Code – Chapter 2 Wiring and Protection, Article 230 Services. 230.50 Protection Against Physical Damage. 230.50(B) All Other Service-Entrance Conductors.

124. Service-entrance cables shall be supported by straps or other approved means within _____ inches of every service head, gooseneck, or connection to a raceway or enclosure and at intervals not exceeding _____ inches.

    A. 12, 24

    B. 12, 30

    C. 15, 30

    D. 18, 36

    Reference: 2017 National Electrical Code – Chapter 2 Wiring and Protection, Article 230 Services. 230.51 Mounting Supports. 230.51(A) Service-entrance Cables.

125. Service disconnecting means shall not be installed in _____.

    A. bathrooms

    B. bedrooms

    C. garages

    D. kitchens

    Reference: 2017 National Electrical Code – Chapter 2 Wiring and Protection, Article 230 Services. 230.70 General. 230.70(A) Location. 230.70(A)(2) Bathrooms

EXAM 5

EXAM 5 ANSWERS

1. **Answer B.** 100

   Feeder conductors shall have an ampacity not less than required to supply the load as calculated in Parts III, IV, and V of Article 220. Conductors shall be sized to carry not less than the larger of 215.2(A)(1)(a) or (b).

   (a) Where a feeder supplies continuous loads or any combination of continuous and noncontinuous loads, the minimum feeder conductor size shall have an allowable ampacity not less than the noncontinuous load plus 125 percent of the continuous load.

   Exception No. 1: If the assembly, including the overcurrent devices protecting the feeder(s), is listed for operation at 100 percent of its rating, the allowable ampacity of the feeder conductors shall be permitted to be not less than the sum of the continuous load plus the noncontinuous load.

   Exception No. 2: Where a portion of a feeder is connected at both its supply and load ends to separately installed pressure connections as covered in 110.14(C)(2), it shall be permitted to have an allowable ampacity not less than the sum of the continuous load plus the noncontinuous load. No portion of a feeder installed under the provisions of this exception shall extend into an enclosure containing either the feeder supply or the feeder load terminations, as covered in 110.14(C)(1).

   Exception No. 3: Grounded conductors that are not connected to an overcurrent device shall be permitted to be sized at 100 percent of the continuous and noncontinuous load.

   (b) The minimum feeder conductor size shall have an allowable ampacity not less than the maximum load to be served after the application of any adjustment or correction factors.

   Informational Note No. 1: See Examples D1 through D11 in Informative Annex D.

   Informational Note No. 2: Conductors for feeders, as defined in Article 100, sized to prevent a voltage drop exceeding 3 percent at the farthest outlet of power, heating, and lighting loads, or combinations of such loads, and where the maximum total voltage drop on both feeders and branch circuits to the farthest outlet does not exceed 5 percent, will provide reasonable efficiency of operation. Informational Note No. 3: See 210.19(A), Informational Note No. 4, for voltage drop for branch circuits.

   Reference: 2017 National Electrical Code – Chapter 2 Wiring and Protection, Article 215 Feeders. 215.2 Minimum Rating and Size. 215.2(A) Feeders Not More Than 600 Volts. 215.2(A)(1) General. Exception No. 1

2. **Answer D.** not be less than

   The feeder conductor ampacity shall not be less than that of the service conductors where the feeder conductors carry the total load supplied by service conductors with an ampacity of 55 amperes or less

   Reference: 2017 National Electrical Code – Chapter 2 Wiring and Protection, Article 215 Feeders. 215.2 Minimum Rating and Size. 215.2(A) Feeders Not More Than 600 Volts. 215.2(A)(3) Ampacity Relative to Service Conductors.

3. **Answer D.** simultaneously

   The ampacity of feeders supplying a combination of transformers and utilization equipment shall not be less than the sum of the nameplate ratings of the transformers and *125 percent of the designed potential load of the utilization equipment that will be operated simultaneously.*

   Reference: 2017 National Electrical Code – Chapter 2 Wiring and Protection, Article 215 Feeders. 215.2 Minimum Rating and Size. 215.2(B) Feeders over 600 Volts. . 215.2(B)(2) Feeders Supplying Transformers and Utilization Equipment.

EXAM 5
EXAM 5 ANSWERS

4. **Answer C.** 125

    Feeders shall be protected against overcurrent in accordance with the provisions of Part I of Article 240. Where a feeder supplies continuous loads or any combination of continuous and noncontinuous loads, the rating of the overcurrent device shall *not be less than the noncontinuous load plus 125 percent of the continuous load.*

    240 amperes X 1.25 = 300 amperes

    Reference: 2017 National Electrical Code – Chapter 2 Wiring and Protection, Article 215 Feeders. 215.3 Overcurrent Protection.

5. **Answer B.** 100

    Feeders shall be protected against overcurrent in accordance with the provisions of Part I of Article 240. Where a feeder supplies continuous loads or any combination of continuous and noncontinuous loads, the rating of the overcurrent device shall not be less than the noncontinuous load plus 125 percent of the continuous load.

    Exception No. 1: Where the assembly, including the overcurrent devices protecting the feeder(s), is listed for operation at 100 percent of its rating, *the ampere rating of the overcurrent device shall be permitted to be not less than the sum of the continuous load plus the noncontinuous load.*

    Reference: 2017 National Electrical Code – Chapter 2 Wiring and Protection, Article 215 Feeders. 215.3 Overcurrent Protection.

6. **Answer D.** 300 amperes

    Feeders shall be protected against overcurrent in accordance with the provisions of Part I of Article 240. Where a feeder supplies continuous loads or any combination of continuous and noncontinuous loads, the rating of *the overcurrent device shall not be less than the noncontinuous load plus 125 percent of the continuous load.*

    Exception No. 1: Where the assembly, including the overcurrent devices protecting the feeder(s), is listed for operation at 100 percent of its rating, the ampere rating of the overcurrent device shall be permitted to be not less than the sum of the continuous load plus the noncontinuous load.

    240 amperes X 1.25 = 300 amperes

    Reference: 2017 National Electrical Code – Chapter 2 Wiring and Protection, Article 215 Feeders. 215.3 Overcurrent Protection.

7. **Answer B.** 3-wire feeders

    Up to three sets of 3-wire feeders or two sets of 4-wire or 5-wire feeders shall be permitted to utilize a common neutral.

    Reference: 2017 National Electrical Code – Chapter 2 Wiring and Protection, Article 215 Feeders. 215.4 Feeders with Common Neutral Conductor. 215.4(A) Feeders with Common Neutral.

EXAM 5

EXAM 5 ANSWERS

8. **Answer A.** diagram showing feeder details

If required by the authority having jurisdiction, a diagram showing feeder details shall be provided prior to the installation of the feeders. Such a diagram shall show the area in square feet of the building or other structure supplied by each feeder, the total calculated load before applying demand factors, the demand factors used, the calculated load after applying demand factors, and the size and type of conductors to be used.

Reference: 2017 National Electrical Code – Chapter 2 Wiring and Protection, Article 215 Feeders. 215.5 Diagrams of Feeders.

9. **Answer B.** equipment grounding conductor

Where a feeder supplies branch circuits in which equipment grounding conductors are required, the feeder shall include *or provide an equipment grounding conductor in accordance with the provisions of 250.134*, to which the equipment grounding conductors of the branch circuits shall be connected. Where the feeder supplies a separate building or structure, the requirements of 250.32(B) shall apply.

Reference: 2017 National Electrical Code – Chapter 2 Wiring and Protection, Article 215 Feeders. 215.6 Feeder Equipment Grounding Conductor.

10. **Answer C.** ungrounded conductors

Two-wire DC circuits and AC circuits of two or more ungrounded conductors shall be permitted to be tapped from the ungrounded conductors of circuits having a grounded neutral conductor. Switching devices in each tapped circuit shall have a pole in each ungrounded conductor.

Reference: 2017 National Electrical Code – Chapter 2 Wiring and Protection, Article 215 Feeders. 215.7 Ungrounded Conductors Tapped from Grounded Systems.

11. **Answer B.** 2

A unit load of not less than that specified in Table 220.12 for occupancies specified shall constitute the minimum lighting load. The floor area for each floor shall be calculated from the outside dimensions of the building, dwelling unit, or other area involved. For dwelling units, the calculated floor area shall not include open porches, garages, or unused or unfinished spaces not adaptable for future use.

Informational Note: The unit values are based on minimum load conditions and 100 percent power factor and may not provide sufficient capacity for the installation contemplated.

Reference: 2017 National Electrical Code – Chapter 2 Wiring and Protection, Article 220 Branch-Circuit, Feeder, and Service Calculations. 220.12 Lighting Load for Specified Occupancies.

EXAM 5

EXAM 5 ANSWERS

Table 220.12 General Lighting Loads by Occupancy

Type of Occupancy	Unit Load	
	Volt-amperes/ m^2	Volt-amperes/ ft^2
Armories and auditoriums	11	1
Banks	39[b]	3½ [b]
Barber shops and beauty parlors	33	3
Churches	11	1
Clubs	22	2
Courtrooms	22	2
Dwelling units[a]	33	3
Garages — commercial (storage)	6	½
Hospitals	22	2
Hotels and motels, including apartment houses without provision for cooking by tenants[a]	22	2
Industrial commercial (loft) buildings	22	2
Lodge rooms	17	1½
Office buildings	39[b]	3½ [b]
Restaurants	22	2
Schools	33	3
Stores	33	3
Warehouses (storage)	3	¼
In any of the preceding occupancies except one-family dwellings and individual dwelling units of two-family and multifamily dwellings:		
Assembly halls and auditoriums	11	1
Halls, corridors, closets, stairways	6	½
Storage spaces	3	¼

EXAM 5

EXAM 5 ANSWERS

12. **Answer C.** five

    A unit load of not less than that specified in Table 220.12 for occupancies specified shall constitute the minimum lighting load. *The floor area for each floor shall be calculated from the outside dimensions of the building*, dwelling unit, or other area involved. For dwelling units, the calculated floor area shall not include open porches, garages, or unused or unfinished spaces not adaptable for future use.

    Informational Note: The unit values are based on minimum load conditions and 100 percent power factor and may not provide sufficient capacity for the installation contemplated.

    Reference: 2017 National Electrical Code – Chapter 2 Wiring and Protection, Article 220 Branch-Circuit, Feeder, and Service Calculations. 220.12 Lighting Load for Special Occupancies

    Reference: 2017 National Electrical Code – Chapter 2 Wiring and Protection, Article 220 Branch-Circuit, Feeder, and Service Calculations. Table 220.12 General Lighting Loads by Occupancy (page 70-68)

    2600 sq. ft. x 3 VA = 7800 VA (total lighting VA of house)

    120 volts x 15 amperes = 1800 VA (one circuit)

    7800 VA (load) = 4.3 = 5 lighting circuits
    1800 VA (one circuit)

13. **Answer C.** four

    A unit load of not less than that specified in Table 220.12 for occupancies specified shall constitute the minimum lighting load. The floor area for each floor shall be calculated from the outside dimensions of the building, dwelling unit, or other area involved. For dwelling units, the calculated floor area shall not include open porches, garages, or unused or unfinished spaces not adaptable for future use.

    Informational Note: The unit values are based on minimum load conditions and 100 percent power factor and may not provide sufficient capacity for the installation contemplated.

    Reference: 2017 National Electrical Code – Chapter 2 Wiring and Protection, Article 220 Branch-Circuit, Feeder, and Service Calculations. 220.12 Lighting Load for Special Occupancies

    Reference: 2017 National Electrical Code – Chapter 2 Wiring and Protection, Article 220 Branch-Circuit, Feeder, and Service Calculations. Table 220.12 General Lighting Loads by Occupancy (page 70-68)

    70 ft. x 30 ft. = 2100 sq. ft. x 3 VA = 6300 VA (house load)

    120 volts x 15 amperes = 1800 VA (one circuit)

    6300 VA (load) = 3.5 = 4 circuits
    1800 VA (one circuit)

14. **Answer C.** 7000

    A unit load of not less than that specified in Table 220.12 for occupancies specified shall constitute the minimum lighting load. The floor area for each floor shall be calculated from the outside dimensions of the building, dwelling unit, or other area involved. For dwelling units, the calculated floor area shall not include open porches, garages, or unused or unfinished spaces not adaptable for future use.

    Informational Note: The unit values are based on minimum load conditions and 100 percent power factor and may not provide sufficient capacity for the installation contemplated.

    24,500%3.5 = 7000

    Reference: 2017 National Electrical Code – Chapter 2 Wiring and Protection, Article 220 Branch-Circuit, Feeder, and Service Calculations. 220.12 Lighting Load for Specified Occupancies.

15. **Answer C.** 3

    A unit load of not less than that specified in *Table 220.12* for occupancies specified shall constitute the minimum lighting load. The floor area for each floor shall be calculated from the outside dimensions of the building, dwelling unit, or other area involved. For dwelling units, the calculated floor area shall not include open porches, garages, or unused or unfinished spaces not adaptable for future use.

    Informational Note: The unit values are based on minimum load conditions and 100 percent power factor and may not provide sufficient capacity for the installation contemplated.

    Reference: 2017 National Electrical Code – Chapter 2 Wiring and Protection, Article 220 Branch-Circuit, Feeder, and Service Calculations. 220.12 Lighting Load for Specified Occupancies.

EXAM 5
EXAM 5 ANSWERS

16. **Answer A.**   2625

    10500 x .25 = 2625

    A unit load of not less than that specified in Table 220.12 for occupancies specified shall constitute the minimum lighting load. The floor area for each floor shall be calculated from the outside dimensions of the building, dwelling unit, or other area involved. For dwelling units, the calculated floor area shall not include open porches, garages, or unused or unfinished spaces not adaptable for future use.

    Informational Note: The unit values are based on minimum load conditions and 100 percent power factor and may not provide sufficient capacity for the installation contemplated.

    Reference: 2017 National Electrical Code – Chapter 2 Wiring and Protection, Article 220 Branch-Circuit, Feeder, and Service Calculations. 220.12 Lighting Load for Specified Occupancies.

17. **Answer A.**   1 VA

    2017 National Electrical Code – Chapter 2 Wiring and Protection, Article 220 Branch-Circuit, Feeder, and Service Calculations. 220.12 Lighting Load for Specified Occupancies.

18. **Answer B.**   2

    See Table

    Reference: 2017 National Electrical Code – Chapter 2 Wiring and Protection, Article 220 Branch-Circuit, Feeder, and Service Calculations. 220.12 Lighting Load for Specified Occupancies.

19. **Answer D.**   10,125 VA

    40,500x.25 = 10,125

    Reference: 2017 National Electrical Code – Chapter 2 Wiring and Protection, Article 220 Branch-Circuit, Feeder, and Service Calculations. 220.12 Lighting Load for Specified Occupancies.

20. **Answer B.**   1,500 volt amps

    Sign and outline lighting outlets shall be calculated at a minimum *of 1200 volt-amperes for each required branch circuit* specified in 600.5(A).

    Reference: 2017 National Electrical Code – Chapter 2 Wiring and Protection, Article 220 Branch-Circuit, Feeder, and Service Calculations. 220.14 Other Loads – All Occupancies. 220.14(F) Sign and Outdoor Lighting. Branch circuits that supply signs shall be rated in accordance with 600.S(B)(1) or (B)(2) and shall be considered to be continuous loads for the purposes of calculations.

    Reference: 2017 National Electrical Code – Chapter 6 Special Equipment, Article 600 Electric Signs and Outline Lighting. 600.5 Branch Circuits. 600.5(B) Rating. Where a branch circuit supplies continuous loads or any combination of continuous and noncontinuous loads, the minimum branch-circuit conductor size shall have an allowable ampacity not less than the *noncontinuous load plus 125 percent of the continuous load.*

    Reference: 2017 National Electrical Code – Chapter 2 Wiring and Protection, Article 210 Branch Circuits. 210.19 Conductors – Minimum Ampacity and Size. 210.19(A) Branch Circuits Not More Than 600 Volts. 210.19(A)(1) General. 210.19(A)(1)(a)

    1,200 VA x 125% = 1,500 VA

EXAM 5

EXAM 5 ANSWERS

21. **Answer A.** 1

    Show windows shall be calculated in accordance with either of the following:

    (1) The unit load per outlet as required in other provisions of this section

    (2) At 200 volt-amperes per linear 300 mm (1 ft) of show window

    Reference: 2017 National Electrical Code – Chapter 2 Wiring and Protection, Article 220 Branch-Circuit, Feeder, and Service Calculations. 220.14 Other Loads - All Occupancies. . 220.14(G) Show Windows.

22. **Answer A.** 1

    Note how the question asks _____ foot not feet. This gives you a clue to the answer. Watch for this on the exam.

    Show windows shall be calculated in accordance with either of the following:

    (1) The unit load per outlet as required in other provisions of this section

    (2) At 200 volt-amperes per linear 300 mm (1 ft) of show window

    Reference: 2017 National Electrical Code – Chapter 2 Wiring and Protection, Article 220 Branch-Circuit, Feeder, and Service Calculations. 220.14 Other Loads - All Occupancies. 220.14(G) Show Windows. 220.14(G)(2)

23. **Answer D.** 180

    Except as covered in 220.14(J) and (K), *receptacle outlets shall be calculated at not less than 180 volt-amperes for each single or for each multiple receptacle on one yoke*. A single piece of equipment consisting of a multiple receptacle comprised of four or more receptacles shall be calculated at not less than 90 volt-amperes per receptacle. This provision shall not be applicable to the receptacle outlets specified in 210.11(C)(1) and (C)(2).

    Reference: 2017 National Electrical Code – Chapter 2 Wiring and Protection, Article 220 Branch-Circuit, Feeder, and Service Calculations. 220.14 Other Loads - All Occupancies. 220.14(I) Receptacle Outlets.

24. **Answer D.** 180 VA

    Except as covered in 220.14(J) and (K), receptacle outlets shall *be calculated at not less than 180 volt-amperes for each single or for each* multiple receptacle on one yoke. A single piece of equipment consisting of a multiple receptacle comprised of four or more receptacles shall be calculated at not less than 90 volt-amperes per receptacle. This provision shall not be applicable to the receptacle outlets specified in 210.11 (C)(1) and (C)(2).

    Reference: 2017 National Electrical Code – Chapter 2 Wiring and Protection, Article 220 Branch-Circuit, Feeder, and Service Calculations. 220.14 Other Loads – All Occupancies. 220.14(I) Receptacle Outlets.

EXAM 5
EXAM 5 ANSWERS

25. Answer A. none

In one-family, two-family, and multifamily dwellings and in guest rooms or guest suites of hotels and motels, the outlets specified in (J)(1), (J)(2), and (J)(3) are included in the general lighting load calculations of 220.12. *No additional load calculations shall be required for such outlets.*

(1) All general-use receptacle outlets of 20-ampere rating or less, including receptacles connected to the circuits in 210.11(C)(3)

Reference: 2017 National Electrical Code – Chapter 2 Wiring and Protection, Article 220 Branch-Circuit, Feeder, and Service Calculations. 220.14 Other Loads – All Occupancies. 220.14(J) Dwelling Occupancies. 220.14(J)(1)

26. Answer D. 125

Where a circuit supplies only motor-operated loads, Article 430 shall apply. Where a circuit supplies only air-conditioning equipment, refrigerating equipment, or both, Article 440 shall apply. For circuits supplying loads consisting of motor-operated utilization equipment that is fastened in place and has a motor larger than ⅛ hp in combination with other loads, *the total calculated load shall be based on 125 percent of the largest motor load plus the sum of the other loads.*

Reference: 2017 National Electrical Code – Chapter 2 Wiring and Protection, Article 220 Branch-Circuit, Feeder, and Service Calculations. 220.18 Maximum Loads. 220.18(A) Motor-Operated and Combination Loads.

27. Answer A. 1/8, 125

Where a circuit supplies only motor-operated loads, Article 430 shall apply. Where a circuit supplies only air-conditioning equipment, refrigerating equipment, or both, Article 440 shall apply. For circuits supplying loads consisting of motor-operated utilization equipment that is *fastened in place and has a motor larger than 1/8 hp in combination with other loads*, t*he total calculated load shall be based on 125 percent of the largest motor load plus the sum of the other loads.*

Reference: 2017 National Electrical Code – Chapter 2 Wiring and Protection, Article 220 Branch-Circuit, Feeder, and Service Calculations. 220.18 Maximum Loads. 220.18(A) Motor-Operated and Combination Loads.

28. Answer C. total ampere ratings of units and not total watts of the lamps

For circuits supplying lighting units that have ballasts, transformers, autotransformers, or LED drivers, *the calculated load shall be based on the total ampere ratings of such units and not on the total watts of the lamps.*

Reference: 2017 National Electrical Code – Chapter 2 Wiring and Protection, Article 220 Branch-Circuit, Feeder, and Service Calculations. 220.18 Maximum Loads. . 220.18(B) Inductive and LED Lighting Loads.

EXAM 5

EXAM 5 ANSWERS

Table 220.42 Lighting Load Demand Factors

Type of Occupancy	Portion of Lighting Load to Which Demand Factor Applies (Volt-Amperes)	Demand Factor (%)
Dwelling units	First 3000 at	100
	From 3001 to 120,000 at	35
	Remainder over 120,000 at	25
Hospitals*	First 50,000 or less at	40
	Remainder over 50,000 at	20
Hotels and motels, including apartment houses without provision for cooking by tenants*	First 20,000 or less at	50
	From 20,001 to 100,000 at	40
	Remainder over 100,000 at	30
Warehouses (storage)	First 12,500 or less at	100
	Remainder over 12,500 at	50
All others	Total volt-amperes	100

*The demand factors of this table shall not apply to the calculated load of feeders or services supplying areas in hospitals, hotels, and motels where the entire lighting is likely to be used at one time, as in operating rooms, ballrooms, or dining rooms.

29. Answer C. 100

See Table 220.42

Reference: 2017 National Electrical Code – Chapter 2 Wiring and Protection, Article 220 Branch-Circuit, Feeder, and Service Calculations. 220.42 General Lighting.

30. Answer C. remainder over 50,000

The demand factors specified in Table 220.42 shall apply to that portion of the total branch-circuit load calculated for general illumination. They shall not be applied in determining the number of branch circuits for general illumination.

Reference: 2017 National Electrical Code – Chapter 2 Wiring and Protection, Article 220 Branch-Circuit, Feeder, and Service Calculations. 220.42 General Lighting.

31. Answer D. 150

Review the exception in this article.

For track lighting in other than dwelling units or guest rooms or guest suites of hotels or motels, an additional load of 150 volt-amperes shall be included for every 600 mm (2 ft.) of lighting track or fraction thereof. Where multi-circuit track is installed, the load shall be considered to be divided equally between the track circuits.

Exception: If the track lighting is supplied through a device that limits the current to the track, the load shall be permitted to be calculated based on the rating of the device used to limit the current.

Reference: 2017 National Electrical Code – Chapter 2 Wiring and Protection, Article 220 Branch-Circuit, Feeder, and Service Calculations. 220.43 Show-Window and Track Lighting. 220.43(B) Track Lighting.

EXAM 5

EXAM 5 ANSWERS

32. Answer C.   1500

In each dwelling unit, the load shall be calculated at 1500 volt-amperes for each 2-wire small-appliance branch circuit as covered by 210.11(C)(1). *Where the load is subdivided through two or more feeders, the calculated load for each shall include not less than 1500 volt-amperes for each 2-wire small-appliance branch circuit*. These loads shall be permitted to be included with the general lighting load and subjected to the demand factors provided in Table 220.42. Table on page 70-70.

Reference: 2017 National Electrical Code – Chapter 2 Wiring and Protection, Article 220 Branch-Circuit, Feeder, and Service Calculations. 220.52 Small-Appliance and Laundry Loads – Dwelling Unit. 220.52(A) Small Appliance Circuit Load.

33. Answer C.   1500 volt-amperes, 1500 volt-amperes

In each dwelling unit, the load shall be calculated at 1500 volt-amperes for each 2-wire small-appliance branch circuit as covered by 210.11(C)(1). Where the load is subdivided through two or more feeders, the *calculated load for each shall include not less than 1500 volt-amperes for each 2-wire small-appliance branch circuit*. These loads shall be permitted to be included with the general lighting load and subjected to the demand factors provided in Table 220.42. . Table on page 70-70.

Reference: 2017 National Electrical Code – Chapter 2 Wiring and Protection, Article 220 Branch-Circuit, Feeder, and Service Calculations. 220.52 Small-Appliance and Laundry Loads – Dwelling Unit. 220.52(A) Small-Appliance Circuit Load.

34. Answer C.   1500

A load of not less than 1500 volt-amperes shall be included for each 2-wire laundry branch circuit installed as covered by 210.11(C)(2). This load shall be permitted to be included with the general lighting load and subjected to the demand factors provided in Table 220.42. Table on page 70-70.

Reference: 2017 National Electrical Code – Chapter 2 Wiring and Protection, Article 220 Branch-Circuit, Feeder, and Service Calculations. 220.52 Small-Appliance and Laundry Loads – Dwelling Unit. 220.52(B) Laundry Circuit Load.

35. Answer A.   general lighting

A load of not less than 1500 volt-amperes shall be included for each 2-wire laundry branch circuit installed as covered by 210.11(C)(2). This load *shall be permitted to be included with the general lighting load* and subjected to the demand factors provided in Table 220.42

Reference: 2017 National Electrical Code – Chapter 2 Wiring and Protection, Article 220 Branch-Circuit, Feeder, and Service Calculations. 220.52 Small-Appliance and Laundry Loads – Dwelling Unit. 220.52(B) Laundry Circuit Load.

EXAM 5

EXAM 5 ANSWERS

36. **Answer D.** four

   It shall be permissible to apply a demand factor of 75 percent to the nameplate rating load of four or more appliances fastened in place, other than electric ranges, clothes dryers, space-heating equipment, or air-conditioning equipment, that are served by the same feeder or service in a one-family, two-family, or multifamily dwelling.

   Reference: 2017 National Electrical Code – Chapter 2 Wiring and Protection, Article 220 Branch-Circuit, Feeder, and Service Calculations. 220.53 Appliance Load - Dwelling Unit(s).

37. **Answer C.** 75%

   It shall be permissible to apply a demand factor of 75 percent to the nameplate rating load of four or more appliances fastened in place, other than electric ranges, clothes dryers, space-heating equipment, or air-conditioning equipment, that are served by the same feeder or service in a one-family, two-family, or multifamily dwelling.

   Reference: 2017 National Electrical Code – Chapter 2 Wiring and Protection, Article 220 Branch-Circuit, Feeder, and Service Calculations. 220.53 Appliance Load – Dwelling Unit(s).

38. **Answer C.** 5000

   Review and know how to use table 220.54 for the open book part of the exam.

   The load for household electric clothes dryers in a dwelling unit(s) shall be either 5000 watts (volt-amperes) or the nameplate rating, whichever is larger, for each dryer served, The use of the demand factors in Table 220.54 shall be permitted. Where two or more single-phase dryers are supplied by a 3-phase, 4-wire feeder or service, the total load shall be calculated on the basis of twice the maximum number connected between any two phases. Kilovolt amperes (kVA) shall be considered equivalent to kilowatts (kW) for loads calculated in this section.

   Reference: 2017 National Electrical Code – Chapter 2 Wiring and Protection, Article 220 Branch-Circuit, Feeder, and Service Calculations. 220.54 Electric Clothes Dryers – Dwelling Unit(s).

EXAM 5 ANSWERS 181

EXAM 5

EXAM 5 ANSWERS

Table 220.54 Demand Factors for Household Electric Clothes Dryers

Number of Dryers	Demand Factor (%)
1–4	100
5	85
6	75
7	65
8	60
9	55
10	50
11	47
12–23	47% minus 1% for each dryer exceeding 11
24–42	35% minus 0.5% for each dryer exceeding 23
43 and over	25%

39. Answer A. 55

The load for household electric clothes dryers in a dwelling unit(s) shall be either 5000 watts (volt-amperes) or the nameplate rating, whichever is larger, for each dryer served, The use of the demand factors in Table 220.54 shall be permitted. Where two or more single-phase dryers are supplied by a 3-phase, 4-wire feeder or service, the total load shall be calculated on the basis of twice the maximum number connected between any two phases. Kilovolt amperes (kVA) shall be considered equivalent to kilowatts (kW) for loads calculated in this section. . Table on page 70-71.

Reference: 2017 National Electrical Code – Chapter 2 Wiring and Protection, Article 220 Branch-Circuit, Feeder, and Service Calculations. 220.54 Electric Clothes Dryers - Dwelling Unit(s).

40. Answer B. 5000

The load for household electric clothes dryers in a dwelling unit(s) shall be either 5000 watts (volt-amperes) or the nameplate rating, whichever is larger, for each dryer served, The use of the demand factors in Table 220.54 shall be permitted. Where two or more single-phase dryers are supplied by a 3-phase, 4-wire feeder or service, the total load shall be calculated on the basis of twice the maximum number connected between any two phases. Kilovolt amperes (kVA) shall be considered equivalent to kilowatts (kW) for loads calculated in this section. . Table on page 70-71.

Reference: 2017 National Electrical Code – Chapter 2 Wiring and Protection, Article 220 Branch-Circuit, Feeder, and Service Calculations. 220.54 Electric Clothes Dryers - Dwelling Unit(s).

EXAM 5

EXAM 5 ANSWERS

41. **Answer C.** 5,000

    The load for household electric clothes dryers in a dwelling unit(s) shall be either 5000 watts (volt-amperes) or the nameplate rating, whichever is larger, for each dryer served, The use of the demand factors in Table 220.54 shall be permitted. Where two or more single-phase dryers are supplied by a 3-phase, 4-wire feeder or service, the total load shall be calculated on the basis of twice the maximum number connected between any two phases. Kilovolt-amperes (kVA) shall be considered equivalent to kilowatts (kW) for loads calculated in this section. Table on page 70-71.

    Reference: 2017 National Electrical Code – Chapter 2 Wiring and Protection, Article 220 Branch-Circuit, Feeder, and Service Calculations. 220.54 Electric Clothes Dryers – Dwelling Unit(s).

42. **Answer B.** twice

    The load for household electric ranges, wall-mounted ovens, counter-mounted cooking units, and other household cooking appliances individually rated in excess of 1-3/4 kW shall be permitted to be calculated in accordance with Table 220.55. Kilovolt-amperes (kVA) shall be considered equivalent to kilowatts (kW) for loads calculated under this section.

    Where two or more single-phase ranges are supplied by a 3-phase, 4-wire feeder or service, the total load shall be calculated on the basis of twice the maximum number connected between any two phases.

    Informational Note No. 1: See the examples in Informative Annex D.

    Informational Note No.2: See Table 220.56 for commercial cooking equipment.

    Reference: 2017 National Electrical Code – Chapter 2 Wiring and Protection, Article 220 Branch-Circuit, Feeder, and Service Calculations. 220.55 Electric Cooking Appliances in Dwelling Units and Household Cooking Appliances Used in Instructional Programs.

43. **Answer A.** 12.2 kW

    Over 1-3/4 kW through 8-3/4 kW. In lieu of the method provided in Column C, it shall be permissible to add the nameplate ratings of all household cooking appliances rated more than 1-3/4 kW but not more than 8-3/4 kW and multiply the sum by the demand factors specified in Column A or Column B for the given number of appliances. Where the rating of cooking appliances falls under both Column A and Column B, the demand factors for each column shall be applied to the appliances for that column, and the results added together.

    Reference: 2017 National Electrical Code – Chapter 2 Wiring and Protection, Article 220 Branch-Circuit, Feeder, and Service Calculations. Table 220.55 Demand Factors and Loads for Household Electric Ranges, Wall-Mounted Ovens, Counter-Mounted Cooking

    Units, and Other Household Cooking Appliances over 1¾ kW Rating (page 70-72)

    (Column C to be used in all cases except as otherwise permitted in Note 3.)

    Note 3

    Use column B – 5 appliances = 45% demand

    6 kW + 8 kW + 3.5 kW + 6 kW + 3.5 kW = 27 kW (total connected load)

    27 kW x 45% = 12.15 kW (demand load)

EXAM 5

EXAM 5 ANSWERS

44. Answer A. 7.8 kW

Over 1-3/4 kW through 8-3/4 kW. In lieu of the method provided in Column C, it shall be permissible to add the nameplate ratings of all household cooking appliances rated more than 1-3/4 kW but not more than 8-3/4 kW and multiply the sum by the demand factors specified in Column A or Column B for the given number of appliances. Where the rating of cooking appliances falls under both Column A and Column B, the demand factors for each column shall be applied to the appliances for that column, and the results added together.

Reference: 2017 National Electrical Code – Chapter 2 Wiring and Protection, Article 220 Branch-Circuit, Feeder, and Service Calculations. Table 220.55 Demand Factors and Loads for Household Electric Ranges, Wall-Mounted Ovens, Counter-Mounted Cooking

Units, and Other Household Cooking Appliances over 1¾ kW Rating (page 70-72)

(Column C to be used in all cases except as otherwise permitted in Note 3.)

Note 3

Use column B - 2 appliances = 65% demand

5 kW + 7 kW = 12 kW (total connected load)

12 kW x 65% (demand) = 7.8 kW (demand load)

45. Answer C. largest

Where it is unlikely that two or more noncoincident loads will be in use simultaneously, *it shall be permissible to use only the largest load(s) that will be used at one time for calculating the total load of a feeder or service.*

Reference: 2017 National Electrical Code – Chapter 2 Wiring and Protection, Article 220 Branch-Circuit, Feeder, and Service Calculations. 220.60 Noncoincident Loads.

46. Answer C. 100, 40

The general calculated load shall be not less than 100 percent of the first 10k VA plus 40 percent of the remainder of the following loads:

(1) 33 volt-amperes/m2 or 3 volt-amperes/ft2 for general lighting and general-use receptacles. The floor area for each floor shall be calculated from the outside dimensions of the dwelling unit. The calculated floor area shall not include open porches, garages, or unused or unfinished spaces not adaptable for future use.

(2) 1500 volt-amperes for each 2-wire, 20-ampere small-appliance branch circuit and each laundry branch circuit covered in 210.11 (C)(1) and (C)(2).

(3) The nameplate rating of the following:

a. All appliances that are fastened in place, permanently connected, or located to be on a specific circuit

b. Ranges, wall-mounted ovens, counter-mounted cooking units

c. Clothes dryers that are not connected to the laundry branch circuit specified in item (2)

d. Water heaters

(4) The nameplate ampere or kVA rating of all permanently connected motors not included in item (3).

Reference: 2017 National Electrical Code – Chapter 2 Wiring and Protection, Article 220 Branch-Circuit, Feeder, and Service Calculations. 220.82 Dwelling Unit. 220.82(B) General Loads.

EXAM 5

EXAM 5 ANSWERS

Table 220.84 Optional Calculations — Demand Factors for Three or More Multifamily Dwelling Units

Number of Dwelling Units	Demand Factor (%)
3–5	45
6–7	44
8–10	43
11	42
12–13	41
14–15	40
16–17	39
18–20	38
21	37
22–23	36
24–25	35
26–27	34
28–30	33
31	32
32–33	31
34–36	30
37–38	29
39–42	28
43–45	27
46–50	26
51–55	25
56–61	24
62 and over	23

47. **Answer D. A and C**

It shall be permissible to calculate the load of a feeder or service that supplies three or more dwelling units of a multifamily dwelling in accordance with Table 220.84 instead of Part III of this article if all the following conditions are met:

(1) No dwelling unit is supplied by more than one feeder.

(2) Each dwelling unit is equipped with electric cooking equipment.

(3) Each dwelling unit is equipped with either electric space heating or air conditioning, or both. Feeders and service conductors whose calculated load is determined by this optional calculation shall be permitted to have the neutral load determined by 220.61. . See Table

Reference: 2017 National Electrical Code – Chapter 2 Wiring and Protection, Article 220 Branch-Circuit, Feeder, and Service Calculations. 220.84 Multifamily Dwelling. 220.84(A) Feeder or Service Load.

EXAM 5

EXAM 5 ANSWERS

48. Answer B. 42

The calculated load to which the demand factors of Table 220.84 apply shall include the following:

(1) 33 volt-amperes/m2 or 3 volt-amperes/ft2 for general lighting and general-use receptacles

(2) 1500 volt-amperes for each 2-wire, 20-ampere small-appliance branch circuit and each laundry branch circuit covered in 210.11(C)(1) and (C)(2)

(3) The nameplate rating of the following:

a. All appliances that are fastened in place, permanently connected, or located to be on a specific circuit

b. Ranges, wall-mounted ovens, counter-mounted cooking units

c. Clothes dryers that are not connected to the laundry branch circuit specified in item (2)

d. Water heaters

(4) The nameplate ampere or kVA rating of all permanently connected motors not included in item (3)

(5) The larger of the air-conditioning load or the fixed electric space-heating load. Table on page 74 of the code.

Reference: 2017 National Electrical Code – Chapter 2 Wiring and Protection, Article 220 Branch-Circuit, Feeder, and Service Calculations. 220.84 Multifamily Dwelling. 220.84(C) Calculated Loads.

49. Answer D. 39.4 kW

All appliances that are fastened in place, permanently connected, or located to be on a specific circuit

Reference: 2017 National Electrical Code – Chapter 2 Wiring and Protection, Article 220 Branch-Circuit, Feeder, and Service Calculations. 220.84 Multifamily Dwelling. 220.84(C) Calculated Loads. 220.84(C)(3). 220.84(C)(3)(a)

Reference: 2017 National Electrical Code – Chapter 2 Wiring and Protection, Article 220 Branch-Circuit, Feeder, and Service Calculations. 220.84 Multifamily Dwelling. Table 220.84 Optional Calculations – Demand Factors for Three or More Multifamily Dwelling Units (page 70-74). *8kW x 12 = 96 kW x 41% (demand) = 39.36kW*

50. Answer D. 12

Overhead conductors for festoon lighting shall not be smaller than 12 AWG unless the conductors are supported by messenger wires. In all spans exceeding 12 m (40 ft.), the conductors shall be supported by messenger wire. The messenger wire shall be supported by strain insulators. Conductors or messenger wires shall not be attached to any fire escape, downspout, or plumbing equipment.

Reference: 2017 National Electrical Code – Chapter 2 Wiring and Protection, Article 225 Outside Branch Circuits and Feeders. 225.6 Conductor Size and Support. 225.6(B) Festoon Lighting.

51. Answer A. 40

Overhead conductors for festoon lighting shall not be smaller than 12 AWG unless the conductors are supported by messenger wires. *In all spans exceeding 12 m (40 ft.)*, the conductors shall be supported by messenger wire. The messenger wire shall be supported by strain insulators. Conductors or messenger wires shall not be attached to any fire escape, downspout, or plumbing equipment.

Reference: 2017 National Electrical Code – Chapter 2 Wiring and Protection, Article 225 Outside Branch Circuits and Feeders. 225.6 Conductor Size and Support. 225.6(B) Festoon Lighting.

EXAM 5

EXAM 5 ANSWERS

52. Answer D.   18

Overhead spans of open conductors and open multiconductor cables of not over 1000 volts, nominal, shall have a clearance of not less than the following:

(1) 3.0 m (10 ft) — above finished grade, sidewalks, or from any platform or projection that will permit personal contact where the voltage does not exceed 150 volts to ground and accessible to pedestrians only

(2) 3.7 m (12 ft) — over residential property and driveways, and those commercial areas not subject to truck traffic where the voltage does not exceed 300 volts to ground

(3) 4.5 m (15 ft) — for those areas listed in the 3.7 m (12 ft) classification where the voltage exceeds 300 volts to ground

(4) 5.5 m (18 ft) — over public streets, alleys, roads, parking areas subject to truck traffic, driveways on other than residential property, and other land traversed by vehicles, such as cultivated, grazing, forest, and orchard

(5) 7.5 m (24 1⁄2 ft) — over track rails of railroads

Reference: 2017 National Electrical Code – Chapter 2 Wiring and Protection, Article 225 Outside Branch Circuits and Feeders. 225.18 Clearance for Overhead Conductors and Cables. 225.18(4)

53. Answer B.   12

Review the other requirements of this article, the same requirements apply for Service Drop Conductors.

Overhead spans of open conductors and open multiconductor cables of not over 1000 volts, nominal, shall have a clearance of not less than the following:

(1) 3.0 m (10 ft) — above finished grade, sidewalks, or from any platform or projection that will permit personal contact where the voltage does not exceed 150 volts to ground and accessible to pedestrians only

(2) 3.7 m (12 ft) — over residential property and driveways, and those commercial areas not subject to truck traffic where the voltage does not exceed 300 volts to ground

(3) 4.5 m (15 ft) — for those areas listed in the 3.7 m (12 ft) classification where the voltage exceeds 300 volts to ground

(4) 5.5 m (18 ft) — over public streets, alleys, roads, parking areas subject to truck traffic, driveways on other than residential property, and other land traversed by vehicles, such as cultivated, grazing, forest, and orchard

(5) 7.5 m (24 1⁄2 ft) — over track rails of railroads**2017 National Electrical Code – Chapter 2 Wiring and Protection, Article 225 Outside Branch Circuits and Feeders. 225.18 Clearance for Overhead Conductors and Cables. . 225.18(2)**

Reference: 2017 National Electrical Code – Chapter 2 Wiring and Protection, Article 225 Outside Branch Circuits and Feeders. 225.18 Clearance for Overhead Conductors and Cables. 225.18(3)

EXAM 5

EXAM 5 ANSWERS

54. Answer C.   15

Overhead spans of open conductors and open multiconductor cables of not over 1000 volts, nominal, shall have a clearance of not less than the following:

(1) 3.0 m (10 ft) — above finished grade, sidewalks, or from any platform or projection that will permit personal contact where the voltage does not exceed 150 volts to ground and accessible to pedestrians only

(2) 3.7 m (12 ft) — over residential property and driveways, and those commercial areas not subject to truck traffic where the voltage does not exceed 300 volts to ground

(3) 4.5 m (15 ft) — for those areas listed in the 3.7 m (12 ft) classification where the voltage exceeds 300 volts to ground

(4) 5.5 m (18 ft) — over public streets, alleys, roads, parking areas subject to truck traffic, driveways on other than residential property, and other land traversed by vehicles, such as cultivated, grazing, forest, and orchard

(5) 7.5 m (24 1⁄2 ft) — over track rails of railroads

Reference: 2017 National Electrical Code – Chapter 2 Wiring and Protection, Article 225 Outside Branch Circuits and Feeders. 225.18 Clearance for Overhead Conductors and Cables. 225.18(3)

55. Answer A.   10

Overhead spans of open conductors and open multiconductor cables of not over 1000 volts, nominal, shall have a clearance of not less than the following:

(1) 3.0 m (10 ft) — above finished grade, sidewalks, or from any platform or projection that will permit personal contact where the voltage does not exceed 150 volts to ground and accessible to pedestrians only

(2) 3.7 m (12 ft) — over residential property and driveways, and those commercial areas not subject to truck traffic where the voltage does not exceed 300 volts to ground

(3) 4.5 m (15 ft) — for those areas listed in the 3.7 m (12 ft) classification where the voltage exceeds 300 volts to ground

(4) 5.5 m (18 ft) — over public streets, alleys, roads, parking areas subject to truck traffic, driveways on other than residential property, and other land traversed by vehicles, such as cultivated, grazing, forest, and orchard

(5) 7.5 m (24 1⁄2 ft) — over track rails of railroads

Reference: 2017 National Electrical Code – Chapter 2 Wiring and Protection, Article 225 Outside Branch Circuits and Feeders. 225.18 Clearance for Overhead Conductors and Cables. 225.18(1)

EXAM 5

EXAM 5 ANSWERS

56. Answer B.   12

Overhead spans of open conductors and open multiconductor cables of not over 1000 volts, nominal, shall have a clearance of not less than the following:

(1) 3.0 m (10 ft) — above finished grade, sidewalks, or from any platform or projection that will permit personal contact where the voltage does not exceed 150 volts to ground and accessible to pedestrians only

(2) 3.7 m (12 ft) — over residential property and driveways, and those commercial areas not subject to truck traffic where the voltage does not exceed 300 volts to ground

(3) 4.5 m (15 ft) — for those areas listed in the 3.7 m (12 ft) classification where the voltage exceeds 300 volts to ground

(4) 5.5 m (18 ft) — over public streets, alleys, roads, parking areas subject to truck traffic, driveways on other than residential property, and other land traversed by vehicles, such as cultivated, grazing, forest, and orchard

(5) 7.5 m (24 1⁄2 ft) — over track rails of railroads

Reference: 2017 National Electrical Code – Chapter 2 Wiring and Protection, Article 225 Outside Branch Circuits and Feeders. 225.18 Clearance for Overhead Conductors and Cables. 225.18(2)

57. Answer B.   12 feet

Overhead spans of open conductors and open multiconductor cables of not over 1000 volts, nominal, shall have a clearance of not less than the following:

(1) 3.0 m (10 ft) — above finished grade, sidewalks, or from any platform or projection that will permit personal contact where the voltage does not exceed 150 volts to ground and accessible to pedestrians only

(2) 3.7 m (12 ft) — over residential property and driveways, and those commercial areas not subject to truck traffic where the voltage does not exceed 300 volts to ground

(3) 4.5 m (15 ft) — for those areas listed in the 3.7 m (12 ft) classification where the voltage exceeds 300 volts to ground

(4) 5.5 m (18 ft) — over public streets, alleys, roads, parking areas subject to truck traffic, driveways on other than residential property, and other land traversed by vehicles, such as cultivated, grazing, forest, and orchard

(5) 7.5 m (24 1⁄2 ft) — over track rails of railroads

Reference: 2017 National Electrical Code – Chapter 2 Wiring and Protection, Article 225 Outside Branch Circuits and Feeders. 225.18 Clearance for Overhead Conductors and Cables. 225.18(2)

EXAM 5 ANSWERS

EXAM 5

EXAM 5 ANSWERS

58. Answer C.   18 feet

Overhead spans of open conductors and open multiconductor cables of not over 1000 volts, nominal, shall have a clearance of not less than the following:

(1) 3.0 m (10 ft) — above finished grade, sidewalks, or from any platform or projection that will permit personal contact where the voltage does not exceed 150 volts to ground and accessible to pedestrians only

(2) 3.7 m (12 ft) — over residential property and driveways, and those commercial areas not subject to truck traffic where the voltage does not exceed 300 volts to ground

(3) 4.5 m (15 ft) — for those areas listed in the 3.7 m (12 ft) classification where the voltage exceeds 300 volts to ground

(4) 5.5 m (18 ft) — over public streets, alleys, roads, parking areas subject to truck traffic, driveways on other than residential property, and other land traversed by vehicles, such as cultivated, grazing, forest, and orchard

(5) 7.5 m (24 1/2 ft) — over track rails of railroads

Reference: 2017 National Electrical Code – Chapter 2 Wiring and Protection, Article 225 Outside Branch Circuits and Feeders. 225.18 Clearance for Overhead Conductors and Cables. 225.18(4)

59. Answer A.   8' 6", 3'

Overhead spans of open conductors and open multiconductor **cables shall have a vertical clearance of not less than 2.7 m (8 ft 6 in.)** above the roof surface. The vertical clearance above the roof level shall be maintained for a **distance not less than 900 mm (3 ft)** in all directions from the edge of the roof.

Reference: 2017 National Electrical Code – Chapter 2 Wiring and Protection, Article 225 Outside Branch Circuits and Feeders. 225.19 Clearances from Buildings for Conductors of Not over 1000 Volts, Nominal. 225.19(A) Above Roofs.

60. Answer A.   3 feet

From signs, chimneys, radio and television antennas, tanks, and other nonbuilding or nonbridge structures, clearances – **vertical, diagonal, and horizontal – shall not be less than 900 mm (3 ft.).**

Reference: 2017 National Electrical Code – Chapter 2 Wiring and Protection, Article 225 Outside Branch Circuits and Feeders. 225.19 Clearances from Buildings for Conductors of Not over 1000 Volts, Nominal. 225.19(B) From Nonbuilding to Nonbridge Structures.

61. Answer B.   3

Final spans to the building they supply, or from which they are fed, **shall be permitted to be attached to the building, but they shall be kept not less than 900 mm (3 ft.) from windows** that are designed to be opened, and from doors, porches, balconies, ladders, stairs, fire escapes, or similar locations.

Reference: 2017 National Electrical Code – Chapter 2 Wiring and Protection, Article 225 Outside Branch Circuits and Feeders. 225.19 Clearances from Buildings for Conductors of Not over 1000 Volts, Nominal. 225.19(D) Final Spans. 225.19(D)(1) Clearance from Windows.

62. Answer B.   protected

Conductors installed on buildings, structures, or poles shall be protected against physical damage as provided for services in 230.50.

Reference: 2017 National Electrical Code – Chapter 2 Wiring and Protection, Article 225 Outside Branch Circuits and Feeders. 225.20 Protection Against Physical Damage.

63. Answer C.   listed or approved

Raceways on exteriors of buildings or other structures shall be arranged to drain and shall be listed or approved for use in wet locations.

Reference: 2017 National Electrical Code – Chapter 2 Wiring and Protection, Article 225 Outside Branch Circuits and Feeders. 225.22 Raceways on Exterior Surfaces of Buildings or Other Structures.

64. Answer C.   staggered.

Where outdoor lampholders are attached as pendants, the connections to the circuit wires shall be staggered. Where such lampholders have terminals of a type that puncture the insulation and make contact with the conductors, they shall be attached only to conductors of the stranded type.

Reference: 2017 National Electrical Code – Chapter 2 Wiring and Protection, Article 225 Outside Branch Circuits and Feeders. 225.24 Outdoor Lampholders.

EXAM 5

EXAM 5 ANSWERS

65. Answer D. all of the above

Locations of lamps for outdoor lighting shall be below all energized conductors, transformers, or other electric utilization equipment, unless either of the following apply:

(1) Clearances or other safeguards are provided for relamping operations.

(2) Equipment is controlled by a disconnecting means that is lockable in accordance with 110.25.

Reference: 2017 National Electrical Code – Chapter 2 Wiring and Protection, Article 225 Outside Branch Circuits and Feeders. 225.25 Location of Outdoor Lamps.

66. Answer D. not be used

Vegetation such as trees *shall not be used for support of overhead conductor spans.*

Reference: 2017 National Electrical Code – Chapter 2 Wiring and Protection, Article 225 Outside Branch Circuits and Feeders. 225.26 Vegetation as Support.

67. Answer D. sealed

Where a raceway enters a building or structure from outside, it shall be sealed. *Spare or unused raceways shall also be sealed.* Sealants shall be identified for use with cable insulation, conductor insulation, bare conductor, shield, or other components.

Reference: 2017 National Electrical Code – Chapter 2 Wiring and Protection, Article 225 Outside Branch Circuits and Feeders. 225.27 Raceway Seal.

68. Answer D. sealed

Where a raceway enters a building or structure from an underground distribution system*, it shall be sealed in accordance with 300.5(G).* Spare or unused raceways shall also be sealed. Sealants shall be identified for use with the cable insulation, conductor insulation, bare conductor, shield, or other components.

Reference: 2017 National Electrical Code – Chapter 2 Wiring and Protection, Article 225 Outside Branch Circuits and Feeders/. 225.27 Raceway Seal.

69. Answer D. only one feeder or branch circuit

A building or other structure that is served by a branch circuit or feeder on the load side of a service disconnecting means **shall be supplied by only one feeder or branch circuit unless permitted** in 225.30(A) through (E). For the purpose of this section, a multiwire branch circuit shall be considered a single circuit.

Where a branch circuit or feeder originates in these additional buildings or other structures, only one feeder or branch circuit shall be permitted to supply power back to the original building or structure, unless permitted in 225.30(A) through (E).

Reference: 2017 National Electrical Code – Chapter 2 Wiring and Protection, Article 225 Outside Branch Circuits and Feeders. 225.30 Number of Supplies.

70. Answer B. disconnecting

Means shall be provided for disconnecting all ungrounded conductors that supply or pass through the building or structure.

Reference: 2017 National Electrical Code – Chapter 2 Wiring and Protection, Article 225 Outside Branch Circuits and Feeders. 225.31 Disconnecting Means.

71. Answer D. ungrounded

Means shall be provided for disconnecting all ungrounded conductors that supply or pass through the building or structure.

Reference: 2017 National Electrical Code – Chapter 2 Wiring and Protection, Article 225 Outside Branch Circuits and Feeders. 225.31 Disconnecting Means.

72. Answer A. either inside or outside

The disconnecting means shall be installed either inside or outside of the building or structure served or where the conductors pass through the building or structure. The disconnecting means shall be at a readily accessible location nearest the point of entrance of the conductors. For the purposes of this section, the requirements in 230.6 shall be utilized.

Reference: 2017 National Electrical Code – Chapter 2 Wiring and Protection, Article 225 Outside Branch Circuits and Feeders. 225.32 Location.

EXAM 5

EXAM 5 ANSWERS

73. **Answer D.** readily

Review the 4 exceptions in this article. Know the difference between accessible and readily accessible.

The disconnecting means shall be installed either inside or outside of the building or structure served or where the conductors pass through the building or structure. ***The disconnecting means shall be at a readily accessible location nearest the point of entrance of the conductors***. For the purposes of this section, the requirements in 230.6 shall be utilized.

Exception No.1: For installations under single management, where documented safe switching procedures are established and maintained for disconnection, and where the installation is monitored by qualified individuals, the disconnecting means shall be permitted to be located elsewhere on the premises.

Exception No.2: For buildings or other structures qualifying under the provisions of Article 685, the disconnecting means shall be permitted to be located elsewhere on the premises.

Exception No.3: For towers or poles used as lighting standards, the disconnecting means shall be permitted to be located elsewhere on the premises.

Exception No.4: For poles or similar structures used only for support of signs installed in accordance with Article 600, the disconnecting means shall be permitted to be located elsewhere 0il the premises.

Reference: 2017 National Electrical Code – Chapter 2 Wiring and Protection, Article 225 Outside Branch Circuits and Feeders. 225.32 Location.

74. **Answer C.** six

(A) General. The disconnecting means for each supply permitted by 225.30 ***shall consist of not more than six switches or six circuit breakers mounted in a single enclosure***, in a group of separate enclosures, or in or on a switchboard or switchgear. There shall be no more than six disconnects per supply grouped in anyone location.

(B) Single-Pole Units. Two or three single-pole switches or breakers capable of individual operation shall be permitted on multiwire circuits, one pole for each ungrounded conductor, as one multipole disconnect, provided they are equipped with identified handle ties or a master handle to disconnect all ungrounded conductors with no more than six operations of the hand.

Reference: 2017 National Electrical Code – Chapter 2 Wiring and Protection, Article 225 Outside Branch Circuits and Feeders. 225.33 Maximum Number of Disconnects.

75. **Answer C.** six, six

The disconnecting means for each supply permitted by 225.30 ***shall consist of not more than six switches or six circuit breakers mounted in a single enclosure, in a group of separate enclosures, or in or on a switchboard or switchgear.*** There shall be no more than six disconnects per supply grouped in anyone location.

Reference: 2017 National Electrical Code – Chapter 2 Wiring and Protection, Article 225 Outside Branch Circuits and Feeders. 225.33 Maximum Number of Disconnects. 225.33(A) General.

76. **Answer B.** six

Two or three single-pole switches or breakers capable of individual operation shall be permitted on multiwire circuits, one pole for each ungrounded conductor, as one multipole disconnect, provided they are equipped with identified handle ties or ***a master handle to disconnect all ungrounded conductors with no more than six operations of the hand.***

Reference: 2017 National Electrical Code – Chapter 2 Wiring and Protection, Article 225 Outside Branch Circuits and Feeders. 225.33 Maximum Number of Disconnects. 225.33(B) Single-Pole Units.

EXAM 5

EXAM 5 ANSWERS

77. Answer C. load

Also see Article 230.2(E)

The two to six disconnects as permitted in 225.33 shall be grouped. *Each disconnect shall be marked to indicate the load served.*

Reference: 2017 National Electrical Code – Chapter 2 Wiring and Protection, Article 225 Outside Branch Circuits and Feeders. 225.34 Grouping of Disconnects. 225.34(A) General.

78. Answer A. access

Review the exception in this section.

In a multiple-occupancy building, each occupant shall have access to the occupant's supply disconnecting means.

Exception: *In a multiple-occupancy building where electric supply and electrical maintenance are provided by the building management and where these are under continuous building management supervision, the supply disconnecting means supplying more than one occupancy shall be permitted to be accessible to authorized management personnel only.*

Reference: 2017 National Electrical Code – Chapter 2 Wiring and Protection, Article 225 Outside Branch Circuits and Feeders. 225.35 Access to Occupants.

79. Answer C. feeder and branch-circuit disconnect location

Where a building or structure has any combination of feeders, branch circuits, or services passing through it or supplying it, a permanent plaque or directory shall be installed at each feeder and branch-circuit disconnect location denoting all other services, feeders, or branch circuits supplying that building or structure or passing through that building or structure and the area served by each.

Reference: 2017 National Electrical Code – Chapter 2 Wiring and Protection, Article 225 Outside Branch Circuits and Feeders. 225.37 Identification.

80. Answer C. simultaneously

Each building or structure disconnecting means shall simultaneously disconnect all ungrounded supply conductors that it controls from the building or structure wiring system.

Reference: 2017 National Electrical Code – Chapter 2 Wiring and Protection, Article 225 Outside Branch Circuits and Feeders. 225.38 Disconnect Construction. 225.38(B) Simultaneous Opening of Poles.

81. Answer A. grounded, grounded

Where the building or structure disconnecting means does not disconnect the grounded conductor from the grounded conductors in the building or structure wiring, other means shall be provided for this purpose at the location of the disconnecting means. *A terminal or bus to which all grounded conductors* can be attached by means of pressure connectors shall be permitted for this purpose.

In a multi section switchboard or switchgear, disconnects for the grounded conductor shall be permitted to be in any section of the switchboard or switchgear, if the switchboard section or switchgear section is marked to indicate a grounded conductor disconnect is contained within the equipment

Reference: 2017 National Electrical Code – Chapter 2 Wiring and Protection, Article 225 Outside Branch Circuits and Feeders. 225.38 Disconnect Construction. . 225.38(C) Disconnection of Grounded Conductor.

82. Answer D. open or closed

The building or structure disconnecting means shall plainly indicate whether it is in the open or closed position.

Reference: 2017 National Electrical Code – Chapter 2 Wiring and Protection, Article 225 Outside Branch Circuits and Feeders. 225.38 Disconnect Construction. . 225.38(D) Indicating.

83. Answer A. 15

Same requirements for Service Disconnecting means, see Article 230.79(A).

For installations to supply only limited loads of a single branch circuit, *the branch circuit disconnecting means shall have a rating of not less than 15 amperes.*

Reference: 2017 National Electrical Code – Chapter 2 Wiring and Protection, Article 225 Outside Branch Circuits and Feeders. 225.39 Rating of Disconnect. 225.39(A) One-Circuit Installation.

84. Answer B. 15

For installations to supply only limited loads of a single branch circuit, *the branch circuit disconnecting means shall have a rating of not less than 15 amperes.*

Reference: 2017 National Electrical Code – Chapter 2 Wiring and Protection, Article 225 Outside Branch Circuits and Feeders. 225.39 Rating of Disconnect. . 225.39(A) One-Circuit Installation.

EXAM 5

EXAM 5 ANSWERS

85. **Answer D.** 30

    Same requirements for Service Disconnecting means, see Article 230.79(B).

    For installations consisting of not more than two 2-wire branch circuits, the feeder or **branch-circuit disconnecting means shall have a rating of not less than 30 amperes.**

    Reference: 2017 National Electrical Code – Chapter 2 Wiring and Protection, Article 225 Outside Branch Circuits and Feeders. 225.39 Rating of Disconnect. 225.39(B) Two-Circuit Installations.

86. **Answer C.** 100

    Same requirements for Service Disconnecting means, see Article 230.79(C).

    For a one-family dwelling, the feeder disconnecting means shall have a rating of not less than 100 amperes, 3-wire.

    Reference: 2017 National Electrical Code – Chapter 2 Wiring and Protection, Article 225 Outside Branch Circuits and Feeders. 225.39 Rating of Disconnect. 225.39(C) One-Family Dwelling.

87. **Answer C.** 100

    For a one-family dwelling, the feeder disconnecting means shall have a rating of not less than 100 amperes, 3-wire.

    Reference: 2017 National Electrical Code – Chapter 2 Wiring and Protection, Article 225 Outside Branch Circuits and Feeders. 225.39 Rating of Disconnect. . 225.39(C) One-Family Dwelling.

88. **Answer C.** a lower

    Where a feeder overcurrent device is not readily accessible, branch-circuit overcurrent devices shall be installed on the load side, shall be mounted in a readily accessible location, and **shall be of a lower ampere rating than the feeder overcurrent device.**

    Reference: 2017 National Electrical Code – Chapter 2 Wiring and Protection, Article 225 Outside Branch Circuits and Feeders. 225.40 Access to Overcurrent Protective Devices.

89. **Answer C.** visible break contacts

    Where oil switches or air, oil, vacuum, or sulfur hexafluoride circuit breakers constitute a building disconnecting means, a**n isolating switch with visible break contacts and meeting the requirements of 230.204(B)**, (C), and (D) shall be installed on the supply side of the disconnecting means and all associated equipment.

    Reference: 2017 National Electrical Code – Chapter 2 Wiring and Protection, Article 225 Outside Branch Circuits and Feeders. 225.51 Isolating Switches.

90. **Answer A.** electrically operated by a remote-control device.

    A building or structure disconnecting means shall be located in accordance with 225.32, or, if not readily accessible, it shall be operable by mechanical linkage from a readily accessible point. For multibuilding industrial installations under single management, *it shall be permitted to be electrically operated by a readily accessible, remote-control device in a separate building or structure.*

    Reference: 2017 National Electrical Code – Chapter 2 Wiring and Protection, Article 225 Outside Branch Circuits and Feeders. 225.52 Disconnecting Means. 225.52(A) Location.

91. **Answer D.** simultaneously

    Each building or structure disconnect shall simultaneously disconnect all ungrounded supply conductors it controls and shall have a fault-closing rating not less than the maximum available short-circuit current available at its supply terminals.

    Reference: 2017 National Electrical Code – Chapter 2 Wiring and Protection, Article 225 Outside Branch Circuits and Feeders. 225.52 Disconnecting Means. 225.52(B) Type.

92. **Answer B.** locked

    Disconnecting means shall be lockable in accordance with 110.25.

    Reference: 2017 National Electrical Code – Chapter 2 Wiring and Protection, Article 225 Outside Branch Circuits and Feeders. 225.52 Disconnecting Means. 225.52(C) Locking

EXAM 5

Chapter 2 Wiring and Protection 02

If a disconnecting means is required to be lockable open elsewhere in this Code, it shall be capable of being locked in the open position. The provisions for locking shall remain in place with or without the lock installed.

Reference: 2017 National Electrical Code – Chapter 1 General, Article 110 - Requirements for Electrical Installations . 110.25 Lockable Disconnecting Means.

93. **Answer C.** in the open position

    Disconnecting means shall be lockable in accordance with 110.25.

    Reference: 2017 National Electrical Code – Chapter 2 Wiring and Protection, Article 225 Outside Branch Circuits and Feeders. 225.52 Disconnecting Means. 225.52(C) Locking.

    If a disconnecting means is required to be lockable open elsewhere in this Code, it shall be capable of being locked in the open position. The provisions for locking shall remain in place with or without the lock installed.

    Reference: 2017 National Electrical Code – Chapter 1 General, Article 110 - Requirements for Electrical Installations . 110.25 Lockable Disconnecting Means.

94. **Answer A.** passing through it

    Where a building or structure has any combination of feeders, branch circuits, or services passing through or supplying it, a permanent plaque or directory shall be installed at each feeder and branch-circuit disconnect location that denotes all other services, feeders, or branch circuits supplying that building or structure or passing through that building or structure and the area served by each.

    Reference: 2017 National Electrical Code – Chapter 2 Wiring and Protection, Article 225 Outside Branch Circuits and Feeders. 225.52 Disconnecting Means. 225.52(F) Identification.

95. **Answer B.** installation violates Code height requirement.

    The clearances over roadways, walkways, rail, water, and open land for conductors and live parts up to 22 kV, nominal, to ground or less shall be not less than the values shown in Table 225.60. Table on page 70-83.

    Reference: 2017 National Electrical Code – Chapter 2 Wiring and Protection, Article 225 Outside Branch Circuits and Feeders. 225.60 Clearances over Roadways, Walkways, Rail, Water, and Open Land. 225.60(A) 22 kV, Nominal, to Ground or Less.

96. **Answer A.** one

    A building or other structure served shall be supplied by only one service unless permitted in 230.2(A) through (D). For the purpose of 230.40, Exception No. 2 only, underground sets of conductors, 1/0 AWG and larger, running to the same location and connected together at their supply end but not connected together at their load end shall be considered to be supplying one service.

    Reference: 2017 National Electrical Code – Chapter 2 Wiring and Protection, Article 230 Services. 230.2 Number of Services.

97. **Answer A.** only one

    A building or other structure served shall be supplied by only one service unless permitted in 230.2(A) through (D). For the purpose of 230.40, Exception No. 2 only, underground sets of conductors, 1/0 AWG and larger, running to the same location and connected together at their supply end but not connected together at their load end shall be considered to be supplying one service.

    Reference: 2017 National Electrical Code – Chapter 2 Wiring and Protection, Article 230 Services. 230.2 Number of Services.

98. **Answer A.** 2, 2

    Conductors shall be considered outside of a building or other structure under any of the following conditions:

    (1) *Where installed under not less than 50 mm (2 in.) of concrete beneath a building or other structure*

    (2) *Where installed within a building or other structure in a raceway that is encased in concrete or brick not less than 50 mm (2 in.) thick*

    (3) Where installed in any vault that meets the construction requirements of Article 450, Part III

    (4) Where installed in conduit and under not less than 450 mm (18 in.) of earth beneath a building or other structure

    (5) Where installed within rigid metal conduit (Type RMC) or intermediate metal conduit (Type IMC) used to accommodate the clearance requirements in 230.24 and routed directly through an eave but not a wall of a building.

    Reference: 2017 National Electrical Code – Chapter 2 Wiring and Protection, Article 230 Services. 230.6 Conductors Considered Outside the Building.

EXAM 5
Chapter 2 Wiring and Protection 02

99. **Answer B.** installed

    Review the 2 exceptions in this article.

    Conductors other than service conductors shall not be installed in the same service raceway or service cable in which the service conductors are installed.

    Exception No. 1: Grounding electrode conductors or supply side bonding jumpers or conductors shall be permitted within service raceways.

    Exception No. 2: Load management control conductors having overcurrent protection shall be permitted within service raceways.

    Reference: 2017 National Electrical Code – Chapter 2 Wiring and Protection, Article 230 Services. 230.7 Other Conductors in Raceway or Cable.

100. **Answer C.** service conductors

    Conductors other than service conductors shall not be installed in the same service raceway or service cable.

    Reference: 2017 National Electrical Code – Chapter 2 Wiring and Protection, Article 230 Services. 230.7 Other Conductors in Raceway or Cable.

101. **Answer A.** 3

    Service conductors installed as open conductors or multiconductor cable without an overall outer jacket shall have a clearance of not less than 900 mm (3 ft.) from windows that are designed to be opened, doors, porches, balconies, ladders, stairs, fire escapes, or similar locations.

    Reference: 2017 National Electrical Code – Chapter 2 Wiring and Protection, Article 230 Services. 230.9 Clearances on Buildings. 230.9(A) Clearances.

102. **Answer A.** 3 feet

    Service conductors installed as open conductors or multiconductor cable **without an overall outer jacket shall have a clearance of not less than 900 mm (3 ft.) from windows** that are designed to be opened, doors, porches, balconies, ladders, stairs, fire escapes, or similar locations.

    Reference: 2017 National Electrical Code – Chapter 2 Wiring and Protection, Article 230 Services. 230.9 Clearances on Buildings. 230.9(A) Clearances.

103. **Answer A.** grounded

    Individual conductors shall be insulated or covered.

    Exception: The grounded conductor of a multiconductor cable shall be permitted to be bare.

    Reference: 2017 National Electrical Code – Chapter 2 Wiring and Protection, Article 230 Services. 230.22 Insulation or Covering.

104. **Answer D.** 8

    The conductors shall not be smaller than 8 AWG copper or 6 AWG aluminum or copper-clad aluminum.

    Reference: 2017 National Electrical Code – Chapter 2 Wiring and Protection, Article 230 Services. 230.23 Size and Rating. 230.23(B) Minimum Size.

105. **Answer D.** 8 AWG copper or 6 AWG aluminum

    The conductors shall not be smaller than 8 AWG copper or 6 AWG aluminum or copper-clad aluminum.

    Reference: 2017 National Electrical Code – Chapter 2 Wiring and Protection, Article 230 Services. 230.23 Size and Rating. 230.23(B) Minimum Size.

106. **Answer D.** 8 AWG copper

    The conductors shall not be smaller than 8 AWG copper or 6 AWG aluminum or copper-clad aluminum.

    Reference: 2017 National Electrical Code – Chapter 2 Wiring and Protection, Article 230 Services. 230.23 Size and Rating. 230.23(B) Minimum Size.

EXAM 5

Chapter 2 Wiring and Protection 02

107. Answer B.   8

Review the 5 exceptions in this article, they seem to apply more often than the 8 ft. requirement.

Conductors shall have a vertical clearance of not less than 2.5 m (8 ft.) above the roof surface. The vertical clearance above the roof level shall be maintained for a distance of not less than 900 mm (3 ft.) in all directions from the edge of the roof.

Exception No.1: The area above a roof surface subject to pedestrian or vehicular traffic shall have a vertical clearance from the roof surface in accordance with the clearance requirements of 230.24(B).

Exception No.2: Where the voltage between conductors does not exceed 300 and the roof has a slope 100 mm in 300 mm (4 in. in 12 in.) or greater; a reduction in clearance to 900 mm (3 ft.) shall be permitted.

Exception No.3: Where the voltage between conductors does not exceed 300, a reduction in clearance above only the overhanging portion of the roof to not less than 450 mm (18 in.) shall be permitted (1) not more than 1.8 m (6 ft.) of overhead service conductors, 1.2 m (4 ft.) horizontally, pass above the roof overhang, and (2) they are terminated at a through-the-roof raceway or approved support.

Informational Note: See 230.28 for mast supports.

Exception No.4: The requirement for maintaining the vertical clearance 900 nun (3 ft.) from the edge of the roof shall not apply to the final conductor span where the service drop or overhead service conductors are attached to the side of a building.

Exception No.5: Where the voltage between conductors does not exceed 300 and the roof area is guarded or isolated, a reduction in clearance to 900 mm (3 ft.) shall be permitted.

Reference: 2017 National Electrical Code – Chapter 2 Wiring and Protection, Article 230 Services. 230.24 Clearances. 230.24(A) Above Roofs.

108. Answer A.   final grade

Overhead service conductors, **where not in excess of 600 volts,** nominal, shall have the following minimum clearance from final grade:

(1) 3.0 m (10 ft.) -- at the electrical service entrance to buildings, also at the lowest point of the drip loop of the building electrical entrance, and above areas or sidewalks accessible only to pedestrians, **measured from final grade** or other accessible surface only for overhead service conductors supported on and cabled together with a grounded bare messenger where the voltage does not exceed 150 volts to ground

(2) 3.7 m (12 ft.) - over residential property and driveways, and those commercial areas not subject to truck traffic where the voltage does not exceed 300 volts to ground

(3) 4.5 m (15 ft.) - for those areas listed in the 3.7 m (12 ft.) classification where the voltage exceeds 300 volts to ground

(4) 5.5 m (18 ft.) - over public streets, alleys, roads. Parking areas subject to truck traffic, driveways on other than residential property, and other land such as cultivated, grazing, forest, and orchard

(5) 7.5 m (24 1⁄2) over tracks of railroads

Reference: 2017 National Electrical Code – Chapter 2 Wiring and Protection, Article 230 Services. 230.24 Clearances. . 230.24(B) Vertical Clearance for Overhead Service Conductors.

109. Answer B.   10 feet

3.0 m (10 ft.) -- at the electrical service entrance to buildings, also at the lowest point of the drip loop of the building electrical entrance, and above areas or sidewalks accessible only to pedestrians, measured from final grade or other accessible surface only for overhead service conductors supported on and cabled together with a grounded bare messenger where the voltage does not exceed 150 volts to ground.

Reference: 2017 National Electrical Code – Chapter 2 Wiring and Protection, Article 230 Services. 230.24 Clearances. 230.24(B) Vertical Clearance for Overhead Service Conductors. 230.24(B)(1)

EXAM 5

Chapter 2 Wiring and Protection 02

110. **Answer C.** 18 feet

    5.5 m (18 ft.) – over public streets, alleys, roads. Parking areas subject to truck traffic, driveways on other than residential property, and other land such as cultivated, grazing, forest, and orchard

    Reference: 2017 National Electrical Code – Chapter 2 Wiring and Protection, Article 230 Services. 230.24 Clearances. 230.24(B) Vertical Clearance for Overhead Service Conductors. 230.24(B)(4)

111. **Answer D.** 18 feet

    5.5 m (18 ft.) – over public streets, alleys, roads. Parking areas subject to truck traffic, driveways on other than residential property, and other land such as cultivated, grazing, forest, and orchard

    Reference: 2017 National Electrical Code – Chapter 2 Wiring and Protection, Article 230 Services. 230.24 Clearances. 230.24(B) Vertical Clearance for Overhead Service Conductors. 230.24(B)(4)

112. **Answer A.** 10

    The point of attachment of the overhead service conductors to a building or other structure shall provide the minimum clearances as specified in 230.9 and 230.24. *In no case shall this point of attachment be less than 3.0 m (10 ft.) above finished grade.*

    Reference: 2017 National Electrical Code – Chapter 2 Wiring and Protection, Article 230 Services. 230.26 Point of Attachment.

113. **Answer B.** 10

    The point of attachment of the overhead service conductors to a building or other structure shall provide the minimum clearances as specified in 230.9 and 230.24. *In no case shall this point of attachment be less than 3.0 m (10 ft.) above finished grade.*

    Reference: 2017 National Electrical Code – Chapter 2 Wiring and Protection, Article 230 Services. 230.26 Point of Attachment.

114. **Answer C.** nonabsorbent

    Multiconductor cables used for overhead service conductors shall be attached to buildings or other structures by fittings identified for use with service conductors. Open conductors shall be attached to fittings identified for use with service conductors or to noncombustible, *nonabsorbent insulators securely attached to the building or other structure.*

    Reference: 2017 National Electrical Code – Chapter 2 Wiring and Protection, Article 230 Services. 230.27 Means of Attachment.

115. **Answer D.** supported by braces or guys

    Only power service-drop or overhead service conductors shall be permitted to be attached to a service mast. Service masts used for the support of service-drop or overhead service conductors shall be installed in accordance with 230.28(A) and (B).

    (A) Strength. *The service mast shall be of adequate strength or be supported by braces or guys to withstand safely the strain imposed by the service-drop or overhead service conductors.* Hubs intended for use with a conduit that serves as a service mast shall be identified for use with service-entrance equipment.

    (B) Attachment. Service-drop or overhead service conductors shall not be attached to a service mast between a weather head or the end of the conduit and a coupling, where the coupling is located above the last point of securement to the building or other structure or is located above the building or other structure.

    Reference: 2017 National Electrical Code – Chapter 2 Wiring and Protection, Article 230 Services. 230.28 Service Masts as Supports.

EXAM 5

Chapter 2 Wiring and Protection 02

116. Answer B. braces or guys

The service mast shall be of adequate strength or be supported by braces or guys to withstand safely the strain imposed by the service-drop or overhead service conductors. Hubs intended for use with a conduit that serves as a service mast shall be identified for use with service-entrance equipment.

Reference: 2017 National Electrical Code – Chapter 2 Wiring and Protection, Article 230 Services. 230.28 Service Masts as Supports. 230.28(a) Attachment.

117. Answer B. independent of the building

Service conductors passing over a roof shall be securely supported by substantial structures. For a grounded system, where the substantial structure is metal, it shall be bonded by means of a bonding jumper and listed connector to the grounded overhead service conductor. Where practicable, *such supports shall be independent of the building.*

Reference: 2017 National Electrical Code – Chapter 2 Wiring and Protection, Article 230 Services. 230.29 Supports over Buildings.

118. Answer C. the applied voltage

Underground service conductors shall be insulated for the applied voltage.

Reference: 2017 National Electrical Code – Chapter 2 Wiring and Protection, Article 230 Services. 230.30 Installation. 230.30(A) Insulation.

119. Answer C. 8 AWG copper or 6 AWG

The conductors shall not be smaller than 8 AWG copper or 6 AWG aluminum or copper-clad aluminum.

Reference: 2017 National Electrical Code – Chapter 2 Wiring and Protection, Article 230 Services. 230.31 Size and Rating. 230.31(B) Minimum Size.

120. Answer D. 8 AWG copper

The conductors shall not be smaller than 8 AWG copper or 6 AWG aluminum or copper-clad aluminum.

2014=7 National Electrical Code – Chapter 2 Wiring and Protection, Article 230 Services. 230.31 Size and Rating. 230.31(B) Minimum Size.

121. Answer D. Type NM cable

Service-entrance conductors shall be installed in accordance with the applicable requirements of this Code covering the type of wiring method used and shall be limited to *the following methods:*

(1) Open wiring on insulators

(2) Type IGS cable

(3) Rigid metal conduit (RMC)

(4) Intermediate metal conduit (IMC)

(5) Electrical metallic tubing (EMT)

(6) Electrical nonmetallic tubing

(7) Service-entrance cables

(8) Wireways

(9) Busways

(10) Auxiliary gutters

(11) Rigid polyvinyl chloride conduit (PVC)

(12) Cablebus

(13) Type MC cable

(14) Mineral-insulated, metal-sheathed cable, Type MI

(15) Flexible metal conduit (FMC) not over 1.8 m (6 ft.) long or liquidtight flexible metal conduit (LFMC) not over 1.8 m (6 ft.) long between a raceway, or between a raceway and service equipment, with a supply-side bonding jumper routed with the flexible metal conduit (FMC) or the liquidtight flexible metal conduit (LFMC) according to the provisions of 250.102(A), (B), (C), and (E)

(16) Liquidtight flexible nonmetallic conduit (LFNC)

(17) High density polyethylene conduit (HDPE)

(18) Nonmetallic underground conduit with conductors (NUCC)

(19) Reinforced thermosetting resin conduit (RTRC)

Reference: 2017 National Electrical Code – Chapter 2 Wiring and Protection, Article 230 Services. 230.43 Wiring Methods for 1000 Volts, Nominal, or Less.

EXAM 5

Chapter 2 Wiring and Protection 02

122. Answer C. service-entrance

Cable tray systems shall be permitted to support service-entrance conductors. *Cable trays used to support service-entrance conductors shall contain only service-entrance conductors* and shall be limited to the following methods:

(1) Type SE cable

(2) Type MC cable

(3) Type MI cable

(4) Type IGS cable

(5) Single conductors 1/0 and larger that are listed for use in cable tray

Such cable trays shall be identified with permanently affixed labels with the wording "Service-Entrance Conductors." The labels shall be located so as to be visible after installation with a spacing not to exceed 3 m (10 ft.) so that the service-entrance conductors are able to be readily traced through the entire length of the cable tray.

Reference: 2017 National Electrical Code – Chapter 2 Wiring and Protection, Article 230 Services. 230.44 Cable Trays.

123. Answer D. all are acceptable

All other service-entrance conductors, other than underground service entrance conductors, shall be protected against physical damage as specified in 230.50(B)(1) or (B)(2).

Reference: 2017 National Electrical Code – Chapter 2 Wiring and Protection, Article 230 Services. 230.50 Protection Against Physical Damage. 230.50(B) All Other Service-Entrance Conductors.

124. Answer B. 12, 30

Service-entrance cables shall be supported by straps or other approved means within 300 mm (12 in.) of every service head, gooseneck, or connection to a raceway or *enclosure and at intervals not exceeding 750 mm (30 in.).*

Reference: 2017 National Electrical Code – Chapter 2 Wiring and Protection, Article 230 Services. 230.51 Mounting Supports. 230.51(A) Service-entrance Cables.

125. Answer A. bathrooms

Service disconnecting means shall not be installed in bathrooms.

Reference: 2017 National Electrical Code – Chapter 2 Wiring and Protection, Article 230 Services. 230.70 General. 230.70(A) Location. 230.70(A)(2) Bathrooms

EXAM 6

Chapter 2 Wiring and Protection 03

1. A means for disconnecting service must not be located in:

    A. basements

    B. bathrooms

    C. hallways

    D. utility rooms

    Reference: 2017 National Electrical Code – Chapter 2 Wiring and Protection, Article 230 Services. 230.70 General. 230.70(A) Location. 230.70(A)(2) Bathrooms.

2. What are the maximum number of switch(es) or set(s) of circuit breakers allowed for service disconnecting means for each residential service?

    A. one

    B. two

    C. four

    D. six

    Reference: 2017 National Electrical Code – Chapter 2 Wiring and Protection, Article 230 Services. 230.71 Maximum Number of Disconnects. 230.71(A) General.

3. What is the minimum rating for a service disconnecting means when supplied with a 120/240-volt, 3-wire, single phase service for a one-family dwelling?

    A. 30 amperes

    B. 60 amperes

    C. 100 amperes

    D. 200 amperes

    Reference: 2017 National Electrical Code – Chapter 2 Wiring and Protection, Article 230 Services. 230.79 Rating of Service Disconnecting Means. 230.79(C) One-Family Dwellings.

4. Overcurrent protection on a residential electric service is required for which of the following?

    A. bonding conductor

    B. grounding conductor

    C. identified conductors

    D. ungrounded conductors

    Reference: 2017 National Electrical Code – Chapter 2 Wiring and Protection, Article 230 Services. 230.90 Where Required. 230.90(A) Ungrounded Conductor.

Chapter 2 Wiring and Protection 03

EXAM 6

Chapter 2 Wiring and Protection 03

5. When it is located in a location to be accessible, an automatic overcurrent device that protects service conductors supplying specific loads, such as water heaters, may be _____ to prevent tampering.

   A. hidden from view

   B. locked or sealed

   C. not labeled

   D. openly accessible only

   Reference: 2017 National Electrical Code – Chapter 2 Wiring and Protection, Article 230 Services. 230.93 Protection of Specific Circuits.

6. All 3-phase, 4-wire, 480Y/227-volt electrical service, disregarding exceptions, require ground-fault protection for each service disconnecting means, when rated for no less than:

   A. 400 amperes

   B. 600 amperes

   C. 1,000 amperes

   D. 1,500 amperes

   Reference: 2017 National Electrical Code – Chapter 2 Wiring and Protection, Article 230 Services. 230.95 Ground-Fault Protection of Equipment.

7. Ground-fault protection shall be provided where a building or structure is supplied with a 3-phase, 480Y/227-volt service with disconnecting means rated at least:

   A. 1000 amperes

   B. 1200 amperes

   C. 1500 amperes

   D. 2000 amperes

   Reference: 2017 National Electrical Code – Chapter 2 Wiring and Protection, Article 230 Services. 230.95 Ground-Fault Protection of Equipment.

EXAM 6

Chapter 2 Wiring and Protection 03

8. Service-entrance conductors to enclosures or buildings must be _____ AWG or larger unless in a multiconductor cable. Multiconductor cables must be _____ AWG or larger.

    A. 4, 6

    B. 6, 4

    C. 6, 8

    D. 8, 10

    Reference: 2017 National Electrical Code – Chapter 2 Wiring and Protection, Article 230 Services. 230.202 Service-Entrance Conductors. . 230.202(A) Conductor Size.

9. When surge arresters are installed in accordance with the requirements of Article 280, they are permitted on each _____ overhead service conductor.

    A. bonding

    B. grounded

    C. grounding

    D. ungrounded

    Reference: 2017 National Electrical Code – Chapter 2 Wiring and Protection, Article 230 Services. 230.209 Surge Arresters.

10. What is the term for a non-service conductor, that has overcurrent protection that exceeds the value allowed for similar conductors, ahead of its point of supply, that are protected as described in 240.4.

    A. branch circuit conductor

    B. overload conductor

    C. tap conductor

    D. ungrounded conductor

    Reference: 2017 National Electrical Code – Chapter 2 Wiring and Protection, Article 240 Overcurrent Protection. 240.2 Definitions.

EXAM 6

Chapter 2 Wiring and Protection 03

11. Conductors must be protected against overcurrent in accordance with their ampacities, except for:

    A. flexible cords, flexible cables, and fixture wires

    B. heating overload conductors

    C. service lateral conductors

    D. variable gauge conductors

    Reference: 2017 National Electrical Code – Chapter 2 Wiring and Protection, Article 240 Overcurrent Protection. 240.4 Protection of Conductors.

12. What is the maximum standard ampere rating of the overcurrent protection device allowed by the NEC to protect a circuit with a computed allowable ampacity of 75 amperes when it is not part of a multioutlet branch circuit supplying more than one receptacle, or a motor circuit?

    A. 70 amperes

    B. 75 amperes

    C. 80 amperes

    D. 85 amperes

    Reference: 2017 National Electrical Code – Chapter 2 Wiring and Protection, Article 240 Overcurrent Protection. 240.6 Standard Ampere Ratings. 240.6(A) Fuses and Fixed-Trip Circuit Breakers.

13. Regardless of the insulation type, after any correction factors for ambient temperature and number of conductors have been applied, the overcurrent protection for size 12 AWG copper conductors is generally no more than:

    A. 15 amperes

    B. 20 amperes

    C. 25 amperes

    D. 30 amperes

    Reference: 2017 National Electrical Code – Chapter 2 Wiring and Protection, Article 240 Overcurrent Protection. 240.4 Protection of Conductors. 240.4(D) Small Conductors. 240.4(D)(5) 12 AWG Copper.

EXAM 6

Chapter 2 Wiring and Protection 03

14. A fixture wire of 18 AWG is allowed to be tapped to a branch circuit conductor of a 20 amp branch circuit, as long as it is not more _____ ft. in length.

    A. 6
    B. 10
    C. 25
    D. 50

    Reference: 2017 National Electrical Code – Chapter 2 Wiring and Protection, Article 240 Overcurrent Protection. 240.5 Protection of Flexible Cords, Flexible Cables, and Fixture Wires. . 240.5(A) Ampacities. 240.5(A)(2) Fixture Wire.

15. What is the smallest size flexible cord allowed to supply a cord-and-plug connected water softener wired to a 20 ampere rated branch circuit?

    A. 14 AWG
    B. 16 AWG
    C. 18 AWG
    D. 20 AWG

    Reference: 2017 National Electrical Code – Chapter 2 Wiring and Protection, Article 240 Overcurrent Protection. 240.5 Protection of Flexible Cords, Flexible Cables, and Fixture Wires. 240.5(B) Branch Circuit Overcurrent Device. 240.5(B)(4) Field Assembled Extension Cord Sets.

16. Of the following, which is not a standard ampere rating for a circuit breaker?

    A. 75 amperes
    B. 90 amperes
    C. 110 amperes
    D. 225 amperes

    Reference: 2017 National Electrical Code – Chapter 2 Wiring and Protection, Article 240 Overcurrent Protection. 240.6 Standard Ampere Ratings. 240.6(A) Fuses and Fixed-Trip Circuit Breakers.

17. Circuit breakers and fuses are allowed to be connected in parallel where they are _____, and listed as a unit. Individual circuit breakers, fuses, or any combination thereof may not be connected otherwise in parallel.

    A. factory assembled in parallel
    B. matched pairs
    C. of the same type and rating
    D. rated equally for amperage and time delay

    Reference: 2017 National Electrical Code – Chapter 2 Wiring and Protection, Article 240 Overcurrent Protection. 240.8 Fuses or Circuit Breakers in Parallel.

EXAM 6

Chapter 2 Wiring and Protection 03

18. When conductors of not over 25 ft. long are being tapped from a service with two (2) parallel size 500 kcmil copper conductors per phase, protected by an 800 ampere overcurrent protection device, terminating in a single breaker, what is the minimum size THW copper conductors required for the tap conductors?

    A. 250 kcmil

    B. 300 kcmil

    C. 400 kcmil

    D. 500 kcmil

    Reference: 2017 National Electrical Code – Chapter 2 Wiring and Protection, Article 240 Overcurrent Protection. 240.21 Location in Circuit. 240.21(B) Feeder Traps. 240.21(B)(2)(1)

19. Overcurrent devices are designed to open all conductors of a circuit, including a grounded conductor, so that no pole can operate _____, so other than overload protection no overcurrent device may be connected in series with any conductor that has been intentionally grounded.

    A. above the open limit

    B. independently

    C. simultaneously

    D. until the circuit breaker for each is closed

    Reference: 2017 National Electrical Code – Chapter 2 Wiring and Protection, Article 240 Overcurrent Protection. 240.22 Grounded Conductor.

20. If a change happens in the size of an ungrounded conductor, a similar change must be allowed to be made in the size of a corresponding _____ conductor.

    A. bonding

    B. grounded

    C. grounding

    D. neutral

    Reference: 2017 National Electrical Code – Chapter 2 Wiring and Protection, Article 240 Overcurrent Protection. 240.23 Change in Size of Grounded Conductor.

EXAM 6

Chapter 2 Wiring and Protection 03

21. Overcurrent devices must be readily accessible and installed so the center of the operating handle grip of the circuit breaker or switch, when in its highest position, is 6 ft. _____ in. above the floor or working platform, or less. Exceptions ignored.

    A. 6
    B. 7
    C. 8
    D. 10

    Reference: 2017 National Electrical Code – Chapter 2 Wiring and Protection, Article 240 Overcurrent Protection. 240.24 Location in or on Premises. 240.24(A) Accessibility.

22. Which of the dwelling unit areas listed below are panelboards NOT allowed to be located in?

    A. bathrooms
    B. garages
    C. hallways
    D. kitchens

    Reference: 2017 National Electrical Code – Chapter 2 Wiring and Protection, Article 240 Overcurrent Protection. 240.24 Location in or on Premises. 240.24(E) Not Located in Bathrooms.

23. If a panelboard contains circuit breakers, they may NOT be located:

    A. over steps of stairways
    B. within 6 feet of a water heater
    C. both A and B
    D. neither A nor B

    Reference: 2017 National Electrical Code – Chapter 2 Wiring and Protection, Article 240 Overcurrent Protection. 240.24 Location in or on Premises. 240.24(F) Not Located over Steps.

24. Unless it is impracticable, overcurrent device enclosures must be mounted in a _____ position.

    A. horizontal
    B. perpendicular
    C. upright
    D. vertical

    Reference: 2017 National Electrical Code – Chapter 2 Wiring and Protection, Article 240 Overcurrent Protection. 240.33 Vertical Position.

EXAM 6

Chapter 2 Wiring and Protection 03

25. All fuses in circuits with a voltage of _____ to ground, minimum, must have a disconnecting means provided on the supply side.

    A. 120 volts
    B. 150 volts
    C. 250 volts
    D. 277 volts

    Reference: 2017 National Electrical Code – Chapter 2 Wiring and Protection, Article 240 Overcurrent Protection. 240.40 Disconnecting Means for Fuses.

26. So that persons will not be burned or otherwise injured by their operation, circuit breakers and fuses must be:

    A. insulated
    B. located or shielded
    C. non-accessible
    D. none of the above

    Reference: 2017 National Electrical Code – Chapter 2 Wiring and Protection, Article 240 Overcurrent Protection. 240.41 Arcing or Suddenly Moving Parts. . 240.41(A) Location.

27. Levers or handles of circuit breakers, and other parts that could suddenly move in a way that individuals in the immediate area might be injured by being struck by such parts, must:

    A. be guarded or isolated
    B. be locked in the open position
    C. be made non-accessible
    D. not be used

    Reference: 2017 National Electrical Code – Chapter 2 Wiring and Protection, Article 240 Overcurrent Protection. 240.41 Arcing or Suddenly Moving Parts. . 240.41(B) Suddenly Moving Parts.

28. Plug fuses of the Edison-base type shall be classified at not over 125 volts and _____ amperes and below.

    A. 20
    B. 30
    C. 40
    D. 50

    Reference: 2017 National Electrical Code – Chapter 2 Wiring and Protection, Article 240 Overcurrent Protection. 240.51 Edison-Base Fuses. 240.51(A) Classification.

EXAM 6

Chapter 2 Wiring and Protection 03

29. Which of the following is only for replacements in existing installations and is NOT allowed in new installations?

    A. Class CC

    B. Class H renewable cartridge

    C. Class K

    D. Time delay

    Reference: 2017 National Electrical Code – Chapter 2 Wiring and Protection, Article 240 Overcurrent Protection. 240.60 General. 240.60(D) Renewable Fuses.

30. Circuit breakers must have their ampere rating marked on them in such a way that is durable and visible after installation. The marking is allowed to be visible after:

    A. markings on the cover

    B. removal of a trim or cover

    C. removing the breaker

    D. tripping the breaker

    Reference: 2017 National Electrical Code – Chapter 2 Wiring and Protection, Article 240 Overcurrent Protection. 240.83 Marking. 240.83(A) Durable and Visible.

31. Circuit breakers used as _____ in 120-volt and 277-volt fluorescent lighting circuits shall be listed and shall be marked SWD or HID.

    A. grounds

    B. interrupts

    C. switches

    D. none of the above

    Reference: 2017 National Electrical Code – Chapter 2 Wiring and Protection, Article 240 Overcurrent Protection. 240.83 Marking. 240.83(D) Used as Switches.

32. Circuit breakers used to switch 120-volt and 277-volt fluorescent lighting circuits, they are required to be marked and listed:

    A. HID

    B. SWD

    C. either A or B

    D. neither A nor B

    Reference: 2017 National Electrical Code – Chapter 2 Wiring and Protection, Article 240 Overcurrent Protection. 240.83 Marking. 240.83(D) Used as Switches.

EXAM 6

Chapter 2 Wiring and Protection 03

33. Overcurrent protection must be located _____, and must be provided in each ungrounded circuit conductor. Exceptions ignored.

    A. at a convent service point in the circuit

    B. at each end of a conductor

    C. at the point where the conductors receive their supply

    D. on the load end of the circuit

    Reference: 2017 National Electrical Code – Chapter 2 Wiring and Protection, Article 240 Overcurrent Protection. 240.92 Location in Circuit. . 240.92(A) Feeder and Branch-Circuit Conductors.

34. Additional ground and bonding requirements for artificial and natural bodies of water may be found in the National Electrical Code (NEC):

    A. Article 230

    B. Article 517

    C. Article 682

    D. Article 690

    Reference: 2017 National Electrical Code – Chapter 2 Wiring and Protection, Article 250 Grounding and Bonding. 250.3 Application of Other Articles.

35. Are there special grounding requirements, for a pipe organ?

    A. Yes

    B. No

    Reference: 2017 National Electrical Code – Chapter 2 Wiring and Protection, Article 250 Grounding and Bonding. 250.3 Application of Other Articles.

36. Electrical systems that are _____ shall be connected to earth in a manner that will limit the voltage imposed by lightning, line surges, or unintentional contact with higher-voltage lines and that will stabilize the voltage to earth during normal operation.

    A. energized

    B. grounded

    C. ungrounded

    D. none of the above

    Reference: 2017 National Electrical Code – Chapter 2 Wiring and Protection, Article 250 Grounding and Bonding. 250.4 General Requirements for Grounding and Bonding. 250.4(A) Grounded Systems. 250.4(A)(1) Electrical System Grounding.

EXAM 6

Chapter 2 Wiring and Protection 03

37. To limit the voltage to ground on normally noncurrent-carrying conductive materials enclosing electrical equipment or conductors, or forming part of said equipment, they must be:

    A. connected to earth

    B. ground fault protected

    C. insulated

    D. marked with a warning label

    Reference: 2017 National Electrical Code – Chapter 2 Wiring and Protection, Article 250 Grounding and Bonding. 250.4 General Requirements for Grounding and Bonding. 250.4(A) Grounded Systems. 250.4(A)(2) Grounding of Electrical Equipment.

38. Normally non-current-carrying conductive materials enclosing electrical conductors or equipment shall be connected together, and to the electrical supply source, in a manner that establishes an effective _____ current path.

    A. ground-fault

    B. grounded

    C. grounding

    D. ungrounded

    Reference: 2017 National Electrical Code – Chapter 2 Wiring and Protection, Article 250 Grounding and Bonding. 250.4 General Requirements for Grounding and Bonding. 250.4(A) Grounded Systems. 250.4(A)(3) Bonding of Electrical Equipment.

39. What term can be defined as connecting together normally noncurrent-carrying conductive materials used to enclose electrical conductors or equipment, or forming part of said equipment, and connecting them to the electrical supply source so that there is an effective ground-fault current path established.

    A. bonding of electrical equipment

    B. ground fault

    C. grounded conductor

    D. ungrounded conductor

    Reference: 2017 National Electrical Code – Chapter 2 Wiring and Protection, Article 250 Grounding and Bonding. 250.4 General Requirements for Grounding and Bonding. 250.4(A) Grounded Systems. 250.4(A)(3) Bonding of Electrical Equipment.

EXAM 6

Chapter 2 Wiring and Protection 03

40. Electrical wiring and equipment and other conductive material that might become energized must be installed in a manner that makes a low-impedance circuit facilitating operation of a ground detector for high-impedance grounded systems or overcurrent device, capable of safely carrying the greatest ground-fault current that may be imposed from any point on the wiring system, where the electrical supply source may have a ground fault is:

    A. Bonding

    B. Effective Ground-Fault Current Path

    C. GFI

    D. grounded conductor

    Reference: 2017 National Electrical Code – Chapter 2 Wiring and Protection, Article 250 Grounding and Bonding. 250.4 General Requirements for Grounding and Bonding. 250.4(A) Grounded Systems. 250.4(A)(5) Effective Ground-Fault Current Path.

41. The earth shall not be considered an _____ ground-fault current path.

    A. acceptable

    B. effective

    C. satisfactory

    D. unacceptable

    Reference: 2017 National Electrical Code – Chapter 2 Wiring and Protection, Article 250 Grounding and Bonding. 250.4 General Requirements for Grounding and Bonding. 250.4(A) Grounded Systems. 250.4(A)(5) Effective Ground-Fault Current Path.

42. Sheet metal screws shall not be permitted to be used to connect _____ conductors or connection devices to enclosures.

    A. energized

    B. grounded

    C. grounding

    D. ungrounded

    Reference: 2017 National Electrical Code – Chapter 2 Wiring and Protection, Article 250 Grounding and Bonding. 250.8 Connection of Grounding and Bonding Equipment. 250.8(A) Permitted Methods.

EXAM 6

Chapter 2 Wiring and Protection 03

43. Nonconductive coatings (such as paint, lacquer, and enamel) on equipment to be grounded shall be _____ from threads and other contact surfaces to ensure good electrical continuity.

    A. dissolved

    B. kept away

    C. removed

    D. scraped

    Reference: 2017 National Electrical Code – Chapter 2 Wiring and Protection, Article 250 Grounding and Bonding. 250.12 Clean Surfaces.

44. Threads and other contact surfaces with nonconductive coatings (enamel, lacquer, paint, etc.) must have the coating removed or use fittings to connect them so that removal is unnecessary, to ensure good electrical:

    A. conduction

    B. continuity

    C. current

    D. voltage

    Reference: 2017 National Electrical Code – Chapter 2 Wiring and Protection, Article 250 Grounding and Bonding. 250.12 Clean Surfaces.

45. A _____ must be connected to ground service conductor, at each service of a premises wiring system supplied by a grounded ac service. Exception ignored.

    A. bonding jumper

    B. circuit breaker

    C. grounding electrode conductor

    D. lightning arrester

    Reference: 2017 National Electrical Code – Chapter 2 Wiring and Protection, Article 250 Grounding and Bonding. 250.24 Grounding Service-Supplied Alternating-Current Systems. 250.24(A) System Grounding Connections.

EXAM 6

Chapter 2 Wiring and Protection 03

46. A grounding electrode conductor for a premises wiring system supplied by a grounded ac electrical service must be connected to:

    A. the equipment grounding conductor

    B. the grounded service conductor

    C. the meter socket enclosure

    D. the service disconnect enclosure

    Reference: 2017 National Electrical Code – Chapter 2 Wiring and Protection, Article 250 Grounding and Bonding. 250.24 Grounding Service-Supplied Alternating-Current Systems. 250.24(A) System Grounding Connections.

47. If an ac system is operating at less than 1000 volts, a main bonding jumper is required to connect the grounded conductor(s) to:

    A. all sub-panels

    B. each meter base only

    C. each service disconnecting means enclosure

    D. the grounding electrode

    Reference: 2017 National Electrical Code – Chapter 2 Wiring and Protection, Article 250 Grounding and Bonding. 250.24 Grounding Service-Supplied Alternating-Current Systems. 250.24(C) Grounded Conductor Brought to Service Equipment.

48. Where the service-entrance phase conductors are *installed in parallel*, in two or more raceways, the size of the grounded conductor in each raceway shall not be smaller than _____ AWG.

    A. 1/0

    B. 2/0

    C. 3/0

    D. 4/0

    Reference: 2017 National Electrical Code – Chapter 2 Wiring and Protection, Article 250 Grounding and Bonding. 250.24 Grounding Service-Supplied Alternating-Current

EXAM 6

Chapter 2 Wiring and Protection 03

49. Where a main bonding jumper is a screw only, the screw shall be identified with a _____ finish that shall be visible with the screw installed.

    A. blue

    B. green

    C. orange

    D. yellow

    Reference: 2017 National Electrical Code – Chapter 2 Wiring and Protection, Article 250 Grounding and Bonding. 250.28 Main Bonding Jumper and System Bonding Jumper. 250.28(B) Construction.

50. Where should the grounding electrode conductor connection to a system be?

    A. as near as practicable to, preferably in the same area

    B. directly adjacent

    C. within 10 feet

    D. within the same general area but in no case more than 30 ft.

    Reference: 2017 National Electrical Code – Chapter 2 Wiring and Protection, Article 250 Grounding and Bonding. 250.30 Grounding Separately Derived Alternating Current Systems: . 250.30(A) Grounded Systems. 250.30(A)(4) Grounding Electrode.

51. A grounding impedance, _____ to limit a ground-fault current to a low value is allowed for 3-phase ac systems of 480 to 1000 volts for a grounding impedance, if certain conditions are fulfilled.

    A. of not greater than 10 mA

    B. of not greater than 240 Volts

    C. of not less than 10 ohms

    D. usually a resistor

    Reference: 2017 National Electrical Code – Chapter 2 Wiring and Protection, Article 250 Grounding and Bonding. 250.36 High-Impedance Grounded Neutral Systems.

EXAM 6

Chapter 2 Wiring and Protection 03

52. What is the minimum length, in feet, for rod and pipe ground electrodes made of specific materials?

    A. 4

    B. 6

    C. 8

    D. 10

    Reference: 2017 National Electrical Code – Chapter 2 Wiring and Protection, Article 250 Grounding and Bonding. 250.50 Grounding Electrode System.

53. Of the following, which may not be used for grounding electrodes?

    A. Aluminum electrodes

    B. Concrete rebar

    C. Metal underground gas piping system

    D. A and C

    Reference: 2017 National Electrical Code – Chapter 2 Wiring and Protection, Article 250 Grounding and Bonding. 250.50 Grounding Electrode System.

54. What is the length, in feet, a metal underground water pipe must be in direct contact with the earth, including any metal well casing effectively bonded to the pipe, and electrically continuous (or made electrically continuous by bonding around insulting joints or pipe), to points of connection of the bonding conductor(s) or jumper(s) and the grounding electrode conductor, if installed?

    A. 8

    B. 10

    C. 12

    D. 15

    Reference: 2017 National Electrical Code – Chapter 2 Wiring and Protection, Article 250 Grounding and Bonding. 250.52 Grounding Electrodes. 250.52(A) Electrodes Permitted for Grounding. 250.52(A)(1) Metal Underground Water Pipe.

EXAM 6

Chapter 2 Wiring and Protection 03

55. For a metal underground water pipe to serve as a grounding electrode, it must be in direct contact with the earth for a minimum of:

    A. 6 feet

    B. 8 feet

    C. 10 feet

    D. 12 feet

    Reference: 2017 National Electrical Code – Chapter 2 Wiring and Protection, Article 250 Grounding and Bonding. 250.52 Grounding Electrodes. 250.52(A) Electrodes Permitted for Grounding. 250.52(A)(1) Metal Underground Water Pipe.

56. Where at least _____ ft. of a single structural member of a metal building or structure frame is in direct contact with the earth or encased in concrete that is in direct contact with the earth, it is allowed to be used as a grounding electrode.

    A. 5

    B. 8

    C. 10

    D. 12

    Reference: 2017 National Electrical Code – Chapter 2 Wiring and Protection, Article 250 Grounding and Bonding. 250.52 Grounding Electrodes. 250.52(A) Electrodes Permitted for Grounding. 250.52(A)(2) Metal Frame of the Building or Structure.

57. A concrete-encased electrode must have 6.0 m (20 ft.) or more of either one or more zinc galvanized or bare or other electrically conductive coated steel reinforcing bars or rods a minimum of 13 mm (1⁄2 in.) in diameter, installed in a unbroken length of _____ feet, or bare copper at least 4 AWG. Metallic components must be encased in _____ or more inches of concrete and be located horizontally within a part of a concrete footing or foundation that is in direct contact with the earth or vertical foundations or structural members or components that are directly connected to the earth. If more than one concrete-encased electrode is in a building or structure, it is allowed to bond only one of them into the grounding electrode system.

    A. 2, 16

    B. 3, 20

    C. 4, 20

    D. 20, 2

    Reference: 2017 National Electrical Code – Chapter 2 Wiring and Protection, Article 250 Grounding and Bonding. 250.52 Grounding Electrodes. 250.52(A) Electrodes Permitted for Grounding. 250.52(A)(3) Concrete-Encased Electrode.

EXAM 6

Chapter 2 Wiring and Protection 03

58. An electrode encased by at least 2 inches of concrete shall be permitted to be 20 feet of bare copper conductor not smaller than _____ AWG.

    A. 4

    B. 8

    C. 10

    D. 12

    Reference: 2017 National Electrical Code – Chapter 2 Wiring and Protection, Article 250 Grounding and Bonding. 250.52 Grounding Electrodes. 250.52(A) Electrodes Permitted for Grounding. 250.52(A)(3) Concrete-Encased Electrode. 250.52(A)(3)(2)

59. To be used as a grounding electrode, a ground ring must encircle a building or structure in direct contact with the earth, and be made up of _____ AWG or larger copper conductor of at 20 feet (6.0 m) or more.

    A. 1

    B. 2

    C. 2/0

    D. 4

    Reference: 2017 National Electrical Code – Chapter 2 Wiring and Protection, Article 250 Grounding and Bonding. 250.52 Grounding Electrodes. 250.52(A) Electrodes Permitted for Grounding. 250.52(A)(4) Ground Ring.

60. Rod and pipe electrodes shall not be less than _____ feet in length.

    A. 8

    B. 10

    C. 14

    D. 20

    Reference: 2017 National Electrical Code – Chapter 2 Wiring and Protection, Article 250 Grounding and Bonding. 250.52 Grounding Electrodes. 250.52(A) Electrodes Permitted for Grounding. 250.52(A)(5) Rod and Pipe Electrodes.

61. What is the minimum electrical trade size for grounding electrodes made of conduit or pipe?

    A. 1/2 in.

    B. 3/4 in.

    C. 1 in.

    D. 1-1/2 in.

    Reference: 2017 National Electrical Code – Chapter 2 Wiring and Protection, Article 250 Grounding and Bonding. 250.52 Grounding Electrodes. 250.52(A) Electrodes Permitted for Grounding. 250.52(A)(5) Rod and Pipe Electrodes. 250.52(A)(5)(a)

EXAM 6

Chapter 2 Wiring and Protection 03

62. For a plate electrode to be used for a grounding electrode, each plate must be _____ sq. ft. of surface or more exposed to exterior soil.

    A. 2

    B. 4

    C. 6

    D. 9

    Reference: 2017 National Electrical Code – Chapter 2 Wiring and Protection, Article 250 Grounding and Bonding. 250.52 Grounding Electrodes. 250.52(A) Electrodes Permitted for Grounding. . 250.52(A)(7) Plate Electrodes.

63. To be used as a grounding electrode, bar or conductively coated iron or steel plates must be _____ in. thick or more, and _____ sq. feet or more contacting exposed earth.

    A. 0.06.2

    B. 0.06.3

    C. 0.06.4

    D. 0.25.2

    Reference: 2017 National Electrical Code – Chapter 2 Wiring and Protection, Article 250 Grounding and Bonding. 250.52 Grounding Electrodes. 250.52(A) Electrodes Permitted for Grounding. . 250.52(A)(7) Plate Electrodes.

64. Pipe, plate, and rod electrodes must be free of nonconductive coatings like enamel or paint, and embedded below _____ where practicable.

    A. footings of the structure

    B. permanent moisture level

    C. surface of the grade line

    D. the average frost line

    Reference: 2017 National Electrical Code – Chapter 2 Wiring and Protection, Article 250 Grounding and Bonding. 250.53 Grounding Electrode System Installation. 250.53(A)Rod, Pipe, and Plate Electrodes. 250.53(A)(1) Below Permanent Moisture Level.

EXAM 6

Chapter 2 Wiring and Protection 03

65. A single electrode consisting of a rod, pipe, or plate that does not have a resistance to ground of _____ ohms or less shall be augmented by one additional electrode.

    A. 10

    B. 20

    C. 25

    D. 50

    Reference: 2017 National Electrical Code – Chapter 2 Wiring and Protection, Article 250 Grounding and Bonding. 250.53 Grounding Electrode System Installation. 250.53(A)Rod, Pipe, and Plate Electrodes. 250.53(A)(2) Supplemental Electrode Required.

66. If multiple rod, pipe, or plate electrodes are installed to meet the grounding requirements shall not be less than _____ feet apart.

    A. 5

    B. 6

    C. 8

    D. 10

    Reference: 2017 National Electrical Code – Chapter 2 Wiring and Protection, Article 250 Grounding and Bonding. 250.53 Grounding Electrode System Installation. 250.53(A)Rod, Pipe, and Plate Electrodes. 250.53(A)(3) Supplemental Electrode.

67. Where more than one, rod and pipe or plate, electrode are used, each electrode of one grounding system shall not be less than _____ feet from any other electrode of another grounding system.

    A. 2

    B. 4

    C. 6

    D. 10

    Reference: 2017 National Electrical Code – Chapter 2 Wiring and Protection, Article 250 Grounding and Bonding. 250.53 Grounding Electrode System Installation. 250.53(B) Electrode Spacing.

EXAM 6

Chapter 2 Wiring and Protection 03

68. Each electrode of one grounding system, where more than one ground rod is used (including any used for strike termination devices), must be at least _____ ft. from any other electrode of a separate grounding system.

   A. 4   C. 8

   B. 6   D. 10

   Reference: 2017 National Electrical Code – Chapter 2 Wiring and Protection, Article 250 Grounding and Bonding. 250.53 Grounding Electrode System Installation. 250.53(B) Electrode Spacing.

69. What is the minimum spacing distance for the installation of multiple ground rods?

   A. 2 feet   C. 6 feet

   B. 4 feet   D. 8 feet

   Reference: 2017 National Electrical Code – Chapter 2 Wiring and Protection, Article 250 Grounding and Bonding. 250.53 Grounding Electrode System Installation. 250.53(B) Electrode Spacing.

70. When more than one grounding electrode is effectively bonded together, they are considered:

   A. a continuous grounding electrode system

   C. a redundant grounding electrode system

   B. a multiple grounding electrode system

   D. a single grounding electrode system

   Reference: 2017 National Electrical Code – Chapter 2 Wiring and Protection, Article 250 Grounding and Bonding. 250.53 Grounding Electrode System Installation. 250.53(B) Electrode Spacing.

Chapter 2 Wiring and Protection 03

EXAM 6

Chapter 2 Wiring and Protection 03

71. What may not be relied on for continuity of ground path or bonding connection to interior piping?

    A. grounding jumpers

    B. patch conductors and connectors

    C. pressure connectors

    D. water meters or filtering devices and similar equipment

    Reference: 2017 National Electrical Code – Chapter 2 Wiring and Protection, Article 250 Grounding and Bonding. 250.53 Grounding Electrode System Installation. 250.53(D) Metal Underground Water Pipe. . 250.53(D)(1) Continuity.

72. Where the supplemental electrode is a rod, pipe, or plate electrode, that portion of the bonding jumper that is the sole connection to the supplemental grounding electrode shall not be required to be larger than _____ copper wire.

    A. 6 AWG

    B. 8 AWG

    C. 10 AWG

    D. 14 AWG

    Reference: 2017 National Electrical Code – Chapter 2 Wiring and Protection, Article 250 Grounding and Bonding. 250.53 Grounding Electrode System Installation. 250.53(E) Supplemental Electrode Bonding Connection Size.

73. A ground ring must be buried at least _____ below the surface of the earth for a grounding electrode system.

    A. 18 in.

    B. 24 in.

    C. 30 in.

    D. 60 in.

    Reference: 2017 National Electrical Code – Chapter 2 Wiring and Protection, Article 250 Grounding and Bonding. 250.53 Grounding Electrode System Installation. 250.53(F) Ground Ring.

EXAM 6

Chapter 2 Wiring and Protection 03

74. When using rod and pipe electrodes, where rock bottom is encountered, the electrode shall be driven at an oblique angle not to exceed _____ degrees from the vertical.

   A. 30   C. 60

   B. 45   D. 90

   Reference: 2017 National Electrical Code – Chapter 2 Wiring and Protection, Article 250 Grounding and Bonding. 250.53 Grounding Electrode System Installation. 250.53(G) Rod and Pipe Electrodes.

75. Unless the grounding electrode conductor attachment and the aboveground end of a grounding rod electrode are protected against physical damage as specified in Article 250.10, the grounding rod electrode may be buried in a trench _____ in. deep or more, and the upper end must be flush with or below ground level.

   A. 30   C. 48

   B. 36   D. 60

   Reference: 2017 National Electrical Code – Chapter 2 Wiring and Protection, Article 250 Grounding and Bonding. 250.53 Grounding Electrode System Installation. 250.53(G) Rod and Pipe Electrodes.

76. What is the minimum length, in feet, of a rod and pipe grounding electrode that must be in contact with the soil when installed?

   A. 6   C. 10

   B. 8   D. 12

   Reference: 2017 National Electrical Code – Chapter 2 Wiring and Protection, Article 250 Grounding and Bonding. 250.53 Grounding Electrode System Installation. 250.53(G) Rod and Pipe Electrodes.

77. What is the maximum oblique angle in degrees for installing a grounding rod electrode when rock bottom has been encountered?

   A. 30   C. 60

   B. 45   D. 75

   Reference: 2017 National Electrical Code – Chapter 2 Wiring and Protection, Article 250 Grounding and Bonding. 250.53 Grounding Electrode System Installation. 250.53(G) Rod and Pipe Electrodes.

EXAM 6

Chapter 2 Wiring and Protection 03

78. What is the minimum distance that a ground rod must be driven into the soil?

    A. 4 feet

    B. 6 feet

    C. 8 feet

    D. 10 feet

    Reference: 2017 National Electrical Code – Chapter 2 Wiring and Protection, Article 250 Grounding and Bonding. 250.53 Grounding Electrode System Installation. 250.53(G) Rod and Pipe Electrodes

79. Under what circumstances are pipe and rod grounding electrodes allowed to be buried in a trench?

    A. under all circumstances

    B. under no circumstances

    C. when rock bottom is encountered

    D. when the trench is 2 feet deep

    Reference: 2017 National Electrical Code – Chapter 2 Wiring and Protection, Article 250 Grounding and Bonding. 250.53 Grounding Electrode System Installation. 250.53(G) Rod and Pipe Electrodes

80. How deep must the trench be that a ground rod is buried in, when solid rock is encountered?

    A. 3 feet

    B. 4 feet

    C. 24 inches

    D. 30 inches

    Reference: 2017 National Electrical Code – Chapter 2 Wiring and Protection, Article 250 Grounding and Bonding. 250.53 Grounding Electrode System Installation. 250.53(G) Rod and Pipe Electrodes

81. Plate electrodes shall be installed not less than _____ inches below the surface of the earth.

    A. 6

    B. 12

    C. 18

    D. 30

    Reference: 2017 National Electrical Code – Chapter 2 Wiring and Protection, Article 250 Grounding and Bonding. 250.53 Grounding Electrode System Installation. 250.53(H) Plate Electrode.

EXAM 6

Chapter 2 Wiring and Protection 03

82. Grounding electrode plates must be _____ in. below the surface of the earth or more.

    A. 30

    B. 45

    C. 60

    D. 95

    Reference: 2017 National Electrical Code – Chapter 2 Wiring and Protection, Article 250 Grounding and Bonding. 250.53 Grounding Electrode System Installation. 250.53(H) Plate Electrode.

83. What is the minimum depth below the surface of the earth for plate grounding electrodes?

    A. 12 inches

    B. 18 inches

    C. 24 inches

    D. 30 inches

    Reference: 2017 National Electrical Code – Chapter 2 Wiring and Protection, Article 250 Grounding and Bonding. 250.53 Grounding Electrode System Installation. 250.53(H) Plate Electrode.

84. If an AC system is connected to a grounding electrode for a building or structure, then _____ electrode(s) must be used to ground equipment and conductor enclosures in or on the same building or structure.

    A. independent

    B. non-bonded

    C. separate

    D. the same

    Reference: 2017 National Electrical Code – Chapter 2 Wiring and Protection, Article 250 Grounding and Bonding. 250.58 Common Grounding Electrode.

85. What material must a grounding electrode conductor be made of?

    A. copper, aluminum, or copper-clad aluminum

    B. solid or stranded, and bare

    C. solid or stranded, and insulated

    D. stranded, insulated, covered, or bare

    Reference: 2017 National Electrical Code – Chapter 2 Wiring and Protection, Article 250 Grounding and Bonding. 250.62 Grounding Electrode Conductor Material.

EXAM 6

Chapter 2 Wiring and Protection 03

86. The material selected for a grounding electrode conductor should be protected from corrosion or resist any _____ condition extant at the installation.

    A. below freezing
    B. corrosive
    C. high temperature
    D. moisture

    Reference: 2017 National Electrical Code – Chapter 2 Wiring and Protection, Article 250 Grounding and Bonding. 250.62 Grounding Electrode Conductor Material.

87. Which of the following materials may a grounding electrode conductor be made of?

    A. aluminum
    B. copper
    C. copper-clad aluminum
    D. any of the above

    Reference: 2017 National Electrical Code – Chapter 2 Wiring and Protection, Article 250 Grounding and Bonding. 250.62 Grounding Electrode Conductor Material.

88. Where used outside, *aluminum or copper-clad aluminum* grounding electrode conductors shall not be terminated within _____ inches of the earth.

    A. 6
    B. 9
    C. 12
    D. 18

    Reference: 2017 National Electrical Code – Chapter 2 Wiring and Protection, Article 250 Grounding and Bonding. 250.64 Grounding Electrode Conductor Installation. 250.64(A) Aluminum or Copper-Clad Aluminum Conductors.

89. Bare aluminum or copper-clad aluminum grounding electrode conductors may not be ended less than _____ in. from the earth if used outside.

    A. 12
    B. 18
    C. 24
    D. 36

    Reference: 2017 National Electrical Code – Chapter 2 Wiring and Protection, Article 250 Grounding and Bonding. 250.64 Grounding Electrode Conductor Installation. 250.64(A) Aluminum or Copper-Clad Aluminum Conductors.

EXAM 6

Chapter 2 Wiring and Protection 03

90. If in direct contact with earth or masonry, or subject to corrosive conditions, bare _____ grounding electrode conductors may not be used.

    A. aluminum

    B. aluminum or copper-clad aluminum

    C. copper

    D. copper-clad aluminum

    Reference: 2017 National Electrical Code – Chapter 2 Wiring and Protection, Article 250 Grounding and Bonding. 250.64 Grounding Electrode Conductor Installation. 250.64(A) Aluminum or Copper-Clad Aluminum Conductors.

91. A 6 AWG grounding electrode conductor may be run along the surface of a building construction without a metal covering or protection, if it is protected from exposure to physical damage, and:

    A. a solid, insulated copper conductor.

    B. a stranded bare copper conductor.

    C. a stranded, insulated copper conductor.

    D. securely fastened to the construction.

    Reference: 2017 National Electrical Code – Chapter 2 Wiring and Protection, Article 250 Grounding and Bonding. 250.64 Grounding Electrode Conductor Installation. . 250.64(B) Securing and Protection Against Physical Damage.

92. When grounding electrode conductors are installed, they must be one continuous length without a joint or splice except that splicing of the wire-type grounding electrode conductor is allowed by _____ or by irreversible compression-type connectors that are indicated for use as grounding and bonding equipment.

    A. arc welding

    B. silver soldering

    C. soldering

    D. the exothermic welding process

    Reference: 2017 National Electrical Code – Chapter 2 Wiring and Protection, Article 250 Grounding and Bonding. 250.64 Grounding Electrode Conductor Installation. 250.64(C) Continuous.

EXAM 6

Chapter 2 Wiring and Protection 03

93. How many times may a grounding electrode conductor be spliced, using a listed split-bolt connector?

    A. once

    B. twice

    C. three times

    D. never

    Reference: 2017 National Electrical Code – Chapter 2 Wiring and Protection, Article 250 Grounding and Bonding. 250.64 Grounding Electrode Conductor Installation. 250.64(C) Continuous. 250.64(C)(1)

94. What is the minimum size for a copper grounding electrode conductor attached to the concrete-encased steel reinforcing bars used as a grounding electrode, when the ungrounded service-entrance conductors for a residence are size 3/0 AWG copper conductors?

    A. 2 AWG

    B. 4 AWG

    C. 6 AWG

    D. 8 AWG

    Reference: 2017 National Electrical Code – Chapter 2 Wiring and Protection, Article 250 Grounding and Bonding. 250.66 Size of Alternating-Current Grounding Electrode Conductor.

95. What is the smallest size copper grounding electrode conductor allowed when connected to concrete encased reinforcing building steel, for an ac electrical service supplied with four (4) parallel sets of size 500 kcmil aluminum ungrounded conductors?

    A. 2/0 AWG

    B. 3/0 AWG

    C. 4/0 AWG

    D. 250 kcmil

    Reference: 2017 National Electrical Code – Chapter 2 Wiring and Protection

228 Chapter 2 Wiring and Protection 03

EXAM 6

Chapter 2 Wiring and Protection 03

96. Grounding electrode conductor or bonding jumper connections to a grounding electrode must be accessible. A buried or encased connection in a _____, buried, or driven grounding electrode is not required to be accessible.

    A. concrete-encased   C. flexible metallic tube

    B. electrical metallic tube   D. rigid metallic tube

Reference: *2017 National Electrical Code – Chapter 2 Wiring and Protection, Article 250 Grounding and Bonding. 250.68 Grounding Electrode Conductor and Bonding Jumper . 250.68(A) Accessibility.*

97. All mechanical elements used to terminate a grounding electrode conductor or bonding jumper to a grounding electrode shall be _____.

    A. accessible   C. enclosed

    B. concealed   D. insulated

Reference: *2017 National Electrical Code – Chapter 2 Wiring and Protection, Article 250 Grounding and Bonding. 250.68 Grounding Electrode Conductor and Bonding Jumper Connection to Grounding Electrodes. 250.68(A) Accessibility.*

98. Which of the following is true of a connection to a buried or driven grounding electrode?

    A. it is not required to be accessible   C. it must be accessible

    B. it may not be buried   D. it must be visible

Reference: *2017 National Electrical Code – Chapter 2 Wiring and Protection, Article 250 Grounding and Bonding. 250.68 Grounding Electrode Conductor and Bonding Jumper Connection to Grounding Electrodes. 250.68(A) Accessibility.*

EXAM 6

Chapter 2 Wiring and Protection 03

99. All metal parts of all service enclosures that are normally noncurrent-carrying must effectively be:

    A. bonded together
    B. insulated
    C. locked
    D. protected

    Reference: 2017 National Electrical Code – Chapter 2 Wiring and Protection, Article 250 Grounding and Bonding. 250.92 Services. 250.92(A) Bonding of Equipment for Services.

100. All _____ that meet the article requirements must be used around impaired connections, such as concentric, eccentric or oversized knockouts or reducing washers. Standard bushings or locknuts may not be the only means for bonding needed according to this section, but will be allowed for installation to make a mechanical connection of the raceway(s).

    A. Bonding Jumpers
    B. Compression fittings
    C. Copper bushings
    D. Locknuts

    Reference: 2017 National Electrical Code – Chapter 2 Wiring and Protection, Article 250 Grounding and Bonding. 250.92 Services. 250.92(B) Method of Bonding at the Service.

101. If any contact points, contact surfaces, or threads have nonconductive coating such as paint or enamel, such coatings must be _____, or they must be connected through the use of fittings designed so that the removal is not necessary.

    A. acid etched
    B. continuity checked
    C. removed
    D. tested

    Reference: 2017 National Electrical Code – Chapter 2 Wiring and Protection, Article 250 Grounding and Bonding. 250.96 Bonding Other Enclosures. 250.96(A) General.

EXAM 6

Chapter 2 Wiring and Protection 03

102. To ensure _____ and the capacity to conduct safely any fault current likely to be imposed on them, all metal raceways, cable armor, cable sheath, cable trays, enclosures, fittings, frames and other metal noncurrent-carrying parts meant to be equipment grounding conductors, with or without using supplementary equipment grounding conductors.

    A. electrical continuity

    B. electrical inductance

    C. electrical insulation

    D. ground stability

    Reference: 2017 National Electrical Code – Chapter 2 Wiring and Protection, Article 250 Grounding and Bonding. 250.96 Bonding Other Enclosures. 250.96(A) General.

103. Metal raceways with telescoping sections and expansion fittings must be made electrically continuous by some means, including:

    A. application of oxidation inhibitors

    B. cleaning bright before assembly

    C. equipment bonding jumpers

    D. the use of bare grounding conductors

    Reference: 2017 National Electrical Code – Chapter 2 Wiring and Protection, Article 250 Grounding and Bonding. 250.98 Bonding Loosely Jointed Metal Raceways.

104. A bonding jumper must be a _____ or similar suitable conductor, made of copper or other corrosion-resistant material.

    A. bus

    B. screw

    C. wire

    D. any of the above

    Reference: 2017 National Electrical Code – Chapter 2 Wiring and Protection, Article 250 Grounding and Bonding. 250.102 Grounded Conductor, Bonding Conductors, and Jumpers. 250.102(A) Material.

Chapter 2 Wiring and Protection 03   231

EXAM 6

Chapter 2 Wiring and Protection 03

105. For a one-family dwelling with a 200 ampere, 120/240-volt, single-phase main service panel, supplied with size 2/0 AWG THW copper ungrounded service-entrance conductors in rigid metal conduit (RMC), what is the minimum allowed size of bonding jumper for the service-entrance conduit?

    A. 1/0 AWG copper

    B. 2 AWG copper

    C. 4 AWG copper

    D. 6 AWG copper

    Reference: 2017 National Electrical Code – Chapter 2 Wiring and Protection, Article 250 Grounding and Bonding. 250.102 Bonding Conductors and Jumpers. 250.102(C) Size – Supply-Side Bonding Jumper. 250.102(C)(1) Size for Supply Conductors in a Single Raceway or Cable.

106. The ground terminals for a lightning protection system must be bonded to the _____ of the building or structure.

    A. foundation rebar

    B. frame

    C. grounding electrode system

    D. lightning rod electrode

    Reference: 2017 National Electrical Code – Chapter 2 Wiring and Protection, Article 250 Grounding and Bonding. 250.106 Lightning Protection Systems

107. Normally noncurrent-carrying exposed metal parts of fixed equipment enclosing or supplied by conductors or components that may become energized must be connected to an equipment grounding conductor under which of the following conditions?

    A. Where any terminal operates at over 150 volts to ground

    B. Where in electrical contact with metal provided with GFI protector

    C. Within 8 ft. of ground or grounded objects & may contact persons

    D. any of these

    Reference: 2017 National Electrical Code – Chapter 2 Wiring and Protection, Article 250 Grounding and Bonding. 250.110 Equipment Fastened in Place (Fixed) or Connected by Permanent Wiring Methods.

EXAM 6

Chapter 2 Wiring and Protection 03

108. If a well casing for a submersible pump is metal, the well casing must be _____ to the grounding conductor for the pump circuit.

    A. bonded

    B. clamped

    C. connected

    D. tied

    Reference: 2017 National Electrical Code – Chapter 2 Wiring and Protection, Article 250 Grounding and Bonding. 250.112 Specific Equipment Fastened in Place (Fixed) or Connected by Permanent Wiring Methods.

109. Equipment such as control, fire alarm, and signaling circuits that are supplied by Class 1 circuits must be grounded, unless operating under:

    A. 25 volts

    B. 50 volts

    C. 120 volts

    D. 150 volts

    Reference: 2017 National Electrical Code – Chapter 2 Wiring and Protection, Article 250 Grounding and Bonding. 250.112 Specific Equipment Fastened in Place (Fixed) or Connected by Permanent Wiring Methods. 250.112(I) Remote-Control, Signaling, and Fire Alarm Circuits.

110. When a metal well casing is used with a submersible pump, the pump equipment grounding conductor must be _____ the well casing.

    A. connected to

    B. exothermic welded to

    C. isolated from

    D. none of these

    Reference: 2017 National Electrical Code – Chapter 2 Wiring and Protection, Article 250 Grounding and Bonding. 250.112 Specific Equipment Fastened in Place (Fixed) or Connected by Permanent Wiring Methods. 250.112(M) Metal Well Casings.

111. When an equipment grounding conductor encloses or is run with the circuit conductors, it is allowed to be either a busbar or wire:

    A. of any metallic element.

    B. of any shape.

    C. of circular copper or aluminum.

    D. within the cable or conduit.

    Reference: 2017 National Electrical Code – Chapter 2 Wiring and Protection, Article 250 Grounding and Bonding. 250.118 Types of Equipment Grounding Conductors.

Chapter 2 Wiring and Protection 03

EXAM 6

Chapter 2 Wiring and Protection 03

112. True or false: when mineral-insulated, metal-sheathed cable has a copper sheath, it may be used as the equipment grounding conductor.

    A. True   B. False

    Reference: 2017 National Electrical Code – Chapter 2 Wiring and Protection, Article 250 Grounding and Bonding. 250.118 Types of Equipment Grounding Conductors.

113. What is the form of equipment grounding conductor run with or enclosing circuit conductors that is NOT allowed?

    A. EMT   C. RMC

    B. IMT   D. RNC

    Reference: 2017 National Electrical Code – Chapter 2 Wiring and Protection, Article 250 Grounding and Bonding. 250.118 Types of Equipment Grounding Conductors.

114. What material is required for an equipment grounding conductor enclosing or run with the circuit conductors?

    A. aluminum   C. copper, aluminum, or copper-clad aluminum

    B. copper   D. copper-clad aluminum

    Reference: 2017 National Electrical Code – Chapter 2 Wiring and Protection, Article 250 Grounding and Bonding. 250.118 Types of Equipment Grounding Conductors.

115. Equipment grounding conductors are allowed to be bare, covered, or _____, unless required elsewhere in the code. Exceptions ignored.

    A. fused   C. insulated

    B. energized   D. painted green

    Reference: 2017 National Electrical Code – Chapter 2 Wiring and Protection, Article 250 Grounding and Bonding. 250.119 Identification of Equipment Grounding Conductors.

EXAM 6

Chapter 2 Wiring and Protection 03

116. An equipment grounding conductor may be uninsulated, but if individually covered, the covering must be have a _____ continuous outer finish.

    A. green

    B. green with yellow stripes

    C. yellow with green stripes

    D. A or B

    Reference: 2017 National Electrical Code – Chapter 2 Wiring and Protection, Article 250 Grounding and Bonding. 250.119 Identification of Equipment Grounding Conductors.

117. For a 50-ampere branch circuit with conductors installed in PVC conduit, what is the minimum size equipment grounding conductor?

    A. 6 AWG

    B. 8 AWG

    C. 10 AWG

    D. 12 AWG

    Reference: 2017 National Electrical Code – Chapter 2 Wiring and Protection, Article 250 Grounding and Bonding. 250.122 Size of Equipment Grounding Conductors. 250.122(A) General.

118. For a 5-hp, 3-phase, 208-volt motor with 20-ampere rated overload protection and branch-circuit, short-circuit and ground fault protection rated at 30 amperes, what is the minimum required size of grounding conductor?

    A. 8 AWG

    B. 10 AWG

    C. 12 AWG

    D. 14 AWG

    Reference: 2017 National Electrical Code – Chapter 2 Wiring and Protection, Article 250 Grounding and Bonding. 250.122 Size of Equipment Grounding Conductors. 250.122(A) General.

Chapter 2 Wiring and Protection 03

EXAM 6

Chapter 2 Wiring and Protection 03

119. Equipment grounding conductors must be run _____, when used with conductors that are run parallel in multiple cables or raceways.

    A. a separate raceway or cable

    B. in one of the conductor raceways or cables

    C. in parallel in each raceway or cable

    D. any of the above

    Reference: 2017 National Electrical Code – Chapter 2 Wiring and Protection, Article 250 Grounding and Bonding. 250.122 Size of Equipment Grounding Conductors. 250.122(F)(1) Conductors in Parallel.

120. On wiring devices (receptacles, switches, etc.) the terminal for the connection of the equipment grounding conductor shall be a _____ screw with a hexagonal head.

    A. blue

    B. green

    C. purple

    D. yellow

    Reference: 2017 National Electrical Code – Chapter 2 Wiring and Protection, Article 250 Grounding and Bonding. 250.126 Identification of Wiring Device Terminals. (2)

121. Where a metal box is mounted on the surface, direct metal-to-metal contact between the device yoke and the box shall be permitted to _____ the receptacle to the box.

    A. encase

    B. ground

    C. penetrate

    D. surround

    Reference: 2017 National Electrical Code – Chapter 2 Wiring and Protection, Article 250 Grounding and Bonding. 250.146 Connecting Receptacle Grounding Terminal to Box. 250.146(A) Surface Mounted Box.

EXAM 6

Chapter 2 Wiring and Protection 03

122. When grounding the secondary of an instrument transformer, what is the minimum size copper wire to be used?

    A. 6 AWG   C. 10 AWG

    B. 8 AWG   D. 12 AWG

    Reference: 2017 National Electrical Code – Chapter 2 Wiring and Protection, Article 250 Grounding and Bonding. 250.178 Instrument Equipment Grounding Conductor.

123. What is the smallest copper equipment grounding conductors that may be used for systems over 1 kV when they are not an integral part of a cable assembly?

    A. 2 AWG   C. 6 AWG

    B. 4 AWG   D. 8 AWG

    Reference: 2017 National Electrical Code – Chapter 2 Wiring and Protection, Article 250 Grounding and Bonding. 250.190 Grounding of Equipment. 250.190(C) Equipment Grounding Conductor. 250.190(C)(1) General.

124. Surge arresters shall be permitted to be located indoors or outdoors.

    A. True   B. False

    Reference: 2017 National Electrical Code – Chapter 2 Wiring and Protection, Article 280 Surge Arrestors, Over 1000 Volts. 280.11 Location.

EXAM 6

EXAM 6 ANSWERS

1. **Answer B.** bathrooms

   Service disconnecting means shall not be installed in bathrooms.

   Reference: 2017 National Electrical Code – Chapter 2 Wiring and Protection, Article 230 Services. 230.70 General. 230.70(A) Location. 230.70(A)(2) Bathrooms.

2. **Answer D.** six

   The service disconnecting means for each service permitted by 230.2, or for each set of service-entrance conductors permitted by 230.40, Exception No.1, 3, 4, or 5, *shall consist of not more than six switches or sets of circuit breakers, or a combination of not more than six switches and sets of circuit breakers*, mounted in a single enclosure, in a group of separate enclosures, or in or on a switchboard or in switchgear. There shall be not more than six sets of disconnects per service grouped in anyone location.

   For the purpose of this section, disconnecting means installed as part of listed equipment and used solely for the following shall not be considered a service disconnecting means:

   (1) Power monitoring equipment

   (2) Surge-protective device(s)

   (3) Control circuit of the ground-fault protection system

   (4) Power-operable service disconnecting means

   Reference: 2017 National Electrical Code – Chapter 2 Wiring and Protection, Article 230 Services. 230.71 Maximum Number of Disconnects. 230.71(A) General.

3. **Answer C.** 100 amperes

   For a one-family dwelling, the service disconnecting means shall have a rating of not less than 100 amperes, 3-wire.

   Reference: 2017 National Electrical Code – Chapter 2 Wiring and Protection, Article 230 Services. 230.79 Rating of Service Disconnecting Means. 230.79(C) One-Family Dwellings.

4. **Answer D.** ungrounded conductors

   Such protection shall be provided by an overcurrent device in series with each ungrounded service conductor that has a rating or setting not higher than the allowable ampacity of the conductor. A set of fuses shall be considered all the fuses required to protect all the ungrounded conductors of a circuit. Single-pole circuit breakers, grouped in accordance with 230.71(B), shall be considered as one protective device.

   Reference: 2017 National Electrical Code – Chapter 2 Wiring and Protection, Article 230 Services. 230.90 Where Required. 230.90(A) Ungrounded Conductor.

5. **Answer B.** locked or sealed

   Where necessary to prevent tampering, an automatic overcurrent device that protects service conductors supplying only a specific load, such as a water heater, *shall be permitted to be locked or sealed where located so as to be accessible.*

   Reference: 2017 National Electrical Code – Chapter 2 Wiring and Protection, Article 230 Services. 230.93 Protection of Specific Circuits.

6. **Answer C.** 1,000 amperes

   Ground-fault protection of equipment shall be provided for solidly grounded wye electric services of more than 150 volts to ground but not exceeding *1000 volts phase-to-phase for each service disconnect rated 1000 amperes or more*. The grounded conductor for the solidly grounded wye system shall be connected directly to ground through a grounding electrode system, as specified in 250.50, without inserting any resistor or impedance device.

   The rating of the service disconnect shall be considered to be the rating of the largest fuse that can be installed or the highest continuous current trip setting for which the actual overcurrent device installed in a circuit breaker is rated or can be adjusted.

   Reference: 2017 National Electrical Code – Chapter 2 Wiring and Protection, Article 230 Services. 230.95 Ground-Fault Protection of Equipment.

EXAM 6

EXAM 6 ANSWERS

7. **Answer A.** 1000 amperes

   Ground-fault protection of equipment shall be provided for solidly grounded wye electric services of more than 150 volts to ground but not exceeding *1000 volts phase-to-phase for each service disconnect rated 1000 amperes or more*. The grounded conductor for the solidly grounded wye system shall be connected directly to ground through a grounding electrode system, as specified in 250.50, without inserting any resistor or impedance device.

   The rating of the service disconnect shall be considered to be the rating of the largest fuse that can be installed or the highest continuous current trip setting for which the actual overcurrent device installed in a circuit breaker is rated or can be adjusted.

   Reference: 2017 National Electrical Code – Chapter 2 Wiring and Protection, Article 230 Services. 230.95 Ground-Fault Protection of Equipment.

8. **Answer C.** 6, 8

   Service-entrance conductors *shall not be smaller than 6 AWG unless in multiconductor cable. Multiconductor cable shall not be smaller than 8 AWG.*

   Reference: 2017 National Electrical Code – Chapter 2 Wiring and Protection, Article 230 Services. 230.202 Service-Entrance Conductors. . 230.202(A) Conductor Size.

9. **Answer D.** ungrounded

   Surge arresters installed in accordance with the requirements of Article 280 *shall be permitted on each ungrounded overhead service conductor.*

   Informational Note: Surge arresters may be referred to as lightning arresters in older documents.

   Reference: 2017 National Electrical Code – Chapter 2 Wiring and Protection, Article 230 Services. 230.209 Surge Arresters.

10. **Answer C.** tap conductor

    As used in this article*, a tap conductor is defined as a conductor*, other than a service conductor, that has overcurrent protection ahead of its point of supply that exceeds the value permitted for similar conductors that are protected as described elsewhere in 240.4.

    Reference: 2017 National Electrical Code – Chapter 2 Wiring and Protection, Article 240 Overcurrent Protection. 240.2 Definitions. Tap Conductors.

11. **Answer A.** flexible cords, flexible cables, and fixture wires

    Conductors, other than flexible cords, flexible cables, and fixture wires, shall be protected against overcurrent in accordance with their ampacities specified in 310.15, unless otherwise permitted or required in 240.4(A) through (G).

    Reference: 2017 National Electrical Code – Chapter 2 Wiring and Protection, Article 240 Overcurrent Protection. 240.4 Protection of Conductors.

EXAM 6

EXAM 6 ANSWERS

Table 240.6(A) Standard Ampere Ratings for Fuses and Inverse Time Circuit Breakers

Standard Ampere Ratings				
15	20	25	30	35
40	45	50	60	70
80	90	100	110	125
150	175	200	225	250
300	350	400	450	500
600	700	800	1000	1200
1600	2000	2500	3000	4000
5000	6000	—	—	—

12. **Answer C.** 80 amperes

    The next higher standard overcurrent device rating (above the ampacity of the conductors being protected) shall be permitted to be used, provided all of the following conditions are met:

    (1) *The conductors being protected are not part of a branch circuit supplying more than one receptacle for cord-and-plug-connected portable loads.*

    (2) The ampacity of the conductors does not correspond with the standard ampere rating of a fuse or a circuit breaker without overload trip adjustments above its rating (but that shall be permitted to have other trip or rating adjustments).

    (3) The next higher standard rating selected does not exceed 800 amperes.

    Reference: 2017 National Electrical Code – Chapter 2 Wiring and Protection, Article 240 Overcurrent Protection. 240.4 Protection of Conductors. 240.4(B) Overcurrent Devices Rated 800 Amperes or Less. 240.4(B)(1),(2)&(3)

    Reference: 2017 National Electrical Code – Chapter 2 Wiring and Protection, Article 240 Overcurrent Protection. 240.6 Standard Ampere Ratings. 240.6(A) Fuses and Fixed-Trip Circuit Breakers.

13. **Answer B.** 20 amperes

    20 amperes.

    Reference: 2017 National Electrical Code – Chapter 2 Wiring and Protection, Article 240 Overcurrent Protection. 240.4 Protection of Conductors. 240.4(D) Small Conductors. 240.4(D)(5) 12 AWG Copper.

14. **Answer D.** 50

    Fixture wire shall be permitted to be tapped to the branch-circuit conductor of a branch circuit in accordance with the following:

    (1) 20-ampere circuits - 18 AWG, up to 15 m (50 ft.) of run length

    (2) 20-ampere circuits - 16 AWG, up to 30 m (100 ft.) of run length

    (3) 20-ampere circuits - 14 AWG and larger

    (4) 30-ampere circuits - 14 AWG and larger

    (5) 40-ampere circuits - 12 AWG and larger

    (6) 50-ampere circuits - 12 AWG and larger

    Reference: 2017 National Electrical Code – Chapter 2 Wiring and Protection, Article 240 Overcurrent Protection. 240.5 Protection of Flexible Cords, Flexible Cables, and Fixture Wires. . 240.5(A) Ampacities. 240.5(A)(2) Fixture Wire.

15. **Answer B.** 16 AWG

    Flexible cord used in extension cords made with separately listed and installed components shall be permitted to be *supplied by a branch circuit in accordance with the following:*

    20-ampere circuits - *16 AWG and larger*

    Reference: 2017 National Electrical Code – Chapter 2 Wiring and Protection, Article 240 Overcurrent Protection. 240.5 Protection of Flexible Cords, Flexible Cables, and Fixture Wires. 240.5(B) Branch Circuit Overcurrent Device. 240.5(B)(4) Field Assembled Extension Cord Sets.

EXAM 6

EXAM 6 ANSWERS

16. **Answer A.** 75 amperes

    See Table

    Reference: 2017 National Electrical Code – Chapter 2 Wiring and Protection, Article 240 Overcurrent Protection. 240.6 Standard Ampere Ratings. 240.6(A) Fuses and Fixed-Trip Circuit Breakers.

17. **Answer A.** factory assembled in parallel

    Fuses and circuit breakers shall be permitted to be connected in parallel where they are *factory assembled in parallel* and listed as a unit. Individual fuses, circuit breakers, or combinations thereof shall not otherwise be connected in parallel.

    Reference: 2017 National Electrical Code – Chapter 2 Wiring and Protection, Article 240 Overcurrent Protection. 240.8 Fuses or Circuit Breakers in Parallel.

18. **Answer B.** 300 kcmil

    The ampacity of the tap conductors is not less than one-third of the rating of the overcurrent device protecting the feeder conductors.

    800 amperes ÷ 3 = 266.6 amperes

    *NOTE: Size 300 kcmil THW conductors with an allowable ampacity of 285 amperes should be selected.

    Reference: 2017 National Electrical Code – Chapter 2 Wiring and Protection, Article 240 Overcurrent Protection. 240.21 Location in Circuit. 240.21(B) Feeder Traps. 240.21(B)(2)(1)

19. **Answer B.** independently

    No overcurrent device shall be connected in series with any conductor that is intentionally grounded, unless one of the following two conditions is met:

    (1) The overcurrent device opens all conductors of the circuit, including the grounded conductor, and *is designed so that no pole can operate independently.*

    (2) Where required by 430.36 or 430.37 for motor overload protection.

    Reference: 2017 National Electrical Code – Chapter 2 Wiring and Protection, Article 240 Overcurrent Protection. 240.22 Grounded Conductor.

20. **Answer B.** grounded

    Where a change occurs in the size of the ungrounded conductor, *a similar change shall be permitted to be made in the size of the grounded conductor.*

    Reference: 2017 National Electrical Code – Chapter 2 Wiring and Protection, Article 240 Overcurrent Protection. 240.23 Change in Size of Grounded Conductor.

21. **Answer B.** 7

    Switches containing fuses and circuit breakers shall be readily accessible and installed so that the center of the grip of the operating handle of the switch or circuit breaker, when in its highest position, *is not more than 2.0 m (6 ft 7 in.) above the floor or working platform, unless one of the following applies:*

    (1) For busways, as provided in 368.17(C).

    (2) For supplementary overcurrent protection, as described in 240.10.

    (3) For overcurrent devices, as described in 225.40 and 230.92.

    (4) For overcurrent devices adjacent to utilization equipment that they supply, access shall be permitted to be by portable means.

    Exception: The use of a tool shall be permitted to access overcurrent devices located within listed industrial control panels or similar enclosures

    Reference: 2017 National Electrical Code – Chapter 2 Wiring and Protection, Article 240 Overcurrent Protection. 240.24 Location in or on Premises. 240.24(A) Accessibility.

EXAM 6

EXAM 6 ANSWERS

22. Answer A. bathrooms

In dwelling units, dormitories, and guest rooms or guest suites, overcurrent devices, other than supplementary overcurrent protection, *shall not be located in bathrooms*.

Reference: 2017 National Electrical Code – Chapter 2 Wiring and Protection, Article 240 Overcurrent Protection. 240.24 Location in or on Premises. 240.24(E) Not Located in Bathrooms.

23. Answer A. over steps of stairways

Overcurrent devices shall not be located over steps of a stairway.

Reference: 2017 National Electrical Code – Chapter 2 Wiring and Protection, Article 240 Overcurrent Protection. 240.24 Location in or on Premises. 240.24(F) Not Located over Steps.

24. Answer D. vertical

Enclosures for overcurrent devices shall be mounted in a vertical position unless that is shown to be impracticable. Circuit breaker enclosures shall be permitted to be installed horizontally where the circuit breaker is installed in accordance with 240.81. Listed busway plug-in units shall be permitted to be mounted in orientations corresponding to the busway mounting position.

Reference: 2017 National Electrical Code – Chapter 2 Wiring and Protection, Article 240 Overcurrent Protection. 240.33 Vertical Position.

25. Answer B. 150 volts

Cartridge fuses in circuits of any voltage where accessible to other than qualified persons, and all fuses in circuits over 150 volts to ground, shall be provided with a disconnecting means on their supply side so that each circuit containing fuses can be independently disconnected from the source of power. A current-limiting device without a disconnecting means shall be permitted on the supply side of the service disconnecting means as permitted by 230.82. A single disconnecting means shall be permitted on the supply side of more than one set of fuses as permitted by 430.112, Exception, for group operation of motors and 424.22(C) for fixed electric space-heating equipment.

Reference: 2017 National Electrical Code – Chapter 2 Wiring and Protection, Article 240 Overcurrent Protection. 240.40 Disconnecting Means for Fuses.

26. Answer B. located or shielded

Fuses and circuit breakers *shall be located or shielded so that persons will not be burned or otherwise injured by their operation*.

Reference: 2017 National Electrical Code – Chapter 2 Wiring and Protection, Article 240 Overcurrent Protection. 240.41 Arcing or Suddenly Moving Parts. . 240.41(A) Location.

EXAM 6

EXAM 6 ANSWERS

27. Answer A. be guarded or isolated

Handles or levers of circuit breakers, and similar parts that may move suddenly in such a way that persons in the vicinity are likely to **be injured by being struck by them, shall be guarded or isolated.**

Reference: 2017 National Electrical Code – Chapter 2 Wiring and Protection, Article 240 Overcurrent Protection. 240.41 Arcing or Suddenly Moving Parts. . 240.41(B) Suddenly Moving Parts.

28. Answer B. 30

Plug fuses of the **Edison-base type shall be classified at not over 125 volts and 30 amperes and below.**

Reference: 2017 National Electrical Code – Chapter 2 Wiring and Protection, Article 240 Overcurrent Protection. 240.51 Edison-Base Fuses. 240.51(A) Classification.

29. Answer B. Class H renewable cartridge

Class H cartridge fuses of the renewable type shall be permitted to be used only for replacement in existing installations where there is no evidence of overfusing or tampering.

Reference: 2017 National Electrical Code – Chapter 2 Wiring and Protection, Article 240 Overcurrent Protection. 240.60 General. 240.60(D) Renewable Fuses.

30. Answer B. removal of a trim or cover

Circuit breakers shall be marked with their ampere rating in a manner that will be durable and visible after installation. **Such marking shall be permitted to be made visible by removal of a trim or cover.**

Reference: 2017 National Electrical Code – Chapter 2 Wiring and Protection, Article 240 Overcurrent Protection. 240.83 Marking. 240.83(A) Durable and Visible.

31. Answer C. switches

Circuit breakers used as switches in 120-volt and 277-volt fluorescent lighting circuits shall be listed and shall be marked SWD or HID. Circuit breakers used as switches in high-intensity discharge lighting circuits shall be listed and shall be marked as HID.

Reference: 2017 National Electrical Code – Chapter 2 Wiring and Protection, Article 240 Overcurrent Protection. 240.83 Marking. 240.83(D) Used as Switches.

32. Answer C. either A or B

Circuit breakers used as switches in 120-volt and 277-volt fluorescent lighting circuits shall be listed and shall be marked SWD or HID. Circuit breakers used as switches in high-intensity discharge lighting circuits shall be listed and shall be marked as HID.

Reference: 2017 National Electrical Code – Chapter 2 Wiring and Protection, Article 240 Overcurrent Protection. 240.83 Marking. 240.83(D) Used as Switches.

33. Answer C. at the point where the conductors receive their supply

Feeder and branch-circuit conductors shall be protected at **the point the conductors receive their supply as permitted** in 240.21 or as otherwise permitted in 240.92(B), (C), CD), or (E).

Reference: 2017 National Electrical Code – Chapter 2 Wiring and Protection, Article 240 Overcurrent Protection. 240.92 Location in Circuit. . 240.92(A) Feeder and Branch-Circuit Conductors.

EXAM 6

EXAM 6 ANSWERS

Table 250.3 see Table 250-3 in Tables folder on CD-ROM

34. **Answer C.** Article 682

    For other articles applying to particular cases of installation of conductors and equipment, grounding and bonding requirements are identified in Table 250.3 that are in addition to, or modifications of, those of this article.

    Reference: 2017 National Electrical Code – Chapter 2 Wiring and Protection, Article 250 Grounding and Bonding. 250.3 Application of Other Articles. Table 250.3 Additional Grounding and Bonding Requirements. (page 70-107)

35. **Answer A.** Yes

    For other articles applying to particular cases of installation of conductors and equipment, grounding and bonding requirements are identified in Table 250.3 that are in addition to, or modifications of, those of this article.

    Reference: 2017 National Electrical Code – Chapter 2 Wiring and Protection, Article 250 Grounding and Bonding. 250.3 Application of Other Articles. Table 250.3 Additional Grounding and Bonding Requirements. (page 70-107)

36. **Answer B.** grounded

    Review the new FPN about unnecessary bends and loops.

    Electrical systems that are grounded shall be connected to earth in a manner that will limit the voltage imposed by lightning, line surges, or unintentional contact with higher-voltage lines and that will stabilize the voltage to earth during normal operation.

    Informational Note: An important consideration for limiting the imposed voltage is the routing of bonding and grounding electrode conductors so that they are not any longer than necessary to complete the connection without disturbing the permanent parts of the installation and so that unnecessary bends and loops are avoided.

    Informational Note No. 2: See NFPA 780-2014, Standard for the

    Installation of Lightning Protection Systems, for information on installation of grounding and bonding for lightning protection systems.

    Reference: 2017 National Electrical Code – Chapter 2 Wiring and Protection, Article 250 Grounding and Bonding. 250.4 General Requirements for Grounding and Bonding. 250.4(A) Grounded Systems. 250.4(A)(1) Electrical System Grounding.

EXAM 6

EXAM 6 ANSWERS

37. Answer A. connected to earth

Normally noncurrent-carrying conductive materials enclosing electrical conductors or equipment, or forming part of such equipment, *shall be connected to earth so as to limit the voltage to ground on these materials.*

Reference: 2017 National Electrical Code – Chapter 2 Wiring and Protection, Article 250 Grounding and Bonding. 250.4 General Requirements for Grounding and Bonding. 250.4(A) Grounded Systems. 250.4(A)(2) Grounding of Electrical Equipment.

38. Answer A. ground-fault

Normally noncurrent-carrying conductive materials enclosing electrical conductors or equipment, or forming part of such equipment, shall be connected together and *to the electrical supply source in a manner that establishes an effective ground-fault current path.*

Reference: 2017 National Electrical Code – Chapter 2 Wiring and Protection, Article 250 Grounding and Bonding. 250.4 General Requirements for Grounding and Bonding. 250.4(A) Grounded Systems. 250.4(A)(3) Bonding of Electrical Equipment.

39. Answer A. bonding of electrical equipment

Normally noncurrent-carrying conductive materials enclosing electrical conductors or equipment, or forming part of such equipment, *shall be connected together and to the electrical supply source in a manner that establishes an effective ground-fault current path.*

Reference: 2017 National Electrical Code – Chapter 2 Wiring and Protection, Article 250 Grounding and Bonding. 250.4 General Requirements for Grounding and Bonding. 250.4(A) Grounded Systems. 250.4(A)(3) Bonding of Electrical Equipment.

40. Answer B. Effective Ground-Fault Current Path

Electrical equipment and wiring and other electrically conductive material likely to become energized shall be installed in a manner that creates a low-impedance circuit facilitating the operation of the overcurrent device or ground detector for high-impedance grounded systems. It shall be capable of safely carrying the maximum ground-fault current likely to be imposed on it from any point on the wiring system where a ground fault may occur to the electrical supply source. *The earth shall not be considered as an effective ground-fault current path.*

Reference: 2017 National Electrical Code – Chapter 2 Wiring and Protection, Article 250 Grounding and Bonding. 250.4 General Requirements for Grounding and Bonding. 250.4(A) Grounded Systems. 250.4(A)(5) Effective Ground-Fault Current Path.

41. Answer B. effective

Electrical equipment and wiring and other electrically conductive material likely to become energized shall be installed in a manner that creates a low-impedance circuit facilitating the operation of the overcurrent device or ground detector for high-impedance grounded systems. It shall be capable of safely carrying the maximum ground-fault current likely to be imposed on it from any point on the wiring system where a ground fault may occur to the electrical supply source. *The earth shall not be considered as an effective ground-fault current path.*

Reference: 2017 National Electrical Code – Chapter 2 Wiring and Protection, Article 250 Grounding and Bonding. 250.4 General Requirements for Grounding and Bonding. 250.4(A) Grounded Systems. 250.4(A)(5) Effective Ground-Fault Current Path.

EXAM 6

EXAM 6 ANSWERS

42. Answer C. grounding

Equipment grounding conductors, grounding electrode conductors, and bonding jumpers shall be connected by one or more of the following means:

(1) Listed pressure connectors

(2) Terminal bars

(3) Pressure connectors listed as grounding and bonding equipment

(4) Exothermic welding process

(5) Machine screw-type fasteners that engage not less than two threads or are secured with a nut

(6) Thread-forming machine screws that engage not less than two threads in the enclosure

(7) Connections that are part of a listed assembly

(8) Other listed means

Reference: 2017 National Electrical Code – Chapter 2 Wiring and Protection, Article 250 Grounding and Bonding. 250.8 Connection of Grounding and Bonding Equipment. 250.8(A) Permitted Methods.

43. Answer C. removed

Nonconductive coatings (such as paint, lacquer, and enamel) on equipment to be grounded shall be removed from threads and other contact surfaces to ensure good electrical continuity or be connected by means of fittings designed so as to make such removal unnecessary.

Reference: 2017 National Electrical Code – Chapter 2 Wiring and Protection, Article 250 Grounding and Bonding. 250.12 Clean Surfaces.

44. Answer B. continuity

Nonconductive coatings (such as paint, lacquer, and enamel) on equipment to be grounded shall be removed from threads and other contact surfaces to *ensure good electrical continuity or be connected by means of fittings designed so as to make such removal unnecessary.*

Reference: 2017 National Electrical Code – Chapter 2 Wiring and Protection, Article 250 Grounding and Bonding. 250.12 Clean Surfaces.

45. Answer C. grounding electrode conductor

A premises wiring system supplied by a grounded ac service *shall have a grounding electrode conductor connected to the grounded service conductor,* at each service, in accordance with 250.24(A)(1) through (A)(5).

Reference: 2017 National Electrical Code – Chapter 2 Wiring and Protection, Article 250 Grounding and Bonding. 250.24 Grounding Service-Supplied Alternating-Current Systems. 250.24(A) System Grounding Connections.

46. Answer B. the grounded service conductor

A premises wiring system supplied by *a grounded ac service shall have a grounding electrode conductor connected to the grounded service conductor,* at each service, in accordance with 250.24(A)(1) through (A)(5).

Reference: 2017 National Electrical Code – Chapter 2 Wiring and Protection, Article 250 Grounding and Bonding. 250.24 Grounding Service-Supplied Alternating-Current Systems. 250.24(A) System Grounding Connections.

EXAM 6

EXAM 6 ANSWERS

47. Answer C. each service disconnecting means enclosure

Where an ac system operating at 1000 volts or less is grounded at any point, the grounded conductor(s) *shall be routed with the ungrounded conductors to each service disconnecting means and shall be connected* to each disconnecting means grounded conductor(s) terminal or bus. A main bonding jumper shall connect the grounded conductor(s) to each service disconnecting means enclosure. The grounded conductor(s) shall be installed in accordance with 250.24(C)(1) through (C)(4).

Reference: 2017 National Electrical Code – Chapter 2 Wiring and Protection, Article 250 Grounding and Bonding. 250.24 Grounding Service-Supplied Alternating-Current Systems. 250.24(C) Grounded Conductor Brought to Service Equipment.

48. Answer A. 1/0

If the ungrounded service-entrance conductors are installed in parallel in two or more raceways or cables, the grounded conductor shall also be installed in parallel. The size of the grounded conductor in each raceway or cable shall be based on the total circular mil area of the parallel ungrounded conductors in the raceway or cable, as indicated in 250.24(C)(1), *but not smaller than 1/0 AWG.*

Informational Note: See 310.10(H) for grounded conductors connected in parallel.

Reference: 2017 National Electrical Code – Chapter 2 Wiring and Protection, Article 250 Grounding and Bonding. 250.24 Grounding Service-Supplied Alternating-Current. Systems. 250.24(C) Grounded Conductor Brought to Service Equipment. 250.24(C)(2) Parallel Conductors in Two or More Raceways.

49. Answer B. green

Where a main bonding jumper or a system bonding jumper is a screw only, *the screw shall be identified with a green finish that shall be visible with the screw installed.*

Reference: 2017 National Electrical Code – Chapter 2 Wiring and Protection, Article 250 Grounding and Bonding. 250.28 Main Bonding Jumper and System Bonding Jumper. 250.28(B) Construction.

50. Answer A. as near as practicable to, preferably in the same area

The grounding electrode shall be as near as practicable to, and preferably in the same area as, the grounding electrode conductor connection to the system. The grounding electrode shall be the nearest of one of the following:

(1) Metal water pipe grounding electrode as specified in 250.52(A)(1)

(2) Structural metal grounding electrode as specified in 250.52(A)(2)

Reference: 2017 National Electrical Code – Chapter 2 Wiring and Protection, Article 250 Grounding and Bonding. 250.30 Grounding Separately Derived Alternating Current Systems. . 250.30(A) Grounded Systems. 250.30(A)(4) Grounding Electrode.

51. Answer D. usually a resistor

High-impedance grounded *neutral systems in which a grounding impedance, usually a resistor*, limits the ground-fault current to a low value shall be permitted for 3-phase ac systems of 480 volts to 1000 volts if all the following conditions are met:

(1) The conditions of maintenance and supervision ensure that only qualified persons service the installation.

(2) Ground detectors are installed on the system.

(3) Line-to-neutral loads are not served.

High-impedance grounded neutral systems shall comply with the provisions of 250.36(A) through (G).

Reference: 2017 National Electrical Code – Chapter 2 Wiring and Protection, Article 250 Grounding and Bonding. 250.36 High-Impedance Grounded Neutral Systems.

52. Answer C. 8

All grounding electrodes as described in 250.52(A)(1) through (A)(7) that are present at each building or structure served shall be bonded together to form the grounding electrode system. Where none of these grounding electrodes exist, one or more of the grounding electrodes specified in 250.52(A)(4) through *(A)(8) shall be installed and used.*

Reference: 2017 National Electrical Code – Chapter 2 Wiring and Protection, Article 250 Grounding and Bonding. 250.50 Grounding Electrode System.

EXAM 6
EXAM 6 ANSWERS

53. Answer D. A and C

All grounding electrodes as described in 250.52(A)(1) through (A)(7) that are present at each building or structure served shall be bonded together to form the grounding electrode system. Where none of these grounding electrodes exist, one or more of the grounding electrodes specified in 250.52(A)(4) through (A)(8) shall be installed and used.

Reference: 2017 National Electrical Code – Chapter 2 Wiring and Protection, Article 250 Grounding and Bonding. 250.50 Grounding Electrode System.

54. Answer B. 10

A metal underground water pipe in direct contact with the earth for 3.0 m (10ft.) or more (including any metal well casing bonded to the pipe) and electrically continuous (or made electrically continuous by bonding around insulating joints or insulating pipe) to the points of connection of the grounding electrode conductor and the bonding conductor(s) or jumper(s), if installed.

Reference: 2017 National Electrical Code – Chapter 2 Wiring and Protection, Article 250 Grounding and Bonding. 250.52 Grounding Electrodes. 250.52(A) Electrodes Permitted for Grounding. 250.52(A)(1) Metal Underground Water Pipe.

55. Answer C. 10 feet

A metal underground water pipe in direct contact with the earth for 3.0 m (10 ft.) or more (including any metal well casing bonded to the pipe) and electrically continuous (or made electrically continuous by bonding around insulating joints or insulating pipe) to the points of connection of the grounding electrode conductor and the bonding conductor(s) or jumper(s), if installed.

Reference: 2017 National Electrical Code – Chapter 2 Wiring and Protection, Article 250 Grounding and Bonding. 250.52 Grounding Electrodes. 250.52(A) Electrodes Permitted for Grounding. 250.52(A)(1) Metal Underground Water Pipe.

56. Answer C. 10

The metal frame of the building or structure that is connected to the earth by one or more of the following methods:

(1) At least one structural metal member that is in direct contact with the earth for 3.0 m (10 ft.) or more, with or without concrete encasement.

(2) Hold-down bolts securing the structural steel column that are connected to a concrete-encased electrode that complies with 250.52(A)(3) and is located in the support footing or foundation. The hold-down bolts shall be connected to the concrete-encased electrode by welding, exothermic welding, the usual steel tie wires, or other approved means.

Reference: 2017 National Electrical Code – Chapter 2 Wiring and Protection, Article 250 Grounding and Bonding. 250.52 Grounding Electrodes. 250.52(A) Electrodes Permitted for Grounding. 250.52(A)(2) Metal Frame of the Building or Structure.

57. Answer D. 20, 2

A concrete-encased electrode shall consist of at least 6.0 m (20 ft.) of either (1) or (2):

(1) One or more bare or zinc galvanized or other electrically conductive coated steel reinforcing bars or rods of not less than 13 mm (V2 in.) in diameter, *installed in one continuous 6.0 m (20 ft.) length, or if in multiple pieces connected together by the usual steel tie wires, exothermic welding, welding, or other effective means to create a 6.0 m (20 ft.) or greater length;* or

(2) Bare copper conductor not smaller than 4 AWG.

Metallic components *shall be encased by at least 50 mm (2 in.) of concrete and shall be located horizontally within that portion of a concrete foundation or footing* that is in direct contact with the earth or within vertical foundations or structural components or members that are in direct contact with the earth. If multiple concrete-encased electrodes are present at a building or structure, it shall be permissible to bond only one into the grounding electrode system.

Informational Note: Concrete installed with insulation, vapor barriers, films or similar items separating the concrete from the earth is not considered to be in "direct contact" with the earth.

Reference: 2017 National Electrical Code – Chapter 2 Wiring and Protection, Article 250 Grounding and Bonding. 250.52 Grounding Electrodes. 250.52(A) Electrodes Permitted for Grounding. 250.52(A)(3) Concrete-Encased Electrode.

EXAM 6

EXAM 6 ANSWERS

58. **Answer A.** 4

A concrete-encased electrode shall consist of at least 6.0 m (20 ft.) of either (1) or (2):

(1) One or more bare or zinc galvanized or other electrically conductive coated steel reinforcing bars or rods of not less than 13 mm (V2 in.) in diameter, installed in one continuous 6.0 m (20 ft.) length, or if in multiple pieces connected together by the usual steel tie wires, exothermic welding, welding, or other effective means to create a 6.0 m (20 ft.) or greater length; or

(2) *Bare copper conductor not smaller than 4 AWG*

Metallic components shall be encased by at least 50 mm (2 in.) of concrete and shall be located horizontally within that portion of a concrete foundation or footing that is in direct contact with the earth or within vertical foundations or structural components or members that are in direct contact with the earth. If multiple concrete-encased electrodes are present at a building or structure, it shall be permissible to bond only one into the grounding electrode system.

Informational Note: Concrete installed with insulation, vapor barriers, films or similar items separating the concrete from the earth is not considered to be in "direct contact" with the earth.

Reference: 2017 National Electrical Code – Chapter 2 Wiring and Protection, Article 250 Grounding and Bonding. 250.52 Grounding Electrodes. 250.52(A) Electrodes Permitted for Grounding. 250.52(A)(3) Concrete-Encased Electrode. 250.52(A)(3)(2)

59. **Answer B.** 2

A ground ring encircling the building or structure, in direct contact with the earth, *consisting of at least 6.0 m (20 ft.) of bare copper conductor not smaller than 2 AWG.*

Reference: 2017 National Electrical Code – Chapter 2 Wiring and Protection, Article 250 Grounding and Bonding. 250.52 Grounding Electrodes. 250.52(A) Electrodes Permitted for Grounding. 250.52(A)(4) Ground Ring.

60. **Answer A.** 8

Rod and pipe electrodes shall not be less than 2.44 m (8 ft.) in length and shall consist of the following materials.

(a) Grounding electrodes of pipe or conduit shall not be smaller than metric designator 21 (trade size 3/4) and, where of steel, shall have the outer surface galvanized or otherwise metal-coated for corrosion protection.

(b) Rod-type grounding electrodes of stainless steel and copper or zinc coated steel shall be at least 15.87 mm (5/8 in.) in diameter, unless listed.

Reference: 2017 National Electrical Code – Chapter 2 Wiring and Protection, Article 250 Grounding and Bonding. 250.52 Grounding Electrodes. 250.52(A) Electrodes Permitted for Grounding. 250.52(A)(5) Rod and Pipe Electrodes.

61. **Answer B.** 3/4 in.

Grounding electrodes of pipe or conduit shall not be smaller than metric designator 21 (trade size 3/4) and, where of steel, shall have the outer surface galvanized or otherwise metal-coated for corrosion protection.

Reference: 2017 National Electrical Code – Chapter 2 Wiring and Protection, Article 250 Grounding and Bonding. 250.52 Grounding Electrodes. 250.52(A) Electrodes Permitted for Grounding. 250.52(A)(5) Rod and Pipe Electrodes. 250.52(A)(5)(a)

62. **Answer A.** 2

Each plate electrode shall expose not less than 0.186 m2 (2 ft2) of surface to exterior soil. Electrodes of bare or electrically conductive coated iron or steel plates shall be at least 6.4 mm (1⁄4 in.) in thickness. Solid, uncoated electrodes of nonferrous metal shall be at least 1.5 mm (0.06 in.) in thickness.

Reference: 2017 National Electrical Code – Chapter 2 Wiring and Protection, Article 250 Grounding and Bonding. 250.52 Grounding Electrodes. 250.52(A) Electrodes Permitted for Grounding. . 250.52(A)(7) Plate Electrodes.

EXAM 6

EXAM 6 ANSWERS

63. Answer C. 0.06.4

Each plate electrode shall expose not less than 0.186 m2 (2 ft2) of surface to exterior soil. *Electrodes of bare or electrically conductive coated iron or steel plates shall be at least 6.4 mm (1⁄4 in.) in thickness.* Solid, uncoated electrodes of nonferrous metal shall be at least 1.5 mm (0.06 in.) in thickness.

Reference: 2017 National Electrical Code – Chapter 2 Wiring and Protection, Article 250 Grounding and Bonding. 250.52 Grounding Electrodes. 250.52(A) Electrodes Permitted for Grounding. . 250.52(A)(7) Plate Electrodes.

64. Answer B. permanent moisture level

If practicable, rod, pipe, and plate electrodes shall be embedded below permanent moisture level. Rod, pipe, and plate electrodes shall be free from nonconductive coatings such as paint or enamel.

Reference: 2017 National Electrical Code – Chapter 2 Wiring and Protection, Article 250 Grounding and Bonding. 250.53 Grounding Electrode System Installation. 250.53(A)Rod, Pipe, and Plate Electrodes. 250.53(A)(1) Below Permanent Moisture Level.

65. Answer C. 25

A single rod, pipe, or plate electrode shall be supplemented by an additional electrode of a type specified in 250.52(A)(2) through (A)(8). The supplemental electrode shall be permitted to be bonded to one of the following:

(1) Rod, pipe, or plate electrode

(2) Grounding electrode conductor

(3) Grounded service-entrance conductor

(4) Nonflexible grounded service raceway

(5) Any grounded service enclosure

Exception: If a single rod, pipe, or plate grounding electrode has a resistance to earth of 25 ohms or less, the supplemental electrode shall not be required.

Reference: 2017 National Electrical Code – Chapter 2 Wiring and Protection, Article 250 Grounding and Bonding. 250.53 Grounding Electrode System Installation. 250.53(A)Rod, Pipe, and Plate Electrodes. 250.53(A)(2) Supplemental Electrode Required.

66. Answer B. 6

If multiple rod, pipe, or plate electrodes are installed to meet the requirements of this section, *they shall not be less than 1.8 m (6 ft.) apart.*

Informational Note: The paralleling efficiency of rods is increased by spacing them twice the length of the longest rod.

Reference: 2017 National Electrical Code – Chapter 2 Wiring and Protection, Article 250 Grounding and Bonding. 250.53 Grounding Electrode System Installation. 250.53(A)Rod, Pipe, and Plate Electrodes. 250.53(A)(3) Supplemental Electrode.

67. Answer C. 6

Where more than one of the electrodes of the type specified in 250.52(A)(5) or (A)(7) are used, *each electrode of one grounding system (including that used for strike termination devices) shall not be less than 1.83 m (6 ft.) from any other electrode of another grounding system.* Two or more grounding electrodes that are bonded together shall be considered a single grounding electrode system.

Reference: 2017 National Electrical Code – Chapter 2 Wiring and Protection, Article 250 Grounding and Bonding. 250.53 Grounding Electrode System Installation. 250.53(B) Electrode Spacing.

68. Answer C. 8

Where more than one of the electrodes of the type specified in 250.52(A)(5) or (A)(7) are used, each electrode of one grounding system (including that used for strike termination devices) shall not be less than 1.83 m (6 ft.) from any other electrode of another grounding system. Two or more grounding electrodes that are bonded together shall be considered a single grounding electrode system.

Reference: 2017 National Electrical Code – Chapter 2 Wiring and Protection, Article 250 Grounding and Bonding. 250.53 Grounding Electrode System Installation. 250.53(B) Electrode Spacing.

EXAM 6

EXAM 6 ANSWERS

69. Answer C.   6 feet

Where more than one of the electrodes of the type specified in 250.52(A)(5) or (A)(7) are used, *each electrode of one grounding system (including that used for strike termination devices) shall not be less than 1.83 m (6 ft.) from any other electrode of another grounding system.* Two or more grounding electrodes that are bonded together shall be considered a single grounding electrode system.

Reference: 2017 National Electrical Code – Chapter 2 Wiring and Protection, Article 250 Grounding and Bonding. 250.53 Grounding Electrode System Installation. 250.53(B) Electrode Spacing.

70. Answer D.   a single grounding electrode system

Where more than one of the electrodes of the type specified in 250.52(A)(5) or (A)(7) are used, each electrode of one grounding system (including that used for strike termination devices) shall not be less than 1.83 m (6 ft.) from any other electrode of another grounding system. *Two or more grounding electrodes that are bonded together shall be considered a single grounding electrode system.*

Reference: 2017 National Electrical Code – Chapter 2 Wiring and Protection, Article 250 Grounding and Bonding. 250.53 Grounding Electrode System Installation. 250.53(B) Electrode Spacing.

71. Answer D.   water meters or filtering devices and similar equipment

Continuity of the grounding path or the bonding connection to interior piping shall not rely *on water meters or filtering devices and similar equipment.*

Reference: 2017 National Electrical Code – Chapter 2 Wiring and Protection, Article 250 Grounding and Bonding. 250.53 Grounding Electrode System Installation. 250.53(D) Metal Underground Water Pipe. . 250.53(D)(1) Continuity.

72. Answer A.   6 AWG

Where the supplemental electrode is a rod, pipe, or plate electrode, that portion of the bonding jumper that is the sole connection to the supplemental grounding *electrode shall not be required to be larger than 6 AWG copper wire or 4 AWG aluminum wire.*

Reference: 2017 National Electrical Code – Chapter 2 Wiring and Protection, Article 250 Grounding and Bonding. 250.53 Grounding Electrode System Installation. 250.53(E) Supplemental Electrode Bonding Connection Size.

73. Answer C.   30 in.

The ground ring shall be installed not less than 750 mm (30 in.) below the surface of the earth.

Reference: 2017 National Electrical Code – Chapter 2 Wiring and Protection, Article 250 Grounding and Bonding. 250.53 Grounding Electrode System Installation. 250.53(F) Ground Ring.

74. Answer B.   45

The electrode shall be installed such that at least 2.44 m (8 ft.) of length is in contact with the soil. It shall be driven to a depth of not less than 2.44 m (8 ft.) except that, *where rock bottom is encountered, the electrode shall be driven at an oblique angle not to exceed 45 degrees from the vertical or, where rock bottom is encountered at an angle up to 45 degrees, the electrode shall be permitted to be buried in a trench that is at least 750 mm (30 in.) deep.* The upper end of the electrode shall be flush with or below ground level unless the aboveground end and the grounding electrode conductor attachment are protected against physical damage as specified in 250.10.

Reference: 2017 National Electrical Code – Chapter 2 Wiring and Protection, Article 250 Grounding and Bonding. 250.53 Grounding Electrode System Installation. 250.53(G) Rod and Pipe Electrodes.

75. Answer A.   30

The electrode shall be installed such that at least 2.44 m (8 ft.) of length is in contact with the soil. It shall be driven to a depth of not less than 2.44 m (8 ft.) except that, where rock bottom is encountered, the electrode shall be driven at an oblique angle not to exceed 45 degrees from the vertical or, where rock bottom is encountered at an angle up to 45 degrees, *the electrode shall be permitted to be buried in a trench that is at least 750 mm (30 in.) deep.* The upper end of the electrode shall be flush with or below ground level unless the aboveground end and the grounding electrode conductor attachment are protected against physical damage as specified in 250.10.

Reference: 2017 National Electrical Code – Chapter 2 Wiring and Protection, Article 250 Grounding and Bonding. 250.53 Grounding Electrode System Installation. 250.53(G) Rod and Pipe Electrodes.

EXAM 6

EXAM 6 ANSWERS

76. Answer B. 8

The electrode shall be installed such that at least 2.44 m (8 ft.) of length is in contact with the soil. It shall be driven to a depth of not less than 2.44 m (8 ft.) except that, where rock bottom is encountered, the electrode shall be driven at an oblique angle not to exceed 45 degrees from the vertical or, where rock bottom is encountered at an angle up to 45 degrees, the electrode shall be permitted to be buried in a trench that is at least 750 mm (30 in.) deep. The upper end of the electrode shall be flush with or below ground level unless the aboveground end and the grounding electrode conductor attachment are protected against physical damage as specified in 250.10.

Reference: 2017 National Electrical Code – Chapter 2 Wiring and Protection, Article 250 Grounding and Bonding. 250.53 Grounding Electrode System Installation. 250.53(G) Rod and Pipe Electrodes.

77. Answer B. 45

The electrode shall be installed such that at least 2.44 m (8 ft.) of length is in contact with the soil. It shall be driven to a depth of not less than 2.44 m (8 ft.) except that, where rock bottom is encountered, the electrode shall be driven at an oblique angle not to exceed 45 degrees from the vertical or, *where rock bottom is encountered at an angle up to 45 degrees*, the electrode shall be permitted to be buried in a trench that is at least 750 mm (30 in.) deep. The upper end of the electrode shall be flush with or below ground level unless the aboveground end and the grounding electrode conductor attachment are protected against physical damage as specified in 250.10.

Reference: 2017 National Electrical Code – Chapter 2 Wiring and Protection, Article 250 Grounding and Bonding. 250.53 Grounding Electrode System Installation. 250.53(G) Rod and Pipe Electrodes.

78. Answer C. 8 feet

The electrode shall be installed such that at least 2.44 m (8 ft.) of length is in contact with the soil. *It shall be driven to a depth of not less than 2.44 m (8 ft.) except that, where rock bottom is encountered*, the electrode shall be driven at an oblique angle not to exceed 45 degrees from the vertical or, where rock bottom is encountered at an angle up to 45 degrees, the electrode shall be permitted to be buried in a trench that is at least 750 mm (30 in.) deep. The upper end of the electrode shall be flush with or below ground level unless the aboveground end and the grounding electrode conductor attachment are protected against physical damage as specified in 250.10.

Reference: 2017 National Electrical Code – Chapter 2 Wiring and Protection, Article 250 Grounding and Bonding. 250.53 Grounding Electrode System Installation. 250.53(G) Rod and Pipe Electrodes

79. Answer C. when rock bottom is encountered

The electrode shall be installed such that at least 2.44 m (8 ft.) of length is in contact with the soil. It shall be driven to a depth of not less than 2.44 m (8 ft.) *except that, where rock bottom is encountered,* the electrode shall be driven at an oblique angle not to exceed 45 degrees from the vertical or, *where rock bottom is encountered at an angle up to 45 degrees, the electrode shall be permitted to be buried in a trench* that is at least 750 mm (30 in.) deep. The upper end of the electrode shall be flush with or below ground level unless the aboveground end and the grounding electrode conductor attachment are protected against physical damage as specified in 250.10.

Reference: 2017 National Electrical Code – Chapter 2 Wiring and Protection, Article 250 Grounding and Bonding. 250.53 Grounding Electrode System Installation. 250.53(G) Rod and Pipe Electrodes

EXAM 6

EXAM 6 ANSWERS

80. **Answer D.** 30 inches

    The electrode shall be installed such that at least 2.44 m (8 ft.) of length is in contact with the soil. It shall be driven to a depth of not less than 2.44 m (8 ft.) except that, where rock bottom is encountered, the electrode shall be driven at an oblique angle not to exceed 45 degrees from the vertical or, where rock bottom is encountered at an angle up to 45 degrees, the electrode *shall be permitted to be buried in a trench that is at least 750 mm (30 in.) deep.* The upper end of the electrode shall be flush with or below ground level unless the aboveground end and the grounding electrode conductor attachment are protected against physical damage as specified in 250.10.

    Reference: 2017 National Electrical Code – Chapter 2 Wiring and Protection, Article 250 Grounding and Bonding. 250.53 Grounding Electrode System Installation. 250.53(G) Rod and Pipe Electrodes

81. **Answer D.** 30

    Plate electrodes shall be installed not less than 750 mm (30 in.) below the surface of the earth.

    Reference: 2017 National Electrical Code – Chapter 2 Wiring and Protection, Article 250 Grounding and Bonding. 250.53 Grounding Electrode System Installation. 250.53(H) Plate Electrode.

82. **Answer A.** 30

    Plate electrodes shall be installed not less than 750 mm (30 in.) below the surface of the earth.

    Reference: 2017 National Electrical Code – Chapter 2 Wiring and Protection, Article 250 Grounding and Bonding. 250.53 Grounding Electrode System Installation. 250.53(H) Plate Electrode.

83. **Answer D.** 30 inches

    Plate electrodes shall be installed not less than 750 mm (30 in.) below the surface of the earth.

    Reference: 2017 National Electrical Code – Chapter 2 Wiring and Protection, Article 250 Grounding and Bonding. 250.53 Grounding Electrode System Installation. 250.53(H) Plate Electrode.

84. **Answer D.** the same

    Where an ac system is connected to a grounding electrode in or at a building or structure, the same electrode shall be used to ground conductor enclosures and equipment in or on that building or structure. Where separate services, feeders, or branch circuits *supply a building and are required to be connected to a grounding electrode(s), the same grounding electrode(s) shall be used.*

    Two or more grounding electrodes that are bonded together shall be considered as a single grounding electrode system in this sense.

    Reference: 2017 National Electrical Code – Chapter 2 Wiring and Protection, Article 250 Grounding and Bonding. 250.58 Common Grounding Electrode.

85. **Answer A.** copper, aluminum, or copper-clad aluminum

    The grounding electrode conductor shall be of copper, aluminum, copper-clad aluminum, or the items as permitted in 250.68(C). The material selected shall be resistant to any corrosive condition existing at the installation or shall be protected against corrosion. Conductors of the wire type shall be solid or stranded, insulated, covered, or bare.

    Reference: 2017 National Electrical Code – Chapter 2 Wiring and Protection, Article 250 Grounding and Bonding. 250.62 Grounding Electrode Conductor Material.

EXAM 6

EXAM 6 ANSWERS

86. **Answer B.** corrosive

The grounding electrode conductor shall be of copper, aluminum, copper-clad aluminum, or the items as permitted in 250.68(C). *The material selected shall be resistant to any corrosive condition existing at the installation or shall be protected against corrosion.* Conductors of the wire type shall be solid or stranded, insulated, covered, or bare.

Reference: 2017 National Electrical Code – Chapter 2 Wiring and Protection, Article 250 Grounding and Bonding. 250.62 Grounding Electrode Conductor Material.

87. **Answer D.** any of the above

The grounding electrode conductor shall be of copper, aluminum, copper-clad aluminum, or the items as permitted in 250.68(C). The material selected shall be resistant to any corrosive condition existing at the installation or shall be protected against corrosion. Conductors of the wire type shall be solid or stranded, insulated, covered, or bare.

Reference: 2017 National Electrical Code – Chapter 2 Wiring and Protection, Article 250 Grounding and Bonding. 250.62 Grounding Electrode Conductor Material.

88. **Answer D.** 18

Bare aluminum or copper-clad aluminum grounding electrode conductors shall not be used where in direct contact with masonry or the earth or where subject to corrosive conditions. *Where used outside, aluminum or copper-clad aluminum grounding electrode conductors shall not be terminated within 450 mm (18 in.) of the earth.*

Reference: 2017 National Electrical Code – Chapter 2 Wiring and Protection, Article 250 Grounding and Bonding. 250.64 Grounding Electrode Conductor Installation. 250.64(A) Aluminum or Copper-Clad Aluminum Conductors.

89. **Answer B.** 18

Bare aluminum or copper-clad aluminum grounding electrode conductors shall not be used where in direct contact with masonry or the earth or where subject to corrosive conditions. *Where used outside, aluminum or copper-clad aluminum grounding electrode conductors shall not be terminated within 450 mm (18 in.) of the earth.*

Reference: 2017 National Electrical Code – Chapter 2 Wiring and Protection, Article 250 Grounding and Bonding. 250.64 Grounding Electrode Conductor Installation. 250.64(A) Aluminum or Copper-Clad Aluminum Conductors.

EXAM 6

EXAM 6 ANSWERS

90. **Answer B.** aluminum or copper-clad aluminum

Bare aluminum or copper-clad aluminum grounding electrode conductors shall not be used where in direct contact with masonry or the earth or where subject to corrosive conditions. *Where used outside, aluminum or copper-clad aluminum grounding electrode conductors shall not be terminated within 450 mm (18 in.) of the earth.*

Reference: 2017 National Electrical Code – Chapter 2 Wiring and Protection, Article 250 Grounding and Bonding. 250.64 Grounding Electrode Conductor Installation. 250.64(A) Aluminum or Copper-Clad Aluminum Conductors.

91. **Answer D.** securely fastened to the construction.

Where exposed, a grounding electrode conductor or its enclosure shall be securely fastened to the surface on which it is carried. Grounding electrode conductors shall be permitted to be installed on or through framing members.

Reference: 2017 National Electrical Code – Chapter 2 Wiring and Protection, Article 250 Grounding and Bonding. 250.64 Grounding Electrode Conductor Installation. . 250.64(B) Securing and Protection Against Physical Damage.

92. **Answer D.** the exothermic welding process

Grounding electrode conductor(s) shall be installed in one continuous length without a splice or joint except splicing of the wire-type grounding electrode conductor shall be permitted by irreversible compression-type connectors listed as grounding and bonding equipment or by:

Except as provided in 250.30(A)(5) and (A)(6), 250.30(B)(1), and 250.68(C), grounding electrode conductor(s) shall be installed in one continuous length without a splice or joint. If necessary, splices or connections shall be made as permitted in (1) through (4):

(1) Splicing of the wire-type grounding electrode conductor shall be permitted only by *irreversible compression-type connectors listed as grounding and bonding equipment or by the exothermic welding process.*

(2) Sections of busbars shall be permitted to be connected together to form a grounding electrode conductor.

(3) Bolted, riveted, or welded connections of structural metal frames of buildings or structures.

(4) Threaded, welded, brazed, soldered or bolted-flange connections of metal water piping.

Reference: 2017 National Electrical Code – Chapter 2 Wiring and Protection, Article 250 Grounding and Bonding. 250.64 Grounding Electrode Conductor Installation. 250.64(C) Continuous.

93. **Answer D.** never

Splicing of the wire-type grounding electrode conductor shall be permitted only by irreversible compression-type connectors listed as grounding and bonding equipment or by *the exothermic welding process.*

Reference: 2017 National Electrical Code – Chapter 2 Wiring and Protection, Article 250 Grounding and Bonding. 250.64 Grounding Electrode Conductor Installation. 250.64(C) Continuous. 250.64(C)(1)

EXAM 6

EXAM 6 ANSWERS

Table 250.102(C)(1) Grounded Conductor, Main Bonding Jumper, System Bonding Jumper, and Supply-Side Bonding Jumper for Alternating-Current Systems

Size of Largest Ungrounded Conductor or Equivalent Area for Parallel Conductors (AWG/kcmil)		Size of Grounded Conductor or Bonding Jumper* (AWG/kcmil)	
Copper	Aluminum or Copper-Clad Aluminum	Copper	Aluminum or Copper-Clad Aluminum
2 or smaller	1/0 or smaller	8	6
1 or 1/0	2/0 or 3/0	6	4
2/0 or 3/0	4/0 or 250	4	2
Over 3/0 through 350	Over 250 through 500	2	1/0
Over 350 through 600	Over 500 through 900	1/0	3/0
Over 600 through 1100	Over 900 through 1750	2/0	4/0
Over 1100	Over 1750	See Notes 1 and 2.	

94. Answer B. 4 AWG

The size of the grounding electrode conductor at the service, at each building or structure where supplied by a feeder(s) or branch circuit(s), or at a separately derived system of a grounded or ungrounded ac system shall not be less than given in *Table 250.66*, except as permitted in 250.66(A) through (C).

Reference: 2017 National Electrical Code – Chapter 2 Wiring and Protection, Article 250 Grounding and Bonding. 250.66 Size of Alternating-Current Grounding Electrode Conductor. Table 250.66 Grounding Electrode Conductor for Alternating-Current Systems (page 70-121)

95. Answer B. 3/0 AWG

Reference: 2017 National Electrical Code – Chapter 2 Wiring and Protection, Article 250 Grounding and Bonding. 250.66 Size of Alternating-Current Grounding Electrode Conductor. Table 250.66 Grounding Electrode Conductor for Alternating-Current Systems (page 70-121)

If the grounding electrode conductor or bonding jumper connected to a single or multiple concrete-encased electrode(s), as described in 250.52(A)(3), does not extend on to other types of electrodes that require a larger size of conductor, the grounding electrode conductor *shall not be required to be larger than 4 AWG copper wire*.

Reference: 2017 National Electrical Code – Chapter 2 Wiring and Protection, Article 250 Grounding and Bonding. 250.64 Size of Alternating-Current Grounding Electrode Conductor. 250.64 (B) Connections to Concrete-Encased Electrodes.

EXAM 6

EXAM 6 ANSWERS

96. Answer A. concrete-encased

All mechanical elements used to terminate a grounding electrode conductor or bonding jumper to a grounding electrode shall be accessible.

Exception No. 1: An encased or buried connection to a concrete-encased, driven, or buried grounding electrode shall not be required to be accessible.

Exception No. 2: Exothermic or irreversible compression connections used at terminations, together with the mechanical means used to

Reference: 2017 National Electrical Code – Chapter 2 Wiring and Protection, Article 250 Grounding and Bonding. 250.68 Grounding Electrode Conductor and Bonding Jumper . 250.68(A) Accessibility.

97. Answer A. accessible

Review the 2 exceptions in this article.

All mechanical elements used to terminate a grounding electrode conductor or bonding jumper to a grounding electrode shall be accessible.

Exception No.1: An encased or buried connection to a concrete-encased, driven, or buried grounding electrode shall not be required to be accessible.

Exception No.2: Exothermic or irreversible compression connections used at terminations, together with the mechanical means used to attach such terminations to fireproofed structural metal whether or not the mechanical means is reversible, shall not be required to be accessible.

Reference: 2017 National Electrical Code – Chapter 2 Wiring and Protection, Article 250 Grounding and Bonding. 250.68 Grounding Electrode Conductor and Bonding Jumper Connection to Grounding Electrodes. 250.68(A) Accessibility.

98. Answer A. it is not required to be accessible

An encased or buried connection to a concrete-encased, driven, or buried grounding electrode shall not be required to be accessible.

Reference: 2017 National Electrical Code – Chapter 2 Wiring and Protection, Article 250 Grounding and Bonding. 250.68 Grounding Electrode Conductor and Bonding Jumper Connection to Grounding Electrodes. 250.68(A) Accessibility. Exception 1

99. Answer A. bonded together

The normally non-current-carrying metal parts of equipment indicated in 250.92(A)(1) and (A)(2) shall be bonded together.

(1) All raceways, cable trays, cablebus framework, auxiliary gutters, or service cable armor or sheath that enclose, contain, or support service conductors, except as permitted in 250.80

(2) All enclosures containing service conductors, including meter fittings, boxes, or the like, interposed in the service raceway or armor

Reference: 2017 National Electrical Code – Chapter 2 Wiring and Protection, Article 250 Grounding and Bonding. 250.92 Services. 250.92(A) Bonding of Equipment for Services.

100. Answer A. Bonding Jumpers

Bonding jumpers meeting the requirements of this article shall be used around impaired connections, such as reducing washers or oversized, concentric, or eccentric knockouts. Standard locknuts or bushings shall not be the only means for the bonding required by this section but shall be permitted to be installed to make a mechanical connection of the raceway(s).

Electrical continuity at service equipment, service raceways, and service conductor enclosures shall be ensured by one of the following methods:

(1) Bonding equipment to the grounded service conductor in a manner provided in 250.8

(2) Connections utilizing threaded couplings or threaded hubs on enclosures if made up wrenchtight

(3) Threadless couplings and connectors if made up tight for metal raceways and metal-clad cables

(4) Other listed devices, such as bonding-type locknuts, bushings, or bushings with bonding jumpers.

Reference: 2017 National Electrical Code – Chapter 2 Wiring and Protection, Article 250 Grounding and Bonding. 250.92 Services. 250.92(B) Method of Bonding at the Service.

EXAM 6

EXAM 6 ANSWERS

101. Answer C.   removed

Metal raceways, cable trays, cable armor, cable sheath, enclosures, frames, fittings, and other metal non-current-carrying parts that are to serve as equipment grounding conductors, with or without the use of supplementary equipment grounding conductors, shall be bonded where necessary to ensure electrical continuity and the capacity to conduct safely any fault current likely to be imposed on them. *Any nonconductive paint, enamel, or similar coating shall be removed at threads,* contact points, and contact surfaces or be connected by means of fittings designed so as to make such removal unnecessary.

Reference: 2017 National Electrical Code – Chapter 2 Wiring and Protection, Article 250 Grounding and Bonding. 250.96 Bonding Other Enclosures. 250.96(A) General.

102. Answer A.   electrical continuity

Metal raceways, cable trays, cable armor, cable sheath, enclosures, frames, fittings, and other metal non-current-carrying parts that are to serve as equipment grounding conductors, with or without the use of supplementary equipment grounding conductors, shall be bonded where *necessary to ensure electrical continuity and the capacity to conduct safely any fault current likely* to be imposed on them. Any nonconductive paint, enamel, or similar coating shall be removed at threads, contact points, and contact surfaces or be connected by means of fittings designed so as to make such removal unnecessary.

Reference: 2017 National Electrical Code – Chapter 2 Wiring and Protection, Article 250 Grounding and Bonding. 250.96 Bonding Other Enclosures. 250.96(A) General.

103. Answer C.   equipment bonding jumpers

Expansion fittings and telescoping sections of metal raceways shall be made electrically continuous by *equipment bonding jumpers or other means.*

Reference: 2017 National Electrical Code – Chapter 2 Wiring and Protection, Article 250 Grounding and Bonding. 250.98 Bonding Loosely Jointed Metal Raceways.

104. Answer D.   any of the above

Bonding jumpers shall be of copper, aluminum, copper-clad aluminum, or other corrosion-resistant material. A bonding jumper shall be a wire, bus, screw, or similar suitable conductor.

Reference: 2017 National Electrical Code – Chapter 2 Wiring and Protection, Article 250 Grounding and Bonding. 250.102 Grounded Conductor, Bonding Conductors, and Jumpers. 250.102(A) Material.

105. Answer C.   4 AWG copper

The supply-side bonding jumper shall not be smaller than specified in Table 250.102(C)(1).

Reference: 2017 National Electrical Code – Chapter 2 Wiring and Protection, Article 250 Grounding and Bonding. 250.102 Bonding Conductors and Jumpers. 250.102(C) Size – Supply-Side Bonding Jumper. 250.102(C)(1) Size for Supply Conductors in a Single Raceway or Cable.

106. Answer C.   grounding electrode system

The lightning protection system ground terminals shall be bonded to the building or structure grounding electrode system.

Informational Note No. 1: See 250.60 for use of strike termination devices. For further information, see NFPA 780-2014. Standard for the Installation of Lightning Protection Systems, which contains detailed information on grounding, bonding, and sideflash distance from lightning protection systems.

Informational Note No.2: Metal raceways, enclosures, frames, and other non-current-carrying metal parts of electrical equipment installed on a building equipped with a lightning protection system may require bonding or spacing from the lightning protection conductors in accordance with NFPA 780-2014, Standard for the Installation of Lightning Protection Systems.

Reference: 2017 National Electrical Code – Chapter 2 Wiring and Protection, Article 250 Grounding and Bonding. 250.106 Lightning Protection Systems

EXAM 6

EXAM 6 ANSWERS

107. Answer D. any of these

Exposed, normally non-current-carrying metal parts of fixed equipment supplied by or enclosing conductors or components that are likely to become energized shall be connected to an equipment grounding conductor under any of the following conditions:

(1) Where within 2.5 m (8 ft.) vertically or 1.5 m (5 ft.) horizontally of ground or *grounded metal objects and subject to contact by persons*

(2) Where located in a wet or damp location and not isolated

(3) Where in electrical contact with metal

(4) Where in a hazardous (classified) location as covered by Articles 500 through 517

(5) Where supplied by a wiring method that provides an equipment grounding conductor, except as permitted by 250.86 Exception No. 2 for short sections of metal enclosures

(6) Where equipment operates with any terminal at over 150 volts to ground

Reference: 2017 National Electrical Code – Chapter 2 Wiring and Protection, Article 250 Grounding and Bonding. 250.110 Equipment Fastened in Place (Fixed) or Connected by Permanent Wiring Methods.

108. Answer C. connected

Except as permitted in 250.112(F) and (I), exposed, normally non-current-carrying metal parts of equipment described in 250.112(A) through (K), and normally non-current-carrying metal parts of equipment and enclosures described in 250.112(L) and (M), *shall be connected to an equipment grounding conductor, regardless of voltage.*

Reference: 2017 National Electrical Code – Chapter 2 Wiring and Protection, Article 250 Grounding and Bonding. 250.112 Specific Equipment Fastened in Place (Fixed) or Connected by Permanent Wiring Methods.

109. Answer B. 50 volts

Equipment supplied by Class 1 circuits shall be grounded unless operating at less than 50 volts. Equipment supplied by Class 1 power-limited circuits, by Class 2 and Class 3 remote-control and signaling circuits, and by fire alarm circuits shall be grounded where system grounding is required by Part II or Part VIII of this article.

Reference: 2017 National Electrical Code – Chapter 2 Wiring and Protection, Article 250 Grounding and Bonding. 250.112 Specific Equipment Fastened in Place (Fixed) or Connected by Permanent Wiring Methods. 250.112(I) Remote-Control, Signaling, and Fire Alarm Circuits.

110. Answer A. connected to

Where a submersible pump is used in a metal well casing, the well casing *shall be connected to the pump circuit equipment grounding conductor.*

Reference: 2017 National Electrical Code – Chapter 2 Wiring and Protection, Article 250 Grounding and Bonding. 250.112 Specific Equipment Fastened in Place (Fixed) or Connected by Permanent Wiring Methods. 250.112(M) Metal Well Casings.

111. Answer B. of any shape.

The equipment grounding conductor run with or enclosing the circuit conductors shall be one or more or a combination of the following:

(1) A copper, aluminum, or copper-clad aluminum conductor. This conductor shall be solid or stranded; insulated, covered, or bare; and *in the form of a wire or a busbar of any shape.*

Reference: 2017 National Electrical Code – Chapter 2 Wiring and Protection, Article 250 Grounding and Bonding. 250.118 Types of Equipment Grounding Conductors.

112. Answer A. True

The equipment grounding conductor run with or enclosing the circuit conductors shall be one or more or a combination of the following:

(9) The copper sheath of mineral-insulated, metal-sheathed cable Type MI.

Reference: 2017 National Electrical Code – Chapter 2 Wiring and Protection, Article 250 Grounding and Bonding. 250.118 Types of Equipment Grounding Conductors.

EXAM 6
EXAM 6 ANSWERS

113. **Answer D.** RNC

The equipment grounding conductor run with or enclosing the circuit conductors shall be one or more or a combination of the following:

(1) A copper, aluminum, or copper-clad aluminum conductor. This conductor shall be solid or stranded; insulated, covered, or bare; and in the form of a wire or a busbar of any shape.

(2) Rigid metal conduit.

(3) Intermediate metal conduit.

(4) Electrical metallic tubing.

(5) Listed flexible metal conduit meeting all the following conditions:

   a. The conduit is terminated in listed fittings.

   b. The circuit conductors contained in the conduit are protected by overcurrent devices rated at 20 amperes or less.

   c. The size of the conduit does not exceed metric designator 35 (trade size 1 1/4).

   d. The combined length of flexible metal conduit and flexible metallic tubing and liquid tight flexible metal conduit in the same ground-fault current path does not exceed 1.8 m (6 ft).

   e. If used to connect equipment where flexibility is necessary to minimize the transmission of vibration from equipment or to provide flexibility for equipment that requires movement after installation, an

(6) Listed liquidtight flexible metal conduit meeting all the following conditions:

   a. The conduit is terminated in listed fittings.

   b. For metric designators 12 through 16 (trade sizes 3/8 through 1/2), the circuit conductors contained in the conduit are protected by overcurrent devices rated at 20 amperes or less.

   c. For metric designators 21 through 35 (trade sizes 3/4 through 1-1/4), the circuit conductors contained in the conduit are protected by overcurrent devices rated not more than 60 amperes and there is no flexible metal conduit, flexible metallic tubing, or liquidtight flexible metal conduit in trade sizes metric designators 12 through 16 (trade sizes 3/8 through 1/2) in the ground-fault current path.

   d. The combined length of flexible metal conduit and flexible metallic tubing and liquidtight flexible metal conduit in the same ground-fault current path does not exceed 1.5 m (6 ft.).

   e. If used to connect equipment where flexibility is necessary to minimize the transmission of vibration from equipment or to provide flexibility for equipment that requires movement after installation, an equipment grounding conductor shall be installed.

(7) Flexible metallic tubing where the tubing is terminated in listed fittings and meeting the following conditions:

   a. The circuit conductors contained in the tubing are protected by overcurrent devices rated at 20 amperes or less.

   b. The combined length of flexible metal conduit and flexible metallic tubing and liquidtight flexible metal conduit in the same ground-fault current path does not exceed 1.5 m (6 ft.).

(8) Armor of Type AC cable as provided in 320.108.

(9) The copper sheath of mineral-insulated, metal-sheathed cable Type MI.

(10) Type MC cable that provides an effective ground-fault current path in accordance with one or more of the following:

   a. It contains an insulated or uninsulated equipment grounding conductor in compliance with 250.115(1)

   b. The combined metallic sheath and uninsulated equipment grounding/bonding conductor of interlocked metal tape-type MC cable that is listed and identified as an equipment grounding conductor

   c. The metallic sheath or the combined metallic sheath and equipment grounding conductors of the smooth or corrugated tube-type MC cable that is listed and identified as an equipment grounding conductor

(11) Cable trays as permitted in 392.10 and 392.60.

(12) Cablebus framework as permitted in 370.60(1).

(13) Other listed electrically continuous metal raceways and listed auxiliary gutters.

(14) Surface metal raceways listed for grounding.

Reference: 2017 National Electrical Code – Chapter 2 Wiring and Protection, Article 250 Grounding and Bonding. 250.118 Types of Equipment Grounding Conductors.

EXAM 6

Chapter 2 Wiring and Protection 03

114. **Answer C.** copper, aluminum, or copper-clad aluminum

The equipment grounding conductor run with or enclosing the circuit conductors shall be one or more or a combination of the following:

(1) A copper, aluminum, or copper-clad aluminum conductor. This conductor shall be solid or stranded; insulated, covered, or bare; and in the form of a wire or a busbar of any shape.

(2) Rigid metal conduit.

(3) Intermediate metal conduit.

(4) Electrical metallic tubing.

(5) Listed flexible metal conduit meeting all the following conditions:

   a. The conduit is terminated in listed fittings.

   b. The circuit conductors contained in the conduit are protected by overcurrent devices rated at 20 amperes or less.

   c. The size of the conduit does not exceed metric designator 35 (trade size 1 1/4).

   d. The combined length of flexible metal conduit and flexible metallic tubing and liquid tight flexible metal conduit in the same ground-fault current path does not exceed 1.8 m (6 ft).

   e. If used to connect equipment where flexibility is necessary to minimize the transmission of vibration from equipment or to provide flexibility for equipment that requires movement after installation, an

(6) Listed liquidtight flexible metal conduit meeting all the following conditions:

   a. The conduit is terminated in listed fittings.

   b. For metric designators 12 through 16 (trade sizes 3/8 through 1/2), the circuit conductors contained in the conduit are protected by overcurrent devices rated at 20 amperes or less.

   c. For metric designators 21 through 35 (trade sizes 3/4 through 1-1/4), the circuit conductors contained in the conduit are protected by overcurrent devices rated not more than 60 amperes and there is no flexible metal conduit, flexible metallic tubing, or liquidtight flexible metal conduit in trade sizes metric designators 12 through 16 (trade sizes 3/8 through 1/2) in the ground-fault current path.

   d. The combined length of flexible metal conduit and flexible metallic tubing and liquidtight flexible metal conduit in the same ground-fault current path does not exceed 1.5 m (6 ft.).

   e. If used to connect equipment where flexibility is necessary to minimize the transmission of vibration from equipment or to provide flexibility for equipment that requires movement after installation, an equipment grounding conductor shall be installed.

(7) Flexible metallic tubing where the tubing is terminated in listed fittings and meeting the following conditions:

   a. The circuit conductors contained in the tubing are protected by overcurrent devices rated at 20 amperes or less.

   b. The combined length of flexible metal conduit and flexible metallic tubing and liquidtight flexible metal conduit in the same ground-fault current path does not exceed 1.5 m (6 ft.).

(8) Armor of Type AC cable as provided in 320.108.

(9) The copper sheath of mineral-insulated, metal-sheathed cable Type MI.

(10) Type MC cable that provides an effective ground-fault current path in accordance with one or more of the following:

   a. It contains an insulated or uninsulated equipment grounding conductor in compliance with 250.115(1)

   b. The combined metallic sheath and uninsulated equipment grounding/bonding conductor of interlocked metal tape-type MC cable that is listed and identified as an equipment grounding conductor

   c. The metallic sheath or the combined metallic sheath and equipment grounding conductors of the smooth or corrugated tube-type MC cable that is listed and identified as an equipment grounding conductor

(11) Cable trays as permitted in 392.10 and 392.60.

(12) Cablebus framework as permitted in 370.60(1).

(13) Other listed electrically continuous metal raceways and listed auxiliary gutters.

(14) Surface metal raceways listed for grounding.

Reference: 2017 National Electrical Code – Chapter 2 Wiring and Protection, Article 250 Grounding and Bonding. 250.118 Types of Equipment Grounding Conductors.

EXAM 6

Chapter 2 Wiring and Protection 03

115. Answer C. insulated

Unless required elsewhere in this Code, equipment *grounding conductors shall be permitted to be bare, covered, or insulated.* Individually covered or insulated equipment grounding conductors shall have a continuous outer finish that is either green or green with one or more yellow stripes except as permitted in this section. Conductors with insulation or individual covering that is green, green with one or more yellow stripes, or otherwise identified as permitted by this section shall not be used for ungrounded or grounded circuit conductors.

Reference: 2017 National Electrical Code – Chapter 2 Wiring and Protection, Article 250 Grounding and Bonding. 250.119 Identification of Equipment Grounding Conductors.

116. Answer D. A or B

Unless required elsewhere in this Code, equipment grounding conductors shall be permitted to be bare, covered, or insulated. Individually covered or insulated equipment grounding conductors shall *have a continuous outer finish that is either green or green with one or more yellow stripes except as permitted in this section*. Conductors with insulation or individual covering that is green, green with one or more yellow stripes, or otherwise identified as permitted by this section shall not be used for ungrounded or grounded circuit conductors.

Reference: 2017 National Electrical Code – Chapter 2 Wiring and Protection, Article 250 Grounding and Bonding. 250.119 Identification of Equipment Grounding Conductors.

117. Answer C. 10 AWG

Copper, aluminum, or copper-clad aluminum equipment grounding conductors of the wire type shall not be smaller than shown in **Table 250.122,** but in no case shall they be required to be larger than the circuit conductors supplying the equipment.

Reference: 2017 National Electrical Code – Chapter 2 Wiring and Protection, Article 250 Grounding and Bonding. 250.122 Size of Equipment Grounding Conductors. 250.122(A) General. Table 250.122 Minimum Size Equipment Grounding Conductors for Grounding Raceway and Equipment (page 70-131)

118. Answer B. 10 AWG

Copper, aluminum, or copper-clad aluminum equipment grounding conductors of the wire type shall not be smaller than shown in **Table 250.122,** but in no case shall they be required to be larger than the circuit conductors supplying the equipment.

Reference: 2017 National Electrical Code – Chapter 2 Wiring and Protection, Article 250 Grounding and Bonding. 250.122 Size of Equipment Grounding Conductors. 250.122(A) General. Table 250.122 Minimum Size Equipment Grounding Conductors for Grounding Raceway and Equipment (page 70-131)

119. Answer C. in parallel in each raceway or cable

For circuits of parallel conductors as permitted in 310.10(H), the equipment grounding conductor shall be installed in accordance with (1) or (2).

Cable Trays.

(a) Single Raceway or Cable *Tray. If conductors are installed in parallel in the same raceway or cable tray, a single wire type conductor shall be permitted as the equipment grounding conductor.* The wire-type equipment grounding conductor shall be sized in accordance with 250.122, based on the overcurrent protective device for the feeder or branch circuit. Wire type equipment grounding conductors installed in cable trays shall meet the minimum requirements of 392.10(B)(1)(c).

Metal raceways or auxiliary gutters in accordance with 250.118 or cable trays complying with 392.60(B) shall be permitted as the equipment grounding conductor.

(b) Multiple Raceways. If conductors are installed in parallel in multiple raceways, wire-type equipment grounding conductors, where used, shall be installed in parallel in each raceway. The equipment grounding conductor installed in each raceway shall be sized in compliance with 250.122 based on the overcurrent protective device for the feeder or branch circuit. Metal raceways or auxiliary gutters in accordance with 250.118 or cable trays complying with 392.60(B) shall be permitted as the equipment grounding conductor.

Reference: 2017 National Electrical Code – Chapter 2 Wiring and Protection, Article 250 Grounding and Bonding. 250.122 Size of Equipment Grounding Conductors. 250.122(F)(1) Conductors in Parallel.

EXAM 6

Chapter 2 Wiring and Protection 03

120. **Answer B.** green

The terminal for the connection of the equipment grounding conductor shall be identified by one of the following:

(1) A green, not readily removable terminal screw with a hexagonal head.

(2) A green, hexagonal, not readily removable terminal nut.

(3) A green pressure wire connector. If the terminal for the equipment grounding conductor is not visible, the conductor entrance hole shall be marked with the word green or ground, the letters G or GR, a grounding symbol, or otherwise identified by a distinctive green color. If the terminal for the equipment grounding conductor is readily removable, the area adjacent to the terminal shall be similarly marked.

Reference: 2017 National Electrical Code – Chapter 2 Wiring and Protection, Article 250 Grounding and Bonding. 250.126 Identification of Wiring Device Terminals. (2)

121. **Answer B.** ground

Where the box is mounted on the surface, direct metal-to-metal contact between the device yoke and the box or a contact yoke or device that complies with 250.146(B) shall be permitted to ground the receptacle to the box. At least one of the insulating washers shall be removed from receptacles that do not have a contact yoke or device that complies with 250.146(B) to ensure direct metal-to-metal contact. This provision shall not apply to cover-mounted receptacles unless the box and cover combination are listed as providing satisfactory ground continuity between the box and the receptacle. A listed exposed work cover shall be permitted to be the grounding and bonding means when (1) the device is attached to the cover with at least two fasteners that are permanent (such as a rivet) or have a thread locking or screw or nut locking means and (2) when the cover mounting holes are located on a flat non-raised portion of the cover.

Reference: 2017 National Electrical Code – Chapter 2 Wiring and Protection, Article 250 Grounding and Bonding. 250.146 Connecting Receptacle Grounding Terminal to Box. 250.146(A) Surface Mounted Box.

122. **Answer D.** 12 AWG

The equipment grounding conductor for secondary circuits of instrument transformers and for instrument cases shall not be smaller than 12 AWG copper or 10 AWG aluminum. Cases of instrument transformers, instruments, meters, and relays that are mounted directly on grounded metal surfaces of enclosures or grounded metal of switchgear or switchboard panels shall be considered to be grounded, and no additional equipment grounding conductor shall be required.

Reference: 2017 National Electrical Code – Chapter 2 Wiring and Protection, Article 250 Grounding and Bonding. 250.178 Instrument Equipment Grounding Conductor.

123. **Answer C.** 6 AWG

Equipment grounding conductors that are not an integral part of a cable assembly shall not be smaller than 6 AWG copper or 4 AWG aluminum.

Reference: 2017 National Electrical Code – Chapter 2 Wiring and Protection, Article 250 Grounding and Bonding. 250.190 Grounding of Equipment. 250.190(C) Equipment Grounding Conductor. 250.190(C)(1) General.

124. **Answer A.** True

Surge arresters shall be permitted to be located indoors or outdoors. Surge arresters shall be made inaccessible to unqualified persons, unless listed for installation in accessible locations.

Reference: 2017 National Electrical Code – Chapter 2 Wiring and Protection, Article 280 Surge Arrestors, Over 1000 Volts. 280.11 Location.

EXAM 7

Chapter 3 Wiring Methods and Materials

1. What inch trade size conduit is the same as metric designator 41?

    A. ½

    B. 1

    C. 1-½

    D. 2

    Reference: 2017 National Electrical Code – Chapter 3 Wiring Methods and Materials, Article 300 General Requirements for Wiring Methods and Materials. 300.1 Scope. 300.1(C) Metric Designators and Trade Sizes.

2. All conductors of the same circuit and, where used, the grounded conductor and all equipment grounding conductors and bonding conductors shall be contained within the same _____.

    A. channel

    B. conduit

    C. pipe

    D. raceway

    Reference: 2017 National Electrical Code – Chapter 3 Wiring Methods and Materials, Article 300 General Requirements for Wiring Methods and Materials. 300.3 Conductors. 300.3(B) Conductors of the Same Circuit.

3. The grounded conductor, all bonding conductors and equipment grounding conductors, where used, and all _____ of the same circuit must be contained in the same auxiliary gutter, cable, cablebus assembly, cable tray, cord, raceway or trench. Exceptions ignored.

    A. communication

    B. conductors

    C. control conductors

    D. relay conductors

    Reference: 2017 National Electrical Code – Chapter 3 Wiring Methods and Materials, Article 300 General Requirements for Wiring Methods and Materials. 300.3 Conductors. 300.3(B) Conductors of the Same Circuit.

EXAM 7

Chapter 3 Wiring Methods and Materials

4. Where subject to physical damage, conductors, raceways and cables shall be _____.

    A. buried
    B. insulated
    C. protected
    D. none of the above

    Reference: 2017 National Electrical Code – Chapter 3 Wiring Methods and Materials, Article 300 General Requirements for Wiring Methods and Materials. 300.4 Protection Against Physical Damage.

5. Where a cable- or raceway-type wiring method is installed through bored holes in joists, rafters, or wood members, holes shall be bored so that the edge of the hole is not less than _____ inches from the nearest edge of the wood member.

    A. 1
    B. 1-¼
    C. 1-½
    D. 2

    Reference: 2017 National Electrical Code – Chapter 3 Wiring Methods and Materials, Article 300 General Requirements for Wiring Methods and Materials. 300.4 Protection Against Physical Damage. 300.4(A) Cables and Raceways Through Wood Members. 300.4(A)(1) Bored Holes.

6. Where a cable or raceway type wiring method is installed through bored holes in joist, rafters, or wood members, in both concealed and exposed locations, holes must be bored so that the edge of the hole is _____ in. or more from the nearest edge of the wood member. Where the distance is not possible, the cable or raceway must be protected from penetration by nails or screws by use of a steel bushing or plate, _____ in thick or more, and of the correct length and width installed to cover the area where the wiring is located.

    A. 1.25, 0.0625
    B. 1.5, 0.125
    C. 1.625, 0.20
    D. 1.75, 0.25

    Reference: 2017 National Electrical Code – Chapter 3 Wiring Methods and Materials, Article 300 General Requirements for Wiring Methods and Materials. 300.4 Protection Against Physical Damage. 300.4(A) Cables and Raceways Through Wood Members. 300.4(A)(1) Bored Holes.

EXAM 7

Chapter 3 Wiring Methods and Materials

7. Generally, Type NM cable can be placed in notches in wooden studs provided the cable is protect against damage from nails or screws by either a steel plate of appropriate length and width, with a thickness of at least:

    A. 1/16 in.

    B. 1/8 in.

    C. 3/16 in.

    D. 1/4 in.

    Reference: 2017 National Electrical Code – Chapter 3 Wiring Methods and Materials, Article 300 General Requirements for Wiring Methods and Materials. 300.4 Protection Against Physical Damage. 300.4(A) Cables and Raceways Through Wood Members. 300.4(A)(2) Notches in Wood.

8. Holes in wooden studs for installation of Type NM cable must be protected by a steel plate with a minimum thickness of 1/16 in., and the hole must be at least _____ from the edge of the wood stud.

    A. 3/4 inch

    B. 1 inch

    C. 1-1/4 inches

    D. 1-1/2 inches

    Reference: 2017 National Electrical Code – Chapter 3 Wiring Methods and Materials, Article 300 General Requirements for Wiring Methods and Materials. 300.4 Protection Against Physical Damage. 300.4(D) Cables and Raceways Parallel to Framing Members and Furring Strips.

9. What is the minimum clearance that must be maintained between electrical metallic tubing (EMT) and the surface of the roof decking when it is installed under metal-corrugated sheet roof decking?

    A. 1 in.

    B. 1-1/4 in.

    C. 1-1/2 in.

    D. 2 in.

    Reference: 2017 National Electrical Code – Chapter 3 Wiring Methods and Materials, Article 300 General Requirements for Wiring Methods and Materials. 300.4 Protection Against Physical Damage. 300.4(E) Cables, Raceways, or Boxes Installed in or Under Roof Decking.

EXAM 7

Chapter 3 Wiring Methods and Materials

10. Of the following, which must be provided for a conductor of a size 4 AWG or larger entering a panelboard?

    A. A bonding jumper.

    B. A grounding clip.

    C. An insulated bushing.

    D. An insulated grounding conductor.

    Reference: 2017 National Electrical Code – Chapter 3 Wiring Methods and Materials, Article 300 General Requirements for Wiring Methods and Materials. 300.4 Protection Against Physical Damage. 300.4(G) Insulated Fittings.

11. Direct burial cables or conductors shall have a minimum cover of _____ inches to finished grade.

    A. 12

    B. 15

    C. 18

    D. 24

    Reference: 2017 National Electrical Code – Chapter 3 Wiring Methods and Materials, Article 300 General Requirements for Wiring Methods and Materials. 300.5 Underground Installations. 300.5(A) Minimum Cover Requirements.

12. What is the minimum burial depth in inches, in a trench below 2 inch thick concrete or equivalent for residential branch circuits rated at up to 120 volts with GFIC protection and overcurrent protection of 20 amperes or less?

    A. 6

    B. 12

    C. 18

    D. 24

    Reference: 2017 National Electrical Code – Chapter 3 Wiring Methods and Materials, Article 300 General Requirements for Wiring Methods and Materials. 300.5 Underground Installations. 300.5(A) Minimum Cover Requirements.

Chapter 3 Wiring Methods and Materials

EXAM 7

Chapter 3 Wiring Methods and Materials

13. What is the minimum direct burial depth in inches of cables or conductors under or in airport runways, as well as adjacent areas where trespassing is prohibited?

    A. 6

    B. 12

    C. 18

    D. 24

    Reference: 2017 National Electrical Code – Chapter 3 Wiring Methods and Materials, Article 300 General Requirements for Wiring Methods and Materials. 300.5 Underground Installations. 300.5(A) Minimum Cover Requirements.

14. Under alleys, driveways, highways, parking lots, roads, and streets, what is the minimum burial depth in inches for wiring in intermediate metal conduit or rigid metal conduit?

    A. 6

    B. 12

    C. 18

    D. 24

    Reference: 2017 National Electrical Code – Chapter 3 Wiring Methods and Materials, Article 300 General Requirements for Wiring Methods and Materials. 300.5 Underground Installations. 300.5(A) Minimum Cover Requirements.

15. What is the minimum cover requirement, in inches, for underground wiring up to 600 volts, in rigid metal conduit under a building?

    A. 0

    B. 6

    C. 12

    D. 18

    Reference: 2017 National Electrical Code – Chapter 3 Wiring Methods and Materials, Article 300 General Requirements for Wiring Methods and Materials. 300.5 Underground Installations. 300.5(A) Minimum Cover Requirements.

EXAM 7

Chapter 3 Wiring Methods and Materials

16. Under alleys, driveways, highways, parking lots, roads, and streets, what is the minimum cover requirement in inches, for underground wiring up to 600 volts, in Type UF cable?

    A. 6

    B. 12

    C. 18

    D. 24

    Reference: 2017 National Electrical Code – Chapter 3 Wiring Methods and Materials, Article 300 General Requirements for Wiring Methods and Materials. 300.5 Underground Installations. 300.5(A) Minimum Cover Requirements.

17. What is the minimum required burial depth in inches for circuits of up to 30 volts, installed with type UF cable under a minimum of 4-in. thick concrete exterior slab with no vehicular traffic, meant for control of landscape and irrigation lighting, with the slab extending at least 6 in. beyond the underground installation?

    A. 6

    B. 12

    C. 18

    D. 24

    Reference: 2017 National Electrical Code – Chapter 3 Wiring Methods and Materials, Article 300 General Requirements for Wiring Methods and Materials. 300.5 Underground Installations. 300.5(A) Minimum Cover Requirements.

18. What is the minimum cover requirement for direct-buried cables or conductors placed in a trench underneath two (2) inch thick concrete or equivalent?

    A. 6 inches

    B. 12 inches

    C. 18 inches

    D. 24 inches

    Reference: 2017 National Electrical Code – Chapter 3 Wiring Methods and Materials, Article 300 General Requirements for Wiring Methods and Materials. 300.5 Underground Installations. 300.5(A) Minimum Cover Requirements.

EXAM 7

Chapter 3 Wiring Methods and Materials

19. For intermediate metal conduit (IMC) with 100 ampere rated, 240-volt, single-phase conductors located underneath a residential gravel driveway, what is the minimum burial depth?

    A. 12 inches

    B. 18 inches

    C. 24 inches

    D. 30 inches

    Reference: 2017 National Electrical Code – Chapter 3 Wiring Methods and Materials, Article 300 General Requirements for Wiring Methods and Materials. 300.5 Underground Installations. 300.5(A) Minimum Cover Requirements.

20. What is the minimum ground cover required when installing a 20-ampere, 120-volt, GFCI protected, direct-buried branch circuit, using Type UF cable to supply landscape lighting for a residence?

    A. 6 inches

    B. 12 inches

    C. 18 inches

    D. 24 inches

    Reference: 2017 National Electrical Code – Chapter 3 Wiring Methods and Materials, Article 300 General Requirements for Wiring Methods and Materials. 300.5 Underground Installations. 300.5(A) Minimum Cover Requirements.

21. What kind of location are the interior of enclosures or raceways installed underground considered to be?

    A. damp

    B. dry

    C. hazardous

    D. wet

    Reference: 2017 National Electrical Code – Chapter 3 Wiring Methods and Materials, Article 300 General Requirements for Wiring Methods and Materials. 300.5 Underground Installations. 300.5(B) Wet Locations.

EXAM 7

Chapter 3 Wiring Methods and Materials

22. When underground cable is installed _____, it must be in a raceway. Exceptions ignored.

    A. in a basement

    B. in a floor

    C. in an attic

    D. under a building

    Reference: *2017 National Electrical Code – Chapter 3 Wiring Methods and Materials, Article 300 General Requirements for Wiring Methods and Materials. 300.5 Underground Installations. 300.5(C) Underground Cables and Conductors Under Buildings.*

23. Direct-buried conductors emerging from grade and specified in columns 1 and 4 of table 300.5 shall be protected extending from the minimum cover required below grade to a point at least _____ feet above finished grade.

    A. 2

    B. 4

    C. 6

    D. 8

    Reference: *2017 National Electrical Code – Chapter 3 Wiring Methods and Materials, Article 300 General Requirements for Wiring Methods and Materials. 300.5 Underground Installations. 300.5(D) Protection from Damage. 300.5(D)(1) Emerging from Grade.*

24. What is the minimum height above grade the direct-buried conductors emerging from grade should be protected by raceways or covers?

    A. 8 feet

    B. 10 feet

    C. 12 feet

    D. 15 feet

    Reference: *2017 National Electrical Code – Chapter 3 Wiring Methods and Materials, Article 300 General Requirements for Wiring Methods and Materials. 300.5 Underground Installations. 300.5(D) Protection from Damage. 300.5(D)(1) Emerging from Grade.*

EXAM 7

Chapter 3 Wiring Methods and Materials

25. Underground service conductors that are *not encased in concrete* and that are buried 18 inches or more below grade shall have their location identified by a warning ribbon that is placed in the trench at least _____ inches above the underground installation.

    A. 4

    B. 6

    C. 9

    D. 12

    Reference: 2017 National Electrical Code – Chapter 3 Wiring Methods and Materials, Article 300 General Requirements for Wiring Methods and Materials. 300.5 Underground Installations. 300.5(D) Protection from Damage. 300.5(D)(3) Service Conductors.

26. Direct-buried conductors or cables shall be _____ to be spliced or tapped without the use of splice boxes.

    A. labeled

    B. not allowed

    C. permitted

    D. none of the above

    Reference: 2017 National Electrical Code – Chapter 3 Wiring Methods and Materials, Article 300 General Requirements for Wiring Methods and Materials. 300.5 Underground Installations. 300.5(E) Splices and Taps.

27. When cables or conductors are direct buried, they are allowed to be spliced or tapped:

    A. and tapped with a minimum of ½" of friction tape

    B. only with the use of splice boxes

    C. only with the use of waterproof splice boxes

    D. without the use of splice boxes

    Reference: 2017 National Electrical Code – Chapter 3 Wiring Methods and Materials, Article 300 General Requirements for Wiring Methods and Materials. 300.5 Underground Installations. 300.5(E) Splices and Taps.

EXAM 7

Chapter 3 Wiring Methods and Materials

28. What does the NEC require when extending to a new service location by splicing existing underground service conductors?

    A. conductors protected with at least two (2) in. of concrete

    B. the use of splice boxes

    C. either A or B

    D. neither A nor B

    Reference: 2017 National Electrical Code – Chapter 3 Wiring Methods and Materials, Article 300 General Requirements for Wiring Methods and Materials. 300.5 Underground Installations. 300.5(E) Splices and Taps.

29. When conduits or raceways may have moisture contacting live parts, they must be:

    A. EMT, RMC, or RNC

    B. RMC

    C. RMC or RNC

    D. sealed or plugged at either or both ends

    Reference: 2017 National Electrical Code – Chapter 3 Wiring Methods and Materials, Article 300 General Requirements for Wiring Methods and Materials. 300.5 Underground Installations. 300.5(G) Raceway Seals.

30. What is the minimum required thickness of concrete encasing for raceways approved for burial only?

    A. 2 inches

    B. 4 inches

    C. 6 inches

    D. 8 inches

    Reference: 2017 National Electrical Code – Chapter 3 Wiring Methods and Materials, Article 300 General Requirements for Wiring Methods and Materials. 300.5 Underground Installation.

Chapter 3 Wiring Methods and Materials

EXAM 7

Chapter 3 Wiring Methods and Materials

31. Auxiliary gutters, cable armor, boxes, cable sheathing, cable trays, cablebus, cabinets, couplings, elbows, fittings, supports, and support hardware must be of materials suitable for the _____ they are to be installed in, to prevent corrosion.

    A. environment

    B. humidity

    C. location

    D. position

    Reference: 2017 National Electrical Code – Chapter 3 Wiring Methods and Materials, Article 300 General Requirements for Wiring Methods and Materials. 300.6 Protection Against Corrosion and Deterioration.

32. Of the following, which requires the use of approved electrically conductive corrosion resistance compound on metal conduit threads?

    A. In Class I Division 1 locations

    B. In Class II Division 1 locations

    C. On field cut threads for indoor locations

    D. On field cut threads in corrosive locations

    Reference: 2017 National Electrical Code – Chapter 3 Wiring Methods and Materials, Article 300 General Requirements for Wiring Methods and Materials. 300.6 Protection Against Corrosion and Deterioration. 300.6(A) Ferrous Metal Equipment.

33. How much space is required between the wall and exposed metallic conduit or metallic panelboard in indoor areas such as canneries, dairy processing facilities or laundries where walls are frequently washed?

    A. 1/8 in.

    B. 1/4 in.

    C. 1/2 in.

    D. 3/4 in.

    Reference: 2017 National Electrical Code – Chapter 3 Wiring Methods and Materials, Article 300 General Requirements for Wiring Methods and Materials. 300.6 Protection Against Corrosion and Deterioration. 300.6(D) Indoor Wet Locations.

EXAM 7

Chapter 3 Wiring Methods and Materials

34. As a method to _____ for thermal expansion and contraction, raceways must have expansion fittings where necessary.

    A. capacitance

    B. compensate

    C. provide enhancement

    D. provide restriction

    Reference: 2017 National Electrical Code – Chapter 3 Wiring Methods and Materials, Article 300 General Requirements for Wiring Methods and Materials. 300.7 Raceways Exposed to Different Temperatures. 300.7(B) Expansion, Expansion-Deflection, and Deflection.

35. If a raceway is installed outdoors, above grade, and exposed to the elements, what kind of location is the interior considered?

    A. Damp

    B. Dry

    C. Moist

    D. Wet

    Reference: 2017 National Electrical Code – Chapter 3 Wiring Methods and Materials, Article 300 General Requirements for Wiring Methods and Materials. 300.9 Raceways in Wet Locations Abovegrade.

36. Cables and raceways shall not be _____ ceiling grids.

    A. secured to

    B. supported by

    C. suspended from

    D. none of the above

    Reference: 2017 National Electrical Code – Chapter 3 Wiring Methods and Materials, Article 300 General Requirements for Wiring Methods and Materials. 300.11 Securing and Supporting. 300.11(A) Secured in Place.

EXAM 7

Chapter 3 Wiring Methods and Materials

37. Support wires that do not provide secure support may not be _____ for boxes, cabinets, cable assemblies, fittings and raceways since they must be fastened securely in place.

    A. may be counted as part of the structural system of fastening

    B. copper or aluminum

    C. permitted

    D. permitted as the sole support

    Reference: 2017 National Electrical Code – Chapter 3 Wiring Methods and Materials, Article 300 General Requirements for Wiring Methods and Materials. 300.11 Securing and Supporting. 300.11(A) Secured in Place.

38. When wiring is located inside the cavity of a fire-rated floor-ceiling or roof-ceiling assembly, it may not be supported by or secured to:

    A. cantilevered floor joists

    B. joists, beams, or columns

    C. metal cross members

    D. the ceiling assembly, including the ceiling support wires

    Reference: 2017 National Electrical Code – Chapter 3 Wiring Methods and Materials, Article 300 General Requirements for Wiring Methods and Materials. 300.11 Securing and Supporting. 300.11(A) Secured in Place. 300.11(A)(1) Fire-Rated Assemblies.

39. Wiring located inside the cavity of a fire-rated floor-ceiling or roof-ceiling assembly may be supported by or secured to an independent means of secure support. If wires for independent support are used, they must be: (Exceptions ignored.)

    A. somehow separated from fire-rated design

    B. distinguishable by twists in the bottom 12" of wire

    C. galvanized steel No. 10 or larger

    D. steel, copper, brass or aluminum

    Reference: 2017 National Electrical Code – Chapter 3 Wiring Methods and Materials, Article 300 General Requirements for Wiring Methods and Materials. 300.11 Securing and Supporting. 300.11(A) Secured in Place. 300.11(A)(1) Fire-Rated Assemblies.

EXAM 7

Chapter 3 Wiring Methods and Materials

40. Between, boxes, cabinets, fittings, or other enclosures or outlets, metal or nonmetallic raceways, cable armors, and cable sheaths must be:

    A. anchored
    B. continuous
    C. horizontal
    D. supported

    Reference: 2017 National Electrical Code – Chapter 3 Wiring Methods and Materials, Article 300 General Requirements for Wiring Methods and Materials. 300.12 Mechanical Continuity - Raceways and Cables.

41. In raceways, between boxes, devices, outlets, and so forth, conductors must be _____. Special exceptions ignored.

    A. continuous
    B. in sections
    C. installed
    D. pulled

    Reference: 2017 National Electrical Code – Chapter 3 Wiring Methods and Materials, Article 300 General Requirements for Wiring Methods and Materials. 300.13 Mechanical and Electrical Continuity - Conductors. 300.13(A) General.

42. In multiwire branch circuits, the continuity of a _____ conductor shall not depend on device connections such as lampholders, receptacles, and so forth.

    A. bare
    B. grounded
    C. insulated
    D. ungrounded

    Reference: 2017 National Electrical Code – Chapter 3 Wiring Methods and Materials, Article 300 General Requirements for Wiring Methods and Materials. 300.13 Mechanical and Electrical Continuity - Conductors. 300.13(B) Device Removal.

43. At least _____ inches of free conductor shall be left at each outlet, junction, and switch point for splices or the connections of luminaries (fixtures) or devices.

    A. 2
    B. 6
    C. 9
    D. 12

    Reference: 2017 National Electrical Code – Chapter 3 Wiring Methods and Materials, Article 300 General Requirements for Wiring Methods and Materials. 300.14 Length of Free Conductors at Outlets, Junctions, and Switch Points.

EXAM 7

Chapter 3 Wiring Methods and Materials

44. _____ in or more of free conductor, as measured from the point where it emerges from its cable sheath or raceway in the box, must be left at each junction, outlet, and switch point for splices or for connection of fixtures (such as luminaries) or devices. Exception ignored.

   A. 3   C. 6

   B. 4   D. 8

   Reference: 2017 National Electrical Code – Chapter 3 Wiring Methods and Materials, Article 300 General Requirements for Wiring Methods and Materials. 300.14 Length of Free Conductors at Outlets, Junctions, and Switch Points.

45. When the opening to a junction, outlet, or switch point is under _____ in. in any dimension, every conductor must have enough length to extend _____ in or more outside the opening. Exception ignored.

   A. 4, 3   C. 6, 6

   B. 6, 4   D. 8, 3

   Reference: 2017 National Electrical Code – Chapter 3 Wiring Methods and Materials, Article 300 General Requirements for Wiring Methods and Materials. 300.14 Length of Free Conductors at Outlets, Junctions, and Switch Points.

46. For the purpose of splicing conductors or connecting luminaires or devices, when the opening to a lighting outlet box or device box is under 8 inches in any dimension, what is the minimum distance that each conductor must be long enough to extend outside the opening of the box?

   A. 3 inches   C. 6 inches

   B. 4 inches   D. 8 inches

   Reference: 2017 National Electrical Code – Chapter 3 Wiring Methods and Materials, Article 300 General Requirements for Wiring Methods and Materials. 300.14 Length of Free Conductors at Outlets, Junctions, and Switch Points.

EXAM 7

Chapter 3 Wiring Methods and Materials

47. If a luminaire (fixture) is being used as a _____, a box or conduit body is not required.

    A. grounding point

    B. junction box

    C. raceway

    D. service panel

    Reference: 2017 National Electrical Code – Chapter 3 Wiring Methods and Materials, Article 300 General Requirements for Wiring Methods and Materials. 300.15 Boxes, Conduit Bodies, or Fittings - Where Required. 300.15(J) Luminaires.

48. A terminal or metal box fitting with separately bushed holes for each conductor is required when changing from conduit to:

    A. knob-and-tube wiring

    B. nonmetallic sheathed cable (NM)

    C. type AC cable

    D. type MC cable

    Reference: 2017 National Electrical Code – Chapter 3 Wiring Methods and Materials, Article 300 General Requirements for Wiring Methods and Materials. 300.16 Raceway or Cable to Open or Concealed Wiring. 300.16(A) Box, Conduit Body, or Fitting.

49. The number and size of conductors in any raceway shall not be more than will permit dissipation of the _____ and ready installation or withdrawal of the conductors without damage to the conductors or to their insulation.

    A. charge

    B. current

    C. heat

    D. none of the above

    Reference: 2017 National Electrical Code – Chapter 3 Wiring Methods and Materials, Article 300 General Requirements for Wiring Methods and Materials. 300.17 Number and Size of Conductors in Raceway.

EXAM 7

Chapter 3 Wiring Methods and Materials

50. Conductors that carry alternating current and are installed in ferrous metal enclosures or raceways may be arranged to avoid heating the surrounding metal by induction by: (Exceptions ignored.)

    A. coiling like phase conductors.

    B. grouping all phase conductors together.

    C. installing conductor spacers.

    D. none of the above.

    Reference: 2017 National Electrical Code – Chapter 3 Wiring Methods and Materials, Article 300 General Requirements for Wiring Methods and Materials. 300.20 Induced Currents in Ferrous Metal Enclosures or Ferrous Metal Raceways. 300.20(A) Conductors Grouped Together.

51. What is being reduced when all phase conductors of the same circuit are required to be in the same ferrous metal raceway?

    A. Expense

    B. Inductive heat

    C. Resistance

    D. Voltage drop

    Reference: 2017 National Electrical Code – Chapter 3 Wiring Methods and Materials, Article 300 General Requirements for Wiring Methods and Materials. 300.20 Induced Currents in Ferrous Metal Enclosures or Ferrous Metal Raceways. 300.20(A) Conductors Grouped Together.

52. The NEC requires that all ungrounded and grounded conductors of a common circuit be grouped together in the same ferrous metal raceway to reduce:

    A. expense

    B. inductive heat

    C. resistance

    D. voltage drop

    Reference: 2017 National Electrical Code – Chapter 3 Wiring Methods and Materials, Article 300 General Requirements for Wiring Methods and Materials. 300.20 Induced Currents in Ferrous Metal Enclosures or Ferrous Metal Raceways. 300.20(A) Conductors Grouped Together.

EXAM 7

Chapter 3 Wiring Methods and Materials

53. When electrical installations are in hollow spaces, ventilation or air-handling ducts and vertical shafts, they must be made so the chance of spread of fire or other products of combustion will not be substantially increased. Openings around electrical penetrations through or into fire-resistant-rated ceilings, floors, partitions, or walls must be _____ with approved methods to maintain the existing fire-resistance rating.

    A. blocked

    B. caulked or taped

    C. firestopped

    D. sealed

    Reference: 2017 National Electrical Code – Chapter 3 Wiring Methods and Materials, Article 300 General Requirements for Wiring Methods and Materials. 300.21 Spread of Fire or Products of Combustion.

54. When electrical wiring and equipment are installed and used in ducts, plenums, and other air-handing spaces, _____ may be installed in ducts or shafts only containing such ducts used for ventilation of commercial-type cooking equipment or for vapor removal.

    A. no flexible type conduit

    B. no wiring systems of any type

    C. only rigid metallic conduit

    D. none of the above

    Reference: 2017 National Electrical Code – Chapter 3 Wiring Methods and Materials, Article 300 General Requirements for Wiring Methods and Materials. 300.22 Wiring in Ducts Not Used for Air Handling, Fabricated Ducts for Environmental Air, and Other Spaces for Environmental Air (Plenums). 300.22(A) Ducts for Dust, Loose Stock, or Vapor Removal.

55. All boxes, fittings, and similar enclosures must have _____ covers installed to prevent either physical damage to parts or insulation, or accidental contact with energized parts.

    A. Metal

    B. Metal or Plastic

    C. Protective

    D. Suitable

    Reference: 2017 National Electrical Code – Chapter 3 Wiring Methods and Materials, Article 300 General Requirements for Wiring Methods and Materials. 300.31 Covers Required.

EXAM 7

Chapter 3 Wiring Methods and Materials

56. For multiconductor or multiplexed single conductor cables having individually shielded conductors, the minimum bending radius is _____ times the diameter of the individually shielded conductors or 7 times the overall diameter, whichever is greater.

    A. 3

    B. 6

    C. 9

    D. 12

    Reference: 2017 National Electrical Code – Chapter 3 Wiring Methods and Materials, Article 300 General Requirements for Wiring Methods and Materials. 300.34 Conductor Bending Radius.

57. Conductors for nonshielded conductors of over 1000 volts, should not be bent to a radius of less than _____ times the overall diameter of the conductor.

    A. six

    B. eight

    C. ten

    D. twelve

    Reference: 2017 National Electrical Code – Chapter 3 Wiring Methods and Materials, Article 300 General Requirements for Wiring Methods and Materials. 300.34 Conductor Bending Radius.

58. Raceways installed in solid rock shall be permitted to be buried at lesser depths than required where covered by _____ inches of concrete, which shall be permitted to extend to the rock surface.

    A. 2

    B. 4

    C. 6

    D. 12

    Reference: 2017 National Electrical Code – Chapter 3 Wiring Methods and Materials, Article 300 General Requirements for Wiring Methods and Materials. 300.50 Underground Installations.

59. Electrical conduits, or other raceways round in cross section, that are suitable for use underground or embedded in concrete.

    A. Capacitors

    B. Conductors

    C. Electrical Ducts

    D. Grounded Conductors

    Reference: 2017 National Electrical Code – Chapter 3 Wiring Methods and Materials, Article 310 Conductors for General Wiring. 310.2 Definitions.

EXAM 7

Chapter 3 Wiring Methods and Materials

60. Aluminum, copper-clad aluminum, or copper conductors, for each phase, polarity, neutral, or grounded circuit shall be permitted to be connected in parallel only in sizes _____ AWG and larger.

   A. 1/0

   B. 2/0

   C. 3/0

   D. 4/0

   Reference: 2017 National Electrical Code – Chapter 3 Wiring Methods and Materials, Article 310 Conductors for General Wiring. 310.10 Uses Permitted. 310.10(H) Conductors in Parallel. 310.10(H)(1) General.

61. Conductors of size 1/0 AWG and larger, made of aluminum, copper, or copper-clad aluminum, comprising each phase, polarity, neutral, or grounded circuit conductor, are allowed to be connected in _____ (electrically joined at both ends). Exceptions ignored.

   A. delta

   B. parallel

   C. series

   D. wye

   Reference: 2017 National Electrical Code – Chapter 3 Wiring Methods and Materials, Article 310 Conductors for General Wiring. 310.10 Uses Permitted. 310.10(H) Conductors in Parallel. 310.10(H)(1) General.

62. Which of the following are required for current-carrying conductors installed in parallel?

   A. be the same size in circular mil area

   B. have the same insulation type

   C. both A and B

   D. neither A nor B

   Reference: 2017 National Electrical Code – Chapter 3 Wiring Methods and Materials, Article 310 Conductors for General Wiring. 310.10 Uses Permitted. 310.10(H) Conductors in Parallel. 310.10(H)(4)

EXAM 7

Chapter 3 Wiring Methods and Materials

63. Where more than one ampacity applies for a given circuit length, the _____ value shall be used.

    A. average

    B. highest

    C. longest used

    D. lowest

    Reference: 2017 National Electrical Code – Chapter 3 Wiring Methods and Materials, Article 310 Conductors for General Wiring. 310.15 Ampacities for Conductors Rated 0-2000 Volts. 310.15(A) General. . 310.15(A)(2) Selection of Ampacity

64. The adjustment factor percentage for over three current-carrying conductors in a cable or raceway, if there are 21 current-carrying conductors in a 2 inch EMT is:

    A. 35

    B. 40

    C. 45

    D. 70

    Reference: 2017 National Electrical Code – Chapter 3 Wiring Methods and Materials, Article 310 Conductors for General Wiring. 310.15 Ampacities for Conductors Rated 0-2000 Volts. 310.15(B) Tables.

65. The maximum allowable ampacity of No. 12 copper conductors of type THHN 167°F rated insulation, with 27 current-carrying conductors in the same raceway, installed in an ambient temperature of 30°C is:

    A. 11.25

    B. 15

    C. 18.75

    D. 25

    Reference: 2017 National Electrical Code – Chapter 3 Wiring Methods and Materials, Article 310 Conductors for General Wiring. 310.15 Ampacities for Conductors Rated 0-2000 Volts. 310.15(B) Tables.

66. The maximum allowable ampacity for No. 2/0 copper conductors of type THHN, 167°F rated insulation, with 2 current-carrying conductors in the cable, installed in an ambient temperature of 30°C is:

    A. 115

    B. 135

    C. 150

    D. 195

    Reference: 2017 National Electrical Code – Chapter 3 Wiring Methods and Materials, Article 310 Conductors for General Wiring. 310.15 Ampacities for Conductors Rated 0-2000 Volts. 310.15(B) Tables.

EXAM 7

Chapter 3 Wiring Methods and Materials

67. For No. 6 aluminum conductors of type THHN, 194°F rated insulation, with 3 current-carrying conductors in the cable, installed in an ambient temperature of 30°C, what is the maximum allowable ampacity?

    A. 50   C. 60

    B. 55   D. 75

    Reference: 2017 National Electrical Code – Chapter 3 Wiring Methods and Materials, Article 310 Conductors for General Wiring. 310.15 Ampacities for Conductors Rated 0-2000 Volts. 310.15(B) Tables.

68. What is the maximum service feeder rating, in amperes, for No. 4 copper service conductors in a service installation for a dwelling?

    A. 100   C. 200

    B. 125   D. 225

    Reference: 2017 National Electrical Code – Chapter 3 Wiring Methods and Materials, Article 310 Conductors for General Wiring. 310.15 Ampacities for Conductors Rated 0-2000 Volts. 310.15(B) Tables.

69. The maximum allowable ampacity for No. 6 aluminum conductors of type THHN, 194°F rated insulation, installed in an ambient temperature of 30°C is:

    A. 55   C. 60.0

    B. 58.2   D. 70

    Reference: 2017 National Electrical Code – Chapter 3 Wiring Methods and Materials, Article 310 Conductors for General Wiring. 310.15 Ampacities for Conductors Rated 0-2000 Volts. 310.15(B) Tables.

EXAM 7

Chapter 3 Wiring Methods and Materials

70. When determining the allowable ampacity of a copper conductor with THWN insulation, installed in a raceway in an area where the ambient temperature reaches 100°F, what is the temperature correction factor that must be applied to the ampacity values given in table 310.15(B)(16) on page 70-158 of the NEC?

    A. 0.75

    B. 0.82

    C. 0.88

    D. 0.94

    Reference: 2017 National Electrical Code – Chapter 3 Wiring Methods and Materials, Article 310 Conductors for General Wiring. 310.15 Ampacities for Conductors Rated 0-2000 Volts. 310.15(B) Tables. 310.15(B)(2) Ambient Temperature Correction Factors.

71. Where the number of current-carrying conductors in a raceway or cable exceeds three (3) the allowable ampacity of each conductor shall be _____.

    A. increased

    B. kept the same

    C. reduced

    D. none of the above

    Reference: 2017 National Electrical Code – Chapter 3 Wiring Methods and Materials, Article 310 Conductors for General Wiring. 310.15 Ampacities for Conductors Rated 0-2000 Volts. 310.15(B) Tables. 310.15(B)(3) Adjustment Factors.

72. The adjustment factor percentage for over three current-carrying conductors in a cable or raceway if there are 4 current-carrying conductors in a 3/4 inch EMT is:

    A. 45

    B. 50

    C. 70

    D. 80

    Reference: 2017 National Electrical Code – Chapter 3 Wiring Methods and Materials, Article 310 Conductors for General Wiring. 310.15 Ampacities for Conductors Rated 0-2000 Volts. 310.15(B) Tables. 310.15(B)(3) Adjustment Factors.

EXAM 7

Chapter 3 Wiring Methods and Materials

73. When the quantity of current-carrying conductors in a cable or raceway is more than _____, or when multiconductor cables or single conductors are installed without preserving spacing for a length of _____ in. or more and are not installed in raceways, the maximum ampacity allowed for each conductor is lowered by a derating adjustment factor. Exceptions ignored.

    A. three, 24

    B. six, 48

    C. twelve, 24

    D. fifteen, 48

    Reference: 2017 National Electrical Code – Chapter 3 Wiring Methods and Materials, Article 310 Conductors for General Wiring. 310.15 Ampacities for Conductors Rated 0-2000 Volts. 310.15(B) Tables. 310.15(B)(3) Adjustment Factors.

74. Where 10-20 current-carrying conductors are installed in the same raceway the ampacity of each conductor shall be reduced _____ percent.

    A. 20

    B. 30

    C. 40

    D. 50

    Reference: 2017 National Electrical Code – Chapter 3 Wiring Methods and Materials, Article 310 Conductors for General Wiring. 310.15 Ampacities for Conductors Rated 0-2000 Volts. 310.15(B) Tables. 310.15(B)(3) Adjustment Factors

75. The allowable ampacity of each conductor in a bundle of Type NM cables bundled together for a length of _____ or more must be reduced as shown in Table 310.15(B)(3)(a) on page 70-160.

    A. 12 inches

    B. 18 inches

    C. 24 inches

    D. 30 inches

    Reference: 2017 National Electrical Code – Chapter 3 Wiring Methods and Materials, Article 310 Conductors for General Wiring. 310.15 Ampacities for Conductors Rated 0-2000 Volts. 310.15(B) Tables. 310.15(B)(3) Adjustment Factors. 310.15(B)(3)(a) More Than Three Current-Carrying Conductors.

Chapter 3 Wiring Methods and Materials

EXAM 7

Chapter 3 Wiring Methods and Materials

76. When a conduit or tubing having a length of more than 24 inches contains four (4) current-carrying conductors, an adjustment factor of _____ must be applied to the conductor ampacity values given in Table 310.15(B)(16) on page 70-161.

    A. 70%
    B. 75%
    C. 80%
    D. 90%

    Reference: 2017 National Electrical Code – Chapter 3 Wiring Methods and Materials, Article 310 Conductors for General Wiring. 310.15 Ampacities for Conductors Rated 0-2000 Volts. 310.15(B) Tables. 310.15(B)(3) Adjustment Factors.

77. For four (4) size 1/0 AWG THW copper current-carrying conductors installed in a common raceway, with an ambient temperature of 86°F, what is the maximum allowable current-carrying capacity?

    A. 105 amperes
    B. 112 amperes
    C. 120 amperes
    D. 150 amperes

    Reference: 2017 National Electrical Code – Chapter 3 Wiring Methods and Materials

78. What is the maximum distance above a rooftop for cables or conductors installed in conduits exposed to direct sunlight, according to Table 310.15(B)(2)(a)?

    A. 6 inches
    B. 12 inches
    C. 24 inches
    D. 36 inches

    Reference: 2017 National Electrical Code – Chapter 3 Wiring Methods and Materials. 310.15 Ampacities for Conductors Rated 0-2000 Volts. 310.15(B) Tables. 310.15(B)(3) Adjustment Factors. 310.15(B)(3)(c) Raceways and Cables Exposed to Sunlight on Rooftops.

EXAM 7

Chapter 3 Wiring Methods and Materials

79. What is the temperature value that should be added to expected outdoor ambient temperature for the allowable ampacity of conductors where the cables or conductors are installed in conduits exposed to direct sunlight, according to Table 310.15(B)(2)(a)?

    A. 25°F

    B. 30°F

    C. 40°F

    D. 60°F

    Reference: 2017 National Electrical Code – Chapter 3 Wiring Methods and Materials. 310.15 Ampacities for Conductors Rated 0-2000 Volts. 310.15(B) Tables. 310.15(B)(3) Adjustment Factors. 310.15(B)(3)(c) Raceways and Cables Exposed to Sunlight on Rooftops.

80. What is the maximum service feeder rating in amperes for 4/0 aluminum service conductors in a service installation for a dwelling?

    A. 150

    B. 175

    C. 200

    D. 225

    Reference: 2017 National Electrical Code – Chapter 3 Wiring Methods and Materials, Article 310 Conductors for General Wiring. 310.15 Ampacities for Conductors Rated 0-2000 Volts. 310.15(B) Tables. 310.15(B)(6) Grounding or Bonding Conductor.

81. For ungrounded service-entrance conductors for a 150 ampere, 120/240-volt, single-phase residential service, what is the minimum size copper SW cable with type THHW insulation?

    A. 1/0 AWG

    B. 1 AWG

    C. 2 AWG

    D. 3 AWG

    Reference: 2017 National Electrical Code – Chapter 3 Wiring Methods and Materials. 310.15 Ampacities for Conductors Rated 0-2000 Volts. 310.15(B) Tables. 310.15(B)(7) 1201240-Volt, Single-Phase Dwelling Services and Feeders.

EXAM 7

Chapter 3 Wiring Methods and Materials

82. What is the minimum size for copper conductors supplying a 7-1/2 hp, 240-volt, single-phase, induction type, ac motor used in a continuous duty application, with a temperature rating of 75°C, according to the NEC?

    A. 4 AWG

    B. 6 AWG

    C. 8 AWG

    D. 10 AWG

    Reference: 2017 National Electrical Code – Chapter 3 Wiring Methods and Materials. 310.15 Ampacities for Conductors Rated 0-2000 Volts. 310.15(B) Tables.

83. For a 200 ampere rated commercial service, what is the minimum size 75°C copper ungrounded (phase) service entrance conductor allowed?

    A. 2/0 THW

    B. 3/0 THHN

    C. 3/0 THW

    D. 4/0 THW

    Reference: 2017 National Electrical Code – Chapter 3 Wiring Methods and Materials, Article 310 Conductors for General Wiring. 310.15 Ampacities for Conductors Rated 0-2000 Volts. 310.15(B) Tables.

84. Given the following information, what is the conductor ampacity?

    A. 178.2 amperes

    B. 199.5 amperes

    C. 294.6 amperes

    D. 380.0 amperes

    Reference: 2017 National Electrical Code – Chapter 3 Wiring Methods and Materials

85. What is the maximum allowable ampacity for a size 8 AWG single copper conductor with type FEPB insulation, installed in free air, when ambient temperature is not a factor?

    A. 45 amperes

    B. 55 amperes

    C. 80 amperes

    D. 83 amperes

    Reference: 2017 National Electrical Code – Chapter 3 Wiring Methods and Materials, Article 310 Conductors for General Wiring. 310.15 Ampacities for Conductors Rated 0-2000 Volts. 310.15(B) Tables.

EXAM 7

Chapter 3 Wiring Methods and Materials

86. What is the allowable ampacity rating of each conductor when twenty (20) size 10 AWG copper current-carrying conductors with THHN insulation are installed in a 50 ft. run of trade size 1-1/2 in. electrical metallic tubing (EMT)?

    A. 15 amperes

    B. 20 amperes

    C. 25 amperes

    D. 30 amperes

    Reference: 2017 National Electrical Code – Chapter 3 Wiring Methods and Materials, Article 310 Conductors for General Wiring. 310.15 Ampacities for Conductors Rated 0-2000 Volts. 310.15(B) Tables.

87. The minimum required size 75°C rated copper conductors for a demand load of 200 amperes when installed in an area with an expected ambient temperature of 120°F is:

    A. 250 kcmil

    B. 300 kcmil

    C. 3/0 AWG

    D. 4/0 AWG

    Reference: 2017 National Electrical Code – Chapter 3 Wiring Methods and Materials, Article 310 Conductors for General Wiring. 310.15 Ampacities for Conductors Rated 0-2000 Volts. 310.15(B) Tables.

88. For an insulated single copper conductor in air, in an ambient temperature of 40°C, with a conductor temperature of 90°C, conductor size No. 4 and voltage 2500 volts, what is the maximum ampere rating?

    A. 100

    B. 110

    C. 115

    D. 145

    Reference: 2017 National Electrical Code – Chapter 3 Wiring Methods and Materials, Article 310 Conductors for General Wiring. 310.60 Conductors Rated 2001 to 35,000 Volts. 310.60(C) Engineering Supervision.

Chapter 3 Wiring Methods and Materials

EXAM 7

Chapter 3 Wiring Methods and Materials

89. What is the characteristic trade name of XHHN insulation?

    A. Extended polytetra-fluoro-ethylene

    B. Modified ethylene tetrafluoro-ethylene

    C. Moisture-resistant thermoset

    D. Thermoset

    Reference: 2017 National Electrical Code – Chapter 3 Wiring Methods and Materials, Article 310 Conductors for General Wiring. 310.104 Conductor Constructions and Applications.

90. What is the typical outer covering for paper insulated conductors?

    A. Copper or alloy steel

    B. Glass braid

    C. Lead sheath

    D. None

    Reference: 2017 National Electrical Code – Chapter 3 Wiring Methods and Materials, Article 310 Conductors for General Wiring. 310.104 Conductor Constructions and Applications.

91. What is the characteristic trade name of THHN insulation?

    A. Heat-resistant thermoplastic

    B. Moisture- and heat-resistant thermoplastic

    C. Moisture, heat, and oil resistant thermoplastic

    D. Moisture-resistant thermoplastic

    Reference: 2017 National Electrical Code – Chapter 3 Wiring Methods and Materials, Article 310 Conductors for General Wiring. 310.104 Conductor Constructions and Applications.

EXAM 7

Chapter 3 Wiring Methods and Materials

92. What does the -2 represent on a conductor with the marking RHW-2 on the insulation?

   A. The cable has 2 conductors.

   B. The cable is double insulated.

   C. The conductor has a maximum operating temperature of 90°C.

   D. The conductor has a nylon outer jacket.

   Reference: 2017 National Electrical Code – Chapter 3 Wiring Methods and Materials, Article 310 Conductors for General Wiring. 310.104 Conductor Constructions and Applications.

93. What is the temperature rating of a conductor with THHN marked on the insulation?

   A. 75 °F

   B. 75 °C

   C. 90 °F

   D. 90 °C

   Reference: 2017 National Electrical Code – Chapter 3 Wiring Methods and Materials, Article 310 Conductors for General Wiring. 310.104 Conductor Constructions and Applications.

94. What would the maximum allowable ampacity be of a 3-conductor size 6 AWG XHHW aluminum SER cable, installed in the attic of a one-family dwelling where the ambient temperature is 44°C?

   A. 41.2 amperes

   B. 47.9 amperes

   C. 52.2 amperes

   D. 56.2 amperes

   Reference: 2017 National Electrical Code – Chapter 3 Wiring Methods and Materials, Article 310 Conductors for General Wiring. 310.15 Ampacities for Conductors Rated 0-2000 Volts. 310.15(B) Tables. 310.15(B)(2) Ambient Temperature Correction Factors.

EXAM 7

Chapter 3 Wiring Methods and Materials

95. Where may Type XHHW insulated conductors be used?

    A. dry locations only

    B. dry or damp locations only

    C. dry, damp, or wet locations

    D. wet locations only

    Reference: 2017 National Electrical Code – Chapter 3 Wiring Methods and Materials, Article 310 Conductors for General Wiring. 310.10 Uses Permitted. 310.10(C)2 Wet Locations.

96. Which insulation gives conductors a greater ampacity when used in a dry location rather than a wet location?

    A. RHW

    B. THHW

    C. THW

    D. THWN

    Reference: 2017 National Electrical Code – Chapter 3 Wiring Methods and Materials, Article 310 Conductors for General Wiring

97. In an existing raceway, what is the largest size insulated solid conductor that the NEC allows to be pulled?

    A. 4 AWG

    B. 6 AWG

    C. 8 AWG

    D. 10 AWG

    Reference: 2017 National Electrical Code – Chapter 3 Wiring Methods and Materials, Article 310 Conductors for General Wiring. 310.106 Conductors. 310.106(C) Stranded Conductors.

98. Durable marking is required on Type NM cables, and the circular mil area or AWG size must be repeated at intervals of _____ in. or less, and all other markings must be repeated at intervals of _____ in. or less.

    A. 12, 24

    B. 18, 48

    C. 24, 40

    D. 40, 24

    Reference: 2017 National Electrical Code – Chapter 3 Wiring Methods and Materials, Article 310 Conductors for General Wiring. 310.120 Marking. 310.120(B) Method of Marking. 310.120(B)(1) Surface Marking.

EXAM 7

Chapter 3 Wiring Methods and Materials

99. What is the minimum allowed air space between metallic surface type cabinets for electrical equipment and the wall or other supporting surface, in a damp or wet location?

   A. ⅛ inch

   B. ¼ inch

   C. ⅜ inch

   D. ½ inch

   Reference: 2017 National Electrical Code – Chapter 3 Wiring Methods and Materials, Article 312 Cabinets, Cutout Boxes, and Meter Socket Enclosures. 312.2 Damp and Wet Locations.

100. When walls are constructed of a combustible material like wood, cabinets must be flush with the finished surface or:

   A. placed on a metal plate

   B. project therefrom

   C. recessed not more than ¼ inch

   D. set off of the surface ¼ inch

   Reference: 2017 National Electrical Code – Chapter 3 Wiring Methods and Materials, Article 312 Cabinets, Cutout Boxes, and Meter Socket Enclosures. 312.3 Position in Wall.

101. When walls are constructed of noncombustible material, such as concrete or tile, cabinets must be installed so that the cabinet's front edge is _____ in from the finished surface or less.

   A. ⅛

   B. ¼

   C. ⅜

   D. ½

   Reference: 2017 National Electrical Code – Chapter 3 Wiring Methods and Materials, Article 312 Cabinets, Cutout Boxes, and Meter Socket Enclosures. 312.3 Position in Wall.

Chapter 3 Wiring Methods and Materials

EXAM 7

Chapter 3 Wiring Methods and Materials

102. When noncombustible surfaces are incomplete or broken, they must be repaired so that any gaps or open spaces are _____ in. or less at the edge of the cabinet or cutout box with a flush-type cover.

    A. 1/16   C. 3/16

    B. 1/8   D. 1/4

    Reference: 2017 National Electrical Code – Chapter 3 Wiring Methods and Materials, Article 312 Cabinets, Cutout Boxes, and Meter Socket Enclosures. 312.4 Repairing Noncombustible Surfaces.

103. Openings in a box where conductors enter must be:

    A. adequately closed   C. open for ventilation

    B. clamped shut   D. sealed

    Reference: 2017 National Electrical Code – Chapter 3 Wiring Methods and Materials, Article 312 Cabinets, Cutout Boxes, and Meter Socket Enclosures. 312.5 Cabinets, Cutout Boxes, and Meter Socket Enclosures. 312.5(A) Openings to Be Closed.

104. Each cable must be _____ to the cutout box, cabinet, or meter socket enclosure, where cable is used. Exceptions ignored.

    A. affixed   C. clamped

    B. bonded   D. secured

    Reference: 2017 National Electrical Code – Chapter 3 Wiring Methods and Materials, Article 312 Cabinets, Cutout Boxes, and Meter Socket Enclosures. 312.5 Cabinets, Cutout Boxes, and Meter Socket Enclosures. 312.5(C) Cables.

105. At a terminal, what is the minimum bending space required, when there are 3 wires per terminal?

    A. 5.5 inches   C. 9 inches

    B. 8.5 inches   D. 10 inches

    Reference: 2017 National Electrical Code – Chapter 3 Wiring Methods and Materials, Article 312 Cabinets, Cutout Boxes, and Meter Socket Enclosures. 312.6 Deflection of Conductors. 312.6(B) Wire-Bending Space at Terminals.

EXAM 7

Chapter 3 Wiring Methods and Materials

106. Sufficient space to accommodate all conductors installed must be available inside a cabinet or cutout box, without:

    A. bending

    B. crowding

    C. kinking

    D. trimming

    Reference: 2017 National Electrical Code – Chapter 3 Wiring Methods and Materials, Article 312 Cabinets, Cutout Boxes, and Meter Socket Enclosures. 312.7 Space in Enclosures.

107. Conductors in enclosures for switches or overcurrent devices shall not fill the wiring space at any cross section to more than _____ percent of the cross-sectional area of the space.

    A. 20

    B. 40

    C. 60

    D. 80

    Reference: 2017 National Electrical Code – Chapter 3 Wiring Methods and Materials, Article 312 Cabinets, Cutout Boxes, and Meter Socket Enclosures. 312.8 Switch and Overcurrent Device Enclosures.

108. _____ boxes shall not be used where conduits or connectors requiring the use of locknuts or bushings are to be connected to the side of the box.

    A. Flat

    B. Octagonal

    C. Round

    D. Square

    Reference: 2017 National Electrical Code – Chapter 3 Wiring Methods and Materials, Article 314 Outlet, Device, Pull, and Junction Boxes; Conduit Bodies; Fittings; and Handhole Enclosures. 314.2 Round Boxes

109. _____ may not be used where conduits or connectors that need bushings or locknuts are going to be attached to the sides of the box.

    A. Handy boxes

    B. Octagon boxes

    C. Round boxes

    D. Square boxes

    Reference: 2017 National Electrical Code – Chapter 3 Wiring Methods and Materials, Article 314 Outlet, Device, Pull, and Junction Boxes; Conduit Bodies; Fittings; and Handhole Enclosures. 314.2 Round Boxes.

Chapter 3 Wiring Methods and Materials

EXAM 7

Chapter 3 Wiring Methods and Materials

110. Nonmetallic boxes are only allowed with flexible cords, open wiring on insulators, cabled wiring methods with entirely nonmetallic sheaths, nonmetallic raceways, and: (Exceptions ignored.)

    A. concealed knob-and-tube wiring

    B. electrical metallic tubing

    C. IMT

    D. rigid metallic tubing

    Reference: 2017 National Electrical Code – Chapter 3 Wiring Methods and Materials, Article 314 Outlet, Device, Pull, and Junction Boxes; Conduit Bodies; Fittings; and Handhole Enclosures. 314.3 Nonmetallic Boxes.

111. All metal boxes shall be _____ or bonded.

    A. concealed

    B. grounded

    C. sealed

    D. secured

    Reference: 2017 National Electrical Code – Chapter 3 Wiring Methods and Materials, Article 314 Outlet, Device, Pull, and Junction Boxes; Conduit Bodies; Fittings; and Handhole Enclosures. 314.4 Metal Boxes.

112. The volume allowance required for each 14 AWG conductor, when calculating box fill, shall be ____ cubic inches.

    A. 1.0

    B. 1.5

    C. 2.0

    D. 3.0

    Reference: 2017 National Electrical Code – Chapter 3 Wiring Methods and Materials, Article 314 Outlet, Device, Pull, and Junction Boxes; Conduit Bodies; Fittings; and Handhole Enclosures. 314.16 Number of Conductors in Outlet, Device, and Junction Boxes, and Conduit Bodies.

113. For a 4 inch square box 2.125" deep, with No. 12 copper conductors, what is the maximum fill allowance?

    A. 10

    B. 12

    C. 13

    D. 15

    Reference: 2017 National Electrical Code – Chapter 3 Wiring Methods and Materials, Article 314 Outlet, Device, Pull, and Junction Boxes; Conduit Bodies; Fittings; and Handhole Enclosures. 314.16 Number of Conductors in Outlet, Device, and Junction Boxes, and Conduit Bodies.

EXAM 7

Chapter 3 Wiring Methods and Materials

114. What is the maximum number of size 14 AWG conductors allowed in an metal octagon 4 in. x 1-1/2 in. box?

    A. six

    B. seven

    C. nine

    D. ten

    Reference: 2017 National Electrical Code – Chapter 3 Wiring Methods and Materials, Article 314 Outlet, Device, Pull, and Junction Boxes; Conduit Bodies; Fittings; and Handhole Enclosures. 314.16 Number of Conductors in Outlet, Device, and Junction Boxes, and Conduit Bodies.

115. What is the maximum number of size 10 AWG conductors allowed in an octagon metal junction box that is 4 in. x 1-1/4 in.?

    A. two

    B. four

    C. five

    D. six

    Reference: 2017 National Electrical Code – Chapter 3 Wiring Methods and Materials, Article 314 Outlet, Device, Pull, and Junction Boxes; Conduit Bodies; Fittings; and Handhole Enclosures. 314.16 Number of Conductors in Outlet, Device, and Junction Boxes, and Conduit Bodies.

116. For an octagon box with 6 No. 12 wires entering and terminating in it, 3 grounding conductors terminating it, a fixture stud and three entry clamps inside, how much free space is required, in cubic inches?

    A. 18.5

    B. 20

    C. 20.25

    D. 21.75

    Reference: 2017 National Electrical Code – Chapter 3 Wiring Methods and Materials, Article 314 Outlet, Device, Pull, and Junction Boxes; Conduit Bodies; Fittings; and Handhole Enclosures. 314.16 Number of Conductors in Outlet, Device, and Junction Boxes, and Conduit Bodies. 314.16(B) Box Fill Calculations.

Chapter 3 Wiring Methods and Materials

EXAM 7

Chapter 3 Wiring Methods and Materials

117. Size 12 AWG THWN copper conductors, for the purpose of determining box fill, are calculated at what volume per conductor?

    A. 1.75 cubic inches

    B. 2.00 cubic inches

    C. 2.25 cubic inches

    D. 2.50 square inches

    Reference: 2017 National Electrical Code – Chapter 3 Wiring Methods and Materials, Article 314 Outlet, Device, Pull, and Junction Boxes; Conduit Bodies; Fittings; and Handhole Enclosures. 314.16 Number of Conductors in Outlet, Device, and Junction Boxes, and Conduit Bodies. 314.16(B) Box Fill Calculations.

118. When calculating box fill requirements, each conductor that originates outside the box and terminates or is spliced within the box shall be counted _____.

    A. once

    B. twice

    C. three times

    D. none of the above

    Reference: 2017 National Electrical Code – Chapter 3 Wiring Methods and Materials, Article 314 Outlet, Device, Pull, and Junction Boxes; Conduit Bodies; Fittings; and Handhole Enclosures. 314.16 Number of Conductors in Outlet, Device, and Junction Boxes, and Conduit Bodies. 314.16(B) Box Fill Calculations. 314.16(B)(1) Conductor Fill.

119. When a conductor originates outside a box, and is spliced or terminates inside the box, it will be counted once, and each conductor that goes through the box without a splice or termination:

    A. does not have to be counted.

    B. shall be counted once.

    C. shall be counted once for all such conductors as a group.

    D. shall be counted twice.

    Reference: 2017 National Electrical Code – Chapter 3 Wiring Methods and Materials, Article 314 Outlet, Device, Pull, and Junction Boxes; Conduit Bodies; Fittings; and Handhole Enclosures. 314.16 Number of Conductors in Outlet, Device, and Junction Boxes, and Conduit Bodies. 314.16(B) Box Fill Calculations. 314.16(B)(1) Conductor Fill.

EXAM 7

Chapter 3 Wiring Methods and Materials

120. For the purposes of calculating conductor fill in a box, each coil or loop of unbroken conductor at least twice the minimum lengths necessary for free conductors gets counted:

    A. as three

    B. as zero

    C. once

    D. twice

Reference: 2017 National Electrical Code – Chapter 3 Wiring Methods and Materials, Article 314 Outlet, Device, Pull, and Junction Boxes; Conduit Bodies; Fittings; and Handhole Enclosures. 314.16 Number of Conductors in Outlet, Device, and Junction Boxes, and Conduit Bodies. 314.16(B) Box Fill Calculations. 314.16(B)(1) Conductor Fill.

121. What is the minimum volume, in inches, required of a two (2) gang device box that is to contain two (2) size 14/2 AWG with ground NM cables and two (2) size 12/2 AWG with ground NM cables connected to a duplex receptacle connected to a single-pole switch, which also contain four (4) cable clamps?

    A. 28 cubic inches

    B. 30 cubic inches

    C. 34 cubic inches

    D. 36 cubic inches

Reference: 2017 National Electrical Code – Chapter 3 Wiring Methods and Materials, Article 314 Outlet, Device, Pull, and Junction Boxes; Conduit Bodies; Fittings; and Handhole Enclosures. 314.16 Number of Conductors in Outlet, Device, and Junction Boxes, and Conduit Bodies.

122. What is the minimum size box, in cubic inches, required by the NEC for a metal junction box that will contain the following?

    A. 16 cubic inches

    B. 18 cubic inches

    C. 20 cubic inches

    D. 23 cubic inches

Reference: 2017 National Electrical Code – Chapter 3 Wiring Methods and Materials, Article 314 Outlet, Device, Pull, and Junction Boxes; Conduit Bodies; Fittings; and Handhole Enclosures. 314.16 Number of Conductors in Outlet, Device, and Junction Boxes, and Conduit Bodies. 314.16(B) Box Fill Calculations. 314.16(B)(1),(2)&(5)

EXAM 7

Chapter 3 Wiring Methods and Materials

123. How many conductors is a luminaire stud in an outlet box considered the equivalent of?

    A. none

    B. one

    C. two

    D. three

    Reference: 2017 National Electrical Code – Chapter 3 Wiring Methods and Materials – Chapter 3 Wiring Methods and Materials, Article 314 Outlet, Device, Pull, and Junction Boxes; Conduit Bodies; Fittings; and Handhole Enclosures. 314.16 Number of Conductors in Outlet, Device, and Junction Boxes, and Conduit Bodies. 314.16(B) Box Fill Calculations. 314.16(B)(3) Support Fittings Fill.

124. A volume allowance of _____ must be made for each yoke or strap based on the largest conductor connected to a device or piece of equipment that is supported by that strap or yoke, for each yoke or strap containing one or more devices or equipment.

    A. zero

    B. single

    C. double

    D. multiple

    Reference: 2017 National Electrical Code – Chapter 3 Wiring Methods and Materials, Article 314 Outlet, Device, Pull, and Junction Boxes; Conduit Bodies; Fittings; and Handhole Enclosures. 314.16 Number of Conductors in Outlet, Device, and Junction Boxes, and Conduit Bodies. 314.16(B) Box Fill Calculations. 314.16(B)(4) Device or Equipment Fill.

125. Based on the largest conductor connected to the switch, for the purpose of determining conductor fill in a device box, how many conductor(s) is a three-way switch counted as equal to?

    A. zero

    B. one

    C. two

    D. three

    Reference: 2017 National Electrical Code – Chapter 3 Wiring Methods and Materials, Article 314 Outlet, Device, Pull, and Junction Boxes; Conduit Bodies; Fittings; and Handhole Enclosures. 314.16 Number of Conductors in Outlet, Device, and Junction Boxes, and Conduit Bodies. 314.16(B) Box Fill Calculations. 314.16(B)(4) Device or Equipment Fill.

EXAM 7

Chapter 3 Wiring Methods and Materials

126. What is the maximum number of size 10 AWG conductors that may be added to a metal junction box with a volume of 24 cubic inches that contains a total of six (6) size 12 AWG conductors, and no grounding conductors, devices or fittings contained in the box?

    A. two

    B. five

    C. six

    D. eight

Reference: 2017 National Electrical Code – Chapter 3 Wiring Methods and Materials, Article 314 Outlet, Device, Pull, and Junction Boxes; Conduit Bodies; Fittings; and Handhole Enclosures. 314.16 Number of Conductors in Outlet, Device, and Junction Boxes, and Conduit Bodies.

127. In an outlet box with a 18 cubic inch volume, where a duplex receptacle is housed in the box, how many size 12/2 AWG Type NM cables with ground are permitted to be installed?

    A. one

    B. two

    C. three

    D. four

Reference: 2017 National Electrical Code – Chapter 3 Wiring Methods and Materials, Article 314 Outlet, Device, Pull, and Junction Boxes; Conduit Bodies; Fittings; and Handhole Enclosures. 314.16 Number of Conductors in Outlet, Device, and Junction Boxes, and Conduit Bodies. 314.16(B) Box Fill Calculations. 314.16(B)(4) Device or Equipment Fill.

128. How many conductors is a single device counted as when it is wider than two (2) inches and installed in a 2-gang divide box?

    A. one

    B. two

    C. three

    D. four

Reference: 2017 National Electrical Code – Chapter 3 Wiring Methods and Materials, Article 314 Outlet, Device, Pull, and Junction Boxes; Conduit Bodies; Fittings; and Handhole Enclosures. 314.16 Number of Conductors in Outlet, Device, and Junction Boxes, and Conduit Bodies. 314.16(B) Box Fill Calculations. 314.16(B)(4) Device or Equipment Fill.

Chapter 3 Wiring Methods and Materials

EXAM 7

Chapter 3 Wiring Methods and Materials

129. In walls or ceilings with a surface of noncombustible material, boxes shall be installed so that the front edge of the box will not be set back of the finished surface more than _____ inch.

   A. ¼

   B. ½

   C. ¾

   D. 1

   Reference: 2017 National Electrical Code – Chapter 3 Wiring Methods and Materials, Article 314 Outlet, Device, Pull, and Junction Boxes; Conduit Bodies; Fittings; and Handhole Enclosures. 314.20 Flush-Mounted Installations.

130. In a wood constructed wall, how far from the surface of the wall should the front edge of a switch box be installed?

   A. flush with or projected out

   B. set back a maximum of ¼ in.

   C. set back a maximum of ½ in.

   D. set back a maximum of ⅜ in.

   Reference: 2017 National Electrical Code – Chapter 3 Wiring Methods and Materials, Article 314 Outlet, Device, Pull, and Junction Boxes; Conduit Bodies; Fittings; and Handhole Enclosures. 314.20 In Wall or Ceiling.

131. Outlet boxes that do not enclose devices or utilization equipment shall have a minimum internal depth of _____ inch.

   A. ¼

   B. ½

   C. ¾

   D. 1

   Reference: 2017 National Electrical Code – Chapter 3 Wiring Methods and Materials, Article 314 Outlet, Device, Pull, and Junction Boxes; Conduit Bodies; Fittings; and Handhole Enclosures. 314.24 Depth of Boxes. 314.24(A) Outlet Boxes Without Enclosed Devices or Utilization Equipment.

EXAM 7

Chapter 3 Wiring Methods and Materials

132. If an outlet box does not encloses a device or utilization equipment, the minimum internal depth must be:

    A. ½ in.

    B. ¾ in.

    C. 1 5/16 in.

    D. 1 in.

    Reference: 2017 National Electrical Code – Chapter 3 Wiring Methods and Materials, Article 314 Outlet, Device, Pull, and Junction Boxes; Conduit Bodies; Fittings; and Handhole Enclosures. 314.24 Depth of Boxes. 314.24(A) Outlet Boxes Without Enclosed Devices or Utilization Equipment.

133. If a luminaire weighs more than _____, unless the outlet box is listed for the weight to be supported, it must be supported independently of the outlet box.

    A. 6 pounds

    B. 25 pounds

    C. 35 pounds

    D. 50 pounds

    Reference: 2017 National Electrical Code – Chapter 3 Wiring Methods and Materials, Article 314 Outlet, Device, Pull, and Junction Boxes; Conduit Bodies; Fittings; and Handhole Enclosures. 314.27 Outlet Boxes. 314.27(A) Boxes at Luminaire or Lampholder Outlets. 314.27(A)(2) Ceiling Outlets.

134. A luminaire (lighting fixture) that weighs more than _____ pounds shall be supported independently of the outlet box.

    A. 10

    B. 25

    C. 40

    D. 50

    Reference: 2017 National Electrical Code – Chapter 3 Wiring Methods and Materials, Article 314 Outlet, Device, Pull, and Junction Boxes; Conduit Bodies; Fittings; and Handhole Enclosures. 314.27 Outlet Boxes. 314.27(A) Boxes at Luminaire or Lampholder Outlets. 314.27(A)(2) Ceiling Outlets.

Chapter 3 Wiring Methods and Materials

EXAM 7

Chapter 3 Wiring Methods and Materials

135. If an outlet box is designed to support ceiling-suspended (paddle) fans weighing more than _____, then the maximum weight to be supported shall be included in the required marking.

    A. 20 pounds   C. 35 pounds

    B. 30 pounds   D. 70 pounds

    Reference: 2017 National Electrical Code – Chapter 3 Wiring Methods and Materials, Article 314 Outlet, Device, Pull, and Junction Boxes; Conduit Bodies; Fittings; and Handhole Enclosures. 314.27 Outlet Boxes. 314.27(C) Boxes at Ceiling-Suspended (Paddle) Fan Outlets.

136. What is the maximum weight for a ceiling-suspended (paddle) fan before it is required to be supported independently of an outlet box?

    A. 35 pounds   C. 50 pounds

    B. 40 pounds   D. 70 pounds

    Reference: 2017 National Electrical Code – Chapter 3 Wiring Methods and Materials, Article 314 Outlet, Device, Pull, and Junction Boxes; Conduit Bodies; Fittings; and Handhole Enclosures. 314.27 Outlet Boxes. 314.27(C) Boxes at Ceiling-Suspended (Paddle) Fan Outlets.

137. The length of a pull box containing conductors of size 4 AWG and larger shall not be less than _____ times the trade diameter of the largest conduit entering the box, when a straight pull of the conductors is to be made.

    A. six   C. eight

    B. four   D. twelve

    Reference: 2017 National Electrical Code – Chapter 3 Wiring Methods and Materials, Article 314 Outlet, Device, Pull, and Junction Boxes; Conduit Bodies; Fittings; and Handhole Enclosures. 314.28 Pull and Junction Boxes and Conduit Bodies. 314.28(A) Minimum Size. 314.28(A)(1) Straight Pulls.

EXAM 7

Chapter 3 Wiring Methods and Materials

138. Where permanent barriers are installed in a box, each section shall be considered as a _____ box.

    A. grounded

    B. secured

    C. separate

    D. ungrounded

    Reference: 2017 National Electrical Code – Chapter 3 Wiring Methods and Materials, Article 314 Outlet, Device, Pull, and Junction Boxes; Conduit Bodies; Fittings; and Handhole Enclosures. 314.28 Pull and Junction Boxes and Conduit Bodies. 314.28(D) Permanent Barriers.

139. When electrical outlet boxes are installed in ceilings or walls, they shall be:

    A. accessible

    B. inaccessible

    C. metal

    D. readily accessible

    Reference: 2017 National Electrical Code – Chapter 3 Wiring Methods and Materials, Article 314 Outlet, Device, Pull, and Junction Boxes; Conduit Bodies; Fittings; and Handhole Enclosures. 314.29 Boxes, Conduit Bodies, and Handhole Enclosures to Be Accessible.

140. Each metal box must provide a means for the connection of an equipment grounding conductor, which is allowed to be a _____ or the equivalent.

    A. cable clamp

    B. strap

    C. tapped hole

    D. toggle bolt

    Reference: 2017 National Electrical Code – Chapter 3 Wiring Methods and Materials, Article 314 Outlet, Device, Pull, and Junction Boxes; Conduit Bodies; Fittings; and Handhole Enclosures. 314.40 Metal Boxes, Conduit Bodies, and Fittings. 314.40(D) Grounding Provisions.

Chapter 3 Wiring Methods and Materials

EXAM 7

Chapter 3 Wiring Methods and Materials

141. The distance between the entry and exit of a cable or conductor from a box must be at least _____ times the outside diameter of the cable or conductor, over sheath.

    A. 24

    B. 30

    C. 36

    D. 40

    Reference: 2017 National Electrical Code – Chapter 3 Wiring Methods and Materials, Article 314 Outlet, Device, Pull, and Junction Boxes; Conduit Bodies; Fittings; and Handhole Enclosures. 314.71 Size of Pull and Junction Boxes, Conduit Bodies, and Handhole Enclosures. 314.71(B) For Angle or U Pulls. 314.71(B)(1) Distance to Opposite Wall.

142. For which of the following situations is Type AC cable permitted?

    A. for feeders

    B. in damp locations

    C. in wet locations

    D. where exposed to physical damage

    Reference: 2017 National Electrical Code – Chapter 3 Wiring Methods and Materials, Article 320 Armored Cable: Type AC. 320.10 Uses Permitted.

143. Where should type AC cable not be used?

    A. in damp or wet locations

    B. masonry block or tile walls exposed to moisture or dampness

    C. where subject to physical damage

    D. all of the above

    Reference: 2017 National Electrical Code – Chapter 3 Wiring Methods and Materials, Article 320 Armored Cable: Type AC. 320.12 Uses Not Permitted.

Chapter 3 Wiring Methods and Materials

EXAM 7

Chapter 3 Wiring Methods and Materials

144. For an individual branch circuit in a flat conductor cable assembly, what is the maximum ampacity?

    A. 10 amperes

    B. 15 amperes

    C. 20 amperes

    D. 30 amperes

    Reference: 2017 National Electrical Code – Chapter 3 Wiring Methods and Materials, Article 324 Flat Conductor Cable: Type FCC. 324.10 Uses Permitted. 324.10(B) Branch-Circuit Ratings. 324.10(B)(2) Current.

145. Type MV cable is allowed for use on power system rated at _____ volts nominal and below.

    A. 600

    B. 2,000

    C. 10,000

    D. 35,000

    Reference: 2017 National Electrical Code – Chapter 3 Wiring Methods and Materials, Article 328 Medium Voltage Cable: Type MV. 328.10 Uses Permitted.

146. Unless identified for such use, where should Type MV cable not be used?

    A. in messenger-supported wiring

    B. in raceways

    C. in wet or dry locations

    D. where exposed to direct sunlight

    Reference: 2017 National Electrical Code – Chapter 3 Wiring Methods and Materials, Article 328 Medium Voltage Cable: Type MV. 328.12 Uses Not Permitted.

147. Where NOT subject to _____, Type MC cables shall be permitted for services, feeders, and branch circuits.

    A. damp conditions

    B. physical damage

    C. power surges

    D. wet conditions

    Reference: 2017 National Electrical Code – Chapter 3 Wiring Methods and Materials, Article 330 Metal-Clad Cable: Type MC. 330.10 Uses Permitted. 330.10(A) General Uses.

EXAM 7

Chapter 3 Wiring Methods and Materials

148. Type MC cable shall be supported and secured at intervals not exceeding _____ feet.

    A. 3   C. 5

    B. 4   D. 6

    Reference: 2017 National Electrical Code – Chapter 3 Wiring Methods and Materials, Article 330 Metal-Clad Cable: Type MC. 330.30 Securing and Supporting. 330.30(B) Securing.

149. Type MC cables containing four or fewer conductors, sized no larger than 10 AWG, shall be secured within _____ inches of every box, cabinet, fitting, or other cable termination.

    A. 6   C. 12

    B. 9   D. 15

    Reference: 2017 National Electrical Code – Chapter 3 Wiring Methods and Materials, Article 330 Metal-Clad Cable: Type MC. 330.30 Securing and Supporting. 330.30(B) Securing.

150. For Type MC cable, the maximum unsupported length used to supply a luminaire in an accessible ceiling is:

    A. 18 inches   C. 6 feet

    B. 4-½ feet   D. 10 feet

    Reference: 2017 National Electrical Code – Chapter 3 Wiring Methods and Materials, Article 330 Metal-Clad Cable: Type MC. 330.30 Securing and Supporting. 330.30(D) Unsupported Cables. 330.30(D)(2)

151. What is the maximum interval for support of Type MI cable?

    A. 2 feet   C. 6 feet

    B. 4 feet   D. 10 feet

    Reference: 2017 National Electrical Code – Chapter 3 Wiring Methods and Materials, Article 332 Mineral-Insulated, Metal-Sheathed Cable: Type MI. 332.30 Securing and Supporting.

EXAM 7

Chapter 3 Wiring Methods and Materials

152. Which of the following is true if the outer sheath of Type MI cable is made of steel?

    A. connect the grounding & grounded conductors together

    B. may be used as an equipment grounding conductor

    C. shall not be longer than 6 feet

    D. provide separate equipment grounding conductor

    Reference: 2017 National Electrical Code – Chapter 3 Wiring Methods and Materials, Article 332 Mineral-Insulated, Metal-Sheathed Cable: Type MI. 332.108 Equipment Grounding Conductor.

153. A factory assembly of two or more insulated conductors enclosed within an overall nonmetallic jacket.

    A. Bundled Cable

    B. Concurrent Cable

    C. Nonmetallic-Sheathed Cable

    D. Parallel Cable

    Reference: 2017 National Electrical Code – Chapter 3 Wiring Methods and Materials, Article 334 Nonmetallic-Sheathed Cable: Types NM, NMC, and NMS. 334.2 Definitions.

154. What kind of cable has insulated conductors inside an overall nonmetallic, corrosion resistant jacket?

    A. Type NMC

    B. Type NMS

    C. Type SE

    D. Type UF

    Reference: 2017 National Electrical Code – Chapter 3 Wiring Methods and Materials, Article 334 Nonmetallic-Sheathed Cable: Types NM, NMC, and NMS. 334.2 Definitions.

155. Where is it not permitted to use Type NM cable?

    A. for exposed work

    B. in any of the above listed installations

    C. in Type V construction

    D. in wet locations

    Reference: 2017 National Electrical Code – Chapter 3 Wiring Methods and Materials, Article 334 Nonmetallic-Sheathed Cable: Types NM, NMC, and NMS. 334.12 Uses Not Permitted. 334.12(B) Types NM and NMS.

EXAM 7

Chapter 3 Wiring Methods and Materials

156. It is allowed to secure Type NM cable run at angles with joists in unfinished basements direct to the lower edges of the joists, if they are at least:

    A. 6/2 AWG

    B. 6/3 AWG

    C. 8/2 AWG

    D. 10/2 AWG

    Reference: 2017 National Electrical Code – Chapter 3 Wiring Methods and Materials, Article 334 Nonmetallic-Sheathed Cable: Types NM, NMC, and NMS. 334.15 Exposed Work. 334.15(C) In Unfinished Basements and Crawl Spaces.

157. Bends in Typed NM, NMC, and NMS cable shall be made so that the cable will not be _____.

    A. compressed

    B. damaged

    C. exposed

    D. folded

    Reference: 2017 National Electrical Code – Chapter 3 Wiring Methods and Materials, Article 334 Nonmetallic-Sheathed Cable: Types NM, NMC, and NMS. 334.24 Bending Radius.

158. Bends in Types NM, NMC, and NMS cables must be made so as not to damage the cable. The radius of the inner edge of the curve on any bend during or after installation must be _____ times the diameter of the cable or more.

    A. five

    B. ten

    C. twenty

    D. thirty six

    Reference: 2017 National Electrical Code – Chapter 3 Wiring Methods and Materials, Article 334 Nonmetallic-Sheathed Cable: Types NM, NMC, and NMS. 334.24 Bending Radius.

159. The tightest bend allowed by the NEC for Type NM cable is a radius of how many times the diameter of the cable?

    A. five

    B. six

    C. seven

    D. eight

    Reference: 2017 National Electrical Code – Chapter 3 Wiring Methods and Materials, Article 334 Nonmetallic-Sheathed Cable: Types NM, NMC, and NMS. 334.24 Bending Radius.

EXAM 7

Chapter 3 Wiring Methods and Materials

160. Nonmetallic-sheathed cable shall be secured by staples, cable ties, straps, hangers or similar fittings at intervals not exceeding _____ feet and within _____ inches of every cabinet, box, or fitting.

    A. 3, 12

    B. 3-½, 18

    C. 4, 18

    D. 4-½, 12

    Reference: 2017 National Electrical Code – Chapter 3 Wiring Methods and Materials, Article 334 Nonmetallic-Sheathed Cable: Types NM, NMC, and NMS. 334.30 Securing and Supporting.

161. When installing nonmetallic sheathed cable (NM), what is the maximum distance allowed between supports, such as cable ties, staples, or straps?

    A. 3 feet

    B. 4-½ feet

    C. 6 feet

    D. 10 feet

    Reference: 2017 National Electrical Code – Chapter 3 Wiring Methods and Materials, Article 334 Nonmetallic-Sheathed Cable: Types NM, NMC, and NMS. 334.30 Securing and Supporting.

162. The ampacity of Types NM, NMC, and NMS cable shall be determined in accordance with the _____ °C (140°F) conductor temperature rating.

    A. 40°C

    B. 50°C

    C. 60°C

    D. 90°C

    Reference: 2017 National Electrical Code – Chapter 3 Wiring Methods and Materials, Article 334 Nonmetallic-Sheathed Cable: Types NM, NMC, and NMS. 334.80 Ampacity.

163. Of the following listed cables, which overall covering is resistant to fungus?

    A. Type MI

    B. Type NM

    C. Type NMC

    D. Type NMS

    Reference: 2017 National Electrical Code – Chapter 3 Wiring Methods and Materials, Article 334 Nonmetallic Sheathed Cable: Types. NM, NMC, and NMS. 334.116 Sheath. 334.116(B) Type NMC.

EXAM 7

Chapter 3 Wiring Methods and Materials

164. For Type TC cables, the insulated conductors for copper, nickel, or nickel-coated copper shall be in sizes _____ to 1000 kcmil.

    A. 12 AWG

    B. 14 AWG

    C. 16 AWG

    D. 18 AWG

    Reference: 2017 National Electrical Code – Chapter 3 Wiring Methods and Materials, Article 336 Power and Control Tray Cable: Type TC. 336.104 Conductors.

165. A single conductor or multiconductor assembly provided with or without an overall covering, primarily used for services.

    A. Nonmetallic Sheathed Cable

    B. Service-Entrance Cable

    C. Type NM Cable

    D. Type NMC Cable

    Reference: 2017 National Electrical Code – Chapter 3 Wiring Methods and Materials, Article 338 Service-Entrance Cable: Types SE and USE. 338.2 Definitions.

166. A factory assembly of one or more insulated conductors with an integral or overall covering of nonmetallic material suitable for direct burial in the earth.

    A. Type NM

    B. Type NMC

    C. Type NSC

    D. Type UF

    Reference: 2017 National Electrical Code – Chapter 3 Wiring Methods and Materials, Article 340 Underground Feeder and Branch-Circuit Cable: Type UF. 340.2 Definition.

167. What describes a factory assembly of one or more insulated conductors suitable for direct burial in the earth, with an integral or overall covering of nonmetallic material?

    A. Type NM

    B. Type SE

    C. Type UF

    D. Type UN

    Reference: 2017 National Electrical Code – Chapter 3 Wiring Methods and Materials, Article 340 Underground Feeder and Branch-Circuit Cable: Type UF. 340.2 Definition.

EXAM 7

Chapter 3 Wiring Methods and Materials

168. Where may a Type UF cable be used?

　　A. As service-entrance cable

　　B. Between a dwelling and separate garage unit

　　C. In storage battery rooms

　　D. Where exposed to direct sun, unless sunlight resistant

　　Reference: 2017 National Electrical Code – Chapter 3 Wiring Methods and Materials, Article 340 Underground Feeder and Branch-Circuit Cable: Type UF. 340.12 Uses Not Permitted.

169. UF cable shall have the ampacity of _____ conductors.

　　A. 60°C

　　B. 75°C

　　C. 85°C

　　D. 90°C

　　Reference: 2017 National Electrical Code – Chapter 3 Wiring Methods and Materials, Article 340 Underground Feeder and Branch-Circuit Cable: Type UF. 340.80 Ampacity.

170. If an IMC is larger than metric designator trade size _____, it may not be used.

　　A. 2

　　B. 3

　　C. 4

　　D. 5

　　Reference: 2017 National Electrical Code – Chapter 3 Wiring Methods and Materials, Article 342 Intermediate Metal Conduit: Type IMC. 342.20 Size. 342.20(B) Maximum.

171. IMC must be securely fastened _____ ft. or less from each cabinet, conduit body, device box, junction box, outlet box, or other conduit termination. Fastening is allowed to increase to _____ ft. or less where structural members interfere with fastening at the standard minimum distance. Exceptions ignored.

　　A. 3, 5

　　B. 4, 8

　　C. 4, 10

　　D. 5, 10

　　Reference: 2017 National Electrical Code – Chapter 3 Wiring Methods and Materials, Article 342 Intermediate Metal Conduit: Type IMC. 342.30 Securing and Supporting. 342.30(A) Securely Fastened.

Chapter 3 Wiring Methods and Materials

EXAM 7

Chapter 3 Wiring Methods and Materials

172. Installation of rigid metal conduit (RMC) is required to be fastened within what minimum distance from a junction box, panel board, or cabinet, where structural members readily permit fastening?

    A. 3 feet

    B. 5 feet

    C. 6 feet

    D. 10 feet

    Reference: 2017 National Electrical Code – Chapter 3 Wiring Methods and Materials, Article 344 Rigid Metal Conduit: Type RMC. 344.30 Securing and Supporting. 344.30(A) Securely Fastened. 344.30(A)(1)

173. The maximum allowable distance, in feet, between trade size 1 RMC supports is:

    A. 10

    B. 12

    C. 14

    D. 16

    Reference: 2017 National Electrical Code – Chapter 3 Wiring Methods and Materials, Article 344 Rigid Metal Conduit: Type RMC. 344.30 Securing and Supporting. 344.30(B) Supports.

174. When RMC threadless connectors and couplings are used with conduit, they must be made tight, and when they are to be buried in concrete or masonry, they must be:

    A. airtight

    B. concrete tight

    C. waterproof

    D. watertight

    Reference: 2017 National Electrical Code – Chapter 3 Wiring Methods and Materials, Article 344 Rigid Metal Conduit: Type RMC. 344.42 Couplings and Connectors. 344.42(A) Threadless.

175. What is the term for a raceway made of helically wound, formed, interlocked metal strip with a circular cross section?

    A. Electrical Metallic Tubing (EMT)

    B. Flexible Metal Conduit (FMC)

    C. Rigid Metal Conduit (RMC)

    D. Rigid Non-metallic Conduit (RNC)

    Reference: 2017 National Electrical Code – Chapter 3 Wiring Methods and Materials, Article 348 Flexible Metal Conduit: Type FMC. 348.2 Definition

EXAM 7

Chapter 3 Wiring Methods and Materials

176. Where is FMC not permitted?

    A. concealed spaces

    B. exposed locations

    C. interior walls

    D. storage battery rooms

    Reference: 2017 National Electrical Code – Chapter 3 Wiring Methods and Materials, Article 348 Flexible Metal Conduit: Type FMC. 348.12 Uses Not Permitted.

177. When is flexible metal conduit (FMC) allowed to be used in wet locations?

    A. When conductors inside have temperature rating of 90°C or more.

    B. When conductors inside are approved for use in wet locations.

    C. Where the length of the FMC is not more than six (6) feet.

    D. Under no circumstances.

    Reference: 2017 National Electrical Code – Chapter 3 Wiring Methods and Materials, Article 348 Flexible Metal Conduit: Type FMC. 348.12 Uses Not Permitted.

178. As long as the length of the flex does not exceed _____, use of electrical trace size 3/8 in. flexible metal conduit (FMC) is allowed for tap conductors to luminaires.

    A. four feet

    B. six feet

    C. eight feet

    D. ten feet

    Reference: 2017 National Electrical Code – Chapter 3 Wiring Methods and Materials, Article 348 Flexible Metal Conduit: Type FMC. 348.20 Size. 348.20(A) Minimum.

EXAM 7

Chapter 3 Wiring Methods and Materials

179. Tap conductors are allowed to be enclosed by trade size 3/8 in. flexible metal conduit (FMC) as long as the length of the FMC is not more than:

    A. 3 feet
    B. 4 feet
    C. 6 feet
    D. 8 feet

    Reference: 2017 National Electrical Code – Chapter 4 Equipment for General Use, Article 410 Luminaries, Lampholders, and Lamps. 410.117 Wiring. 410.117(C) Tap Conductors.

180. The maximum percent of FMC conduit interior total area the may be filled if more than 2 conductors are used in the tube is:

    A. 31
    B. 40
    C. 53
    D. 60

    Reference: 2017 National Electrical Code – Chapter 3 Wiring Methods and Materials, Article 348 Flexible Metal Conduit: Type FMC. 348.22 Number of Conductors.

181. What is the maximum number of size 14 AWG THHN conductors allowed to be installed in a trade size 3/8 in. flexible metal conduit (FMC) containing bare size 114 AWG grounding conductor, if the FMC has external fittings?

    A. two
    B. three
    C. four
    D. five

    Reference: 2017 National Electrical Code – Chapter 3 Wiring Methods and Materials, Article 348 Flexible Metal Conduit: Type FMC. 348.22 Number of Conductors.

182. Which kind of FMC connectors may not be concealed?

    A. 45 degree offset
    B. angle
    C. rigid
    D. XLT

    Reference: 2017 National Electrical Code – Chapter 3 Wiring Methods and Materials, Article 348 Flexible Metal Conduit: Type FMC. 348.42 Couplings and Connectors.

EXAM 7

Chapter 3 Wiring Methods and Materials

183. Where is LFMC (Liquidtight Flexible Metal Conduit) allowed to be used?

    A. direct burial where listed and marked for the purpose

    B. If total operating temperatures are over the approved level

    C. Where subject to physical damage

    D. Where total bends exceeds 360 degrees

    Reference: 2017 National Electrical Code – Chapter 3 Wiring Methods and Materials, Article 350 Liquidtight Flexible Metal Conduit: Type LFMC. 350.10 Uses Permitted

184. Where shall liquidtight flexible metallic conduit (LFMC) not be used?

    A. in concealed work.

    B. in hazardous locations.

    C. in lengths in excess of 6 feet.

    D. where subject to physical damage.

    Reference: 2017 National Electrical Code – Chapter 3 Wiring Methods and Materials, Article 350 Liquidtight Flexible Metal Conduit: Type LFMC. 350.12 Uses Not Permitted.

185. LFMC must be fastened in place securely by an approved means _____ in. or less of each box, cabinet, conduit body, or other conduit termination and must be secured and supported at intervals of _____ ft. or less. Exceptions ignored.

    A. 8, 4

    B. 12, 4-½

    C. 12, 6

    D. 18, 4.5

    Reference: 2017 National Electrical Code – Chapter 3 Wiring Methods and Materials, Article 350 Liquidtight Flexible Metal Conduit: Type LFMC. 350.30 Securing and Supporting. 350.30(A) Securely Fastened.

186. What is the maximum distance between a box or other conduit termination for securely fastening liquidtight flexible metal conduit (LFMC)?

    A. 3 feet

    B. 4-½ feet

    C. 12 inches

    D. 18 inches

    Reference: 2017 National Electrical Code – Chapter 3 Wiring Methods and Materials, Article 350 Liquidtight Flexible Metal Conduit: Type LFMC. 350.30 Securing and Supporting. 350.30(A) Securely Fastened.

EXAM 7

Chapter 3 Wiring Methods and Materials

187. What are the maximum number of bends allowed for an underground rigid polyvinyl chloride conduit system consisting of 50 ft. lengths between pulling points?

    A. two (2) – 90 degree

    B. four (4) – 90 degree

    C. four (4) – 120 degree

    D. six (6) – 90 degree

    Reference: 2017 National Electrical Code – Chapter 3 Wiring Methods and Materials, Article 352 Rigid Polyvinyl Chloride Conduit: Type PVC. 352.26 Bends – Number in One Run.

188. What is the maximum allowed distance between supports for trade size 3/4 in. Schedule 40 PVC conduit?

    A. 3 feet

    B. 4 feet

    C. 6 feet

    D. 8 feet

    Reference: 2017   National Electrical Code – Chapter 3 Wiring Methods and Materials, Article 352 Rigid Polyvinyl Chloride Conduit: Type PVC. 352.30 Securing and Supporting.

189. What is the maximum distance between supports for standard trade size 2 in. right Schedule 40 polyvinyl chloride conduit (PVC)?

    A. 3 feet

    B. 5 feet

    C. 6 feet

    D. 8 feet

    Reference: 2017 National Electrical Code – Chapter 3 Wiring Methods and Materials, Article 352 Rigid Polyvinyl Chloride Conduit: Type PVC. 352.30 Securing and Supporting.

190. When a conduit enters an enclosure such as a box or fitting, _____ must be provided to protect the wire from damage such as abrasion unless the design of the box, fitting, or enclosure gives protection that is equivalent.

    A. a bushing or adapter

    B. an insulated collar

    C. end clamp

    D. pipe nipple

    Reference: 2017 National Electrical Code – Chapter 3 Wiring Methods and Materials, Article 352 Rigid Polyvinyl Chloride Conduit: Type PVC. 352.46 Bushings.

EXAM 7

Chapter 3 Wiring Methods and Materials

191. Where is HDPE (High Density Polyethylene) conduit, and associated connectors, couplings and fittings for installing electrical conductors not allowed for installation?

    A. in cinder fill

    B. in corrosive areas as covered in 300.6

    C. in discrete lengths or in continuous lengths from a reel

    D. within a building

    Reference: 2017 National Electrical Code – Chapter 3 Wiring Methods and Materials, Article 353 High Density Polyethylene Conduit: Type HDPE Conduit. 353.12 Uses Not Permitted.

192. Where is LFNC (Liquidtight Flexible Nonmetallic Conduit) allowed to be used? (Exceptions ignored.)

    A. If protection is needed from vapors, liquids, or solids.

    B. If the conductor operating voltage is over of 600 volts, nominal.

    C. In any conditions of extreme cold or heat.

    D. In lengths longer than 100 ft.

    Reference: 2017 National Electrical Code – Chapter 3 Wiring Methods and Materials, Article 356 Liquidtight Flexible Nonmetallic Conduit: Type LFNC. 356.10 Uses Permitted.

193. What kind of work is EMT allowed to be used for?

    A. concealed

    B. exposed

    C. underwater

    D. both A and B

    Reference: 2017 National Electrical Code – Chapter 3 Wiring Methods and Materials, Article 358 Electrical Metallic Tubing: Type EMT. 358.10 Uses Permitted. 358.10(A) Exposed and Concealed.

Chapter 3 Wiring Methods and Materials   321

EXAM 7

Chapter 3 Wiring Methods and Materials

194. EMT smaller than _____ inch shall not be used.

    A. ¼

    B. ½

    C. ¾

    D. 1

    Reference: 2017 National Electrical Code – Chapter 3 Wiring Methods and Materials, Article 358 Electrical Metallic Tubing: Type EMT. 358.20 Size. 358.20(A) Minimum.

195. Bends in tubing must be made so that there is no damage, and so that the diameter of the inside of the tubing is not:

    A. increased

    B. lengthened

    C. reduced

    D. none of the above

    Reference: 2017 National Electrical Code – Chapter 3 Wiring Methods and Materials, Article 358 Electrical Metallic Tubing: Type EMT. 358.24 Bends - How Made.

196. There shall not be more than the equivalent of four quarter bends (_____ degrees total) between pull points, for example, conduit bodies and boxes.

    A. 180

    B. 270

    C. 350

    D. 360

    Reference: 2017 National Electrical Code – Chapter 3 Wiring Methods and Materials, Article 358 Electrical Metallic Tubing: Type EMT. 358.26 Bends – Number in One Run.

197. Between pull points, conduit bodies and boxes for example, there must be no more than the equivalent of four quarter bends, _____ degrees total.

    A. 180

    B. 270

    C. 360

    D. 450

    Reference: 2017 National Electrical Code – Chapter 3 Wiring Methods and Materials, Article 358 Electrical Metallic Tubing: Type EMT. 358.26 Bends - Number in One Run.

EXAM 7

Chapter 3 Wiring Methods and Materials

198. What is the maximum number of 90 degree bends in electrical metallic tubing (EMT), between boxes and/or pull points?

    A. three

    B. four

    C. five

    D. six

    Reference: *2017 National Electrical Code – Chapter 3 Wiring Methods and Materials, Article 358 Electrical Metallic Tubing: Type EMT. 358.26 Bends – Number in One Run.*

199. EMT shall be securely fastened in place at least every _____ feet.

    A. 6

    B. 8

    C. 10

    D. 12

    Reference: *2017 National Electrical Code – Chapter 3 Wiring Methods and Materials, Article 358 Electrical Metallic Tubing: Type EMT. 358.30 Securing and Supporting. 358.30(A) Securely Fastened.*

200. Electrical metallic tubing (EMT) shall be fastened securely within what distance of each junction box, panelboard, or other conduit termination?

    A. 3 feet

    B. 6 feet

    C. 8 feet

    D. 10 feet

    Reference: *2017 National Electrical Code – Chapter 3 Wiring Methods and Materials, Article 358 Electrical Metallic Tubing: Type EMT. 358.30 Securing and Supporting. 358.30(A) Securely Fastened.*

201. The run of electrical metallic tubing (EMT) shall be securely fastened a minimum of every:

    A. 6 feet

    B. 10 feet

    C. 15 feet

    D. 20 feet

    Reference: *2017 National Electrical Code – Chapter 3 Wiring Methods and Materials, Article 358 Electrical Metallic Tubing: Type EMT. 358.30 Securing and Supporting. 358.30(A) Securely Fastened.*

Chapter 3 Wiring Methods and Materials

EXAM 7

Chapter 3 Wiring Methods and Materials

202. EMT shall be permitted as an equipment _____ conductor.

    A. ground-fault

    B. grounded

    C. grounding

    D. lightning protection

    Reference: 2017 National Electrical Code – Chapter 3 Wiring Methods and Materials, Article 358 Electrical Metallic Tubing: Type EMT. 358.60 Grounding.

203. In which conditions or places is FMT (Flexible Metallic Tubing) allowed to be used?

    A. for direct earth burial, or embedded in concrete or aggregate

    B. for system voltages of 1000 volts maximum

    C. in hoistways

    D. in lengths over 100 ft.

    Reference: 2017 National Electrical Code – Chapter 3 Wiring Methods and Materials, Article 360 Flexible Metallic Tubing: Type FMT. 360.10 Uses Permitted.

204. Unless a fire sprinkler system is installed on all floors in accordance with NFPA 13-2013, Standard for the Installation of Sprinkler Systems, ENT (Electrical Nonmetallic Tubing) is not allowed to be used in a building _____ stories above grade or less.

    A. one

    B. two

    C. three

    D. five

    Reference: 2017 National Electrical Code – Chapter 3 Wiring Methods and Materials, Article 362 Electrical Nonmetallic Tubing: Type ENT. 362.10 Uses Permitted.

EXAM 7

Chapter 3 Wiring Methods and Materials

205. Where is it allowed to use ENT (Electrical Nonmetallic Tubing)? Exceptions ignored.

    A. for direct earth burial

    B. in a two story building

    C. where subject to physical damage

    D. where the voltage is over 600 volts

    Reference: 2017 National Electrical Code – Chapter 3 Wiring Methods and Materials, Article 362 Electrical Nonmetallic Tubing: Type ENT. 362.10 Uses Permitted.

206. ENT may not be used to _____ luminaries and other equipment.

    A. conductors

    B. connection

    C. support

    D. wiring method

    Reference: 2017 National Electrical Code – Chapter 3 Wiring Methods and Materials, Article 362 Electrical Nonmetallic Tubing: Type ENT. 362.12 Uses Not Permitted.

207. What is the maximum voltage that current-carrying conductors installed within electrical nonmetallic tubing (ENT) may carry?

    A. 300 volts

    B. 450 volts

    C. 500 volts

    D. 600 volts

    Reference: 2017 National Electrical Code – Chapter 3 Wiring Methods and Materials, Article 362 Electrical Nonmetallic Tubing: Type ENT. 362.12 Uses Not Permitted.

208. What is the maximum distance between secure fastenings for electrical nonmetallic tubing (ENT)?

    A. 3 feet

    B. 4 feet

    C. 6 feet

    D. 10 feet

    Reference: 2017 National Electrical Code – Chapter 3 Wiring Methods and Materials, Article 362 Electrical Nonmetallic Tubing: Type ENT. 362.30 Securing and Supporting. 362.30(A) Securely Fastened.

Chapter 3 Wiring Methods and Materials

EXAM 7

Chapter 3 Wiring Methods and Materials

209. Electrical nonmetallic tubing (ENT) shall be securely fastened in place within _____ of each cabinet, device box, fitting, junction box, or outlet box where it terminates.

    A. 12 inches

    B. 18 inches

    C. 24 inches

    D. 36 inches

    Reference: 2017 National Electrical Code – Chapter 3 Wiring Methods and Materials, Article 362 Electrical Nonmetallic Tubing: Type ENT. 362.30 Securing and Supporting. 362.30(A) Securely Fastened.

210. The sum of the cross-sectional areas of all contained conductors at any cross section of a sheet metal auxiliary gutter shall not exceed _____ percent of the interior cross-sectional area of the sheet metal auxiliary gutter.

    A. 10

    B. 20

    C. 30

    D. 40

    Reference: 2017 National Electrical Code – Chapter 3 Wiring Methods and Materials, Article 366 Auxiliary Gutters. 366.22 Number of Conductors. 366.22(A) Sheet Metal Auxiliary Gutters.

211. Auxiliary gutters made of sheet metal must be secured and supported at intervals of _____ ft. or less along their entire length.

    A. 3

    B. 5

    C. 6

    D. 8

    Reference: 2017 National Electrical Code – Chapter 3 Wiring Methods and Materials, Article 366 Auxiliary Gutters. 366.30 Securing and Supporting. 366.30(A) Sheet Metal Auxiliary Gutters.

212. Conductors, including splices and taps, shall not fill gutters to more than _____ percent of its area.

    A. 25

    B. 50

    C. 60

    D. 75

    Reference: 2017 National Electrical Code – Chapter 3 Wiring Methods and Materials, Article 366 Auxiliary Gutters. 366.56 Splices and Taps. 366.56(A) Within Gutters.

EXAM 7

Chapter 3 Wiring Methods and Materials

213. Where they are accessible by means of removable covers or doors, splices or taps are allowed. Including splices and taps, all conductors must not fill more than _____ percent of the gutter area.

    A. 25

    B. 50

    C. 75

    D. 90

    Reference: 2017 National Electrical Code – Chapter 3 Wiring Methods and Materials, Article 366 Auxiliary Gutters. 366.56 Splices and Taps. 366.56(A) Within Gutters.

214. Conductors must not come into contact with uninsulated current-carrying parts of different potential, and taps from bare conductors must leave the gutter _____ their terminal connections.

    A. bare from

    B. opposite

    C. parallel to

    D. within 3 inches of

    Reference: 2017 National Electrical Code – Chapter 3 Wiring Methods and Materials, Article 366 Auxiliary Gutters. 366.56 Splices and Taps. 366.56(B) Bare Conductors.

215. What is the term for a grounded metal enclosure containing bare, factory-mounted or insulated conductors, which are usually aluminum or copper bars, rods, or tubes.

    A. Busway

    B. Collector

    C. Grounding Bus

    D. Raceway

    Reference: 2017 National Electrical Code – Chapter 3 Wiring Methods and Materials, Article 368 Busways. 368.2 Definition.

216. Lengths of busway are allowed to extend through _____ if they are unbroken.

    A. damp locations

    B. dry walls

    C. hazardous locations

    D. hoistways

    Reference: 2017 National Electrical Code – Chapter 3 Wiring Methods and Materials, Article 368 Busways. 368.10 Uses Permitted. 368.10(C) Through Walls and Floors. 368.10(C)(1) Walls.

Chapter 3 Wiring Methods and Materials

EXAM 7

Chapter 3 Wiring Methods and Materials

217. Lighting and trolley busway must be installed _____ ft. or more above the floor or working platform, unless a cover is provided that is identified for the purpose.

    A. 8   C. 12

    B. 10   D. 14

Reference: 2017 National Electrical Code – Chapter 3 Wiring Methods and Materials, Article 368 Busways. 368.12 Uses Not Permitted. 368.12(E) Working Platform.

218. Busways shall be securely supported at intervals not exceeding _____ feet.

    A. 3   C. 7

    B. 5   D. 10

Reference: 2017 National Electrical Code – Chapter 3 Wiring Methods and Materials, Article 368 Busways. 368.30 Support.

219. What kind of locations is cable bus installed for?

    A. Commercial   C. Exposed

    B. Concealed   D. Hazardous

Reference: 2017 National Electrical Code – Chapter 3 Wiring Methods and Materials, Article 370 Cablebus. 370.10 Uses Permitted.

220. Other than for supplying _____ outlets or extension to the area below the floor but not above it, Cellular Concrete Floor Raceways may not be used in commercial garages.

    A. ceiling   C. roof

    B. floor   D. wall

Reference: 2017 National Electrical Code – Chapter 3 Wiring Methods and Materials, Article 372 Cellular Concrete Floor Raceways. 372.12 Uses Not Permitted.

EXAM 7

Chapter 3 Wiring Methods and Materials

221. The combined cross-sectional area of all cables or conductors in a Cellular Metal Floor Raceway may not be more than _____ percent of the interior cross-sectional area of the cell or header.

   A. 25
   B. 40
   C. 60
   D. 75

   Reference: 2017 National Electrical Code – Chapter 3 Wiring Methods and Materials, Article 374 Cellular Metal Floor Raceways. 374.22 Maximum Number of Conductors in Raceway.

222. On a metal wireway cross-section, what is the maximum percent that may be occupied by conductors, splices, and taps at any point?

   A. 20%
   B. 30%
   C. 40%
   D. 75%

   Reference: 2017 National Electrical Code – Chapter 3 Wiring Methods and Materials, Article 376 Metal Wireways. 376.56 Splices, Taps, and Power Distribution Blocks. 376.56(A) Splices and Taps.

223. Where sizes 1/0 AWG to 4/0 AWG single conductor cables are installed in industrial establishments, what is the maximum allowable rung spacing for the cable tray?

   A. 6 inches
   B. 9 inches
   C. 12 inches
   D. 15 inches

   Reference: 2017 National Electrical Code – Chapter 3 Wiring Methods and Materials, Article 392 Cable Trays. 392.10 Uses Permitted. 392.10(B) In Industrial Establishments. 392.10(B)(1)

224. Unless special permission is granted by the local inspector, concealed knob-and-tube wiring is only allowed to be used for:

   A. accessible installations
   B. dwellings
   C. extensions of existing installations
   D. temporary wiring

   Reference: 2017 National Electrical Code – Chapter 3 Wiring Methods and Materials, Article 394 Concealed Knob-and-Tube Wiring. 394.10 Uses Permitted.

EXAM 7

EXAM 7 ANSWERS

Table 300.1(C) Metric Designators and Trade Sizes

Metric Designator	Trade Size
12	3/8
16	1/2
21	3/4
27	1
35	1¼
41	1½
53	2
63	2½
78	3
91	3½
103	4
129	5
155	6

Note: The metric designators and trade sizes are for identification purposes only and are not actual dimensions.

---

1. **Answer C.** 1-1/2

   Metric designators and trade sizes for conduit, tubing, and associated fittings and accessories shall be as designated in Table 300.1 (C).

   Reference: 2017 National Electrical Code – Chapter 3 Wiring Methods and Materials, Article 300 General Requirements for Wiring Methods and Materials. 300.1 Scope. 300.1(C) Metric Designators and Trade Sizes. Table 300.1(C) Metric Designators and Trade Sizes (page 70-142)

2. **Answer D.** raceway

   All conductors of the same circuit and, where used, the grounded conductor and all equipment grounding conductors and bonding conductors shall be contained within the same raceway, auxiliary gutter, cable tray, cablebus assembly, trench, cable, or cord, unless otherwise permitted in accordance with 300.3(B)(1) through (B)(4).

   Reference: 2017 National Electrical Code – Chapter 3 Wiring Methods and Materials, Article 300 General Requirements for Wiring Methods and Materials. 300.3 Conductors. 300.3(B) Conductors of the Same Circuit.

3. **Answer B.** conductors

   All conductors of the same circuit and, where used, the grounded conductor and all equipment grounding conductors and bonding conductors shall be contained within the same raceway, auxiliary gutter, cable tray, cablebus assembly, trench, cable, or cord, unless otherwise permitted in accordance with 300.3(B)(1) through (B)(4).

   Reference: 2017 National Electrical Code – Chapter 3 Wiring Methods and Materials, Article 300 General Requirements for Wiring Methods and Materials. 300.3 Conductors. 300.3(B) Conductors of the Same Circuit.

4. **Answer C.** protected

   Where subject to physical damage, conductors, raceways, and cables shall be protected.

   Informational note: Minor damage to a raceway, cable armor, or cable insulation does not necessarily violate the integrity of either the contained conductors or the conductors' insulation.

   Reference: 2017 National Electrical Code – Chapter 3 Wiring Methods and Materials, Article 300 General Requirements for Wiring Methods and Materials. 300.4 Protection Against Physical Damage.

EXAM 7

EXAM 7 ANSWERS

5. **Answer B.**   1-1/4

   In both exposed and concealed locations, where a cable- or raceway-type wiring method is installed through bored holes in joists, rafters, or wood members, *holes shall be bored so that the edge of the hole is not less than 32 mm (1-1/4 in.) from the nearest edge of the wood member.* Where this distance cannot be maintained, the cable or raceway shall be protected from penetration by screws or nails by a steel plate(s) or bushing(s), at least 1.6 mm (1/16 in.) thick, and of appropriate length and width installed to cover the area of the wiring.

   Reference: 2017 National Electrical Code – Chapter 3 Wiring Methods and Materials, Article 300 General Requirements for Wiring Methods and Materials. 300.4 Protection Against Physical Damage. 300.4(A) Cables and Raceways Through Wood Members. 300.4(A)(1) Bored Holes.

6. **Answer A.**   1.25, 0.0625

   In both exposed and concealed locations, where a cable- or raceway-type wiring method is installed through bored holes in joists, rafters, or *wood members, holes shall be bored so that the edge of the hole is not less than 32 mm (1-1/4 in.) from the nearest edge of the wood member.* Where this distance cannot be maintained, the cable or raceway shall be protected from penetration by screws or nails by a steel plate(s) or bushing(s), at least 1.6 mm (1/16 in.) thick, and of appropriate length and width installed to cover the area of the wiring.

   Reference: 2017 National Electrical Code – Chapter 3 Wiring Methods and Materials, Article 300 General Requirements for Wiring Methods and Materials. 300.4 Protection Against Physical Damage. 300.4(A) Cables and Raceways Through Wood Members. 300.4(A)(1) Bored Holes.

7. **Answer A.**   1/16 in.

   Where there is no objection because of weakening the building structure, in both exposed and concealed locations, cables or raceways shall be permitted to be laid in notches in wood studs, joists, rafters, or other wood members *where the cable or raceway at those points is protected against nails or screws by a steel plate at least 1.6 mm (1/16 in.) thick,* and of appropriate length and width, installed to cover the area of the wiring. The steel plate shall be installed before the building finish is applied.

   Reference: 2017 National Electrical Code – Chapter 3 Wiring Methods and Materials, Article 300 General Requirements for Wiring Methods and Materials. 300.4 Protection Against Physical Damage. 300.4(A) Cables and Raceways Through Wood Members. 300.4(A)(2) Notches in Wood.

8. **Answer C.**   1-1/4 inches

   In both exposed and concealed locations, where a cable- or raceway-type wiring method is installed parallel to framing members, such as joists, rafters, or studs, or is installed parallel to furring strips, the cable or raceway shall be installed and supported so that the nearest outside *surface of the cable or raceway is not less than 32 mm (1-1/4 in.) from the nearest edge of the framing member or furring strips where nails or screws are likely to penetrate.* Where this distance cannot be maintained, the cable or raceway shall be protected from penetration by nails or screws by a steel plate, sleeve, or equivalent at least 1.6 mm (1/16 in.) thick.

   Reference: 2017 National Electrical Code – Chapter 3 Wiring Methods and Materials, Article 300 General Requirements for Wiring Methods and Materials. 300.4 Protection Against Physical Damage. 300.4(D) Cables and Raceways Parallel to Framing Members and Furring Strips.

EXAM 7

EXAM 7 ANSWERS

9. **Answer C.** 1-1/2 in.

    A cable, raceway, or box, installed in exposed or concealed locations under metal-corrugated sheet roof decking, shall be installed and supported so there is not less *than 38 mm (1/2 in.) measured from the lowest surface of the roof decking to the top of the cable*, raceway, or box. A cable, raceway, or box shall not be installed in concealed locations in metal-corrugated, sheet decking-type roof.

    Informational Note: Roof decking material is often repaired or replaced after the initial raceway or cabling and roofing installation and may be penetrated by the screws or other mechanical devices designed to provide "hold down" strength of the waterproof membrane or roof insulating material.

    Reference: 2017 National Electrical Code – Chapter 3 Wiring Methods and Materials, Article 300 General Requirements for Wiring Methods and Materials. 300.4 Protection Against Physical Damage. 300.4(E) Cables, Raceways, or Boxes Installed in or Under Roof Decking.

10. **Answer C.** An insulated bushing.

    Where raceways contain 4 AWG or larger insulated circuit conductors, and these conductors enter a cabinet, a box, an enclosure, or a raceway, the conductors shall be protected by an identified fitting providing a smoothly rounded insulating surface, unless the conductors are separated from the fitting or raceway by identified insulating material that is securely fastened in place.

    Conduit bushings constructed wholly of insulating material shall not be used to secure a fitting or raceway. The insulating fitting or insulating material shall have a temperature rating not less than the insulation temperature rating of the installed conductors.

    Reference: 2017 National Electrical Code – Chapter 3 Wiring Methods and Materials, Article 300 General Requirements for Wiring Methods and Materials. 300.4 Protection Against Physical Damage. 300.4(G) Insulated Fittings.

EXAM 7

EXAM 7 ANSWERS

Table 300.5 Minimum Cover Requirements, 0 to 1000 Volts, Nominal, Burial in Millimeters (Inches)

Location of Wiring Method or Circuit	Column 1 Direct Burial Cables or Conductors		Column 2 Rigid Metal Conduit or Intermediate Metal Conduit		Column 3 Nonmetallic Raceways Listed for Direct Burial Without Concrete Encasement or Other Approved Raceways		Column 4 Residential Branch Circuits Rated 120 Volts or Less with GFCI Protection and Maximum Overcurrent Protection of 20 Amperes		Column 5 Circuits for Control of Irrigation and Landscape Lighting Limited to Not More Than 30 Volts and Installed with Type UF or in Other Identified Cable or Raceway	
	mm	in.	mm	in.	mm	in.	mm	in.	mm	in.
All locations not specified below	600	24	150	6	450	18	300	12	150	6
In trench below 50 mm (2 in.) thick concrete or equivalent	450	18	150	6	300	12	150	6	150	6
Under a building	0 (in raceway or Type MC or Type MI cable identified for direct burial)	0	0	0	0	0	0 (in raceway or Type MC or Type MI cable identified for direct burial)	0	0 (in raceway or Type MC or Type MI cable identified for direct burial)	0
Under minimum of 102 mm (4 in.) thick concrete exterior slab with no vehicular traffic and the slab extending not less than 152 mm (6 in.) beyond the underground installation	450	18	100	4	100	4	150 (direct burial) 100 (in raceway)	6 4	150 (direct burial) 100 (in raceway)	6 4
Under streets, highways, roads, alleys, driveways, and parking lots	600	24	600	24	600	24	600	24	600	24
One- and two-family dwelling driveways and outdoor parking areas, and used only for dwelling-related purposes	450	18	450	18	450	18	300	12	450	18
In or under airport runways, including adjacent areas where trespassing prohibited	450	18	450	18	450	18	450	18	450	18

11. **Answer D.** 24

Direct-buried cable or conduit or other raceways shall be installed to meet the minimum cover requirements of Table 300.5.

Reference: 2017 National Electrical Code – Chapter 3 Wiring Methods and Materials, Article 300 General Requirements for Wiring Methods and Materials. 300.5 Underground Installations. 300.5(A) Minimum Cover Requirements. Table 300.5 Minimum Cover Requirements, 0 to 1000 Volts, Nominal, Burial in Millimeters (Inches)

12. **Answer A.** 6

Direct-buried cable or conduit or other raceways shall be installed to meet the minimum cover requirements of Table 300.5.

Reference: 2017 National Electrical Code – Chapter 3 Wiring Methods and Materials, Article 300 General Requirements for Wiring Methods and Materials. 300.5 Underground Installations. 300.5(A) Minimum Cover Requirements. Table 300.5 Minimum Cover Requirements, 0 to 1000 Volts, Nominal, Burial in Millimeters (Inches)

EXAM 7

EXAM 7 ANSWERS

13. Answer C.   18

Direct-buried cable or conduit or other raceways shall be installed to meet the minimum cover requirements of Table 300.5.

Reference: 2017 National Electrical Code – Chapter 3 Wiring Methods and Materials, Article 300 General Requirements for Wiring Methods and Materials. 300.5 Underground Installations. 300.5(A) Minimum Cover Requirements. Table 300.5 Minimum Cover Requirements, 0 to 1000 Volts, Nominal, Burial in Millimeters (Inches)

14. Answer D.   24

Direct-buried cable or conduit or other raceways shall be installed to meet the minimum cover requirements of Table 300.5.

Reference: 2017 National Electrical Code – Chapter 3 Wiring Methods and Materials, Article 300 General Requirements for Wiring Methods and Materials. 300.5 Underground Installations. 300.5(A) Minimum Cover Requirements. Table 300.5 Minimum Cover Requirements, 0 to 1000 Volts, Nominal, Burial in Millimeters (Inches)

15. Answer A.   0

Direct-buried cable or conduit or other raceways shall be installed to meet the minimum cover requirements of Table 300.5.

Reference: 2017 National Electrical Code – Chapter 3 Wiring Methods and Materials, Article 300 General Requirements for Wiring Methods and Materials. 300.5 Underground Installations. 300.5(A) Minimum Cover Requirements. Table 300.5 Minimum Cover Requirements, 0 to 1000 Volts, Nominal, Burial in Millimeters (Inches)

16. Answer D.   24

Direct-buried cable or conduit or other raceways shall be installed to meet the minimum cover requirements of Table 300.5.

Reference: 2017 National Electrical Code – Chapter 3 Wiring Methods and Materials, Article 300 General Requirements for Wiring Methods and Materials. 300.5 Underground Installations. 300.5(A) Minimum Cover Requirements. Table 300.5 Minimum Cover Requirements, 0 to 1000 Volts, Nominal, Burial in Millimeters (Inches)

17. Answer A.   6

Direct-buried cable or conduit or other raceways shall be installed to meet the minimum cover requirements of Table 300.5.

Reference: 2017 National Electrical Code – Chapter 3 Wiring Methods and Materials, Article 300 General Requirements for Wiring Methods and Materials. 300.5 Underground Installations. 300.5(A) Minimum Cover Requirements. Table 300.5 Minimum Cover Requirements, 0 to 1000 Volts, Nominal, Burial in Millimeters (Inches)

18. Answer C.   18 inches

Direct-buried cable or conduit or other raceways shall be installed to meet the minimum cover requirements of Table 300.5.

Reference: 2017 National Electrical Code – Chapter 3 Wiring Methods and Materials, Article 300 General Requirements for Wiring Methods and Materials. 300.5 Underground Installations. 300.5(A) Minimum Cover Requirements. Table 300.5 Minimum Cover Requirements, 0 to 1000 Volts, Nominal, Burial in Millimeters (Inches)

19. Answer B.   18 inches

Direct-buried cable or conduit or other raceways shall be installed to meet the minimum cover requirements of Table 300.5.

Reference: 2017 National Electrical Code – Chapter 3 Wiring Methods and Materials, Article 300 General Requirements for Wiring Methods and Materials. 300.5 Underground Installations. 300.5(A) Minimum Cover Requirements. Table 300.5 Minimum Cover Requirements, 0 to 1000 Volts, Nominal, Burial in Millimeters (Inches)

20. Answer B.   12 inches

Direct-buried cable or conduit or other raceways shall be installed to meet the minimum cover requirements of Table 300.5.

Reference: 2017 National Electrical Code – Chapter 3 Wiring Methods and Materials, Article 300 General Requirements for Wiring Methods and Materials. 300.5 Underground Installations. 300.5(A) Minimum Cover Requirements. Table 300.5 Minimum Cover Requirements, 0 to 1000 Volts, Nominal, Burial in Millimeters (Inches)

EXAM 7

EXAM 7 ANSWERS

21. **Answer D.** wet

    The interior of enclosures or raceways installed underground shall be considered to be a wet location. Insulated conductors and cables installed in these enclosures or raceways in underground installations shall comply with 310.10(C).

    Reference: 2017 National Electrical Code – Chapter 3 Wiring Methods and Materials, Article 300 General Requirements for Wiring Methods and Materials. 300.5 Underground Installations. 300.5(B) Wet Locations.

22. **Answer D.** under a building

    Underground cable and conductors installed under a building shall be in a raceway.

    Reference: 2017 National Electrical Code – Chapter 3 Wiring Methods and Materials, Article 300 General Requirements for Wiring Methods and Materials. 300.5 Underground Installations. 300.5(C) Underground Cables and Conductors Under Buildings.

23. **Answer D.** 8

    Direct-buried conductors and cables emerging from grade and specified in columns 1 and 4 of Table 300.5 shall be protected by enclosures or raceways extending from the minimum cover distance below grade required by 300.5(A) *to a point at least 2.5 m (8 ft.) above finished grade. In no case shall the protection be required to exceed 450 mm (18 in.) below finished grade.*

    Reference: 2017 National Electrical Code – Chapter 3 Wiring Methods and Materials, Article 300 General Requirements for Wiring Methods and Materials. 300.5 Underground Installations. 300.5(D) Protection from Damage. 300.5(D)(1) Emerging from Grade.

24. **Answer A.** 8 feet

    Direct-buried conductors and cables emerging from grade and specified in columns 1 and 4 of Table 300.5 shall be protected by enclosures or raceways extending from the minimum cover distance below grade required by 300.5(A) *to a point at least 2.5 m (8 ft.) above finished grade. In no case shall the protection be required to exceed 450 mm (18 in.) below finished grade.*

    Reference: 2017 National Electrical Code – Chapter 3 Wiring Methods and Materials, Article 300 General Requirements for Wiring Methods and Materials. 300.5 Underground Installations. 300.5(D) Protection from Damage. 300.5(D)(1) Emerging from Grade.

25. **Answer D.** 12

    Underground service conductors that are not encased in concrete and that are buried 450 mm (18 in.) or more below grade shall have their location identified *by a warning ribbon that is placed in the trench at least 300 mm (12 in.) above the underground installation.*

    Reference: 2017 National Electrical Code – Chapter 3 Wiring Methods and Materials, Article 300 General Requirements for Wiring Methods and Materials. 300.5 Underground Installations. 300.5(D) Protection from Damage. 300.5(D)(3) Service Conductors.

26. **Answer C.** permitted

    Direct-buried conductors or cables shall be permitted to be spliced or tapped without the use of splice boxes. The splices or taps shall be made in accordance with 110.14(B).

    Reference: 2017 National Electrical Code – Chapter 3 Wiring Methods and Materials, Article 300 General Requirements for Wiring Methods and Materials. 300.5 Underground Installations. 300.5(E) Splices and Taps.

27. **Answer D.** without the use of splice boxes

    Direct-buried conductors or cables shall be permitted to be spliced or tapped without the use of splice boxes. The splices or taps shall be made in accordance with 110.14(B).

    Reference: 2017 National Electrical Code – Chapter 3 Wiring Methods and Materials, Article 300 General Requirements for Wiring Methods and Materials. 300.5 Underground Installations. 300.5(E) Splices and Taps.

28. **Answer D.** neither A nor B

    Direct-buried conductors or cables shall be permitted to be spliced or tapped without the use of splice boxes. The splices or taps shall be made in accordance with 110.14(B).

    Reference: 2017 National Electrical Code – Chapter 3 Wiring Methods and Materials, Article 300 General Requirements for Wiring Methods and Materials. 300.5 Underground Installations. 300.5(E) Splices and Taps.

EXAM 7

EXAM 7 ANSWERS

29. Answer D. sealed or plugged at either or both ends

Conduits or raceways through which moisture may contact live parts shall be sealed or plugged at either or both ends. *Spare or unused raceways shall also be sealed. Sealants shall be identified for use with the cable insulation, conductor insulation, bare conductor, shield, or other components.*

Informational Note: Presence of hazardous gases or vapors may also necessitate sealing of underground conduits or raceways entering buildings.

Reference: 2017 National Electrical Code – Chapter 3 Wiring Methods and Materials, Article 300 General Requirements for Wiring Methods and Materials. 300.5 Underground Installations. 300.5(G) Raceway Seals.

30. Answer A. 2 inches

Raceways approved for burial only where concrete encased shall require concrete envelope not less than 50 mm (2 in.) thick.

Reference: 2017 National Electrical Code – Chapter 3 Wiring Methods and Materials, Article 300 General Requirements for Wiring Methods and Materials. 300.5 Underground Installation. Table 300.5 Minimum Cover Requirements, 0 to 1000 Volts, Nominal, Burial in Millimeters (Inches). Note 2

31. Answer A. environment

Raceways, cable trays, cablebus, auxiliary gutters, cable armor, boxes, cable sheathing, cabinets, elbows, couplings, fittings, supports, and *support hardware shall be of materials suitable for the environment in which they are to be installed.*

Reference: 2017 National Electrical Code – Chapter 3 Wiring Methods and Materials, Article 300 General Requirements for Wiring Methods and Materials. 300.6 Protection Against Corrosion and Deterioration.

32. Answer D. On field cut threads in corrosive locations

Ferrous metal raceways, cable trays, cablebus, auxiliary gutters, cable armor, boxes, cable sheathing, cabinets, metal elbows, couplings, nipples, fittings, supports, and support hardware shall be suitably protected against corrosion inside and outside (except threads at joints) by a coating of approved corrosion-resistant material. *Where corrosion protection is necessary and the conduit is threaded in the field, the threads shall be coated with an approved electrically conductive, corrosion-resistant compound.*

Informational Note: Field-cut threads are those threads that are cut in conduit, elbows, or nipples anywhere other than at the factory where the product is listed.

Reference: 2017 National Electrical Code – Chapter 3 Wiring Methods and Materials, Article 300 General Requirements for Wiring Methods and Materials. 300.6 Protection Against Corrosion and Deterioration. 300.6(A) Ferrous Metal Equipment.

33. Answer B. 1/4 in.

In portions of dairy processing facilities, laundries, canneries, and other indoor wet locations, and in locations *where walls are frequently washed or where there are surfaces of absorbent materials, such as damp paper or wood, the entire wiring system, where installed exposed, including all boxes, fittings, raceways, and cable used therewith, shall be mounted so that there is at least a 6-mm (1/4-in.) airspace between it and the wall or supporting surface.*

Reference: 2017 National Electrical Code – Chapter 3 Wiring Methods and Materials, Article 300 General Requirements for Wiring Methods and Materials. 300.6 Protection Against Corrosion and Deterioration. 300.6(D) Indoor Wet Locations.

EXAM 7

EXAM 7 ANSWERS

34. **Answer B.** compensate

    Raceways shall be provided with expansion, expansion deflection, or deflection fittings where necessary to *compensate for thermal expansion, deflection, and contraction.*

    Informational Note: Table 352.44 and Table 355.44 provide the expansion information for polyvinyl chloride (PVC) and for reinforced thermosetting resin conduit (RTRC), respectively. A nominal number for steel conduit can be determined by multiplying the expansion length in Table 352.44 by 0.20. The coefficient of expansion for steel electrical metallic tubing, intermediate metal conduit, and rigid metal conduit is 1.170×10^{-5} (0.0000117 mm per mm of conduit for each °C in temperature change) [0.650×10^{-5} (0.0000065 in. per inch of conduit for each °F in temperature change)].

    A nominal number for aluminum conduit and aluminum electrical metallic tubing can be determined by multiplying the expansion length in Table 352.44 by 0.40. The coefficient of expansion for aluminum electrical metallic tubing and aluminum rigid metal conduit is 2.34×10^{-5} (0.0000234 mm per mm of conduit for each °C in temperature change) [1.30×10^{-5}

    (0.000013 in. per inch of conduit for each °F in temperature change)].

    Reference: 2017 National Electrical Code – Chapter 3 Wiring Methods and Materials, Article 300 General Requirements for Wiring Methods and Materials. 300.7 Raceways Exposed to Different Temperatures. 300.7(B) Expansion, Expansion-Deflection, and Deflection.

35. **Answer D.** Wet

    Where raceways are installed in wet locations abovegrade, *the interior of these raceways shall be considered to be a wet location. Insulated conductors and cables installed in raceways in wet locations above grade shall comply with 310.10(C).*

    Reference: 2017 National Electrical Code – Chapter 3 Wiring Methods and Materials, Article 300 General Requirements for Wiring Methods and Materials. 300.9 Raceways in Wet Locations Abovegrade.

36. **Answer B.** supported by

    Raceways, cable assemblies, boxes, cabinets, and fittings shall be securely fastened in place. Support wires that do not provide secure support shall not be permitted as the sole support. Support wires and associated fittings that provide secure support and that are installed in addition to the ceiling grid support wires shall be permitted as the sole support. *Where independent support wires are used, they shall be secured at both ends. Cables and raceways shall not be supported by ceiling grids.*

    Reference: 2017 National Electrical Code – Chapter 3 Wiring Methods and Materials, Article 300 General Requirements for Wiring Methods and Materials. 300.11 Securing and Supporting. 300.11(A) Secured in Place.

EXAM 7

EXAM 7 ANSWERS

37. Answer D. permitted as the sole support

Raceways, cable assemblies, boxes, cabinets, and fittings shall be securely fastened in place. ***Support wires that do not provide secure support shall not be permitted as the sole support.*** Support wires and associated fittings that provide secure support and that are installed in addition to the ceiling grid support wires shall be permitted as the sole support. Where independent support wires are used, they shall be secured at both ends. Cables and raceways shall not be supported by ceiling grids.

Reference: 2017 National Electrical Code – Chapter 3 Wiring Methods and Materials, Article 300 General Requirements for Wiring Methods and Materials. 300.11 Securing and Supporting. 300.11(A) Secured in Place.

38. Answer D. the ceiling assembly, including the ceiling support wires

Wiring located within the cavity of a fire-rated floor-ceiling or roof-ceiling assembly shall not be secured to, or supported by, the ceiling assembly, including the ceiling support wires. An independent means of secure support shall be provided and shall be permitted to be attached to the assembly. Where independent support wires are used, they shall be distinguishable by color, tagging, or other effective means from those that are part of the fire-rated design.

Informational Note: One method of determining fire rating is testing in accordance with ANSI/ASTM E119-2012a, Method for Fire Tests of Building Construction and Materials.

Reference: 2017 National Electrical Code – Chapter 3 Wiring Methods and Materials, Article 300 General Requirements for Wiring Methods and Materials. 300.11 Securing and Supporting. 300.11(A) Secured in Place. 300.11(A)(1) Fire-Rated Assemblies.

39. Answer A. somehow separated from fire-rated design

Wiring located within the cavity of a fire-rated floor-ceiling or roof-ceiling assembly shall not be secured to, or supported by, the ceiling assembly, including the ceiling support wires. An independent means of secure support shall be provided and shall be permitted to be attached to the assembly. ***Where independent support wires are used, they shall be distinguishable by color, tagging, or other effective means from those that are part of the fire-rated design.***

Informational Note: One method of determining fire rating is testing in accordance with ANSI/ASTM E119-2012a, Method for Fire Tests of Building Construction and Materials.

Reference: 2017 National Electrical Code – Chapter 3 Wiring Methods and Materials, Article 300 General Requirements for Wiring Methods and Materials. 300.11 Securing and Supporting. 300.11(A) Secured in Place. 300.11(A)(1) Fire-Rated Assemblies.

40. Answer B. continuous

Raceways, cable armors, and cable sheaths shall be continuous between cabinets, boxes, fittings, or other enclosures or outlets.

Exception No. 1: Short sections of raceways used to provide support or protection of cable assemblies from physical damage shall not be required to be mechanically continuous.

Exception No. 2: Raceways and cables installed into the bottom of open bottom equipment, such as switchboards, motor control centers, and floor or pad-mounted transformers, shall not be required to be mechanically secured to the equipment.

Reference: 2017 National Electrical Code – Chapter 3 Wiring Methods and Materials, Article 300 General Requirements for Wiring Methods and Materials. 300.12 Mechanical Continuity - Raceways and Cables.

EXAM 7

EXAM 7 ANSWERS

41. **Answer A.** continuous

    Conductors in raceways shall be continuous between outlets, boxes, devices, and so forth. There shall be no splice or tap within a raceway unless permitted by 300.15; 368.56(A); 376.56; 378.56; 384.56; 386.56; 388.56; or 390.7.

    Reference: 2017 National Electrical Code – Chapter 3 Wiring Methods and Materials, Article 300 General Requirements for Wiring Methods and Materials. 300.13 Mechanical and Electrical Continuity - Conductors. 300.13(A) General.

42. **Answer B.** grounded

    *In multi wire branch circuits, the continuity of a grounded conductor shall not depend on device connections such as lampholders, receptacles, and so fo*rth, where the removal of such devices would interrupt the continuity.

    Reference: 2017 National Electrical Code – Chapter 3 Wiring Methods and Materials, Article 300 General Requirements for Wiring Methods and Materials. 300.13 Mechanical and Electrical Continuity - Conductors. 300.13(B) Device Removal.

43. **Answer B.** 6

    At least 150 mm (6 in.) of free conductor, measured from the point in the box where it emerges from its raceway or cable sheath, shall be left at each outlet, junction, and switch point for splices or the connection of luminaires or devices. Where the opening to an outlet, junction, or switch point is less than 200 mm (8 in.) in any dimension, each conductor shall be long enough to extend at least 75 mm (3 in.) outside the opening.

    Reference: 2017 National Electrical Code – Chapter 3 Wiring Methods and Materials, Article 300 General Requirements for Wiring Methods and Materials. 300.14 Length of Free Conductors at Outlets, Junctions, and Switch Points.

44. **Answer C.** 6

    At least 150 mm (6 in.) of free conductor, measured from the point in the box where it emerges from its raceway or cable sheath, shall be left at each outlet, junction, and switch point for splices or the connection of luminaires or devices. Where the opening to an outlet, junction, or switch point is less than 200 mm (8 in.) in any dimension, each conductor shall be long enough to extend at least 75 mm (3 in.) outside the opening.

    Reference: 2017 National Electrical Code – Chapter 3 Wiring Methods and Materials, Article 300 General Requirements for Wiring Methods and Materials. 300.14 Length of Free Conductors at Outlets, Junctions, and Switch Points.

45. **Answer D.** 8, 3

    At least 150 mm (6 in.) of free conductor, measured from the point in the box where it emerges from its raceway or cable sheath, shall be left at each outlet, junction, and switch point for splices or the connection of luminaires or devices. *Where the opening to an outlet, junction, or switch point is less than 200 mm (8 in.) in any dimension, each conductor shall be long enough to extend at least 75 mm (3 in.) outside the opening.*

    Reference: 2017 National Electrical Code – Chapter 3 Wiring Methods and Materials, Article 300 General Requirements for Wiring Methods and Materials. 300.14 Length of Free Conductors at Outlets, Junctions, and Switch Points.

EXAM 7

EXAM 7 ANSWERS

46. Answer A. 3 inches

At least 150 mm (6 in.) of free conductor, measured from the point in the box where it emerges from its raceway or cable sheath, shall be left at each outlet, junction, and switch point for splices or the connection of luminaires or devices. Where the opening to an outlet, junction, or switch point is less than 200 mm (8 in.) in any dimension, *each conductor shall be long enough to extend at least 75 mm (3 in.) outside the opening.*

Reference: 2017 National Electrical Code – Chapter 3 Wiring Methods and Materials, Article 300 General Requirements for Wiring Methods and Materials. 300.14 Length of Free Conductors at Outlets, Junctions, and Switch Points.

47. Answer C. raceway

A box or conduit body shall not be required where a luminaire is used as a raceway as permitted in 410.64.

Reference: 2017 National Electrical Code – Chapter 3 Wiring Methods and Materials, Article 300 General Requirements for Wiring Methods and Materials. 300.15 Boxes, Conduit Bodies, or Fittings - Where Required. 300.15(J) Luminaires.

48. Answer A. knob-and-tube wiring

A box, conduit body, or terminal fitting having a separately bushed hole for each conductor shall be used wherever a change is made *from conduit, electrical metallic tubing, electrical nonmetallic tubing, nonmetallic-sheathed cable, Type AC cable, Type MC cable, or mineral-insulated, metal-sheathed cable and surface raceway wiring to open wiring or to concealed knob-and-tube wiring.* A fitting used for this purpose shall contain no taps or splices and shall not be used at luminaire outlets. A conduit body used for this purpose shall contain no taps or splices, unless it complies with 314.16(C)(2).

Reference: 2017 National Electrical Code – Chapter 3 Wiring Methods and Materials, Article 300 General Requirements for Wiring Methods and Materials. 300.16 Raceway or Cable to Open or Concealed Wiring. 300.16(A) Box, Conduit Body, or Fitting.

49. Answer C. heat

The number and size of conductors in any raceway shall not be more than will permit dissipation of the heat and ready installation or withdrawal of the conductors without damage to the conductors or to their insulation.

Informational Note: See the following sections of this Code: intermediate metal conduit, 342.22; rigid metal conduit, 344.22; flexible metal conduit, 348.22; liquidtight flexible metal conduit, 350.22; PVC conduit, 352.22; HDPE conduit, 353.22; RTRC, 355.22; liquidtight nonmetallic flexible conduit, 356.22; electrical metallic tubing, 358.22; flexible metallic tubing, 360.22; electrical nonmetallic tubing, 362.22; cellular concrete floor raceways, 372.11; cellular metal floor raceways, 374.5; metal wireways, 376.22; nonmetallic wireways, 378.22; surface metal raceways, 386.22; surface nonmetallic raceways, 388.22; underfloor raceways, 390.6; fixture wire, 402.7; theaters, 520.6; signs, 600.31(C); elevators, 620.33; audio signal processing, amplification, and reproduction equipment, 640.23(A) and 640.24; Class 1, Class 2, and Class 3 circuits, Article 725; fire alarm circuits, Article 760; and optical fiber cables and raceways, Article 770.

Reference: 2017 National Electrical Code – Chapter 3 Wiring Methods and Materials, Article 300 General Requirements for Wiring Methods and Materials. 300.17 Number and Size of Conductors in Raceway.

50. Answer B. grouping all phase conductors together.

Where conductors carrying alternating current are installed in ferrous metal enclosures or ferrous metal raceways, they shall be arranged so as to avoid heating the surrounding ferrous metal by induction. To accomplish this, all phase conductors and, *where used, the grounded conductor and all equipment grounding conductors shall be grouped together.*

Reference: 2017 National Electrical Code – Chapter 3 Wiring Methods and Materials, Article 300 General Requirements for Wiring Methods and Materials. 300.20 Induced Currents in Ferrous Metal Enclosures or Ferrous Metal Raceways. 300.20(A) Conductors Grouped Together.

EXAM 7

EXAM 7 ANSWERS

51. **Answer B.** Inductive heat

    Where conductors carrying alternating current are installed in ferrous metal enclosures or ferrous metal raceways, they shall be arranged so as to avoid heating the surrounding ferrous metal by induction. To accomplish this, all phase conductors and, where used, the grounded conductor and all equipment grounding conductors shall be grouped together.

    Reference: 2017 National Electrical Code – Chapter 3 Wiring Methods and Materials, Article 300 General Requirements for Wiring Methods and Materials. 300.20 Induced Currents in Ferrous Metal Enclosures or Ferrous Metal Raceways. 300.20(A) Conductors Grouped Together.

52. **Answer B.** inductive heat

    Where conductors carrying alternating current are installed in ferrous metal enclosures or ferrous metal raceways, they shall be arranged so as to avoid heating the surrounding ferrous metal by induction. To accomplish this, all phase conductors and, where used, the grounded conductor and all equipment grounding conductors shall be grouped together.

    Reference: 2017 National Electrical Code – Chapter 3 Wiring Methods and Materials, Article 300 General Requirements for Wiring Methods and Materials. 300.20 Induced Currents in Ferrous Metal Enclosures or Ferrous Metal Raceways. 300.20(A) Conductors Grouped Together.

53. **Answer C.** firestopped

    Electrical installations in hollow spaces, vertical shafts, and ventilation or air-handling ducts shall be made so that the possible spread of fire or products of combustion will not be substantially increased. *Openings around electrical penetrations into or through fire-resistant-rated walls, partitions, floors, or ceilings shall be firestopped using approved methods to maintain the fire resistance rating.*

    Informational Note: Directories of electrical construction materials published by qualified testing laboratories contain many listing installation restrictions necessary to maintain the fire-resistive rating of assemblies where penetrations or openings are made. Building codes also contain restrictions on membrane penetrations on opposite sides of a fire-resistance-rated wall assembly. An example is the 600-mm (24-in.) minimum horizontal separation that usually applies between boxes installed on opposite sides of the wall. Assistance in complying with 300.21 can be found in building codes, fire resistance directories, and product listings.

    Reference: 2017 National Electrical Code – Chapter 3 Wiring Methods and Materials, Article 300 General Requirements for Wiring Methods and Materials. 300.21 Spread of Fire or Products of Combustion.

54. **Answer B.** no wiring systems of any type

    No wiring systems of any type shall be installed in ducts used to transport dust, loose stock, or flammable vapors. No wiring system of any type shall be installed in any duct, or shaft containing only such ducts, used for vapor removal or for ventilation of commercial-type cooking equipment.

    Reference: 2017 National Electrical Code – Chapter 3 Wiring Methods and Materials, Article 300 General Requirements for Wiring Methods and Materials. 300.22 Wiring in Ducts Not Used for Air Handling, Fabricated Ducts for Environmental Air, and Other Spaces for Environmental Air (Plenums). 300.22(A) Ducts for Dust, Loose Stock, or Vapor Removal.

EXAM 7

EXAM 7 ANSWERS

55. Answer D. Suitable

Suitable covers shall be installed on all boxes, fittings, and similar enclosures to prevent accidental contact with energized parts or physical damage to parts or insulation.

Reference: 2017 National Electrical Code – Chapter 3 Wiring Methods and Materials, Article 300 General Requirements for Wiring Methods and Materials. 300.31 Covers Required.

56. Answer D. 12

The conductor shall not be bent to a radius less than 8 times the overall diameter for nonshielded conductors or 12 times the overall diameter for shielded or lead-covered conductors during or after installation. For multiconductor or multiplexed single-conductor cables having individually shielded conductors, *the minimum bending radius is 12 times the diameter of the individually shielded conductors or 7 times the overall diameter, whichever is greater.*

Reference: 2017 National Electrical Code – Chapter 3 Wiring Methods and Materials, Article 300 General Requirements for Wiring Methods and Materials. 300.34 Conductor Bending Radius.

57. Answer B. eight

The conductor shall not be bent to a radius less than 8 times the overall diameter for nonshielded conductors or 12 times the overall diameter for shielded or lead-covered conductors during or after installation. For multiconductor or multiplexed single-conductor cables having individually shielded conductors, the minimum bending radius is 12 times the diameter of the individually shielded conductors or 7 times the overall diameter, whichever is greater.

Reference: 2017 National Electrical Code – Chapter 3 Wiring Methods and Materials, Article 300 General Requirements for Wiring Methods and Materials. 300.34 Conductor Bending Radius.

58. Answer A. 2

Review and know how to use this table and notes.

Note 2. Where solid rock prevents compliance with the cover depths specified in this table, the wiring shall be installed in a metal or nonmetallic raceway permitted for direct burial. *The raceways shall be covered by a minimum of 50 mm (2 in.)* of concrete extending down to rock.

Reference: 2017 National Electrical Code – Chapter 3 Wiring Methods and Materials, Article 300 General Requirements for Wiring Methods and Materials. 300.50 Underground Installations. Table 300.50 Minimum Cover Requirements (page 70-154)

59. Answer C. Electrical Ducts

Electrical conduits, or other raceways round in cross section, that are suitable for use underground or embedded in concrete.

Reference: 2017 National Electrical Code – Chapter 3 Wiring Methods and Materials, Article 310 Conductors for General Wiring. 310.2 Definitions. Electrical Ducts.

60. Answer A. 1/0

Aluminum, copper-clad aluminum, or copper conductors, for each phase, polarity, neutral, or grounded circuit shall be permitted to be connected in parallel (electrically joined at both ends) *only in sizes 1/0 AWG and larger where installed in accordance with 310.10(H)(2) through (H)(6).*

Reference: 2017 National Electrical Code – Chapter 3 Wiring Methods and Materials, Article 310 Conductors for General Wiring. 310.10 Uses Permitted. 310.10(H) Conductors in Parallel. 310.10(H)(1) General.

61. Answer B. parallel

Aluminum, copper-clad aluminum, or copper conductors, for each phase, polarity, neutral, or grounded circuit shall be *permitted to be connected in parallel* (electrically joined at both ends) only in sizes 1/0 AWG and larger where installed in accordance with 310.10(H)(2) through (H)(6).

Reference: 2017 National Electrical Code – Chapter 3 Wiring Methods and Materials, Article 310 Conductors for General Wiring. 310.10 Uses Permitted. 310.10(H) Conductors in Parallel. 310.10(H)(1) General.

EXAM 7

EXAM 7 ANSWERS

62. **Answer C.** both A and B

    The paralleled conductors in each phase, polarity, neutral, grounded circuit conductor, equipment grounding conductor, or equipment bonding jumper shall comply with all of the following:

    (1) Be the same length.

    (2) Consist of the same conductor material.

    (3) Be the same size in circular mil area.

    (4) Have the same insulation type.

    (5) Be terminated in the same manner.

    Reference: 2017 National Electrical Code – Chapter 3 Wiring Methods and Materials, Article 310 Conductors for General Wiring. 310.10 Uses Permitted. 310.10(H) Conductors in Parallel. 310.10(H)(2)

    Where run in separate cables or raceways, the cables or raceways with conductors shall have the same number of conductors and shall have the same electrical characteristics. Conductors of one phase, polarity, neutral, grounded circuit conductor, or equipment grounding conductor shall not be required to have the same physical characteristics as those of another phase, polarity, neutral, grounded circuit conductor, or equipment grounding conductor.

    Reference: 2017 National Electrical Code – Chapter 3 Wiring Methods and Materials, Article 310 Conductors for General Wiring. 310.10 Uses Permitted. 310.10(H) Conductors in Parallel. 310.10(H)(3)

    Conductors installed in parallel shall comply with the provisions of 310.15(B)(3)(a).

    Reference: 2017 National Electrical Code – Chapter 3 Wiring Methods and Materials, Article 310 Conductors for General Wiring. 310.10 Uses Permitted. 310.10(H) Conductors in Parallel. 310.10(H)(4)

63. **Answer D.** lowest

    Where more than one ampacity applies for a given circuit length, the lowest value shall be used.

    Exception: Where different ampacities apply to portions of a circuit, the higher ampacity shall be permitted to be used if the total portion(s) of the circuit with lower ampacity does not exceed the lesser of 3.0 m (10 ft) or 10 percent of the total circuit.

    Informational Note: See 110.14(C) for conductor temperature limitations due to termination provisions.

    Reference: 2017 National Electrical Code – Chapter 3 Wiring Methods and Materials, Article 310 Conductors for General Wiring. 310.15 Ampacities for Conductors Rated 0-2000 Volts. 310.15(A) General. . 310.15(A)(2) Selection of Ampacity

EXAM 7

EXAM 7 ANSWERS

Table 310.15(B)(2)(a) Ambient Temperature Correction Factors Based on 30°C (86°F)

For ambient temperatures other than 30°C (86°F), multiply the allowable ampacities specified in the ampacity tables by the appropriate correction factor shown below.

Ambient Temperature (°C)	Temperature Rating of Conductor			Ambient Temperature (°F)
	60°C	75°C	90°C	
10 or less	1.29	1.20	1.15	50 or less
11–15	1.22	1.15	1.12	51–59
16–20	1.15	1.11	1.08	60–68
21–25	1.08	1.05	1.04	69–77
26–30	1.00	1.00	1.00	78–86
31–35	0.91	0.94	0.96	87–95
36–40	0.82	0.88	0.91	96–104
41–45	0.71	0.82	0.87	105–113
46–50	0.58	0.75	0.82	114–122
51–55	0.41	0.67	0.76	123–131
56–60	—	0.58	0.71	132–140
61–65	—	0.47	0.65	141–149
66–70	—	0.33	0.58	150–158
71–75	—	—	0.50	159–167
76–80	—	—	0.41	168–176
81–85	—	—	0.29	177–185

64. Answer C. 45

Ampacities for conductors rated 0 to 2000 volts shall be as specified in the Allowable Ampacity Table 310.15(B)(16) through Table 310.15(B)(19), and Ampacity **Table 310.15(B)(20) and Table 310.15(B)(21) as modified by 310.15(B)(1) through (B)(7).**

The temperature correction and adjustment factors shall be permitted to be applied to the ampacity for the temperature rating of the conductor, if the corrected and adjusted ampacity does not exceed the ampacity for the temperature rating of the termination in accordance with the provisions of 110.14(C).

Reference: 2017 National Electrical Code – Chapter 3 Wiring Methods and Materials, Article 310 Conductors for General Wiring. 310.15 Ampacities for Conductors Rated 0-2000 Volts. 310.15(B) Tables. Table 310.15(B)(2)(a) Ambient Temperature Correction Factors Based on 30°C (86°F) (page 70-158)

65. Answer A. 11.25

Ampacities for conductors rated 0 to 2000 volts shall be as specified in the Allowable Ampacity Table 310.15(B)(16) through Table 310.15(B)(19), and Ampacity Table 310.15(B)(20) and Table 310.15(B)(21) as modified by 310.15(B)(1) through (B)(7).

The temperature correction and adjustment factors shall be permitted to be applied to the ampacity for the temperature rating of the conductor, if the corrected and adjusted ampacity does not exceed the ampacity for the temperature rating of the termination in accordance with the provisions of 110.14(C).

Reference: 2017 National Electrical Code – Chapter 3 Wiring Methods and Materials, Article 310 Conductors for General Wiring. 310.15 Ampacities for Conductors Rated 0-2000 Volts. 310.15(B) Tables. Table 310.15(B)(16) (formerly Table 310.16) Allowable Ampacities of Insulated Conductors Rated Up to and Including 2000 Volts, 60°C Through 90°C (140°F Through 194°F), Not More Than Three Current-Carrying Conductors in Raceway, Cable, or Earth (Directly Buried), Based on Ambient Temperature of 30°C (86°F) (page 70-161)

EXAM 7

EXAM 7 ANSWERS

66. Answer A. 115

Ampacities for conductors rated 0 to 2000 volts shall be as specified in the Allowable Ampacity Table 310.15(B)(16) through Table 310.15(B)(19), and Ampacity Table 310.15(B)(20) and Table 310.15(B)(21) as modified by 310.15(B)(1) through (B)(7).

The temperature correction and adjustment factors shall be permitted to be applied to the ampacity for the temperature rating of the conductor, if the corrected and adjusted ampacity does not exceed the ampacity for the temperature rating of the termination in accordance with the provisions of 110.14(C).

Reference: 2017 National Electrical Code – Chapter 3 Wiring Methods and Materials, Article 310 Conductors for General Wiring. 310.15 Ampacities for Conductors Rated 0-2000 Volts. 310.15(B) Tables. Table 310.15(B)(16) (formerly Table 310.16) Allowable Ampacities of Insulated Conductors Rated Up to and Including 2000 Volts, 60°C Through 90°C (140°F Through 194°F), Not More Than Three Current-Carrying Conductors in Raceway, Cable, or Earth (Directly Buried), Based on Ambient Temperature of 30°C (86°F) (page 70-161)

67. Answer B. 55

Ampacities for conductors rated 0 to 2000 volts shall be as specified in the Allowable Ampacity Table 310.15(B)(16) through Table 310.15(B)(19), and Ampacity Table 310.15(B)(20) and Table 310.15(B)(21) as modified by 310.15(B)(1) through (B)(7).

The temperature correction and adjustment factors shall be permitted to be applied to the ampacity for the temperature rating of the conductor, if the corrected and adjusted ampacity does not exceed the ampacity for the temperature rating of the termination in accordance with the provisions of 110.14(C).

Reference: 2017National Electrical Code – Chapter 3 Wiring Methods and Materials, Article 310 Conductors for General Wiring. 310.15 Ampacities for Conductors Rated 0-2000 Volts. 310.15(B) Tables. Table 310.15(B)(16) (formerly Table 310.16) Allowable Ampacities of Insulated Conductors Rated Up to and Including 2000 Volts, 60°C Through 90°C (140°F Through 194°F), Not More Than Three Current-Carrying Conductors in Raceway, Cable, or Earth (Directly Buried), Based on Ambient Temperature of 30°C (86°F) (page 70-161)

EXAM 7

EXAM 7 ANSWERS

68. Answer A. 100

Ampacities for conductors rated 0 to 2000 volts shall be as specified in the Allowable Ampacity Table 310.15(B)(16) through Table 310.15(B)(19), and Ampacity Table 310.15(B)(20) and Table 310.15(B)(21) as modified by 310.15(B)(1) through (B)(7).

The temperature correction and adjustment factors shall be permitted to be applied to the ampacity for the temperature rating of the conductor, if the corrected and adjusted ampacity does not exceed the ampacity for the temperature rating of the termination in accordance with the provisions of 110.14(C).

Reference: 2017 National Electrical Code – Chapter 3 Wiring Methods and Materials, Article 310 Conductors for General Wiring. 310.15 Ampacities for Conductors Rated 0-2000 Volts. 310.15(B) Tables. Table 310.15(B)(16) (formerly Table 310.16) Allowable Ampacities of Insulated Conductors Rated Up to and Including 2000 Volts, 60°C Through 90°C (140°F Through 194°F), Not More Than Three Current-Carrying Conductors in Raceway, Cable, or Earth (Directly Buried), Based on Ambient Temperature of 30°C (86°F) (page 70-161)

69. Answer A. 55

Ampacities for conductors rated 0 to 2000 volts shall be as specified in the Allowable Ampacity Table 310.15(B)(16) through Table 310.15(B)(19), and Ampacity Table 310.15(B)(20) and Table 310.15(B)(21) as modified by 310.15(B)(1) through (B)(7).

The temperature correction and adjustment factors shall be permitted to be applied to the ampacity for the temperature rating of the conductor, if the corrected and adjusted ampacity does not exceed the ampacity for the temperature rating of the termination in accordance with the provisions of 110.14(C).

Reference: 2017 National Electrical Code – Chapter 3 Wiring Methods and Materials, Article 310 Conductors for General Wiring. 310.15 Ampacities for Conductors Rated 0-2000 Volts. 310.15(B) Tables. Table 310.15(B)(16) (formerly Table 310.16) Allowable Ampacities of Insulated Conductors Rated Up to and Including 2000 Volts, 60°C Through 90°C (140°F Through 194°F), Not More Than Three Current-Carrying Conductors in Raceway, Cable, or Earth (Directly Buried), Based on Ambient Temperature of 30°C (86°F) (page 70-161)

70. Answer C. 0.88

Ampacities for ambient temperatures other than those shown in the ampacity tables shall be corrected in accordance with Table 310.l5(B)(2)(a) or Table 310.l5(B)(2)(b) , or shall be permitted to be calculated using the equation on page 70-157.

Reference: 2017 National Electrical Code – Chapter 3 Wiring Methods and Materials, Article 310 Conductors for General Wiring. 310.15 Ampacities for Conductors Rated 0-2000 Volts. 310.15(B) Tables. 310.15(B)(2) Ambient Temperature Correction Factors. Table 310.15(B)(2)(a) Ambient Temperature Correction Factors Based on 30°C (86°F) (page 70-158)

71. Answer C. reduced

(a) More than Three Current-Carrying Conductors. Where the number of current-carrying conductors in a raceway or cable exceeds three, or where single conductors or multiconductor cables are installed without maintaining spacing for a continuous length longer than 600 mm (24 in.) and are not installed in raceways, the allowable ampacity of each conductor shall be reduced as shown in Table 310.15(B)(3)(a). Each current carrying conductor of a paralleled set of conductors shall be counted as a current-carrying conductor. Where conductors of different systems, as provided in 300.3, are installed in a common raceway or cable, the adjustment factors shown in Table 310.15(B)(3)(a) shall apply only to the number of power and lighting conductors (Articles 210, 215, 220, and 230).

Informational Note No. 1: See Annex B for adjustment factors for more than three current-carrying conductors in a raceway or cable with load diversity.

Informational Note No. 2: See 366.23 for adjustment factors for conductors and ampacity for bare copper and aluminum bars in auxiliary gutters and 376.22(B) for adjustment factors for conductors in metal wire ways.

Reference: 2017 National Electrical Code – Chapter 3 Wiring Methods and Materials, Article 310 Conductors for General Wiring. 310.15 Ampacities for Conductors Rated 0-2000 Volts. 310.15(B) Tables. 310.15(B)(3) Adjustment Factors.

EXAM 7

EXAM 7 ANSWERS

Table 310.15(B)(3)(a) Adjustment Factors for More Than Three Current-Carrying Conductors

Number of Conductors[1]	Percent of Values in Table 310.15(B)(16) Through Table 310.15(B)(19) as Adjusted for Ambient Temperature if Necessary
4–6	80
7–9	70
10–20	50
21–30	45
31–40	40
41 and above	35

72. Answer D. 80

(a) More than Three Current-Carrying Conductors. Where the number of current-carrying conductors in a raceway or cable exceeds three, or where single conductors or multiconductor cables are installed without maintaining spacing for a continuous length longer than 600 mm (24 in.) and are not installed in raceways, the allowable ampacity of each conductor shall be reduced as shown in *Table 310.15(B)(3)(a). Each current carrying conductor of a paralleled set of conductors shall be counted as a current-carrying conductor. Where conductors of different systems, as provided in 300.3, are installed in a common raceway or cable, the adjustment factors shown in Table 310.15(B)(3)(a) shall apply only to the number of power and lighting conductors (Articles 210, 215, 220, and 230).*

Informational Note No. 1: See Annex B for adjustment factors for more than three current-carrying conductors in a raceway or cable with load diversity.

Informational Note No. 2: See 366.23 for adjustment factors for conductors and ampacity for bare copper and aluminum bars in auxiliary gutters and 376.22(B) for adjustment factors for conductors in metal wire ways.

Reference: 2017 National Electrical Code – Chapter 3 Wiring Methods and Materials, Article 310 Conductors for General Wiring. 310.15 Ampacities for Conductors Rated 0-2000 Volts. 310.15(B) Tables. 310.15(B)(3) Adjustment Factors. Table 310.15(B)(3)(a) Adjustment Factors for More Than Three Current-Carrying Conductors (page 70-160)

73. Answer A. three, 24

(a) More Than Three Current-Carrying Conductors.

Where the number of current-carrying conductors in a raceway or cable exceeds three, or where single conductors or multiconductor cables are installed without maintaining spacing for a continuous length longer than 600 mm (24 in.) and are not installed in raceways, the allowable ampacity of each conductor shall be reduced as shown in Table 310.15(B)(3)(a). Each current-carrying conductor of a paralleled set of conductors shall be counted as a current-carrying conductor.

Where conductors of different systems, as provided in 300.3, are installed in a common raceway or cable, the adjustment factors shown in Table 310.15(B)(3)(a) shall apply only to the number of power and lighting conductors (Articles 210, 215, 220, and 230).

Informational Note No.1: See Annex B for adjustment factors for more than three current-carrying conductors in a raceway or cable with load diversity.

Informational Note No.2: See 366.23(A) for adjustment factors for conductors and ampacity for bare copper and aluminum bars in sheet metal auxiliary gutters and 376.22(B) for adjustment factors for conductors in metal wireways.

Reference: 2017 National Electrical Code – Chapter 3 Wiring Methods and Materials, Article 310 Conductors for General Wiring. 310.15 Ampacities for Conductors Rated 0-2000 Volts. 310.15(B) Tables. 310.15(B)(3) Adjustment Factors.

EXAM 7

EXAM 7 ANSWERS

74. Answer D. 50

(a) More Than Three Current-Carrying Conductors.

Where the number of current-carrying conductors in a raceway or cable exceeds three, or where single conductors or multiconductor cables are installed without maintaining spacing for a continuous length longer than 600 mm (24 in.) and are not installed in raceways, the allowable ampacity of each conductor shall be reduced as shown in Table 310.15(B)(3)(a). Each current-carrying conductor of a paralleled set of conductors shall be counted as a current-carrying conductor.

Where conductors of different systems, as provided in 300.3, are installed in a common raceway or cable, the adjustment factors shown in Table 310.15(B)(3)(a) shall apply only to the number of power and lighting conductors (Articles 210, 215, 220, and 230).

Informational Note No.1: See Annex B for adjustment factors for more than three current-carrying conductors in a raceway or cable with load diversity.

Informational Note No.2: See 366.23(A) for adjustment factors for conductors and ampacity for bare copper and aluminum bars in sheet metal auxiliary gutters and 376.22(B) for adjustment factors for conductors in metal wireways.

Reference: 2017 National Electrical Code – Chapter 3 Wiring Methods and Materials, Article 310 Conductors for General Wiring. 310.15 Ampacities for Conductors Rated 0-2000 Volts. 310.15(B) Tables. 310.15(B)(3) Adjustment Factors . Table 310.15(B)(3)(a) Adjustment Factors for More Than Three Current-Carrying Conductors (page 70-160)

75. Answer C. 24 inches

(a) More Than Three Current-Carrying Conductors.

Where the number of current-carrying conductors in a raceway or cable exceeds three, or where single conductors or multiconductor cables are installed without maintaining spacing for a continuous length longer than 600 mm (24 in.) and are not installed in raceways, the allowable ampacity of each conductor shall be reduced as shown in Table 310.15(B)(3)(a). Each current-carrying conductor of a paralleled set of conductors shall be counted as a current-carrying conductor.

Where conductors of different systems, as provided in 300.3, are installed in a common raceway or cable, the adjustment factors shown in Table 310.15(B)(3)(a) shall apply only to the number of power and lighting conductors (Articles 210, 215, 220, and 230).

Informational Note No.1: See Annex B for adjustment factors for more than three current-carrying conductors in a raceway or cable with load diversity.

Informational Note No.2: See 366.23(A) for adjustment factors for conductors and ampacity for bare copper and aluminum bars in sheet metal auxiliary gutters and 376.22(B) for adjustment factors for conductors in metal wireways.

Reference: 2017 National Electrical Code – Chapter 3 Wiring Methods and Materials, Article 310 Conductors for General Wiring. 310.15 Ampacities for Conductors Rated 0-2000 Volts. 310.15(B) Tables. 310.15(B)(3) Adjustment Factors. 310.15(B)(3)(a) More Than Three Current-Carrying Conductors. Table 310.15(B)(3)(a) Adjustment Factors for More Than Three Current-Carrying Conductors (page 70-160)

EXAM 7

EXAM 7 ANSWERS

Table 310.15(B)(16) (formerly Table 310.16) Allowable Ampacities of Insulated Conductors Rated Up to and Including 2000 Volts, 60°C Through 90°C (140°F Through 194°F), Not More Than Three Current-Carrying Conductors in Raceway, Cable, or Earth (Directly Buried), Based on Ambient Temperature of 30°C (86°F)*

Size AWG or kcmil	Temperature Rating of Conductor [See Table 310.104(A).]						Size AWG or kcmil
	60°C (140°F)	75°C (167°F)	90°C (194°F)	60°C (140°F)	75°C (167°F)	90°C (194°F)	
	Types TW, UF	Types RHW, THHW, THW, THWN, XHHW, USE, ZW	Types TBS, SA, SIS, FEP, FEPB, MI, RHH, RHW-2, THHN, THHW, THW-2, THWN-2, USE-2, XHH, XHHW, XHHW-2, ZW-2	Types TW, UF	Types RHW, THHW, THW, THWN, XHHW, USE	Types TBS, SA, SIS, THHN, THHW, THW-2, THWN-2, RHH, RHW-2, USE-2, XHH, XHHW, XHHW-2, ZW-2	
	COPPER			ALUMINUM OR COPPER-CLAD ALUMINUM			
18**	—	—	14	—	—	—	—
16**	—	—	18	—	—	—	—
14**	15	20	25	—	—	—	—
12**	20	25	30	15	20	25	12**
10**	30	35	40	25	30	35	10**
8	40	50	55	35	40	45	8
6	55	65	75	40	50	55	6
4	70	85	95	55	65	75	4
3	85	100	115	65	75	85	3
2	95	115	130	75	90	100	2
1	110	130	145	85	100	115	1
1/0	125	150	170	100	120	135	1/0
2/0	145	175	195	115	135	150	2/0
3/0	165	200	225	130	155	175	3/0
4/0	195	230	260	150	180	205	4/0
250	215	255	290	170	205	230	250
300	240	285	320	195	230	260	300
350	260	310	350	210	250	280	350
400	280	335	380	225	270	305	400
500	320	380	430	260	310	350	500
600	350	420	475	285	340	385	600
700	385	460	520	315	375	425	700
750	400	475	535	320	385	435	750
800	410	490	555	330	395	445	800
900	435	520	585	355	425	480	900
1000	455	545	615	375	445	500	1000
1250	495	590	665	405	485	545	1250
1500	525	625	705	435	520	585	1500
1750	545	650	735	455	545	615	1750
2000	555	665	750	470	560	630	2000

*Refer to 310.15(B)(2) for the ampacity correction factors where the ambient temperature is other than 30°C (86°F). Refer to 310.15(B)(3)(a) for more than three current-carrying conductors.
**Refer to 240.4(D) for conductor overcurrent protection limitations.

EXAM 7
EXAM 7 ANSWERS

76. **Answer C.**   80%

    (a) More Than Three Current-Carrying Conductors.

    Where the number of current-carrying conductors in a raceway or cable exceeds three, or where single conductors or multiconductor cables are installed without maintaining spacing for a continuous length longer than 600 mm (24 in.) and are not installed in raceways, the allowable ampacity of each conductor shall be reduced as shown in Table 310.15(B)(3)(a). Each current-carrying conductor of a paralleled set of conductors shall be counted as a current-carrying conductor.

    Where conductors of different systems, as provided in 300.3, are installed in a common raceway or cable, the adjustment factors shown in Table 310.15(B)(3)(a) shall apply only to the number of power and lighting conductors (Articles 210, 215, 220, and 230).

    Informational Note No.1: See Annex B for adjustment factors for more than three current-carrying conductors in a raceway or cable with load diversity.

    Informational Note No.2: See 366.23(A) for adjustment factors for conductors and ampacity for bare copper and aluminum bars in sheet metal auxiliary gutters and 376.22(B) for adjustment factors for conductors in metal wireways.

    Reference: 2017 National Electrical Code – Chapter 3 Wiring Methods and Materials, Article 310 Conductors for General Wiring. 310.15 Ampacities for Conductors Rated 0-2000 Volts. 310.15(B) Tables. 310.15(B)(3) Adjustment Factors. Table 310.15(B)(3)(a) Adjustment Factors for More Than Three Current-Carrying Conductors (page 70-160)

77. **Answer C.**   120 amperes

    Where the number of current-carrying conductors in a raceway or cable exceeds three, or where single conductors or multiconductor cables are installed without maintaining spacing for a continuous length longer than 600 mm (24 in.) and are not installed in raceways, the allowable ampacity of each conductor shall be reduced as shown in Table 310.l5(B)(3)(a). Each current-carrying conductor of a paralleled set of conductors shall be counted as a current-carrying conductor.

    Where conductors of different systems, as provided in 300.3, are installed in a common raceway or cable, the adjustment factors shown in Table 310.15(B)(3)(a) shall apply only to the number of power and lighting conductors (Articles 210, 215, 220, and 230).

    Informational Note No.1: See Annex B for adjustment factors for more than three current-carrying conductors in a raceway or cable with load diversity.

    Informational Note No.2: See 366.23(A) for adjustment factors for conductors and ampacity for bare copper and aluminum bars in sheet metal auxiliary gutters and 376.22(B) for adjustment factors for conductors in metal wireways.

    Reference: 2017 National Electrical Code – Chapter 3 Wiring Methods and Materials, Article 310 Conductors for General Wiring. 310.15 Ampacities for Conductors Rated 0-2000 Volts. 310.15(B) Tables. 310.15(B)(3) Adjustment Factors. 310.15(B)(3)(a) More Than Three Current-Carrying Conductors.

    Reference: 2017 National Electrical Code – Chapter 3 Wiring Methods and Materials. Table 310.15(B)(16) (formerly Table 310.16) Allowable Ampacities of Insulated Conductors Rated Up to and Including 2000 Volts, 60°C Through 90°C (140°F Through 194°F), Not More Than Three Current-Carrying Conductors in Raceway, Cable, or Earth (Directly Buried), Based on Ambient Temperature of 30°C (86°F)* (page 70-161)

    Size 1/0 AWG THW ampacity = 150 amperes before derating

    150 amperes x 80% (adjustment factor) = 120 amperes

EXAM 7

EXAM 7 ANSWERS

Table 310.15(B)(2)(b) Ambient Temperature Correction Factors Based on 40°C (104°F)

For ambient temperatures other than 40°C (104°F), multiply the allowable ampacities specified in the ampacity tables by the appropriate correction factor shown below.

Ambient Temperature (°C)	Temperature Rating of Conductor						Ambient Temperature (°F)
	60°C	75°C	90°C	150°C	200°C	250°C	
10 or less	1.58	1.36	1.26	1.13	1.09	1.07	50 or less
11–15	1.50	1.31	1.22	1.11	1.08	1.06	51–59
16–20	1.41	1.25	1.18	1.09	1.06	1.05	60–68
21–25	1.32	1.2	1.14	1.07	1.05	1.04	69–77
26–30	1.22	1.13	1.10	1.04	1.03	1.02	78–86
31–35	1.12	1.07	1.05	1.02	1.02	1.01	87–95
36–40	1.00	1.00	1.00	1.00	1.00	1.00	96–104
41–45	0.87	0.93	0.95	0.98	0.98	0.99	105–113
46–50	0.71	0.85	0.89	0.95	0.97	0.98	114–122
51–55	0.50	0.76	0.84	0.93	0.95	0.96	123–131
56–60	—	0.65	0.77	0.90	0.94	0.95	132–140
61–65	—	0.53	0.71	0.88	0.92	0.94	141–149
66–70	—	0.38	0.63	0.85	0.90	0.93	150–158
71–75	—	—	0.55	0.83	0.88	0.91	159–167
76–80	—	—	0.45	0.80	0.87	0.90	168–176
81–90	—	—	—	0.74	0.83	0.87	177–194
91–100	—	—	—	0.67	0.79	0.85	195–212
101–110	—	—	—	0.60	0.75	0.82	213–230
111–120	—	—	—	0.52	0.71	0.79	231–248
121–130	—	—	—	0.43	0.66	0.76	249–266
131–140	—	—	—	0.30	0.61	0.72	267–284
141–160	—	—	—	—	0.50	0.65	285–320
161–180	—	—	—	—	0.35	0.58	321–356
181–200	—	—	—	—	—	0.49	357–392
201–225	—	—	—	—	—	0.35	393–437

78. Answer D. 36 inches

Where raceways or cables are exposed to direct sunlight on or above rooftops, the adjustments shown in Table 310.15(B)(3)(c) shall be added to the outdoor temperature to determine the applicable ambient temperature for application of the correction factors in Table 310.15(B)(2)(a) or Table 310.15(B)(2)(b).

Reference: 2017 National Electrical Code – Chapter 3 Wiring Methods and Materials. 310.15 Ampacities for Conductors Rated 0-2000 Volts. 310.15(B) Tables. 310.15(B)(3) Adjustment Factors. 310.15(B)(3)(c) Raceways and Cables Exposed to Sunlight on Rooftops. Table 310.15(B)(3)(c) Ambient Temperature Adjustment for Raceways or Cables Exposed to Sunlight on or Above Rooftops (page 70-160)

79. Answer B. 30°F

Where raceways or cables are exposed to direct sunlight on or above rooftops, the adjustments shown in Table 310.15(B)(3)(c) shall be added to the outdoor temperature to determine the applicable ambient temperature for application of the correction factors in Table 310.15(B)(2)(a) or Table 310.15(B)(2)(b).

Reference: 2017 National Electrical Code – Chapter 3 Wiring Methods and Materials. 310.15 Ampacities for Conductors Rated 0-2000 Volts. 310.15(B) Tables. 310.15(B)(3) Adjustment Factors. 310.15(B)(3)(c) Raceways and Cables Exposed to Sunlight on Rooftops. Table 310.15(B)(3)(c) Ambient Temperature Adjustment for Raceways or Cables Exposed to Sunlight on or Above Rooftops (page 70-160)

80. Answer C. 200

A grounding or bonding conductor shall not be counted when applying the provisions of 310.15(B)(3)(a)

Reference: 2017 National Electrical Code – Chapter 3 Wiring Methods and Materials, Article 310 Conductors for General Wiring. 310.15 Ampacities for Conductors Rated 0-2000 Volts. 310.15(B) Tables. 310.15(B)(6) Grounding or Bonding Conductor.

EXAM 7

EXAM 7 ANSWERS

Table 310.15(B)(3)(a) Adjustment Factors for More Than Three Current-Carrying Conductors

Number of Conductors[1]	Percent of Values in Table 310.15(B)(16) Through Table 310.15(B)(19) as Adjusted for Ambient Temperature if Necessary
4–6	80
7–9	70
10–20	50
21–30	45
31–40	40
41 and above	35

[1]Number of conductors is the total number of conductors in the raceway or cable, including spare conductors. The count shall be adjusted in accordance with 310.15(B)(5) and (6). The count shall not include conductors that are connected to electrical components that cannot be simultaneously energized.

Table 310.15(B)(3)(a) see Table -15-B-3-a in Tables folder on CD-ROM

---

81. Answer B. 1 AWG

For one family dwellings and the individual dwelling units of two-family and multifamily dwellings, service and feeder conductors supplied by a single-phase, 120/240-volt system shall be permitted to be sized in accordance with 310.15(B)(7)(1) through (4). For one-family dwellings and the individual dwelling units of two-family and multifamily dwellings, single-phase feeder conductors consisting of 2 ungrounded conductors and the neutral conductor from a 208Y/120 volt system shall be permitted to be sized in accordance with 310.15(B)(7)(1) through (3).

(1) *For a service rated 100 through 400 amperes, the service conductors supplying the entire load associated with a one-family dwelling, or the service conductors supplying the entire load associated with an individual dwelling unit in a two-family or multifamily dwelling, shall be permitted to have an ampacity not less than 83 percent of the service rating.*

(2) For a feeder rated 100 through 400 amperes, the feeder conductors supplying the entire load associated with a one-family dwelling, or the feeder conductors supplying the entire load associated with an individual dwelling unit in a two-family or multifamily dwelling, shall be permitted to have an ampacity not less than 83 percent of the feeder rating.

(3) In no case shall a feeder for an individual dwelling unit be required to have an ampacity greater than that specified in 310.15(B)(7)(1) or (2).

(4) Grounded conductors shall be permitted to be sized smaller than the ungrounded conductors, if the requirements of 220.61 and 230.42 for service conductors or the requirements of 215.2 and 220.61 for feeder conductors are met.

Where correction or adjustment factors are required by. 310.15(B)(2) or (3), they shall be permitted to be applied to the ampacity associated with the temperature rating of the conductor.

Informational Note No. 1: The service or feeder ratings addressed by this section

150 amperes x 83% = 124.5 amperes

*NOTE- Size 1 AWG THHW copper conductors with an ampacity of 130 amperes should be selected from Table 310.15(B)(16).

Reference: 2017 National Electrical Code – Chapter 3 Wiring Methods and Materials. 310.15 Ampacities for Conductors Rated 0-2000 Volts. 310.15(B) Tables. 310.15(B)(7) 1201240-Volt, Single-Phase Dwelling Services and Feeders. Table 310.15(B)(16) (formerly Table 310.16) Allowable Ampacities of Insulated Conductors Rated Up to and Including 2000 Volts, 60°C Through 90°C (140°F Through 194°F), Not More Than Three Current-Carrying Conductors in Raceway, Cable, or Earth (Directly Buried), Based on Ambient Temperature of 30°C (86°F)* (page 70-161)

EXAM 7

EXAM 7 ANSWERS

Table 310.15(B)(20) (formerly Table 310.20) Ampacities of Not More Than Three Single Insulated Conductors, Rated Up to and Including 2000 Volts, Supported on a Messenger, Based on Ambient Air Temperature of 40°C (104°F)*

Size AWG or kcmil	Temperature Rating of Conductor [See Table 310.104(A).]				Size AWG or kcmil
	75°C (167°F)	90°C (194°F)	75°C (167°F)	90°C (194°F)	
	Types RHW, THHW, THW, THWN, XHHW, ZW	Types MI, THHN, THHW, THW-2, THWN-2, RHH, RHW-2, USE-2, XHHW, XHHW-2, ZW-2	Types RHW, THW, THWN, THHW, XHHW	Types THHN, THHW, RHH, XHHW, RHW-2, XHHW-2, THW-2, THWN-2, USE-2, ZW-2	
	COPPER		ALUMINUM OR COPPER-CLAD ALUMINUM		
8	57	66	44	51	8
6	76	89	59	69	6
4	101	117	78	91	4
3	118	138	92	107	3
2	135	158	106	123	2
1	158	185	123	144	1
1/0	183	214	143	167	1/0
2/0	212	247	165	193	2/0
3/0	245	287	192	224	3/0
4/0	287	335	224	262	4/0
250	320	374	251	292	250
300	359	419	282	328	300
350	397	464	312	364	350
400	430	503	339	395	400
500	496	580	392	458	500
600	553	647	440	514	600
700	610	714	488	570	700
750	638	747	512	598	750
800	660	773	532	622	800
900	704	826	572	669	900
1000	748	879	612	716	1000

*Refer to 310.15(B)(2) for the ampacity correction factors where the ambient temperature is other than 40°C (104°F). Refer to 310.15(B)(3)(a) for more than three current-carrying conductors.

Table 310.15 (B)(20) see Table 310-15-B-20 in Tables folder on CD-ROM

82. **Answer C.** 8 AWG

Ampacities for conductors rated 0 to 2000 volts shall be as specified in the Allowable Ampacity Table 310.15(B)(16) through Table 310.15(B)(19), and Ampacity *Table 310.15(B)(20) and Table 310.15(B)(21) as modified by 310.15(B)(1) through (B)(7).*

The temperature correction and adjustment factors shall be permitted to be applied to the ampacity for the temperature rating of the conductor, if the corrected and adjusted ampacity does not exceed the ampacity for the temperature rating of the termination in accordance with the provisions of 110.14(C).

Reference: 2017 National Electrical Code – Chapter 3 Wiring Methods and Materials. 310.15 Ampacities for Conductors Rated 0-2000 Volts. 310.15(B) Tables. Table 310.15(B)(16) (formerly Table 310.16) Allowable Ampacities of Insulated Conductors Rated Up to and Including 2000 Volts, 60°C Through 90°C (140°F Through 194°F), Not More Than Three Current-Carrying Conductors in Raceway, Cable, or Earth (Directly Buried), Based on Ambient Temperature of 30°C (86°F)

EXAM 7

EXAM 7 ANSWERS

83. **Answer C.**   3/0 THW

Ampacities for conductors rated 0 to 2000 volts shall be as specified in the Allowable Ampacity Table 310.15(B)(16) through Table 310.15(B)(19), and Ampacity Table 310.15(B)(20) and Table 310.15(B)(21) as modified by 310.15(B)(1) through (B)(7).

The temperature correction and adjustment factors shall be permitted to be applied to the ampacity for the temperature rating of the conductor, if the corrected and adjusted ampacity does not exceed the ampacity for the temperature rating of the termination in accordance with the provisions of 110.14(C).

* conductors are size 500 kcmil copper

* conductor insulation is THWN

* eight (8) current-carrying conductors are in the raceway

* ambient temperature is 125 deg. F

* conduit length is 50 feet

* installation is a wet location

Reference: 2017 National Electrical Code – Chapter 3 Wiring Methods and Materials, Article 310 Conductors for General Wiring. 310.15 Ampacities for Conductors Rated 0-2000 Volts. 310.15(B) Tables. Table 310.15(B)(16) (formerly Table 310.16) Allowable Ampacities of Insulated Conductors Rated Up to and Including 2000 Volts, 60°C Through 90°C (140°F Through 194°F), Not More Than Three Current-Carrying Conductors in Raceway, Cable, or Earth (Directly Buried), Based on Ambient Temperature of 30°C (86°F)* (page 70-161)

84. **Answer A.**   178.2 amperes

Ampacities for conductors rated 0 to 2000 volts shall be as specified in the Allowable Ampacity Table 310.15(B)(16) through Table 310.15(B)(19), and Ampacity Table 310.15(B)(20) and Table 310.15(B)(21) as modified by 310.15(B)(1) through (B)(7).

The temperature correction and adjustment factors shall be permitted to be applied to the ampacity for the temperature rating of the conductor, if the corrected and adjusted ampacity does not exceed the ampacity for the temperature rating of the termination in accordance with the provisions of 110.14(C).

Reference: 2017 National Electrical Code – Chapter 3 Wiring Methods and Materials. Table 310.15(B)(16) (formerly Table 310.16) Allowable Ampacities of Insulated Conductors Rated Up to and Including 2000 Volts, 60°C Through 90°C (140°F Through 194°F), Not More Than Three Current-Carrying Conductors in Raceway, Cable, or Earth (Directly Buried), Based on Ambient Temperature of 30°C (86°F)* (page 70-161)

Reference: 2017 National Electrical Code – Chapter 3 Wiring Methods and Materials, Article 310 Conductors for General Wiring. 310.15 Ampacities for Conductors Rated 0-2000 Volts. 310.15(B) Tables. 310.15(B)(2) Ambient Temperature Correction Factors. Table 310.15(B)(2)(a) Ambient Temperature Correction Factors Based on 30°C (86°F) (page 70-158)

380 amperes x .67 (temp. correction) x .7 (adjustment factor) = 178.22 amperes

Reference: 2017 National Electrical Code – Chapter 3 Wiring Methods and Materials, Article 310 Conductors for General Wiring. 310.15 Ampacities for Conductors Rated 0-2000 Volts. 310.15(B) Tables. 310.15(B)(3) Adjustment Factors. Table 310.15(B)(3)(a) Adjustment Factors for More Than Three Current-Carrying Conductors (page 70-160). *Size 500 KCMIL THWN copper ampacity before derating = 380 amperes*

85. **Answer C.**   80 amperes

Ampacities for conductors rated 0 to 2000 volts shall be as specified in the Allowable Ampacity Table 310.15(B)(16) through Table 310.15(B)(19), and Ampacity Table 310.15(B)(20) and Table 310.15(B)(21) as modified by 310.15(B)(1) through (B)(7).

The temperature correction and adjustment factors shall be permitted to be applied to the ampacity for the temperature rating of the conductor, if the corrected and adjusted ampacity does not exceed the ampacity for the temperature rating of the termination in accordance with the provisions of 110.14(C).

Reference: 2017 National Electrical Code – Chapter 3 Wiring Methods and Materials, Article 310 Conductors for General Wiring. 310.15 Ampacities for Conductors Rated 0-2000 Volts. 310.15(B) Tables. Table 310.15(B)(17) (formerly Table 310.17) Allowable Ampacities of Single-Insulated Conductors Rated Up to and Including 2000 Volts in Free Air, Based on Ambient Temperature of 30°C (86°F)* (page 70-162)

EXAM 7

EXAM 7 ANSWERS

86. **Answer B.** 20 amperes

Ampacities for conductors rated 0 to 2000 volts shall be as specified in the Allowable Ampacity Table 310.15(B)(16) through Table 310.15(B)(19), and Ampacity Table 310.15(B)(20) and Table 310.15(B)(21) as modified by 310.15(B)(1) through (B)(7).

The temperature correction and adjustment factors shall be permitted to be applied to the ampacity for the temperature rating of the conductor, if the corrected and adjusted ampacity does not exceed the ampacity for the temperature rating of the termination in accordance with the provisions of 110.14(C).

Reference: 2017 National Electrical Code – Chapter 3 Wiring Methods and Materials, Article 310 Conductors for General Wiring. 310.15 Ampacities for Conductors Rated 0-2000 Volts. 310.15(B) Tables. Table 310.15(B)(16) (formerly Table 310.16) Allowable Ampacities of Insulated Conductors Rated Up to and Including 2000 Volts, 60°C Through 90°C (140°F Through 194°F), Not More Than Three Current-Carrying Conductors in Raceway, Cable, or Earth (Directly Buried), Based on Ambient Temperature of 30°C (86°F)* (page 70-161)

Reference: 2017 National Electrical Code – Chapter 3 Wiring Methods and Materials, Article 310 Conductors for General Wiring. 310.15 Ampacities for Conductors Rated 0-2000 Volts. 310.15(B) Tables. Table 310.15(B)(3)(a) Adjustment Factors for More Than Three Current-Carrying Conductors (page 70-160)

87. **Answer B.** 300 kcmil

Ampacities for conductors rated 0 to 2000 volts shall be as specified in the Allowable Ampacity Table 310.15(B)(16) through Table 310.15(B)(19), and Ampacity Table 310.15(B)(20) and Table 310.15(B)(21) as modified by 310.15(B)(1) through (B)(7).

The temperature correction and adjustment factors shall be permitted to be applied to the ampacity for the temperature rating of the conductor, if the corrected and adjusted ampacity does not exceed the ampacity for the temperature rating of the termination in accordance with the provisions of 110.14(C).

Reference: 2017 National Electrical Code – Chapter 3 Wiring Methods and Materials, Article 310 Conductors for General Wiring. 310.15 Ampacities for Conductors Rated 0-2000 Volts. 310.15(B) Tables. Table 310.15(B)(16) (formerly Table 310.16) Allowable Ampacities of Insulated Conductors Rated Up to and Including 2000 Volts, 60°C Through 90°C (140°F Through 194°F), Not More Than Three Current-Carrying Conductors in Raceway, Cable, or Earth (Directly Buried), Based on Ambient Temperature of 30°C (86°F)* (page 70-161)

Reference: 2017 National Electrical Code – Chapter 3 Wiring Methods and Materials, Article 310 Conductors for General Wiring. 310.15 Ampacities for Conductors Rated 0-2000 Volts. 310.15(B) Tables. Table 310.15(B)(2)(a) Ambient Temperature Correction Factors Based on 30°C (86°F) (page 70-158)

200 amperes (load) = 266.6 amperes

.75 (temp. correction)

*NOTE: Size 300 kcmil conductors with an allowable ampacity of 285 amperes should be selected.

EXAM 7

EXAM 7 ANSWERS

Table 310.60(C)(69) Ampacities of Insulated Single Copper Conductor Isolated in Air Based on Conductor Temperatures of 90°C (194°F) and 105°C (221°F) and Ambient Air Temperature of 40°C (104°F)*

Conductor Size (AWG or kcmil)	Temperature Rating of Conductor [See Table 310.104(C).]					
	2001–5000 Volts Ampacity		5001–15,000 Volts Ampacity		15,001–35,000 Volts Ampacity	
	90°C (194°F) Type MV-90	105°C (221°F) Type MV-105	90°C (194°F) Type MV-90	105°C (221°F) Type MV-105	90°C (194°F) Type MV-90	105°C (221°F) Type MV-105
8	83	93	—	—	—	—
6	110	120	110	125	—	—
4	145	160	150	165	—	—
2	190	215	195	215	—	—
1	225	250	225	250	225	250
1/0	260	290	260	290	260	290
2/0	300	330	300	335	300	330
3/0	345	385	345	385	345	380
4/0	400	445	400	445	395	445
250	445	495	445	495	440	490
350	550	615	550	610	545	605
500	695	775	685	765	680	755
750	900	1000	885	990	870	970
1000	1075	1200	1060	1185	1040	1160
1250	1230	1370	1210	1350	1185	1320
1500	1365	1525	1345	1500	1315	1465
1750	1495	1665	1470	1640	1430	1595
2000	1605	1790	1575	1755	1535	1710

*Refer to 310.60(C)(4) for the ampacity correction factors where the ambient air temperature is other than 40°C (104°F).

88. **Answer D.** 145

Under engineering supervision, conductor ampacities shall be permitted to be calculated by using a general equation on page 70-165.

Reference: 2017 National Electrical Code – Chapter 3 Wiring Methods and Materials, Article 310 Conductors for General Wiring. 310.60 Conductors Rated 2001 to 35,000 Volts. 310.60(C) Engineering Supervision. Table 310.60(C)(69) Ampacities of Insulated Single Copper Conductor Isolated in Air Based on Conductor Temperatures of 90°C (194°F) and 105°C (221°F) and Ambient Air Temperature of 40°C (104°F) (page 70-167)

EXAM 7

EXAM 7 ANSWERS

Table 310.104(A) Continued

Trade Name	Type Letter	Maximum Operating Temperature	Application Provisions	Insulation	Thickness of Insulation AWG or kcmil	mm	mils	Outer Covering[2]
Underground service-entrance cable — single conductor (for Type USE cable employing more than one conductor, see Article 338).	USE	75°C (167°F)[5]	See Article 338.	Heat- and moisture-resistant	14–10	1.14	45	Moisture-resistant nonmetallic covering (See 338.2.)
	USE-2	90°C (194°F)	Dry and wet locations		8–2	1.52	60	
					1–4/0	2.03	80	
					213–500	2.41	95[7]	
					501–1000	2.79	110	
					1001–2000	3.18	125	
Thermoset	XHH	90°C (194°F)	Dry and damp locations	Flame-retardant thermoset	14–10	0.76	30	None
					8–2	1.14	45	
					1–4/0	1.40	55	
					213–500	1.65	65	
					501–1000	2.03	80	
					1001–2000	2.41	95	
Thermoset	XHHN	90°C (194°F)	Dry and damp locations	Flame-retardant thermoset	14–12	0.38	15	Nylon jacket or equivalent
					10	0.51	20	
					8–6	0.76	30	
					4–2	1.02	40	
					1–4/0	1.27	50	
					250–500	1.52	60	
					501–1000	1.78	70	
Moisture-resistant thermoset	XHHW	90°C (194°F)	Dry and damp locations	Flame-retardant, moisture-resistant thermoset	14–10	0.76	30	None
		75°C (167°F)	Wet locations		8–2	1.14	45	
					1–4/0	1.40	55	
					213–500	1.65	65	
					501–1000	2.03	80	
					1001–2000	2.41	95	
Moisture-resistant thermoset	XHHW-2	90°C (194°F)	Dry and wet locations	Flame-retardant, moisture-resistant thermoset	14–10	0.76	30	None
					8–2	1.14	45	
					1–4/0	1.40	55	
					213–500	1.65	65	
					501–1000	2.03	80	
					1001–2000	2.41	95	
Moisture-resistant thermoset	XHWN	75°C (167°F)	Dry and wet locations	Flame-retardant, moisture-resistant thermoset	14–12	0.38	15	Nylon jacket or equivalent
	XHWN-2	90°C (194°F)			10	0.51	20	
					8–6	0.76	30	
					4–2	1.02	40	
					1–4/0	1.27	50	
					250–500	1.52	60	
					501–1000	1.78	70	
Modified ethylene tetrafluoro-ethylene	Z	90°C (194°F)	Dry and damp locations	Modified ethylene tetrafluoro-ethylene	14–12	0.38	15	None
					10	0.51	20	
		150°C (302°F)	Dry locations — special applications[3]		8–4	0.64	25	
					3–1	0.89	35	
					1/0–4/0	1.14	45	
Modified ethylene tetrafluoro-ethylene	ZW	75°C (167°F)	Wet locations	Modified ethylene tetrafluoro-ethylene	14–10	0.76	30	None
		90°C (194°F)	Dry and damp locations		8–2	1.14	45	
		150°C (302°F)	Dry locations — special applications[3]					
	ZW-2	90°C (194°F)	Dry and wet locations					

[1] Conductors can be rated up to 1000 V if listed and marked.
[2] Some insulations do not require an outer covering.
[3] Where design conditions require maximum conductor operating temperatures above 90°C (194°F).
[4] For signaling circuits permitting 300-volt insulation.
[5] For ampacity limitation, see 340.80.
[6] Includes integral jacket.
[7] Insulation thickness shall be permitted to be 2.03 mm (80 mils) for listed Type USE conductors that have been subjected to special investigations. The nonmetallic covering over individual rubber-covered conductors of aluminum-sheathed cable and of lead-sheathed or multiconductor cable shall not be required to be flame retardant. For Type MC cable, see 330.104. For nonmetallic-sheathed cable, see Article 334, Part III. For Type UF cable, see Article 340, Part III.

Table 310.104(A) see Table 310-104-A in Tables folder on CD-ROM

EXAM 7

EXAM 7 ANSWERS

89. Answer D. Thermoset

Insulated conductors shall comply with the applicable provisions of Table 310.I04(A) through Table 310.104(E).

Informational Note: Thermoplastic insulation may stiffen at temperatures lower than -10°C (+14°F). Thermoplastic insulation may also be deformed at normal temperatures where subjected to pressure, such as at points of support.

Reference: 2017 National Electrical Code – Chapter 3 Wiring Methods and Materials, Article 310 Conductors for General Wiring. 310.104 Conductor Constructions and Applications. Table 310.104(A) Conductor Applications and Insulations Rated 600 Volts (page 70-175)

90. Answer C. Lead sheath

Insulated conductors shall comply with the applicable provisions of Table 310.104(A) through Table 310.104(E).

Informational Note: Thermoplastic insulation may stiffen at temperatures lower than -10°C (+14°F). Thermoplastic insulation may also be deformed at normal temperatures where subjected to pressure, such as at points of support.

Reference: 2017 National Electrical Code – Chapter 3 Wiring Methods and Materials, Article 310 Conductors for General Wiring. 310.104 Conductor Constructions and Applications. Table 310.104(A) Conductor Applications and Insulations Rated 600 Volts (page 70-175)

91. Answer A. Heat-resistant thermoplastic

Insulated conductors shall comply with the applicable provisions of Table 310.104(A) through Table 310.104(E).

Informational Note: Thermoplastic insulation may stiffen at temperatures lower than -10°C (+14°F). Thermoplastic insulation may also be deformed at normal temperatures where subjected to pressure, such as at points of support.

Reference: 2017 National Electrical Code – Chapter 3 Wiring Methods and Materials, Article 310 Conductors for General Wiring. 310.104 Conductor Constructions and Applications. Table 310.104(A) Conductor Applications and Insulations Rated 600 Volts (page 70-175)

92. Answer C. The conductor has a maximum operating temperature of 90°C.

Insulated conductors shall comply with the applicable provisions of Table 310.104(A) through Table 310.104(E).

Informational Note: *Thermoplastic insulation may stiffen at temperatures lower than -10°C (+14°F). Thermoplastic insulation may also be deformed at normal temperatures where subjected to pressure, such as at points of support.*

Reference: 2017 National Electrical Code – Chapter 3 Wiring Methods and Materials, Article 310 Conductors for General Wiring. 310.104 Conductor Constructions and Applications. Table 310.104(A) Conductor Applications and Insulations Rated 600 Volts (page 70-175)

EXAM 7

EXAM 7 ANSWERS

93. Answer D. 90 °C

Insulated conductors shall comply with the applicable provisions of Table 310.104(A) through Table 310.104(E).

Informational Note: Thermoplastic insulation may stiffen at temperatures lower than -10°C (+14°F). Thermoplastic insulation may also be deformed at normal temperatures where subjected to pressure, such as at points of support.

Reference: 2017 National Electrical Code – Chapter 3 Wiring Methods and Materials, Article 310 Conductors for General Wiring. 310.104 Conductor Constructions and Applications. Table 310.104(A) Conductor Applications and Insulations Rated 600 Volts (page 70-175)

94. Answer B. 47.9 amperes

Insulated conductors shall comply with the applicable provisions of Table 310.104(A) through Table 310.104(E).

Informational Note: Thermoplastic insulation may stiffen at temperatures lower than -10°C (+14°F). Thermoplastic insulation may also be deformed at normal temperatures where subjected to pressure, such as at points of support.

Reference: 2017 National Electrical Code – Chapter 3 Wiring Methods and Materials, Article 310 Conductors for General Wiring. 310.104 Conductor Constructions and Applications. Table 310.104(A) Conductor Applications and Insulations Rated 600 Volts (page 70-175)

Reference: 2017 National Electrical Code – Chapter 3 Wiring Methods and Materials. Table 310.15(B)(16) (formerly Table 310.16) Allowable Ampacities of Insulated Conductors Rated Up to and Including 2000 Volts, 60°C Through 90°C (140°F Through 194°F), Not More Than Three Current-Carrying Conductors in Raceway, Cable, or Earth (Directly Buried), Based on Ambient Temperature of 30°C (86°F)* (page 70-161)

Reference: 2017 National Electrical Code – Chapter 3 Wiring Methods and Materials, Article 310 Conductors for General Wiring. 310.15 Ampacities for Conductors Rated 0-2000 Volts. 310.15(B) Tables. 310.15(B)(2) Ambient Temperature Correction Factors. Table 310.15(B)(2)(a) Ambient Temperature Correction Factors Based on 30°C (86°F) (page 70-158)

95. Answer C. dry, damp, or wet locations

Insulated conductors shall comply with the applicable provisions of Table 310.104(A) through Table 310.104(E).

Informational Note: Thermoplastic insulation may stiffen at temperatures lower than -10°C (+14°F). Thermoplastic insulation may also be deformed at normal temperatures where subjected to pressure, such as at points of support.

Reference: 2017 National Electrical Code – Chapter 3 Wiring Methods and Materials, Article 310 Conductors for General Wiring. 310.104 Conductor Constructions and Applications. Table 310.104(A) Conductor Applications and Insulations Rated 600 Volts (page 70-175)

Insulated conductors and cables used in dry and damp locations shall be Types FEP, FEPB, MTW, PFA, RHH, RHW, RHW-2, SA, THHN, THW, THW-2, THHW, THWN, THWN-2, TW, XHH, XHHW, XHHW-2, Z, or ZW.

Reference: 2017 National Electrical Code – Chapter 3 Wiring Methods and Materials, Article 310 Conductors for General Wiring. 310.10 Uses Permitted. 310.10(B) Dry and Damp Locations.

Insulated conductors and cables used in wet locations shall comply with one of the following:

(1) Be moisture-impervious metal-sheathed

(2) Be types MTW, RHW, RHW-2, TW, THW, THW-2, THHW, THWN, THWN-2, XHHW, XHHW-2, ZW

(3) Be of a type listed for use in wet locations

Reference: 2017 National Electrical Code – Chapter 3 Wiring Methods and Materials, Article 310 Conductors for General Wiring. 310.10 Uses Permitted. 310.10(C)2 Wet Locations. 95.Which insulation gives conductors a greater ampacity when used in a dry location rather than a wet location?

EXAM 7

EXAM 7 ANSWERS

96. Answer B.   THHW

Insulated conductors shall comply with the applicable provisions of Table 310.104(A) through Table 310.104(E).

Informational Note: Thermoplastic insulation may stiffen at temperatures lower than -10°C (+14°F). Thermoplastic insulation may also be deformed at normal temperatures where subjected to pressure, such as at points of support.

Reference: 2017 National Electrical Code – Chapter 3 Wiring Methods and Materials, Article 310 Conductors for General Wiring. 310.104 Conductor Constructions and Applications. Table 310.104(A) Conductor Applications and Insulations Rated 600 Volts (page 70-175)

Reference: 2017 National Electrical Code – Chapter 3 Wiring Methods and Materials, Article 310 Conductors for General Wiring. Table 310.15(B)(16) (formerly Table 310.16) Allowable Ampacities of Insulated Conductors Rated Up to and Including 2000 Volts, 60°C Through 90°C (140°F Through 194°F), Not More Than Three Current-Carrying Conductors in Raceway, Cable, or Earth (Directly Buried), Based on Ambient Temperature of 30°C (86°F)* (page 70-161)

97. Answer D.   10 AWG

Where installed in raceways, conductors 8 AWG and larger, not specifically permitted or required elsewhere in this Code to be solid, shall be stranded.

Reference: 2017 National Electrical Code – Chapter 3 Wiring Methods and Materials, Article 310 Conductors for General Wiring. 310.106 Conductors. 310.106(C) Stranded Conductors.

98. Answer C.   24, 40

The following conductors and cables shall be durably marked on the surface. *The AWG size or circular mil area shall be repeated at intervals not exceeding 610 mm (24 in.). All other markings shall be repeated at intervals not exceeding 1.0 m (40 in.).*

(1) Single-conductor and multiconductor rubber- and thermoplastic-insulated wire and cable

(2) Nonmetallic-sheathed cable

(3) Service-entrance cable

(4) Underground feeder and branch-circuit cable

(5) Tray cable

(6) Irrigation cable

(7) Power-limited tray cable

(8) Instrumentation tray cable

Reference: 2017 National Electrical Code – Chapter 3 Wiring Methods and Materials, Article 310 Conductors for General Wiring. 310.120 Marking. 310.120(B) Method of Marking. 310.120(B)(1) Surface Marking.

99. Answer B.   1/4 inch

In damp or wet locations, surface-type enclosures within the scope of this article shall be placed or equipped so as to prevent moisture or water from entering and accumulating within the cabinet or cutout box, and *shall be mounted so there is at least 6 mm (1/4 in.) airspace between the enclosure and the wall or other supporting surface. Enclosures installed in wet locations shall be weatherproof.* For enclosures in wet locations, raceways or cables entering above the level of uninsulated live parts shall use fittings listed for wet locations.

Informational Note: For protection against corrosion, see 300.6.

Reference: 2017 National Electrical Code – Chapter 3 Wiring Methods and Materials, Article 312 Cabinets, Cutout Boxes, and Meter Socket Enclosures. 312.2 Damp and Wet Locations.

EXAM 7

EXAM 7 ANSWERS

100. Answer B. project therefrom

In walls of concrete, tile, or other noncombustible material, cabinets shall be installed so that the front edge of the cabinet is not set back of the finished surface more than 6 mm (1/4 in.). *In walls constructed of wood or other combustible material, cabinets shall be flush with the finished surface or project therefrom.*

Reference: 2017 National Electrical Code – Chapter 3 Wiring Methods and Materials, Article 312 Cabinets, Cutout Boxes, and Meter Socket Enclosures. 312.3 Position in Wall.

101. Answer B. 1/4

In walls of concrete, tile, or other noncombustible material, cabinets shall be installed so that the front edge of the cabinet is not set back of the finished surface more than 6 mm (1/4 in.). In walls constructed of wood or other combustible material, cabinets shall be flush with the finished surface or project therefrom.

Reference: 2017 National Electrical Code – Chapter 3 Wiring Methods and Materials, Article 312 Cabinets, Cutout Boxes, and Meter Socket Enclosures. 312.3 Position in Wall.

102. Answer B. 1/8

Noncombustible surfaces that are broken or incomplete shall be repaired so there will be *no gaps or open spaces greater than 3 mm (1/8 in.) at the edge of the cabinet or cutout box employing a flush-type cover.*

Reference: 2017 National Electrical Code – Chapter 3 Wiring Methods and Materials, Article 312 Cabinets, Cutout Boxes, and Meter Socket Enclosures. 312.4 Repairing Noncombustible Surfaces.

103. Answer A. adequately closed

Openings through which conductors enter shall be closed in an approved manner.

Reference: 2017 National Electrical Code – Chapter 3 Wiring Methods and Materials, Article 312 Cabinets, Cutout Boxes, and Meter Socket Enclosures. 312.5 Cabinets, Cutout Boxes, and Meter Socket Enclosures. 312.5(A) Openings to Be Closed.

EXAM 7 ANSWERS

EXAM 7

EXAM 7 ANSWERS

Wire Size (AWG or kcmil)		Wires per Terminal							
		1		2		3		4 or More	
All Other Conductors	Compact Stranded AA-8000 Aluminum Alloy Conductors (See Note 5.)	mm	in.	mm	in.	mm	in.	mm	in.
14–10	12–8	Not specified		—	—	—	—	—	—
8	6	38.1	1½	—	—	—	—	—	—
6	4	50.8	2	—	—	—	—	—	—
4	2	76.2	3	—	—	—	—	—	—
3	1	76.2	3	—	—	—	—	—	—
2	1/0	88.9	3½	—	—	—	—	—	—
1	2/0	114	4½	—	—	—	—	—	—
1/0	3/0	140	5½	140	5½	178	7	—	—
2/0	4/0	152	6	152	6	190	7½	—	—
3/0	250	165ª	6½ª	165ª	6½ª	203	8	—	—
4/0	300	178ᵇ	7ᵇ	190ᶜ	7½ᶜ	216ª	8½ª	—	—
250	350	216ᵈ	8½ᵈ	229ᵈ	8½ᵈ	254ᵇ	9ᵇ	254	10
300	400	254ᵉ	10ᵉ	254ᵈ	10ᵈ	279ᵇ	11ᵇ	305	12
350	500	305ᵉ	12ᵉ	305ᵉ	12ᵉ	330ᵉ	13ᵉ	356ᵈ	14ᵈ
400	600	330ᵉ	13ᵉ	330ᵉ	13ᵉ	356ᵉ	14ᵉ	381ᵉ	15ᵉ
500	700–750	356ᵉ	14ᵉ	356ᵉ	14ᵉ	381ᵉ	15ᵉ	406ᵉ	16ᵉ
600	800–900	381ᵉ	15ᵉ	406ᵉ	16ᵉ	457ᵉ	18ᵉ	483ᵉ	19ᵉ
700	1000	406ᵉ	16ᵉ	457ᵉ	18ᵉ	508ᵉ	20ᵉ	559ᵉ	22ᵉ
750	—	432ᵉ	17ᵉ	483ᵉ	19ᵉ	559ᵉ	22ᵉ	610ᵉ	24ᵉ
800	—	457	18	508	20	559	22	610	24
900	—	483	19	559	22	610	24	610	24
1000	—	508	20	—	—	—	—	—	—
1250	—	559	22	—	—	—	—	—	—
1500	—	610	24	—	—	—	—	—	—
1750	—	610	24	—	—	—	—	—	—
2000	—	610	24	—	—	—	—	—	—

104. Answer D. secured

Where cable is used, each cable shall be secured to the cabinet, cutout box, or meter socket enclosure.

Informational Note: See Table 1 in Chapter 9, including Note 9, for allowable cable fill in circular raceways. See 310.15(8)(3)(a) for required ampacity reductions for multiple cables installed in a common raceway.

Reference: 2017 National Electrical Code – Chapter 3 Wiring Methods and Materials, Article 312 Cabinets, Cutout Boxes, and Meter Socket Enclosures. 312.5 Cabinets, Cutout Boxes, and Meter Socket Enclosures. 312.5(C) Cables.

105. Answer B. 8.5 inches

Wire-bending space at each terminal shall be provided in accordance with 312.6(B)(1) or (B)(2).

(1) Conductors Not Entering or Leaving Opposite Wall. Table 312.6(A) shall apply where the conductor does not enter or leave the enclosure through the wall opposite its terminal.

(2) Conductors Entering or Leaving Opposite Wall. *Table 312.6(B) shall* apply where the conductor does enter or leave the enclosure through the wall opposite its terminal.

Reference: 2017 National Electrical Code – Chapter 3 Wiring Methods and Materials, Article 312 Cabinets, Cutout Boxes, and Meter Socket Enclosures. 312.6 Deflection of Conductors. 312.6(B) Wire-Bending Space at Terminals.

EXAM 7

EXAM 7 ANSWERS

106. Answer B. crowding

Cabinets and cutout boxes shall have approved space to accommodate all conductors installed in them without crowding.

Reference: 2017 National Electrical Code – Chapter 3 Wiring Methods and Materials, Article 312 Cabinets, Cutout Boxes, and Meter Socket Enclosures. 312.7 Space in Enclosures.

107. Answer B. 40

The wiring space within enclosures for switches and overcurrent devices shall be permitted for other wiring and equipment subject to limitations for specific equipment as provided in (A) and (B).

(A) Splices, Taps, and Feed-Through Conductors. The wiring space of enclosures for switches or overcurrent devices shall be permitted for conductors feeding through, spliced, or tapping off to other enclosures, switches, or overcurrent devices where all of the following conditions are met:

(1) The total of all conductors installed at any cross section of the wiring space does not exceed 40 percent of the cross sectional area of that space.

(2) The total area of all conductors, splices, and taps installed at any cross section of the wiring space does not exceed 75 percent of the cross-sectional area of that space.

(3) A warning label complying with 110.21(B) is applied to the enclosure that identifies the closest disconnecting means for any feed-through conductors.

Reference: 2017 National Electrical Code – Chapter 3 Wiring Methods and Materials, Article 312 Cabinets, Cutout Boxes, and Meter Socket Enclosures. 312.8 Switch and Overcurrent Device Enclosures.

108. Answer C. Round

Round boxes shall not be used where conduits or connectors requiring the use of locknuts or bushings are to be connected to the side of the box.

Reference: 2017 National Electrical Code – Chapter 3 Wiring Methods and Materials, Article 314 Outlet, Device, Pull, and Junction Boxes; Conduit Bodies; Fittings; and Handhole Enclosures. 314.2 Round Boxes

109. Answer C. Round boxes

Round boxes shall not be used where conduits or connectors requiring the use of locknuts or bushings are to be connected to the side of the box.

Reference: 2017 National Electrical Code – Chapter 3 Wiring Methods and Materials, Article 314 Outlet, Device, Pull, and Junction Boxes; Conduit Bodies; Fittings; and Handhole Enclosures. 314.2 Round Boxes.

110. Answer A. concealed knob-and-tube wiring

Nonmetallic boxes shall be permitted only with open wiring on insulators, concealed knob-and tube wiring, cabled wiring methods with entirely nonmetallic sheaths, flexible cords, and nonmetallic raceways. Exception No. 1: Where internal bonding means are provided between all entries, nonmetallic boxes shall be permitted to be used with metal raceways or metal-armored cables.

Exception No. 2: Where integral bonding means with a provision for attaching an equipment bonding jumper inside the box are provided between all threaded entries in nonmetallic boxes listed for the purpose, nonmetallic boxes shall be permitted to be used with metal raceways or metal-armored cables.

Reference: 2017 National Electrical Code – Chapter 3 Wiring Methods and Materials, Article 314 Outlet, Device, Pull, and Junction Boxes; Conduit Bodies; Fittings; and Handhole Enclosures. 314.3 Nonmetallic Boxes.

111. Answer B. grounded

Metal boxes shall be grounded and bonded in accordance with Parts I, IV, V, VI, VII, and X of Article 250 as applicable, except as permitted in 250.112(I).

Reference: 2017 National Electrical Code – Chapter 3 Wiring Methods and Materials, Article 314 Outlet, Device, Pull, and Junction Boxes; Conduit Bodies; Fittings; and Handhole Enclosures. 314.4 Metal Boxes.

EXAM 7

EXAM 7 ANSWERS

Table 314.16(B) Volume Allowance Required per Conductor

Size of Conductor (AWG)	Free Space Within Box for Each Conductor	
	cm³	in.³
18	24.6	1.50
16	28.7	1.75
14	32.8	2.00
12	36.9	2.25
10	41.0	2.50
8	49.2	3.00
6	81.9	5.00

112. Answer C. 2.0

Review and know how to use this table.

Boxes and conduit bodies shall be of an approved size to provide free space for all enclosed conductors. In no case shall the volume of the box, as calculated in 314.16(A), be less than the fill calculation as calculated in 314.16(B). The minimum volume for conduit bodies shall be as calculated in 314.16(C).

The provisions of this section shall not apply to terminal housings supplied with motors or generators.

Informational Note: For volume requirements of motor or generator terminal housings, see 430.12.

Boxes and conduit bodies enclosing conductors 4 AWG or larger shall also comply with the provisions of 314.28.

Reference: 2017 National Electrical Code – Chapter 3 Wiring Methods and Materials, Article 314 Outlet, Device, Pull, and Junction Boxes; Conduit Bodies; Fittings; and Handhole Enclosures. 314.16 Number of Conductors in Outlet, Device, and Junction Boxes, and Conduit Bodies. Table 314.16(B) Volume Allowance Required per Conductor (page 70-186)

113. Answer C. 13

Review and know how to use this table.

Boxes and conduit bodies shall be of an approved size to provide free space for all enclosed conductors. In no case shall the volume of the box, as calculated in 314.16(A), be less than the fill calculation as calculated in 314.16(B). The minimum volume for conduit bodies shall be as calculated in 314.16(C).

The provisions of this section shall not apply to terminal housings supplied with motors or generators.

Informational Note: For volume requirements of motor or generator terminal housings, see 430.12.

Boxes and conduit bodies enclosing conductors 4 AWG or larger shall also comply with the provisions of 314.28.

Reference: 2017 National Electrical Code – Chapter 3 Wiring Methods and Materials, Article 314 Outlet, Device, Pull, and Junction Boxes; Conduit Bodies; Fittings; and Handhole Enclosures. 314.16 Number of Conductors in Outlet, Device, and Junction Boxes, and Conduit Bodies.

EXAM 7 ANSWERS

Table 314.16(A) Metal Boxes

Box Trade Size			Minimum Volume		Maximum Number of Conductors* (arranged by AWG size)						
mm	in.		cm³	in.³	18	16	14	12	10	8	6
100 × 32	(4 × 1¼)	round/octagonal	205	12.5	8	7	6	5	5	5	2
100 × 38	(4 × 1½)	round/octagonal	254	15.5	10	8	7	6	6	5	3
100 × 54	(4 × 2⅛)	round/octagonal	353	21.5	14	12	10	9	8	7	4
100 × 32	(4 × 1¼)	square	295	18.0	12	10	9	8	7	6	3
100 × 38	(4 × 1½)	square	344	21.0	14	12	10	9	8	7	4
100 × 54	(4 × 2⅛)	square	497	30.3	20	17	15	13	12	10	6
120 × 32	(4$^{11}/_{16}$ × 1¼)	square	418	25.5	17	14	12	11	10	8	5
120 × 38	(4$^{11}/_{16}$ × 1½)	square	484	29.5	19	16	14	13	11	9	5
120 × 54	(4$^{11}/_{16}$ × 2⅛)	square	689	42.0	28	24	21	18	16	14	8
75 × 50 × 38	(3 × 2 × 1½)	device	123	7.5	5	4	3	3	3	2	1
75 × 50 × 50	(3 × 2 × 2)	device	164	10.0	6	5	5	4	4	3	2
75 × 50 × 57	(3 × 2 × 2¼)	device	172	10.5	7	6	5	4	4	3	2
75 × 50 × 65	(3 × 2 × 2½)	device	205	12.5	8	7	6	5	5	4	2
75 × 50 × 70	(3 × 2 × 2¾)	device	230	14.0	9	8	7	6	5	4	2
75 × 50 × 90	(3 × 2 × 3½)	device	295	18.0	12	10	9	8	7	6	3
100 × 54 × 38	(4 × 2⅛ × 1½)	device	169	10.5	6	5	5	4	4	3	2
100 × 54 × 48	(4 × 2⅛ × 1⅞)	device	213	13.0	8	7	6	5	5	4	2
100 × 54 × 54	(4 × 2⅛ × 2⅛)	device	238	14.5	9	8	7	6	5	4	2
95 × 50 × 65	(3¾ × 2 × 2½)	masonry box	230	14.0	9	8	7	6	5	4	2
95 × 50 × 90	(3¾ × 2 × 3½)	masonry box	344	21.0	14	12	10	9	8	7	4
min. 44.5 depth	FS — single cover (1¾)		221	13.5	9	7	6	6	5	4	2
min. 60.3 depth	FD — single cover (2⅜)		295	18.0	12	10	9	8	7	6	3
min. 44.5 depth	FS — multiple cover (1¾)		295	18.0	12	10	9	8	7	6	3
min. 60.3 depth	FD — multiple cover (2⅜)		395	24.0	16	13	12	10	9	8	4

114. **Answer B.** seven

Review and know how to use this table.

Boxes and conduit bodies shall be of an approved size to provide free space for all enclosed conductors. In no case shall the volume of the box, as calculated in 314.16(A), be less than the fill calculation as calculated in 314.16(B). The minimum volume for conduit bodies shall be as calculated in 314.16(C).

The provisions of this section shall not apply to terminal housings supplied with motors or generators.

Informational Note: For volume requirements of motor or generator terminal housings, see 430.12.

Boxes and conduit bodies enclosing conductors 4 AWG or larger shall also comply with the provisions of 314.28.

Reference: 2017 National Electrical Code – Chapter 3 Wiring Methods and Materials, Article 314 Outlet, Device, Pull, and Junction Boxes; Conduit Bodies; Fittings; and Handhole Enclosures. 314.16 Number of Conductors in Outlet, Device, and Junction Boxes, and Conduit Bodies. Table 314.16(A) Metal Boxes (page 70-186)

115. **Answer C.** five

Review and know how to use this table.

Boxes and conduit bodies shall be of an approved size to provide free space for all enclosed conductors. In no case shall the volume of the box, as calculated in 314.16(A), be less than the fill calculation as calculated in 314.16(B). The minimum volume for conduit bodies shall be as calculated in 314.16(C).

The provisions of this section shall not apply to terminal housings supplied with motors or generators.

Informational Note: For volume requirements of motor or generator terminal housings, see 430.12.

Boxes and conduit bodies enclosing conductors 4 AWG or larger shall also comply with the provisions of 314.28.

Reference: 2017 National Electrical Code – Chapter 3 Wiring Methods and Materials, Article 314 Outlet, Device, Pull, and Junction Boxes; Conduit Bodies; Fittings; and Handhole Enclosures. 314.16 Number of Conductors in Outlet, Device, and Junction Boxes, and Conduit Bodies. Table 314.16(A) Metal Boxes (page 70-186)

EXAM 7

EXAM 7 ANSWERS

116. Answer C. 20.25

The volumes in paragraphs 314.16(B)(1) through (B)(5), as applicable, shall be added together. No allowance shall be required for small fittings such as locknuts and bushings.

Size 12 AWG = 2.25 cu.in x 6= 13.5 clamps=2.25cu. in. x 3= 6.75

Total=20.25

Reference: 2017 National Electrical Code – Chapter 3 Wiring Methods and Materials, Article 314 Outlet, Device, Pull, and Junction Boxes; Conduit Bodies; Fittings; and Handhole Enclosures. 314.16 Number of Conductors in Outlet, Device, and Junction Boxes, and Conduit Bodies. 314.16(B) Box Fill Calculations. Table 314.16(A) Metal Boxes and Table 314.16(B) Volume Allowance Required per Conductor (page 70-186)

117. Answer C. 2.25 cubic inches

The volumes in paragraphs 314.16(B)(1) through (B)(5), as applicable, shall be added together. No allowance shall be required for small fittings such as locknuts and bushings.

Reference: 2017 National Electrical Code – Chapter 3 Wiring Methods and Materials, Article 314 Outlet, Device, Pull, and Junction Boxes; Conduit Bodies; Fittings; and Handhole Enclosures. 314.16 Number of Conductors in Outlet, Device, and Junction Boxes, and Conduit Bodies. 314.16(B) Box Fill Calculations. Table 314.16(B) Volume Allowance Required per Conductor (page 70-186)

118. Answer A. once

Each conductor that originates outside the box and terminates or is spliced within the box shall be counted once, and each conductor that passes through the box without splice or termination shall be counted once. Each loop or coil of unbroken conductor not less than twice the minimum length required for free conductors in 300.14 shall be counted twice. The conductor till shall be calculated using Table 314.16(B). A conductor, no part of which leaves the box, shall not be counted.

Exception: An equipment grounding conductor or conductors or not over four fixture wires smaller than 14 AWG, or both, shall be permitted to be omitted from the calculations where they enter a box from a domed luminaire or similar canopy and terminate within that box.

Reference: 2017 National Electrical Code – Chapter 3 Wiring Methods and Materials, Article 314 Outlet, Device, Pull, and Junction Boxes; Conduit Bodies; Fittings; and Handhole Enclosures. 314.16 Number of Conductors in Outlet, Device, and Junction Boxes, and Conduit Bodies. 314.16(B) Box Fill Calculations. 314.16(B)(1) Conductor Fill.

119. Answer B. shall be counted once.

Each conductor that originates outside the box and terminates or is spliced within the box shall be counted once, *and each conductor that passes through the box without splice or termination shall be counted once*. Each loop or coil of unbroken conductor not less than twice the minimum length required for free conductors in 300.14 shall be counted twice. The conductor till shall be calculated using Table 314.16(B). A conductor, no part of which leaves the box, shall not be counted.

Exception: An equipment grounding conductor or conductors or not over four fixture wires smaller than 14 AWG, or both, shall be permitted to be omitted from the calculations where they enter a box from a domed luminaire or similar canopy and terminate within that box.

Reference: 2017 National Electrical Code – Chapter 3 Wiring Methods and Materials, Article 314 Outlet, Device, Pull, and Junction Boxes; Conduit Bodies; Fittings; and Handhole Enclosures. 314.16 Number of Conductors in Outlet, Device, and Junction Boxes, and Conduit Bodies. 314.16(B) Box Fill Calculations. 314.16(B)(1) Conductor Fill.

120. Answer D. twice

Each conductor that originates outside the box and terminates or is spliced within the box shall be counted once, and each conductor that passes through the box without splice or termination shall be counted once. *Each loop or coil of unbroken conductor not less than twice the minimum length required for free* conductors in 300.14 shall be counted twice. The conductor till shall be calculated using Table 314.16(B). A conductor, no part of which leaves the box, shall not be counted.

Exception: An equipment grounding conductor or conductors or not over four fixture wires smaller than 14 AWG, or both, shall be permitted to be omitted from the calculations where they enter a box from a domed luminaire or similar canopy and terminate within that box.

Reference: 2017 National Electrical Code – Chapter 3 Wiring Methods and Materials, Article 314 Outlet, Device, Pull, and Junction Boxes; Conduit Bodies; Fittings; and Handhole Enclosures. 314.16 Number of Conductors in Outlet, Device, and Junction Boxes, and Conduit Bodies. 314.16(B) Box Fill Calculations. 314.16(B)(1) Conductor Fill.

EXAM 7

EXAM 7 ANSWERS

121. **Answer B.** 30 cubic inches

Each conductor that originates outside the box and terminates or is spliced within the box shall be counted once, and each conductor that passes through the box without splice or termination shall be counted once. Each loop or coil of unbroken conductor not less than twice the minimum length required for free conductors in 300.14 shall be counted twice. The conductor till shall be calculated using Table 314.16(B). A conductor, no part of which leaves the box, shall not be counted.

Exception: An equipment grounding conductor or conductors or not over four fixture wires smaller than 14 AWG, or both, shall be permitted to be omitted from the calculations where they enter a box from a domed luminaire or similar canopy and terminate within that box.

Reference: 2017 National Electrical Code – Chapter 3 Wiring Methods and Materials, Article 314 Outlet, Device, Pull, and Junction Boxes; Conduit Bodies; Fittings; and Handhole Enclosures. 314.16 Number of Conductors in Outlet, Device, and Junction Boxes, and Conduit Bodies. 314.16(B) Box Fill Calculations. 314.16(B)(1) Conductor Fill.

Where one or more internal cable clamps, whether factory or field supplied, are present in the box, a single volume allowance in accordance with Table 314.16(B) shall be made based on the largest conductor present in the box. No allowance shall be required for a cable connector with its clamping mechanism outside the box.

A clamp assembly that incorporates a cable termination for the cable conductors shall be listed and marked for use with specific nonmetallic boxes. Conductors that originate within the clamp assembly sha11 be included in conductor fill calculations covered in 314.16(B)(1) as though they entered from outside the box. The clamp assembly shall not require a fill a11owance, but the volume of the portion of the assembly that remains within the box after installation shall be excluded from the box volume as marked in 314.16(A)(2).

Reference: 2017 National Electrical Code – Chapter 3 Wiring Methods and Materials, Article 314 Outlet, Device, Pull, and Junction Boxes; Conduit Bodies; Fittings; and Handhole Enclosures. 314.16 Number of Conductors in Outlet, Device, and Junction Boxes, and Conduit Bodies. 314.16(B) Box Fill Calculations. 314.16(B)(2) Clamp Fill.

For each yoke or strap containing one or more devices or equipment, a double volume allowance in accordance with Table 314.16(B) shall be made for each yoke or strap based on the largest conductor connected to a device(s) or equipment supported by that yoke or strap. A device or utilization equipment wider than a single 50 mm (2 in.) device box as described in Table 314.16(A) shall have double volume allowances provided for each gang required for mounting.

Reference: 2017 National Electrical Code – Chapter 3 Wiring Methods and Materials, Article 314 Outlet, Device, Pull, and Junction Boxes; Conduit Bodies; Fittings; and Handhole Enclosures. 314.16 Number of Conductors in Outlet, Device, and Junction Boxes, and Conduit Bodies. 314.16(B) Box Fill Calculations. 314.16(B)(4) Device or Equipment Fill.

Where one or more equipment grounding conductors or equipment bonding jumpers enter a box, a single volume allowance in accordance with Table 314.16(B) shall be made based on the largest equipment grounding conductor or equipment bonding jumper present in the box. Where an additional set of equipment grounding conductors, as permitted by 250.146(D), is present in the box, an additional volume allowance shall be made based on the largest equipment grounding conductor in the additional set.

Reference: 2017 National Electrical Code – Chapter 3 Wiring Methods and Materials, Article 314 Outlet, Device, Pull, and Junction Boxes; Conduit Bodies; Fittings; and Handhole Enclosures. 314.16 Number of Conductors in Outlet, Device, and Junction Boxes, and Conduit Bodies. 314.16(B) Box Fill Calculations. 314.16(B)(5) Equipment Grounding Conductor Fill.

Size 14 AWG= 2.00 cu. in. x 4 = 8.00 cubic inches

Size 12 AWG= 2.25 cu. in. x 4 = 9.00 cubic inches

equip grnd.= 2.25 cu. in. x 1 = 2.25 cubic inches

clamps= 2.25 cu. in. x 1 = 2.25 cubic inches

recept.= 2.25 cu. in. x 2 = 4.50 cubic inches

switch= 2.00 cu. in. x 2 = 4.00 cubic inches

TOTAL =30.00 cubic inches

* Three - 6 AWG wires, 2 ungrounded & 1 grounded conductors

*One - 8 AWG equipment grounding conductor

*Two - internal clamps

*One – pigtail

Reference: 2017 National Electrical Code – Chapter 3 Wiring Methods and Materials, Article 314 Outlet, Device, Pull, and Junction Boxes; Conduit Bodies; Fittings; and Handhole Enclosures. 314.16 Number of Conductors in Outlet, Device, and Junction Boxes, and Conduit Bodies. Table 314.16(B) Volume Allowance Required per Conductor (page 70-186)

EXAM 7
EXAM 7 ANSWERS

122. **Answer D.** 23 cubic inches

The volumes in paragraphs 314.16(B)(1) through (B)(5), as applicable, shall be added together. No allowance shall be required for small fittings such as locknuts and bushings.

(1) **Conductor Fill.** Each conductor that originates outside the box and terminates or is spliced within the box shall be counted once, and each conductor that passes through the box without splice or termination shall be counted once. Each loop or coil of unbroken conductor not less than twice the minimum length required for free conductors in 300.14 shall be counted twice. The conductor till shall be calculated using Table 314.16(B). A conductor, no part of which leaves the box, shall not be counted.

(2) **Clamp Fill.** Where one or more internal cable clamps, whether factory or field supplied, are present in the box, a single volume allowance in accordance with Table 314.16(B) shall be made based on the largest conductor present in the box. No allowance shall be required for a cable connector with its clamping mechanism outside the box.

A clamp assembly that incorporates a cable termination for the cable conductors shall be listed and marked for use with specific nonmetallic boxes. Conductors that originate within the clamp assembly shall be included in conductor fill calculations covered in 314.16(B)(1) as though they entered from outside the box. The clamp assembly shall not require a fill allowance, but the volume of the portion of the assembly that remains within the box after installation shall be excluded from the box volume as marked in 314.16(A)(2).

(5) **Equipment Grounding Conductor Fill.** Where one or more equipment grounding conductors or equipment bonding jumpers enter a box, a single volume allowance in accordance with Table 314.16(B) shall be made based on the largest equipment grounding conductor or equipment bonding jumper present in the box. Where an additional set of equipment grounding conductors, as permitted by 250.146(D), is present in the box, an additional volume allowance shall be made based on the largest equipment grounding conductor in the additional set.

Reference: 2017 National Electrical Code – Chapter 3 Wiring Methods and Materials, Article 314 Outlet, Device, Pull, and Junction Boxes; Conduit Bodies; Fittings; and Handhole Enclosures. 314.16 Number of Conductors in Outlet, Device, and Junction Boxes, and Conduit Bodies. 314.16(B) Box Fill Calculations. 314.16(B)(1),(2)&(5). Table 314.16(B) Volume Allowance Required by Conductor (page 70-186)

2 – 6 AWG ungrounded conductors = 2 x 5.00 cu. in. = 10 cu. in.

1 – 6 AWG grounded conductor = 1 x 5.00 cu. in. = 5 cu. in.

1 – 8 AWG equipment Grounding = 1 x 3.00 cu. in. = 3 cu. in.

2 – Internal clamps = 1 x 5.00 cu. in. = 5 cu. in.

1 – pigtail = -0- = 0 cu. in.

TOTAL 23 cu. in.

123. **Answer B.** one

Where one or more luminaire studs or hickeys are present in the box, a single volume allowance in accordance with Table 314.16(B) shall be made for each type of fitting based on the largest conductor present in the box.

Reference: 2017 National Electrical Code – Chapter 3 Wiring Methods and Materials – Chapter 3 Wiring Methods and Materials, Article 314 Outlet, Device, Pull, and Junction Boxes; Conduit Bodies; Fittings; and Handhole Enclosures. 314.16 Number of Conductors in Outlet, Device, and Junction Boxes, and Conduit Bodies. 314.16(B) Box Fill Calculations. 314.16(B)(3) Support Fittings Fill.

124. **Answer C.** double

For each yoke or strap containing one or more devices or equipment, a double volume allowance in accordance with Table 314.16(B) shall be made for each yoke or strap based on the largest conductor connected to a device(s) or equipment supported by that yoke or strap. A device or utilization equipment wider than a single 50 mm (2 in.) device box as described in Table 314.16(A) shall have double volume allowances provided for each gang required for mounting.

Reference: 2017 National Electrical Code – Chapter 3 Wiring Methods and Materials, Article 314 Outlet, Device, Pull, and Junction Boxes; Conduit Bodies; Fittings; and Handhole Enclosures. 314.16 Number of Conductors in Outlet, Device, and Junction Boxes, and Conduit Bodies. 314.16(B) Box Fill Calculations. 314.16(B)(4) Device or Equipment Fill.

EXAM 7

EXAM 7 ANSWERS

125. Answer C. two

For each yoke or strap containing one or more devices or equipment, a double volume allowance in accordance with Table 314.16(B) shall be made for each yoke or strap based on the largest conductor connected to a device(s) or equipment supported by that yoke or strap. *A device or utilization equipment wider than a single 50 mm (2 in.) device box as described in Table 314.16(A) shall have double volume allowances* provided for each gang required for mounting.

Reference: 2017 National Electrical Code – Chapter 3 Wiring Methods and Materials, Article 314 Outlet, Device, Pull, and Junction Boxes; Conduit Bodies; Fittings; and Handhole Enclosures. 314.16 Number of Conductors in Outlet, Device, and Junction Boxes, and Conduit Bodies. 314.16(B) Box Fill Calculations. 314.16(B)(4) Device or Equipment Fill.

126. Answer B. five

The volumes in paragraphs 314.16(B)(1) through (B)(5), as applicable, shall be added together. No allowance shall be required for small fittings such as locknuts and bushings.

Reference: 2017 National Electrical Code – Chapter 3 Wiring Methods and Materials, Article 314 Outlet, Device, Pull, and Junction Boxes; Conduit Bodies; Fittings; and Handhole Enclosures. 314.16 Number of Conductors in Outlet, Device, and Junction Boxes, and Conduit Bodies. Table 314.16(B) Volume Allowance Required per Conductor (page 70-186)

Size 12 AWG = 2.25 cu. in. x 6 (existing wire in box) = 13.5 cu. in.

24.0 cu. in. (allowable fill of box)

-13.5 cu. in. (existing wire in box)

13.5 cu. in. (remaining space available)

127. Answer B. two

The volumes in paragraphs 314.16(B)(1) through (B)(5), as applicable, shall be added together. No allowance shall be required for small fittings such as locknuts and bushings.

Reference: 2017 National Electrical Code – Chapter 3 Wiring Methods and Materials, Article 314 Outlet, Device, Pull, and Junction Boxes; Conduit Bodies; Fittings; and Handhole Enclosures. 314.16 Number of Conductors in Outlet, Device, and Junction Boxes, and Conduit Bodies. Table 314.16(B) Volume Allowance Required per Conductor (page 70-186)

For each yoke or strap containing one or more devices or equipment, a double volume allowance in accordance with Table 314.16(B) shall be made for each yoke or strap based on the largest conductor connected to a device(s) or equipment supported by that yoke or strap. A device or utilization equipment wider than a single 50 mm (2 in.) device box as described in Table 314.16(A) shall have double volume allowances provided for each gang required for mounting.

Reference: 2017 National Electrical Code – Chapter 3 Wiring Methods and Materials, Article 314 Outlet, Device, Pull, and Junction Boxes; Conduit Bodies; Fittings; and Handhole Enclosures. 314.16 Number of Conductors in Outlet, Device, and Junction Boxes, and Conduit Bodies. 314.16(B) Box Fill Calculations. 314.16(B)(4) Device or Equipment Fill.

18 cu. in. (box) / 2.25 cu. in. (#12 wire) =8 wires (allowable fill)

-2 wires (device)

6 wires may be installed

NOTE: A size 12/2 AWG with ground NM cable contains three (3) conductors.

6 wires (may be added)

3 (wires in NM cable)= 2 size 12/2 NM cables may be installed

128. Answer D. four

For each yoke or strap containing one or more devices or equipment, a double volume allowance in accordance with Table 314.16(B) shall be made for each yoke or strap based on the largest conductor connected to a device(s) or equipment supported by that yoke or strap. *A device or utilization equipment wider than a single 50 mm (2 in.) device box as described in Table 314.16(A) shall have double volume allowances provided for each gang required for mounting.*

Reference: 2017 National Electrical Code – Chapter 3 Wiring Methods and Materials, Article 314 Outlet, Device, Pull, and Junction Boxes; Conduit Bodies; Fittings; and Handhole Enclosures. 314.16 Number of Conductors in Outlet, Device, and Junction Boxes, and Conduit Bodies. 314.16(B) Box Fill Calculations. 314.16(B)(4) Device or Equipment Fill.

EXAM 7

EXAM 7 ANSWERS

129. Answer A. 1/4

Installations within or behind a surface of concrete, tile, gypsum, plaster, or other noncombustible material, including boxes employing a flush type cover or faceplate, shall be made *so that the front edge of the box, plaster ring, extension ring, or listed extender will not be set back of the finished surface more than 6 mm (1⁄4 in.).*

Installations within a surface of wood or other combustible surface material, boxes, plaster rings, extension rings, or listed extenders shall extend to the finished surface or project therefrom.

Reference: 2017 National Electrical Code – Chapter 3 Wiring Methods and Materials, Article 314 Outlet, Device, Pull, and Junction Boxes; Conduit Bodies; Fittings; and Handhole Enclosures. 314.20 Flush-Mounted Installations.

130. Answer A. flush with or projected out

Installations within or behind a surface of concrete, tile, gypsum, plaster, or other noncombustible material, including boxes employing a flush type cover or faceplate, shall be made so that the front edge of the box, plaster ring, extension ring, or listed extender will not be set back of the finished surface more than 6 mm (1⁄4 in.).

Installations within a surface of wood or other combustible surface material, boxes, plaster rings, extension rings, or listed extenders shall extend to the finished surface or project therefrom.

Reference: 2017 National Electrical Code – Chapter 3 Wiring Methods and Materials, Article 314 Outlet, Device, Pull, and Junction Boxes; Conduit Bodies; Fittings; and Handhole Enclosures. 314.20 In Wall or Ceiling.

131. Answer B. 1/2

Outlet boxes that do not enclose devices or utilization *equipment shall have a minimum internal depth of 12.7 mm (1/2 in.).*

Reference: 2017 National Electrical Code – Chapter 3 Wiring Methods and Materials, Article 314 Outlet, Device, Pull, and Junction Boxes; Conduit Bodies; Fittings; and Handhole Enclosures. 314.24 Depth of Boxes. 314.24(A) Outlet Boxes Without Enclosed Devices or Utilization Equipment.

132. Answer A. 1/2 in.

Outlet boxes that do not enclose devices or utilization equipment shall have a minimum internal depth of 12.7 mm (1/2 in.).

Reference: 2017 National Electrical Code – Chapter 3 Wiring Methods and Materials, Article 314 Outlet, Device, Pull, and Junction Boxes; Conduit Bodies; Fittings; and Handhole Enclosures. 314.24 Depth of Boxes. 314.24(A) Outlet Boxes Without Enclosed Devices or Utilization Equipment.

133. Answer D. 50 pounds

Boxes used at luminaire or lampholder outlets in or on a vertical surface shall be identified and marked on the interior of the box to *indicate the maximum weight of the luminaire that is permitted to be supported by the box if other than 23 kg (50 lb.).*

Exception: A vertically mounted luminaire or lamp holder weighing not more than 3 kg (6 lb) shall be permitted to be supported on other boxes or plaster rings that are secured to other boxes, provided that the luminaire or its supporting yoke, or the lamp holder, is secured to the box with no fewer than two No. 6 or larger screws.

Reference: 2017 National Electrical Code – Chapter 3 Wiring Methods and Materials, Article 314 Outlet, Device, Pull, and Junction Boxes; Conduit Bodies; Fittings; and Handhole Enclosures. 314.27 Outlet Boxes. 314.27(A) Boxes at Luminaire or Lampholder Outlets. 314.27(A)(1) Vertical Surface Outlets.

At every outlet used exclusively for lighting, the box shall be designed or installed so that a luminaire or lamp holder may be attached. Boxes shall be required to support a luminaire weighing a minimum of 23 kg (50 lb). *A luminaire that weighs more than 23 kg (50 lb) shall be supported independently of the outlet box*, unless the outlet box is listed for not less than the weight to be supported. The interior of the box shall be marked by the manufacturer to indicate the maximum weight the box shall be permitted to support.

Reference: 2017 National Electrical Code – Chapter 3 Wiring Methods and Materials, Article 314 Outlet, Device, Pull, and Junction Boxes; Conduit Bodies; Fittings; and Handhole Enclosures. 314.27 Outlet Boxes. 314.27(A) Boxes at Luminaire or Lampholder Outlets. 314.27(A)(2) Ceiling Outlets.

EXAM 7

EXAM 7 ANSWERS

134. **Answer D.** 50

At every outlet used exclusively for lighting, the box shall be designed or installed so that a luminaire or lamp holder may be attached. Boxes shall be required to support a luminaire weighing a minimum of 23 kg (50 lb). *A luminaire that weighs more than 23 kg (50 lb) shall be supported independently of the outlet box*, unless the outlet box is listed for not less than the weight to be supported. The interior of the box shall be marked by the manufacturer to indicate the maximum weight the box shall be permitted to support.

Reference: 2017 National Electrical Code – Chapter 3 Wiring Methods and Materials, Article 314 Outlet, Device, Pull, and Junction Boxes; Conduit Bodies; Fittings; and Handhole Enclosures. 314.27 Outlet Boxes. 314.27(A) Boxes at Luminaire or Lampholder Outlets. 314.27(A)(2) Ceiling Outlets.

135. **Answer C.** 35 pounds

Outlet boxes or outlet box systems used as the sole support of a ceiling-suspended (paddle) fan shall be listed, shall be marked by their manufacturer as suitable for this purpose, and shall not support ceiling-suspended (paddle) fans that weigh more than 32 kg (70 lb). *For outlet boxes or outlet box systems designed to support ceiling-suspended (paddle) fans that weigh more than 16 kg (35 lb), the required marking shall include the maximum weight to be supported.*

Where spare, separately switched, ungrounded conductors are provided to a ceiling-mounted outlet box, in a location acceptable for a ceiling-suspended (paddle) fan in one-family, two-family, or multifamily dwellings, the outlet box or outlet box system shall be listed for sole support of a ceiling suspended (paddle) fan.

Reference: 2017 National Electrical Code – Chapter 3 Wiring Methods and Materials, Article 314 Outlet, Device, Pull, and Junction Boxes; Conduit Bodies; Fittings; and Handhole Enclosures. 314.27 Outlet Boxes. 314.27(C) Boxes at Ceiling-Suspended (Paddle) Fan Outlets.

136. **Answer D.** 70 pounds

Outlet boxes or outlet box systems used as the sole support of a ceiling-suspended (paddle) fan shall be listed, shall be marked by their manufacturer as suitable for this purpose, and shall not support ceiling-suspended (paddle) fans that weigh more than 32 kg (70 lb). For outlet boxes or outlet box systems designed to support ceiling-suspended (paddle) fans that weigh more than 16 kg (35 lb), the required marking shall include the maximum weight to be supported.

Where spare, separately switched, ungrounded conductors are provided to a ceiling-mounted outlet box, in a location acceptable for a ceiling-suspended (paddle) fan in one-family, two-family, or multifamily dwellings, the outlet box or outlet box system shall be listed for sole support of a ceiling suspended (paddle) fan.

Reference: 2017 National Electrical Code – Chapter 3 Wiring Methods and Materials, Article 314 Outlet, Device, Pull, and Junction Boxes; Conduit Bodies; Fittings; and Handhole Enclosures. 314.27 Outlet Boxes. 314.27(C) Boxes at Ceiling-Suspended (Paddle) Fan Outlets.

137. **Answer C.** eight

In straight pulls, the length of the box or conduit body shall not be less than eight times the metric designator (trade size) of the largest raceway.

Reference: 2017 National Electrical Code – Chapter 3 Wiring Methods and Materials, Article 314 Outlet, Device, Pull, and Junction Boxes; Conduit Bodies; Fittings; and Handhole Enclosures. 314.28 Pull and Junction Boxes and Conduit Bodies. 314.28(A) Minimum Size. 314.28(A)(1) Straight Pulls.

138. **Answer C.** separate

Where permanent barriers are installed in a box, *each section shall be considered as a separate box.*

Reference: 2017 National Electrical Code – Chapter 3 Wiring Methods and Materials, Article 314 Outlet, Device, Pull, and Junction Boxes; Conduit Bodies; Fittings; and Handhole Enclosures. 314.28 Pull and Junction Boxes and Conduit Bodies. 314.28(D) Permanent Barriers.

EXAM 7

EXAM 7 ANSWERS

139. Answer A.   accessible

Boxes, conduit bodies, and handhole enclosures shall be installed so that the wiring contained in them can be rendered accessible without removing any part of the building or structure or, in underground circuits, without excavating sidewalks, paving, earth, or other substance that is to be used to establish the finished grade.

Exception: Listed boxes and hand hole enclosures shall be permitted where covered by gravel, light aggregate, or no cohesive granulated soil if their location is effectively identified and accessible for excavation.

Reference: 2017 National Electrical Code – Chapter 3 Wiring Methods and Materials, Article 314 Outlet, Device, Pull, and Junction Boxes; Conduit Bodies; Fittings; and Handhole Enclosures. 314.29 Boxes, Conduit Bodies, and Handhole Enclosures to Be Accessible.

140. Answer C.   tapped hole

A means shall be provided in each metal box for the connection of an equipment grounding conductor. *The means shall be permitted to be a tapped hole or equivalent.*

Informational Note: See 300.6 for limitation in the use of boxes and fittings protected from corrosion solely by enamel.

Reference: 2017 National Electrical Code – Chapter 3 Wiring Methods and Materials, Article 314 Outlet, Device, Pull, and Junction Boxes; Conduit Bodies; Fittings; and Handhole Enclosures. 314.40 Metal Boxes, Conduit Bodies, and Fittings. 314.40(D) Grounding Provisions.

141. Answer C.   36

The distance between each cable or conductor entry inside the box and the opposite wall of the box shall not be less than 36 times the outside diameter, over sheath, of the largest cable or conductor. This distance shall be increased for additional entries by the amount of the sum of the outside diameters, over sheath, of all other cables or conductor entries through the same wall of the box.

Exception No. 1: Where a conductor or cable entry is in the wall of a box opposite a removable cover, the distance from that wall to the cover shall be permitted to be not less than the bending radius for the conductors as provided in 300.34.

Exception No. 2: Where cables are nonshielded and not lead covered, the distance of 36 times the outside diameter shall be permitted to be reduced to 24 times the outside diameter.

Reference: 2017 National Electrical Code – Chapter 3 Wiring Methods and Materials, Article 314 Outlet, Device, Pull, and Junction Boxes; Conduit Bodies; Fittings; and Handhole Enclosures. 314.71 Size of Pull and Junction Boxes, Conduit Bodies, and Handhole Enclosures. 314.71(B) For Angle or U Pulls. 314.71(B)(1) Distance to Opposite Wall.

142. Answer A.   for feeders

Type AC cable shall be permitted as follows:

(1) For feeders and branch circuits in both exposed and concealed installations

(2) In cable trays

(3) In dry locations

(4) Embedded in plaster finish on brick or other masonry, except in damp or wet locations

(5) To be run or fished in the air voids of masonry block or tile walls where such walls are not exposed or subject to excessive moisture or dampness

Informational Note: The "Uses Permitted" is not an all-inclusive list.

Reference: 2017 National Electrical Code – Chapter 3 Wiring Methods and Materials, Article 320 Armored Cable: Type AC. 320.10 Uses Permitted.

EXAM 7

EXAM 7 ANSWERS

143. Answer D.   all of the above

Type AC cable shall not be used as follows:

(1) *Where subject to physical damage*

(2) *In damp or wet locations*

(3) *In air voids of masonry block or tile walls where such walls are exposed or subject to excessive moisture or dampness*

(4) Where exposed to corrosive conditions

(5) Embedded in plaster finish on brick or other masonry in damp or wet locations

Reference: 2017 National Electrical Code – Chapter 3 Wiring Methods and Materials, Article 320 Armored Cable: Type AC. 320.12 Uses Not Permitted.

144. Answer D.   30 amperes

General-purpose and appliance branch circuits shall have ratings not exceeding 20 amperes. *Individual branch circuits shall have ratings not exceeding 30 amperes.*

Reference: 2017 National Electrical Code – Chapter 3 Wiring Methods and Materials, Article 324 Flat Conductor Cable: Type FCC. 324.10 Uses Permitted. 324.10(B) Branch-Circuit Ratings. 324.10(B)(2) Current.

145. Answer D.   35,000

Type MV cable shall be permitted for use on power systems rated up to and including 35,000 volts, nominal, as follows:

(1) In wet or dry locations.

(2) In raceways.

(3) In cable trays, where identified for the use, in accordance with 392.10, 392.20(B), (C), and (D), 392.22(C), 392.30(B)(1), 392.46, 392.56, and 392.60. Type MV cable that has an overall metallic sheath or armor, complies with the requirements for Type MC cable, and is identified as "MV or MC" shall be permitted to be installed in cable trays in accordance with 392.10(B)(2).

(4) Direct buried in accordance with 300.50.

(5) In messenger-supported wiring in accordance with Part II of Article 396.

(6) As exposed runs in accordance with 300.37. Type MV cable that has an overall metallic sheath or armor, complies with the requirements for Type MC cable, and is identified as "MV or MC" shall be permitted to be installed as exposed runs of metal-clad cable in accordance with 300.37.

Reference: 2017 National Electrical Code – Chapter 3 Wiring Methods and Materials, Article 328 Medium Voltage Cable: Type MV. 328.10 Uses Permitted.

146. Answer D.   where exposed to direct sunlight

Type MV cable shall not be used where exposed to direct sunlight, unless identified for the use.

Reference: 2017 National Electrical Code – Chapter 3 Wiring Methods and Materials, Article 328 Medium Voltage Cable: Type MV. 328.12 Uses Not Permitted.

EXAM 7

EXAM 7 ANSWERS

147. **Answer B.** physical damage

Review all of the other uses permitted.

Type MC cable shall be permitted as follows:

(1) For services, feeders, and branch circuits.

(2) For power, lighting, control, and signal circuits.

(3) Indoors or outdoors.

(4) Exposed or concealed.

(5) To be direct buried where identified for such use.

(6) In cable tray where identified for such use.

(7) In any raceway.

(8) As aerial cable on a messenger.

(9) In hazardous (classified) locations where specifically permitted by other articles in this Code.

(10) In dry locations and embedded in plaster finish on brick or other masonry except in damp or wet locations.

(11) In wet locations where a corrosion-resistant jacket is provided over the metallic covering and any of the following conditions are met:

a. The metallic covering is impervious to moisture.

b. A jacket resistant to moisture is provided under the metal covering.

c. The insulated conductors under the metallic covering are listed for use in wet locations.

(12) Where single-conductor cables are used, all phase conductors and, where used, the grounded conductor shall be grouped together to minimize induced voltage on the sheath.

Reference: 2017 National Electrical Code – Chapter 3 Wiring Methods and Materials, Article 330 Metal-Clad Cable: Type MC. 330.10 Uses Permitted. 330.10(A) General Uses.

148. **Answer D.** 6

Unless otherwise provided, cables shall be secured at intervals not exceeding 1.8 m (6 ft.). Cables containing four or fewer conductors sized no larger than 10 AWG shall be secured within 300 mm (12 in.) of every box, cabinet, fitting, or other cable termination. In vertical installations, listed cables with ungrounded conductors 250 kc mil and larger shall be permitted to be secured at intervals not exceeding 3 m (10 ft.).

Reference: 2017 National Electrical Code – Chapter 3 Wiring Methods and Materials, Article 330 Metal-Clad Cable: Type MC. 330.30 Securing and Supporting. 330.30(B) Securing.

149. **Answer C.** 12

Unless otherwise provided, cables shall be secured at intervals not exceeding 1.8 m (6 ft.). *Cables containing four or fewer conductors sized no larger than 10 AWG shall be secured within 300 mm (12 in.) of every box, cabinet, fitting, or other cable termination.* In vertical installations, listed cables with ungrounded conductors 250 kc mil and larger shall be permitted to be secured at intervals not exceeding 3 m (10 ft.).

Reference: 2017 National Electrical Code – Chapter 3 Wiring Methods and Materials, Article 330 Metal-Clad Cable: Type MC. 330.30 Securing and Supporting. 330.30(B) Securing.

150. **Answer C.** 6 feet

Is not more than 1.8 m (6 ft.) in length from the last point of cable support to the point of connection to luminaires or other electrical equipment and the cable and point of connection are within an accessible ceiling. For the purpose of this section, Type MC cable fittings shall be permitted as a means of cable support.

Reference: 2017 National Electrical Code – Chapter 3 Wiring Methods and Materials, Article 330 Metal-Clad Cable: Type MC. 330.30 Securing and Supporting. 330.30(D) Unsupported Cables. 330.30(D)(2)

151. **Answer C.** 6 feet

Type MI cable shall be supported and secured by staples, straps, hangers, or similar fittings, designed and installed so as not to damage the cable, at intervals not exceeding 1.8 m (6 ft.).

Reference: 2017 National Electrical Code – Chapter 3 Wiring Methods and Materials, Article 332 Mineral-Insulated, Metal-Sheathed Cable: Type MI. 332.30 Securing and Supporting.

EXAM 7

EXAM 7 ANSWERS

152. Answer D. provide separate equipment grounding conductor

Where the outer sheath is made of copper, it shall provide an adequate path to serve as an equipment grounding conductor. *Where the outer sheath is made of steel, a separate equipment grounding conductor shall be provided.*

Reference: 2017 National Electrical Code – Chapter 3 Wiring Methods and Materials, Article 332 Mineral-Insulated, Metal-Sheathed Cable: Type MI. 332.108 Equipment Grounding Conductor.

153. Answer C. Nonmetallic-Sheathed Cable

A factory assembly of two or more insulated conductors enclosed within an overall nonmetallic jacket.

Reference: 2017 National Electrical Code – Chapter 3 Wiring Methods and Materials, Article 334 Nonmetallic-Sheathed Cable: Types NM, NMC, and NMS. 334.2 Definitions. Nonmetallic-Sheathed Cable.

154. Answer A. Type NMC

A factory assembly of two or more insulated conductors enclosed within an overall nonmetallic jacket.

Reference: 2017 National Electrical Code – Chapter 3 Wiring Methods and Materials, Article 334 Nonmetallic-Sheathed Cable: Types NM, NMC, and NMS. 334.2 Definitions. Nonmetallic-Sheathed Cable.

155. Answer D. in wet locations

Types NM and NMS cables *shall not be used under the following conditions or in the following locations:*

(1) Where exposed to corrosive fumes or vapors

(2) Where embedded in masonry, concrete, adobe, fill, or plaster

(3) In a shallow chase in masonry, concrete, or adobe and covered with plaster, adobe, or similar finish

(4) In wet or damp locations

Reference: 2017 National Electrical Code – Chapter 3 Wiring Methods and Materials, Article 334 Nonmetallic-Sheathed Cable: Types NM, NMC, and NMS. 334.12 Uses Not Permitted. 334.12(B) Types NM and NMS.

156. Answer A. 6/2 AWG

Where cable is run at angles with joists in unfinished basements and crawl spaces, it shall be permissible to secure cables not smaller than two 6 AWG or three 8 AWG conductors directly to the lower edges of the joists. Smaller cables shall be run either through bored holes in joists or on running boards. Nonmetallic-sheathed cable installed on the wall of an unfinished basement shall be permitted to be installed in a listed conduit or tubing or shall be protected in accordance with 300.4. Conduit or tubing shall be provided with a suitable insulating bushing or adapter at the point the cable enters the raceway. The sheath of the nonmetallic-sheathed cable shall extend through the conduit or tubing and into the outlet or device box not less than 6 mm (1/4 in.). The cable shall be secured within 300 mm (12 in.) of the point where the cable enters the conduit or tubing. Metal conduit, tubing, and metal outlet boxes shall be connected to an equipment grounding conductor complying with the provisions of 250.86 and 250.148.

Reference: 2017 National Electrical Code – Chapter 3 Wiring Methods and Materials, Article 334 Nonmetallic-Sheathed Cable: Types NM, NMC, and NMS. 334.15 Exposed Work. 334.15(C) In Unfinished Basements and Crawl Spaces.

157. Answer B. damaged

Bends in Types NM, NMC, and NMS cable shall be so made that the cable will not be damaged. The radius of the curve of the inner edge of any bend during or after installation shall not be less than five times the diameter of the cable.

Reference: 2017 National Electrical Code – Chapter 3 Wiring Methods and Materials, Article 334 Nonmetallic-Sheathed Cable: Types NM, NMC, and NMS. 334.24 Bending Radius.

158. Answer A. five

Bends in Types NM, NMC, and NMS cable shall be so made that the cable will not be damaged. *The radius of the curve of the inner edge of any bend during or after installation shall not be less than five times the diameter of the cable.*

Reference: 2017 National Electrical Code – Chapter 3 Wiring Methods and Materials, Article 334 Nonmetallic-Sheathed Cable: Types NM, NMC, and NMS. 334.24 Bending Radius.

EXAM 7 ANSWERS

EXAM 7

EXAM 7 ANSWERS

159. Answer A.   five

Bends in Types NM, NMC, and NMS cable shall be so made that the cable will not be damaged. *The radius of the curve of the inner edge of any bend during or after installation shall not be less than five times the diameter of the cable.*

Reference: 2017 National Electrical Code – Chapter 3 Wiring Methods and Materials, Article 334 Nonmetallic-Sheathed Cable: Types NM, NMC, and NMS. 334.24 Bending Radius.

160. Answer D.   4-1/2, 12

Nonmetallic-sheathed cable shall be supported and secured by staples; *cable ties listed and identified for securement and support; or straps, hangers, or similar fittings designed and installed so as not to damage the cable, at intervals not exceeding 1.4 m (4 1/2 ft)* and within 300 mm (12 in.) of every cable entry into enclosures such as outlet boxes, junction boxes, cabinets, or fittings. Flat cables shall not be stapled on edge.

Sections of cable protected from physical damage by raceway shall not be required to be secured within the raceway.

Reference: 2017 National Electrical Code – Chapter 3 Wiring Methods and Materials, Article 334 Nonmetallic-Sheathed Cable: Types NM, NMC, and NMS. 334.30 Securing and Supporting.

161. Answer B.   4-1/2 feet

Nonmetallic-sheathed cable shall be supported and secured by staples; cable ties listed and identified for securement and support; or straps, hangers, or similar fittings designed and installed so as not to damage the cable, at intervals not exceeding 1.4 m (4 1/2 ft) and within 300 mm (12 in.) of every cable entry into enclosures such as outlet boxes, junction boxes, cabinets, or fittings. Flat cables shall not be stapled on edge.

Sections of cable protected from physical damage by raceway shall not be required to be secured within the raceway.

Reference: 2017 National Electrical Code – Chapter 3 Wiring Methods and Materials, Article 334 Nonmetallic-Sheathed Cable: Types NM, NMC, and NMS. 334.30 Securing and Supporting.

162. Answer C.   60°C

The ampacity of Types NM, NMC, and NMS cable shall be determined in accordance with 310.15. The allowable ampacity shall not exceed that of a 60°C (140°F) rated conductor. The 90°C (194°F) rating shall be permitted to be used for ampacity adjustment and correction calculations, provided the final calculated ampacity does not exceed that of a 60°C (140°F) rated conductor. The ampacity of Types NM, NMC, and NMS cable installed in cable trays shall be determined in accordance with 392.80(A).

Where more than two NM cables containing two or more current-carrying conductors are installed, without maintaining spacing between the cables, through the same opening in wood0020framing that is to be sealed with thermal insulation, caulk, or sealing foam, the allowable ampacity of each conductor shall be adjusted in accordance with Table 310.15(B)(3)(a) and the provisions of 310.15(A)(2), Exception, shall not apply.

Where more than two NM cables containing two or more current-carrying conductors are installed in contact with thermal insulation without maintaining spacing between cables, the allowable ampacity of each conductor shall be adjusted in accordance with Table 310.15(B)(3)(a).

Reference: 2017 National Electrical Code – Chapter 3 Wiring Methods and Materials, Article 334 Nonmetallic-Sheathed Cable: Types NM, NMC, and NMS. 334.80 Ampacity.

163. Answer C.   Type NMC

The overall covering shall be flame retardant, moisture resistant, fungus resistant, and corrosion resistant.

Reference: 2017 National Electrical Code – Chapter 3 Wiring Methods and Materials, Article 334 Nonmetallic Sheathed Cable: Types. NM, NMC, and NMS. 334.116 Sheath. 334.116(B) Type NMC.

EXAM 7

EXAM 7 ANSWERS

164. Answer D.   18 AWG

The insulated conductors of Type TC cables shall be in sizes 18 AWG to 1000 kcmil copper, nickel, or nickel-coated copper, and sizes 12 AWG through 1000 kcmil aluminum or copper-clad aluminum. Insulated conductors of sizes 14 AWG, and larger copper, nickel, or nickel-coated copper, and sizes 12 AWG through 1000 kcmil aluminum or copper-clad aluminum shall be one of the types listed in Table 310.104(A) or Table 310.104(B) that is suitable for branch circuit and feeder circuits or one that is identified for such use.

Reference: 2017 National Electrical Code – Chapter 3 Wiring Methods and Materials, Article 336 Power and Control Tray Cable: Type TC. 336.104 Conductors.

165. Answer B.   Service-Entrance Cable

A single conductor or multiconductor assembly provided with or without an overall covering, primarily used for services, and of the following types:

Type SE. Service-entrance cable having a flame-retardant, moisture-resistant covering.

Type USE. Service-entrance cable, identified for underground use, having a moisture-resistant covering, but not required to have a flame-retardant covering.

Reference: 2017 National Electrical Code – Chapter 3 Wiring Methods and Materials, Article 338 Service-Entrance Cable: Types SE and USE. 338.2 Definitions. Service-Entrance Cable.

166. Answer D.   Type UF

A factory assembly of one or more insulated conductors with an integral or an overall covering of nonmetallic material suitable for direct burial in the earth.

Reference: 2017 National Electrical Code – Chapter 3 Wiring Methods and Materials, Article 340 Underground Feeder and Branch-Circuit Cable: Type UF. 340.2 Definition. Underground Feeder and Branch-Circuit Cable, Type UF.

167. Answer C.   Type UF

A factory assembly of one or more insulated conductors with an integral or an overall covering of nonmetallic material suitable for direct burial in the earth.

Reference: 2017 National Electrical Code – Chapter 3 Wiring Methods and Materials, Article 340 Underground Feeder and Branch-Circuit Cable: Type UF. 340.2 Definition. Underground Feeder and Branch-Circuit Cable, Type UF.

168. Answer B.   Between a dwelling and separate garage unit

Type UF cable shall not be used as follows:

(1) As service-entrance cable

(2) In commercial garages

(3) In theaters and similar locations

(4) In motion picture studios

(5) In storage battery rooms

(6) In hoistways or on elevators or escalators

(7) In hazardous (classified) locations, except as specifically permitted by other articles in this Code

(8) Embedded in poured cement, concrete, or aggregate, except where embedded in plaster as nonheating leads where permitted in 424.43

(9) Where exposed to direct rays of the sun, unless identified as sunlight resistant

(10) Where subject to physical damage

(11) As overhead cable, except where installed as messenger-supported wiring in accordance with Part II of Article 396

Reference: 2017 National Electrical Code – Chapter 3 Wiring Methods and Materials, Article 340 Underground Feeder and Branch-Circuit Cable: Type UF. 340.12 Uses Not Permitted.

EXAM 7

EXAM 7 ANSWERS

169. **Answer A.** 60°C

The ampacity of Type UF cable shall be that of 60°C (140°F) conductors in accordance with 310.15.

Reference: 2017 National Electrical Code – Chapter 3 Wiring Methods and Materials, Article 340 Underground Feeder and Branch-Circuit Cable: Type UF. 340.80 Ampacity.

170. **Answer C.** 4

IMC larger than metric designator 103 (trade size 4) shall not be used.

Reference: 2017 National Electrical Code – Chapter 3 Wiring Methods and Materials, Article 342 Intermediate Metal Conduit: Type IMC. 342.20 Size. 342.20(B) Maximum.

171. **Answer A.** 3, 5

IMC shall be secured in accordance with one of the following:

(1) IMC shall be securely fastened within 900 mm (3 ft.) of each outlet box, junction box, device box, cabinet, conduit body, or other conduit termination.

(2) Where structural members do not readily permit fastening within 900 mm (3 ft.), *fastening shall be permitted to be increased to a distance of 1.5 m (5 ft.).*

(3) Where approved, conduit shall not be required to be securely fastened within 900 mm (3 ft.) of the service head for above-the-roof termination of a mast.

Reference: 2017 National Electrical Code – Chapter 3 Wiring Methods and Materials, Article 342 Intermediate Metal Conduit: Type IMC. 342.30 Securing and Supporting. 342.30(A) Securely Fastened.

172. **Answer A.** 3 feet

RMC shall be securely fastened within 900 mm (3 ft.) of each outlet box, junction box, device box, cabinet, conduit body, or other conduit termination.

Reference: 2017 National Electrical Code – Chapter 3 Wiring Methods and Materials, Article 344 Rigid Metal Conduit: Type RMC. 344.30 Securing and Supporting. 344.30(A) Securely Fastened. 344.30(A)(1)

EXAM 7

EXAM 7 ANSWERS

Table 314.16(B) Volume Allowance Required per Conductor

Size of Conductor (AWG)	Free Space Within Box for Each Conductor	
	cm^3	$in.^3$
18	24.6	1.50
16	28.7	1.75
14	32.8	2.00
12	36.9	2.25
10	41.0	2.50
8	49.2	3.00
6	81.9	5.00

173. Answer B. 12

RMC shall be supported in accordance with one of the following:

(1) Conduit shall be supported at intervals not exceeding 3 m (10 ft.).

(2) The distance between supports for straight runs of conduit shall be permitted in accordance with Table 344.30(B)(2), provided the conduit is made up with threaded couplings and such supports prevent transmission of stresses to termination where conduit is deflected between supports.

(3) Exposed vertical risers from industrial machinery or fixed equipment shall be permitted to be supported at intervals not exceeding 6 m (20 ft.) if the conduit is made up with threaded couplings, the conduit is supported and securely fastened at the top and bottom of the riser, and no other means of intermediate support is readily available.

(4) Horizontal runs of RMC supported by openings through framing members at intervals not exceeding 3 m (10 ft.) and securely fastened within 900 mm (3 ft.) of termination points shall be permitted.

Reference: 2017 National Electrical Code – Chapter 3 Wiring Methods and Materials, Article 344 Rigid Metal Conduit: Type RMC. 344.30 Securing and Supporting. 344.30(B) Supports. Table 344.30(B)(2) Supports for Rigid Metal Conduit (page 70-212)

EXAM 7

EXAM 7 ANSWERS

174. Answer B.   concrete tight

Threadless couplings and connectors used with conduit shall be made tight. **Where buried in masonry or concrete, they shall be the concrete tight type.** Where installed in wet locations, they shall comply with 314.15. Threadless couplings and connectors shall not be used on threaded conduit ends unless listed for the purpose.

Reference: 2017 National Electrical Code – Chapter 3 Wiring Methods and Materials, Article 344 Rigid Metal Conduit: Type RMC. 344.42 Couplings and Connectors. 344.42(A) Threadless.

175. Answer B.   Flexible Metal Conduit (FMC)

A raceway of circular cross section made of helically wound, formed, interlocked metal strip.

Reference: 2017 National Electrical Code – Chapter 3 Wiring Methods and Materials, Article 348 Flexible Metal Conduit: Type FMC. 348.2 Definition

176. Answer D.   storage battery rooms

FMC shall not be used in the following:

(1) In wet locations

(2) In hoistways, other than as permitted in 620.21(A)(l)

(3) In storage battery rooms

(4) In any hazardous (classified) location except as permitted by other articles in this Code

(5) Where exposed to materials having a deteriorating effect on the installed conductors, such as oil or gasoline

(6) Underground or embedded in poured concrete or aggregate

(7) Where subject to physical damage

Reference: 2017 National Electrical Code – Chapter 3 Wiring Methods and Materials, Article 348 Flexible Metal Conduit: Type FMC. 348.12 Uses Not Permitted.

177. Answer D.   Under no circumstances.

FMC shall *not* be used in the following:

(1) In wet locations

(2) In hoistways, other than as permitted in 620.21(A)(l)

(3) In storage battery rooms

(4) In any hazardous (classified) location except as permitted by other articles in this Code

(5) Where exposed to materials having a deteriorating effect on the installed conductors, such as oil or gasoline

(6) Underground or embedded in poured concrete or aggregate

(7) Where subject to physical damage

Reference: 2017 National Electrical Code – Chapter 3 Wiring Methods and Materials, Article 348 Flexible Metal Conduit: Type FMC. 348.12 Uses Not Permitted.

EXAM 7

EXAM 7 ANSWERS

178. Answer B. six feet

FMC less than metric designator 16 (trade size 1/2) shall not be used unless permitted in 348.20(A)(1) through (A)(5) for metric designator 12 (trade size 3/8).

(1) For enclosing the leads of motors as permitted in 430.245(B)

(2) In lengths not in excess of 1.8 m (6 ft.) for any of the following uses:

a. For utilization equipment

b. As part of a listed assembly

c. For tap connections to luminaires as permitted in 410.117(C)

(3) For manufactured wiring systems as permitted in 604.6(A)

(4) In hoistways as permitted in 620.21(A)(1)

(5) As part of a listed assembly to connect wired luminaire sections as permitted in 410.137(C)

Reference: 2017 National Electrical Code – Chapter 3 Wiring Methods and Materials, Article 348 Flexible Metal Conduit: Type FMC. 348.20 Size. 348.20(A) Minimum.

179. Answer C. 6 feet

FMC less than metric designator 16 (trade size 1/2) shall not be used unless permitted in 348.20(A)(1) through (A)(5) for metric designator 12 (trade size 3/8).

(1) For enclosing the leads of motors as permitted in 430.245(B)

(2) In lengths not in excess of 1.8 m (6 ft.) for any of the following uses:

a. For utilization equipment

b. As part of a listed assembly

c. For tap connections to luminaires as permitted in 410.117(C)

(3) For manufactured wiring systems as permitted in 604.6(A)

(4) In hoistways as permitted in 620.21(A)(1)

(5) As part of a listed assembly to connect wired luminaire sections as permitted in 410.137(C)

Reference: 2017 National Electrical Code – Chapter 3 Wiring Methods and Materials, Article 348 Flexible Metal Conduit: Type FMC. 348.20 Size. 348.20(A) Minimum.

Tap conductors of a type suitable for the temperature encountered shall be permitted to run from the luminaire terminal connection to an outlet box placed at least 300 mm (1 ft.) from the luminaire. *Such tap conductors shall be in suitable raceway or Type AC or MC cable of at least 450 mm (18 in.) but not more than 1.8 m (6 ft.) in length.*

Reference: 2017 National Electrical Code – Chapter 4 Equipment for General Use, Article 410 Luminaries, Lampholders, and Lamps. 410.117 Wiring. 410.117(C) Tap Conductors.

EXAM 7

EXAM 7 ANSWERS

Table 314.16(B) Volume Allowance Required per Conductor

Size of Conductor (AWG)	Free Space Within Box for Each Conductor	
	cm³	in.³
18	24.6	1.50
16	28.7	1.75
14	32.8	2.00
12	36.9	2.25
10	41.0	2.50
8	49.2	3.00
6	81.9	5.00

180. **Answer B.** 40

The number of conductors shall not exceed that permitted by the percentage fill specified in Table 1, Chapter 9, or as permitted in Table 348.22, or for metric designator 12 (trade size ⅜).

Cables shall be permitted to be installed where such use is not prohibited by the respective cable articles. The number of cables shall not exceed the allowable percentage fill specified in *Table 1, Chapter 9.*

Reference: 2017 National Electrical Code – Chapter 3 Wiring Methods and Materials, Article 348 Flexible Metal Conduit: Type FMC. 348.22 Number of Conductors.

Reference: 017 National Electrical Code – Chapter 9 Tables. Table 1 Percent of Cross Section of Conduit and Tubing for Conductors and Cables (page 70-756)

181. **Answer C.** four

The number of conductors shall not exceed that permitted by the percentage fill specified in Table 1, Chapter 9, or as permitted in *Table 348.22,* or for metric designator 12 (trade size 3/8).

Cables shall be permitted to be installed where such use is not prohibited by the respective cable articles. The number of cables shall not exceed the allowable percentage fill specified in Table 1, Chapter 9.

Reference: 2017 National Electrical Code – Chapter 3 Wiring Methods and Materials, Article 348 Flexible Metal Conduit: Type FMC. 348.22 Number of Conductors. Table 348.22 Maximum Number of Insulated Conductors in Metric Designator 12 (Trade Size 3/8) Flexible Metal Conduit (FMC) (page 70-213). – Chapter 9 Tables. Table 1 Percent of Cross Section of Conduit and Tubing for Conductors and Cables (page 70-756)

182. **Answer B.** angle

Angle connectors shall not be concealed.

Reference: 2017 National Electrical Code – Chapter 3 Wiring Methods and Materials, Article 348 Flexible Metal Conduit: Type FMC. 348.42 Couplings and Connectors.

183. **Answer A.** direct burial where listed and marked for the purpose

LFMC shall be permitted to be used in exposed or concealed locations as follows:

(1) Where conditions of installation, operation, or maintenance require flexibility or protection from liquids, vapors, or solids

(2) In hazardous (classified) locations where specifically permitted by Chapter 5

(3) For direct burial where listed and marked for the purpose

Reference: 2017 National Electrical Code – Chapter 3 Wiring Methods and Materials, Article 350 Liquidtight Flexible Metal Conduit: Type LFMC. 350.10 Uses Permitted

EXAM 7

EXAM 7 ANSWERS

Table 348.22 Maximum Number of Insulated Conductors in Metric Designator 12 (Trade Size ⅜) Flexible Metal Conduit (FMC)*

Size (AWG)	Types RFH-2, SF-2		Types TF, XHHW, TW		Types TFN, THHN, THWN		Types FEP, FEBP, PF, PGF	
	Fittings Inside Conduit	Fittings Outside Conduit	Fittings Inside Conduit	Fittings Outside Conduit	Fittings Inside Conduit	Fittings Outside Conduit	Fittings Inside Conduit	Fittings Outside Conduit
18	2	3	3	5	5	8	5	8
16	1	2	3	4	4	6	4	6
14	1	2	2	3	3	4	3	4
12	—	—	1	2	2	3	2	3
10	—	—	1	1	1	1	1	2

*In addition, one insulated, covered, or bare equipment grounding conductor of the same size shall be permitted.

Table 348.22 see Table 348-22 in Tables folder on CD-ROM

Table 1 Percent of Cross Section of Conduit and Tubing for Conductors and Cables

Number of Conductors and/or Cables	Cross-Sectional Area (%)
1	53
2	31
Over 2	40

184. Answer D. where subject to physical damage.

LFMC shall *not* be used as follows:

(1) Where subject to physical damage

(2) Where any combination of ambient and conductor temperature produces an operating temperature in excess of that for which the material is approved

Reference: 2017 National Electrical Code – Chapter 3 Wiring Methods and Materials, Article 350 Liquidtight Flexible Metal Conduit: Type LFMC. 350.12 Uses Not Permitted.

185. Answer B. 12, 4-1/2

LFMC shall be securely fastened in place by an approved means *within 300 mm (12 in.) of each box, cabinet, conduit body, or other conduit termination and shall be supported and secured at intervals not to exceed 1.4 m (4-1/2 ft.).* Where used, cable ties shall be listed and be identified for securement and support.

Reference: 2017 National Electrical Code – Chapter 3 Wiring Methods and Materials, Article 350 Liquidtight Flexible Metal Conduit: Type LFMC. 350.30 Securing and Supporting. 350.30(A) Securely Fastened.

186. Answer C. 12 inches

LFMC shall be securely fastened in place by an approved means within 300 mm (12 in.) of each box, cabinet, conduit body, or other conduit termination and shall be supported and secured at intervals not to exceed 1.4 m (4-1/2 ft.). Where used, cable ties shall be listed and be identified for securement and support.

Reference: 2017 National Electrical Code – Chapter 3 Wiring Methods and Materials, Article 350 Liquidtight Flexible Metal Conduit: Type LFMC. 350.30 Securing and Supporting. 350.30(A) Securely Fastened.

187. Answer B. four (4) – 90 degree

There shall not be more than the equivalent of four quarter bends (360 degrees total) between pull points, for example, conduit bodies and boxes.

Reference: 2017 National Electrical Code – Chapter 3 Wiring Methods and Materials, Article 352 Rigid Polyvinyl Chloride Conduit: Type PVC. 352.26 Bends – Number in One Run.

EXAM 7

EXAM 7 ANSWERS

Table 352.30 Support of Rigid Polyvinyl Chloride Conduit (PVC)

Conduit Size		Maximum Spacing Between Supports	
Metric Designator	Trade Size	mm or m	ft
16–27	½–1	900 mm	3
35–53	1¼–2	1.5 m	5
63–78	2½–3	1.8 m	6
91–129	3½–5	2.1 m	7
155	6	2.5 m	8

188. Answer A. 3 feet

PVC conduit shall be installed as a complete system as provided in 300.18 and shall be fastened so that movement from thermal expansion or contraction is permitted. PVC conduit shall be securely fastened and supported in accordance with 352.30(A) and (B).

Reference: 2017 National Electrical Code – Chapter 3 Wiring Methods and Materials, Article 352 Rigid Polyvinyl Chloride Conduit: Type PVC. 352.30 Securing and Supporting. Table 352.30 Support of Rigid Polyvinyl Chloride Conduit (PVC) (page 70-217)

189. Answer B. 5 feet

PVC conduit shall be installed as a complete system as provided in 300.18 and shall be fastened so that movement from thermal expansion or contraction is permitted. PVC conduit shall be securely fastened and supported in accordance with 352.30(A) and (B).

Reference: 2017 National Electrical Code – Chapter 3 Wiring Methods and Materials, Article 352 Rigid Polyvinyl Chloride Conduit: Type PVC. 352.30 Securing and Supporting. Table 352.30 Support of Rigid Polyvinyl Chloride Conduit (PVC) (page 70-217)

190. Answer A. a bushing or adapter

Where a conduit enters a box, fitting, or other enclosure, a bushing or adapter shall be provided to protect the wire from abrasion unless the box, fitting, or enclosure design provides equivalent protection.

Informational Note: See 300.4(G) for the protection of conductors 4 AWG and larger at bushings.

Reference: 2017 National Electrical Code – Chapter 3 Wiring Methods and Materials, Article 352 Rigid Polyvinyl Chloride Conduit: Type PVC. 352.46 Bushings.

191. Answer D. within a building

HDPE conduit shall not be used under the following conditions:

(1) Where exposed

(2) Within a building

(3) In any hazardous (classified) location, except as permitted by other articles in this Code

(4) Where subject to ambient temperatures in excess of 50°C (122°F) unless listed otherwise

Reference: 2017 National Electrical Code – Chapter 3 Wiring Methods and Materials, Article 353 High Density Polyethylene Conduit: Type HDPE Conduit. 353.12 Uses Not Permitted.

EXAM 7

EXAM 7 ANSWERS

192. Answer A. If protection is needed from vapors, liquids, or solids.

LFNC shall be permitted to be used in exposed or concealed locations for the following purposes:

Informational Note: Extreme cold can cause some types of nonmetallic conduits to become brittle and therefore more susceptible to damage from physical contact.

(1) Where flexibility is required for installation, operation, or maintenance.

(2) Where protection of the contained conductors is required from vapors, liquids, or solids.

(3) For outdoor locations where listed and marked as suitable for the purpose.

(4) For direct burial where listed and marked for the purpose.

(5) Type LFNC shall be permitted to be installed in lengths longer than 1.8 m (6 ft) where secured in accordance with 356.30.

(6) Type LFNC-B as a listed manufactured prewired assembly, metric designator 16 through 27 (trade size 1/2 through 1) conduit.

(7) For encasement in concrete where listed for direct burial and installed in compliance with 356.42.

Reference: 2017 National Electrical Code – Chapter 3 Wiring Methods and Materials, Article 356 Liquidtight Flexible Nonmetallic Conduit: Type LFNC. 356.10 Uses Permitted.

193. Answer D. both A and B

The use of EMT shall be permitted for both exposed and concealed work for the following:

(1) In concrete, in direct contact with the earth or in areas subject to severe corrosive influences where installed in accordance with 358.10(B)

(2) In dry, damp, and wet locations

(3) In any hazardous (classified) location as permitted by other articles in this *Code*

Reference: 2017 National Electrical Code – Chapter 3 Wiring Methods and Materials, Article 358 Electrical Metallic Tubing: Type EMT. 358.10 Uses Permitted. 358.10(A) Exposed and Concealed.

194. Answer B. 1/2

EMT smaller than metric designator 16 (trade size 1/2) shall not be used.

Exception: For enclosing the leads of motors as permitted in 430.245(B).

Reference: 2017 National Electrical Code – Chapter 3 Wiring Methods and Materials, Article 358 Electrical Metallic Tubing: Type EMT. 358.20 Size. 358.20(A) Minimum.

195. Answer C. reduced

Bends shall be made so that the tubing is not damaged and the internal diameter of the tubing is not effectively reduced. The radius of the curve of any field bend to the centerline of the tubing shall not be less than shown in Table 2, Chapter 9 for one-shot and full shoe benders.

Reference: 2017 National Electrical Code – Chapter 3 Wiring Methods and Materials, Article 358 Electrical Metallic Tubing: Type EMT. 358.24 Bends - How Made.

196. Answer D. 360

There shall not be more than the equivalent of four quarter bends (360 degrees total) between pull points, for example, conduit bodies and boxes.

Reference: 2017 National Electrical Code – Chapter 3 Wiring Methods and Materials, Article 358 Electrical Metallic Tubing: Type EMT. 358.26 Bends – Number in One Run.

197. Answer C. 360

There shall not be more than the equivalent of four quarter bends (*360 degrees total) between pull points, for example, conduit bodies and boxes.*

Reference: 2017 National Electrical Code – Chapter 3 Wiring Methods and Materials, Article 358 Electrical Metallic Tubing: Type EMT. 358.26 Bends - Number in One Run.

198. Answer B. four

There shall not be more than the equivalent of four quarter bends (360 degrees total) between pull points, for example, conduit bodies and boxes.

Reference: 2017 National Electrical Code – Chapter 3 Wiring Methods and Materials, Article 358 Electrical Metallic Tubing: Type EMT. 358.26 Bends – Number in One Run.

EXAM 7
EXAM 7 ANSWERS

199. Answer C. 10

EMT shall be securely fastened in place at intervals not to exceed 3 m (10 ft). In addition, each EMT run between termination points shall be securely fastened within 900 mm (3 ft) of each outlet box, junction box, device box, cabinet, conduit body, or other tubing termination.

Reference: 2017 National Electrical Code – Chapter 3 Wiring Methods and Materials, Article 358 Electrical Metallic Tubing: Type EMT. 358.30 Securing and Supporting. 358.30(A) Securely Fastened.

200. Answer A. 3 feet

EMT shall be securely fastened in place at intervals not to exceed 3 m (10 ft). *In addition, each EMT run between termination points shall be securely fastened within 900 mm (3 ft) of each outlet box, junction box, device box, cabinet, conduit body, or other tubing termination.*

Reference: 2017 National Electrical Code – Chapter 3 Wiring Methods and Materials, Article 358 Electrical Metallic Tubing: Type EMT. 358.30 Securing and Supporting. 358.30(A) Securely Fastened.

201. Answer B. 10 feet

EMT shall be securely fastened in place at intervals not to exceed 3 m (10 ft). In addition, each EMT run between termination points shall be securely fastened within 900 mm (3 ft) of each outlet box, junction box, device box, cabinet, conduit body, or other tubing termination.

Reference: 2017 National Electrical Code – Chapter 3 Wiring Methods and Materials, Article 358 Electrical Metallic Tubing: Type EMT. 358.30 Securing and Supporting. 358.30(A) Securely Fastened.

202. Answer C. grounding

EMT shall be permitted as an equipment grounding conductor.

Reference: 2017 National Electrical Code – Chapter 3 Wiring Methods and Materials, Article 358 Electrical Metallic Tubing: Type EMT. 358.60 Grounding.

203. Answer B. for system voltages of 1000 volts maximum

FMT shall be permitted to be used for branch circuits as follows:

(1) In dry locations

(2) Where concealed

(3) In accessible locations

(4) For system voltages of 1000 volts maximum

Reference: 2017 National Electrical Code – Chapter 3 Wiring Methods and Materials, Article 360 Flexible Metallic Tubing: Type FMT. 360.10 Uses Permitted.

EXAM 7

EXAM 7 ANSWERS

204. Answer C. three

For the purpose of this article, the first floor of a building shall be that floor that has 50 percent or more of the exterior wall surface area level with or above finished grade. One additional level that is the first level and not designed for human habitation and used only for vehicle parking, storage, or similar use shall be permitted. The use of ENT and fittings shall be permitted in the following:

(1) In any building not exceeding three floors above grade as follows:

a. For exposed work, where not prohibited by 362.12

b. Concealed within walls, floors, and ceilings

(2) In any building exceeding three floors above grade, ENT shall be concealed within walls, floors. and ceilings where the walls, floors, and ceilings provide a thermal barrier of material that has at least a 15-minute finish rating as identified in listings of fire-rated assemblies. The 15-minute-finish-rated thermal barrier shall be permitted to be used for combustible or noncombustible walls, floors, and ceilings.

(3) In locations subject to severe corrosive influences as covered in 300.6 and where subject to chemicals for which the materials are specifically approved.

(4) In concealed, dry, and damp locations not prohibited by 362.12.

(5) Above suspended ceilings where the suspended ceilings provide a thermal barrier of material that has at least a 15-minute finish rating as identified in listings of fire-rated assemblies, except as permitted in 362.10(1)(a).

(6) Encased in poured concrete, or embedded in a concrete slab on grade where ENT is placed on sand or approved screenings, provided fittings identified for this purpose are used for connections.

(7) For wet locations indoors as permitted in this section or in a concrete slab on or belowgrade, with fittings listed for the purpose.

(8) Metric designator 16 through 27 (trade size 1/2 through 1) as listed manufactured prewired assembly.

(9) Conductors or cables rated at a temperature higher than the listed temperature rating of ENT shall be permitted to be installed in ENT, if the conductors or cables are not operated at a temperature higher than the listed temperature rating of the ENT.

Reference: 2017 National Electrical Code – Chapter 3 Wiring Methods and Materials, Article 362 Electrical Nonmetallic Tubing: Type ENT. 362.10 Uses Permitted.

EXAM 7

EXAM 7 ANSWERS

205. Answer B. in a two story building

For the purpose of this article, the first floor of a building shall be that floor that has 50 percent or more of the exterior wall surface area level with or above finished grade. One additional level that is the first level and not designed for human habitation and used only for vehicle parking, storage, or similar use shall be permitted. The use of ENT and fittings shall be permitted in the following:

(1) *In any building not exceeding three floors above grade as follows:*

a. *For exposed work, where not prohibited by 362.12*

b. *Concealed within walls, floors, and ceilings*

(2) In any building exceeding three floors above grade, ENT shall be concealed within walls, floors. and ceilings where the walls, floors, and ceilings provide a thermal barrier of material that has at least a 15-minute finish rating as identified in listings of fire-rated assemblies. The 15-minute-finish-rated thermal barrier shall be permitted to be used for combustible or noncombustible walls, floors, and ceilings.

(3) In locations subject to severe corrosive influences as covered in 300.6 and where subject to chemicals for which the materials are specifically approved.

(4) In concealed, dry, and damp locations not prohibited by 362.12.

(5) Above suspended ceilings where the suspended ceilings provide a thermal barrier of material that has at least a 15-minute finish rating as identified in listings of fire-rated assemblies, except as permitted in 362.10(1)(a).

(6) Encased in poured concrete, or embedded in a concrete slab on grade where ENT is placed on sand or approved screenings, provided fittings identified for this purpose are used for connections.

(7) For wet locations indoors as permitted in this section or in a concrete slab on or belowgrade, with fittings listed for the purpose.

(8) Metric designator 16 through 27 (trade size 1/2 through 1) as listed manufactured prewired assembly.

(9) Conductors or cables rated at a temperature higher than the listed temperature rating of ENT shall be permitted to be installed in ENT, if the conductors or cables are not operated at a temperature higher than the listed temperature rating of the ENT.

Reference: 2017 National Electrical Code – Chapter 3 Wiring Methods and Materials, Article 362 Electrical Nonmetallic Tubing: Type ENT. 362.10 Uses Permitted.

206. Answer C. support

ENT shall not be used in the following:

(1) In any hazardous (classified) location, except as permitted by other articles in this Code

(2) For the support of luminaires and other equipment

(3) Where subject to ambient temperatures in excess of 50°C

(122°F) unless listed otherwise

(4) For direct earth burial

(5) In exposed locations, except as permitted by 362.10(1), 362.10(5), and 362.10(7)

(6) In theaters and similar locations, except as provided in 518.4 and 520.5 (7) Where exposed to the direct rays of the sun, unless identified as sunlight resistant

(8) Where subject to physical damage

(9) Where the voltage is over 600 volts

Reference: 2017 National Electrical Code – Chapter 3 Wiring Methods and Materials, Article 362 Electrical Nonmetallic Tubing: Type ENT. 362.12 Uses Not Permitted.

EXAM 7

EXAM 7 ANSWERS

207. Answer D. 600 volts

ENT shall not be used in the following:

(1) In any hazardous (classified) location, except as permitted by other articles in this Code

(2) For the support of luminaires and other equipment

(3) Where subject to ambient temperatures in excess of 50°C

(122°F) unless listed otherwise

(4) For direct earth burial

(5) In exposed locations, except as permitted by 362.10(1), 362.10(5), and 362.10(7)

(6) In theaters and similar locations, except as provided in 518.4 and 520.5 (7) Where exposed to the direct rays of the sun, unless identified as sunlight resistant

(8) Where subject to physical damage

(9) Where the voltage is over 600 volts

Reference: 2017 National Electrical Code – Chapter 3 Wiring Methods and Materials, Article 362 Electrical Nonmetallic Tubing: Type ENT. 362.12 Uses Not Permitted.

208. Answer A. 3 feet

ENT shall be securely fastened at intervals not exceeding 900 mm (3 ft). In addition, ENT shall be securely fastened in place within 900 mm (3 ft) of each outlet box, device box, junction box, cabinet, or fitting where it terminates. Where used, cable ties shall be listed as suitable for the application and for securing and supporting.

Exception No. 1: Lengths not exceeding a distance of 1.8 m (6 ft) from a luminaire terminal connection for tap connections to lighting luminaires shall be permitted without being secured.

Exception No. 2: Lengths not exceeding 1.8 m (6 ft) from the last point where the raceway is securely fastened for connections within an accessible ceiling to luminaire(s) or other equipment.

Exception No. 3: For concealed work in finished buildings or prefinished wall panels where such securing is impracticable, unbroken lengths (without coupling) of ENT shall be permitted to be fished.

Reference: 2017 National Electrical Code – Chapter 3 Wiring Methods and Materials, Article 362 Electrical Nonmetallic Tubing: Type ENT. 362.30 Securing and Supporting. 362.30(A) Securely Fastened.

209. Answer D. 36 inches

ENT shall be securely fastened at intervals not exceeding 900 mm (3 ft*). In addition, ENT shall be securely fastened in place within 900 mm (3 ft) of each outlet box, device box, junction box, cabinet, or fitting where it terminates. Where used, cable ties shall be listed as suitable for the application and for securing and supporting.*

Exception No. 1: Lengths not exceeding a distance of 1.8 m (6 ft) from a luminaire terminal connection for tap connections to lighting luminaires shall be permitted without being secured.

Exception No. 2: Lengths not exceeding 1.8 m (6 ft) from the last point where the raceway is securely fastened for connections within an accessible ceiling to luminaire(s) or other equipment.

Exception No. 3: For concealed work in finished buildings or prefinished wall panels where such securing is impracticable, unbroken lengths (without coupling) of ENT shall be permitted to be fished.

Reference: 2017 National Electrical Code – Chapter 3 Wiring Methods and Materials, Article 362 Electrical Nonmetallic Tubing: Type ENT. 362.30 Securing and Supporting. 362.30(A) Securely Fastened.

210. Answer B. 20

The sum of the cross sectional areas of all contained conductors and cables at any cross section of a **sheet metal auxiliary gutter shall not exceed 20 percent of the interior cross-sectional area of the sheet metal auxiliary gutter.** The adjustment factors in 310.15(B)(3)(a) shall be applied only where the number of current-carrying conductors, including neutral conductors classified as current-carrying under the provisions of 310.15(B)(5), exceeds 30. Conductors for signaling circuits or controller conductors between a motor and its starter and used only for starting duty shall not be considered as current-carrying conductors.

Reference: 2017 National Electrical Code – Chapter 3 Wiring Methods and Materials, Article 366 Auxiliary Gutters. 366.22 Number of Conductors. 366.22(A) Sheet Metal Auxiliary Gutters.

211. Answer B. 5

Sheet metal auxiliary gutters shall be supported and secured throughout their entire length at intervals not exceeding 1.5 m (5 ft).

Reference: 2017 National Electrical Code – Chapter 3 Wiring Methods and Materials, Article 366 Auxiliary Gutters. 366.30 Securing and Supporting. 366.30(A) Sheet Metal Auxiliary Gutters.

EXAM 7

EXAM 7 ANSWERS

212. Answer D. 75

Splices or taps shall be permitted within gutters where they are accessible by means of removable covers or doors. *The conductors, including splices and taps, shall not fill the gutter to more than 75 percent of its area.*

Reference: 2017 National Electrical Code – Chapter 3 Wiring Methods and Materials, Article 366 Auxiliary Gutters. 366.56 Splices and Taps. 366.56(A) Within Gutters.

213. Answer C. 75

Splices or taps shall be permitted within gutters where they are accessible by means of removable covers or doors. The conductors, including splices and taps, shall not fill the gutter to more than 75 percent of its area.

Reference: 2017 National Electrical Code – Chapter 3 Wiring Methods and Materials, Article 366 Auxiliary Gutters. 366.56 Splices and Taps. 366.56(A) Within Gutters.

214. Answer B. opposite

Taps from bare conductors shall leave the gutter opposite their terminal connections, and conductors shall not be brought in contact with uninsulated current carrying parts of different voltages.

Reference: 2017 National Electrical Code – Chapter 3 Wiring Methods and Materials, Article 366 Auxiliary Gutters. 366.56 Splices and Taps. 366.56(B) Bare Conductors.

215. Answer A. Busway

A raceway consisting of a metal enclosure containing factory-mounted, bare or insulated conductors, which are usually copper or aluminum bars, rods, or tubes.

Informational Note: For cablebus. refer to Article 370.

Reference: 2017 National Electrical Code – Chapter 3 Wiring Methods and Materials, Article 368 Busways. 368.2 Definition. Busway.

216. Answer B. dry walls

Unbroken lengths of busway shall be permitted to be extended through dry walls.

Informational Note: See 300.21 for information concerning the spread of fire or products of combustion

Reference: 2017 National Electrical Code – Chapter 3 Wiring Methods and Materials, Article 368 Busways. 368.10 Uses Permitted. 368.10(C) Through Walls and Floors. 368.10(C)(1) Walls.

217. Answer A. 8

Lighting busway and trolley busway shall not be installed less than 2.5 m (8 ft.) above the floor or working platform unless provided with an identified cover.

Reference: 2017 National Electrical Code – Chapter 3 Wiring Methods and Materials, Article 368 Busways. 368.12 Uses Not Permitted. 368.12(E) Working Platform.

218. Answer B. 5

Busways shall be securely supported at intervals not exceeding 1.5 m (5 ft.) unless otherwise designed and marked.

Reference: 2017 National Electrical Code – Chapter 3 Wiring Methods and Materials, Article 368 Busways. 368.30 Support.

219. Answer C. Exposed

Approved cablebus shall be permitted:

(1) At any voltage or current for which spaced conductors are rated and where installed only for exposed work, except as permitted in 370.18

(2) For branch circuits, feeders, and services

(3) To be installed outdoors or in corrosive, wet, or damp locations where. identified for the use

Reference: 2017 National Electrical Code – Chapter 3 Wiring Methods and Materials, Article 370 Cablebus. 370.10 Uses Permitted.

220. Answer A. ceiling

Conductors shall not be installed in precast cellular concrete floor raceways as follows:

(1) Where subject to corrosive vapor

(2) In any hazardous (classified) location, except as permitted by other articles in this Code

(3) In commercial garages, other than for supplying ceiling outlets or extensions to the area below the floor but not above

Informational Note: See 300.8 for installation of conductors with other systems

Reference: 2017 National Electrical Code – Chapter 3 Wiring Methods and Materials, Article 372 Cellular Concrete Floor Raceways. 372.12 Uses Not Permitted.

EXAM 7

EXAM 7 ANSWERS

221. Answer B.   40

The combined cross-sectional area of all conductors or cables shall not exceed 40 percent of the interior cross-sectional area of the cell or header.

Reference: 2017 National Electrical Code – Chapter 3 Wiring Methods and Materials, Article 374 Cellular Metal Floor Raceways. 374.22 Maximum Number of Conductors in Raceway.

222. Answer D.   75%

Splices and taps shall be permitted within a wireway, provided they are accessible. *The conductors, including splices and taps, shall not fill the wireway to more than 75 percent of its area at that point.*

Reference: 2017 National Electrical Code – Chapter 3 Wiring Methods and Materials, Article 376 Metal Wireways. 376.56 Splices, Taps, and Power Distribution Blocks. 376.56(A) Splices and Taps.

223. Answer B.   9 inches

Single-conductor cables shall be permitted to be installed in accordance with (B)(1)(a) through (B)(1)(c).

(a) *Single-conductor cable shall be 1/0 AWG or larger and shall be of a type listed and marked on the surface for use in cable trays. Where 110 AWG through 4/0 AWG single-conductor cables are installed in ladder cable tray, the maximum allowable rung spacing for the ladder cable tray shall be 225 mm (9 in.).*

(b) Welding cables shall comply with the provisions of Article 630, Part IV.

(c) Single conductors used as equipment grounding conductors shall be insulated, covered, or bare, and they shall be 4 AWG or larger.

Reference: 2017 National Electrical Code – Chapter 3 Wiring Methods and Materials, Article 392 Cable Trays. 392.10 Uses Permitted. 392.10(B) In Industrial Establishments. 392.10(B)(1)

224. Answer C.   extensions of existing installations

Concealed knob-and-tube wiring shall be permitted to be installed in the hollow spaces of walls and ceilings, or in unfinished attics and roof spaces as provided by 394.23, only as follows:

(1) For extensions of existing installations

(2) Elsewhere by special permission

Reference: 2017 National Electrical Code – Chapter 3 Wiring Methods and Materials, Article 394 Concealed Knob-and-Tube Wiring. 394.10 Uses Permitted.

EXAM 8

Chapter 4 Equipment for General Use

1. The ampacity rating of a two-conductor copper No. 8 Type SCE flexible cord with an ambient temperature of 30°C, rated at 60°C is:

    A. 48

    B. 55

    C. 60

    D. 65

    Reference: 2017 National Electrical Code – Chapter 4 Equipment for General Use, Article 400 Flexible Cords and Cables. 400.5 Ampacities for Flexible Cords and Cables.

2. The maximum allowable ampacity of size 14/2 AWG Type SJT cord is:

    A. 13 amperes

    B. 15 amperes

    C. 18 amperes

    D. 20 amperes

    Reference: 2017 National Electrical Code – Chapter 4 Equipment for General Use, Article 400 Flexible Cords and Cables. 400.5 Ampacities for Flexible Cords and Cables. 400.5(A) Ampacity Tables.

3. Flexible cords and cables shall not be run through holes in walls, structural ceilings, suspended ceilings, dropped ceilings, or floors.

    A. True

    B. False

    Reference: 2017 National Electrical Code – Chapter 4 Equipment for General Use, Article 400 Flexible Cords and Cables. 400.12 Uses Not Permitted.1.

4. Where may flexible cords and cables not be used?

    A. as data processing cables

    B. as elevator cables

    C. to prevent transmission of vibration

    D. when run through holes in walls

    Reference: 2017 National Electrical Code – Chapter 4 Equipment for General Use, Article 400 Flexible Cords and Cables. 400.8 Uses Not Permitted.1.

EXAM 8

Chapter 4 Equipment for General Use

5. What kind of conductor is identified by a ridge on the exterior of a flexible cord?

   A. equipment grounding

   B. grounded

   C. phase

   D. ungrounded

   Reference: *2017 National Electrical Code – Chapter 4 Equipment for General Use, Article 400 Flexible Cords and Cables. 400.22 Grounded-Conductor Identification. 400.22 (F) Surface Marking.1.*

6. What is the smallest size copper conductor, along with flexible stranding, allowed in multiconductor portable cables of over 600 volts, that are used to connect mobile equipment and machinery?

   A. 8 AWG

   B. 10 AWG

   C. 12 AWG

   D. 14 AWG

   Reference: *2017 National Electrical Code – Chapter 4 Equipment for General Use, Article 400 Flexible Cords and Cables. 400.31 Construction. 400.31(A) Conductors.1.*

7. Type HFF wiring is normally used for what application?

   A. fixture wiring

   B. Heat, Fire and Flame resistant

   C. hydrogen atmosphere applications

   D. underground

   Reference: *2017 National Electrical Code – Chapter 4 Equipment for General Use, Article 402 Fixture Wires. 402.3 Types.1.*

8. A No. 14 fixture wire has an allowable ampacity of:

   A. 15

   B. 17

   C. 20

   D. 25

   Reference: *2017 National Electrical Code – Chapter 4 Equipment for General Use, Article 402 Fixture Wires. 402.5 Allowable Ampacities for Fixture Wires.1.*

EXAM 8

Chapter 4 Equipment for General Use

9. Fixture wires shall not be smaller than _____ AWG.

   A. 10

   B. 12

   C. 14

   D. 18

   Reference: 2017 National Electrical Code – Chapter 4 Equipment for General Use, Article 402 Fixture Wires. 402.6 Minimum Size.1.

10. Three-way and four-way switches shall be so wired that all switching is done:

    A. either in the grounded or ungrounded circuit conductor.

    B. only in the grounded circuit conductor.

    C. only in the ungrounded circuit conductor.

    D. only in the white circuit conductor.

    Reference: 2017 National Electrical Code – Chapter 4 Equipment for General Use, Article 404 Switches. 404.2 Switch Connections. 404.2(A) Three-Way and Four-Way Switches.1.

11. Switches or circuit breakers shall not disconnect the _____ conductor of a circuit.

    A. grounded

    B. grounding

    C. insulated

    D. ungrounded

    Reference: 2017 National Electrical Code – Chapter 4 Equipment for General Use, Article 404 Switches. 404.2 Switch Connections. 404.2(B) Grounded Conductors.1.

12. Under what circumstances are switches allowed to be installed inside shower or tub spaces?

    A. under any circumstances

    B. unless installed as part of a listed tub or shower assembly

    C. unless they are grounded, bonded and GFI protected

    D. unless they have a watertight cover

    Reference: 2017 National Electrical Code – Chapter 4 Equipment for General Use, Article 404 Switches. 404.4 Damp or Wet Locations. 404.4(C) Switches in Tub or Shower Spaces.1.

EXAM 8

Chapter 4 Equipment for General Use

13. Circuit breakers used as switches, and switches, must be in a location so that they can be operated from a readily accessible place, and must be placed so that when the center of the grip of the operating handle of the circuit breaker or switch is in its highest position, it is _____ or less above the working platform or floor. Exceptions ignored.

    A. 4 ft. 7 in.

    B. 5 ft. 2 in.

    C. 6 ft. 6 in.

    D. 6 ft. 7 in.

    Reference: 2017 National Electrical Code – Chapter 4 Equipment for General Use, Article 404 Switches. 404.8 Accessibility and Grouping. 404.8(A) Location.1.

14. All switches and circuit breakers used as switches shall be located so the operating handle, *when in its highest position*, is not more than _____ above the floor or working platform.

    A. 5 ft. 6 in.

    B. 6 ft.

    C. 6 ft. 7 in.

    D. 7 ft.

    Reference: 2017 National Electrical Code – Chapter 4 Equipment for General Use, Article 404 Switches. 404.8 Accessibility and Grouping. 404.8(A) Location.1.

15. What is the maximum height to the center of the operating handle of a disconnect switch when it is in the ON position, above the floor or working platform?

    A. 5 ft., 6 in.

    B. 6 ft.

    C. 6 ft., 6 in.

    D. 6 ft., 7 in.

    Reference: 2017 National Electrical Code – Chapter 4 Equipment for General Use, Article 404 Switches. 404.8 Accessibility and Grouping. 404.8(A) Location.1.

EXAM 8

Chapter 4 Equipment for General Use

16. Snap switches must not be ganged or grouped in enclosures with other receptacles, snap switches, or similar devices, unless they are placed so that voltage is _____ volts or less between adjacent devices, or unless placed in enclosures with securely installed, identified barriers between adjacent devices.

    A. 120
    B. 240
    C. 300
    D. 600

    Reference: 2017 National Electrical Code – Chapter 4 Equipment for General Use, Article 404 Switches. 404.8 Accessibility and Grouping. 404.8(B) Voltage Between Adjacent Devices.1.

17. True or false: all snap switches, including dimmer switches and similar control switches, must be connected to an equipment grounding conductor, and must have a way to connect metal faceplates to the equipment grounding conductor, whether a metal faceplate is installed or not. Exceptions ignored.

    A. True
    B. False

    Reference: 2017 National Electrical Code – Chapter 4 Equipment for General Use, Article 404 Switches. 404.9 Provisions for General-Use Snap Switches. 404.9(B) Grounding.1.

18. Any hand-operable circuit breaker that is equipped with a handle or lever, or a power operated circuit breaker that can be opened by hand in a power failure, is allowed to serve as a switch if it has:

    A. a plastic insulated handle
    B. been mounted in a panelboard
    C. not been mounted in a panelboard
    D. the required number of poles

    Reference: 2017 National Electrical Code – Chapter 4 Equipment for General Use, Article 404 Switches. 404.11 Circuit Breakers as Switches.1.

EXAM 8

Chapter 4 Equipment for General Use

19. What is the maximum of the ampere rating of the switch for general use snap switches supplying inductive loads, at the applied voltage?

   A. 50%
   B. 60%
   C. 75%
   D. 80%

   Reference: 2017 National Electrical Code – Chapter 4 Equipment for General Use, Article 404 Switches. 404.14 Rating and Use of Snap Switches. 404.14(B) Alternating-Current General-Use Snap Switch.1.

20. General-use dimmer switches shall be used only to control permanently installed _____ luminaries (lighting fixtures).

   A. compact fluorescent
   B. fluorescent
   C. halogen
   D. incandescent

   Reference: 2017 National Electrical Code – Chapter 4 Equipment for General Use, Article 404 Switches. 404.14 Rating and Use of Snap Switches. 404.14(E) Dimmer Switches.1.

21. Unless listed for controlling other loads and installed accordingly, general-use dimmer switches may be used to for permanently installed:

   A. fluorescent lights
   B. incandescent luminaries
   C. lighting receptacle outlets
   D. paddle fans

   Reference: 2017 National Electrical Code – Chapter 4 Equipment for General Use, Article 404 Switches. 404.14 Rating and Use of Snap Switches. . 404.14(E) Dimmer Switches.1.

22. What is the only use for general-use dimmer switches, unless listed to control other loads?

   A. a ceiling (paddle) fan with a luminaire
   B. holiday decorative lighting
   C. permanently installed incandescent luminaires
   D. switched receptacles for cord-connected incandescent luminaries

   Reference: 2017 National Electrical Code – Chapter 4 Equipment for General Use, Article 404 Switches. 404.14 Rating and Use of Snap Switches. 404.14(E) Dimmer Switches.1.

Chapter 4 Equipment for General Use   397

EXAM 8

Chapter 4 Equipment for General Use

23. What is the minimum ampere rating for cord connectors and receptacles, of a type not suitable for use as lampholders, that are also rated for 125 volts or 250 volts?

    A. 12   C. 20

    B. 15   D. 25

    Reference: 2017 National Electrical Code – Chapter 4 Equipment for General Use, Article 406 Receptacles, Cord Connectors, and Attachment Plugs. 406.3 Receptacle Rating and Type. 406.3(B) Rating.1.

24. What marking must be on receptacles rated for up to 20 amperes and designed for directly connecting aluminum conductors?

    A. Aluminum   C. Bi-Metal

    B. Any Metal   D. CO/ALR

    Reference: 2017 National Electrical Code – Chapter 4 Equipment for General Use, Article 406 Receptacles, Cord Connectors, and Attachment Plugs. 406.3 Receptacle Rating and Type. 406.3(C) Receptacles for Aluminum Conductors.1.

25. Receptacles incorporating an isolated grounding conductor connection, shall be identified by an _____ triangle located on the face of the receptacle.

    A. green   C. yellow

    B. orange   D. white

    Reference: 2017 National Electrical Code – Chapter 4 Equipment for General Use, Article 406 Receptacles, Cord Connectors, and Attachment Plugs. 406.3 Receptacle Rating and Type. 406.3(D) Isolated Ground Receptacles.1.

EXAM 8

Chapter 4 Equipment for General Use

26. Receptacles installed on 15- and 20-ampere branch circuits shall be of the _____ type.

    A. grounded

    B. grounding

    C. insulated

    D. ungrounded

    Reference: 2017 National Electrical Code – Chapter 4 Equipment for General Use, Article 406 Receptacles, Cord Connectors, and Attachment Plugs. 406.4 General Installation Requirements. 406.4(A) Grounding Type.1.

27. Receptacles shall not be installed in a _____ - ___ position in countertops or similar work surfaces.

    A. face-up

    B. horizontal

    C. sideways

    D. vertical

    Reference: 2017 National Electrical Code – Chapter 4 Equipment for General Use, Article 406 Receptacles, Cord Connectors, and Attachment Plugs. 406.5 Receptacle Mounting. 406.5(G) Receptacle Orientation. 1.

28. When a receptacle is installed in a location outdoors that is protected from weather or in damp locations, it must have an enclosure that is weatherproof when the receptacle is:

    A. being used by a cord plugged into it

    B. covered

    C. energized

    D. open

    Reference: 2017 National Electrical Code – Chapter 4 Equipment for General Use, Article 406 Receptacles, Cord Connectors, and Attachment Plugs. 406.9 Receptacles in Damp or Wet Locations. . 406.9(A) Damp Locations.1.

Chapter 4 Equipment for General Use

EXAM 8

Chapter 4 Equipment for General Use

29. Receptacle installations suitable for wet locations are also considered suitable for _____ locations.

    A. corrosive vapor

    B. damp

    C. exposed

    D. underwater

    Reference: 2017 National Electrical Code – Chapter 4 Equipment for General Use, Article 406 Receptacles, Cord Connectors, and Attachment Plugs. 406.9 Receptacles in Damp or Wet Locations. . 406.9(A) Damp Locations.1.

30. Receptacles installed outdoors in a wet location shall have an enclosure that is _____ whether or not the attachment plug cap is inserted.

    A. rainproof

    B. water resistant

    C. waterproof

    D. weatherproof

    Reference: 2017 National Electrical Code – Chapter 4 Equipment for General Use, Article 406 Receptacles, Cord Connectors, and Attachment Plugs. 406.9 Receptacles in Damp or Wet Locations. 406.9(B) Wet Locations. 406.9(B)(1) Receptacles of 15 and 20 Amperes in a Wet Location.1.

31. A receptacle shall not be installed within or directly over a _____.

    A. bathtub

    B. bathtub or shower stall

    C. shower

    D. sink

    Reference: 2017 National Electrical Code – Chapter 4 Equipment for General Use, Article 406 Receptacles, Cord Connectors, and Attachment Plugs. 406.9 Receptacles in Damp or Wet Locations. 406.9(C) Bathtub and Shower Space.1.

32. What are the uses of a grounding-type device or a grounding terminal?

    A. be used by grounded conductor

    B. be used in lieu of a GFI

    C. bond the grounded conductor to the neutral

    D. not be used for purposes other than grounding

    Reference: 2017 National Electrical Code – Chapter 4 Equipment for General Use, Article 406 Receptacles, Cord Connectors, and Attachment Plugs. 406.10 Grounding-Type Receptacles, Adapters, Cord Connectors, and Attachment Plugs. 406.10(C) Grounding Terminal Use.1.

EXAM 8

Chapter 4 Equipment for General Use

33. The B phase shall be that phase having the _____ voltage to ground on 3-phase, 4-wire, delta-connected systems.

    A. higher

    B. lower

    C. median

    D. nominal

    Reference: 2017 National Electrical Code – Chapter 4 Equipment for General Use, Article 408 Switchboards, Switchgear, and Panelboards. 408.3 Support and Arrangement of Busbars and Conductors. 408.3(E) Bus Arrangement. 408.3(E)(1) AC Phase Arrangement1.

34. Where conduits enter a switchboard or floor-standing panelboard at the bottom, the conduit including their end fittings, shall not rise more than _____ inches above the bottom of the enclosure.

    A. 2

    B. 3

    C. 6

    D. 8

    Reference: 2017 National Electrical Code – Chapter 4 Equipment for General Use, Article 408 Switchboards, Switchgear, and Panelboards. 408.5 Clearance for Conductor Entering Bus Enclosures.1.

35. Unless a non-combustible shield is placed between a switchboard and the ceiling, or _____, the space between a switchboard and any combustible ceiling must be 3 feet or more.

    A. the switchboard has no conductor with voltages over 300 V

    B. the switchboard is in a controlled area

    C. the switchboard is totally enclosed

    D. none of the above

    Reference: 2017 National Electrical Code – Chapter 4 Equipment for General Use, Article 408 Switchboards, Switchgear, and Panelboards. 408.18 Clearances. 408.18(A) From Ceiling.1.

EXAM 8

Chapter 4 Equipment for General Use

36. Switchboards that have any exposed live parts shall be located in permanently dry locations and then only where under competent supervision and accessible only to qualified persons.

    A. True
    B. False

    Reference: 2017 National Electrical Code – Chapter 4 Equipment for General Use, Article 408 Switchboards, Switchgear, and Panelboards. 408.20 Location of Switchboards.1.

37. Panelboards shall be required to have overcurrent protection, except for:

    A. existing panelboards used for single-family service equipment
    B. panelboards containing less than 42 overcurrent devices
    C. panelboards containing only single-pole overcurrent devices
    D. panelboards supplying another structure within the same panelboard

    Reference: 2017 National Electrical Code – Chapter 4 Equipment for General Use, Article 408 Switchboards, Switchgear, and Panelboards. 408.36 Overcurrent Protection.

38. Each grounded conductor shall terminate within the panelboard in an _____ terminal that is not also used for another conductor.

    A. bundled
    B. grounded
    C. individual
    D. ungrounded

    Reference: 2017 National Electrical Code – Chapter 4 Equipment for General Use, Article 408 Switchboards, Switchgear, and Panelboards. 408.41 Grounded Conductor Terminations.1.

39. The distance between bare metal parts, busbars, and other such parts in a panelboard when the voltage is 240V must be _____ or more.

    A. 1/4 inch
    B. 1/2 inch
    C. 3/4 inch
    D. 1 inch

    Reference: 2017 National Electrical Code – Chapter 4 Equipment for General Use, Article 408 Switchboards, Switchgear, and Panelboards. 408.56 Minimum Spacings.

EXAM 8

Chapter 4 Equipment for General Use

40. On an industrial control panel supplied from a 3-phase, 4-wire, delta-connected electrical system, the higher voltage to ground is:

    A. permitted to be any phase

    B. required to be the "A" phase

    C. required to be the "B" phase

    D. required to be the "C" phase

    Reference: 2017 National Electrical Code – Chapter 4 Equipment for General Use, Article 409 Industrial Control Panels. 409.102 Busbars and Conductors. 409.102(B) Phase Arrangement.1.

41. No parts of cord-connected luminaries (fixtures), hanging luminaries, lighting track, pendants, or ceiling-suspended (paddle) fans shall be located within a zone measured _____ feet horizontally and _____ feet vertically from the top of the bathtub rim or shower stall threshold.

    A. 2, 6

    B. 3, 8

    C. 4, 8

    D. 6, 6

    Reference: 2017 National Electrical Code – Chapter 4 Equipment for General Use, Article 410 Luminaires, Lampholders, and Lamps. 410.10 Luminaires in Specific Locations. 410.10(D) Bathtub and Shower Areas.1.

42. The clear zone distance from the top of a bathtub rim or a shower stall threshold must be at least _____ ft. horizontally and _____ ft. vertically for any parts of chain-, cable- or cord-suspended luminaries, cord-connected luminaries (fixtures), lighting track, pendant, or ceiling-suspended (paddle) fans.

    A. 3, 8

    B. 5, 8

    C. 5, 10

    D. 8, 8

    Reference: 2017 National Electrical Code – Chapter 4 Equipment for General Use, Article 410 Luminaires, Lampholders, and Lamps. 410.10 Luminaires in Specific Locations. 410.10(D) Bathtub and Shower Areas.1.

EXAM 8

Chapter 4 Equipment for General Use

43. Surface-mounted incandescent luminaries (fixtures) installed on the wall above the door or on the ceiling in clothes closets shall have a minimum clearance of _____ inches between the luminaire and the nearest point of storage.

    A. 10

    B. 12

    C. 15

    D. 18

    Reference: 2017 National Electrical Code – Chapter 4 Equipment for General Use, Article 410 Luminaires, Lampholders, and Lamps. 410.16 Luminaires in Clothes Closets. 410.16(C) Location.1.

44. What is the minimum clearance required between a surface mounted incandescent luminaire installed above the door or on the ceiling of a clothes closet, and the nearest shelf?

    A. 6 inches

    B. 8 inches

    C. 12 inches

    D. 18 inches

    Reference: 2017 National Electrical Code – Chapter 4 Equipment for General Use, Article 410 Luminaires, Lampholders, and Lamps. 410.16 Luminaires in Clothes Closets. 410.16(C) Location.1.

45. A luminaire (fixture) that weighs more than _____ pounds or exceeds 16 inches in any dimension shall not be supported by the screw shell of a lampholder.

    A. 6

    B. 8

    C. 10

    D. 12

    Reference: 2017 National Electrical Code – Chapter 4 Equipment for General Use, Article 410 Luminaires, Lampholders, and Lamps. 410.30 Supports. 410.30(A) General.1.

EXAM 8

Chapter 4 Equipment for General Use

46. Pendant conductors on a pendant mounted luminaire shall be twisted together where not cabled in a listed assembly during installation if they are longer than:

    A. 18 inches
    B. 24 inches
    C. 30 inches
    D. 36 inches

    Reference: 2017 National Electrical Code – Chapter 4 Equipment for General Use, Article 410 Luminaries, Lampholders, and Lamps. 410.54 Pendant Conductors for Incandescent Filament Lamps. 410.54(C) Twisted or Cabled.1.

47. _____ conductors shall be used for wiring on luminaire (fixture) chains and on other movable or flexible parts.

    A. Cabled
    B. Grounded
    C. Insulated
    D. Stranded

    Reference: 2017 National Electrical Code – Chapter 4 Equipment for General Use, Article 410 Luminaries, Lampholders, and Lamps. 410.56 Protection of Conductors and Insulation. 410.56(E) Stranding.1.

48. When is a fluorescent luminaire allowed to be cord connected?

    A. Where the flexible cord is at least size 12 AWG.
    B. Where the flexible cord is contained in an approved raceway.
    C. Where the flexible cord is visible for its entire length.
    D. Never

    Reference: 2017 National Electrical Code – Chapter 4 Equipment for General Use, Article 410 Luminaries, Lampholders, and Lamps. 410.62 Cord-Connected Lampholders and Luminaires. 410.62(C) Electric-Discharge and LED Luminaires. 410.62(C)(1) Cord-Connected Installation.1.

EXAM 8

Chapter 4 Equipment for General Use

49. Luminaries (fixtures) shall not be used as a _____ for circuit conductors.

    A. conduit

    B. ground-fault

    C. raceway

    D. support

    Reference: 2017 National Electrical Code – Chapter 4 Equipment for General Use, Article 410 Luminaires, Lampholders, and Lamps. 410.64 Luminaires as Raceways.1.

50. What is the minimum temperature rating for branch circuit conductors installed inside a ballast enclosure of a luminaire that are within three (3) inches of the ballast?

    A. 60°C

    B. 75°C

    C. 90°C

    D. 105°C

    Reference: 2017 National Electrical Code – Chapter 4 Equipment for General Use, Article 410 Luminaires, Lampholders, and Lamps. 410.68 Feeder and Branch-Circuit Conductors and Ballasts.1.

51. When the branch circuit conductor passes within three (3) inches of the ballast, which of the following conductor insulation types are acceptable for fluorescent luminaire wiring?

    A. THW

    B. THWN

    C. Both A and B

    D. Neither A nor B

    Reference: 2017 National Electrical Code – Chapter 4 Equipment for General Use, Article 410 Luminaires, Lampholders, and Lamps. 410.68 Feeder and Branch-Circuit Conductors and Ballasts.

52. Screw-shell type lampholders must be installed to be used as lampholders only, and where the supply circuit has a grounded conductor, the grounded conductor must be attached to the:

    A. center terminal

    B. green terminal

    C. grounding terminal

    D. screw shell

    Reference: 2017 National Electrical Code – Chapter 4 Equipment for General Use, Article 410 Luminaires, Lampholders, and Lamps. 410.90 Screw Shell Type.1.

EXAM 8

Chapter 4 Equipment for General Use

53. Recessed portions of lighting fixture enclosures must be spaced from combustible material at least _____, when not identified for contact with insulation.

    A. 3/8 in.

    B. 1/2 in.

    C. 3/4 in.

    D. 1 in.

    Reference: 2017 National Electrical Code – Chapter 4 Equipment for General Use, Article 410 Luminaires, Lampholders, and Lamps. 410.116 Clearance and Installation. 410.116(A) Clearance. 410.116(A)(1) Non-Type IC.1.

54. Thermal insulation shall not be installed above a recessed luminaire (fixture) or within _____ inches of the recessed luminaires (fixtures) enclosure, wiring compartment, or ballast unless it is identified for contact with insulation, Type IC.

    A. 2

    B. 3

    C. 6

    D. 8

    Reference: 2017 National Electrical Code – Chapter 4 Equipment for General Use, Article 410 Luminaires, Lampholders, and Lamps. 410.116 Clearance and Installation. 410.116(B) Installation.1.

55. What is the minimum length for a suitable raceway to enclose tap conductors for recessed luminaires?

    A. 18 inches

    B. 2 feet

    C. 4 feet

    D. 6 feet

    Reference: 2017 National Electrical Code – Chapter 4 Equipment for General Use, Article 410 Luminaires, Lampholders, and Lamps. 410.117 Wiring. 410.117(C) Tap Conductors.1.

56. _____ used for constructing a luminaire (fixture) box.

    A. No solder shall be

    B. Only silver solder may be

    C. Screws, crimps or solder may be

    D. none of the above

    Reference: 2017 National Electrical Code – Chapter 4 Equipment for General Use, Article 410 Luminaires, Lampholders, and Lamps. 410.121 Solder Prohibited.1.

Chapter 4 Equipment for General Use   407

EXAM 8

Chapter 4 Equipment for General Use

57. For required disconnecting means for a fluorescent luminaire, which of the following statements is true?

    A. Disconnecting simultaneously breaks all conductors to branch circuit.

    B. The disconnecting means shall be external to the luminaire.

    C. The disconnecting means shall not be external to the luminaire.

    D. Ungrounded conductor disconnects from multi-wire branch circuits.

    Reference: 2017 National Electrical Code – Chapter 4 Equipment for General Use, Article 410 Luminaires, Lampholders, and Lamps. 410.130 General. 410.130(G) Disconnecting Means.1.

58. What is the minimum distance that a surface-mounted luminaire with a ballast, transformer, LED driver or power supply shall be from combustible low-density cellulose fiberboard, unless marked for such conditions?

    A. 3/4 in.

    B. 1 in.

    C. 1-1/4 in.

    D. 1-1/2 in.

    Reference: 2017 National Electrical Code – Chapter 4 Equipment for General Use, Article 410 Luminaires, Lampholders, and Lamps. 410.136 Luminaire Mounting. 410.136(B) Combustible Low-Density Cellulose Fiberboard.1.

59. If equipment has an open-circuit voltage of over _____ volts may not be installed in or on dwelling occupancies.

    A. 208

    B. 240

    C. 1000

    D. 1200

    Reference: 2017 National Electrical Code – Chapter 4 Equipment for General Use, Article 410 Luminaires, Lampholders, and Lamps. 410.140 General. 410.140(B) Dwelling Occupancies.1.

EXAM 8

Chapter 4 Equipment for General Use

60. Which of the following locations may have lighting track installed?

    A. In storage battery rooms.

    B. In wet or damp locations.

    C. Where concealed.

    D. None of the above.

    Reference: 2017 National Electrical Code – Chapter 4 Equipment for General Use, Article 410 Luminaires, Lampholders, and Lamps. 410.151 Installation. 410.151(C) Locations Not Permitted.1.

61. Heavy-duty lighting track is lighting track identified for use exceeding _____ amperes.

    A. 10

    B. 20

    C. 30

    D. 40

    Reference: 2017 National Electrical Code – Chapter 4 Equipment for General Use, Article 410 Luminaires, Lampholders, and Lamps. 410.153 Heavy-Duty Lighting Track.1.

62. A single section (of track for lighting) 4 feet or shorter in length shall have _____ supports.

    A. two

    B. four

    C. six

    D. none of the above

    Reference: 2017 National Electrical Code – Chapter 4 Equipment for General Use, Article 410 Luminaires, Lampholders, and Lamps. 410.154 Fastening.1.

63. Lighting systems for fountains, pools, spas, and similar locations must be installed _____ or more horizontally from the nearest water's edge, unless Article 680 permits otherwise.

    A. 3 m (10 ft.)

    B. 6 m (20 ft.)

    C. 9 m (30 ft.)

    D. 12 m (40 ft.)

    Reference: 2017 National Electrical Code – Chapter 4 Equipment for General Use, Article 411 Lighting Systems Operating at 30 Volts or Less and Lighting Equipment Connected to Class-2 Power Sources. 411.5 Specific Location Requirements. 411.5(B) Pools, Spas, Fountains, and Similar Locations.1.

EXAM 8

Chapter 4 Equipment for General Use

64. When an appliance other than a motor-operated appliance is a continuous load, the branch-circuit rating must be _____ percent of the marked rating or more, or 100 percent of the marked branch-circuit rating or less, and its assembly listed for continuous loading at 100 percent of its rating.

    A. 100

    B. 125

    C. 150

    D. 175

    Reference: 2017 National Electrical Code – Chapter 4 Equipment for General Use, Article 422 Appliances. 422.10 Branch-Circuit Rating. . 422.10(A) Individual Circuits.1.

65. If a branch-circuit conductor is supplying a fixed storage-type electric water heater with a capacity of up to 120 gallons, the minimum ampacity must be what percentage of the full-load current of the water heater?

    A. 80%

    B. 100%

    C. 125%

    D. 150%

    Reference: 2017 National Electrical Code – Chapter 4 Equipment for General Use, Article 422 Appliances. 422.10 Branch-Circuit Rating. 422.10(A) Individual Circuits.

66. A household-type appliance with surface heating elements shall have its power supply subdivided into two (2) or more circuits if the maximum demand is over:

    A. 30 amperes

    B. 40 amperes

    C. 50 amperes

    D. 60 amperes

    Reference: 2017 National Electrical Code – Chapter 4 Equipment for General Use, Article 422 Appliances. 422.11 Overcurrent Protection. 422.11(B) Household-Type Appliances with Surface Heating Elements.1.

EXAM 8

Chapter 4 Equipment for General Use

67. What is the maximum overcurrent protection for infrared commercial and industrial heating appliances?

    A. 20 amperes

    B. 40 amperes

    C. 50 amperes

    D. 60 amperes

    Reference: 2017 National Electrical Code – Chapter 4 Equipment for General Use, Article 422 Appliances. 422.11 Overcurrent Protection. 422.11(C) Infrared Lamp Commercial and Industrial Heating Appliances.1.

68. Which of the following is not to be taken into consideration when sizing the overcurrent protection for a single non-motor operated appliance?

    A. The full-load current marked on the appliance.

    B. The length of time the appliance operates.

    C. The voltage rating of the appliance.

    D. Where selected overcurrent protection is not a standard size.

    Reference: 2017 National Electrical Code – Chapter 4 Equipment for General Use, Article 422 Appliances. 422.11 Overcurrent Protection. 422.11(E) Single Non-Motor-Operated Appliance.1.

69. Which of the following is not a consideration when sizing the overcurrent protection for a single non-motor operated appliance such as a cook top, range, or storage-type water heater?

    A. The full-load current marked on the appliance.

    B. The length of time the appliance operates.

    C. The voltage rating of the appliance.

    D. Where the overcurrent protection device selected is not a standard size.

    Reference: 2017 National Electrical Code – Chapter 4 Equipment for General Use, Article 422 Appliances. 422.11 Overcurrent Protection. 422.11(E) Single Non-Motor-Operated Appliances. 422.11(E)(3)1.

EXAM 8

Chapter 4 Equipment for General Use

70. What is the maximum standard size overcurrent protection device to protect an installed 40 gallon electric water heater with a nameplate rating of 4,500 watts at 240 volts, single phase?

    A. 20 amperes

    B. 25 amperes

    C. 30 amperes

    D. 45 amperes

    Reference: 2017 National Electrical Code – Chapter 2 Wiring and Protection, Article 240 Overcurrent Protection. 240.6 Standard Ampere Ratings. 240.6(A) Fuses and Fixed-Trip Circuit Breakers.

71. Which of the following shall be done for gas or oil central space heating equipment?

    A. may be supplied from a branch circuit supplying other equipment

    B. provided with GFCI protection

    C. provided with LCDI protection

    D. supplied from an individual branch circuit

    Reference: 2017 National Electrical Code – Chapter 4 Equipment for General Use, Article 422 Appliances. 422.12 Central Heating Equipment.1.

72. The length of cord for electrically operated kitchen waste disposers shall not be less than _____ inches and not over _____ inches.

    A. 12, 24

    B. 15, 30

    C. 18, 36

    D. 24, 48

    Reference: 2017 National Electrical Code – Chapter 4 Equipment for General Use, Article 422 Appliances. 422.16 Flexible Cords. 422.16(B) Specific Appliances. 422.16(B)(1) Electrically Operated In-Sink Waste Disposers. (2) 1.

EXAM 8

Chapter 4 Equipment for General Use

73. A kitchen waste disposer cord must be at least _____ in, and not over _____ in. in length.

    A. 18, 36

    B. 24, 42

    C. 30, 48

    D. 36, 72

    Reference: 2017 National Electrical Code – Chapter 4 Equipment for General Use, Article 422 Appliances. 422.16 Flexible Cords. 422.16(B) Specific Appliances. 422.16(B)(1) Electrically Operated In-Sink Waste Disposers.1.

74. The length of cord for built-in dishwashers and trash compactors shall not be less than _____ feet and not over _____ feet.

    A. 1, 3

    B. 2, 3

    C. 2, 4

    D. 3, 4

    Reference: 2017 National Electrical Code – Chapter 4 Equipment for General Use, Article 422 Appliances. 422.16 Flexible Cords. 422.16(B) Specific Appliances. 422.16(B)(2) Built-in Dishwashers and Trash Compactors. (2)1.

75. A cord-and-plug-connected dishwasher installed under a counter in a dwelling unit has a maximum allowed cord length of:

    A. 1 1/2 feet

    B. 3 1/2 feet

    C. 4 1/2 feet

    D. 6 1/2 feet

    Reference: 2017 National Electrical Code – Chapter 4 Equipment for General Use, Article 422 Appliances. 422.16 Flexible Cords. 422.16(B) Specific Appliances. 422.16(B)(2) Built-in Dishwashers and Trash Compactors. (2)1.

76. Ceiling-suspended (paddle) fans shall be supported _____ of the outlet box.

    A. alongside

    B. by use

    C. dependent

    D. independently

    Reference: 2017 National Electrical Code – Chapter 4 Equipment for General Use, Article 422 Appliances. 422.18 Support of Ceiling-Suspended (Paddle) Fans.1.

EXAM 8

Chapter 4 Equipment for General Use

77. For permanently connected appliances rated at not over _____ horsepower, the branch-circuit overcurrent device shall be permitted to serve as the disconnecting means.

    A. 1/8

    B. 1/4

    C. 1/2

    D. 3/4

    Reference: 2017 National Electrical Code – Chapter 4 Equipment for General Use, Article 422 Appliances. 422.31 Disconnection of Permanently Connected Appliances. 422.31(A) Rated at Not over 300 Volt-Amperes or 1/8 Horsepower.1.

78. Permanently connected appliances that are rated at 300 volt amperes or less, or 1/8 hp must have a branch-circuit overcurrent device that will:

    A. be permitted to serve as the disconnecting means

    B. be within sight of the appliance

    C. not be permitted to serve as the disconnecting means

    D. none of the above

    Reference: 2017 National Electrical Code – Chapter 4 Equipment for General Use, Article 422 Appliances. 422.31 Disconnection of Permanently Connected Appliances. 422.31(A) Rated at Not over 300 Volt-Amperes or 1/8 Horsepower.1.

79. All water heaters, both instantaneous-type and storage, must have a temperature-limiting device as well as its control thermostat, to disconnect all:

    A. connected conductors

    B. ungrounded conductors

    C. water supply systems

    D. none of the above

    Reference: 2017 National Electrical Code – Chapter 4 Equipment for General Use, Article 422 Appliances. 422.47 Water Heater Controls.1.

EXAM 8

Chapter 4 Equipment for General Use

80. What is the maximum rating on a branch circuit supplying more than one electric baseboard heater in a residential occupancy?

    A. 15 amperes

    B. 20 amperes

    C. 30 amperes

    D. 50 amperes

    Reference: 2017 National Electrical Code – Chapter 4 Equipment for General Use, Article 424 Fixed Electric Space-Heating Equipment. 424.3 Branch Circuits. 424.3(A) Branch-Circuit Requirements.1.

81. What percentage of the load should be the minimum ampacity of branch-circuit conductors for a residential central heating electric furnace?

    A. 80%

    B. 100%

    C. 115%

    D. 125%

    Reference: 2017 National Electrical Code – Chapter 2 Wiring and Protection, Article 210 Branch Circuits. 210.19 Conductors – Minimum Ampacity and Size. 210.19(A) Branch Circuits Not More Than 600 Volts. 210.19(A)(1) General. 210.19(A)(1)(a)1.

82. For supplying a fixed electric space heating unit with heating elements having a full-load current rating of 125 amperes and a blower motor with a full-load current rating of 2.5 amperes, what is the minimum size 75°C rated copper conductors required?

    A. 1 AWG

    B. 2 AWG

    C. 2/0 AWG

    D. 3/0 AWG

    Reference: 2017 National Electrical Code – Chapter 3 Wiring Methods and Materials, Article 310 Conductors for General Wiring. 310.15 Ampacities for Conductors Rated 0-2000 Volts. 310.15(B) Tables.

EXAM 8

Chapter 4 Equipment for General Use

83. Circuit breakers and switches to be used as a means of disconnection must be of the _____ type.

    A. grounded disconnect conductor

    B. indicating

    C. T

    D. toggle

    Reference: 2017 National Electrical Code – Chapter 4 Equipment for General Use, Article 424 Fixed Electric Space-Heating Equipment. 424.21 Switch and Circuit Breaker to Be Indicating.1.

84. For the protection of resistance-type electric space heating equipment, what is the maximum overcurrent protection allowed?

    A. 30 amperes

    B. 40 amperes

    C. 48 amperes

    D. 60 amperes

    Reference: 2017 National Electrical Code – Chapter 4 Equipment for General Use, Article 424 Fixed Electric Space-Heating Equipment. 424.22 Overcurrent Protection. 424.22(B) Resistance Elements.1.

85. What is considered the ambient temperature of wiring located 2 inches above a heated ceiling?

    A. 50°C

    B. 60°C

    C. 75°C

    D. 99°F

    Reference: 2017 National Electrical Code – Chapter 4 Equipment for General Use, Article 424 Fixed Electric Space-Heating Equipment. 424.36 Clearances of Wiring in Ceilings.1.

86. Ground-fault circuit-interrupter protection for personnel shall be provided for cables installed in electrically heated _____ of bathrooms, kitchens, and in hydromassage bathtub locations.

    A. floors

    B. linens

    C. water

    D. none of the above

    Reference: 2017 National Electrical Code – Chapter 4 Equipment for General Use, Article 424 Fixed Electric Space-Heating Equipment. 424.44 Installation of Cables in Concrete or Poured Masonry Floors. 424.44(E) Ground-Fault Circuit-Interrupter Protection.1.

EXAM 8

Chapter 4 Equipment for General Use

87. Which of the following is a requirement for electrically heated floors in bathrooms, kitchens, and in hydromassage bathtub locations?

    A. AFCI protected

    B. GFCI protected

    C. grounded

    D. isolated

    Reference: 2017 National Electrical Code – Chapter 4 Equipment for General Use, Article 424 Fixed Electric Space-Heating Equipment. 424.44 Installation of Cables in Concrete or Poured Masonry Floors. 424.44(G) Ground-Fault Circuit-Interrupter Protection.1.

88. Fixed outdoor electric deicing and snow-melting equipment shall be considered as a _____ load.

    A. continuous

    B. grounded

    C. noncontinuous

    D. ungrounded

    Reference: 2017 National Electrical Code – Chapter 4 Equipment for General Use, Article 426 Fixed Outdoor Electric Deicing and Snow-Melting Equipment. 426.4 Continuous Load.1.

89. For fixed outdoor electric deicing equipment, the ampacity of branch-circuit conductors and the rating or setting of overcurrent protective devices supplying the equipment shall be a minimum of _____ of the full-load current.

    A. 80%

    B. 100%

    C. 125%

    D. 150%

    Reference: 2017 National Electrical Code – Chapter 2 Wiring and Protection, Article 210 Branch Circuits. 210.20 Overcurrent Protection. 210.20(A) Continuous and Noncontinuous Loads.1.

90. What section governs the minimum size of conductors to be used when flexible cord is used for wiring to supply ac motors?

    A. Table 310.15(B)(16)

    B. Table 31.015(B)(17)

    C. Table 310.15(B)(18)

    D. Section 400.5

    Reference: 2017 National Electrical Code – Chapter 4 Equipment for General Use, Article 430 Motors, Motor Circuits, and Controllers. 430.6 Ampacity and Motor Rating Determination.1.

Chapter 4 Equipment for General Use

EXAM 8

Chapter 4 Equipment for General Use

91. What table is used for current values to determine the required ampacity of the branch circuit conductors to supply a 3-phase, continuous duty ac motor?

    A. the motors nameplate
    B. Table 430.52 of the NEC
    C. Table 430.248 of the NEC
    D. Table 430.250 of the NEC

    Reference: 2017 National Electrical Code – Chapter 4 Equipment for General Use, Article 430 Motors, Motor Circuits, and Controllers. 430.6 Ampacity and Motor Rating Determination. 430.6(A) General Motor Applications. 430.6(A)(1) Table Values. 1.

92. What is the minimum ampacity of the branch-circuit conductors used to supply a 7-1/2 hp, 230-volt, single-phase induction type, ac motor for continuous duty application?

    A. 40 amperes
    B. 50 amperes
    C. 60 amperes
    D. 75 amperes

    Reference: 2017 National Electrical Code – Chapter 4 Equipment for General Use, Article 430 Motors, Motor Circuits, and Controllers. 430.22 Single Motor.

93. The motor nameplate current rating on a motor used in a continuous-duty application is used to determine the requirement of the motor for:

    A. branch-circuit conductors
    B. disconnecting means
    C. motor overload protection
    D. short-circuit protection

    Reference: 2017 National Electrical Code – Chapter 4 Equipment for General Use, Article 430 Motors, Motor Circuits, and Controllers. 430.6 Ampacity and Motor Rating Determination. 430.6(A) General Motor Applications. 1.

94. If a feeder supplies two (2) continuous-duty, 3-phase, 208-volt motors, one 7-1/2 hp and one 10 hp, what is the minimum ampacity?

    A. 38.50 amperes
    B. 55.00 amperes
    C. 62.70 amperes
    D. 68.75 amperes

    Reference: 2017 National Electrical Code – Chapter 4 Equipment for General Use, Article 430 Motors, Motor Circuits, and Controllers. 430.24 Several Motors or a Motor(s) and Other Load(s). 1.

EXAM 8

Chapter 4 Equipment for General Use

95. What is the minimum ampacity, in relation to the full-load current rating of the motor, for branch circuit conductors that supply a continuous-duty ac motor?

    A. 100%

    B. 115%

    C. 125%

    D. 150%

    Reference: 2017 National Electrical Code – Chapter 4 Equipment for General Use, Article 430 Motors, Motor Circuits, and Controllers. 430.22 Single Motor.1.

96. What is the minimum size THW copper branch-circuit conductor required by the NEC for a 3-phase, continuous-duty, ac motor drawing 70 amperes for phase, when all terminations are rated for 75°C?

    A. 1 AWG

    B. 2 AWG

    C. 3 AWG

    D. 4 AWG

    Reference: 2017 National Electrical Code – Chapter 3 Wiring Methods and Materials

97. What percentage of the nameplate rating of a varying duty motor with a 30 minute and/or 60 minute rating should the ampacity of the supplying branch circuit conductors have?

    A. 85%

    B. 110%

    C. 120%

    D. 150%

    Reference: 2017 National Electrical Code – Chapter 4 Equipment for General Use, Article 430 Motors, Motor Circuits, and Controllers. 430.22 Single Motor. 430.22(E) Other Than Continuous Duty.

98. When a branch-circuit conductor supplies more than one motor, it shall have an ampacity of at least _____ of the highest rated motor in the group, and a minimum of 100% of the remaining motor(s) FLC.

    A. 25%

    B. 80%

    C. 100%

    D. 125%

    Reference: 2017 National Electrical Code – Chapter 4 Equipment for General Use, Article 430 Motors, Motor Circuits, and Controllers . 430.24 Several Motors or a Motor(s) and Other Load(s).1.

Chapter 4 Equipment for General Use

EXAM 8

Chapter 4 Equipment for General Use

99. Given the information below for a listed 3-phase, 230-volt motor, what is the minimum size 75°C copper feeder conductors required?

    A. 2 AWG THW

    B. 3 AWG THW

    C. 4 AWG THHN

    D. 4 AWG THWN

    Reference: 2017 National Electrical Code – Chapter 3 Wiring Methods and Materials

100. For the purposes of selecting the overload device on a motor of more than 1 horsepower with a temperature rise of 50°C on the nameplate, the device shall be selected to trip at no higher than what percentage of the motor's full-load ampere rating? (Assume no modification of this value is necessary.)

    A. 100%

    B. 115%

    C. 125%

    D. 130%

    Reference: 2017 National Electrical Code – Chapter 4 Equipment for General Use, Article 430 Motors, Motor Circuits, and Controllers . 430.32 Continuous-Duty Motors. 430.32(A) More than 1 Horsepower. 430.32(A)(1) Separate Overload Device.1.

101. What does a motor overload device function in direct response to?

    A. Ambient temperature

    B. Motor current

    C. Temperature rise of the motor

    D. Voltage

    Reference: 2017 National Electrical Code – Chapter 4 Equipment for General Use, Article 430 Motors, Motor Circuits, and Controllers. 430.32 Continuous-Duty Motors. 430.32(A) More Than 1 Horsepower. 430.32(A)(1) Separate Overload Device.1.

102. What is the maximum percentage of the full-load current of a thermally protected 2 horsepower, single-phase, 240-volt motor where a thermal protector is integral with the motor?

    A. 115 percent

    B. 125 percent

    C. 140 percent

    D. 156 percent

    Reference: 2017 National Electrical Code – Chapter 4 Equipment for General Use, Article 430 Motors, Motor Circuits, and Controllers. 430.6 Ampacity and Motor Rating Determination.

EXAM 8

Chapter 4 Equipment for General Use

103. Besides a motor short-circuit protector, what shall be used to protect overhead relays and other devices for motor overload protection that are not capable of opening ground-faults or short-circuits?

    A. a ground-fault circuit interrupter

    B. an instantaneous trip circuit breaker only

    C. Class CC fuses only

    D. fuses or circuit breakers

    Reference: 2017 National Electrical Code – Chapter 4 Equipment for General Use, Article 430 Motors, Motor Circuits, and Controllers. 430.40 Overload Relays.1.

104. For a pump motor control-circuit protected by a motor branch circuit protection device, with size 14 AWG conductors extending beyond the enclosure, what is the maximum size required overcurrent protection device?

    A. 15 amperes

    B. 20 amperes

    C. 45 amperes

    D. 100 amperes

    Reference: 2017 National Electrical Code – Chapter 4 Equipment for General Use, Article 430 Motors, Motor Circuits, and Controllers. 430.72 Overcurrent Protection.

105. What should the minimum horsepower rating of a motor controller that is not an inverse time circuit breaker or molded case switch, controlling a 120 hp, continuous-duty, ac motor of up to 600 volts?

    A. 120 hp

    B. 150 hp

    C. 175 hp

    D. 200 hp

    Reference: 2017 National Electrical Code – Chapter 4 Equipment for General Use, Article 430 Motors, Motor Circuits, and Controllers. 430.83 Ratings. 430.83(A) General. 430.83(A)(1) Horsepower Ratings.1.

EXAM 8

Chapter 4 Equipment for General Use

106. A motor controller that also serves as a disconnecting means shall open all of which conductors to the motor?

    A. grounded

    B. grounding

    C. neutral

    D. ungrounded

    Reference: 2017 National Electrical Code – Chapter 4 Equipment for General Use, Article 430 Motors, Motor Circuits, and Controllers . 430.84 Need Not Open All Conductors. 430.84, Exception1.

107. Which of the following is required when a circuit breaker serves as the control for a motor that is not in sight of the breaker?

    A. The breaker be able to be locked in the open position.

    B. The breaker to be rated 25,000 AIC.

    C. The motor to be Code letter "E".

    D. The motor to be less than 2 hp.

    Reference: 2017 National Electrical Code – Chapter 4 Equipment for General Use, Article 430 Motors, Motor Circuits, and Controllers . 430.102 Location. 430.102(B) Motor. 430.102(B)(2) Controller Disconnect. 430.102(B)(2), Exception1.

108. The disconnecting means for motor circuits rated 600 volts, nominal, or less shall have an ampere rating of at least _____ percent of the full-load current rating of the motor.

    A. 75

    B. 80

    C. 100

    D. 115

    Reference: 2017 National Electrical Code – Chapter 4 Equipment for General Use, Article 430 Motors, Motor Circuits, and Controllers. 430.110 Ampere Rating and Interrupting Capacity. 430.110(A) General.1.

EXAM 8

Chapter 4 Equipment for General Use

109. The disconnecting means for motor circuits rated 1000 volts nominal, or less, must have an ampere rating of at least _____ of the full-load current rating of the motor.

    A. 80%

    B. 100%

    C. 115%

    D. 125%

    Reference: 2017 National Electrical Code – Chapter 4 Equipment for General Use, Article 430 Motors, Motor Circuits, and Controllers. 430.110 Ampere Rating and Interrupting Capacity. 430.110(A) General.1.

110. Flexible metal conduit or liquidtight flexible metal conduit not exceeding _____ feet in length shall be permitted to be employed for raceway connection to a motor terminal enclosure.

    A. 4

    B. 5

    C. 6

    D. 8

    Reference: 2017 National Electrical Code – Chapter 4 Equipment for General Use, Article 430 Motors, Motor Circuits, and Controllers. 430.223 Raceway Connection To Motors.1.

111. For a 3 hp, 208-volt, single-phase, ac motor used in a continuous duty application, the full-load running current is:

    A. 10.6 amperes

    B. 13.2 amperes

    C. 18.7 amperes

    D. 19.6 amperes

    Reference: 2017 National Electrical Code – Chapter 4 Equipment for General Use, Article 430 Motors, Motor Circuits, and Controllers. 430.110 Ampere Rating and Interrupting

112. What is the full-load current rating of a 3/4 hp, 115-volt, single-phase AC motor?

    A. 7.9 amperes

    B. 9.8 amperes

    C. 13.8 amperes

    D. 16.0 amperes

    Reference: 2017 National Electrical Code – Chapter 4 Equipment for General Use, Article 430 Motors, Motor Circuits, and Controllers

EXAM 8

Chapter 4 Equipment for General Use

113. What is the full-load running current rating of a 208-volt, 3-phase, 50 hp, squirrel-cage, continuous-duty, ac motor?

    A. 130 amperes

    B. 143 amperes

    C. 162 amperes

    D. 195 amperes

    Reference: 2017 National Electrical Code – Chapter 4 Equipment for General Use, Article 430 Motors, Motor Circuits, and Controllers

114. What is the full-load running current rating of a 30 hp, 480-volt, 3-phase wound-rotor, ac motor?

    A. 27 amperes

    B. 32 amperes

    C. 40 amperes

    D. 50 amperes

    Reference: 2017 National Electrical Code – Chapter 4 Equipment for General Use, Article 430 Motors, Motor Circuits, and Controllers

115. Disconnecting means shall be located within _____ from and readily accessible from air-conditioning or refrigerating equipment.

    A. 3 feet

    B. 5 feet

    C. 10 feet

    D. sight

    Reference: 2017 National Electrical Code – Chapter 4 Equipment for General Use, Article 440 Air-Conditioning and Refrigeration Equipment. 440.14 Location.1.

116. The total marked rating of a cord-and-attachment-plug-connected room air conditioner shall not exceed _____ percent of the rating of a branch circuit where no other loads are supplied.

    A. 40

    B. 60

    C. 75

    D. 80

    Reference: 2017 National Electrical Code – Chapter 4 Equipment for General Use, Article 440 Air-Conditioning and Refrigeration Equipment. 440.62 Branch-Circuit Requirements. 440.62(B) Where No Other Loads Are Supplied.1.

EXAM 8

Chapter 4 Equipment for General Use

117. For a branch-circuit where lighting outlets or general-use receptacles are also supplied, what is the maximum percentage of the rating that may not be exceeded by a cord-and-attachment-plug connected room air-conditioner?

    A. 50%

    B. 60%

    C. 75%

    D. 80%

    Reference: 2017 National Electrical Code – Chapter 4 Equipment for General Use, Article 440 Air-Conditioning and Refrigerating Equipment. 440.62 Branch-Circuit Requirements. 440.62(C) Where Lighting Units or Other Appliances Are Also Supplied. 1.

118. Where a flexible cord is used to supply a room air conditioner, the length of such cord shall not exceed _____ feet for a nominal, 120-volt rating or _____ feet for a nominal, 208- or 240-volt rating.

    A. 5, 3

    B. 10, 6

    C. 15, 9

    D. 20, 12

    Reference: 2017 National Electrical Code – Chapter 4 Equipment for General Use, Article 440 Air-Conditioning and Refrigeration Equipment. 440.64 Supply Cords. 1.

EXAM 8

Chapter 4 Equipment for General Use

119. If a room air conditioner uses a flexible cord to supply it, the cord may not be more than _____ ft. for a rating of 120-volts, nominal, or _____ ft. for a rating of 208- or 240-volts, nominal.

   A. 6, 3
   B. 6, 4
   C. 8, 10
   D. 10, 6

   Reference: 2017 National Electrical Code – Chapter 4 Equipment for General Use, Article 440 Air-Conditioning and Refrigeration Equipment. 440.64 Supply Cords.1.

120. What is the maximum allowed length for a flexible cord supplying a 208-volt, single-phase, room air-conditioner?

   A. 4 feet
   B. 6 feet
   C. 8 feet
   D. 10 feet

   Reference: 2017 National Electrical Code – Chapter 4 Equipment for General Use, Article 440 Air-Conditioning and Refrigerating Equipment. 440.64 Supply Cords.1.

121. Of the following, which is not a requirement for marking on a transformer's nameplate?

   A. kVA rating
   B. manufacturer
   C. overcurrent protection
   D. voltage

   Reference: 2017 National Electrical Code – Chapter 4 Equipment for General Use, Article 450 Transformers and Transformer Vaults (including Secondary Ties). 450.11 Marking. 450.11(A)General.1.

EXAM 8

Chapter 4 Equipment for General Use

122. What is the minimum fire-resistance rating of the materials of a transformer vault that is not protected with an automatic fire-suppression system?

    A. 1 hour

    B. 2 hours

    C. 3 hours

    D. 4 hours

    Reference: 2017 National Electrical Code – Chapter 4 Equipment for General Use, Article 450 Transformers and Transformer Vaults (including Secondary Ties). 450.42 Walls, Roofs, and Floors.1.

123. What is required for a control transformer when a 240-volt wye-connected motor gets power from a converted single-phase source, and it is intended to connect a 120/240-volt transformer to control the motor on the load side of the converter?

    A. Be connected to the manufactured phase

    B. Be disconnected after start-up of the motor

    C. Have separate overcurrent protection

    D. Not be connected to the manufactured phase

    Reference: 2017 National Electrical Code – Chapter 4 Equipment for General Use, Article 455 Phase Converters. 455.9 Connection of Single-Phase Loads.

Chapter 4 Equipment for General Use 427

EXAM 8

EXAM 8 ANSWERS

Table 400.5(A)(2) Ampacity of Cable Types SC, SCE, SCT, PPE, G, G-GC, and W [Based on Ambient Temperature of 30°C (86°F). See Table 400.4.]

Copper Conductor Size (AWG or kcmil)	Temperature Rating of Cable								
	60°C (140°F)			75°C (167°F)			90°C (194°F)		
	D¹	E²	F³	D¹	E²	F³	D¹	E²	F³
12	—	31	26	—	37	31	—	42	35
10	—	44	37	—	52	43	—	59	49
8	60	55	48	70	65	57	80	74	65
6	80	72	63	95	88	77	105	99	87
4	105	96	84	125	115	101	140	130	114
3	120	113	99	145	133	118	165	152	133
2	140	128	112	170	152	133	190	174	152
1	165	150	131	195	178	156	220	202	177
1/0	195	173	151	230	207	181	260	234	205
2/0	225	199	174	265	238	208	300	271	237
3/0	260	230	201	310	275	241	350	313	274
4/0	300	265	232	360	317	277	405	361	316
250	340	296	259	405	354	310	455	402	352
300	375	330	289	445	395	346	505	449	393
350	420	363	318	505	435	381	570	495	433
400	455	392	343	545	469	410	615	535	468
500	515	448	392	620	537	470	700	613	536
600	575	—	—	690	—	—	780	—	—
700	630	—	—	755	—	—	855	—	—
750	655	—	—	785	—	—	885	—	—
800	680	—	—	815	—	—	920	—	—
900	730	—	—	870	—	—	985	—	—
1000	780	—	—	935	—	—	1055	—	—

1. **Answer B. 55**

    Table 400.5(A)(1) provides the allowable ampacities, and **Table 400.5(A)(2)** provides the ampacities for flexible cords and flexible cables with not more than three current-carrying conductors. These tables shall be used in conjunction with applicable end-use product standards to ensure selection of the proper size and type. Where cords and cables are used in ambient temperatures other than 30°C (86°F), the temperature correction factors from Table 310.15(B)(2)(a) that correspond to the temperature rating of the cord or cable shall be applied to the ampacity in Table 400.5(A)(1) and Table 400.5(A)(2). Cords and cables rated 105°C shall use correction factors in the 90°C column of. Table 310.15(B)(2)(a) for temperature correction. Where the number of current-carrying conductors exceeds three, the allowable ampacity or the ampacity of each conductor shall be reduced from the three-conductor rating as shown in Table 400.5(A)(3).

    Informational Note: See Informative Annex B, Table B.310.15(B)(2)(11), for adjustment factors for more than three current-carrying conductors in a raceway or cable with load diversity.

    A neutral conductor that carries only the unbalanced current from other conductors of the same circuit shall not be required to meet the requirements of a current-carrying conductor.

    In a 3-wire circuit consisting of two phase conductors and the neutral conductor of a 4-wire, 3-phase, wye-connected system, a common conductor carries approximately the same current as the line-to-neutral currents of the other conductors and shall be considered to be a current-carrying conductor.

    On a 4-wire, 3-phase, wye circuit where more than 50 percent of the load consists of nonlinear loads, there are harmonic currents present in the neutral conductor and the neutral conductor shall be considered to be a current-carrying conductor.

    An equipment grounding conductor shall not be considered a current-carrying conductor.

    Where a single conductor is used for both equipment grounding and to carry unbalanced current from other conductors, as provided for in 250.140 for electric ranges and electric clothes dryers, it shall not be considered as a current carrying conductor.

    Reference: 2017 National Electrical Code – Chapter 4 Equipment for General Use, Article 400 Flexible Cords and Cables. 400.5 Ampacities for Flexible Cords and Cables. **(A) Ampacity Tables.**1.

EXAM 8

EXAM 8 ANSWERS

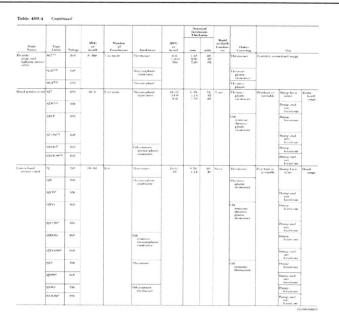

Table 400.4 (pg 3) see page 70-244 in the Code

2. Answer C.   18 amperes

Table 400.5(A)(1) provides the allowable ampacities, and Table 400.5(A)(2) provides the ampacities for flexible cords and cables with not more than three current-carrying conductors. These tables shall be used in conjunction with applicable end-use product standards to ensure selection of the proper size and type. Where cords and cables are used in ambient temperatures other than 30°C (86°F), the temperature connection factors from Table 310.15(B)(2)(a) that correspond to the temperature rating of the cord or cable shall be applied to the ampacity in Table 400.5(A)(1) and Table 400.5(A)(2). Cords and cables rated 105°C. shall use connection factors in the 90°C column of Table310.15(B)(2)(a) for temperature correction. Where the number of current-carrying conductors exceeds three, the allowable ampacity or the ampacity of each conductor shall be reduced from the three-conductor rating as shown in Table 400.5(A)(3).

Reference: 2017 National Electrical Code – Chapter 4 Equipment for General Use, Article 400 Flexible Cords and Cables. 400.5 Ampacities for Flexible Cords and Cables. 400.5(A) Ampacity Tables. Table 400.5(A)(1) Allowable Ampacity for Flexible Cords and Cables [Based on Ambient Temperature of 30°C (86°F). See 400.13 and Table 400.4., Column B (page 70-269)1.

3. Answer A.   True

Unless specifically permitted in 400.10, flexible cables, flexible cord sets, and power supply cords shall not be used for the following:

(1) As a substitute for the fixed wiring of a structure

(2) Where run through holes in walls, structural ceilings, suspended ceilings, dropped ceilings, or floors

(3) Where run through doorways, windows, or similar openings

(4) Where attached to building surfaces

Exception to (4): Flexible cord and flexible cable shall be permitted to be attached to building surfaces in accordance with 368.56(B) .

(5) Where concealed by walls, floors, or ceilings or located above suspended or dropped ceilings

Exception to (5): Flexible cord and flexible cable shall be permitted if contained within an enclosure for use in Other Spaces Used for Environmental Air as permitted by 300.22(C)(3).

(6) Where installed in raceways, except as otherwise permitted in this Code

(7) Where subject to physical damage

Reference: 2017 National Electrical Code – Chapter 4 Equipment for General Use, Article 400 Flexible Cords and Cables. 400.12 Uses Not Permitted.1.

EXAM 8

EXAM 8 ANSWERS

ECTFE — flexible stranding	HFF	Ethylene chlorotrifluoroethylene	18–14	0.88	15	None	150°C (302°F)	Fixture wiring

Table 402.3 see Table 402-3 in the Tables folder on CD-ROM

4. **Answer D.** when run through holes in walls

Unless specifically permitted in 400.10, flexible cables, flexible cord sets, and power supply cords shall not be used for the following:

(1) As a substitute for the fixed wiring of a structure

(2) Where run through holes in walls, structural ceilings, suspended ceilings, dropped ceilings, or floors

(3) Where run through doorways, windows, or similar openings

(4) Where attached to building surfaces
Exception to (4): Flexible cord and flexible cable shall be permitted to be attached to building surfaces in accordance with 368.56(B).

(5) Where concealed by walls, floors, or ceilings or located above suspended or dropped ceilings

Exception to (5): Flexible cord and flexible cable shall be permitted if contained within an enclosure for use in Other Spaces Used for Environmental Air as permitted by 300.22(C)(3).

(6) Where installed in raceways, except as otherwise permitted in this Code

(7) Where subject to physical damage

Reference: 2017 National Electrical Code – Chapter 4 Equipment for General Use, Article 400 Flexible Cords and Cables. 400.8 Uses Not Permitted.1.

5. **Answer B.** grounded

One or more ridges, grooves, or white stripes located on the exterior of the cord so as to identify one conductor for cords having insulation on the individual conductors integral with the jacket.

Reference: 2017 National Electrical Code – Chapter 4 Equipment for General Use, Article 400 Flexible Cords and Cables. 400.22 *Grounded-Conductor* Identification. 400.22 (F) Surface Marking.1.

6. **Answer C.** 12 AWG

The conductors shall be 12 AWG copper or larger and shall employ flexible stranding.

Reference: 2017 National Electrical Code – Chapter 4 Equipment for General Use, Article 400 Flexible Cords and Cables. 400.31 Construction. 400.31(A) Conductors.1.

7. **Answer A.** fixture wiring

Fixture wires shall be of a type listed in Table 402.3, and they shall comply with all requirements of that table. The fixture wires listed in Table 402.3 are all suitable for service at 600 volts, nominal, unless otherwise specified.

Informational Note: Thermoplastic insulation may stiffen at temperatures lower than −10°C (+14°F). Thermoplastic insulation may also be deformed at normal temperatures where subjected to pressure, such as at points of support.

Reference: 2017 National Electrical Code – Chapter 4 Equipment for General Use, Article 402 Fixture Wires. 402.3 Types.1.

Table 402.5 Allowable Ampacity for Fixture Wires

Size (AWG)	Allowable Ampacity
18	6
16	8
14	17
12	23
10	28

8. **Answer B.** 17

The allowable ampacity of fixture wire shall be as specified in Table 402.5.

No conductor shall be used under such conditions that its operating temperature exceeds the temperature specified in Table 402.3 for the type of insulation involved.

Informational Note: See 310.15(A)(3) for temperature limitation of conductors. Table 402.5 Allowable Ampacity for Fixture Wires on page 70-277.

Reference: 2017 National Electrical Code – Chapter 4 Equipment for General Use, Article 402 Fixture Wires. 402.5 Allowable Ampacities for Fixture Wires.1.

EXAM 8

EXAM 8 ANSWERS

9. **Answer D.** 18

   Fixture wires shall not be smaller than 18 AWG.

   Reference: 2017 National Electrical Code – Chapter 4 Equipment for General Use, Article 402 Fixture Wires. 402.6 Minimum Size.1.

10. **Answer C.** only in the ungrounded circuit conductor.

    Three-way and four-way switches shall be wired so that all switching is done only in the ungrounded circuit conductor. Where in metal raceways or metal-armored cables, wiring between switches and outlets shall be in accordance with 300.20(A).

    Reference: 2017 National Electrical Code – Chapter 4 Equipment for General Use, Article 404 Switches. 404.2 Switch Connections. 404.2(A) Three-Way and Four-Way Switches.1.

11. **Answer A.** grounded

    Review the exception in this article.

    Switches or circuit breakers shall not disconnect the grounded conductor of a circuit.

    Exception: A switch or circuit breaker shall be permitted to disconnect a grounded circuit conductor where all circuit conductors are disconnected simultaneously, or where the device is arranged so that the grounded conductor cannot be disconnected until all the ungrounded conductors of the circuit have been disconnected.

    Reference: 2017 National Electrical Code – Chapter 4 Equipment for General Use, Article 404 Switches. 404.2 Switch Connections. 404.2(B) Grounded Conductors.1.

12. **Answer B.** unless installed as part of a listed tub or shower assembly

    Switches shall not be installed within tubs or shower spaces *unless installed as part of a listed tub or shower assembly.*

    Reference: 2017 National Electrical Code – Chapter 4 Equipment for General Use, Article 404 Switches. 404.4 Damp or Wet Locations. 404.4(C) Switches in Tub or Shower Spaces.1.

13. **Answer D.** 6 ft. 7 in.

    All switches and circuit breakers used as switches shall be located so that they may be operated from a readily accessible place. They shall be installed such that the center of the grip of the operating handle of the switch or circuit breaker, when in its highest position, *is not more than 2.0 m (6 ft. 7 in.) above the floor or working platform.*

    Reference: 2017 National Electrical Code – Chapter 4 Equipment for General Use, Article 404 Switches. 404.8 Accessibility and Grouping. 404.8(A) Location.1.

14. **Answer C.** 6 ft. 7 in.

    Review the three exceptions in this article.

    All switches and circuit breakers used as switches shall be located so that they may be operated from a readily accessible place. **They shall be installed such that the center of the grip of the operating handle of the switch or circuit breaker, when in its highest position, is not more than 2.0 m (6 ft. 7 in.) above the floor or working platform.**

    Exception No.1: On busway installations, fused switches and circuit breakers shall be permitted to be located at the same level as the busway. Suitable means shall be provided to operate the handle of the device from the floor.

    Exception No.2: Switches and circuit breakers installed adjacent to motors, appliances, or other equipment that they supply shall be permitted to be located higher than 2.0 m (6 ft. 7 in.) and to be accessible by portable means.

    Exception No.3: Hookstick operable isolating switches shall be permitted at greater heights.

    Reference: 2017 National Electrical Code – Chapter 4 Equipment for General Use, Article 404 Switches. 404.8 Accessibility and Grouping. 404.8(A) Location.1.

15. **Answer D.** 6 ft., 7 in.

    All switches and circuit breakers used as switches shall be located so that they may be operated from a readily accessible place. **They shall be installed such that the center of the grip of the operating handle of the switch or circuit breaker, when in its highest position, is not more than 2.0 m (6 ft. 7 in.) above the floor or working platform.**

    Reference: 2017 National Electrical Code – Chapter 4 Equipment for General Use, Article 404 Switches. 404.8 Accessibility and Grouping. 404.8(A) Location.1.

EXAM 8

EXAM 8 ANSWERS

16. **Answer C.** 300

    A snap switch shall not be grouped or ganged in enclosures with other snap switches, *receptacles, or similar devices, unless they are arranged so that the voltage between adjacent devices does not exceed 300 volts,* or unless they are installed in enclosures equipped with identified, securely installed barriers between adjacent devices.

    Reference: 2017 National Electrical Code – Chapter 4 Equipment for General Use, Article 404 Switches. 404.8 Accessibility and Grouping. 404.8(B) Voltage Between Adjacent Devices.1.

17. **Answer A.** True

    Snap switches, including dimmer and similar control switches, shall be connected to an equipment grounding conductor and shall provide a means to connect metal faceplates to the equipment grounding conductor, whether or not a metal faceplate is installed. Metal faceplates shall be grounded. Snap switches shall be considered to be part of an effective ground-fault current path if either of the following conditions is met:

    (1) The switch is mounted with metal screws to a metal box or metal cover that is connected to an equipment grounding conductor or to a nonmetallic box with integral means for connecting to an equipment grounding conductor.

    (2) An equipment grounding conductor or equipment bonding jumper is connected to an equipment grounding termination of the snap switch.

    Reference: 2017 National Electrical Code – Chapter 4 Equipment for General Use, Article 404 Switches. 404.9 Provisions for General-Use Snap Switches. 404.9(B) Grounding.1.

18. **Answer D.** the required number of poles

    A hand-operable circuit breaker equipped with a lever or handle, or a power-operated circuit breaker capable of being opened by hand in the event of a power failure, shall be permitted to serve as a switch if it has the required number of poles.

    Informational Note: See the provisions contained in 240.81 and 240.83.

    Reference: 2017 National Electrical Code – Chapter 4 Equipment for General Use, Article 404 Switches. 404.11 Circuit Breakers as Switches.1.

19. **Answer A.** 50%

    A form of general-use snap switch suitable for use on either ac or dc circuits for controlling the following:

    (1) Resistive loads not exceeding the ampere rating of the switch at the voltage applied.

    (2) *Inductive loads not exceeding 50 percent of the ampere rating of the switch at the applied voltage. Switches rated in horsepower are suitable for controlling motor loads within their rating at the voltage applied.*

    (3) Tungsten-filament lamp loads not exceeding the ampere rating of the switch at the applied voltage if T-rated.

    Reference: 2017 National Electrical Code – Chapter 4 Equipment for General Use, Article 404 Switches. 404.14 Rating and Use of Snap Switches. 404.14(B) Alternating-Current General-Use Snap Switch.1.

20. **Answer D.** incandescent

    General-use dimmer switches shall be used only to control permanently installed incandescent luminaires unless listed for the control of other loads and installed accordingly.

    Reference: 2017 National Electrical Code – Chapter 4 Equipment for General Use, Article 404 Switches. 404.14 Rating and Use of Snap Switches. 404.14(E) Dimmer Switches.1.

21. **Answer B.** incandescent luminaries

    General-use dimmer switches shall be used only to control *permanently installed incandescent luminaries unless listed for the control of other loads and installed accordingly.*

    Reference: 2017 National Electrical Code – Chapter 4 Equipment for General Use, Article 404 Switches. 404.14 Rating and Use of Snap Switches. . 404.14(E) Dimmer Switches.1.

22. **Answer C.** permanently installed incandescent luminaries

    General-use dimmer switches shall be used only to control *permanently installed incandescent luminaries unless listed for the control of other loads and installed accordingly.*

    Reference: 2017 National Electrical Code – Chapter 4 Equipment for General Use, Article 404 Switches. 404.14 Rating and Use of Snap Switches. 404.14(E) Dimmer Switches.1.

EXAM 8

EXAM 8 ANSWERS

23. Answer B. 15

Receptacles and cord connectors shall be rated not less than 15 amperes, 125 volts, or 15 amperes, 250 volts, and shall be of a type not suitable for use as lampholders.

Informational Note: See 210.21(B) for receptacle ratings where installed on branch circuits.

Reference: 2017 National Electrical Code – Chapter 4 Equipment for General Use, Article 406 Receptacles, Cord Connectors, and Attachment Plugs. 406.3 Receptacle Rating and Type. 406.3(B) Rating.1.

24. Answer D. CO/ALR

Receptacles rated 20 amperes or less and designed for the direct connection of aluminum conductors shall be marked CO/ALR.

Reference: 2017 National Electrical Code – Chapter 4 Equipment for General Use, Article 406 Receptacles, Cord Connectors, and Attachment Plugs. 406.3 Receptacle Rating and Type. 406.3(C) Receptacles for Aluminum Conductors.1.

25. Answer B. orange

Receptacles incorporating an isolated grounding conductor connection intended for the reduction of electrical noise (electromagnetic interference) as permitted in 250.146(D) *shall be identified by an orange triangle located on the face of the receptacle.*

Reference: 2017 National Electrical Code – Chapter 4 Equipment for General Use, Article 406 Receptacles, Cord Connectors, and Attachment Plugs. 406.3 Receptacle Rating and Type. 406.3(D) Isolated Ground Receptacles.1.

26. Answer B. grounding

Except as provided in 406.4(D), receptacles installed on 15- and 20-ampere branch circuits shall be of the grounding type. Grounding-type receptacles shall be installed only on circuits of the voltage class and current for which they are rated, except as provided in Table 210.21(B)(2) and Table 210.21(B)(3).

Reference: 2017 National Electrical Code – Chapter 4 Equipment for General Use, Article 406 Receptacles, Cord Connectors, and Attachment Plugs. 406.4 General Installation Requirements. 406.4(A) Grounding Type.1.

27. Answer A. face-up

Receptacles shall not be installed in a face-up position in or on countertop surfaces or work surfaces unless listed for countertop or work surface applications.

Reference: 2017 National Electrical Code – Chapter 4 Equipment for General Use, Article 406 Receptacles, Cord Connectors, and Attachment Plugs. 406.5 Receptacle Mounting. 406.5(G) Receptacle Orientation. 1.

EXAM 8

EXAM 8 ANSWERS

28. **Answer B.** covered

    A receptacle installed outdoors in a location protected from the weather or in other damp locations shall have an enclosure for the receptacle that is weatherproof when the receptacle is covered (attachment plug cap not inserted and receptacle covers closed).

    An installation suitable for wet locations shall also be considered suitable for damp locations.

    A receptacle shall be considered to be in a location protected from the weather where located under roofed open porches, canopies, marquees, and the like, and will not be subjected to a beating rain or water runoff. All 15- and 20-ampere, 125- and 250-volt non locking receptacles shall be a listed weather-resistant type.

    Informational Note: The types of receptacles covered by this requirement are identified as 5-15, 5-20, 6-15, and 6-20 in ANSI/

    NEMA WD 6–2012, Wiring Devices — Dimensional Specifications.

    Reference: 2017 National Electrical Code – Chapter 4 Equipment for General Use, Article 406 Receptacles, Cord Connectors, and Attachment Plugs. 406.9 Receptacles in Damp or Wet Locations. . 406.9(A) Damp Locations.1.

29. **Answer B.** damp

    A receptacle installed outdoors in a location protected from the weather or in other damp locations shall have an enclosure for the receptacle that is weatherproof when the receptacle is covered (attachment plug cap not inserted and receptacle covers closed).

    An installation suitable for wet locations shall also be considered suitable for damp locations.

    A receptacle shall be considered to be in a location protected from the weather where located under roofed open porches, canopies, marquees, and the like, and will not be subjected to a beating rain or water runoff. All 15- and 20-ampere, 125- and 250-volt non locking receptacles shall be a listed weather-resistant type.

    Informational Note: The types of receptacles covered by this requirement are identified as 5-15, 5-20, 6-15, and 6-20 in ANSI/

    NEMA WD 6–2012, Wiring Devices — Dimensional Specifications.

    Reference: 2017 National Electrical Code – Chapter 4 Equipment for General Use, Article 406 Receptacles, Cord Connectors, and Attachment Plugs. 406.9 Receptacles in Damp or Wet Locations. . 406.9(A) Damp Locations.1.

30. **Answer D.** weatherproof

    Receptacles of 15 and 20 amperes, 125 and 250 volts installed in a wet location shall have an enclosure that is weatherproof whether or not the attachment plug cap is inserted. An outlet box hood installed for this purpose shall be listed and shall be identified as "extra-duty." Other listed products, enclosures, or assemblies providing weatherproof protection that do not utilize an outlet box hood need not be marked "extra duty."

    Informational Note No. 1: Requirements for extra-duty outlet box hoods are found in ANSI/UL 514D–2013, Cover Plates for Flush-Mounted Wiring Devices. "Extra duty" identification and requirements are not applicable to listed receptacles, faceplates, outlet boxes, enclosures, or assemblies that are identified as either being suitable for wet locations or rated as one of the outdoor enclosure–type numbers of Table 110.28 that does not utilize an outlet box hood.

    Exception: 15- and 20-ampere, 125- through 250-volt receptacles installed in a wet location and subject to routine high-pressure spray washing shall be permitted to have an enclosure that is weatherproof when the attachment plug is removed.

    All 15- and 20-ampere, 125- and 250-volt non locking-type receptacles shall be listed and so identified as the weather resistant type.

    Informational Note No. 2: The configuration of weather resistant receptacles covered by this requirement are identified as 5-15, 5-20, 6-15, and 6-20 in ANSI/NEMA WD 6–2012, Wiring Devices — Dimensional Specifications.

    Reference: 2017 National Electrical Code – Chapter 4 Equipment for General Use, Article 406 Receptacles, Cord Connectors, and Attachment Plugs. 406.9 Receptacles in Damp or Wet Locations. 406.9(B) Wet Locations. 406.9(B)(1) Receptacles of 15 and 20 Amperes in a Wet Location.1.

31. **Answer B.** bathtub or shower stall

    Receptacles shall not be installed within or directly over a bathtub or shower stall.

    Reference: 2017 National Electrical Code – Chapter 4 Equipment for General Use, Article 406 Receptacles, Cord Connectors, and Attachment Plugs. 406.9 Receptacles in Damp or Wet Locations. 406.9(C) Bathtub and Shower Space.1.

EXAM 8

EXAM 8 ANSWERS

32. Answer D. not be used for purposes other than grounding

A grounding terminal shall not be used for purposes other than grounding.

Reference: 2017 National Electrical Code – Chapter 4 Equipment for General Use, Article 406 Receptacles, Cord Connectors, and Attachment Plugs. 406.10 Grounding-Type Receptacles, Adapters, Cord Connectors, and Attachment Plugs. 406.10(C) Grounding Terminal Use.1.

33. Answer A. higher

Alternating-current phase arrangement on 3-phase buses shall be A, B, C from front to back, top to bottom, or left to right, as viewed from the front of the switchboard, switchgear, or panelboard. *The B phase shall be that phase having the higher voltage to ground on 3-phase, 4-wire, delta-connected systems.* Other busbar arrangements shall be permitted for additions to existing installations and shall be marked.

Exception: Equipment within the same single section or multi section switchboard, switchgear, or panelboard as the meter on 3-phase, 4-wire, delta-connected systems shall be permitted to have the same phase configuration as the metering equipment.

Informational Note: See 110.15 for requirements on marking the busbar or phase conductor having the higher voltage to ground where supplied from a 4-wire, delta-connected system.

Reference: 2017 National Electrical Code – Chapter 4 Equipment for General Use, Article 408 Switchboards, Switchgear, and Panelboards. 408.3 Support and Arrangement of Busbars and Conductors. 408.3(E) Bus Arrangement. 408.3(E)(1) AC Phase Arrangement1.

34. Answer B. 3

Where conduits or other raceways enter a switchboard, switchgear, floor-standing panelboard, or similar enclosure at the bottom, approved space shall be provided to permit installation of conductors in the enclosure. The wiring space shall not be less than shown in Table 408.5 where the conduit or raceways enter or leave the enclosure below the bus bars, their supports, or other obstructions. *The conduit or raceways, including their end fittings, shall not rise more than 75 mm (3 in.) above the bottom of the enclosure.*

Reference: 2017 National Electrical Code – Chapter 4 Equipment for General Use, Article 408 Switchboards, Switchgear, and Panelboards. 408.5 Clearance for Conductor Entering Bus Enclosures.1.

35. Answer C. the switchboard is totally enclosed

For other than a totally enclosed switchboard or switchgear, a space not less than 900 mm (3 ft.) shall be provided between the top of the switchboard or switchgear and any combustible ceiling, unless a noncombustible shield is provided between the switchboard or switchgear and the ceiling.

Reference: 2017 National Electrical Code – Chapter 4 Equipment for General Use, Article 408 Switchboards, Switchgear, and Panelboards. 408.18 Clearances. 408.18(A) From Ceiling.1.

EXAM 8

EXAM 8 ANSWERS

36. **Answer A.** True

Switchboards and switchgear that have any exposed live parts shall be located in permanently dry locations and then only where under competent supervision and accessible only to qualified persons. Switchboards and switchgear shall be located such that the probability of damage from equipment or processes is reduced to a minimum.

Reference: 2017 National Electrical Code – Chapter 4 Equipment for General Use, Article 408 Switchboards, Switchgear, and Panelboards. 408.20 Location of Switchboards.1.

37. **Answer A.** existing panelboards used for single-family service equipment

In addition to the requirement of 408.30, a panelboard shall be protected by an overcurrent protective device having a rating not greater than that of the panelboard. This overcurrent protective device shall be located within or at any point on the supply side of the panelboard.

Exception No.1: Individual protection shall not be required for a panelboard used as service equipment with multiple disconnecting means in accordance with 230.71. In panelboards protected by three or more main circuit breakers or sets of fuses, the circuit breakers or sets of fuses shall not supply a second bus structure within the same panelboard assembly.

Exception No.2: Individual protection shall not be required for a panelboard protected on its supply side by two main circuit breakers or two sets of fuses having a combined rating not greater than that of the panelboard. A panelboard constructed or wired under this exception shall not contain more than 42 overcurrent devices. For the purposes of determining the maximum of 42 overcurrent devices, a 2-pole or a 3-pole circuit breaker shall be considered as two or three overcurrent devices, respectively.

Exception 3: For existing panelboards, individual protection shall not be required for a panelboard used as service equipment for an individual residential occupancy.

Reference: 2017 National Electrical Code – Chapter 4 Equipment for General Use, Article 408 Switchboards, Switchgear, and Panelboards. 408.36 Overcurrent Protection. Exception 31.

38. **Answer C.** individual

Each grounded conductor shall terminate within the panelboard in an individual terminal that is not also used f2or another conductor.

Reference: 2017 National Electrical Code – Chapter 4 Equipment for General Use, Article 408 Switchboards, Switchgear, and Panelboards. 408.41 Grounded Conductor Terminations.1.

EXAM 8 ANSWERS

EXAM 8

EXAM 8 ANSWERS

Table 408.56 Minimum Spacings Between Bare Metal Parts

AC or DC Voltage	Opposite Polarity Where Mounted on the Same Surface		Opposite Polarity Where Held Free in Air		Live Parts to Ground*	
	mm	in.	mm	in.	mm	in.
Not over 125 volts, nominal	19.1	¾	12.7	½	12.7	½
Not over 250 volts, nominal	31.8	1¼	19.1	¾	12.7	½
Not over 1000 volts, nominal	50.8	2	25.4	1	25.4	1

*For spacing between live parts and doors of cabinets, see 312.11(A) (1), (2), and (3).

Table 408.46 see Table 408-45 file in Tables folder on CD-ROM

39. **Answer B.** 1/2 inch

The distance between bare metal parts, busbars, and so forth shall not be less than specified in **Table 408.56**.

Where close proximity does not cause excessive heating, parts of the same polarity at switches, enclosed fuses, and so forth shall be permitted to be placed as close together as convenience in handling will allow.

Reference: 2017 National Electrical Code – Chapter 4 Equipment for General Use, Article 408 Switchboards, Switchgear, and Panelboards. 408.56 Minimum Spacings. Table 408.56 Minimum Spacings Between Bare Metal Parts (page 70-290)1.

40. **Answer C.** required to be the "B" phase

The phase arrangement on 3-phase horizontal common power and vertical buses shall be A, B, C from front to back, top to bottom, or left to right, as viewed from the front of the industrial control panel. *The B phase shall be that phase having the higher voltage to ground on 3-phase, 4-wire, delta-connected systems*. Other busbar arrangements shall be permitted for additions to existing installations, and the phases shall be permanently marked.

Reference: 2017 National Electrical Code – Chapter 4 Equipment for General Use, Article 409 Industrial Control Panels. 409.102 Busbars and Conductors. 409.102(B) Phase Arrangement.1.

EXAM 8

EXAM 8 ANSWERS

41. **Answer B.** 3, 8

    No parts of cord-connected luminaires, chain-, cable-, or cord-suspended luminaires, lighting track, pendants, or ceiling-suspended (paddle) fans shall be located within a zone measured 900 mm (3 ft.) horizontally and 2.5 m (8 ft.) vertically from the top of the bathtub rim or shower stall threshold. This zone is all encompassing and includes the space directly over the tub or shower stall. Luminaires located within the actual outside dimension of the bathtub or shower to a height of 2.5 m (8 ft.) vertically from the top of the bathtub rim or shower threshold shall be marked for damp locations, or marked for wet locations where subject to shower spray.

    Reference: 2017 National Electrical Code – Chapter 4 Equipment for General Use, Article 410 Luminaires, Lampholders, and Lamps. 410.10 Luminaires in Specific Locations. 410.10(D) Bathtub and Shower Areas.1.

42. **Answer A.** 3, 8

    No parts of cord-connected luminaires, chain-, cable-, or cord-suspended luminaires, lighting track, pendants, or ceiling-suspended (paddle) fans shall be located within *a zone measured 900 mm (3 ft.) horizontally and 2.5 m (8 ft.) vertically from the top of the bathtub rim or shower stall threshold. This zone is all encompassing and includes the space directly over the tub or shower stall.* Luminaires located within the actual outside dimension of the bathtub or shower to a height of 2.5 m (8 ft.) vertically from the top of the bathtub rim or shower threshold shall be marked for damp locations, or marked for wet locations where subject to shower spray.

    Reference: 2017 National Electrical Code – Chapter 4 Equipment for General Use, Article 410 Luminaires, Lampholders, and Lamps. 410.10 Luminaires in Specific Locations. 410.10(D) Bathtub and Shower Areas.1.

43. **Answer B.** 12

    The minimum clearance between luminaires installed in clothes closets and the nearest point of a closet storage space shall be as follows:

    (1) 300 mm (12 in.) for surface-mounted incandescent or LED luminaires with a completely enclosed light source installed on the wall above the door or on the ceiling.

    (2) 150 mm (6 in.) for surface-mounted fluorescent luminaires installed on the wall above the door or on the ceiling.

    (3) 150 mm (6 in.) for recessed incandescent or LED luminaires with a completely enclosed light source installed in the wall or the ceiling.

    (4) 150 mm (6 in.) for recessed fluorescent luminaires installed in the wall or the ceiling.

    (5) Surface-mounted fluorescent or LED luminaires shall be permitted to be installed within the closet storage space where identified for this use.

    Reference: 2017 National Electrical Code – Chapter 4 Equipment for General Use, Article 410 Luminaires, Lampholders, and Lamps. 410.16 Luminaires in Clothes Closets. 410.16(C) Location.1.

44. **Answer C.** 12 inches

    The minimum clearance between luminaires installed in clothes closets and the nearest point of a closet storage space shall be as follows:

    (1) 300 mm (12 in.) for surface-mounted incandescent or LED luminaires with a completely enclosed light source installed on the wall above the door or on the ceiling.

    (2) 150 mm (6 in.) for surface-mounted fluorescent luminaires installed on the wall above the door or on the ceiling.

    (3) 150 mm (6 in.) for recessed incandescent or LED luminaires with a completely enclosed light source installed in the wall or the ceiling.

    (4) 150 mm (6 in.) for recessed fluorescent luminaires installed in the wall or the ceiling.

    (5) Surface-mounted fluorescent or LED luminaires shall be permitted to be installed within the closet storage space where identified for this use.

    Reference: 2017 National Electrical Code – Chapter 4 Equipment for General Use, Article 410 Luminaires, Lampholders, and Lamps. 410.16 Luminaires in Clothes Closets. 410.16(C) Location.1.

EXAM 8

EXAM 8 ANSWERS

45. **Answer A.** 6

    Luminaires and lampholders shall be securely supported. A luminaire that weighs more than 3 kg (6 lb.) or exceeds 400 mm (16 in.) in any dimension shall not be supported by the screw shell of a lampholder.

    Reference: 2017 National Electrical Code – Chapter 4 Equipment for General Use, Article 410 Luminaires, Lampholders, and Lamps. 410.30 Supports. 410.30(A) General.1.

46. **Answer D.** 36 inches

    Pendant conductors longer than 900 mm (3 ft.) shall be twisted together where not cabled in a listed assembly.

    Reference: 2017 National Electrical Code – Chapter 4 Equipment for General Use, Article 410 Luminaires, Lampholders, and Lamps. 410.54 Pendant Conductors for Incandescent Filament Lamps. 410.54(C) Twisted or Cabled.1.

47. **Answer D.** Stranded

    Stranded conductors shall be used for wiring on luminaire chains and on other movable or flexible parts.

    Reference: 2017 National Electrical Code – Chapter 4 Equipment for General Use, Article 410 Luminaires, Lampholders, and Lamps. 410.56 Protection of Conductors and Insulation. 410.56(E) Stranding.1.

48. **Answer C.** Where the flexible cord is visible for its entire length.

    A luminaire or a listed assembly in compliance with any of the conditions in (a) through (c) **shall be permitted** to be cord connected provided the luminaire is located directly below the outlet or busway, the cord is not subject to strain or physical damage, and the **cord is visible over its entire length except at terminations.**

    (a) A luminaire shall be permitted to be connected with a cord terminating in a grounding-type attachment plug or busway plug.

    (b) A luminaire assembly equipped with a strain relief and canopy shall be permitted to use a cord connection between the luminaire assembly and the canopy. The canopy shall be permitted to include a section of raceway not over 150 mm (6 in.) in length and intended to facilitate the connection to an outlet box mounted above a suspended ceiling.

    (c) Listed luminaires connected using listed assemblies that incorporate manufactured wiring system connectors in accordance with 604.100(C) shall be permitted to be cord connected.

    Reference: 2017 National Electrical Code – Chapter 4 Equipment for General Use, Article 410 Luminaires, Lampholders, and Lamps. 410.62 Cord-Connected Lampholders and Luminaires. 410.62(C) Electric-Discharge and LED Luminaires. 410.62(C)(1) Cord-Connected Installation.1.

49. **Answer C.** raceway

    Luminaires shall not be used as a raceway for circuit conductors unless they comply with 410.64(A), (B), or (C).

    Reference: 2017 National Electrical Code – Chapter 4 Equipment for General Use, Article 410 Luminaires, Lampholders, and Lamps. 410.64 Luminaries as Raceways.1.

50. **Answer C.** 90°C

    Feeder and branch-circuit conductors within 75 mm (3 in.) of a ballast, LED driver, power supply, or transformer shall have an insulation temperature rating not lower than 90°C (194°F), unless supplying a luminaire marked as suitable for a different insulation temperature.

    Reference: 2017 National Electrical Code – Chapter 4 Equipment for General Use, Article 410 Luminaires, Lampholders, and Lamps. 410.68 Feeder and Branch-Circuit Conductors and Ballasts.1.

EXAM 8

EXAM 8 ANSWERS

Moisture- and heat-resistant thermoplastic	THW	75°C (167°F) 90°C (194°F)	Dry and wet locations Special applications within electric discharge lighting equipment. Limited to 1000 open-circuit volts or less. (Size 14-8 only as permitted in 410.68.)	Flame-retardant, moisture- and heat-resistant thermoplastic	14–10 8 6–2 1–4/0 213–500 501–1000 1001–2000	0.76 1.14 1.52 2.03 2.41 2.79 3.18	30 45 60 80 95 110 125	None
	THW-2	90°C (194°F)	Dry and wet locations					

Table 310.104(A) see Table 310-104-A in Tables folder on CD-ROM

51. Answer A. THW

Feeder and branch-circuit conductors within 75 mm (3 in.) of a ballast, LED driver, power supply, or transformer shall have an insulation temperature rating not lower than 90°C (194°F), unless supplying a luminaire marked as suitable for a different insulation temperature.

Reference: 2017 National Electrical Code – Chapter 4 Equipment for General Use, Article 410 Luminaires, Lampholders, and Lamps. 410.68 Feeder and Branch-Circuit Conductors and Ballasts.

Reference: 2017 National Electrical Code – Chapter 3 Wiring Methods and Materials, Article 310 Conductors for General Wiring. 310.104 Conductor Constructions and Applications. Table 310.104(A) Conductor Applications and Insulations Rated 600 Volts (page 70-175)1.

52. Answer D. screw shell

Lampholders of the screw shell type shall be installed for use as lampholders only. Where supplied by a circuit having a grounded conductor, the grounded conductor shall be connected to the screw shell.

Reference: 2017 National Electrical Code – Chapter 4 Equipment for General Use, Article 410 Luminaires, Lampholders, and Lamps. 410.90 Screw Shell Type.1.

53. Answer B. 1/2 in.

A recessed luminaire that is not identified for contact with insulation shall have all recessed parts spaced not less than 13 mm (1/2 in.) from combustible materials. The points of support and the trim finishing off the openings in the ceiling, wall, or other finished surface shall be permitted to be in contact with combustible materials.

Reference: 2017 National Electrical Code – Chapter 4 Equipment for General Use, Article 410 Luminaires, Lampholders, and Lamps. 410.116 Clearance and Installation. 410.116(A) Clearance. 410.116(A)(1) Non-Type IC.1.

54. Answer B. 3

Thermal insulation shall not be installed above a recessed luminaire or within 75 mm (3 in.) of the recessed luminaire's enclosure, wiring compartment, ballast, transformer, LED driver, or power supply unless the luminaire is identified as Type IC for insulation contact.

Reference: 2017 National Electrical Code – Chapter 4 Equipment for General Use, Article 410 Luminaires, Lampholders, and Lamps. 410.116 Clearance and Installation. 410.116(B) Installation.1.

55. Answer A. 18 inches

Tap conductors of a type suitable for the temperature encountered shall be permitted to run from the luminaire terminal connection to an outlet box placed at least 300 mm (1 ft.) from the luminaire. *Such tap conductors shall be in suitable raceway or Type AC or MC cable of at least 450 mm (18 in.)* but not more than 1.8 m (6 ft.) in length.

Reference: 2017 National Electrical Code – Chapter 4 Equipment for General Use, Article 410 Luminaires, Lampholders, and Lamps. 410.117 Wiring. 410.117(C) Tap Conductors.1.

56. Answer A. No solder shall be

No solder shall be used in the construction of a luminaire recessed housing.

Reference: 2017 National Electrical Code – Chapter 4 Equipment for General Use, Article 410 Luminaires, Lampholders, and Lamps. 410.121 Solder Prohibited.1.

EXAM 8

EXAM 8 ANSWERS

57. Answer A. Disconnecting simultaneously breaks all conductors to branch circuit.

(1) General. In indoor locations other than dwellings and associated accessory structures, fluorescent luminaires that utilize double-ended lamps and contain ballast(s) that can be serviced in place shall have a disconnecting means either internal or external to each luminaire. For existing installed luminaires without disconnecting means, at the time a ballast is replaced, a disconnecting means shall be installed. The line side terminals of the disconnecting means shall be guarded.

Exception No. 1: A disconnecting means shall not be required for luminaires installed in hazardous (classified) location(s).

Exception No. 2: A disconnecting means shall not be required for luminaires that provide emergency illumination required in 700.16.

Exception No. 3: For cord-and-plug-connected luminaires, an accessible separable connector or an accessible plug and receptacle shall be permitted to serve as the disconnecting means.

Exception No. 4: Where more than one luminaire is installed and supplied by other than a multi wire branch circuit, a disconnecting means shall not be required for every luminaire when the design of the installation includes disconnecting means, such that the illuminated space cannot be left in total darkness.

(2) Multi wire Branch Circuits. *When connected to multi wire branch circuits, the disconnecting means shall simultaneously break all the supply conductors to the ballast, including the grounded conductor.*

(3) Location. The disconnecting means shall be located so as to be accessible to qualified persons before servicing or maintaining the ballast. Where the disconnecting means is external to the luminaire, it shall be a single device, and shall be attached to the luminaire or the luminaire shall be located within sight of the disconnecting means.

Reference: 2017 National Electrical Code – Chapter 4 Equipment for General Use, Article 410 Luminaires, Lampholders, and Lamps. 410.130 General. 410.130(G) Disconnecting Means.1.

58. Answer D. 1-1/2 in.

Where a surface-mounted luminaire containing a ballast, transformer, LED driver, or power supply is to be installed on combustible low-density cellulose fiberboard, *it shall be marked for this condition or shall be spaced not less than 38 mm (1 1/2 in.) from the surface of the fiberboard.* Where such luminaires are partially or wholly recessed, the provisions of 410.110 through 410.122 shall apply.

Informational Note: Combustible low-density cellulose fiberboard includes sheets, panels, and tiles that have a density of 320 kg/m3 (20 lb/ft3) or less and that are formed of bonded plant fiber material but does not include solid or laminated wood or fiberboard that has a density in excess of 320 kg/m3 (20 lb/ft3) or is a material that has been integrally treated with fire-retarding chemicals to the degree that the flame spread index in any plane of the material will not exceed 25, determined in accordance with tests for surface burning characteristics of building materials. See ANSI/ASTM E84–2015a, Standard Test Method for Surface Burning Characteristics of Building Materials or ANSI/UL 723–2013, Standard for Test for Surface Burning Characteristics of Building Materials.

Reference: 2017 National Electrical Code – Chapter 4 Equipment for General Use, Article 410 Luminaires, Lampholders, and Lamps. 410.136 Luminaire Mounting. 410.136(B) Combustible Low-Density Cellulose Fiberboard.1.

59. Answer C. 1000

Equipment that has an open-circuit voltage exceeding 1000 volts shall not be installed in or on dwelling occupancies.

Reference: 2017 National Electrical Code – Chapter 4 Equipment for General Use, Article 410 Luminaires, Lampholders, and Lamps. 410.140 General. 410.140(B) Dwelling Occupancies.1.

EXAM 8

EXAM 8 ANSWERS

60. **Answer D.** None of the above.

    Lighting track shall not be installed in the following locations:

    (1) Where likely to be subjected to physical damage

    (2) In wet or damp locations

    (3) Where subject to corrosive vapors

    (4) In storage battery rooms

    (5) In hazardous (classified) locations

    (6) Where concealed

    (7) Where extended through walls or partitions

    (8) Less than 1.5 m (5 ft.) above the finished floor except where protected from physical damage or track operating at less than 30 volts rms open-circuit voltage

    (9) Where prohibited by 410.10(D)

    Reference: 2017 National Electrical Code – Chapter 4 Equipment for General Use, Article 410 Luminaires, Lampholders, and Lamps. 410.151 Installation. 410.151(C) Locations Not Permitted.1.

61. **Answer B.** 20

    Heavy-duty lighting track is lighting track identified for use exceeding 20 amperes. Each fitting attached to a heavy-duty lighting track shall have individual overcurrent protection.

    Reference: 2017 National Electrical Code – Chapter 4 Equipment for General Use, Article 410 Luminaires, Lampholders, and Lamps. 410.153 Heavy-Duty Lighting Track.1.

62. **Answer A.** two

    Lighting track shall be securely mounted so that each fastening is suitable for supporting the maximum weight of luminaires that can be installed. Unless identified for supports at greater intervals, *a single section 1.2 m (4 ft.) or shorter in length shall have two supports*, and, where installed in a continuous row, each individual section of not more than 1.2 m (4 ft.) in length shall have one additional support.

    Reference: 2017 National Electrical Code – Chapter 4 Equipment for General Use, Article 410 Luminaires, Lampholders, and Lamps. 410.154 Fastening.1.

63. **Answer A.** 3 m (10 ft.)

    Lighting systems shall be installed not less than 3 m (10 ft.) horizontally from the nearest edge of the water, unless permitted by Article 680.

    Reference: 2017 National Electrical Code – Chapter 4 Equipment for General Use, Article 411 Lighting Systems Operating at 30 Volts or Less and Lighting Equipment Connected to Class-2 Power Sources. 411.5 Specific Location Requirements. 411.5(B) Pools, Spas, Fountains, and Similar Locations.1.

64. **Answer B.** 125

    The rating of an individual branch circuit shall not be less than the marked rating of the appliance or the marked rating of an appliance having combined loads as provided in 422.62.

    The rating of an individual branch circuit for motor-operated appliances not having a marked rating shall be in accordance with Part II of Article 430.

    The branch-circuit rating for an appliance that is a continuous load, other than a motor-operated appliance, shall not be less than 125 percent of the marked rating, or not less than 100 percent of the marked rating if the branch-circuit device and its assembly are listed for continuous loading at 100 percent of its rating.

    Branch circuits and branch-circuit conductors for household ranges and cooking appliances shall be permitted to be in accordance with Table 220.55 and shall be sized in accordance with 210.19(A)(3).

    Reference: 2017 National Electrical Code – Chapter 4 Equipment for General Use, Article 422 Appliances. 422.10 Branch-Circuit Rating. . 422.10(A) Individual Circuits.1.

EXAM 8

EXAM 8 ANSWERS

65. **Answer C.** 125%

    The rating of an individual branch circuit shall not be less than the marked rating of the appliance or the marked rating of an appliance having combined loads as provided in 422.62.

    The rating of an individual branch circuit for motor-operated appliances not having a marked rating shall be in accordance with Part II of Article 430.

    The branch-circuit rating for an appliance that is a continuous load, other than a motor-operated appliance, shall not be less than 125 percent of the marked rating, or not less than 100 percent of the marked rating if the branch-circuit device and its assembly are listed for continuous loading at 100 percent of its rating.

    Branch circuits and branch-circuit conductors for household ranges and cooking appliances shall be permitted to be in accordance with Table 220.55 and shall be sized in accordance with 210.19(A)(3).

    Reference: 2017 National Electrical Code – Chapter 4 Equipment for General Use, Article 422 Appliances. 422.10 Branch-Circuit Rating. 422.10(A) Individual Circuits.

    A fixed storage-type water heater that has a capacity of 450 L (120 gal) or less shall be *considered a continuous load for the purposes of sizing branch circuits.*

    Informational Note: For branch-circuit rating, see 422.10.

    Reference: 2017 National Electrical Code – Chapter 4 Equipment for General Use, Article 422 Appliances. 422.13 Storage-Type Water Heaters.1.

66. **Answer D.** 60 amperes

    Household-type appliances with surface heating elements having a maximum demand of more than 60 amperes calculated in accordance with Table 220.55 shall have their power supply subdivided into two or more circuits, each of which shall be provided with overcurrent protection rated at not over 50 amperes.

    Reference: 2017 National Electrical Code – Chapter 4 Equipment for General Use, Article 422 Appliances. 422.11 Overcurrent Protection. 422.11(B) Household-Type Appliances with Surface Heating Elements.1.

67. **Answer C.** 50 amperes

    Infrared lamp commercial and industrial heating appliances shall have overcurrent protection not exceeding 50 amperes.

    Reference: 2017 National Electrical Code – Chapter 4 Equipment for General Use, Article 422 Appliances. 422.11 Overcurrent Protection. 422.11(C) Infrared Lamp Commercial and Industrial Heating Appliances.1.

68. **Answer D.** Where selected overcurrent protection is not a standard size.

    If the branch circuit supplies a single non-motor-operated appliance, the rating of overcurrent protection shall comply with the following:

    (1) Not exceed that marked on the appliance.

    (2) Not exceed 20 amperes if the overcurrent protection rating is not marked and the appliance is rated 13.3 amperes or less; or

    (3) Not exceed 150 percent of the appliance rated current if the overcurrent protection rating is not marked and the appliance is rated over 13.3 amperes. *Where 150 percent of the appliance rating does not correspond to a standard overcurrent device ampere rating, the next higher standard rating shall be permitted.*

    Reference: 2017 National Electrical Code – Chapter 4 Equipment for General Use, Article 422 Appliances. 422.11 Overcurrent Protection. 422.11(E) Single Non-Motor-Operated Appliance.1.

EXAM 8
EXAM 8 ANSWERS

69. Answer B. The length of time the appliance operates.

Not exceed 150 percent of the appliance rated current if the overcurrent protection rating is not marked and the appliance is rated over 13.3 amperes. Where 150 percent of the appliance rating does not correspond to a standard overcurrent device ampere rating, the next higher standard rating shall be permitted.

Reference: 2017 National Electrical Code – Chapter 4 Equipment for General Use, Article 422 Appliances. 422.11 Overcurrent Protection. 422.11(E) Single Non-Motor-Operated Appliances. 422.11(E)(3)1.

70. Answer C. 30 amperes

(3) Not exceed 150 percent of the appliance rated current if the overcurrent protection rating is not marked and the appliance is rated over 13.3 amperes. Where 150 percent of the appliance rating does not correspond to a standard overcurrent device ampere rating, the next higher standard rating shall be permitted.

Reference: 2017 National Electrical Code – Chapter 4 Equipment for General Use, Article 422 Appliances. 422.11 Overcurrent Protection. 422.11(E) Single Non-Motor-Operated Appliance. 422.11(E)(3)

Single-Phase Current Formula

$I = P \div E$ $I = 4500 \text{ VA} \div 240 \text{ V} = 18.75 \text{ amps} \times 150\% = 28.1 \text{ amperes}$

*NOTE: The next size circuit breaker with a rating of 30 amperes should be selected.*1.

The standard ampere ratings for fuses and inverse time circuit breakers shall be considered 15, 20, 25, 30, 35, 40, 45, 50, 60, 70, 80, 90, 100, 110, 125, 150, 175, 200, 225, 250, 300, 350, 400, 450, 500, 600, 700, 800, 1000, 1200, 1600, 2000, 2500, 3000, 4000, 5000, and 6000 amperes. Additional standard ampere ratings for fuses shall be 1, 3, 6, 10, and 601. The use of fuses and inverse time circuit breakers with nonstandard ampere ratings shall be permitted.

Reference: 2017 National Electrical Code – Chapter 2 Wiring and Protection, Article 240 Overcurrent Protection. 240.6 Standard Ampere Ratings. 240.6(A) Fuses and Fixed-Trip Circuit Breakers.

71. Answer D. supplied from an individual branch circuit

Central heating equipment other than fixed electric space-heating equipment shall be supplied by an individual branch circuit.

Exception No. 1: Auxiliary equipment, such as a pump, valve, humidifier, or electrostatic air cleaner directly associated with the heating equipment, shall be permitted to be connected to the same branch circuit.

Exception No. 2: Permanently connected air-conditioning equipment shall be permitted to be connected to the same branch circuit.

Reference: 2017 National Electrical Code – Chapter 4 Equipment for General Use, Article 422 Appliances. 422.12 Central Heating Equipment.1.

72. Answer C. 18, 36

Electrically operated in-sink waste disposers shall be permitted to be cord and- plug-connected with a flexible cord identified as suitable in the installation instructions of the appliance manufacturer where all of the following conditions are met:

(1) The flexible cord shall be terminated with a grounding type attachment plug.

Exception: A listed in-sink waste disposer distinctly marked to identify it as protected by a system of double insulation shall not be required to be terminated with a grounding-type attachment plug.

(2) The length of the cord shall not be less than 450 mm (18 in.) and not over 900 mm (36 in.).

(3) Receptacles shall be located to protect against physical damage to the flexible cord.

(4) The receptacle shall be accessible.

Reference: 2017 National Electrical Code – Chapter 4 Equipment for General Use, Article 422 Appliances. 422.16 Flexible Cords. 422.16(B) Specific Appliances. 422.16(B)(1) Electrically Operated In-Sink Waste Disposers. (2) 1.

EXAM 8

EXAM 8 ANSWERS

73. Answer A. 18, 36

Electrically operated in-sink waste disposers shall be permitted to be cord and- plug-connected with a flexible cord identified as suitable in the installation instructions of the *appliance manufacturer where all of the following conditions are met:*

(1) The flexible cord shall be terminated with a grounding type attachment plug.

Exception: A listed in-sink waste disposer distinctly marked to identify it as protected by a system of double insulation shall not be required to be terminated with a grounding-type attachment plug.

(2) The length of the cord shall not be less than 450 mm (18 in.) and not over 900 mm (36 in.).

(3) Receptacles shall be located to protect against physical damage to the flexible cord.

(4) The receptacle shall be accessible.

Reference: 2017 National Electrical Code – Chapter 4 Equipment for General Use, Article 422 Appliances. 422.16 Flexible Cords. 422.16(B) Specific Appliances. 422.16(B)(1) Electrically Operated In-Sink Waste Disposers.1.

74. Answer D. 3, 4

Built-in dishwashers and trash compactors shall be permitted to be cord and- plug-connected with a flexible cord identified as suitable for the purpose in the installation instructions of the appliance manufacturer where all of the following conditions are met:

(1) The flexible cord shall be terminated with a grounding type attachment plug.

Exception: A listed dishwasher or trash compactor distinctly marked to identify it as protected by a system of double insulation shall not be required to be terminated with a grounding-type attachment plug.

(2) For a trash compactor, the length of the cord shall be 0.9 m to 1.2 m (3 ft to 4 ft) measured from the face of the attachment plug to the plane of the rear of the appliance.

(3) For a built-in dishwasher, the length of the cord shall be 0.9 m to 2.0 m (3 ft to 6.5 ft) measured from the face of the attachment plug to the plane of the rear of the appliance.

(4) Receptacles shall be located to protect against physical damage to the flexible cord.

(5) The receptacle for a trash compactor shall be located in the space occupied by the appliance or adjacent thereto.

(6) The receptacle for a built-in dishwasher shall be located in the space adjacent to the space occupied by the dishwasher

(7) The receptacle shall be accessible.

Reference: 2017 National Electrical Code – Chapter 4 Equipment for General Use, Article 422 Appliances. 422.16 Flexible Cords. 422.16(B) Specific Appliances. 422.16(B)(2) Built-in Dishwashers and Trash Compactors. (2)1.

EXAM 8

EXAM 8 ANSWERS

75. Answer D. 6 1/2 feet

Built-in dishwashers and trash compactors shall be permitted to be cord and- plug-connected with a flexible cord identified as suitable for the purpose in the installation instructions of the appliance manufacturer where all of the following conditions are met:

(1) The flexible cord shall be terminated with a grounding type attachment plug.

Exception: A listed dishwasher or trash compactor distinctly marked to identify it as protected by a system of double insulation shall not be required to be terminated with a grounding-type attachment plug.

(2) For a trash compactor, the length of the cord shall be 0.9 m to 1.2 m (3 ft to 4 ft) measured from the face of the attachment plug to the plane of the rear of the appliance.

(3) For a built-in dishwasher, the length of the cord shall be 0.9 m to 2.0 m (3 ft to **6.5 ft) measured from the face of the attachment plug to the plane of the rear of the appliance.**

(4) Receptacles shall be located to protect against physical damage to the flexible cord.

(5) The receptacle for a trash compactor shall be located in the space occupied by the appliance or adjacent thereto.

(6) The receptacle for a built-in dishwasher shall be located in the space adjacent to the space occupied by the dishwasher

(7) The receptacle shall be accessible.

Reference: 2017 National Electrical Code – Chapter 4 Equipment for General Use, Article 422 Appliances. 422.16 Flexible Cords. 422.16(B) Specific Appliances. 422.16(B)(2) Built-in Dishwashers and Trash Compactors. (2)1.

76. Answer D. independently

Ceiling suspended (paddle) fans shall be supported independently of an outlet box or by one of the following:

(1) A listed outlet box or listed outlet box system identified for the use and installed in accordance with 314.27(C)

(2) A listed outlet box system, a listed locking support and mounting receptacle, and a compatible factory installed attachment fitting designed for support, identified for the use and installed in accordance with 314.27(E)

Reference: 2017 National Electrical Code – Chapter 4 Equipment for General Use, Article 422 Appliances. 422.18 Support of Ceiling-Suspended (Paddle) Fans.1.

77. Answer A. 1/8

For permanently connected appliances rated at not over 300 volt-amperes or 1/8 hp, the branch-circuit overcurrent device shall be permitted to serve as the disconnecting means where the switch or circuit breaker is within sight from the appliance or is lockable in accordance with 110.25.

Reference: 2017 National Electrical Code – Chapter 4 Equipment for General Use, Article 422 Appliances. 422.31 Disconnection of Permanently Connected Appliances. 422.31(A) Rated at Not over 300 Volt-Amperes or 1/8 Horsepower.1.

78. Answer A. be permitted to serve as the disconnecting means

For permanently connected appliances rated at not over 300 volt-amperes or 1/8 hp, *the branch-circuit overcurrent device shall be permitted to serve as the disconnecting means where the switch or circuit breake*r is within sight from the appliance or is lockable in accordance with 110.25.

Reference: 2017 National Electrical Code – Chapter 4 Equipment for General Use, Article 422 Appliances. 422.31 Disconnection of Permanently Connected Appliances. 422.31(A) Rated at Not over 300 Volt-Amperes or 1/8 Horsepower.1.

EXAM 8

EXAM 8 ANSWERS

79. **Answer B.** ungrounded conductors

All storage or instantaneous-type water heaters shall be equipped with a temperature-limiting means in addition to its control thermostat to disconnect all ungrounded conductors. Such means shall comply with both of the following:

(1) Installed to sense maximum water temperature.

(2) Be either a trip-free, manually reset type or a type having a replacement element. Such water heaters shall be marked to require the installation of a temperature and pressure relief valve.

Exception No. 1: Storage water heaters that are identified as being suitable for use with a supply water temperature of 82°C (180°F) or above and a capacity of 60 kW or above.

Exception No. 2: Instantaneous-type water heaters that are identified as being suitable for such use, with a capacity of 4 L (1 gal) or less.

Informational Note: See ANSI Z21.22-1999/CSA 4.4-M99, Relief Valves for Hot Water Supply Systems.

Reference: 2017 National Electrical Code – Chapter 4 Equipment for General Use, Article 422 Appliances. 422.47 Water Heater Controls.1.

80. **Answer C.** 30 amperes

Individual branch circuits shall be permitted to supply any volt-ampere or wattage rating of fixed electric space-heating equipment for which they are rated.

Branch circuits supplying two or more outlets for fixed electric space-heating equipment shall be rated not over 30 amperes. In other than a dwelling unit, fixed infrared heating equipment shall be permitted to be supplied from branch circuits rated not over 50 amperes.

Reference: 2017 National Electrical Code – Chapter 4 Equipment for General Use, Article 424 Fixed Electric Space-Heating Equipment. 424.3 Branch Circuits. 424.3(A) Branch-Circuit Requirements.1.

EXAM 8 ANSWERS 447

EXAM 8

EXAM 8 ANSWERS

Table 310.15(B)(16) (formerly Table 310.16) Allowable Ampacities of Insulated Conductors Rated Up to and Including 2000 Volts, 60°C Through 90°C (140°F Through 194°F), Not More Than Three Current-Carrying Conductors in Raceway, Cable, or Earth (Directly Buried), Based on Ambient Temperature of 30°C (86°F)*

	Temperature Rating of Conductor [See Table 310.104(A).]						
	60°C (140°F)	75°C (167°F)	90°C (194°F)	60°C (140°F)	75°C (167°F)	90°C (194°F)	
Size AWG or kcmil	Types TW, UF	Types RHW, THHW, THW, THWN, XHHW, USE, ZW	Types TBS, SA, SIS, FEP, FEPB, MI, RHH, RHW-2, THHN, THHW, THW-2, THWN-2, USE-2, XHH, XHHW, XHHW-2, ZW-2	Types TW, UF	Types RHW, THHW, THW, THWN, XHHW, USE	Types TBS, SA, SIS, THHN, THHW, THW-2, THWN-2, RHH, RHW-2, USE-2, XHH, XHHW, XHHW-2, ZW-2	Size AWG or kcmil
	COPPER			ALUMINUM OR COPPER-CLAD ALUMINUM			
18**	—	—	14	—	—	—	—
16**	—	—	18	—	—	—	—
14**	15	20	25	—	—	—	—
12**	20	25	30	15	20	25	12**
10**	30	35	40	25	30	35	10**
8	40	50	55	35	40	45	8
6	55	65	75	40	50	55	6
4	70	85	95	55	65	75	4
3	85	100	115	65	75	85	3
2	95	115	130	75	90	100	2
1	110	130	145	85	100	115	1
1/0	125	150	170	100	120	135	1/0
2/0	145	175	195	115	135	150	2/0
3/0	165	200	225	130	155	175	3/0
4/0	195	230	260	150	180	205	4/0
250	215	255	290	170	205	230	250
300	240	285	320	195	230	260	300
350	260	310	350	210	250	280	350
400	280	335	380	225	270	305	400
500	320	380	430	260	310	350	500
600	350	420	475	285	340	385	600
700	385	460	520	315	375	425	700
750	400	475	535	320	385	435	750
800	410	490	555	330	395	445	800
900	435	520	585	355	425	480	900
1000	455	545	615	375	445	500	1000
1250	495	590	665	405	485	545	1250
1500	525	625	705	435	520	585	1500
1750	545	650	735	455	545	615	1750
2000	555	665	750	470	560	630	2000

*Refer to 310.15(B) (2) for the ampacity correction factors where the ambient temperature is other than 30°C (86°F). Refer to 310.15(B)(3)(a) for more than three current-carrying conductors.
**Refer to 240.4(D) for conductor overcurrent protection limitations.

| Underground feeder and branch-circuit cable — single conductor (for Type UF cable employing more than one conductor, see Article 340). | UF | 60°C (140°F) 75°C (167°F)³ | See Article 340. | Moisture-resistant Moisture- and heat-resistant | 14–10 8–2 1–4/0 | 1.52 2.03 2.41 | 60⁶ 80⁶ 95⁶ | Integral with insulation |

(continues)

Table 310.15(B)(16) see Table 310-15-B-16 in Tables folder on CD-ROM

81. **Answer D.**   125%

Fixed electric space-heating equipment and motors shall be considered continuous load.

Reference: 2017 National Electrical Code – Chapter 4 Equipment for General Use, Article 424 Fixed Electric Space-Heating Equipment. 424.3 Branch Circuits. 424.3(B) Branch-Circuit Sizing.

Where a branch circuit supplies continuous loads or any combination of continuous and noncontinuous loads, the minimum branch-circuit conductor size shall have an allowable ampacity not less than the noncontinuous load plus 125 percent of the continuous load.

Reference: 2017 National Electrical Code – Chapter 2 Wiring and Protection, Article 210 Branch Circuits. 210.19 Conductors – Minimum Ampacity and Size. 210.19(A) Branch Circuits Not More Than 600 Volts. 210.19(A)(1) General. 210.19(A)(1)(a)1.

EXAM 8

EXAM 8 ANSWERS

82. **Answer C.** 2/0 AWG

    Fixed electric space-heating equipment and motors shall be considered continuous load.

    Reference: 2017 National Electrical Code – Chapter 4 Equipment for General Use, Article 424 Fixed Electric Space-Heating Equipment. 424.3 Branch Circuit. 424.3(B) Branch-Circuit Sizing.

    Where a branch circuit supplies continuous loads or any combination of continuous and noncontinuous loads, the minimum branch-circuit conductor size shall have an allowable ampacity not less than the noncontinuous load plus 125 percent of the continuous load.

    Reference: 2017 National Electrical Code – Chapter 2 Wiring and Protection, Article 210 Branch Circuits. 210.19 Conductors – Minimum Ampacity and Size. 210.19(A) Branch Circuits Not More Than 600 Volts. 210.19(A)(1) General. 210.19(A)(1)(a)

    Reference: 2017 National Electrical Code – Chapter 3 Wiring Methods and Materials, Article 310 Conductors for General Wiring. 310.15 Ampacities for Conductors Rated 0-2000 Volts. 310.15(B) Tables. Table 310.15(B)(16) (formerly Table 310.16) Allowable Ampacities of Insulated Conductors Rated Up to and Including 2000 Volts, 60°C Through 90°C (140°F Through 194°F), Not More Than Three Current-Carrying Conductors in Raceway, Cable, or Earth (Directly Buried), Based on Ambient Temperature of 30°C (86°F)* (page 70-161)1.

83. **Answer B.** indicating

    Switches and circuit breakers used as disconnecting means shall be of the indicating type.

    Reference: 2017 National Electrical Code – Chapter 4 Equipment for General Use, Article 424 Fixed Electric Space-Heating Equipment. 424.21 Switch and Circuit Breaker to Be Indicating.1.

84. **Answer D.** 60 amperes

    Resistance-type heating elements in electric space-heating equipment shall be protected at not more than 60 amperes. Equipment rated more than 48 amperes and employing such elements shall have the heating elements subdivided, and each subdivided load shall not exceed 48 amperes. Where a subdivided load is less than 48 amperes, the rating of the supplementary overcurrent protective device shall comply with 424.3(B). A boiler employing resistance-type immersion heating elements contained in an ASME-rated and stamped vessel shall be permitted to comply with 424.72(A).

    Reference: 2017 National Electrical Code – Chapter 4 Equipment for General Use, Article 424 Fixed Electric Space-Heating Equipment. 424.22 Overcurrent Protection. 424.22(B) Resistance Elements.1.

85. **Answer A.** 50°C

    Wiring located above heated ceilings shall be spaced not less than 50 mm (2 in.) above the heated ceiling. *The ampacity of conductors shall be calculated on the basis of an assumed ambient temperature of 50°C (122°F)*, applying the correction factors shown in the 0–2000 volt ampacity tables of Article 310. If this wiring is located above thermal insulation having a minimum thickness of 50 mm (2 in.), the wiring shall not require correction for temperature.

    Reference: 2017 National Electrical Code – Chapter 4 Equipment for General Use, Article 424 Fixed Electric Space-Heating Equipment. 424.36 Clearances of Wiring in Ceilings.1.

86. **Answer A.** floors

    Ground fault circuit-interrupter protection for personnel shall be provided for cables installed in electrically heated floors of bathrooms and kitchens and in hydro massage bathtub locations.

    Reference: 2017 National Electrical Code – Chapter 4 Equipment for General Use, Article 424 Fixed Electric Space-Heating Equipment. 424.44 Installation of Cables in Concrete or Poured Masonry Floors. 424.44(E) Ground-Fault Circuit-Interrupter Protection.1.

87. **Answer B.** GFCI protected

    Ground fault circuit-interrupter protection for personnel shall be provided for cables installed in electrically heated floors of bathrooms and kitchens and in hydro massage bathtub locations.

    Reference: 2017 National Electrical Code – Chapter 4 Equipment for General Use, Article 424 Fixed Electric Space-Heating Equipment. 424.44 Installation of Cables in Concrete or Poured Masonry Floors. 424.44(G) Ground-Fault Circuit-Interrupter Protection.1.

EXAM 8

EXAM 8 ANSWERS

88. **Answer A.** continuous

    Fixed outdoor electric deicing and snow-melting equipment shall be considered a continuous load.

    Reference: 2017 National Electrical Code – Chapter 4 Equipment for General Use, Article 426 Fixed Outdoor Electric Deicing and Snow-Melting Equipment. 426.4 Continuous Load.1.

89. **Answer C.** 125%

    Fixed outdoor electric deicing and snow-melting equipment shall be considered as a continuous load.

    Reference: 2017 National Electrical Code – Chapter 4 Equipment for General Use, Article 426 Fixed Outdoor Electric Deicing and Snow-Melting Equipment. 426.4 Continuous Load.

    Where a branch circuit supplies *continuous loads or any combination of continuous and noncontinuous loads*, the minimum branch-circuit conductor size shall have an allowable ampacity not less than the noncontinuous load *plus 125 percent of the continuous load.*

    Reference: 2017 National Electrical Code – Chapter 2 Wiring and Protection, Article 210 Branch Circuits. 210.19 Conductors – Minimum Ampacity and Size. 210.19(A) Branch Circuits Not More Than 600 Volts. 210.19(A)(1) General. 210.19(A)(1)(a)

    Where a branch circuit supplies continuous loads or any combination of continuous and noncontinuous loads, the rating of the overcurrent device shall not be less than the noncontinuous load plus *125 percent of the continuous load.*

    Reference: 2017 National Electrical Code – Chapter 2 Wiring and Protection, Article 210 Branch Circuits. 210.20 Overcurrent Protection. 210.20(A) Continuous and Noncontinuous Loads.1.

90. **Answer D.** Section 400.5

    The size of conductors supplying equipment covered by Article 430 shall be selected from the allowable ampacity tables in accordance with 310.15(B) or shall be calculated in accordance with 310.15(C). *Where flexible cord is used, the size of the conductor shall be selected in accordance with 400.5*. The required ampacity and motor ratings shall be determined as specified in 430.6(A), (B), (C), and (D).

    Reference: 2017 National Electrical Code – Chapter 4 Equipment for General Use, Article 430 Motors, Motor Circuits, and Controllers. 430.6 Ampacity and Motor Rating Determination.1.

EXAM 8

EXAM 8 ANSWERS

Table 430.248 Full-Load Currents in Amperes, Single-Phase Alternating-Current Motors

The following values of full-load currents are for motors running at usual speeds and motors with normal torque characteristics. The voltages listed are rated motor voltages. The currents listed shall be permitted for system voltage ranges of 110 to 120 and 220 to 240 volts.

Horsepower	115 Volts	200 Volts	208 Volts	230 Volts
1/6	4.4	2.5	2.4	2.2
1/4	5.8	3.3	3.2	2.9
1/3	7.2	4.1	4.0	3.6
1/2	9.8	5.6	5.4	4.9
3/4	13.8	7.9	7.6	6.9
1	16	9.2	8.8	8.0
1½	20	11.5	11.0	10
2	24	13.8	13.2	12
3	34	19.6	18.7	17
5	56	32.2	30.8	28
7½	80	46.0	44.0	40
10	100	57.5	55.0	50

91. **Answer D.** Table 430.250 of the NEC

Other than for motors built for low speeds (less than 1200 RPM) or high torques, and for multispeed motors, the values given in Table 430.247, Table 430.248, Table 430.249, and *Table 430.250 shall be used to determine the ampacity of conductors or ampere ratings of switches, branch-circuit short-circuit and ground-fault protection,* instead of the actual current rating marked on the motor nameplate. Where a motor is marked in amperes, but not horsepower, the horsepower rating shall be assumed to be that corresponding to the value given in Table 430.247, Table 430.248, Table 430.249, and Table 430.250, interpolated if necessary. Motors built for low speeds (less than 1200 RPM) or high torques may have higher full-load currents, and multispeed motors will have full-load current varying with speed, in which case the nameplate current ratings shall be used.

Reference: 2017 National Electrical Code – Chapter 4 Equipment for General Use, Article 430 Motors, Motor Circuits, and Controllers. 430.6 Ampacity and Motor Rating Determination. 430.6(A) General Motor Applications. 430.6(A)(1) Table Values. 1.

EXAM 8

EXAM 8 ANSWERS

92. **Answer B.** 50 amperes

Other than for motors built for low speeds (less than 1200 RPM) or high torques, and for multispeed motors, the values given in Table 430.247, **Table 430.248,** Table 430.249, and Table 430.250 shall be used to determine the ampacity of conductors or ampere ratings of switches, branch-circuit short-circuit and ground-fault protection, instead of the actual current rating marked on the motor nameplate. Where a motor is marked in amperes, but not horsepower, the horsepower rating shall be assumed to be that corresponding to the value given in Table 430.247, Table 430.248, Table 430.249, and Table 430.250, interpolated if necessary. Motors built for low speeds (less than 1200 RPM) or high torques may have higher full-load currents, and multispeed motors will have full-load current varying with speed, in which case the nameplate current ratings shall be used.

Reference: 2017 National Electrical Code – Chapter 4 Equipment for General Use, Article 430 Motors, Motor Circuits, and Controllers. 430.6 Ampacity and Motor Rating Determination. 430.6(A) General Motor Applications. 430.6(A)(1) Table Values.

Reference: 2017 National Electrical Code – Chapter 4 Equipment for General Use, Article 430 Motors, Motor Circuits, and Controllers. Table 430.248 Full-Load Currents in Amperes, Single-Phase. Alternating-Current Motors (page 70-350)

Conductors that supply a single motor used in a continuous duty application shall have an ampacity of not less than 125 percent of the motor full-load current rating, as determined by 430.6(A)(1), or not less than specified in 430.22(A) through (G).

Reference: 2017 National Electrical Code – Chapter 4 Equipment for General Use, Article 430 Motors, Motor Circuits, and Controllers. 430.22 Single Motor.

93. **Answer C.** motor overload protection

(A) General Motor Applications. For general motor applications, current ratings shall be determined based on (A)(1) and (A)(2).

(1) Table Values. Other than for motors built for low speeds (less than 1200 RPM) or high torques, and for multispeed motors, the values given in Table 430.247, Table 430.248, Table 430.249, and Table 430.250 shall be used to determine the ampacity of conductors or ampere ratings of switches, branch-circuit short-circuit and ground-fault protection, instead of the actual current rating marked on the motor nameplate. Where a motor is marked in amperes, but not horsepower, the horsepower rating shall be assumed to be that corresponding to the value given in Table 430.247, Table 430.248, Table 430.249, and Table 430.250, interpolated if necessary. Motors built for low speeds (less than 1200 RPM) or high torques may have higher full-load currents, and multispeed motors will have full-load current varying with speed, in which case the nameplate current ratings shall be used.

Exception No. 1: Multispeed motors shall be in accordance with 430.22(B) and 430.52.

Exception No. 2: For equipment that employs a shaded-pole or permanent-split capacitor-type fan or blower motor that is marked with the motor type, the full load current for such motor marked on the nameplate of the equipment in which the fan or blower motor is employed shall be used instead of the horsepower rating to determine the ampacity or rating of the disconnecting means, the branch-circuit conductors, the controller, the branch-circuit short-circuit and ground fault protection, and the separate overload protection. This marking on the equipment nameplate shall not be less than the current marked on the fan or blower motor nameplate.

EXAM 8

EXAM 8 ANSWERS

Exception No. 3: For a listed motor-operated appliance that is marked with both motor horsepower and full-load current, the motor full-load current marked on the nameplate of the appliance shall be used instead of the horsepower rating on the appliance nameplate to determine the ampacity or rating of the disconnecting means, the branch-circuit conductors, the controller, the branch-circuit short-circuit and ground fault protection, and any separate overload protection.

(2) Nameplate Values. Separate motor overload protection shall be based on the motor nameplate current rating.

Reference: 2017 National Electrical Code – Chapter 4 Equipment for General Use, Article 430 Motors, Motor Circuits, and Controllers. 430.6 Ampacity and Motor Rating Determination. 430.6(A) General Motor Applications.1.

94. Answer C. 62.70 amperes

The size of conductors supplying equipment covered by Article 430 shall be selected from the allowable ampacity tables in accordance with 310.15(B) or shall be calculated in accordance with 310.15(C). Where flexible cord is used, the size of the conductor shall be selected in accordance with 400.5. The required ampacity and motor ratings shall be determined as specified in 430.6(A), (B), (C), and (D).

Reference: 2017 National Electrical Code – Chapter 4 Equipment for General Use, Article 430 Motors, Motor Circuits, and Controllers. 430.6 Ampacity and Motor Rating Determination. Table 430.250 Full-Load Current, Three-Phase Alternating-Current Motors (page 70-351)

Conductors supplying several motors, or a motor(s) and other load(s), shall have an ampacity not less than the sum of each of the following:

(1) 125 percent of the full-load current rating of the highest rated motor, as determined by 430.6(A)

(2) Sum of the full-load current ratings of all the other motors in the group, as determined by 430.6(A)

(3) 100 percent of the noncontinuous non-motor load

(4) 125 percent of the continuous non-motor load.

Informational Note: See Informative Annex D, Example No. D8.

Reference: 2017 National Electrical Code – Chapter 4 Equipment for General Use, Article 430 Motors, Motor Circuits, and Controllers. 430.24 Several Motors or a Motor(s) and Other Load(s).1.

95. Answer C. 125%

Conductors that supply a single motor used in a continuous duty application shall have an ampacity of not less than 125 percent of the motor full-load current rating, as determined by 430.6(A)(1), or not less than specified in 430.22(A) through (G).

Reference: 2017 National Electrical Code – Chapter 4 Equipment for General Use, Article 430 Motors, Motor Circuits, and Controllers. 430.22 Single Motor.1.

EXAM 8

EXAM 8 ANSWERS

Table 430.72(B) Maximum Rating of Overcurrent Protective Device in Amperes

Control Circuit Conductor Size (AWG)	Column A Separate Protection Provided		Protection Provided by Motor Branch-Circuit Protective Device(s)			
			Column B Conductors Within Enclosure		Column C Conductors Extend Beyond Enclosure	
	Copper	Aluminum or Copper-Clad Aluminum	Copper	Aluminum or Copper-Clad Aluminum	Copper	Aluminum or Copper-Clad Aluminum
18	7	—	25	—	7	—
16	10	—	40	—	10	—
14	(Note 1)	—	100	—	45	—
12	(Note 1)	(Note 1)	120	100	60	45
10	(Note 1)	(Note 1)	160	140	90	75
Larger than 10	(Note 1)	(Note 1)	(Note 2)	(Note 2)	(Note 3)	(Note 3)

Notes:
1. Value specified in 310.15 as applicable.
2. 400 percent of value specified in Table 310.15(B)(17) for 60°C conductors.
3. 300 percent of value specified in Table 310.15(B)(16) for 60°C conductors.

Table 430.72(B) see Tables folder on CD-ROM

96. Answer C.   3 AWG

Conductors that supply a single motor used in a continuous duty application shall have an ampacity of not less than 125 percent of the motor full-load current rating, as determined by 430.6(A)(1), or not less than specified in 430.22(A) through (G).

Reference: 2017 National Electrical Code – Chapter 4 Equipment for General Use, Article 430 Motors, Motor Circuits, and Controllers. 430.22 Single Motor.

Reference: 2017 National Electrical Code – Chapter 3 Wiring Methods and Materials. Table 310.15(B)(16) (formerly Table 310.16) Allowable Ampacities of Insulated Conductors Rated Up to and Including 2000 Volts, 60°C Through 90°C (140°F Through 194°F), Not More Than Three Current-Carrying Conductors in Raceway, Cable, or Earth (Directly Buried), Based on Ambient Temperature of 30°C (86°F)* (page 70-161)

FLC of motor = 70 amperes x 125% = 87.5 amperes

*Size 3 AWG THW with an ampacity of 100 amperes should be selected.*1.

97. Answer D.   150%

Conductors for a motor used in a short-time, intermittent, periodic, or varying duty application shall have an ampacity of not less than the percentage of the motor nameplate current rating shown in Table 430.22(E), unless the authority having jurisdiction grants special permission for conductors of lower ampacity.

Reference: 2017 National Electrical Code – Chapter 4 Equipment for General Use, Article 430 Motors, Motor Circuits, and Controllers. 430.22 Single Motor. 430.22(E) Other Than Continuous Duty. Table 430.22(E) Duty-Cycle Service (page 70-329)1.

EXAM 8

EXAM 8 ANSWERS

98. **Answer D.   125%**

Conductors supplying several motors, or a motor(s) and other load(s), shall have an ampacity not less than the sum of each of the following:

(1) *125 percent of the full-load current rating of the highest rated motor, as determined by 430.6(A)*

(2) *Sum of the full-load current ratings of all the other motors in the group, as determined by 430.6(A)*

(3) 100 percent of the noncontinuous non-motor load

(4) 125 percent of the continuous non-motor load.

Reference: 2017 National Electrical Code – Chapter 4 Equipment for General Use, Article 430 Motors, Motor Circuits, and Controllers . 430.24 Several Motors or a Motor(s) and Other Load(s).1.

99. **Answer D.   4 AWG THWN**

Conductors supplying several motors, or a motor(s) and other load(s), shall have an ampacity not less than the sum of each of the following:

(1) 125 percent of the full-load current rating of the highest rated motor, as determined by 430.6(A)

(2) Sum of the full-load current ratings of all the other motors in the group, as determined by 430.6(A)

(3) 100 percent of the noncontinuous non-motor load

(4) 125 percent of the continuous non-motor load.

Reference: 2017 National Electrical Code – Chapter 4 Equipment for General Use, Article 430 Motors, Motor Circuits, and Controllers . 430.24 Several Motors or a Motor(s) and Other Load(s).

Reference: 2017 National Electrical Code – Chapter 4 Equipment for General Use, Article 430 Motors, Motor Circuits, and Controllers . Table 430.250 Full-Load Current, Three-Phase Alternating-Current Motors (page 70-351)

Reference: 2017 National Electrical Code – Chapter 3 Wiring Methods and Materials. Table 310.15(B)(16) (formerly Table 310.16) Allowable Ampacities of Insulated Conductors Rated Up to and Including 2000 Volts, 60°C Through 90°C (140°F Through 194°F), Not More Than Three Current-Carrying Conductors in Raceway, Cable, or Earth (Directly Buried), Based on Ambient Temperature of 30°C (86°F)* (page 70-161)

15 hp FLC – 42 amperes x 125% = 52.5 amperes

7-1/2 hp FLC – 22 amperes x 100% = 22.0 amperes

3 hp FLC – 9.6 amperes x 100% = 9.6 amperes

Total = 84.1 amperes

*NOTE: Size 4 AWG THWN conductors with an allowable ampacity of 85 amperes should be selected.1.

EXAM 8

EXAM 8 ANSWERS

Table 430.250 Full-Load Current, Three-Phase Alternating-Current Motors
The following values of full-load currents are typical for motors running at speeds usual for belted motors and motors with normal torque characteristics. The voltages listed are rated motor voltages. The currents listed shall be permitted for system voltage ranges of 110 to 120, 220 to 240, 440 to 480, and 550 to 600 volts.

Horsepower	Induction-Type Squirrel Cage and Wound Rotor (Amperes)							Synchronous-Type Unity Power Factor* (Amperes)			
	115 Volts	200 Volts	208 Volts	230 Volts	460 Volts	575 Volts	2300 Volts	230 Volts	460 Volts	575 Volts	2300 Volts
½	4.4	2.5	2.4	2.2	1.1	0.9	—	—	—	—	—
¾	6.4	3.7	3.5	3.2	1.6	1.3	—	—	—	—	—
1	8.4	4.8	4.6	4.2	2.1	1.7	—	—	—	—	—
1½	12.0	6.9	6.6	6.0	3.0	2.4	—	—	—	—	—
2	13.6	7.8	7.5	6.8	3.4	2.7	—	—	—	—	—
3	—	11.0	10.6	9.6	4.8	3.9	—	—	—	—	—
5	—	17.5	16.7	15.2	7.6	6.1	—	—	—	—	—
7½	—	25.3	24.2	22	11	9	—	—	—	—	—
10	—	32.2	30.8	28	14	11	—	—	—	—	—
15	—	48.3	46.2	42	21	17	—	—	—	—	—
20	—	62.1	59.4	54	27	22	—	—	—	—	—
25	—	78.2	74.8	68	34	27	—	53	26	21	—
30	—	92	88	80	40	32	—	63	32	26	—
40	—	120	114	104	52	41	—	83	41	33	—
50	—	150	143	130	65	52	—	104	52	42	—
60	—	177	169	154	77	62	16	123	61	49	12
75	—	221	211	192	96	77	20	155	78	62	15
100	—	285	273	248	124	99	26	202	101	81	20
125	—	359	343	312	156	125	31	253	126	101	25
150	—	414	396	360	180	144	37	302	151	121	30
200	—	552	528	480	240	192	49	400	201	161	40
250	—	—	—	—	302	242	60	—	—	—	—
300	—	—	—	—	361	289	72	—	—	—	—
350	—	—	—	—	414	336	83	—	—	—	—
400	—	—	—	—	477	382	95	—	—	—	—
450	—	—	—	—	515	412	103	—	—	—	—
500	—	—	—	—	590	472	118	—	—	—	—

EXAM 8

EXAM 8 ANSWERS

100. **Answer B.** 115%

A separate overload device that is responsive to motor current. *This device shall be selected to trip or shall be rated at no more than the following percent of the motor nameplate full-load current rating:*

Motors with a marked service factor 1.15 or greater125%

Motors with a marked temperature rise 40°C or less125%

All other motors115%

Modification of this value shall be permitted as provided in 430.32(C). For a multispeed motor, each winding connection shall be considered separately.

Where a separate motor overload device is connected so that it does not carry the total current designated on the motor nameplate, such as for wye-delta starting, the proper percentage of nameplate current applying to the selection or setting of the overload device shall be clearly designated on the equipment, or the manufacturer's selection table shall take this into account.

Informational Note: Where power factor correction capacitors are installed on the load side of the motor overload device, see 460.9.

Reference: 2017 National Electrical Code – Chapter 4 Equipment for General Use, Article 430 Motors, Motor Circuits, and Controllers. 430.32 Continuous-Duty Motors. 430.32(A) More than 1 Horsepower. 430.32(A)(1) Separate Overload Device.1.

101. **Answer B.** Motor current

A separate overload device that is responsive to motor current. This device shall be selected to trip or shall be rated at no more than the following percent of the motor nameplate full-load current rating:

Motors with a marked service factor 1.15 or greater125%

Motors with a marked temperature rise 40°C or less125%

All other motors115%

Modification of this value shall be permitted as provided in 430.32(C). For a multispeed motor, each winding connection shall be considered separately.

Where a separate motor overload device is connected so that it does not carry the total current designated on the motor nameplate, such as for wye-delta starting, the proper percentage of nameplate current applying to the selection or setting of the overload device shall be clearly designated on the equipment, or the manufacturer's selection table shall take this into account.

Informational Note: Where power factor correction capacitors are installed on the load side of the motor overload device, see 460.9.

Reference: 2017 National Electrical Code – Chapter 4 Equipment for General Use, Article 430 Motors, Motor Circuits, and Controllers. 430.32 Continuous-Duty Motors. 430.32(A) More Than 1 Horsepower. 430.32(A)(1) Separate Overload Device.1.

EXAM 8

EXAM 8 ANSWERS

Table 430.72(B) Maximum Rating of Overcurrent Protective Device in Amperes

Control Circuit Conductor Size (AWG)	Column A Separate Protection Provided		Protection Provided by Motor Branch-Circuit Protective Device(s)			
			Column B Conductors Within Enclosure		Column C Conductors Extend Beyond Enclosure	
	Copper	Aluminum or Copper-Clad Aluminum	Copper	Aluminum or Copper-Clad Aluminum	Copper	Aluminum or Copper-Clad Aluminum
18	7	—	25	—	7	—
16	10	—	40	—	10	—
14	(Note 1)	—	100	—	45	—
12	(Note 1)	(Note 1)	120	100	60	45
10	(Note 1)	(Note 1)	160	140	90	75
Larger than 10	(Note 1)	(Note 1)	(Note 2)	(Note 2)	(Note 3)	(Note 3)

Notes:
1. Value specified in 310.15 as applicable.
2. 400 percent of value specified in Table 310.15(B)(17) for 60°C conductors.
3. 300 percent of value specified in Table 310.15(B)(16) for 60°C conductors.

Table 430.72(B) seeTable 430-72B in the Tables folder on CD-ROM

102. Answer D. 156 percent

A thermal protector integral with the motor, approved for use with the motor it protects on the basis that it will prevent dangerous overheating of the motor due to overload and failure to start. The ultimate trip current of a thermally protected motor shall not exceed the following percentage of motor full-load current given in Table 430.248, Table 430.249, and Table 430.250:

Motor full-load current 9 amperes or less170%

Motor full-load current from 9.1 to, and156%

including, 20 amperes

Motor full-load current greater than 20 amperes140%

If the motor current-interrupting device is separate from the motor and its control circuit is operated by a protective device integral with the motor, it shall be arranged so that the opening of the control circuit will result in interruption of current to the motor.

Reference: 2017 National Electrical Code – Chapter 4 Equipment for General Use, Article 430 Motors, Motor Circuits, and Controllers. 430.32 Continuous-Duty Motors. 430.32(A) More Than 1 Horsepower. 430.32(A)(2) Thermal Protector.

Reference: 2017 National Electrical Code – Chapter 4 Equipment for General Use, Article 430 Motors, Motor Circuits, and Controllers. 430.6 Ampacity and Motor Rating Determination. Table 430.248 Full-Load Currents in Amperes, Single-Phase Alternating-Current Motors (page 70-350)1.

103. Answer D. fuses or circuit breakers

Overload relays and other devices for motor overload protection that are not capable of opening short circuits or ground faults shall be protected by fuses or circuit breakers with ratings or settings in accordance with 430.52 or by a motor short-circuit protector in accordance with 430.52.

Reference: 2017 National Electrical Code – Chapter 4 Equipment for General Use, Article 430 Motors, Motor Circuits, and Controllers. 430.40 Overload Relays.1.

EXAM 8

EXAM 8 ANSWERS

Table 430.72(B) Maximum Rating of Overcurrent Protective Device in Amperes

Control Circuit Conductor Size (AWG)	Column A Separate Protection Provided		Protection Provided by Motor Branch-Circuit Protective Device(s)			
			Column B Conductors Within Enclosure		Column C Conductors Extend Beyond Enclosure	
	Copper	Aluminum or Copper-Clad Aluminum	Copper	Aluminum or Copper-Clad Aluminum	Copper	Aluminum or Copper-Clad Aluminum
18	7	—	25	—	7	—
16	10	—	40	—	10	—
14	(Note 1)	—	100	—	45	—
12	(Note 1)	(Note 1)	120	100	60	45
10	(Note 1)	(Note 1)	160	140	90	75
Larger than 10	(Note 1)	(Note 1)	(Note 2)	(Note 2)	(Note 3)	(Note 3)

Notes:
1. Value specified in 310.15 as applicable.
2. 400 percent of value specified in Table 310.15(B)(17) for 60°C conductors.
3. 300 percent of value specified in Table 310.15(B)(16) for 60°C conductors.

Table 430.72(B) seeTable 430-72B in the Tables folder on CD-ROM

104. Answer C.   45 amperes

Conductors shall be permitted to be protected by the motor branch-circuit short-circuit and ground-fault protective device and shall require only short-circuit and ground-fault protection. Where the conductors do not extend beyond the motor control equipment enclosure, the rating of the protective device(s) shall not exceed the value specified in Column B of Table 430.72(B). *Where the conductors extend beyond the motor control equipment enclosure, the rating of the protective device(s) shall not exceed the value specified in Column C of Table 430.72(B).*

Reference: 2017 National Electrical Code – Chapter 4 Equipment for General Use, Article 430 Motors, Motor Circuits, and Controllers. 430.72 Overcurrent Protection. 430.72(B) Conductor Protection. 430.72(B)(2) Branch-Circuit Overcurrent Protective Device.

Reference: 2017 National Electrical Code – Chapter 4 Equipment for General Use, Article 430 Motors, Motor Circuits, and Controllers. 430.72 Overcurrent Protection. Table 430.72(B) Maximum Rating of Overcurrent Protective Device in Amperes (page 70-339)1.

105. Answer A.   120 hp

Controllers, other than inverse time circuit breakers and molded case switches, shall have horsepower ratings at the application voltage not lower than the horsepower rating of the motor.

Reference: 2017 National Electrical Code – Chapter 4 Equipment for General Use, Article 430 Motors, Motor Circuits, and Controllers. 430.83 Ratings. 430.83(A) General. 430.83(A)(1) Horsepower Ratings.1.

106. Answer D.   ungrounded

The controller shall not be required to open all conductors to the motor.

Exception: Where the controller serves also as a disconnecting means, it shall open all ungrounded conductors to the motor as provided *in 430.111*

Reference: 2017 National Electrical Code – Chapter 4 Equipment for General Use, Article 430 Motors, Motor Circuits, and Controllers . 430.84 Need Not Open All Conductors. 430.84, Exception1.

EXAM 8

EXAM 8 ANSWERS

107. **Answer A.** The breaker be able to be locked in the open position.

The controller disconnecting means required in accordance with 430.]02(A) shall be permitted to serve as the disconnecting means for the motor if it is in sight from the motor location and the driven machinery location.

Exception to (1) and (2): The disconnecting means for the motor shall not be required under either condition (a) or condition (b), which follow, provided that the controller disconnecting means required in 430.102(A) is lockable in accordance with 110.25.

  (a) Where such a location of the disconnecting means for the motor is impracticable or introduces additional or increased hazards' to persons or property

Informational Note: Some examples of increased or additional hazards include, but are not limited to, motors rated in excess of 100 hp, multi motor equipment, submersible motors, motors associated with adjustable speed drives, and motors located in hazardous (classified) locations.

  (b) In industrial installations, with written safety procedures, where conditions of maintenance and supervision ensure that only qualified persons service the equipment

Informational Note: For information on lockout/tag out procedures, see NFPA 70E-2015, Standard for Electrical Safety in the Workplace.

Reference: 2017 National Electrical Code – Chapter 4 Equipment for General Use, Article 430 Motors, Motor Circuits, and Controllers . 430.102 Location. 430.102(B) Motor. 430.102(B)(2) Controller Disconnect. 430.102(B)(2), Exception1.

108. **Answer D.** 115

The disconnecting means for motor circuits rated 1000 volts, nominal, or less shall have an ampere rating not less than 115 percent of the full-load current rating of the motor.

Exception: A listed unfused motor-circuit switch having a horsepower rating not less than the motor horsepower shall be permitted to have an ampere rating less than 115 percent of the full-load current rating of the motor.

Reference: 2017 National Electrical Code – Chapter 4 Equipment for General Use, Article 430 Motors, Motor Circuits, and Controllers. 430.110 Ampere Rating and Interrupting Capacity. 430.110(A) General.1.

109. **Answer C.** 115%

The disconnecting means for motor circuits rated 1000 volts, nominal, or less shall have an ampere rating not less than 115 percent of the full-load current rating of the motor.

Exception: A listed unfused motor-circuit switch having a horsepower rating not less than the motor horsepower shall be permitted to have an ampere rating less than 115 percent of the full-load current rating of the motor.

Reference: 2017 National Electrical Code – Chapter 4 Equipment for General Use, Article 430 Motors, Motor Circuits, and Controllers. 430.110 Ampere Rating and Interrupting Capacity. 430.110(A) General.1.

110. **Answer C.** 6

Flexible metal conduit or liquidtight flexible metal conduit not exceeding 1.8 m (6 ft.) in length shall be permitted to be employed for raceway connection to a motor terminal enclosure.

Reference: 2017 National Electrical Code – Chapter 4 Equipment for General Use, Article 430 Motors, Motor Circuits, and Controllers. 430.223 Raceway Connection To Motors.1.

EXAM 8

EXAM 8 ANSWERS

Table 430.248 Full-Load Currents in Amperes, Single-Phase Alternating-Current Motors
The following values of full-load currents are for motors running at usual speeds and motors with normal torque characteristics. The voltages listed are rated motor voltages. The currents listed shall be permitted for system voltage ranges of 110 to 120 and 220 to 240 volts.

Horsepower	115 Volts	200 Volts	208 Volts	230 Volts
1/6	4.4	2.5	2.4	2.2
1/4	5.8	3.3	3.2	2.9
1/3	7.2	4.1	4.0	3.6
1/2	9.8	5.6	5.4	4.9
3/4	13.8	7.9	7.6	6.9
1	16	9.2	8.8	8.0
1 1/2	20	11.5	11.0	10
2	24	13.8	13.2	12
3	34	19.6	18.7	17
5	56	32.2	30.8	28
7 1/2	80	46.0	44.0	40
10	100	57.5	55.0	50

Table 430.248 see Table 430-248 in Tables folder on CD-ROM

111. Answer C.   18.7 amperes

The following values of full-load currents are for motors running at usual speeds and motors with normal torque characteristics. The voltages listed are rated motor voltages. T*he currents listed shall be permitted for system voltage ranges of 110 to 120 and 220 to 240 volts.*

Reference: 2017 National Electrical Code – Chapter 4 Equipment for General Use, Article 430 Motors, Motor Circuits, and Controllers. 430.110 Ampere Rating and Interrupting . Table 430.248 Full-Load Currents in Amperes, Single-Phase Alternating-Current Motors (page 70-350)1.

112. Answer C.   13.8 amperes

The following values of full-load currents are for motors running at usual speeds and motors with normal torque characteristics. The voltages listed are rated motor voltages. The currents listed shall be permitted for system voltage ranges of 110 to 120 and 220 to 240 volts.

Reference: 2017 National Electrical Code – Chapter 4 Equipment for General Use, Article 430 Motors, Motor Circuits, and Controllers . Table 430.248 Full-Load Currents in Amperes, Single-Phase Alternating-Current Motors (page 70-350)1.

113. Answer B.   143 amperes

The following values of full-load currents are typical for motors running at speeds usual for belted motors and motors with normal torque characteristics.

The voltages listed are rated motor voltages. The currents listed shall be permitted for system voltage ranges of 110 to 120, 220 to 240, 440 to 480, and 550 to 1000 volts.

Reference: 2017 National Electrical Code – Chapter 4 Equipment for General Use, Article 430 Motors, Motor Circuits, and Controllers . Table 430.250 Full-Load Current, Three-Phase Alternating-Current Motors (page 70-351)1.

114. Answer C.   40 amperes

The following values of full-load currents are typical for motors running at speeds usual for belted motors and motors with normal torque characteristics.

The voltages listed are rated motor voltages. The currents listed shall be permitted for system voltage ranges of 110 to 120, 220 to 240, 440 to 480, and 550 to 1000 volts.

Reference: 2017 National Electrical Code – Chapter 4 Equipment for General Use, Article 430 Motors, Motor Circuits, and Controllers . Table 430.250 Full-Load Current, Three-Phase Alternating-Current Motors (page 70-351)1.

EXAM 8

EXAM 8 ANSWERS

Table 430.250 Full-Load Current, Three-Phase Alternating-Current Motors
The following values of full-load currents are typical for motors running at speeds usual for belted motors and motors with normal torque characteristics. The voltages listed are rated motor voltages. The currents listed shall be permitted for system voltage ranges of 110 to 120, 220 to 240, 440 to 480, and 550 to 600 volts.

Horsepower	Induction-Type Squirrel Cage and Wound Rotor (Amperes)							Synchronous-Type Unity Power Factor* (Amperes)			
	115 Volts	200 Volts	208 Volts	230 Volts	460 Volts	575 Volts	2300 Volts	230 Volts	460 Volts	575 Volts	2300 Volts
½	4.4	2.5	2.4	2.2	1.1	0.9	—	—	—	—	—
¾	6.4	3.7	3.5	3.2	1.6	1.3	—	—	—	—	—
1	8.4	4.8	4.6	4.2	2.1	1.7	—	—	—	—	—
1½	12.0	6.9	6.6	6.0	3.0	2.4	—	—	—	—	—
2	13.6	7.8	7.5	6.8	3.4	2.7	—	—	—	—	—
3	—	11.0	10.6	9.6	4.8	3.9	—	—	—	—	—
5	—	17.5	16.7	15.2	7.6	6.1	—	—	—	—	—
7½	—	25.3	24.2	22	11	9	—	—	—	—	—
10	—	32.2	30.8	28	14	11	—	—	—	—	—
15	—	48.3	46.2	42	21	17	—	—	—	—	—
20	—	62.1	59.4	54	27	22	—	—	—	—	—
25	—	78.2	74.8	68	34	27	—	53	26	21	—
30	—	92	88	80	40	32	—	63	32	26	—
40	—	120	114	104	52	41	—	83	41	33	—
50	—	150	143	130	65	52	—	104	52	42	—
60	—	177	169	154	77	62	16	123	61	49	12
75	—	221	211	192	96	77	20	155	78	62	15
100	—	285	273	248	124	99	26	202	101	81	20
125	—	359	343	312	156	125	31	253	126	101	25
150	—	414	396	360	180	144	37	302	151	121	30
200	—	552	528	480	240	192	49	400	201	161	40
250	—	—	—	—	302	242	60	—	—	—	—
300	—	—	—	—	361	289	72	—	—	—	—
350	—	—	—	—	414	336	83	—	—	—	—
400	—	—	—	—	477	382	95	—	—	—	—
450	—	—	—	—	515	412	103	—	—	—	—
500	—	—	—	—	590	472	118	—	—	—	—

*For 90 and 80 percent power factor, the figures shall be multiplied by 1.1 and 1.25, respectively.

Table 430.250 see Table 430-250 in Tables folder on CD-ROM

115. Answer D.   sight

Disconnecting means shall be located within sight from and readily accessible from the air-conditioning or refrigerating equipment. The disconnecting means shall be permitted to be installed on or within the air-conditioning or refrigerating equipment.

The disconnecting means shall not be located on panels that are designed to allow access to the air-conditioning or refrigeration equipment or to obscure the equipment nameplate(s).

Exception No. 1: Where the disconnecting means provided in accordance with 430.102(A) is lockable in accordance with 110.25 and the refrigerating or air-conditioning equipment is essential to an industrial process in a facility with written safety procedures, and where the conditions of maintenance and supervision ensure that only qualified persons service the equipment, a disconnecting means within sight from the equipment shall not be required.

Exception No. 2: Where an attachment plug and receptacle serve as the disconnecting means in accordance with 440.13, their location shall be accessible but shall not be required to be readily accessible.

Informational Note No. 1: See Parts VII and IX of Article 430 for additional requirements.

Informational Note No. 2: See 110.26.

Reference: 2017 National Electrical Code – Chapter 4 Equipment for General Use, Article 440 Air-Conditioning and Refrigeration Equipment. 440.14 Location.1.

116. Answer D.   80

The total marked rating of a cord- and attachment-plug-connected room air conditioner shall not exceed 80 percent of the rating of a branch circuit where no other loads are supplied.

Reference: 2017 National Electrical Code – Chapter 4 Equipment for General Use, Article 440 Air-Conditioning and Refrigeration Equipment. 440.62 Branch-Circuit Requirements. 440.62(B) Where No Other Loads Are Supplied.1.

117. Answer A.   50%

The total marked rating of a cord- and attachment-plug-connected room air conditioner shall not exceed 50 percent of the rating of a branch circuit where lighting outlets, other appliances, or general-use receptacles are also supplied. Where the circuitry is interlocked to prevent simultaneous operation of the room air conditioner and energization of other outlets on the same branch circuit, a cord- and attachment-plug-connected room air conditioner shall not exceed 80 percent of the branch-circuit rating.

Reference: 2017 National Electrical Code – Chapter 4 Equipment for General Use, Article 440 Air-Conditioning and Refrigerating Equipment. 440.62 Branch-Circuit Requirements. 440.62(C) Where Lighting Units or Other Appliances Are Also Supplied.1.

118. Answer B.   10, 6

Where a flexible cord is used to supply a room air conditioner, the length of such cord shall not exceed 3.0 m (10 ft.) for a nominal, 120-volt rating or 1.8 m (6 ft.) for a nominal, 208- or 240-volt rating.

Reference: 2017 National Electrical Code – Chapter 4 Equipment for General Use, Article 440 Air-Conditioning and Refrigeration Equipment. 440.64 Supply Cords.1.

EXAM 8

EXAM 8 ANSWERS

119. Answer D.   10, 6

Where a flexible cord is used to supply a room air conditioner, the length of such cord shall not exceed 3.0 m (10 ft.) for a nominal, 120-volt rating or 1.8 m (6 ft.) for a nominal, 208- or 240-volt rating.

Reference: 2017 National Electrical Code – Chapter 4 Equipment for General Use, Article 440 Air-Conditioning and Refrigeration Equipment. 440.64 Supply Cords.1.

120. Answer B.   6 feet

Where a flexible cord is used to supply a room air conditioner, the length of such cord shall not exceed 3.0 m (10 ft.) for a nominal, ***120-volt rating or 1.8 m (6 ft.) for a nominal, 208- or 240-volt rating.***

Reference: 2017 National Electrical Code – Chapter 4 Equipment for General Use, Article 440 Air-Conditioning and Refrigerating Equipment. 440.64 Supply Cords.1.

121. Answer C.   overcurrent protection

Each transformer shall be provided with a nameplate giving the following information:

(1) Name of manufacturer

(2) Rated kilovolt-amperes

(3) Frequency

(4) Primary and secondary voltage

(5) Impedance of transformers 25 kVA and larger

(6) Required clearances for transformers with ventilating openings

(7) Amount and kind of insulating liquid where used

(8) For dry-type transformers, temperature class for the insulation system

Reference: 2017 National Electrical Code – Chapter 4 Equipment for General Use, Article 450 Transformers and Transformer Vaults (including Secondary Ties). 450.11 Marking. 450.11(A)General.1.

122. Answer C.   3 hours

The walls and roofs of vaults shall be constructed of materials that have approved structural strength for the conditions with a minimum fire resistance of 3 hours. The floors of vaults in contact with the earth shall be of concrete that is not less than 100 mm (4 in.) thick, but, where the vault is constructed with a vacant space or other stories below it, the floor shall have approved structural strength for the load imposed thereon and a minimum fire resistance of 3 hours. For the purposes of this section, studs and wallboard construction shall not be permitted.

Exception: Where transformers are protected with automatic sprinkler, water spray, carbon dioxide, or halon, construction of 1-hour rating shall be permitted.

Informational Note No. 1: For additional information, see ANSI/ASTM E119-15, Method for Fire Tests of Building Construction and Materials.

Informational Note No. 2: A typical 3-hour construction is 150 mm (6 in.) thick reinforced concrete.

Reference: 2017 National Electrical Code – Chapter 4 Equipment for General Use, Article 450 Transformers and Transformer Vaults (including Secondary Ties). 450.42 Walls, Roofs, and Floors.1.

123. Answer D.   Not be connected to the manufactured phase

Where single-phase loads are connected on the load side of a phase converter, they shall not be connected to the manufactured phase.

Reference: 2017 National Electrical Code – Chapter 4 Equipment for General Use, Article 455 Phase Converters. 455.9 Connection of Single-Phase Loads.

EXAM 9

Chapter 5 Special Occupancies

1. True or False: Locating much of the equipment in unclassified or less hazardous locations and thereby reducing the amount of required special equipment is frequently possible.

    A. True
    B. False

    Reference: 2017 National Electrical Code – Chapter 5 Special Occupancies, Article 500 Hazardous (Classified) Locations, Classes I, II, and III, Divisions 1 and 2. 500.5 Classifications of Locations. 500.5(A) General.

2. Which class of hazardous locations are the ones with combustible liquid-produced vapors, or flammable liquid-produced vapors that may be present in the air in sufficient quantities to be an ignitable or explosive mixture?

    A. I
    B. II
    C. III
    D. IV

    Reference: 2017 National Electrical Code – Chapter 5 Special Occupancies, Article 500 Hazardous (Classified) Locations, Classes I, II, and III, Divisions 1 and 2. 500.5 Classifications of Locations. 500.5(B) Class I Locations.

3. What is present at a Class II locations that makes them hazardous?

    A. combustible dust
    B. flammable gas
    C. ignitable fibers
    D. ignitable vapors

    Reference: 2017 National Electrical Code – Chapter 5 Special Occupancies, Article 500 Hazardous (Classified) Locations, Classes I, II, and III, Divisions 1 and 2. 500.5 Classifications of Locations. 500.5(C) Class II Locations.

EXAM 9

Chapter 5 Special Occupancies

4. Which Class locations is hazardous because of the presence of materials producing combustible flyings, or having the presence of easily ignitable fibers, but where they are not expected to be in sufficient quantities to create an ignitable mixture?

    A. I

    B. II

    C. III

    D. IV

    Reference: 2017 National Electrical Code – Chapter 5 Special Occupancies, Article 500 Hazardous (Classified) Locations, Classes I, II, and III, Divisions 1 and 2. 500.5 Classifications of Locations. 500.5(D) Class III Locations.

5. What is present that makes Class III locations hazardous?

    A. combustible dust

    B. easily ignitable fibers or materials producing combustible flyings

    C. flammable gases or liquids

    D. flammable vapors or gases

    Reference: 2017 National Electrical Code – Chapter 5 Special Occupancies, Article 500 Hazardous (Classified) Locations, Classes I, II, and III, Divisions 1 and 2. 500.5 Classifications of Locations. 500.5(D) Class III Locations

6. Identification of equipment should be for the combustible, explosive, or ignitible properties of a specific _____ present, as well as the class of hazardous (classified) location.

    A. dust

    B. fibers/flyings

    C. gas or vapor

    D. any of these

    Reference: 2017 National Electrical Code – Chapter 5 Special Occupancies, Article 500 Hazardous (Classified) Locations, Classes I, II, and III, Divisions 1 and 2. 500.8 Equipment. 500.8(B) Approval for Class and Properties.

Chapter 5 Special Occupancies

EXAM 9

Chapter 5 Special Occupancies

7. In equipment for hazardous (classified) locations, all unused openings are required to be closed with which kind of listed close-up plugs?

   A. composition

   B. metal

   C. nonmetallic

   D. Either A or B

   Reference: 2017 National Electrical Code – Chapter 5 Special Occupancies, Article 500 Hazardous (Classified) Locations, Classes I, II, and III, Divisions 1 and 2. 500.8 Equipment.

8. Which of the following requirements must be met for MC-HL cable being used in a Class I, Division 1 location in an industrial establishment with restricted public access, where only qualified persons will service an installation, in addition to being required to be terminated with fittings that are listed for the application? Cable must comply with Part II of Article 330.

   A. listed for Class I, Zone 1, or Division 1 locations

   B. gas/vaportight metallic sheath & jacket of polymeric material

   C. equipment grounding conductor(s) complying with 250.122

   D. A through C

   Reference: 2017 National Electrical Code – Chapter 5 Special Occupancies, Article 501 Class I Locations. 501.10 Wiring Methods. 501.10(A) Class I, Division 1. 501.10(A)(1)(C) General.

9. Where in Class I, Division 2 locations is Schedule 80 PVC conduit or reinforced thermosetting resin conduit (RTRC with an –XW suffix) permitted?

   A. if metal conduit has insufficient corrosion resistance

   B. only qualified persons service the installation

   C. installed in industrial locations

   D. A through C

   Reference: 2017 National Electrical Code – Chapter 5 Special Occupancies, Article 501 Class I Locations. 501.10 Wiring Methods. 501.10(B) Class I, Division 2. 501.10(B)(1) General.

466 Chapter 5 Special Occupancies

EXAM 9

Chapter 5 Special Occupancies

10. Class I, Division 2 locations may have general purpose enclosures and fittings unless otherwise required by Section 51.105(B)(1), Section 501.115(B)(1), or 501.105(B)(1), for which of the following?

    A. meters, instruments, and relays

    B. circuit breakers, or motor controllers

    C. signaling, alarm, remote-control, and communications

    D. A through C

    Reference: 2017 National Electrical Code – Chapter 5 Special Occupancies, Article 501 Class I Locations. 501.10 Wiring Methods. 501.10(B) Class I, Division 2. 501.10(B)(4) Boxes and Fittings.

11. For an enclosure in a Class I, Division 1 location that contains components with arcing devices, they must have an approved seal within at least what distance of each conduit run leaving or entering those enclosures?

    A. 12 inches

    B. 18 inches

    C. 24 inches

    D. 4-1/2 feet

    Reference: 2017 National Electrical Code – Chapter 5 Special Occupancies, Article 501 Class I Locations. 501.15 Sealing and Drainage. 501.15(A) Conduit Seals, Class I, Division 1. 501.15(A)(1) Entering Enclosures.

12. Which of the following rules must be complied with for sealing fittings required for Class I locations?

    A. Be listed for Class I locations and be accessible

    B. Minimum thickness of the compound not be less than 5/8 in.

    C. Splices and taps shall not be made in the conduit seal

    D. A through C

    Reference: 2017 National Electrical Code – Chapter 5 Special Occupancies, Article 501 Class I Locations. 501.15 Sealing and Drainage. 501.15(C) Class I, Divisions 1 and 2. 501.15(C)(1) Fittings.

Chapter 5 Special Occupancies

EXAM 9

Chapter 5 Special Occupancies

13. What is the minimum thickness of sealing compound on a seal for trade size 1/2 in. rigid metal conduit (RMC) installed in a Class I location?

    A. 3/8 inch

    B. 1/2 inch

    C. 5/8 inch

    D. 3/4 inch

    Reference: 2017 National Electrical Code – Chapter 5 Special Occupancies, Article 501 Class I Locations. 501.15 Sealing and Drainage. 501.15(C) Class I, Divisions 1 and 2. 501.15(C)(3) Thickness of Compounds.

14. The cross-sectional area of the conductors or optical fiber tubes allowed in a seal shall not exceed _____ of the cross-sectional area of a rigid metal conduit of the same trade side, unless specifically identified for a higher fill percentage.

    A. 25%

    B. 40%

    C. 50%

    D. 60%

    Reference: 2017 National Electrical Code – Chapter 5 Special Occupancies, Article 501 Class I Locations. 501.15 Sealing and Drainage. 501.15(C) Class I, Divisions 1 and 2. 501.15(C)(6) Conductor or Optical Fiber Fill.

15. True or False: For bonding purposes, locknut-bushing and double-locknut contact types in Class I locations must not be depended on.

    A. True

    B. False

    Reference: 2017 National Electrical Code – Chapter 5 Special Occupancies, Article 501 Class I Locations. 501.30 Grounding and Bonding, Class I, Division 1 and 2. 501.30(A) Bonding.

16. What is required to be done with current-interrupting contacts for instruments, meters and relays to have circuit breakers, make-and-break contacts, and switches installed in general purpose enclosures in Class I, Division 2 locations?

    A. enclosed within a hermetically sealed chamber

    B. immersed in oil

    C. Both A and B

    D. Either A or B

    Reference: 2017 National Electrical Code – Chapter 5 Special Occupancies, Article 501 Class I Locations. 501.105 Meters, Instruments, and Relays. 501.105(B) Class I, Division 2. 501.105(B)(2) Contacts.

EXAM 9

Chapter 5 Special Occupancies

17. True or False: In a Class I, Division 1 location, totally enclosed motors like those specified in 501.125(A)(2) or (A)(3) must have a device designed to provide an alarm or de-energize the motor if the temperature of the motor increases beyond designed limits.

    A. True
    B. False

    Reference: 2017 National Electrical Code – Chapter 5 Special Occupancies, Article 501 Class I Locations. 501.125 Motors and Generators. 501.125(A) Class I, Division 1.

18. Which of the following is a suitable protection from physical damage for luminaires installed in Class I, Division 2 locations?

    A. guard or by location
    B. pendant
    C. warning label
    D. A through C

    Reference: 2017 National Electrical Code – Chapter 5 Special Occupancies, Article 501 Class I Locations. 501.130 Luminaires. 501.130(B) Class I, Division 2. 501.130(B)(2) Physical Damage.

19. Flexible cords in Class I locations that apply 501.140(A)(5) must be _____ between the utilization equipment to the temporary portable assembly and between the temporary portable assembly and the power source.

    A. installed in a metal raceway
    B. of continuous length
    C. permitted to be spliced
    D. spliced only using listed splicing kits

    Reference: 2017 National Electrical Code – Chapter 5 Special Occupancies, Article 501 Class I Locations. 501.140 Flexible Cords, Class I, Divisions 1 and 2. 501.140(B)(5) Installation.

20. When installed in Class II, Division 1 locations, boxes and fittings used for joints, taps, or terminal connections must be:

    A. explosionproof
    B. identified for Class II locations
    C. dusttight
    D. weatherproof

    Reference: 2017 National Electrical Code – Chapter 5 Special Occupancies, Article 502 Class II Locations. 502.10 Wiring Methods. 502.10(A) Class II, Division 1. 502.10(A)(3) Boxes and Fittings.

EXAM 9

Chapter 5 Special Occupancies

21. In a Class II, Division 2 location, an installed disconnect switch enclosure shall be:

    A. dusttight

    B. general duty type

    C. heavy duty type

    D. raintight

    Reference: 2017 National Electrical Code – Chapter 5 Special Occupancies, Article 502 Class II Locations. 502.10 Wiring Methods. 502.10(B) Class II, Division 2. 502.10(B)(4) Boxes and Fittings.

22. True or False: Seals for Class II hazardous (classified) locations are not required to be explosion proof.

    A. True

    B. False

    Reference: 2017 National Electrical Code – Chapter 5 Special Occupancies, Article 502 Class II Locations. 502.15 Sealing, Class II, Divisions 1 and 2.

23. Control transformers, impedance coils and resistors, solenoids, and any overcurrent devices and switching mechanisms associated with those that are installed in Class II, Division 1 locations must have enclosures identified for:

    A. Class I, Division 1 locations

    B. Class II, Division 1 locations

    C. control transformer duty

    D. general duty

    Reference: 2017 National Electrical Code – Chapter 5 Special Occupancies, Article 502 Class II Locations. 502.120 Control Transformers and Resistors. 502.120(A) Class II, Division 1.

24. If pendant luminaires are installed in Class II, Division 1 locations, they must be suspended by chains with approved fittings, steel IMC or threaded RMC conduit stems, or other approved means, and to prevent loosening, stems must have _____ or some other effective means.

    A. set-screws

    B. welded joints

    C. expansion joints

    D. explosionproof flex

    Reference: 2017 National Electrical Code – Chapter 5 Special Occupancies, Article 502 Class II Locations. 502.130 Luminaires. 502.130(A) Class II, Division 1. 502.130(A)(3) Pendant Luminaires.

EXAM 9

Chapter 5 Special Occupancies

25. Receptacles in Class II, Division 1 locations must be part of the premises wiring and any attachment plugs must be the sort that provides connection of the flexible cord to the:

    A. building grounding electrode system

    B. equipment bonding conductor

    C. equipment grounding conductor

    D. any of these

    Reference: 2017 National Electrical Code – Chapter 5 Special Occupancies, Article 502 Class II Locations. 502.145 Receptacles and Attachment Plugs. 502.145(A) Class II, Division 1.

26. True or False: Double-locknut and locknut-bushing types of fittings shall be relied on for bonding purposes.

    A. True

    B. False

    Reference: 2017 National Electrical Code – Chapter 5 Special Occupancies, Article 503 Class III Locations. 503.30 Grounding and Bonding - Class III, Divisions 1 and 2. 503.30(A) Bonding.

27. If luminaires are installed in Class III locations, and exposed to physical damage what kind of guard is required?

    A. explosionproof

    B. metal

    C. plastic

    D. suitable

    Reference: 2017 National Electrical Code – Chapter 5 Special Occupancies, Article 503 Class III Locations. 503.130 Luminaires - Class III, Divisions 1 and 2. 503.130(B) Physical Damage.

28. Intrinsically safe apparatus, associated apparatus, and other equipment shall be installed:

    A. in a dedicated enclosure

    B. in accordance with the control drawings

    C. in the electrical equipment room

    D. on a backboard of at least 3/4 in. thick plywood

    Reference: 2017 National Electrical Code – Chapter 5 Special Occupancies, Article 504 Intrinsically Safe Systems. 504.10 Equipment Installation. 504.10(A) Control Drawing.

Chapter 5 Special Occupancies   471

EXAM 9

Chapter 5 Special Occupancies

29. Who determined the classification of hazardous areas and zones?

    A. engineers

    B. licensed electricians

    C. qualified persons

    D. the local authority having jurisdiction

    Reference: 2017 National Electrical Code – Chapter 5 Special Occupancies, Article 505 Zone 0, 1, and 2 Locations. 505.7 Special Precaution. 505.7(A) Implementation of Zone Classification System.

30. Which Article of the NEC has the wiring requirements for service and repair operations involving self-propelled vehicles that use flammable gases or volatile flammable liquids for fuel or power?

    A. Article 500

    B. Article 501

    C. Article 511

    D. Article 514

    Reference: 2017 National Electrical Code – Chapter 5 Special Occupancies, Article 511 Commercial Garages, Repair and Storage. 511.1 Scope.

31. Any pit or depression below floor level in a major repair garage that does not provide ventilation in compliance with 511.3(C)(3)(a) will be a Class I, _____ location, extending to the floor level.

    A. Division 1

    B. Division 2

    C. Both A and B

    D. Either A or B

    Reference: 2017 National Electrical Code – Chapter 5 Special Occupancies, Article 511 Commercial Garages, Repair and Storage. 511.3 Area Classification, General. 511.3(C) Major Repair Garages. 511.3(C)(3) Repair Garages, Major and Minor.

32. True or False: In a commercial garage, Type NM cable may be installed above a Class I location.

    A. True

    B. False

    Reference: 2017 National Electrical Code – Chapter 5 Special Occupancies, Article 511 Commercial Garages, Repair and Storage. 511.7 Wiring and Equipment Installed Above Class I Locations. 511.7(A) Wiring in Spaces Above Class I Locations. 511.7(A)(1) Fixed Wiring Above Class I Locations.

EXAM 9

Chapter 5 Special Occupancies

33. For fixed wiring in an area above Class I locations in a commercial garage, which wiring method is/are approved?

    A. Type MC cable

    B. Type MI cable

    C. Type TC cable

    D. all of the above

    Reference: 2017 National Electrical Code – Chapter 5 Special Occupancies, Article 511 Commercial Garages, Repair and Storage. 511.7 Wiring and Equipment Installed Above Class I Locations. 511.7(A) Wiring in Spaces Above Class I Locations. 511.7(A)(1) Fixed Wiring Above Class I Locations.

34. GFCI protection for personnel is required to be provided in commercial garages on all 15A and 20A, 125V receptacles that are installed where which of the following is used?

    A. electrical diagnostic equipment

    B. electrical hand tools

    C. portable lighting equipment

    D. any of these

    Reference: 2017 National Electrical Code – Chapter 5 Special Occupancies, Article 511 Commercial Garages, Repair and Storage. 511.12 Ground-Fault Circuit-Interrupter Protection for Personnel.

35. True or False: If a circuit leads to or through motor fuel dispensing equipment, it must be provided with a readily accessible and clearly identified switch or other approved means to disconnect all conductors of the circuit, including the grounded conductor, located remote from the dispensing devices.

    A. True

    B. False

    Reference: 2017 National Electrical Code – Chapter 5 Special Occupancies, Article 514 Motor Fuel Dispensing Facilities. 514.11 Circuit Disconnects. 514.11(A) Emergency Electrical Disconnects.

EXAM 9

Chapter 5 Special Occupancies

36. The area around motor fuel dispensing pumps at a service station is considered a hazardous location. How far horizontally from the enclosure of the outdoor motor fuel dispensing pumps does this extend?

    A. 5 feet

    B. 10 feet

    C. 16 feet

    D. 20 feet

    Reference: 2017 National Electrical Code – Chapter 5 Special Occupancies, Article 514 Motor Fuel Dispensing Facilities. 514.3 Classification of Locations. 514.3(B) Classified Locations. 514.3(B)(1) Class I Locations.

37. What is the first fitting that should be installed in the raceway that emerges from below ground or concrete into the base of a gasoline dispenser, when wiring motor fuel dispensing pumps?

    A. Automatic cut-off breakaway valve.

    B. Disconnect

    C. Sealing fitting

    D. No fittings of any kind are permitted in this location.

    Reference: 2017 National Electrical Code – Chapter 5 Special Occupancies, Article 514 Motor Fuel Dispensing Facilities. 514.9 Sealing. 514.9(A) At Dispenser.

38. True or False: During periods of maintenance and service of motor fuel dispensing equipment, each device must be provided with a means to remove all external sources of voltage, including communications, data, feedback, power, and video circuits.

    A. True

    B. False

    Reference: 2017 National Electrical Code – Chapter 5 Special Occupancies, Article 514 Motor Fuel Dispensing Facilities. 514.13 Provisions for Maintenance and Service of Dispensing Equipment.

EXAM 9

Chapter 5 Special Occupancies

39. A location used to house four or more persons incapable of self-preservation due to age; mental limitations, mental illness or chemical dependency; or physical limitation due to accident or illness on a(n) _____ basis is a limited care facility.

    A. 10-hour or less per day

    B. 24-hour

    C. occasional

    D. temporary

    Reference: 2017 National Electrical Code – Chapter 5 Special Occupancies, Article 517 Health Care Facilities. 517.2 Definitions.

40. True or False: Except as modified by Article 517, wiring used in health care locations are required to comply with the provisions of Chapter 1 through 4 of the NEC.

    A. True

    B. False

    Reference: 2017 National Electrical Code, Article 90 Introduction. 90.3 Code Arrangement.

41. True or False: Receptacles in health care facilities that have insulated grounding terminals as described in 250.146(D) are allowed in the vicinity of patient care areas.

    A. True

    B. False

    Reference: 2017 National Electrical Code – Chapter 5 Special Occupancies, Article 517 Health Care Facilities. 517.16 Use of Isolated Ground Receptacles.

42. What is the minimum number of hospital grade receptacles required for each patient bed location in general care areas of hospitals, disregarding exceptions?

    A. Eight

    B. Ten

    C. Twelve

    D. Fourteen

    Reference: 2017 National Electrical Code – Chapter 5 Special Occupancies, Article 517 Health Care Facilities. 517.18 General Care Areas. 517.18(B) Patient Bed Location Receptacles.

EXAM 9

Chapter 5 Special Occupancies

43. Of the following, which is required for a patient bed location in a critical care area of a health care facility?

    A. Four single receptacles or two duplex receptacles.

    B. Six duplex receptacles or twelve single receptacles.

    C. Eight single receptacles or four duplex receptacles.

    D. Fourteen single receptacles or seven duplex receptacles.

    Reference: 2017 National Electrical Code – Chapter 5 Special Occupancies, Article 517 Health Care Facilities. 517.19 Critical Care Areas. 517.19(B) Patient Bed Location Receptacles.

44. Essential electrical systems for hospitals are comprised of which branches?

    A. The emergency, life safety, and the standby

    B. The essential, the emergency, and the equipment

    C. The life safety, equipment, and the critical

    D. The normal, life safety, and the alternate

    Reference: 2017 National Electrical Code – Chapter 5 Special Occupancies, Article 517 Health Care Facilities. 517.31 Requirements for the Essential Electrical System. 517.30(A) Separate Branches. A.

45. What is required for the installation of wiring for the essential electrical system in patient care areas of hospitals?

    A. Flexible metal raceways

    B. Flexible nonmetallic raceways

    C. Nonflexible metal raceways

    D. Nonflexible nonmetallic raceways

    Reference: 2017 National Electrical Code – Chapter 5 Special Occupancies, Article 517 Health Care Facilities. 517.31 Requirements for the Essential Electrical System. 517.31(C) Wiring Requirements. 517.31(C)(3) Mechanical Protection of the Essential Electrical System. 517.31(C)(3)(1)

EXAM 9

Chapter 5 Special Occupancies

46. What is the maximum operating voltage for low-voltage equipment that is frequently in contact with the bodies of persons, or has exposed current-carrying elements?

    A. 10 volts

    B. 24 volts

    C. 100 volts

    D. 120 volts

    Reference: 2017 National Electrical Code – Chapter 5 Special Occupancies, Article 517 Health Care Facilities. 517.64 Low-Voltage Equipment and Instruments. 517.64(A) Equipment Requirements.

47. What is the minimum number of people that a hospital conference room must be designed to hold to be an assembly occupancy?

    A. 25

    B. 50

    C. 75

    D. 100

    Reference: 2017 National Electrical Code – Chapter 5 Special Occupancies, Article 518 Assembly Occupancies. 518.1 Scope.

48. In accordance with Article 590, temporary wiring for display booths in exhibition halls is allowed, except:

    A. when requirements of Article 590 are not required

    B. flexible cords & cables can be laid on floors away from general public

    C. GFCI protection is required except for Article 590 requirements

    D. A through C

    Reference: 2017 National Electrical Code – Chapter 5 Special Occupancies. 518.3 Other Articles. 518.3(B) Temporary Wiring.

EXAM 9
Chapter 5 Special Occupancies

49. What is the maximum load that may be carried by branch circuits for luminaires installed as border lighting for stages in theaters?

    A. 10 amperes

    B. 15 amperes

    C. 20 amperes

    D. 30 amperes

    Reference: 2017 National Electrical Code – Chapter 5 Special Occupancies, Article 520 Theaters, Audience Areas of Motion Picture and Television Studios, Performance Areas, and Similar Locations. 520.41 Circuit Loads. 520.41(A) Circuits Rated 20 Amperes or Less.

50. Which Article covers the installation of portable wiring and equipment for functions such as carnivals, circuses, exhibitions, fairs, and traveling attractions?

    A. Article 518

    B. Article 525

    C. Article 590

    D. A through C

    Reference: 2017 National Electrical Code – Chapter 5 Special Occupancies, Article 525 Carnivals, Circuses, Fairs, and Similar Events. 525.1 Scope.

51. At carnivals and circuses, electrical service equipment must not be accessible to unqualified persons unless it is:

    A. accessible

    B. lockable

    C. readily accessible

    D. none of these

    Reference: 2017 National Electrical Code – Chapter 5 Special Occupancies, Article 525 Carnivals, Circuses, Fairs, and Similar Events. 525.10 Services. 525.10(A) Guarding.

52. At a carnival, circus or fair, wiring for amusement rides, attractions, tents, or similar structures may not be supported by any other ride or structure unless it is designed specifically for that purpose.

    A. True

    B. False

    Reference: 2017 National Electrical Code – Chapter 5 Special Occupancies, Article 525 Carnivals, Circuses, Fairs, and Similar Events. 525.20 Wiring Methods. 525.20(F) Support.

EXAM 9

Chapter 5 Special Occupancies

53. On a portable carnival ride, the maximum distance that a disconnect switch is allowed to be located from the operator's station is:

    A. 6 feet

    B. 10 feet

    C. 25 feet

    D. 50 feet

    Reference: 2017 National Electrical Code – Chapter 5 Special Occupancies, Article 525 Carnivals, Circuses, Fairs, and Similar Events. 525.21 Rides, Tents, and Concessions. 525.21(A) Disconnecting Means.

54. True or False: GFCI protection is not required on receptacles of the locking type at carnivals and fairs that are not accessible from grade level and facilitate quick disconnecting and reconnecting of electrical equipment.

    A. True

    B. False

    Reference: 2017 National Electrical Code – Chapter 5 Special Occupancies, Article 525 Carnivals, Circuses, Fairs, and Similar Events. 525.23 Ground-Fault Circuit-Interrupter (GFCI) Protection. 525.23(B) Where GFCI Protection Is Not Required.

55. Compliance with Article 547 is required for all agricultural buildings for _____ confinement systems where excessive dust and dust with water may accumulate, or where litter dust or feed dust may accumulate.

    A. fish

    B. livestock

    C. poultry

    D. A through C

    Reference: 2017 National Electrical Code – Chapter 5 Special Occupancies, Article 547 Agricultural Buildings. 547.1 Scope. 547.1(A) Excessive Dust and Dust with Water.

56. What is the maximum distance from a box, cabinet, or fitting for cables installed in agricultural buildings to be secured?

    A. 8 in.

    B. 12 in.

    C. 18 in.

    D. 24 in.

    Reference: 2017 National Electrical Code – Chapter 5 Special Occupancies, Article 547 Agricultural Buildings. 547.5 Wiring Methods. 547.5(B) Mounting.

EXAM 9
Chapter 5 Special Occupancies

57. What kind of conductor must be used for an equipment grounding conductor installed underground inside an agricultural building?

    A. bare

    B. copper

    C. insulated or covered

    D. any of these

    Reference: 2017 National Electrical Code – Chapter 5 Special Occupancies, Article 547 Agricultural Buildings. 547.5 Wiring Methods. 547.5(F) Separate Equipment Grounding Conductor.

58. True or False: In outdoor concrete slabs where metallic equipment is accessible to livestock other than poultry and may become energized, equipotential plans are required to be installed.

    A. True

    B. False

    Reference: 2017 National Electrical Code – Chapter 5 Special Occupancies, Article 547 Agricultural Buildings. 547.10 Equipotential Planes and Bonding of Equipotential

59. What is the maximum rating of the power supply cord to a mobile home?

    A. 50 amperes

    B. 60 amperes

    C. 100 amperes

    D. 150 amperes

    Reference: 2017 National Electrical Code – Chapter 5 Special Occupancies, Article 550 Mobile Homes, Manufactured Homes, and Mobile Home Parks. 550.10 Power Supply. 550.10(A) Feeder.

60. What is the maximum trade size conduit allowed to enclose a mobile home supply cord between the underside of a mobile home floor and the branch circuit panelboard?

    A. 1 in.

    B. 1-1/4 in.

    C. 1-1/2 in.

    D. 2 in.

    Reference: 2017 National Electrical Code – Chapter 5 Special Occupancies, Article 550 Mobile Homes, Manufactured Homes, and Mobile Home Parks. 550.10 Power Supply. 550.10(G) Protected.

EXAM 9

Chapter 5 Special Occupancies

61. Where are receptacle outlets for manufactured and mobile homes not allowed to be installed?

    A. in a face-up position in any countertop

    B. underneath the skirting of the home

    C. within or directly over a bathtub or shower space

    D. either A or C

    Reference: 2017 National Electrical Code – Chapter 5 Special Occupancies, Article 550 Mobile Homes, Manufactured Homes, and Mobile Home Parks. 550.13 Receptacle Outlets. 550.13(F) Receptacle Outlets Not Permitted.

62. What is the minimum rating allowed for 120/240 volt, single-phase service equipment for a mobile home?

    A. 50 amperes

    B. 60 amperes

    C. 100 amperes

    D. 150 amperes

    Reference: 2017 National Electrical Code – Chapter 5 Special Occupancies, Article 550 Mobile Homes, Manufactured Homes, and Mobile Home Parks. 550.32 Service Equipment. 550.32(C) Rating.

63. The disconnecting means for a mobile home is installed outdoors, and what is the minimum height of the bottom of the enclosure above finished grade?

    A. two feet

    B. three feet

    C. four feet

    D. six feet

    Reference: 2017 National Electrical Code – Chapter 5 Special Occupancies, Article 550 Mobile Homes, Manufactured Homes, and Mobile Home Parks. 550.32 Service Equipment. 550.32(F) Mounting Height.

EXAM 9

Chapter 5 Special Occupancies

64. For a mobile home, an outdoor disconnecting means must be installed so that the bottom of the enclosure is above the finished grade or working platform by at least:

    A. 1 ft.

    B. 2 ft.

    C. 3 ft.

    D. 6 ft.

    Reference: 2017 National Electrical Code – Chapter 5 Special Occupancies, Article 550 Mobile Homes, Manufactured Homes, and Mobile Home Parks. 550.32 Service Equipment. 550.32(F) Mounting Height.

65. Where flexible connections are required, feeders to floating buildings may be installed in:

    A. MC cable

    B. AC cable

    C. NMC cable

    D. Portable power cable

    Reference: 2017 National Electrical Code – Chapter 5 Special Occupancies, Article 553 Floating Buildings. 553.7 Installation of Services and Feeders. 553.7(B) Wiring Methods.

66. What is defined as an enclosed assembly that can include equipment such as circuit breakers, fused switches, fuses, panelboards, receptacles, watt-hour meter(s), and monitoring means approved for marine use?

    A. marine outlet

    B. marine power outlet

    C. marine power receptacle

    D. any of these

    Reference: 2017 National Electrical Code – Chapter 5 Special Occupancies, Article 555 Marinas and Boatyards. 555.2 Definitions.

67. True or False: Substantial support by structural members, independent of a connected raceway, is required of electrical equipment enclosures at marinas.

    A. True

    B. False

    Reference: 2017 National Electrical Code – Chapter 5 Special Occupancies, Article 555 Marinas and Boatyards. 555.10 Electrical Equipment Enclosures. 555.10(A) Securing and Supporting.

EXAM 9

Chapter 5 Special Occupancies

68. Disconnecting means, consisting of a circuit breaker, switch, or both, that identifies which receptacle it controls, is required to _____ each boat from the connection to its electrical supply.

    A. control

    B. guard

    C. isolate

    D. separate

    Reference: 2017 National Electrical Code – Chapter 5 Special Occupancies, Article 555 Marinas and Boatyards. 555.17 Disconnecting Means for Shore Power Connection(s).

69. What is the maximum distance that an accessible disconnecting means may be from a boat receptacle in a marina?

    A. 30 inches

    B. 6 feet

    C. 10 feet

    D. 50 feet

    Reference: 2017 National Electrical Code – Chapter 5 Special Occupancies, Article 555 Marinas and Boatyards. 555.17 Disconnecting Means for Shore Power Connection(s). 555.17(B) Location.

70. What is the minimum rating for single receptacle shore power for boats?

    A. 20 amperes

    B. 30 amperes

    C. 50 amperes

    D. 60 amperes

    Reference: 2017 National Electrical Code – Chapter 5 Special Occupancies, Article 555 Marinas and Boatyards. 555.19 Receptacles. 555.19(A) Shore Power Receptacles. 555.19(A)(4) Ratings.

71. What is the minimum rating for receptacles that provide shore power for boats?

    A. 15A

    B. 20A

    C. 30A

    D. 60A

    Reference: 2017 National Electrical Code – Chapter 5 Special Occupancies, Article 555 Marinas and Boatyards. 555.19 Receptacles. 555.19(A) Shore Power Receptacles. 555.19(A)(4) Ratings.

EXAM 9

Chapter 5 Special Occupancies

72. Temporary electric power and lighting installations for holiday decorative lighting and similar purposes is allowed for a maximum of:

    A. 30 days

    B. 60 days

    C. 90 days

    D. four months

    Reference: 2017 National Electrical Code – Chapter 5 Special Occupancies, Article 590 Temporary Installations. 590.3 Time Constraints. 590.3(B) 90 Days.

73. Other than emergencies, what is temporary electrical power and lighting allowed for?

    A. developmental work

    B. experiments

    C. tests

    D. A through C

    Reference: 2017 National Electrical Code – Chapter 5 Special Occupancies, Article 590 Temporary Installations. 590.3 Time Constraints. 590.3(C) Emergencies and Tests.

74. On construction sites, receptacles must not be installed on the same _____ as temporary lighting.

    A. same branch circuit

    B. the same feeders

    C. Either A or B

    D. none of these

    Reference: 2017 National Electrical Code – Chapter 5 Special Occupancies, Article 590 Temporary Installations. 590.4 General. 590.4(D) Receptacles. 590.4(D)(1) All Receptacles.

75. For temporary installations, vegetation must not be used as a support for overhead conductor spans of:

    A. branch circuits

    B. feeders

    C. Either A or B

    D. none of these

    Reference: 2017 National Electrical Code – Chapter 5 Special Occupancies, Article 590 Temporary Installations. 590.4 General. 590.4(J) Support.

Chapter 5 Special Occupancies

EXAM 9

Chapter 5 Special Occupancies

76. On portable generators manufactured before _____, listed cord sets or adapters incorporating listed GFCI protection are allowed to be used to meet the GFCI requirement.

    A. January 1, 2005   C. January 1, 2014

    B. January 1, 2011   D. January 1, 2015

Reference: 2017 National Electrical Code – Chapter 5 Special Occupancies, Article 590 Temporary Installations. 590.6 Ground-Fault Protection for Personnel. 590.6(A) Receptacle Outlets. 590.6(A)(3) Receptacles on 15-kW or less Portable Generators.

EXAM 9

EXAM 9 ANSWERS

1. **Answer A.** True

   Locations shall be classified depending on the properties of the flammable gas, flammable liquid–produced vapor, combustible liquid–produced vapors, combustible dusts, or fibers/flyings that could be present, and the likelihood that a flammable or combustible concentration or quantity is present. Each room, section, or area shall be considered individually in determining its classification. Where pyrophoric materials are the only materials used or handled, these locations are outside the scope of this article.

   Informational Note No. 1: *Through the exercise of ingenuity in the layout of electrical installations for hazardous (classified) locations, it is frequently possible to locate much of the equipment in a reduced level of classification or in an unclassified location and, thus, to reduce the amount of special equipment required.*

   Refrigerant machinery rooms that contain ammonia refrigeration systems and are equipped with adequate mechanical ventilation that operates continuously or is initiated by a detection system at a concentration not exceeding 150 ppm shall be permitted to be classified as "unclassified" locations.

   Informational Note No. 2: For further information regarding classification and ventilation of areas involving closed-circuit ammonia refrigeration systems, see ANSI/ASHRAE 15-2013, Safety Standard for Refrigeration Systems, and ANSI/IIAR 2–2014, Standard for Safe Design of Closed-Circuit Ammonia Refrigeration Systems.

   Reference: 2017 National Electrical Code – Chapter 5 Special Occupancies, Article 500 Hazardous (Classified) Locations, Classes I, II, and III, Divisions 1 and 2. 500.5 Classifications of Locations. 500.5(A) General.

2. **Answer A.** I

   Class I locations are those in which flammable gases, flammable liquid-produced vapors, or combustible liquid-produced vapors are or may be present in the air in quantities sufficient to produce explosive or ignitable mixtures. Class I locations shall include those specified in 500.5(B)(1) and (B)(2).

   Reference: 2017 National Electrical Code – Chapter 5 Special Occupancies, Article 500 Hazardous (Classified) Locations, Classes I, II, and III, Divisions 1 and 2. 500.5 Classifications of Locations. 500.5(B) Class I Locations.

3. **Answer A.** combustible dust

   Class II locations are those that are hazardous because of the presence of combustible dust. Class II locations shall include those specified in 500.5(C)(1) and (C)(2).

   Reference: 2017 National Electrical Code – Chapter 5 Special Occupancies, Article 500 Hazardous (Classified) Locations, Classes I, II, and III, Divisions 1 and 2. 500.5 Classifications of Locations. 500.5(C) Class II Locations.

4. **Answer C.** III

   Class III locations are those that are hazardous because of the presence of easily ignitable fibers or where materials producing combustible flyings are handled, manufactured, or used, but in which such fibers/flyings are not likely to be in suspension in the air in quantities sufficient to produce ignitable mixtures. Class III locations shall include those specified in 500.5(D)(1) and (D)(2).

   Reference: 2017 National Electrical Code – Chapter 5 Special Occupancies, Article 500 Hazardous (Classified) Locations, Classes I, II, and III, Divisions 1 and 2. 500.5 Classifications of Locations. 500.5(D) Class III Locations.

5. **Answer B.** easily ignitable fibers or materials producing combustible flyings

   Class III locations are those that are hazardous because of *the presence of easily ignitable fibers or where materials producing combustible flyings are handled, manufactured, or used,* but in which such fibers/flyings are not likely to be in suspension in the air in quantities sufficient to produce ignitable mixtures. Class III locations shall include those specified in 500.5(D)(1) and (D)(2).

   Reference: 2017 National Electrical Code – Chapter 5 Special Occupancies, Article 500 Hazardous (Classified) Locations, Classes I, II, and III, Divisions 1 and 2. 500.5 Classifications of Locations. 500.5(D) Class III Locations

EXAM 9

EXAM 9 ANSWERS

6. **Answer D.** any of these

   (1) Equipment shall be identified not only for the class of location but also for the explosive, combustible, or ignitible properties of the specific gas, vapor, dust, or fibers/flyings that will be present. In addition, Class I equipment shall not have any exposed surface that operates at a temperature in excess of the autoignition temperature of the specific gas or vapor. Class II equipment shall not have an external temperature higher than that specified in 500.8(D)(2). Class III equipment shall not exceed the maximum surface temperatures specified in 503.5.

   Informational Note: Luminaires and other heat-producing apparatus, switches, circuit breakers, and plugs and receptacles are potential sources of ignition and are investigated for suitability in classified locations. Such types of equipment, as well as cable terminations for entry into explosionproof enclosures, are available as listed for Class I, Division 2 locations. Fixed wiring, however, may utilize wiring methods that are not evaluated with respect to classified locations. Wiring products such as cable, raceways, boxes, and fittings, therefore, are not marked as being suitable for Class I, Division 2 locations. Also see 500.8(C)(6)(a).

   Reference: 2017 National Electrical Code – Chapter 5 Special Occupancies, Article 500 Hazardous (Classified) Locations, Classes I, II, and III, Divisions 1 and 2. 500.8 Equipment. 500.8(B) Approval for Class and Properties.

7. **Answer B.** metal

   All unused openings shall be closed with listed metal close-up plugs. The plug engagement shall comply with 500.8(E)(1) or (E)(2).

   Reference: 2017 National Electrical Code – Chapter 5 Special Occupancies, Article 500 Hazardous (Classified) Locations, Classes I, II, and III, Divisions 1 and 2. 500.8 Equipment.

8. **Answer D.** A through C

   (c) In industrial establishments with restricted public access, where the conditions of maintenance and supervision ensure that only qualified persons service the installation, *Type MC-HL cable listed for use in Class I, Zone 1 or Division 1 locations, with a gas/vaportight continuous corrugated metallic sheath, an overall jacket of suitable polymeric material and a separate equipment grounding conductor(s) in accordance with 250.122, and terminated with fittings listed for the application.*

   Type MC-HL cable shall be installed in accordance with the provisions of Article 330, Part II.

   Reference: 2017 National Electrical Code – Chapter 5 Special Occupancies, Article 501 Class I Locations. 501.10 Wiring Methods. 501.10(A) Class I, Division 1. 501.10(A)(1)(C) General.

9. **Answer D.** A through C

   (6) In industrial establishments with restricted public access, where the conditions of maintenance and supervision ensure that only qualified persons service the installation and where metallic conduit does not provide sufficient corrosion resistance, listed reinforced thermosetting resin conduit (RTRC), factory elbows, and associated fittings, all marked with the suffix -XW, and Schedule 80 PVC conduit, factory elbows, and associated fittings shall be permitted.

   Where seals are required for boundary conditions as defined in 501.I5(A)(4), the Division 1 wiring method shall extend into the Division 2 area to the seal, which shall be located on the Division 2 side of the Division 1-Division 2 boundary.

   Reference: 2017 National Electrical Code – Chapter 5 Special Occupancies, Article 501 Class I Locations. 501.10 Wiring Methods. 501.10(B) Class I, Division 2. 501.10(B)(1) General.

EXAM 9

EXAM 9 ANSWERS

10. **Answer D.** A through C

    Boxes and fittings shall not be required to be explosion proof except as required by 501.105(B)(2), 501.115(B)(1) and 501.150(B)(1).

    Informational Note: *For entry into enclosures required to be explosionproof, see the information on construction, testing, and marking of cables, explosionproof cable fittings, and explosionproof cord connectors in ANSI/UL 2225-2011, Cables and Cable-Fittings for Use in Hazardous (Classified) Locations.*

    Reference: 2017 National Electrical Code – Chapter 5 Special Occupancies, Article 501 Class I Locations. 501.10 Wiring Methods. 501.10(B) Class I, Division 2. 501.10(B)(4) Boxes and Fittings.

11. **Answer B.** 18 inches

    Each Conduit entry into an explosionproof enclosure shall have a conduit seal where either of the following conditions apply:

    (1) The enclosure contains apparatus, such as switches, circuit breakers, fuses, relays, or resistors that may produce arcs, sparks, or temperatures that exceed 80 percent of the auto ignition temperature, in degrees Celsius, of the gas or vapor involved in normal operation.

    Exception: Seals shall not be required for conduit entering an enclosure under any one of the following conditions:

    b. The switch, circuit breaker, fuse, relay, or resistor is immersed in oil in accordance with 501.115(B)(1)(2).

    c. The switch, circuit breaker, fuse, relay, or resistor is enclosed within an enclosure, identified for the location, and marked "Leads Factory Sealed," or "Factory Sealed," "Seal not Required," or equivalent.

    d. The switch, circuit breaker, fuse, relay, or resistor is part of a non incendive circuit.

    (2) The entry is metric designator 53 (trade size 2) or larger, and the enclosure contains terminals, splices, or taps. An enclosure, identified for the location, and marked "Leads Factory Sealed", or "Factory Sealed," or "Seal not Required," or equivalent shall not be considered to serve as a seal for another adjacent enclosure that is required to have a conduit seal.

    Conduit seals shall be installed within 450 mm (18 in.) from the enclosure or as required by the enclosure marking. Only explosionproof unions, couplings, reducers, elbows, and capped elbows that are not larger than the trade size of the conduit shall be permitted between the sealing fitting and the explosionproof enclosure.

    Reference: 2017 National Electrical Code – Chapter 5 Special Occupancies, Article 501 Class I Locations. 501.15 Sealing and Drainage. 501.15(A) Conduit Seals, Class I, Division 1. 501.15(A)(1) Entering Enclosures.

12. **Answer D.** A through C

    Enclosures that contain connections or equipment shall be provided with an integral sealing means, or sealing fittings listed for the location shall be used. Sealing fittings shall be listed for use with one or more specific compounds and shall be accessible.

    Reference: 2017 National Electrical Code – Chapter 5 Special Occupancies, Article 501 Class I Locations. 501.15 Sealing and Drainage. 501.15(C) Class I, Divisions 1 and 2. 501.15(C)(1) Fittings. The thickness of the sealing compound installed in completed seals, other than listed cable sealing fittings, shall not be less than the metric designator (trade size) of the sealing fitting expressed in the units of measurement employed; *however, in no case shall the thickness of the compound be less than 16 mm (5/8 in.).*

    Reference: 2017 National Electrical Code – Chapter 5 Special Occupancies, Article 501 Class I Locations. 501.15 Sealing and Drainage. 501.15(C) Class I, Divisions 1 and 2. 501.15(C)(3) Thickness of Compounds. *Splices and taps shall not be made in fittings intended only for sealing with compound; nor shall other fittings in which splices or taps are made be filled with compound.*

    Reference: 2017 National Electrical Code – Chapter 5 Special Occupancies, Article 501 Class I Locations. 501.15 Sealing and Drainage. 501.15(C) Class I, Divisions 1 and 2. 501.15(C)(4) Splices and Taps.

13. **Answer C.** 5/8 inch

    The thickness of the sealing compound installed in completed seals, other than listed cable sealing fittings, shall not be less than the metric designator (trade size) of the sealing fitting expressed in the units of measurement employed; however, in no case shall the thickness of the compound be less than 16 mm (5/8 in.).

    Reference: 2017 National Electrical Code – Chapter 5 Special Occupancies, Article 501 Class I Locations. 501.15 Sealing and Drainage. 501.15(C) Class I, Divisions 1 and 2. 501.15(C)(3) Thickness of Compounds.

EXAM 9

EXAM 9 ANSWERS

14. **Answer A.** 25%

    The cross-sectional area of the conductors or optical fiber tubes (metallic or nonmetallic) permitted in a seal shall not exceed 25 percent of the cross-sectional area of a rigid metal conduit of the same trade size unless the seal is specifically identified for a higher percentage of fill.

    Reference: 2017 National Electrical Code – Chapter 5 Special Occupancies, Article 501 Class I Locations. 501.15 Sealing and Drainage. 501.15(C) Class I, Divisions 1 and 2. 501.15(C)(6) Conductor or Optical Fiber Fill.

15. **Answer A.** True

    The locknut-bushing and double-locknut types of contacts shall not be depended on for bonding purposes, but bonding jumpers with proper fittings or other approved means of bonding shall be used. Such means of bonding shall apply to all intervening raceways, fittings, boxes, enclosures, and so forth between Class I locations and the point of grounding for service equipment or point of grounding of a separately derived system.

    Reference: 2017 National Electrical Code – Chapter 5 Special Occupancies, Article 501 Class I Locations. 501.30 Grounding and Bonding, Class I, Division 1 and 2. 501.30(A) Bonding.

16. **Answer D.** Either A or B

    Switches, circuit breakers, and make-and-break contacts of pushbuttons, relays, alarm bells, and horns shall have enclosures identified for Class I, Division 1 locations in accordance with 501.105(A).

    Exception: General-purpose enclosures shall be permitted if current-interrupting contacts comply with one of the following:

    (1) Are immersed in oil

    (2) Are enclosed within a chamber that is hermetically sealed against the entrance of gases or vapors

    (3) Are in nonincendive circuits

    (4) Are listed for Division 2

    Reference: 2017 National Electrical Code – Chapter 5 Special Occupancies, Article 501 Class I Locations. 501.105 Meters, Instruments, and Relays. 501.105(B) Class I, Division 2. 501.105(B)(2) Contacts.

17. **Answer A.** True

    Class I, Division 1 locations, motors, generators, and other rotating electrical machinery shall be one of the following:

    (1) Identified for Class I, Division 1 locations

    (2) Of the totally enclosed type supplied with positive pressure ventilation from a source of clean air with discharge to a safe area, so arranged to prevent energizing of the machine until ventilation has been **established and the enclosure has been purged with at least 10 volumes of air, and also arranged to automatically de-energize the equipment when the air supply fails**

    (3) Of the totally enclosed inert gas–filled type supplied with a suitable reliable source of inert gas for pressurizing the enclosure, **with devices provided to ensure a positive pressure in the enclosure and arranged to automatically de-energize the equipment when the gas supply fails**

    (4) For machines that are for use only in industrial establishments with restricted public access, where the conditions of maintenance and supervision ensure that only qualified persons service the installation, the machine is permitted to be of a type designed to be submerged in a liquid that is flammable only when vaporized and mixed with air, or in a gas or vapor at a pressure greater than atmospheric and that is flammable only when mixed with air; and the machine is so arranged to prevent energizing it until it has been purged with the liquid or gas to exclude air, and also arranged to automatically de-energize the equipment when the supply of liquid or gas or vapor fails or the pressure is reduced to atmospheric Totally enclosed motors of the types specified in 501.125(A)(2) or (A)(3) shall have no external surface with an operating temperature in degrees Celsius in excess of 80 percent of the auto ignition temperature of the gas or vapor involved. Appropriate devices shall be provided to detect and automatically de-energize the motor or provide an adequate alarm if there is any increase in temperature of the motor beyond designed limits. Auxiliary equipment shall be of a type identified for the location in which it is installed.

    Reference: 2017 National Electrical Code – Chapter 5 Special Occupancies, Article 501 Class I Locations. 501.125 Motors and Generators. 501.125(A) Class I, Division 1.

EXAM 9

EXAM 9 ANSWERS

18. **Answer A.** guard or by location

    Luminaires shall be protected from physical damage by suitable guards or by location. Where there is danger that falling sparks or hot metal from lamps or luminaires might ignite localized concentrations of flammable vapors or gases, suitable enclosures or other effective protective means shall be provided.

    Reference: 2017 National Electrical Code – Chapter 5 Special Occupancies, Article 501 Class I Locations. 501.130 Luminaires. 501.130(B) Class I, Division 2. 501.130(B)(2) Physical Damage.

19. **Answer B.** of continuous length

    (5) *Be of continuous length. Where 501.140(A)(5) is applied, cords shall be of continuous length* from the power source to the temporary portable assembly and from the temporary portable assembly to the utilization equipment.

    Informational Note: See 501.20 for flexible cords exposed to liquids having a deleterious effect on the conductor insulation.

    Reference: 2017 National Electrical Code – Chapter 5 Special Occupancies, Article 501 Class I Locations. 501.140 Flexible Cords, Class I, Divisions 1 and 2. 501.140(B)(5) Installation.

20. **Answer B.** identified for Class II locations

    Boxes and fittings shall be provided with threaded bosses for connection to conduit or cable terminations and shall be dusttight. *Boxes and fittings in which taps, joints, or terminal connections are made, or that are used in Group E locations, shall be identified for Class II locations.*

    Informational Note: For entry into enclosures required to be dust-ignitionproof, see the information on construction, testing, and marking of cables, dust-ignitionproof cable fittings, and dust-ignitionproof cord connectors in ANSI/UL 2225-2011, Cables and Cable-Fittings for Use in Hazardous (Class(fied) Locations.

    Reference: 2017 National Electrical Code – Chapter 5 Special Occupancies, Article 502 Class II Locations. 502.10 Wiring Methods. 502.10(A) Class II, Division 1. 502.10(A)(3) Boxes and Fittings.

21. **Answer A.** dusttight

    All boxes and fittings shall be dusttight.

    Reference: 2017 National Electrical Code – Chapter 5 Special Occupancies, Article 502 Class II Locations. 502.10 Wiring Methods. 502.10(B) Class II, Division 2. 502.10(B)(4) Boxes and Fittings.

22. **Answer B.** False

    Where a raceway provides communication between an enclosure that is required to be dust-ignitionproof and one that is not, suitable means shall be provided to prevent the entrance of dust into the dust-ignitionproof enclosure through the raceway. One of the following means shall be permitted:

    (1) A permanent and effective seal

    (2) A horizontal raceway not less than 3.05 m (10 ft.) long

    (3) A vertical raceway not less than 1.5 m (5 ft.) long and extending downward from the dust-ignitionproof enclosure

    (4) A raceway installed in a manner equivalent to (2) or (3) that extends only horizontally and downward from the dust-ignition proof enclosures.

    Where a raceway provides communication between an enclosure that is required to be dust-ignitionproof and an enclosure in an unclassified location, seals shall not be required.

    Sealing fittings shall be accessible.

    Seals shall not be required to be explosion proof.

    Informational Note: Electrical sealing putty is a method of sealing.

    Reference: 2017 National Electrical Code – Chapter 5 Special Occupancies, Article 502 Class II Locations. 502.15 Sealing, Class II, Divisions 1 and 2.

23. **Answer B.** Class II, Division 1 locations

    In Class II, Division 1 locations, control transformers, solenoids, impedance coils, resistors, and any overcurrent devices or switching mechanisms associated with them shall be provided with enclosures identified for the location.

    Reference: 2017 National Electrical Code – Chapter 5 Special Occupancies, Article 502 Class II Locations. 502.120 Control Transformers and Resistors. 502.120(A) Class II, Division 1.

EXAM 9

EXAM 9 ANSWERS

24. Answer A. set-screws

Pendant luminaires shall be suspended by threaded rigid metal conduit stems, by threaded steel intermediate metal conduit stems, by chains with approved fittings, or by other approved means. For rigid stems longer than 300 mm (12 in.), permanent and effective bracing against lateral displacement shall be provided at a level not more than 300 mm (12 in.) above the lower end of the stem, or flexibility in the form of a fitting or a flexible connector listed for the location shall be provided not more than 300 mm (12 in.) from the point of attachment to the supporting box or fitting. *Threaded joints shall be provided with set screws or other effective means to prevent loosening.* Where wiring between an outlet box or fitting and a pendant luminaire is not enclosed in conduit, flexible cord listed for hard usage shall be permitted to be used in accordance with 502.10(A)(2)(5). Flexible cord shall not serve as the supporting means for a luminaire.

Reference: 2017 National Electrical Code – Chapter 5 Special Occupancies, Article 502 Class II Locations. 502.130 Luminaires. 502.130(A) Class II, Division 1. 502.130(A)(3) Pendant Luminaires.

25. Answer C. equipment grounding conductor

(1) Receptacles. In Class II, Division 1 locations, receptacles shall be part of the premises wiring.

(2) *Attachment Plugs. Attachment plugs shall be of the type that provides for connection to the equipment grounding conductor of the flexible cord.*

Reference: 2017 National Electrical Code – Chapter 5 Special Occupancies, Article 502 Class II Locations. 502.145 Receptacles and Attachment Plugs. 502.145(A) Class II, Division 1.

26. Answer B. False

The locknut-bushing *and double-locknut types of contacts shall not be depended on for bonding purposes*, but bonding jumpers with proper fittings or other approved means of bonding shall be used. Such means of bonding shall apply to all intervening raceways. fittings, boxes, enclosures, and so forth, between Class III locations and the point of grounding for service equipment or point of grounding of a separately derived system.

Exception: The specific bonding means shall only be required to the nearest point where the grounded circuit conductor and the grounding electrode conductor are connected together on the line side of the building or structure disconnecting means as specified in 250.32(B) if the branch-circuit overcurrent protection is located on the load side of the disconnecting means.

Reference: 2017 National Electrical Code – Chapter 5 Special Occupancies, Article 503 Class III Locations. 503.30 Grounding and Bonding - Class III, Divisions 1 and 2. 503.30(A) Bonding.

EXAM 9
EXAM 9 ANSWERS

27. **Answer D.** suitable

    A luminaire that may be exposed to physical damage shall be protected by a suitable guard.

    Reference: 2017 National Electrical Code – Chapter 5 Special Occupancies, Article 503 Class III Locations. 503.130 Luminaires - Class III, Divisions 1 and 2. 503.130(B) Physical Damage.

28. **Answer B.** in accordance with the control drawings

    Intrinsically safe apparatus, associated apparatus, and other equipment shall be installed in accordance with the control drawing(s).

    A simple apparatus, whether or not shown on the control drawing(s), shall be permitted to be installed provided the simple apparatus does not interconnect intrinsically safe circuits.

    Informational Note No. 1: The control drawing identification is marked on the apparatus.

    Informational Note No. 2: Associated apparatus with a marked Um of less than 250 V may require additional overvoltage protection at the inputs to limit any possible fault voltages to less than the Um marked on the product.

    Reference: 2017 National Electrical Code – Chapter 5 Special Occupancies, Article 504 Intrinsically Safe Systems. 504.10 Equipment Installation. 504.10(A) Control Drawing.

29. **Answer C.** qualified persons

    Classification of areas, engineering and design, selection of equipment and wiring methods, installation, and inspection shall be performed by qualified persons.

    Reference: 2017 National Electrical Code – Chapter 5 Special Occupancies, Article 505 Zone 0, 1, and 2 Locations. 505.7 Special Precaution. 505.7(A) Implementation of Zone Classification System.

30. **Answer C.** Article 511

    These occupancies shall include locations used for service and repair operations in connection with self-propelled vehicles (including, but not limited to, passenger automobiles, buses, trucks, and tractors) in which volatile flammable liquids or flammable gases are used for fuel or power.

    Reference: 2017 National Electrical Code – Chapter 5 Special Occupancies, Article 511 Commercial Garages, Repair and Storage. 511.1 Scope.

EXAM 9

EXAM 9 ANSWERS

Table 511.3(C) see Table 511-3-C in Tables folder on CD-ROM

31. Answer A. Division 1

Where vehicles using Class I liquids or heavier-than-air gaseous fuels (such as LPG) are repaired, hazardous area classification guidance is found in Table 511.3(C).

Informational Note: For additional information, see NFPA 30A-2015, Code for Motor Fuel Dispensing Facilities and Repair Garages, Table 8.3.2.

Reference: 2017 National Electrical Code – Chapter 5 Special Occupancies, Article 511 Commercial Garages, Repair and Storage. 511.3 Area Classification, General. 511.3(C) Major Repair Garages. 511.3(C)(3) Repair Garages, Major and Minor. Table 511.3(C)(3) Extent of Classified Locations for Major and Minor Repair Garages with Heavier-Than-Air Fuel (70-304)

32. Answer B. False

All fixed wiring above Class I locations shall be in metal raceways, rigid nonmetallic conduit electrical nonmetallic tubing, flexible metal conduit, liquidtight flexible metal conduit, or liquidtight flexible nonmetallic conduit, or shall be Type MC, AC, MI, manufactured wiring systems, or PLTC cable in accordance with Article 725, or Type TC cable or Type ITC cable in accordance with Article 727. **Cellular metal floor raceways or cellular concrete floor raceways shall be permitted to be used only for supplying ceiling outlets or extensions to the area below the floor, but such raceways shall have no connections leading into or through any Class I location above the floor.**

Reference: 2017 National Electrical Code – Chapter 5 Special Occupancies, Article 511 Commercial Garages, Repair and Storage. 511.7 Wiring and Equipment Installed Above Class I Locations. 511.7(A) Wiring in Spaces Above Class I Locations. 511.7(A)(1) Fixed Wiring Above Class I Locations.

EXAM 9

EXAM 9 ANSWERS

33. **Answer D.** all of the above

   All fixed wiring above Class I locations shall be in metal raceways, rigid nonmetallic conduit electrical nonmetallic tubing, flexible metal conduit, liquidtight flexible metal conduit, or liquidtight flexible nonmetallic conduit, or shall be Type MC, AC, MI, manufactured wiring systems, or PLTC cable in accordance with Article 725, or Type TC cable or Type ITC cable in accordance with Article 727. Cellular metal floor raceways or cellular concrete floor raceways shall be permitted to be used only for supplying ceiling outlets or extensions to the area below the floor, but such raceways shall have no connections leading into or through any Class I location above the floor.

   Reference: 2017 National Electrical Code – Chapter 5 Special Occupancies, Article 511 Commercial Garages, Repair and Storage. 511.7 Wiring and Equipment Installed Above Class I Locations. 511.7(A) Wiring in Spaces Above Class I Locations. 511.7(A)(1) Fixed Wiring Above Class I Locations.

34. **Answer D.** any of these

   All 125-volt, single-phase, 15- and 20-ampere receptacles installed in areas where electrical diagnostic equipment, electrical hand tools, or portable lighting equipment are to be used shall have ground-fault circuit-interrupter protection for personnel.

   Reference: 2017 National Electrical Code – Chapter 5 Special Occupancies, Article 511 Commercial Garages, Repair and Storage. 511.12 Ground-Fault Circuit-Interrupter Protection for Personnel.

35. **Answer A.** True

   Fuel dispensing systems shall be provided with one or more clearly identified emergency shutoff devices or electrical disconnects. Such devices or disconnects shall be installed in approved locations but not less than 6 m (20 ft) or more than 30 m (100 ft) from the fuel dispensing devices that they serve. Emergency shutoff devices or electrical disconnects shall disconnect power to all dispensing devices; to all remote pumps serving the dispensing devices; to all associated power, control, and signal circuits; and to all other electrical equipment in the hazardous (classified) locations surrounding the fuel dispensing devices. When more than one emergency shutoff device or electrical disconnect is provided, all devices shall be interconnected. Resetting from an emergency shutoff condition shall require manual intervention and the manner of resetting shall be approved by the authority having jurisdiction. [30A:6.7]

   Exception: Intrinsically safe electrical equipment need not meet this requirement. [30A:6.7]

   Reference: 2017 National Electrical Code – Chapter 5 Special Occupancies, Article 514 Motor Fuel Dispensing Facilities. 514.11 Circuit Disconnects. 514.11(A) Emergency Electrical Disconnects.

EXAM 9

EXAM 9 ANSWERS

Table 514.3(B)(1) Class I Locations — Motor Fuel Dispensing Facilities

Location	Division (Group D)	Zone (Group IIA)	Extent of Classified Location[1]
Dispensing Device (except Overhead Type)[2,3]			
Under dispenser containment	1	1	Entire space within and under dispenser pit or containment
Dispenser	2	2	Within 450 mm (18 in.) of dispenser enclosure or that portion of dispenser enclosure containing liquid-handling components, extending horizontally in all directions and down to grade level
Outdoor	2	2	Up to 450 mm (18 in.) above grade level, extending 6 m (20 ft) horizontally in all directions from dispenser enclosure
Indoor			
-with mechanical ventilation	2	2	Up to 450 mm (18 in.) above floor level, extending 6 m (20 ft) horizontally in all directions from dispenser enclosure
-with gravity ventilation	2	2	Up to 450 mm (18 in.) above floor level, extending 7.5 m (25 ft) horizontally in all directions from dispenser enclosure

36. Answer D.   20 feet

Table 514.3(B)(1) shall be applied where Class I liquids are stored, handled, or dispensed and shall be used to delineate and classify motor fuel dispensing facilities and commercial garages as defined in Article 511. Table 515.3 shall be used for the purpose of delineating and classifying aboveground tanks. A Class I location shall not extend beyond an unpierced wall, roof, or other solid partition. **[30A:8.1, 8.3]**

Reference: 2017 National Electrical Code – Chapter 5 Special Occupancies, Article 514 Motor Fuel Dispensing Facilities. 514.3 Classification of Locations. 514.3(B) Classified Locations. 514.3(B)(1) Class I Locations. Table 514.3(B)(1) Class I Locations – Motor Fuel Dispensing Facilities (page 70-445)

37. Answer C.   Sealing fitting

A listed seal shall be provided in each conduit run entering or leaving a dispenser or any cavities or enclosures in direct communication therewith. *The sealing fitting or listed explosion proof reducer at the seal shall be the first fitting after the conduit emerges from the earth or concrete.*

Reference: 2017 National Electrical Code – Chapter 5 Special Occupancies, Article 514 Motor Fuel Dispensing Facilities. 514.9 Sealing. 514.9(A) At Dispenser.

38. Answer A.   True

Each dispensing device shall be provided with a means to remove all external voltage sources, including power, communications, data, and video circuits and including feedback, during periods of maintenance and service of the dispensing equipment. The location of this means shall be permitted to be other than inside or adjacent to the dispensing device. The means shall be capable of being locked in the open position in accordance with 110.25.

Reference: 2017 National Electrical Code – Chapter 5 Special Occupancies, Article 514 Motor Fuel Dispensing Facilities. 514.13 Provisions for Maintenance and Service of Dispensing Equipment.

39. Answer B.   24-hour

A building or portion thereof used on a 24-hour basis for the housing of four or more persons who are incapable of self-preservation because of age; physical limitation due to accident or illness; or limitations such as mental retardation/developmental disability, mental illness, or chemical dependency. **[99:3.3.4]**

Reference: 2017 National Electrical Code – Chapter 5 Special Occupancies, Article 517 Health Care Facilities. 517.2 Definitions.

EXAM 9 ANSWERS

EXAM 9

EXAM 9 ANSWERS

40. **Answer A.** True

    Except as modified in this article, wiring methods shall comply with the applicable provisions of Chapters 1 through 4 of this Code.

    Reference: 2017 National Electrical Code – Chapter 5 Special Occupancies, Article 517 Health Care Facilities. 517.12 Wiring Methods. This *Code* is divided into the introduction and nine chapters, as shown in Figure 90.3. Chapters 1, 2, 3, and 4 apply generally. Chapters 5, 6, and 7 apply to special occupancies, special equipment, or other special conditions and may supplement or modify the requirements in Chapters 1 through 7 .

    Chapter 8 covers communications systems and is not subject to the requirements of Chapters 1 through 7 except where the requirements are specifically referenced in Chapter 8.

    Chapter 9 consists of tables that are applicable as referenced.

    Informative annexes are not part of the requirements of this Code but are included for informational purposes only.

    Reference: 2017 National Electrical Code, Article 90 Introduction. 90.3 Code Arrangement.

41. **Answer D.** False

    ***An isolated grounding receptacle shall not be installed within a patient care vicinity.* [99:6.3.2.2.7.1(B)]**

    Reference: 2017 National Electrical Code – Chapter 5 Special Occupancies, Article 517 Health Care Facilities. 517.16 Use of Isolated Ground Receptacles.

42. **Answer A.** Eight

    Each patient bed location shall be provided with a minimum of eight receptacles. They shall be permitted to be of the single, duplex, or quadruplex type or any combination of the three. All receptacles shall be listed "hospital grade" and shall be so identified. The grounding terminal of each receptacle shall be connected to an insulated copper equipment grounding conductor sized in accordance with Table 250.122.

    Informational Note: It is not intended that there be a total, immediate replacement of existing non-hospital grade receptacles. It is intended, however, that non-hospital grade receptacles be replaced with hospital grade receptacles upon modification of use, renovation, or as existing receptacles need replacement.

    Reference: 2017 National Electrical Code – Chapter 5 Special Occupancies, Article 517 Health Care Facilities. 517.18 General Care Areas. 517.18(B) Patient Bed Location Receptacles.

43. **Answer D.** Fourteen single receptacles or seven duplex receptacles.

    (1) Minimum Number and Supply. *Each patient bed location shall be provided with a minimum of 14 receptacles, at least one of which shall be connected to either of the following:*

    (1) The normal system branch circuit required in 517.19(A)

    (2) A critical branch circuit supplied by a different transfer switch than the other receptacles at the same patient bed location

    (2) Receptacle Requirements. T*he receptacles required in 517.19(B)(1) shall be permitted to be single, duplex, or quadruplex type or any combination thereof.* All receptacles shall be listed "hospital grade" and shall be so identified. The grounding terminal of each receptacle shall be connected to the reference grounding point by means of an insulated copper equipment grounding conductor.

    Reference: 2017 National Electrical Code – Chapter 5 Special Occupancies, Article 517 Health Care Facilities. 517.19 Critical Care Areas. 517.19(B) Patient Bed Location Receptacles.

EXAM 9

EXAM 9 ANSWERS

44. Answer C. The life safety, equipment, and the critical

Essential electrical systems for hospitals shall be comprised of three separate branches capable of supplying a limited amount of lighting and power service that is considered essential for life safety and effective hospital operation during the time the normal electrical service is interrupted for any reason. *The three branches are life safety, critical, and equipment.*

The division between the branches shall occur at transfer switches where more than one transfer switch is required [**99:**6.4.2.2.1.2

Reference: 2017 National Electrical Code – Chapter 5 Special Occupancies, Article 517 Health Care Facilities. 517.31 Requirements for the Essential Electrical System. 517.30(A) Separate Branches.

45. Answer C. Nonflexible metal raceways

Nonflexible metal raceways, Type MI cable, Type RTRC marked with the suffix -XW, or Schedule 80 PVC conduit. Nonmetallic raceways shall not be used for branch circuits that supply patient care areas.

Reference: 2017 National Electrical Code – Chapter 5 Special Occupancies, Article 517 Health Care Facilities. 517.31 Requirements for the Essential Electrical System. 517.31(C) Wiring Requirements. 517.31(C)(3) Mechanical Protection of the Essential Electrical System. 517.31(C)(3)(1)

46. Answer A. 10 volts

Low-voltage equipment that is frequently in contact with the bodies of persons or has exposed current-carrying elements shall comply with one of the following:

(1) Operate on an electrical potential of 10 volts or less

(2) Be approved as intrinsically safe or double-insulated equipment

(3) Be moisture resistant

Reference: 2017 National Electrical Code – Chapter 5 Special Occupancies, Article 517 Health Care Facilities. 517.64 Low-Voltage Equipment and Instruments. 517.64(A) Equipment Requirements.

47. Answer D. 100

Except for the assembly occupancies explicitly covered by 520.1, *this article covers all buildings or portions of buildings or structures designed or intended for the gathering together of 100 or more persons for such purposes as deliberation,* worship, entertainment, eating, drinking, amusement, awaiting transportation, or similar purposes.

Reference: 2017 National Electrical Code – Chapter 5 Special Occupancies, Article 518 Assembly Occupancies. 518.1 Scope.

48. Answer D. A through C

In exhibition halls used for display booths, as in trade shows, *the temporary wiring shall be permitted to be installed in accordance with Article 590. Flexible cables and cords approved for hard or extra-hard usage shall be permitted to be laid on floors where protected from contact by the general public. The ground-fault circuit-interrupter requirements of 590.6 shall not apply.* All other ground-fault circuit-interrupter requirements of this Code shall apply.

Where ground-fault circuit interrupter protection for personnel is supplied by plug-and-cord-connection to the branch circuit or to the feeder, the ground fault circuit interrupter protection shall be listed as portable ground fault circuit interrupter protection or provide a level of protection equivalent to a portable ground fault circuit interrupter, whether assembled in the field or at the factory.

Reference: 2017 National Electrical Code – Chapter 5 Special Occupancies. 518.3 Other Articles. 518.3(B) Temporary Wiring.

49. Answer C. 20 amperes

Footlights, border lights, and proscenium sidelights shall be arranged so that no branch circuit supplying such equipment carries a load exceeding 20 amperes.

Reference: 2017 National Electrical Code – Chapter 5 Special Occupancies, Article 520 Theaters, Audience Areas of Motion Picture and Television Studios, Performance Areas, and Similar Locations. 520.41 Circuit Loads. 520.41(A) Circuits Rated 20 Amperes or Less.

50. Answer B. Article 525

This article covers the installation of portable wiring and equipment for carnivals, circuses, fairs, and similar functions, including wiring in or on all structures.

Reference: 2017 National Electrical Code – Chapter 5 Special Occupancies, Art*icle 525 Carnivals, Circuses, Fairs, and Similar Events*. 525.1 Scope.

EXAM 9

EXAM 9 ANSWERS

51. **Answer B.** lockable

    Service equipment shall not be installed in a location that is accessible to unqualified persons, unless the equipment is lockable.

    Reference: 2017 National Electrical Code – Chapter 5 Special Occupancies, Article 525 Carnivals, Circuses, Fairs, and Similar Events. 525.10 Services. 525.10(A) Guarding.

52. **Answer A.** True

    Wiring for an amusement ride, attraction, tent, or similar structure shall not be supported by any other ride or structure unless specifically designed for the purpose.

    Reference: 2017 National Electrical Code – Chapter 5 Special Occupancies, Article 525 Carnivals, Circuses, Fairs, and Similar Events. 525.20 Wiring Methods. 525.20(F) Support.

53. **Answer A.** 6 feet

    A means to disconnect each portable structure from all ungrounded conductors shall be provided. The disconnecting means shall be located within sight of and within 1.8 m (6 ft.) of the operator's station. The disconnecting means shall be readily accessible to the operator, including when the ride is in operation. Where accessible to unqualified persons, the disconnecting means shall be lockable. A shunt trip device that opens the fused disconnect or circuit breaker when a switch located in the ride operator's console is closed shall be a permissible method of opening the circuit.

    Reference: 2017 National Electrical Code – Chapter 5 Special Occupancies, Article 525 Carnivals, Circuses, Fairs, and Similar Events. 525.21 Rides, Tents, and Concessions. 525.21(A) Disconnecting Means.

54. **Answer A.** True

    Receptacles that are not accessible from grade level and that only facilitate quick disconnecting and reconnecting of electrical equipment shall not be required to be provided with GFCI protection. These receptacles shall be of the locking type.

    Reference: 2017 National Electrical Code – Chapter 5 Special Occupancies, Article 525 Carnivals, Circuses, Fairs, and Similar Events. 525.23 Ground-Fault Circuit-Interrupter (GFCI) Protection. 525.23(B) Where GFCI Protection Is Not Required.

55. **Answer D.** A through C

    Agricultural buildings where excessive dust and dust with water may accumulate, including all areas of poultry, livestock, and fish confinement systems, where litter dust or feed dust, including mineral feed particles, may accumulate.

    Reference: 2017 National Electrical Code – Chapter 5 Special Occupancies, Article 547 Agricultural Buildings. 547.1 Scope. 547.1(A) Excessive Dust and Dust with Water.

56. **Answer A.** 8 in.

    All cables shall be secured within 200 mm (8 in.) of each cabinet, box, or fitting. Nonmetallic boxes, fittings, conduit, and cables shall be permitted to be mounted directly to any building surface covered by this article without maintaining the 6 mm (1/4 in.) airspace in accordance with 300.6(D).

    Reference: 2017 National Electrical Code – Chapter 5 Special Occupancies, Article 547 Agricultural Buildings. 547.5 Wiring Methods. 547.5(B) Mounting.

57. **Answer C.** insulated or covered

    Where an equipment grounding conductor is installed underground within a location falling under the scope of Article 547, it shall be insulated.

    Informational Note: For further information on aluminum and copper-clad aluminum conductors, see 250.120(B).

    Reference: 2017 National Electrical Code – Chapter 5 Special Occupancies, Article 547 Agricultural Buildings. 547.5 Wiring Methods. 547.5(F) Separate Equipment Grounding Conductor.

EXAM 9

EXAM 9 ANSWERS

58. Answer A. True

Equipotential planes shall be Installed where required in (A)(1) and (A)(2).

(1) Indoors. Equipotential planes shall be installed in confinement areas with concrete floors where metallic equipment is located that may become energized and is accessible to livestock.

(2) Outdoors. *Equipotential planes shall be installed in concrete slabs where metallic equipment is located that may become energized and is accessible to livestock.*

The equipotential plane shall encompass the area where the livestock stands while accessing metallic equipment that may become energized.

Reference: 2017 National Electrical Code – Chapter 5 Special Occupancies, Article 547 Agricultural Buildings. 547.10 Equipotential Planes and Bonding of Equipotential Planes. 547.10(A) Where Required. 547.10(A)(1) Indoors. 547.10(A)(2) Outdoors.

59. Answer A. 50 amperes

The power supply to the mobile home shall be a feeder assembly consisting of not more than one listed 50- ampere mobile home power-supply cord or a permanently installed feeder.

Exception No. 1: A mobile home that is factory equipped with gas or oil fired central heating equipment and cooking appliances shall be permitted to be provided with a listed mobile home power-supply cord rated 40 amperes.

Exception No. 2: A feeder assembly shall not be required for manufactured homes constructed in accordance with 550.32(B).

Reference: 2017 National Electrical Code – Chapter 5 Special Occupancies, Article 550 Mobile Homes, Manufactured Homes, and Mobile Home Parks. 550.10 Power Supply. 550.10(A) Feeder.

60. Answer B. 1-1/4 in.

Where the cord passes through walls or floors, it shall be protected by means of conduits and bushings or equivalent. The cord shall be permitted to be *installed within the mobile home walls, provided a continuous raceway having a maximum size of 32 mm (1-1/4 in.)* is installed from the branch-circuit panel board to the underside of the mobile home floor.

Reference: 2017 National Electrical Code – Chapter 5 Special Occupancies, Article 550 Mobile Homes, Manufactured Homes, and Mobile Home Parks. 550.10 Power Supply. 550.10(G) Protected.

61. Answer D. either A or C

Receptacle outlets shall not be permitted in the following locations:

(1) Receptacle outlets shall not be installed within or directly over a bathtub or shower space.

(2) A receptacle shall not be installed in a face-up position in any countertop.

(3) Receptacle outlets shall not be installed above electric baseboard heaters, unless provided for in the listing or manufacturer's instructions.

Reference: 2017 National Electrical Code – Chapter 5 Special Occupancies, Article 550 Mobile Homes, Manufactured Homes, and Mobile Home Parks. 550.13 Receptacle Outlets. 550.13(F) Receptacle Outlets Not Permitted.

62. Answer C. 100 amperes

Mobile home service equipment shall be rated at not less than 100 amperes at 120/240 volts, and provisions shall be made for connecting a mobile home feeder assembly by a permanent wiring method. Power outlets used as mobile home service equipment shall also be permitted to contain receptacles rated up to 50 amperes with appropriate overcurrent protection. Fifty-ampere receptacles shall conform to the configuration shown in Figure 550.10(C).

Informational Note: Complete details of the 50-ampere plug and receptacle configuration can be found in ANSI/NEMA WD 6-2002 (Rev. 2008), Standard for Wiring Devices - Dimensional Requirements, Figure 14-50.

Reference: 2017 National Electrical Code – Chapter 5 Special Occupancies, Article 550 Mobile Homes, Manufactured Homes, and Mobile Home Parks. 550.32 Service Equipment. 550.32(C) Rating.

63. Answer A. two feet

Outdoor mobile home disconnecting means shall be installed so the bottom of the enclosure containing the disconnecting means is not less than 600 mm (2 ft.) above finished grade or working platform. The disconnecting means shall be installed so that the center of the grip of the operating handle, when in the highest position, is not more than 2.0 m (6 ft. 7 in.) above the finished grade or working platform.

Reference: 2017 National Electrical Code – Chapter 5 Special Occupancies, Article 550 Mobile Homes, Manufactured Homes, and Mobile Home Parks. 550.32 Service Equipment. 550.32(F) Mounting Height.

EXAM 9

EXAM 9 ANSWERS

64. Answer B. 2 ft.

Outdoor mobile home disconnecting means shall be installed so the bottom of the enclosure containing the disconnecting means is not less than 600 mm (2 ft.) above finished grade or working platform. The disconnecting means shall be installed so that the center of the grip of the operating handle, when in the highest position, is not more than 2.0 m (6 ft. 7 in.) above the finished grade or working platform.

Reference: 2017 National Electrical Code – Chapter 5 Special Occupancies, Article 550 Mobile Homes, Manufactured Homes, and Mobile Home Parks. 550.32 Service Equipment. 550.32(F) Mounting Height.

65. Answer D. Portable power cable

Liquid tight flexible metal conduit or liquid tight flexible nonmetallic conduit with approved fittings shall be permitted for feeders and where flexible connections are required for services. *Extra-hard usage portable power cable listed for both wet locations and sunlight resistance shall be permitted for a feeder to a floating building where flexibility is required.* Other raceways suitable for the location shall be permitted to be installed where flexibility is not required.

Reference: 2017 National Electrical Code – Chapter 5 Special Occupancies, Article 553 Floating Buildings. 553.7 Installation of Services and Feeders. 553.7(B) Wiring Methods.

66. Answer B. marine power outlet

An enclosed assembly that can include equipment such as receptacles, circuit breakers, fused switches, fuses, a watt-hour meter(s), panelboards, and monitoring means approved for marine use.

Reference: 2017 National Electrical Code – Chapter 5 Special Occupancies, Article 555 Marinas and Boatyards. 555.2 Definitions.

67. Answer A. True

Electrical equipment enclosures installed on piers above deck level shall be securely and substantially supported by structural members, independent of any conduit connected to them. If enclosures are not attached to mounting surfaces by means of external ears or lugs, the internal screw heads shall be sealed to prevent seepage of water through mounting holes.

Reference: 2017 National Electrical Code – Chapter 5 Special Occupancies, Article 555 Marinas and Boatyards. 555.10 Electrical Equipment Enclosures. 555.10(A) Securing and Supporting.

68. Answer C. isolate

Disconnecting means shall be provided to isolate each boat from its supply connection(s).

(A) Type. *The disconnecting means shall consist of a circuit breaker, switch, or both, and shall be properly identified as to which receptacle it controls.*

Reference: 2017 National Electrical Code – Chapter 5 Special Occupancies, Article 555 Marinas and Boatyards. 555.17 Disconnecting Means for Shore Power Connection(s).

69. Answer A. 30 inches

The disconnecting means shall be readily accessible, located not more than 762 mm (30 in.) from the receptacle it controls, and shall be located in the supply circuit ahead of the receptacle. Circuit breakers or switches located in marine power outlets complying with this section shall be permitted as the disconnecting means.

Reference: 2017 National Electrical Code – Chapter 5 Special Occupancies, Article 555 Marinas and Boatyards. 555.17 Disconnecting Means for Shore Power Connection(s). 555.17(B) Location.

70. Answer B. 30 amperes

Shore power for boats shall be provided by single receptacles rated not less than 30 amperes.

Informational Note: For locking- and grounding-type receptacles for auxiliary power to boats, see NFPA 303-2011, Fire Protection Standard for Marinas and Boatyards.

Reference: 2017 National Electrical Code – Chapter 5 Special Occupancies, Article 555 Marinas and Boatyards. 555.19 Receptacles. 555.19(A) Shore Power Receptacles. 555.19(A)(4) Ratings.

EXAM 9

EXAM 9 ANSWERS

71. Answer C. 30A

Shore power for boats shall be provided by single receptacles rated not less than 30 amperes.

Informational Note: For locking- and grounding-type receptacles for auxiliary power to boats, see NFPA 303-2011, Fire Protection Standard for Marinas and Boatyards.

(a) Receptacles rated 30 amperes and 50 amperes shall be of the locking and grounding type.

Informational Note: For various configurations and ratings of locking- and grounding-type receptacles and caps, see ANSI/ NEMA WD 6-2002 (Rev. 2008), Standard for Dimensions of Attachment Plugs and Receptacles.

(b) Receptacles rated 60 amperes or higher shall be of the pin and sleeve type.

Informational Note: For various configurations and ratings of pin and sleeve receptacles, see ANSI/ UL 1686, UL Standard for Safety Pin and Sleeve Configurations.

Reference: 2017 National Electrical Code – Chapter 5 Special Occupancies, Article 555 Marinas and Boatyards. 555.19 Receptacles. 555.19(A) Shore Power Receptacles. 555.19(A)(4) Ratings.

72. Answer C. 90 days

Temporary electric power and lighting installations shall be permitted for a period not to exceed 90 days for holiday decorative lighting and similar purposes.

Reference: 2017 National Electrical Code – Chapter 5 Special Occupancies, Article 590 Temporary Installations. 590.3 Time Constraints. 590.3(B) 90 Days.

73. Answer D. A through C

Temporary electric power and lighting installations shall be permitted during emergencies and for tests, experiments, and developmental work.

Reference: 2017 National Electrical Code – Chapter 5 Special Occupancies, Article 590 Temporary Installations. 590.3 Time Constraints. 590.3(C) Emergencies and Tests.

74. Answer A. same branch circuit

All receptacles shall be of the grounding type. Unless installed in a continuous metal raceway that qualifies as an equipment grounding conductor in accordance with 250.118 or a continuous metal-covered cable that qualifies as an equipment grounding conductor in accordance with 250.118, all branch circuits shall include a separate equipment grounding conductor, and all receptacles shall be electrically connected to the equipment grounding conductor(s). *Receptacles on construction sites shall not be installed on any branch circuit that supplies temporary lighting.*

Reference: 2017 National Electrical Code – Chapter 5 Special Occupancies, Article 590 Temporary Installations. 590.4 General. 590.4(D) Receptacles. 590.4(D)(1) All Receptacles.

75. Answer C. Either A or B

Cable assemblies and flexible cords and cables shall be supported in place at intervals that ensure that they will be protected from physical damage. Support shall be in the form of staples, cable ties, straps, or similar type fittings installed so as not to cause damage. Cable assemblies and flexible cords and cables installed as branch circuits or feeders shall not be installed on the floor or on the ground. Extension cords shall not be required to comply with 590.4(J). *Vegetation shall not be used for support of overhead spans of branch circuits or feeders.*

Reference: 2017 National Electrical Code – Chapter 5 Special Occupancies, Article 590 Temporary Installations. 590.4 General. 590.4(J) Support.

76. Answer B. January 1, 2011

All 125-volt and 125/250-volt, single-phase, 15-, 20-, and 30-ampere receptacle outlets that are a part of a 15-kW or smaller portable generator shall have listed ground-fault circuit-interrupter protection for personnel. All 15- and 20-ampere, 125- and 250-volt receptacles, including those that are part of a portable generator, used in a damp or wet location shall comply with 406.9(A) and (B). *Listed cord sets or devices incorporating listed ground-fault circuit-interrupter protection for personnel identified for portable use shall be permitted for use with 15-kW or less portable generators manufactured or remanufactured prior to January I, 2011.*

Reference: 2017 National Electrical Code – Chapter 5 Special Occupancies, Article 590 Temporary Installations. 590.6 Ground-Fault Protection for Personnel. 590.6(A) Receptacle Outlets. 590.6(A)(3) Receptacles on 15-kW or less Po rtable Generators.

EXAM 10

Chapter 6 Special Equipment

1. Regardless of voltage, an electric sign, whether fixed, mobile or portable, must be _____ and installed in conformance with its listing, unless given special permission or otherwise approved by the Authority Having Jurisdiction.

    A. listed

    B. provided with installation instructions

    C. both A and B

    D. neither A nor B

    Reference: 2017 National Electrical Code, Article 90 Introduction. 90.4 Enforcement.

2. As long as it is installed in compliance with the NEC, field-installed skeleton tubing is not required to be:

    A. labeled

    B. listed

    C. either A or B

    D. neither A nor B

    Reference: 2017 National Electrical Code – Chapter 6 Special Equipment, Article 600 Electric Signs and Outline Lighting. 600.3 Listing. 600.3(A) Field-Installed Skeleton Tubing.

3. True or False: When it is installed with listed luminaires, outline lighting must be listed as a system.

    A. True

    B. False

    Reference: 2017 National Electrical Code – Chapter 6 Special Equipment, Article 600 Electric Signs and Outline Lighting. 600.3 Listing. 600.3(B) Outline Lighting.

4. What rating must be provided at the time of installation, along with input voltage, for electric signs and outline lighting systems?

    A. amperage

    B. current

    C. resistance

    D. none of these

    Reference: 2017 National Electrical Code – Chapter 6 Special Equipment, Article 600 Electric Signs and Outline Lighting. 600.4 Markings. 600.4(A) Signs and Outline Lighting Systems.

502   Chapter 6 Special Equipment

EXAM 10

Chapter 6 Special Equipment

5. All signs and outline lighting systems must have marking with the manufacturer's name, trademark, _____, and other means of identification.

    A. current rating

    B. date of manufacturing

    C. input voltage

    D. A and C

    Reference: 2017 National Electrical Code – Chapter 6 Special Equipment, Article 600 Electric Signs and Outline Lighting. 600.4 Markings. 600.4(A) Signs and Outline Lighting Systems.

6. How high must the permanently installed letters on incandescent lampholders be when indicating the maximum allowed lamp wattage?

    A. 1/8 in.

    B. 1/4 in.

    C. 1/2 in.

    D. 3/4 in.

    Reference: 2017 National Electrical Code – Chapter 6 Special Equipment, Article 600 Electric Signs and Outline Lighting. 600.4 Markings. 600.4(C) Signs with Lampholders for Incandescent Lamps.

7. True or False: Loads other than electric signs or outline lighting systems may be supplied by the required 20 amp circuits required for each commercial building and occupancy.

    A. True

    B. False

    Reference: 2017 National Electrical Code – Chapter 6 Special Equipment, Article 600 Electric Signs and Outline Lighting. 600.5 Branch Circuits. 600.5(A) Required Branch Circuit.

8. For each commercial building and occupancy that is accessible to pedestrians, there must be at least one outlet provided in an accessible location at the _____ to every tenant space, for the use of an outline or sign lighting system.

    A. entrance

    B. exit

    C. store front

    D. window

    Reference: 2017 National Electrical Code – Chapter 6 Special Equipment, Article 600 Electric Signs and Outline Lighting. 600.5 Branch Circuits. 600.5(A) Required Branch Circuit.

EXAM 10

Chapter 6 Special Equipment

9. What should service hallways or corridors not be considered, where pedestrians are concerned?

    A. accessible

    B. closed

    C. restricted

    D. none of these

    Reference: 2017 National Electrical Code – Chapter 6 Special Equipment, Article 600 Electric Signs and Outline Lighting. 600.5 Branch Circuits. 600.5(A) Required Branch Circuit.

10. At the entrance to each tenant space on a commercial building or occupancy that is accessible to pedestrians, at least one outlet must be installed in an accessible location, rated at:

    A. 15 amps

    B. 20 amps

    C. 25 amps

    D. 30 amps

    Reference: 2017 National Electrical Code – Chapter 6 Special Equipment, Article 600 Electric Signs and Outline Lighting. 600.5 Branch Circuits. 600.5(A) Required Branch Circuit.

11. The load for an electric sign or outline lighting system should be computed at a minimum of _____ volt-amps when sizing the service calculation.

    A. 1000

    B. 1200

    C. 1500

    D. 1800

    Reference: 2017 National Electrical Code – Chapter 2 Wiring and Protection, Article 220 Branch-Circuit, Feeder, and Service Calculations. 220.14 Other Loads - All Occupancies. 220.14(F) Sign and Outline Lighting.

12. What should the load for a sign be multiplied by for continuous operation, if a sign burns for three hours or more?

    A. 100%

    B. 125%

    C. 150%

    D. 175%

    Reference: 2017 National Electrical Code – Chapter 1 General, Article 100 Definitions

EXAM 10

Chapter 6 Special Equipment

13. What is the maximum number of amps that a branch-circuit supplying a neon tubing installation should have?

    A. 20   C. 30

    B. 25   D. 50

    Reference: 2017 National Electrical Code – Chapter 6 Special Equipment, Article 600 Electric Signs and Outline Lighting. 600.5 Branch Circuits. 600.5(B) Rating. 600.5(B)(1) Neon Signs.

14. If branch circuits supply neon tubing installations, they must be rated for over _____ amperes.

    A. 15   C. 30

    B. 20   D. 40

    Reference: 2017 National Electrical Code – Chapter 6 Special Equipment, Article 600 Electric Signs and Outline Lighting. 600.5 Branch Circuits. 600.5(B) Rating. . 600.5(B)(1) Neon Signs.

15. What is the maximum number of amps allowed for electrical signs and outline lighting systems containing either fluorescent or incandescent lighting?

    A. 20   C. 30

    B. 25   D. 40

    Reference: 2017 National Electrical Code – Chapter 6 Special Equipment, Article 600 Electric Signs and Outline Lighting. 600.5 Branch Circuits. 600.5(B) Rating. 600.5(B)(2) All Other Signs.

16. True or False: Wiring methods that supply a sign enclosure or cabinet must terminate inside the sign or outline lighting system enclosure.

    A. True   B. False

    Reference: 2017 National Electrical Code – Chapter 6 Special Equipment, Article 600 Electric Signs and Outline Lighting. 600.5 Branch Circuits. 600.5(C) Wiring Methods. 600.5(C)(1) Supply.

Chapter 6 Special Equipment 505

EXAM 10

Chapter 6 Special Equipment

17. True or False: It is not allowed for electric signs to contain both branch and secondary circuit conductors that are used for supplying the components of the sign.

    A. True   B. False

    Reference: 2017 National Electrical Code – Chapter 6 Special Equipment, Article 600 Electric Signs and Outline Lighting. 600.5 Branch Circuits. 600.5(C) Wiring Methods. 600.5(C)(2) Enclosures as Pull Boxes.

18. When a sign system has adjacent signs, outline lighting systems, or floodlights that are an integral part of the sign system they are attached to, the sign may be used as a pull box or:

    A. junction box   C. either A or B

    B. outlet box   D. neither A nor B

    Reference: 2017 National Electrical Code – Chapter 6 Special Equipment, Article 600 Electric Signs and Outline Lighting. 600.5 Branch Circuits. 600.5(C) Wiring Methods. 600.5(C)(2) Enclosures as Pull Boxes.

19. True or False: It is permissible to use a metal pole supporting a sign cabinet or sign system to enclose the supply conductors.

    A. True   B. False

    Reference: 2017 National Electrical Code – Chapter 6 Special Equipment, Article 600 Electric Signs and Outline Lighting. 600.5 Branch Circuits. 600.5(C) Wiring Methods. 600.5(C)(3) Metal or Nonmetallic Poles.

20. True or False: For a metal pole under 8 ft. in height that encloses supply conductors, a grounding terminal must be accessible.

    A. True   B. False

    Reference: 2017 National Electrical Code – Chapter 4 Equipment for General Use, Article 410 Luminaires, Lampholders, and Lamps. 410.30 Supports. 410.30(B) Metal or Nonmetallic Poles Supporting Luminaires

506   Chapter 6 Special Equipment

COPYRIGHT 2020 BUILDER'S BOOK, INC. ALL RIGHTS RESERVED • 1-800-273-7375 • WWW.BUILDERSBOOK.COM

EXAM 10

Chapter 6 Special Equipment

21. If a pole over 8 ft. in height, a _____ terminal must be accessible from a handhole.

    A. connector

    B. equipment

    C. grounding

    D. wiring

    Reference: 2017 National Electrical Code – Chapter 4 Equipment for General Use, Article 410 Luminaires, Lampholders, and Lamps. 410.30 Supports. 410.30(B) Metal or Nonmetallic Poles Supporting Luminaires

22. For a metal pole over 8 ft. tall, what is the minimum size for the handhole?

    A. 1 in. x 2 in.

    B. 2 in. x 2 in.

    C. 2 in. x 4 in.

    D. 2 in. x 6 in.

    Reference: 2017 National Electrical Code – Chapter 4 Equipment for General Use, Article 410 Luminaires, Lampholders, and Lamps. 410.30 Supports. 410.30(B) Metal or Nonmetallic Poles Supporting Luminaires

23. If a metal pole is less than _____ ft. in height, then a handhole is not required.

    A. 6

    B. 8

    C. 10

    D. 12

    Reference: 2017 National Electrical Code – Chapter 4 Equipment for General Use, Article 410 Luminaires, Lampholders, and Lamps. 410.30 Supports. 410.30(B) Metal or Nonmetallic Poles Supporting Luminaires

24. True or False: If an electric sign is cord-connected with an attachment plug, it must have an additional means of disconnecting.

    A. True

    B. False

    Reference: 2017 National Electrical Code – Chapter 6 Special Equipment, Article 600 Electric Signs and Outline Lighting. 600.6 Disconnects.

Chapter 6 Special Equipment

EXAM 10

Chapter 6 Special Equipment

25. Inside a building, which directional sign is not required to have a disconnect?

    A. exit

    B. restroom

    C. either A or B

    D. neither A nor B

    Reference: 2017 National Electrical Code – Chapter 6 Special Equipment, Article 600 Electric Signs and Outline Lighting. 600.6 Disconnects.

26. The disconnecting means for electric signs or outline lighting systems must be visible and _____ of any part of the sign display.

    A. in line of sight

    B. out of sight

    C. within sight

    D. any of these

    Reference: 2017 National Electrical Code – Chapter 1 General, Article 100 Definitions

27. What is the maximum distance from any section of the sign display for the disconnecting means to be from electric signs or outline lighting systems?

    A. 25

    B. 40

    C. 50

    D. 60

    Reference: 2017 National Electrical Code – Chapter 1 General, Article 100 Definitions

28. True or False: If an electric sign or outline lighting system may be controlled by an electric control outside of the sign, it is allowed to have the disconnect located in the controller's enclosure.

    A. True

    B. False

    Reference: 2017 National Electrical Code – Chapter 6 Special Equipment, Article 600 Electric Signs and Outline Lighting. 600.6 Disconnects. 600.6(A) Location. 600.6(A)(3) Within Sight of the Controller.

EXAM 10

Chapter 6 Special Equipment

29. If an electric sign or outline lighting system is supplied by more than one feeder-circuit or branch-circuit, they must have multiple disconnects and all _____ conductors must be opened by them.

    A. grounded

    B. ungrounded

    C. both A and B

    D. neither A nor B

    Reference: 2017 National Electrical Code – Chapter 6 Special Equipment, Article 600 Electric Signs and Outline Lighting. 600.6 Disconnects. 600.6(A) Location. 600.6(A)(3) Within Sight of the Controller.

30. True or False: Flashers, switches, and similar devices that control electronic power supplies and transformers must have a rating equal to the transformer's rating.

    A. True

    B. False

    Reference: 2017 National Electrical Code – Chapter 6 Special Equipment, Article 600 Electric Signs and Outline Lighting. 600.6 Disconnects. 600.6(B) Control Switch Rating.

31. An AC-DC general-use snap switch must have a rating at least how much of the output of the transformer?

    A. 1.25 times

    B. 1.5 times

    C. equal to

    D. twice

    Reference: 2017 National Electrical Code – Chapter 6 Special Equipment, Article 600 Electric Signs and Outline Lighting. 600.6 Disconnects. 600.6(B) Control Switch Rating.

32. True or False: It is not required to ground metal equipment of outline lighting, signs, and skeleton tubing systems.

    A. True

    B. False

    Reference: 2017 National Electrical Code – Chapter 6 Special Equipment, Article 600 Electric Signs and Outline Lighting. 600.7 Grounding and Bonding. 600.7(A) Grounding. 600.7(A)(1) Equipment Grounding.

Chapter 6 Special Equipment

EXAM 10
Chapter 6 Special Equipment

33. True or False: It is permitted to use the metal parts of buildings for grounding conductors for equipment.

    A. True

    B. False

    Reference: 2017 National Electrical Code – Chapter 6 Special Equipment, Article 600 Electric Signs and Outline Lighting. 600.7 Grounding and Bonding. 600.7(A) Grounding. 600.7(A)(5) Metal Building Parts.

34. What is the maximum length for listed flexible metal conduit or listed liquidtight flexible metal conduit that is allowed to be used as a bonding jumper for electric sign or outline lighting systems?

    A. 50 ft.

    B. 100 ft.

    C. 125 ft.

    D. 150 ft.

    Reference: 2017 National Electrical Code – Chapter 6 Special Equipment, Article 600 Electric Signs and Outline Lighting. 600.7 Grounding and Bonding. 600.7(B) Bonding. 600.7(B)(4) Flexible Metal Conduit Length.

35. Small metal parts under 2 in. in any direction are not required to be bonded in an electric sign or outline lighting system, provided they are not likely to become energized and their spacing from neon tubing is a minimum of:

    A. 1/8 in.

    B. 1/4 in.

    C. 1/2 in.

    D. 3/4 in.

    Reference: 2017 National Electrical Code – Chapter 6 Special Equipment, Article 600 Electric Signs and Outline Lighting. 600.7 Grounding and Bonding. 600.7(B) Bonding. 600.7(B)(5) Small Metal Parts.

36. What is the minimum distance that a bonding conductor from a separately and remotely routed nonmetallic conduit when the circuit is operating for electric signs or outline lighting systems and 100 Hz or less?

    A. 1-1/8 in.

    B. 1-1/4 in.

    C. 1-1/2 in.

    D. 1-3/4 in.

    Reference: 2017 National Electrical Code – Chapter 6 Special Equipment, Article 600 Electric Signs and Outline Lighting. 600.7 Grounding and Bonding. 600.7(B) Bonding. 600.7(B)(6) Nonmetallic Conduit.

EXAM 10

Chapter 6 Special Equipment

37. What is the minimum distance that a bonding conductor from a separately and remotely routed nonmetallic conduit when the circuit is operating for electric signs or outline lighting systems and over 100 Hz?

   A. 1-1/8 in.

   B. 1-1/4 in.

   C. 1-1/2 in.

   D. 1-3/4 in.

   Reference: 2017 National Electrical Code – Chapter 6 Special Equipment, Article 600 Electric Signs and Outline Lighting. 600.7 Grounding and Bonding. 600.7(B) Bonding. 600.7(B)(6) Nonmetallic Conduit.

38. For electric signs or outline lighting systems, what is the smallest that bonding conductors should be sized to in copper?

   A. 14 AWG

   B. 12 AWG

   C. 10 AWG

   D. 8 AWG

   Reference: 2017 National Electrical Code – Chapter 6 Special Equipment, Article 600 Electric Signs and Outline Lighting. 600.7 Grounding and Bonding. 600.7(B) Bonding. 600.7(B)(7) Bonding Conductors.

39. True or False: A transformer is required to be in an additional enclosure if it is provided in an integral enclosure that includes both a primary and secondary circuit splice.

   A. True

   B. False

   Reference: 2017 National Electrical Code – Chapter 6 Special Equipment, Article 600 Electric Signs and Outline Lighting. 600.8 Enclosures.

40. Other than those for lamps and neon tubing, all live parts of an enclosure must be:

   A. enclosed

   B. grounded

   C. open

   D. ungrounded

   Reference: 2017 National Electrical Code – Chapter 6 Special Equipment, Article 600 Electric Signs and Outline Lighting. 600.8 Enclosures.

Chapter 6 Special Equipment

EXAM 10

Chapter 6 Special Equipment

41. True or False: Electric sign enclosures are required to have ample rigidity and strength.

    A. True
    B. False

    Reference: 2017 National Electrical Code – Chapter 6 Special Equipment, Article 600 Electric Signs and Outline Lighting. 600.8 Enclosures. 600.8(A) Strength.

42. To prevent _____ from abnormally corrosive conditions, all metal parts for electric signs or outline lighting systems must be coated or otherwise protected.

    A. corrosion
    B. etching
    C. oxidation
    D. stress

    Reference: 2017 National Electrical Code – Chapter 6 Special Equipment, Article 600 Electric Signs and Outline Lighting. 600.8 Enclosures. 600.8 (D) Protection of Metal.

43. Electric signs and outline lighting systems must be _____ or more in height to in areas accessible to vehicles, unless protected from physical damage.

    A. 8 ft.
    B. 10 ft.
    C. 12 ft.
    D. 14 ft.

    Reference: 2017 National Electrical Code – Chapter 6 Special Equipment, Article 600 Electric Signs and Outline Lighting. 600.9 Location. 600.9(A) Vehicles

44. Other than dry location portable signs, where neon tubing is _____ to pedestrians, it must be protected from physical damage.

    A. accessible
    B. protected
    C. dangerous
    D. unprotected

    Reference: 2017 National Electrical Code – Chapter 6 Special Equipment, Article 600 Electric Signs and Outline Lighting. 600.9 Location. 600.9(B) Pedestrians.

EXAM 10

Chapter 6 Special Equipment

45. Combustible materials adjacent to installed electric signs and outline lighting system must not be subjected to temperatures over:

    A. 90°C
    B. 100°C
    C. 105°C
    D. 110°C

    Reference: 2017 National Electrical Code – Chapter 6 Special Equipment, Article 600 Electric Signs and Outline Lighting. 600.9 Location. 600.9(C) Adjacent to Combustible Materials.

46. Wood and other combustible materials and incandescent or HID lamps or lampholders for electric signs or outline lighting systems must be a minimum of:

    A. 1 in.
    B. 2 in.
    C. 4 in.
    D. 6 in.

    Reference: 2017 National Electrical Code – Chapter 6 Special Equipment, Article 600 Electric Signs and Outline Lighting. 600.9 Location. 600.9(C) Adjacent to Combustible Materials.

47. Unless they are listed as a watertight type, what is the smallest size allowed for the minimum one allowed drain hole if installed in wet locations?

    A. 1/4 in. to 1/2 in.
    B. 1/2 in. to 3/4 in.
    C. 3/4 in. to 1 in.
    D. 1 in. to 1-1/4 in.

    Reference: 2017 National Electrical Code – Chapter 6 Special Equipment, Article 600 Electric Signs and Outline Lighting. 600.9 Location. 600.9(D) Wet Location.

48. All mobile or portable signs must be adequately _____ and connected with an attachment plug.

    A. braced
    B. grounded
    C. secured
    D. supported

    Reference: 2017 National Electrical Code – Chapter 6 Special Equipment, Article 600 Electric Signs and Outline Lighting. 600.10 Portable or Mobile Signs.

EXAM 10
Chapter 6 Special Equipment

49. True or False: It must be possible to move portable or mobile signs without specialized equipment or tools.

    A. True   B. False

    Reference: 2017 National Electrical Code – Chapter 6 Special Equipment, Article 600 Electric Signs and Outline Lighting. 600.10 Portable or Mobile Signs. 600.10(A) Support.

50. If a portable or mobile sign is installed in a wet location, it must have GFCI-protection in the power supply and within what distance of the attachment cord?

    A. 6 in.   C. 10 in.

    B. 8 in.   D. 12 in.

    Reference: 2017 National Electrical Code – Chapter 6 Special Equipment, Article 600 Electric Signs and Outline Lighting. 600.10 Portable or Mobile Signs. 600.10(C) Wet or Damp Location.

51. True or False: Only junior hard service or hard service type cords with an equipment grounding conductor should be used to connect portable or mobile signs.

    A. True   B. False

    Reference: 2017 National Electrical Code – Chapter 6 Special Equipment, Article 600 Electric Signs and Outline Lighting. 600.10 Portable or Mobile Signs. 600.10(C) Wet or Damp Location. 600.10(C)(1) Cords.

52. All portable or mobile signs must have a factory-installed _____ device for protection of personnel.

    A. ground-fault-circuit-interrupter   C. either A or B

    B. grounding   D. neither A nor B

    Reference: 2017 National Electrical Code – Chapter 6 Special Equipment, Article 600 Electric Signs and Outline Lighting. 600.10 Portable or Mobile Signs. 600.10(C) Wet or Damp Location. 600.10(C)(2) Ground-Fault Circuit Interrupter.

EXAM 10

Chapter 6 Special Equipment

53. What is the maximum length for the SP-2, SPE-2, SPT-2 or heavier cords for portable or mobile signs in dry locations?

    A. 6 ft.

    B. 10 ft.

    C. 15 ft.

    D. 20 ft.

    Reference: *2017 National Electrical Code – Chapter 6 Special Equipment, Article 600 Electric Signs and Outline Lighting. 600.10 Portable or Mobile Signs. 600.10(D) Dry Location.*

54. For electric signs or outline lighting systems the transformer must be in an accessible and firmly installed location as _____ to lamps and neon tubing as practicable.

    A. close

    B. distant

    C. far

    D. near

    Reference: *2017 National Electrical Code – Chapter 6 Special Equipment, Article 600 Electric Signs and Outline Lighting. 600.21 Ballasts, Transformers, Electronic Power Supplies, and Class 2 Power Sources. 600.21(B) Location.*

55. If electronic power supplies for outline lighting systems are to be used in wet locations, they must be either weatherproof or _____ and protected from the weather by being installed in the sign cabinet or in an enclosure.

    A. insulated

    B. outdoor

    C. rainproof

    D. none of these

    Reference: *2017 National Electrical Code – Chapter 6 Special Equipment, Article 600 Electric Signs and Outline Lighting. 600.21 Ballasts, Transformers, Electronic Power Supplies, and Class 2 Power Sources. 600.21(C) Wet Location.*

Chapter 6 Special Equipment   515

EXAM 10

Chapter 6 Special Equipment

56. An electric sign or outline lighting system transformer that is not installed inside a sign cabinet must have a working area of at least:

    A. 2 ft. high x 2 ft. wide x 2 ft. deep

    B. 2 ft. high x 3 ft. wide x 3 ft. deep

    C. 3 ft. high x 3 ft. wide x 3 ft. deep

    D. 3 ft. high x 4 ft. wide x 3 ft. deep

    Reference: *2017 National Electrical Code – Chapter 6 Special Equipment, Article 600 Electric Signs and Outline Lighting. 600.21 Ballasts, Transformers, Electronic Power Supplies, and Class 2 Power Sources. 600.21(D) Workings Space.*

57. If a transformer is installed in an attic, an access door must be provided that is a minimum of:

    A. 24 in. x 24 in.

    B. 36 in. x 22-1/2 in.

    C. 36 in. x 36 in.

    D. 48 in. x 24 in.

    Reference: *2017 National Electrical Code – Chapter 6 Special Equipment, Article 600 Electric Signs and Outline Lighting. 600.21 Ballasts, Transformers, Electronic Power Supplies, and Class 2 Power Sources. 600.21(E) Attic and Soffit Locations.*

58. If ballasts have been installed in an attic, a passageway must be provided that is a minimum of:

    A. 3 ft. x 2 ft.

    B. 3 ft. x 3 ft.

    C. 4 ft. x 4 ft.

    D. 4 ft. x 6 ft.

    Reference: *2017 National Electrical Code – Chapter 6 Special Equipment, Article 600 Electric Signs and Outline Lighting. 600.21 Ballasts, Transformers, Electronic Power Supplies, and Class 2 Power Sources. 600.21(E) Attic and Soffit Locations.*

EXAM 10

Chapter 6 Special Equipment

59. If ballasts have been installed in an attic, a permanent walkway must be provided that is a minimum of:

    A. 10 in.
    B. 12 in.
    C. 18 in.
    D. 24 in.

    Reference: 2017 National Electrical Code – Chapter 6 Special Equipment, Article 600 Electric Signs and Outline Lighting. 600.21 Ballasts, Transformers, Electronic Power Supplies, and Class 2 Power Sources. 600.21(E) Attic and Soffit Locations.

60. True or False: It is permissible to connect transformers located above a suspended ceiling to the grid of the suspended ceiling for support.

    A. True
    B. False

    Reference: 2017 National Electrical Code – Chapter 6 Special Equipment, Article 600 Electric Signs and Outline Lighting. 600.21 Ballasts, Transformers, Electronic Power Supplies, and Class 2 Power Sources. 600.21(F) Suspended Ceilings.

61. Ballasts must be identified for the conditions of their use and _____ protected.

    A. electrically
    B. mechanically
    C. physically
    D. thermally

    Reference: 2017 National Electrical Code – Chapter 6 Special Equipment, Article 600 Electric Signs and Outline Lighting. 600.22 Ballasts.

62. Electronic power supplies and transformers must have a secondary-circuit current rating that is not over:

    A. 150 mA
    B. 200 mA
    C. 300 mA
    D. 450 mA

    Reference: 2017 National Electrical Code – Chapter 6 Special Equipment, Article 600 Electric Signs and Outline Lighting. 600.23 Transformers and Electronic Power Supplies. 600.23(D) Rating.

EXAM 10

Chapter 6 Special Equipment

63. What kind of item is used to protect wires passing through metal openings for field-installed skeletal tubing?

    A. bushing

    B. collar

    C. insulation

    D. sheath

    Reference: 2017 National Electrical Code – Chapter 6 Special Equipment, Article 600 Electric Signs and Outline Lighting. 600.31 Neon Secondary-Circuit Wiring, 1000 Volts or Less, Nominal. 600.31(E) Protection of Leads.

64. True or False: It is permissible for high-voltage secondary wiring on a neon system to be enclosed by nonmetallic conduit.

    A. True

    B. False

    Reference: 2017 National Electrical Code – Chapter 6 Special Equipment, Article 600 Electric Signs and Outline Lighting. 600.32 Neon Secondary-Circuit Wiring, over 1000 Volts, Nominal. 600.32(A) Wiring Methods. 600.32(A)(1) Installation.

65. Conductors used to wire skeleton tubing must not only be insulated for such use, but also:

    A. designed

    B. labeled

    C. licensed

    D. listed

    Reference: 2017 National Electrical Code – Chapter 6 Special Equipment, Article 600 Electric Signs and Outline Lighting. 600.32 Neon Secondary-Circuit Wiring, over 1000 Volts, Nominal. 600.32(B) Insulation and Size.

66. What is the minimum size for listed and insulated conductors used to wire field-installed skeleton tubing?

    A. 10 AWG

    B. 12 AWG

    C. 14 AWG

    D. 18 AWG

    Reference: 2017 National Electrical Code – Chapter 6 Special Equipment, Article 600 Electric Signs and Outline Lighting. 600.32 Neon Secondary-Circuit Wiring, over 1000 Volts, Nominal. 600.32(B) Insulation and Size.

EXAM 10

Chapter 6 Special Equipment

67. What is the minimum temperature rating required for rated conductors used to wire field-installed skeleton tubing?

    A. 75°C

    B. 90°C

    C. 100°C

    D. 105°C

    Reference: 2017 National Electrical Code – Chapter 6 Special Equipment, Article 600 Electric Signs and Outline Lighting. 600.32 Neon Secondary-Circuit Wiring, over 1000 Volts, Nominal. 600.32(B) Insulation and Size.

68. What is the minimum distance that must be between conductors for field-installed skeleton tubing and from all other objects?

    A. 1-1/8 in.

    B. 1-1/4 in.

    C. 1-1/2 in.

    D. 1-3/4 in.

    Reference: 2017 National Electrical Code – Chapter 6 Special Equipment, Article 600 Electric Signs and Outline Lighting. 600.32 Neon Secondary-Circuit Wiring, over 1000 Volts, Nominal. 600.32(E) Spacing.

69. True or False: It is not required for bushings used with neon conductors to be listed for such use when used for field-installed skeleton tubing.

    A. True

    B. False

    Reference: 2017 National Electrical Code – Chapter 6 Special Equipment, Article 600 Electric Signs and Outline Lighting. 600.32 Neon Secondary-Circuit Wiring, over 1000 Volts, Nominal. 600.32(F) Insulators and Bushings.

70. What is the minimum distance that insulation on conductors for field-installed skeleton tubing should extend beyond a metal raceway or conduit?

    A. 2-1/2 in.

    B. 3 in.

    C. 4 in.

    D. 6-1/2 in.

    Reference: 2017 National Electrical Code – Chapter 6 Special Equipment, Article 600 Electric Signs and Outline Lighting. 600.32 Neon Secondary-Circuit Wiring, over 1000 Volts, Nominal. 600.32(G) Conductors in Raceways.

EXAM 10

Chapter 6 Special Equipment

71. Conductors shall be permitted to run between the ends of neon tubing or to the secondary circuit _____ return of listed transformers.

    A. anchor

    B. end

    C. midpoint

    D. wire

    Reference: 2017 National Electrical Code – Chapter 6 Special Equipment, Article 600 Electric Signs and Outline Lighting. 600.32 Neon Secondary-Circuit Wiring, over 1000 Volts, Nominal. 600.32(H) Between Neon Tubing and Midpoint Return.

72. True or False: It is allowed to install equipment with an open circuit voltage of over 1000 volts in or on dwelling occupancies.

    A. True

    B. False

    Reference: 2017 National Electrical Code – Chapter 6 Special Equipment, Article 600 Electric Signs and Outline Lighting. 600.32 Neon Secondary-Circuit Wiring, over 1000 Volts, Nominal. 600.32(I) Dwelling Occupancies.

73. If skeleton tubing and equipment has and open circuit voltage of more than _____ volts, it may not be installed in or on a dwelling occupancy.

    A. 600

    B. 1000

    C. 1200

    D. 15,000.

    Reference: 2017 National Electrical Code – Chapter 6 Special Equipment, Article 600 Electric Signs and Outline Lighting. 600.32 Neon Secondary-Circuit Wiring, over 1000 Volts, Nominal. 600.32(I) Dwelling Occupancies.

74. What is the minimum length of high-voltage cabling for field-installed skeleton tubing installed in metal conduit, between the first neon tube and a high-voltage terminal of the transformer?

    A. 10 ft.

    B. 20 ft.

    C. 40 ft.

    D. 50 ft.

    Reference: 2017 National Electrical Code – Chapter 6 Special Equipment, Article 600 Electric Signs and Outline Lighting. 600.32 Neon Secondary-Circuit Wiring, over 1000 Volts, Nominal. 600.32(J) Length of Secondary Circuit Conductors. 600.32(J) (1) Secondary Conductor to the First Electrode.

EXAM 10

Chapter 6 Special Equipment

75. Other than its listed tube support, what is the minimum distance that field-installed skeleton tubing must be spaced from any surface?

    A. 1/4 in.   C. 3/4 in.

    B. 1/2 in.   D. 1 in.

Reference: 2017 National Electrical Code – Chapter 6 Special Equipment, Article 600 Electric Signs and Outline Lighting. 600.41 Neon Tubing. 600.41(C) Spacing.

76. For field-installed skeleton tubing, the connection between high-voltage cable and neon electrodes must not only be electrically secure, but also:

    A. mechanically   C. both A and B

    B. physically   D. neither A nor B

Reference: 2017 National Electrical Code – Chapter 6 Special Equipment, Article 600 Electric Signs and Outline Lighting. 600.42 Electrode Connections. 600.42(C) Electrode Connections.

77. What is the maximum distance allowed of a supported, mechanically secure attachment between the electrode terminals of the electrode and the neon tubing and conductor for field-installed skeleton tubing?

    A. 2 in.   C. 4 in.

    B. 3 in.   D. 6 in.

Reference: 2017 National Electrical Code – Chapter 6 Special Equipment, Article 600 Electric Signs and Outline Lighting. 600.42 Electrode Connections. 600.42(D) Support.

78. If a conductor for field-installed skeleton tubing is required to penetrate a metal opening, if _____ are not used, then bushings are required to protect the conductors.

    A. receptacles   C. either A or B

    B. sleeves   D. neither A nor B

Reference: 2017 National Electrical Code – Chapter 6 Special Equipment, Article 600 Electric Signs and Outline Lighting. 600.42 Electrode Connections. 600.42(F) Bushings.

Chapter 6 Special Equipment

EXAM 10

Chapter 6 Special Equipment

79. The minimum size 60°C rated copper conductors required for an ac transformer arc welder with a 50 ampere rated primary current and a 60 percent duty cycle is:

    A. 4 AWG

    B. 6 AWG

    C. 8 AWG

    D. 10 AWG

    Reference: 2017 National Electrical Code – Chapter 3 Wiring Methods and Materials

80. What is required of a designated information technology equipment room?

    A. equipped with walls at least 6 inches thick

    B. provided with at least two exit doors

    C. separated by fire-resistant-rate walls, floors, and ceilings

    D. sound-proofed

    Reference: 2017 National Electrical Code – Chapter 6 Special Equipment, Article 645 Information Technology Equipment. 645.4 Special Requirements for Information Technology Equipment Room. 645.4(5)

81. Where branch-circuit conductors supply one or more units of information technology equipment, they must have an ampacity of at least _____ percent of the total load that is connected.

    A. 80

    B. 100

    C. 125

    D. 150

    Reference: 2017 National Electrical Code – Chapter 6 Special Equipment, Article 645 Information Technology Equipment. 645.5 Supply Circuits and Interconnecting Cables.

82. What is the maximum length for a listed power-supply cord connected to a branch circuit for information technology equipment?

    A. 10 feet

    B. 12 feet

    C. 15 feet

    D. 20 feet

    Reference: 2017 National Electrical Code – Chapter 6 Special Equipment, Article 645 Information Technology Equipment. 645.5 Supply Circuits and Interconnecting Cables. 645.5(B) Power Supply Cords.

EXAM 10

Chapter 6 Special Equipment

83. What is the maximum required voltage to ground for wiring installation for sensitive electronic equipment?

    A. 30 volts

    B. 60 volts

    C. 120 volts

    D. 277 volts

    Reference: 2017 National Electrical Code – Chapter 6 Special Equipment, Article 647 Sensitive Electronic Equipment. 647.1 Scope.

84. For a permanently installed pool, fixed or stationary equipment other than an underwater luminaire (lighting fixture), is allowed to have a _____ for the supply connection.

    A. 6 ft. long flexible cord

    B. flexible cord to facilitate disconnection for maintenance

    C. overhead service drop

    D. none of the above

    Reference: 2017 National Electrical Code – Chapter 6 Special Equipment, Article 680 Swimming Pools, Fountains, and Similar Installations. 680.8 Cord-and-Plug-Connected Equipment.

85. In other than storable pools, cord-and-plug-connected equipment must have a flexible cord that is _____ ft. in length or less.

    A. 3

    B. 6

    C. 10

    D. 15

    Reference: 2017 National Electrical Code – Chapter 6 Special Equipment, Article 680 Swimming Pools, Fountains, and Similar Installations. 680.8 Cord-and-Plug-Connected Equipment. . 680.8(A) Length.

Chapter 6 Special Equipment

EXAM 10

Chapter 6 Special Equipment

86. What is the clearance near a swimming pool for insulated cables, 0-750 volts to ground, cabled together with and supported on an effectively grounded bare messenger or effectively grounded neutral conductor, in relation to a diving platform, observation stand, or tower?

    A. 14.5 feet

    B. 17 feet

    C. 22.5 feet

    D. 25 feet

    Reference: 2017 National Electrical Code – Chapter 6 Special Equipment, Article 680 Swimming Pools, Fountains, and Similar Installations. 680.9 Overhead Conductor Clearances. . 680.9(A) Power.

87. Heating elements for electric pool water heaters must be subdivided in to loads of _____ amperes or less, and protected for _____ amperes or less.

    A. 20, 40

    B. 40, 80

    C. 48, 60

    D. 50, 80

    Reference: 2017 National Electrical Code – Chapter 6 Special Equipment, Article 680 Swimming Pools, Fountains, and Similar Installations. 680.10 Electric Pool Water Heaters.

88. underground wiring shall be encased in _____.

    A. rigid metal conduit

    B. intermediate metal conduit

    C. rigid polyvinyl

    D. any of the above

    Reference: 2017 National Electrical Code – Chapter 6 Special Equipment, Article 680 Swimming Pools, Fountains, and Similar Installations. 680.11 Underground Wiring Location.

89. If there is not enough space to allow wiring to be routed a minimum of 5 ft. from a pool. The wiring is allowed where the complete raceway systems are:

    A. thermosetting resign conduit

    B. Thermoplastic high-heat resistant nylon-coated wire

    C. chloride conduit

    D. Either A or C

    Reference: 2017 National Electrical Code – Chapter 6 Special Equipment, Article 680 Swimming Pools, Fountains, and Similar Installations. 680.10 Underground Wiring Location.

EXAM 10

Chapter 6 Special Equipment

90. True or False: Unless the wiring is supplying the associated pool equipment, underground wiring is not allowed under a permanently installed swimming pool or within a distance of it.

    A. True

    B. False

    Reference: 2017 National Electrical Code – Chapter 6 Special Equipment, Article 680 Swimming Pools, Fountains, and Similar Installations. 680.10 Underground Wiring Location.

91. For a recirculating motor on a residential swimming pool, what is the longest that the flexible cord may be?

    A. 3 feet

    B. 4 feet

    C. 6 feet

    D. 8 feet

    Reference: 2017 National Electrical Code – Chapter 6 Special Equipment, Article 680 Swimming Pools, Fountains, and Similar Installations. 680.21 Motors. 680.21(A) Wiring Methods. 680.21(A)(3) Cord-and-Plug Connections.

92. All 15- and 20-ampere, single-phase, 125-volt receptacles shall be protected by a GFCI if they are within what minimum distance to the inside walls of a permanently installed swimming pool?

    A. 10 feet

    B. 15 feet

    C. 20 feet

    D. 25 feet

    Reference: 2017 National Electrical Code – Chapter 4 Equipment for General Use, Article 680 Swimming Pools, Fountains, and Similar Installations. 680.22 Lighting, Receptacles, and Equipment. 680.22(A) Receptacles. 680.22(A)(1) Required Receptacle, Location.

Chapter 6 Special Equipment   525

EXAM 10

Chapter 6 Special Equipment

93. Receptacles providing power for water-pump motors and other loads directly related to water circulation and sanitation of a pool must be 10 ft. or more from the inside walls, and are only allowed to be as little as 6 ft. from the inside walls if they:

    A. Consist of single receptacles

    B. Employ a locking configuration

    C. Have GFCI protection

    D. All of the above

    Reference: 2017 National Electrical Code – Chapter 6 Special Equipment, Article 680 Swimming Pools, Fountains, and Similar Installations. 680.22 Lighting, Receptacles, and Equipment. 680.22(A) Receptacles. 680.22(A)(2) Circulation and Sanitation System, Location.

94. Receptacle providing power for swimming pool recirculating pump motors must be single receptacles, GFCI protected, and must be at least how far from the inside walls of the pool?

    A. 5 feet

    B. 6 feet

    C. 10 feet

    D. 12 feet

    Reference: 2017 National Electrical Code – Chapter 6 Special Equipment, Article 680 Swimming Pools, Fountains, and Similar Installations. 680.22 Lighting, Receptacles, and Equipment. 680.22(A) Receptacles. 680.22(A)(2) Circulation and Sanitation System, Location.

95. Generally, receptacles are required to be _____ ft. or more from the inside walls of a pool.

    A. 5

    B. 6

    C. 15

    D. 25

    Reference: 2017 National Electrical Code – Chapter 6 Special Equipment, Article 680 Swimming Pools, Fountains, and Similar Installations. 680.22 Lighting, Receptacles, and Equipment. 680.22(A) Receptacles. 680.22(A)(3) Other Receptacles, Location.

EXAM 10

Chapter 6 Special Equipment

96. Luminaires installed outdoors above a pool or horizontally within five (5) feet of the inside wall of a pool, must be above the maximum water level by at least:

    A. 8 feet

    B. 10 feet

    C. 12 feet

    D. 15 feet

    Reference: 2017 National Electrical Code – Chapter 6 Special Equipment, Article 680 Swimming Pools, Fountains, and Similar Installations. 680.22 Lighting, Receptacles, and Equipment. 680.22(B) Luminaires, Lighting Outlets, and Ceiling-Suspended (Paddle) Fans. 680.22(B)(1) New Outdoor Installation Clearances.

97. Switching devices must be _____ ft. or more horizontally from the inside walls of a pool unless they are separated by a solid fence, wall, or other permanent barrier. A switch listed as being acceptable for use inside this distance is allowed.

    A. 5

    B. 10

    C. 15

    D. 20

    Reference: 2017 National Electrical Code – Chapter 6 Special Equipment, Article 680 Swimming Pools, Fountains, and Similar Installations. 680.22 Lighting, Receptacles, and Equipment. 680.22(C) Switching Devices.

98. Wet niche swimming pool luminaries must be removable from the water for normal maintenance including relamping. Luminaries must be installed in a way that personnel can reach them for inspection, maintenance, or relamping while on the deck or a similarly:

    A. accessible location

    B. dry location

    C. wet location

    D. none of the above

    Reference: 2017 National Electrical Code – Chapter 6 Special Equipment, Article 680 Swimming Pools, Fountains, and Similar Installations. 680.23 Underwater Luminaires. . 680.23(B) Wet-Niche Luminaires. 680.23(B)(6) Servicing.

EXAM 10

Chapter 6 Special Equipment

99. For wet-niche underwater pool luminaires, which of the following listed conduits are allowed to enclose the conductors?

    A. electrical metallic tubing (EMT)

    B. electrical nonmetallic tubing (ENT)

    C. galvanized rigid metal conduit (RMC)

    D. Schedule 40 rigid polyvinyl chloride conduit (PVC)

    Reference: 2017 National Electrical Code – Chapter 6 Special Equipment, Article 680 Swimming Pools, Fountains, and Similar Installations. 680.23 Underwater Luminaires. 680.23(B) Wet-Niche Luminaires. 680.23(B)(2) Wiring Extending Directly to the Forming Shell.

100. What is the smallest size grounding conductor allowed for grounding the structural reinforcing steel of a swimming pool?

    A. 6 AWG

    B. 8 AWG

    C. 10 AWG

    D. 12 AWG

    Reference: 2017 National Electrical Code – Chapter 6 Special Equipment, Article 680 Swimming Pools, Fountains, and Similar Installations. 680.26 Equipotential Bonding. 680.26(B) Bonded Parts. 680.26(B)(1) Conductive Pool Shells. 680.26(B)(1)(b)(a)

101. If an equipotential bonding grid is required to be installed in the deck around a permanently installed swimming pool, what is the minimum horizontal distance for it to be beyond the inside walls of the pool?

    A. 3 feet

    B. 5 feet

    C. 6 feet

    D. 10 feet

    Reference: 2017 National Electrical Code – Chapter 6 Special Equipment, Article 680 Swimming Pools, Fountains, and Similar Installations. 680.26 Equipotential Bonding. 680.26(B) Bonded Parts. 680.26(B)(2) Perimeter Surfaces.

EXAM 10

Chapter 6 Special Equipment

102. If spa and hot tub equipment is installed in a non-dwelling occupancy, it shall be provided with an emergency control switch or shutoff within sight of the unit(s), and at least how far from the inside wall of the spa or hot tub?

    A. 5 feet
    B. 6 feet
    C. 10 feet
    D. 12 feet

    Reference: 2017 National Electrical Code – Chapter 6 Special Equipment, Article 680 Swimming Pools, Fountains, and Similar Installations. 680.41 Emergency Switch for Spas and Hot Tubs.

103. What is the longest cord permitted for a cord-and-plug connected, listed packaged spa or hot tub installed outdoors, protected by a GFCI?

    A. 6 feet
    B. 10 feet
    C. 15 feet
    D. 20 feet

    Reference: 2017 National Electrical Code – Chapter 6 Special Equipment, Article 680 Swimming Pools, Fountains, and Similar Installations. 680.42 Outdoor Installations. 680.42(A) Flexible Connections. 680.42(A)(2) Cord-and-Plug Connections.

104. From the inside walls of an indoor installed spa or hot tub, to the wall switches, what is the minimum distance?

    A. 5 feet
    B. 10 feet
    C. 15 feet
    D. 18 feet

    Reference: 2017 National Electrical Code – Chapter 6 Special Equipment, Article 680 Swimming Pools, Fountains, and Similar Installations. 680.43 Indoor Installations. 680.43(C) Switches.

105. All metal parts associated with a hot tub must be bonded to a bonding conductor at least what size?

    A. 6 AWG
    B. 8 AWG
    C. 10 AWG
    D. 12 AWG

    Reference: 2017 National Electrical Code – Chapter 6 Special Equipment, Article 680 Swimming Pools, Fountains, and Similar Installations. 680.43 Indoor Installations. 680.43(E) Methods of Bonding.

Chapter 6 Special Equipment

EXAM 10

Chapter 6 Special Equipment

106. For a fixed for stationary electric sign installed in a fountain, the disconnecting means must be at least how far horizontally from the inside wall of the fountain?

    A. 5 ft.

    B. 10 ft.

    C. 15 ft.

    D. 20 ft.

    Reference: 2017 National Electrical Code – Chapter 6 Special Equipment, Article 680 Swimming Pools, Fountains, and Similar Installations. 680.57 Signs. 680.57(C) Location. 680.57(C)(1) Fixed or Stationary.

107. What is the minimum distance for all 125-volt, single-phase receptacles up to 30 amperes, from the inside wall of a GFCI protected hydromassage tub?

    A. 3 feet

    B. 5 feet

    C. 6 feet

    D. 10 feet

    Reference: 2017 National Electrical Code – Chapter 6 Special Equipment, Article 680 Swimming Pools, Fountains, and Similar Installations. 680.71 Protection.

108. What is the minimum distance from the shoreline, horizontally, for on land service equipment for a submersible pump located in a pond of a water treatment plant?

    A. 3 feet

    B. 5 feet

    C. 6 feet

    D. 10 feet

    Reference: 2017 National Electrical Code – Chapter 6 Special Equipment, Article 682 Naturally and Artificially Made Bodies of Water. 682.11 Location of Service Equipment.

109. Service equipment for floating structures and submersible electrical equipment that is located on land must be at least how far horizontally from the shoreline?

    A. 5 feet

    B. 10 feet

    C. 15 feet

    D. 20 feet

    Reference: 2017 National Electrical Code – Chapter 6 Special Equipment, Article 682 Natural and Artificially Made Bodies of Water. 682.11 Location of Service Equipment.

EXAM 10

Chapter 6 Special Equipment

110. What kind of systems, including inverter(s), array circuit(s), and controllers for such systems, are covered by Article 690?

    A. solar photoconductive

    B. solar photogenic

    C. solar photosynthesis

    D. solar PV

Reference: 2017 National Electrical Code – Chapter 6 Special Equipment, Article 690 Solar Photovoltaic (PV) Systems. 690.1 Scope

111. What kind of exposure is required for an alternating-current photovoltaic module to generate ac power?

    A. electromagnetic induction

    B. heat

    C. hysteresis

    D. sunlight

Reference: 2017 National Electrical Code – Chapter 6 Special Equipment, Article 690 Solar Photovoltaic (PV) Systems. 690.2 Definitions.

112. What is the correct term for a mechanically integrated assembly of PV modules or panels with support structure, foundation, tracker, and other components as required to form a dc power-producing unit?

    A. array

    B. alternating-current photovoltaic module

    C. capacitive supply bank

    D. pulse width modulator

Reference: 2017 National Electrical Code – Chapter 6 Special Equipment, Article 690 Solar Photovoltaic (PV) Systems. 690.2 Definitions.

113. In a PV system, a _____ is a device meant to change direct-current input to alternating-current output.

    A. diode

    B. inverter

    C. rectifier

    D. transistor

Reference: 2017 National Electrical Code – Chapter 6 Special Equipment, Article 690 Solar Photovoltaic (PV) Systems. 690.2 Definitions.

EXAM 10

Chapter 6 Special Equipment

114. Which of the following terms encompasses the conductors between the battery and the inverter in a stand-alone system, or the conductors between the PV output circuits and the inverter in a network that produces and distributes electrical power?

    A. feeder

    B. inverter input circuit

    C. inverter output circuit

    D. overcurrent protection

    Reference: 2017 National Electrical Code – Chapter 6 Special Equipment, Article 690 Solar Photovoltaic (PV) Systems. 690.2 Definitions.

115. The conductors the inverter in a stand-alone system, or the conductors between the service equipment or another electric power production source such as a utility, and the inverter for an electrical production and distribution network are all part of:

    A. a bipolar photovoltaic array

    B. a monopole subarray

    C. an inverter output circuit

    D. emergency standby power

    Reference: 2017 National Electrical Code – Chapter 6 Special Equipment, Article 690 Solar Photovoltaic (PV) Systems. 690.2 Definitions.

116. Which of the following terms refers to a complete, environmentally protected unit that consist of solar cells and other components, excluding a tracker, that is designed, when exposed to sunlight, to generate direct-current electricity?

    A. battery

    B. cell bank

    C. interface

    D. module

    Reference: 2017 National Electrical Code – Chapter 6 Special Equipment, Article 690 Solar Photovoltaic (PV) Systems. 690.2 Definitions.

EXAM 10

Chapter 6 Special Equipment

117. What are the circuit conductors that are between the direct-current utilization equipment or inverter and the PV source circuit(s) part of?

    A. inverter input circuit

    B. inverter output circuit

    C. photovoltaic input circuit

    D. photovoltaic output circuit

Reference: 2017 National Electrical Code – Chapter 6 Special Equipment, Article 690 Solar Photovoltaic (PV) Systems. 690.2 Definitions.

118. What is the correct term for a single array or aggregate of arrays generating direct-current power at system voltage and current?

    A. array source

    B. output source

    C. power source

    D. source circuit

Reference: 2017 National Electrical Code – Chapter 6 Special Equipment, Article 690 Solar Photovoltaic (PV) Systems. 690.2 Definitions.

119. The term for the circuit(s) between modules and from modules in a PV system to the common connection point(s) of the direct-current system is:

    A. photovoltaic array circuit

    B. photovoltaic input circuit

    C. photovoltaic output circuit

    D. photovoltaic source circuit

Reference: 2017 National Electrical Code – Chapter 6 Special Equipment, Article 690 Solar Photovoltaic (PV) Systems. 690.2 Definitions.

120. True or False: The system voltage of a photovoltaic system is the direct-current voltage of any PV output circuit or source.

    A. True

    B. False

Reference: 2017 National Electrical Code – Chapter 6 Special Equipment, Article 690 Solar Photovoltaic (PV) Systems. 690.2 Definitions.

EXAM 10

Chapter 6 Special Equipment

121. What is the basic PV device used to generate electricity when exposed to light?

    A. solar atom

    B. solar battery

    C. solar cell

    D. solar ray

    Reference: 2017 National Electrical Code – Chapter 6 Special Equipment, Article 690 Solar Photovoltaic (PV) Systems. 690.2 Definitions.

122. True or False: Power from a stand-alone PV system is supplied with and in supplement to a network for electrical production and distribution.

    A. True

    B. False

    Reference: 2017 National Electrical Code – Chapter 6 Special Equipment, Article 690 Solar Photovoltaic (PV) Systems. 690.2 Definitions.

123. PV systems are allowed to supply a building or other structure along with any other systems to supply:

    A. electricity

    B. plumbing service

    C. telephone service

    D. none of these

    Reference: 2017 National Electrical Code – Chapter 6 Special Equipment, Article 690 Solar Photovoltaic (PV) Systems. 690.4 General Requirements. 690.4(A) Photovoltaic Systems.

124. If equipment is intended to be used in a PV power system, then it must be _____ for the application.

    A. approved

    B. field labeled

    C. listed

    D. both B and C

    Reference: 2017 National Electrical Code – Chapter 6 Special Equipment, Article 690 Solar Photovoltaic (PV) Systems. 690.4 General Requirements. 690.4(B) Equipment.

EXAM 10

Chapter 6 Special Equipment

125. True or False: A directory showing where all ac and dc PV system disconnecting means in a building are located must be provided when multiple utility-interactive inverters are remotely located from one another, at each dc PV system disconnecting means, ac disconnecting means, and the main service disconnecting means.

    A. True
    B. False

    Reference: 2017 National Electrical Code – Chapter 6 Special Equipment, Article 690 Solar Photovoltaic (PV) Systems. 690.4 General Requirements. 690.4(D) Multiple Inverters.

126. True or False: The requirements of Article 690 that pertain to dc PV source circuits do not apply to ac PV modules since they have no dc output. The internal wiring of an ac module is considered to include the PV source circuit, conductors, and inverters.

    A. True
    B. False

    Reference: 2017 National Electrical Code – Chapter 6 Special Equipment, Article 690 Solar Photovoltaic (PV) Systems. 690.6 Alternating-Current (ac) Modules. 690.6(A) Photovoltaic Source Circuits.

127. As defined in 690.2, the output of an ac module is considered to be what kind of output circuit?

    A. inverter
    B. module
    C. PV
    D. subarray

    Reference: 2017 National Electrical Code – Chapter 6 Special Equipment, Article 690 Solar Photovoltaic (PV) Systems. 690.6 Alternating-Current (ac) Modules. 690.6(B) Inverter Output Circuit.

Chapter 6 Special Equipment 535

EXAM 10

Chapter 6 Special Equipment

128. What on a dc PV output circuit or source circuit is used to calculate the sum of the rated open-circuit voltage of series-connected PV modules, when multiplied by the correction factor provided in Table 690.7?

    A. maximum allowed conductor ampacity

    B. maximum PV system voltage

    C. minimum allowed conductor ampacity

    D. minimum PV system voltage

    Reference: 2017 National Electrical Code – Chapter 6 Special Equipment, Article 690 Solar Photovoltaic (PV) Systems. 690.7 Maximum Voltage. 690.7(A) Maximum Photovoltaic System Voltage.

129. True or False: One of the sources for lowest-expected ambient temperature for PV systems is found in the ASHRAE Handbook Fundamentals under 'Extreme Annual Mean Minimum Design Dry Bulb Temperature'.

    A. True

    B. False

    Reference: 2017 National Electrical Code – Chapter 6 Special Equipment, Article 690 Solar Photovoltaic (PV) Systems. 690.7 Maximum Voltage. 690.7(A) Maximum Photovoltaic System Voltage.

130. The maximum voltage for PV circuits or PV source for one- and two-family dwellings is:

    A. 150V

    B. 300V

    C. 450V

    D. 600V

    Reference: 2017 National Electrical Code – Chapter 6 Special Equipment, Article 690 Solar Photovoltaic (PV) Systems. 690.7 Maximum Voltage.

131. In one-and two-family dwelling PV systems, who may not access live parts over 150V to ground while they are energized?

    A. electrician

    B. inspector

    C. unqualified person

    D. A through C

    Reference: 2017 National Electrical Code – Chapter 6 Special Equipment, Article 690 Solar Photovoltaic (PV) Systems. 694.10 Maximum Voltage. 694.10(C) Circuits over 150 Volts to Ground.

EXAM 10

Chapter 6 Special Equipment

132. True or False: Current for the PV source circuit is calculated by multiplying by 125 percent the sum of the ratings for the parallel module nameplate short-circuit currents (Isc).

    A. True   B. False

Reference: 2017 National Electrical Code – Chapter 6 Special Equipment, Article 690 Solar Photovoltaic (PV) Systems. 690.8 Circuit Sizing and Current. 690.8(A) Calculation of Maximum Circuit Current. 690.8(A)(1) Photovoltaic Source Circuit Currents.

133. PV output circuit current is equal to the sum of parallel PV source circuit maximum currents, which is detailed in which Article?

    A. 690.8(A)(1)   C. 690.8(A)(3)

    B. 690.8(A)(2)   D. none of these

Reference: 2017 National Electrical Code – Chapter 6 Special Equipment, Article 690 Solar Photovoltaic (PV) Systems. 690.8 Circuit Sizing and Current. 690.8(A) Calculation of Maximum Circuit Current. 690.8(A)(2) Photovoltaic Output Circuit Currents.

134. Which output current rating is the maximum PV inverter output circuit current equal to?

    A. average   C. intermittent

    B. continuous   D. peak

Reference: 2017 National Electrical Code – Chapter 6 Special Equipment, Article 690 Solar Photovoltaic (PV) Systems. 690.8 Circuit Sizing and Current. 690.8(A) Calculation of Maximum Circuit Current. 690.8(A)(3) Inverter Output Circuit Current.

135. Which of the following are currents of PV systems considered?

    A. continuous   C. noncontinuous

    B. inverted   D. safe

Reference: 2017 National Electrical Code – Chapter 6 Special Equipment, Article 690 Solar Photovoltaic (PV) Systems. 690.8 Circuit Sizing and Current. 690.8(B) Conductor Ampacity

EXAM 10

Chapter 6 Special Equipment

136. What is the minimum percent of the maximum current rating for PV system overcurrent devices, as calculated in 690.8(A)?

    A. 75%

    B. 100%

    C. 125%

    D. 150%

    Reference: 2017 National Electrical Code – Chapter 6 Special Equipment, Article 690 Solar Photovoltaic (PV) Systems. 690.9 Overcurrent Protection. 690.9(B) Overcurrent Device Ratings.

137. A single _____ protective device, where required, shall be permitted to protect the PV modules and conductors of each source circuit or the conductors of each output circuit.

    A. warning

    B. conductor

    C. overcurrent

    D. GFCI

    Reference: 2017 National Electrical Code – Chapter 6 Special Equipment, Article 690 Solar Photovoltaic (PV) Systems. 690.9 Overcurrent Protection. 690.9(C) Photovoltaic Source and Output Circuits.

138. True or False: PV source circuit overcurrent devices are required to be readily accessible.

    A. True

    B. False

    Reference: 2017 National Electrical Code – Chapter 6 Special Equipment, Article 690 Solar Photovoltaic (PV) Systems. 690.9 Overcurrent Protection. 690.9(C) Photovoltaic Source and Output Circuits.

139. True or False: One overcurrent protection device is not permitted in grounded PV source circuits, to protect the PV modules and interconnecting conductors.

    A. True

    B. False

    Reference: 2017 National Electrical Code – Chapter 6 Special Equipment, Article 690 Solar Photovoltaic (PV) Systems. 690.9 Overcurrent Protection. 690.9(C) Photovoltaic Source and Output Circuits.

EXAM 10

Chapter 6 Special Equipment

140. The ac current output from a stand-alone system may be _____ than the calculated load attached to the disconnect, but may not be less than the single largest piece of equipment attached to the system

    A. greater

    B. less

    C. more

    D. any of these

    Reference: 2017 National Electrical Code – Chapter 7 Special Conditions, Article 712 Stand-Alone Systems. 710.15 General.

141. True or False: Backup power supplies or energy storage are required for stand-alone systems.

    A. True

    B. False

    Reference: 2017 National Electrical Code – Chapter 7 Special Conditions, Article 712 Stand-Alone Systems. 710.15 General. 710.15(D) Energy Storage or Backup Power System Requirements

142. True or False: To open ungrounded dc circuit conductors of a PV system requires a disconnecting means.

    A. True

    B. False

    Reference: 2017 National Electrical Code – Chapter 6 Special Equipment, Article 690 Solar Photovoltaic (PV) Systems. 690.13 Building or Other Structure Supplied by a Photovoltaic System.

143. For an ungrounded PV system on a building or structure, in what readily accessible location should the system to disconnect the dc circuit conductors?

    A. anywhere inside

    B. inside, closest to entrance

    C. outside

    D. either A or B

    Reference: 2017 National Electrical Code – Chapter 6 Special Equipment, Article 690 Solar Photovoltaic (PV) Systems. 690.13 Building or Other Structure Supplied by a Photovoltaic System. 690.13(A) Location.

EXAM 10

Chapter 6 Special Equipment

144. True or False: Where all terminals of a disconnecting means for a PV system might be energized when the switch is in the open position, a warning sign saying something like: WARNING ELECTRIC SHOCK HAZARD. DO NOT TOUCH TERMINALS. TERMINALS ON BOTH THE LINE AND LOAD SIDES MAY BE ENERGIZED IN THE OPEN POSITION is required to be placed on or adjacent to the disconnecting means.

   A. True   B. False

   Reference: 2017 National Electrical Code – Chapter 6 Special Equipment, Article 690 Solar Photovoltaic (PV) Systems. 690.17 Disconnect Type. 690.17(E) Interrupting Rating.

145. To identify it properly, the PV system disconnecting means is required to be:

   A. approved   C. permanently marked

   B. listed   D. temporarily marked

   Reference: 2017 National Electrical Code – Chapter 6 Special Equipment, Article 690 Solar Photovoltaic (PV) Systems. 690.13 Building or Other Structure Supplied by a Photovoltaic System. 690.13(B) Marking.

146. True or False: Means must be provided for PV systems to disconnect batteries, charge controllers, inverters, and other such equipment from all sources of ungrounded conductors.

   A. True   B. False

   Reference: 2017 National Electrical Code – Chapter 6 Special Equipment, Article 690 Solar Photovoltaic (PV) Systems. 690.15 Disconnection of Photovoltaic Equipment

147. True or False: If a fuse is energized from both directions, it is required to have a disconnecting means provided to sever all sources of supply, and it must operate independently of other PV source circuit fuses.

   A. True   B. False

   Reference: 2017 National Electrical Code – Chapter 6 Special Equipment, Article 690 Solar Photovoltaic (PV) Systems. 694.26 Fuses. 694.26 Disconnecting Means.

EXAM 10

Chapter 6 Special Equipment

148. Each PV system disconnecting means shall consist of not more than _____ or _____ of circuit breakers, or a combination of not more than six switches and sets of circuit breakers, mounted in a single enclosure, or in a group of separate enclosures.

    A. 3 Switches/3 sets

    B. 6 Switches/6 sets

    C. 9 Switches/ 9 sets

    D. 12 Switches/ 12 sets

    Reference: 2017 National Electrical Code – Chapter 6 Special Equipment, Article 690 Solar Photovoltaic (PV) Systems. 690.13 Photovoltaic System Disconnecting Means. 690.13(D) Maximum Number of Disconnects.

149. True or False: Devices marked with "line" and "load" shall not be permitted for backfeed or reverse current.

    A. True

    B. False

    Reference: 2017 National Electrical Code – Chapter 6 Special Equipment, Article 690 Solar Photovoltaic (PV) Systems. 690.13 Fuses. 690.13(F)(2) Devices Marked "Line" and "Load"

150. True or False: The disconnecting means for PV must indicate whether it is in the open or closed position, and must be externally operable so that the operator is not exposed to contact with live parts.

    A. True

    B. False

    Reference: 2017 National Electrical Code – Chapter 6 Special Equipment, Article 690 Solar Photovoltaic (PV) Systems. 694.22 Additional Provisions. 694.22(A) Disconnecting Means.

151. PV arrays with not more than _____ and with all PV system dc circuits not on or in buildings shall be permitted without ground-fault protection where solidly grounded

    A. one PV source circuits

    B. two PV source circuits

    C. three PV source circuits

    D. four PV source circuits

    Reference: 2017 National Electrical Code – Chapter 6 Special Equipment, Article 690 Solar Photovoltaic (PV) Systems. 690.41 System Grounding. 690.41(B)Ground-Fault Protection

Chapter 6 Special Equipment

EXAM 10

Chapter 6 Special Equipment

152. An Isolating device shall be which of the following?

    A. a finger safe fuse holder

    B. a overcurrent protector

    C. an isolating switch that requires a tool to open

    D. A and C

    Reference: 2017 National Electrical Code – Chapter 6 Special Equipment, Article 690 Solar Photovoltaic (PV) Systems. 690.18 Installation and Service of an Array.

153. True or False: It is permitted to use all raceway and cable wiring methods included in the NEC, wiring as part of a listed system, and other wiring fittings and systems specifically listed for PV arrays.

    A. True

    B. False

    Reference: 2017 National Electrical Code – Chapter 6 Special Equipment, Article 690 Solar Photovoltaic (PV) Systems. 690.31 Methods Permitted. 690.31(A) Wiring Systems.

154. Circuit conductors are required to be guarded or installed in a Chapter 3 wiring method if they are in a(n) _____ location or operate at more than _____.

    A. accessible, 30V

    B. accessible, 60V

    C. readily accessible, 30V

    D. readily accessible, 60V

    Reference: 2017 National Electrical Code – Chapter 6 Special Equipment, Article 690 Solar Photovoltaic (PV) Systems. 690.31 Methods Permitted. 690.31(A) Wiring Systems.

155. True or False: It is not permitted to contain PV output and source circuits in the same cable, cable tray, junction box, outlet box, raceway, or similar fitting with non-PV systems unless there is a partition between the two systems.

    A. True

    B. False

    Reference: 2017 National Electrical Code – Chapter 6 Special Equipment, Article 690 Solar Photovoltaic (PV) Systems. 690.31 Methods Permitted. 690.31(B) Identification and Grouping.

EXAM 10

Chapter 6 Special Equipment

156. True or False: Conductors for PV systems must be identified by separate color coding, tagging, marking tape, or some other approved method.

    A. True   B. False

    Reference: 2017 National Electrical Code – Chapter 6 Special Equipment, Article 690 Solar Photovoltaic (PV) Systems. 690.31 Methods Permitted. 690.31(B) Identification and Grouping.

157. True or False: All points of connection, splices, and termination for PV source circuits must be identified.

    A. True   B. False

    Reference: 2017 National Electrical Code – Chapter 6 Special Equipment, Article 690 Solar Photovoltaic (PV) Systems. 690.31 Methods Permitted. 690.31(B) Identification and Grouping. 690.31(B)(1) Identification.

158. True or False: PV output circuit conductors and input and output circuits for inverters must be identified at all points of connection, splices, and termination.

    A. True   B. False

    Reference: 2017 National Electrical Code – Chapter 6 Special Equipment, Article 690 Solar Photovoltaic (PV) Systems. 690.31 Methods Permitted. 690.31(B) Identification and Grouping. 690.31(B)(1) PV Output and Inverter Circuits.

159. True or False: If the conductors of more than one PV system are in the same equipment, junction box, or raceway, each system's conductors must be identified at all connection, splice, and termination points.

    A. True   B. False

    Reference: 2017 National Electrical Code – Chapter 6 Special Equipment, Article 690 Solar Photovoltaic (PV) Systems. 690.31 Methods Permitted. 690.31(B) Identification and Grouping. 690.31(B)(2 Grouping.

EXAM 10

Chapter 6 Special Equipment

160. If more than one PV system's conductors are in the same raceway or junction box with removable cover(s), then each system's ac and dc conductors must be separately grouped with cable ties or a similar approved method a minimum of one time, and grouped at intervals of no more than:

    A. 6 in.

    B. 12 in.

    C. 36 in.

    D. 6 ft.

    Reference: 2017 National Electrical Code – Chapter 6 Special Equipment, Article 690 Solar Photovoltaic (PV) Systems. 690.31 Methods Permitted. 690.31(B) Identification and Grouping. 690.31(B)(2) Grouping.

161. Grouping PV output and source circuits is not required if the circuit enters from a unique cable or raceway that makes the grouping clearly evident.

    A. True

    B. False

    Reference: 2017 National Electrical Code – Chapter 6 Special Equipment, Article 690 Solar Photovoltaic (PV) Systems. 690.31 Methods Permitted. 690.31(B) Identification and Grouping. 690.31(B)(2) Grouping.

162. If single-conductor Type USE-2 and single conductor cable are _____ as PV wire, then it is allowed to be run exposed for PV source circuits within the PV array, for PV module interconnections at outdoor locations.

    A. approved

    B. listed and labeled

    C. listed or labeled

    D. none of these

    Reference: 2017 National Electrical Code – Chapter 6 Special Equipment, Article 690 Solar Photovoltaic (PV) Systems. 690.31 Methods Permitted. 690.31(C) Single-Conductor Cable. 690.31(C)(1) General.

163. True or False: Single-conductor Type USE-2 or listed and labeled PV wires located in a readily accessible location are required to be installed in a raceway if the source circuits operates at more than 30V.

    A. True

    B. False

    Reference: 2017 National Electrical Code – Chapter 6 Special Equipment, Article 690 Solar Photovoltaic (PV) Systems. 690.31 Methods Permitted. 690.31(A) Wiring Systems.

EXAM 10

Chapter 6 Special Equipment

164. Which of the following must dc PV source or output circuits be contained in if they are run inside a building or other structure?

    A. metal enclosures

    B. metal raceways

    C. Type MC cables

    D. any of these

    Reference: 2017 National Electrical Code – Chapter 6 Special Equipment, Article 690 Solar Photovoltaic (PV) Systems. 690.31 Methods Permitted. 690.31(G) Direct-Current Photovoltaic Source and Direct-Current Output Circuits on or Inside a Building.

165. True or False: It is required to clearly mark the location of PV source and output conductors if embedded in built-up, laminate, or membrane roofing materials, if the area is not covered by PV modules or other associated equipment.

    A. True

    B. False

    Reference: 2017 National Electrical Code – Chapter 6 Special Equipment, Article 690 Solar Photovoltaic (PV) Systems. 690.31 Methods Permitted. 690.31(G) Direct-Current Photovoltaic Source and Direct-Current Output Circuits on or Inside a Building. 690.31(G)(1) Embedded in Building Surfaces.

166. Labels or markings for PV system raceways and enclosures must be suitable for the environment they are placed in. What is the maximum distance between labels or markings?

    A. 5 ft.

    B. 10 ft.

    C. 20 ft.

    D. 25 ft.

    Reference: 2017 National Electrical Code – Chapter 6 Special Equipment, Article 690 Solar Photovoltaic (PV) Systems. 690.31 Methods Permitted. 690.31(G) Direct-Current Photovoltaic Source and Direct-Current Output Circuits on or Inside a Building. 690.31(G)(4) Marking and Labeling Methods and Locations.

167. Which type of photovoltaic wiring method must be terminated only with identified and listed connectors, devices, lugs, or terminals?

    A. flexible, fine-stranded cables

    B. flexible raceways

    C. solid conductors

    D. A through C

    Reference: 2017 National Electrical Code – Chapter 6 Special Equipment, Article 690 Solar Photovoltaic (PV) Systems. 690.31 Methods Permitted. 690.31(H) Flexible, Fine-Stranded Cables.

Chapter 6 Special Equipment   545

EXAM 10

Chapter 6 Special Equipment

168. If the sum of PV system voltages of two monopole subarrays in a bipolar PV system exceeds the rating of the conductors and connected equipment, they must be:

    A. connected

    B. joined

    C. separated

    D. together

    Reference: 2017 National Electrical Code – Chapter 6 Special Equipment, Article 690 Solar Photovoltaic (PV) Systems. 690.31 Methods Permitted. 690.31(I) Bipolar Photovoltaic Systems.

169. PV system dc circuits that run inside of buildings shall be contained in what?

    A. Type MC metal-clad cable

    B. wooden raceways

    C. metal raceways

    D. A and C

    Reference: 2017 National Electrical Code – Chapter 6 Special Equipment, Article 690 Solar Photovoltaic (PV) Systems. 690.31 Methods Permitted. 690.31(G) Module Connection Arrangement.

170. Which of the following applies to connectors allowed under Article 690?

    A. guard against accidental contact with live parts by persons

    B. polarized

    C. require tools to open if the circuit operates at over 30V

    D. A through C

    Reference: 2017 National Electrical Code – Chapter 6 Special Equipment, Article 690 Solar Photovoltaic (PV) Systems. 690.33 Connectors.

171. True or False: If PV modules are secured by removable fasteners, then junction, outlet, and pull boxes can be located behind them.

    A. True

    B. False

    Reference: 2017 National Electrical Code – Chapter 6 Special Equipment, Article 690 Solar Photovoltaic (PV) Systems. 690.34 Access to Boxes.

EXAM 10

Chapter 6 Special Equipment

172. All grounded dc PV arrays shall have direct-current _____ provided to reduce fire hazards, and such must meet the requirements of 690.5(a) through (c).

    A. arc-fault protection
    B. ground-fault monitors
    C. ground-fault protection
    D. rectifier protection

    Reference: 2017 National Electrical Code – Chapter 6 Special Equipment, Article 690 Solar Photovoltaic (PV) Systems. 690.41(b) Ground-Fault Protection.

173. a grounding system of _____ PV array with more than one functional grounded conductor shall be employed.

    A. 2-wire
    B. 3-wire
    C. 4-wire
    D. any of these

    Reference: 2017 National Electrical Code – Chapter 6 Special Equipment, Article 690 Solar Photovoltaic (PV) Systems. 690.41 System Grounding.

174. At how many point(s) on a PV output circuit must a dc system grounding connection be made?

    A. single
    B. two
    C. three
    D. four

    Reference: 2017 National Electrical Code – Chapter 6 Special Equipment, Article 690 Solar Photovoltaic (PV) Systems. 690.42 Point of' System Grounding Connection.

175. If a device and system used for mounting PV modules also provides grounding of the module frames, it must be _____ for bonding PV modules.

    A. identified
    B. labeled
    C. listed
    D. both A and B

    Reference: 2017 National Electrical Code – Chapter 6 Special Equipment, Article 690 Solar Photovoltaic (PV) Systems. 690.43 Equipment Grounding. 690.43(A) Photovoltaic Mounting Systems and Devices.

Chapter 6 Special Equipment   547

EXAM 10

Chapter 6 Special Equipment

176. If a device is permitted to bond the exposed metallic frames of PV modules to the metallic frames of adjacent PV modules, it must be:

    A. identified
    B. labeled
    C. listed
    D. All of the above

    Reference: 2017 National Electrical Code – Chapter 6 Special Equipment, Article 690 Solar Photovoltaic (PV) Systems. 690.43 Equipment Grounding. 690.43(E) Adjacent Modules.

177. Which of the following must be installed between a photovoltaic array and other equipment?

    A. equipment grounding conductor
    B. grounded conductor
    C. main bonding jumper
    D. system bonding jumper

    Reference: 2017 National Electrical Code – Chapter 6 Special Equipment, Article 690 Solar Photovoltaic (PV) Systems. 690.43 Equipment Grounding. 690.43(B) Equipment Grounding Conductor Required.

178. What is required for a device to be permitted to bond the exposed metal surfaces of PV modules or other equipment to the mounting structures?

    A. approved
    B. identified
    C. listed
    D. both B and C

    Reference: 2017 National Electrical Code – Chapter 6 Special Equipment, Article 690 Solar Photovoltaic (PV) Systems. 690.43 Equipment Grounding. 690.43(C) Structure as Equipment Grounding Conductor.

179. Metallic mounting structures for PV systems that are used for grounding must have _____ bonding devices or jumpers connected between the separate metallic sections and bonded to the grounding system, or be _____ as equipment grounding conductors.

    A. identified, identified
    B. labeled, listed
    C. listed, labeled
    D. both A and B

    Reference: 2017 National Electrical Code – Chapter 6 Special Equipment, Article 690 Solar Photovoltaic (PV) Systems. 690.43 Equipment Grounding. 690.43(C) Structure as Equipment Grounding Conductor.

EXAM 10

Chapter 6 Special Equipment

180. True or False: All conductors of a circuit must be installed in the same raceway or cable, including the equipment grounding conductor, or otherwise run with the PV array circuit conductors when they leave the vicinity of the PV array.

    A. True   B. False

    Reference: 2017 National Electrical Code – Chapter 6 Special Equipment, Article 690 Solar Photovoltaic (PV) Systems. 690.43 Equipment Grounding. 690.43(C) With Circuit Conductors.

181. Which section governs the sizing of equipment grounding conductors for PV circuits with overcurrent protection?

    A. 250.122   C. Table 250.122
    B. 250.66   D. Table 250.66

    Reference: 2017 National Electrical Code – Chapter 6 Special Equipment, Article 690 Solar Photovoltaic (PV) Systems. 690.45 Size of Equipment Grounding Conductors.

182. Where no overcurrent protective device is used in the circuit, an assumed overcurrent device rated at the PV maximum circuit current shall be used when applying:

    A. 250.122   C. Table 250.122
    B. 250.66   D. Table 250.66

    Reference: 2017 National Electrical Code – Chapter 6 Special Equipment, Article 690 Solar Photovoltaic (PV) Systems. 690.45 Size of Equipment Grounding Conductors.

183. True or False: PV array equipment grounding conductors smaller than 4 AWG require protection by raceway or cable armor where subject to or exposed to physical damage.

    A. True   B. False

    Reference: 2017 National Electrical Code – Chapter 2 Wiring and Protection, Article 250 Grounding and Bonding. 250.120(C)

EXAM 10

Chapter 6 Special Equipment

184. Grounding electrodes shall be permitted to be installed in accordance with 250.52 and 250.54 at the location of _____ and _____ PV Arrays

    A. wall-mounted and roof-mounted

    B. ground and floor

    C. window and wall-mounted

    D. ground and roof-mounted

    Reference: 2017 National Electrical Code – Chapter 6 Special Equipment, Article 690 Solar Photovoltaic (PV) Systems. 690.47 Grounding Electrode System. 690.47(B) Additional Auxiliary Electrodes for Array Grounding.

185. what ratings shall modules be marked with for identification?

    A. Open-circuit voltage

    B. operating current

    C. Maximum power

    D. All of the above

    Reference: 2017 National Electrical Code – Chapter 6 Special Equipment, Article 690 Solar Photovoltaic (PV) Systems. 690.51 Modules.

186. Which of the following is true if a solar photovoltaic system has both ac and dc systems that require grounding?

    A. ac grounding electrodes must be isolated from the dc electrodes.

    B. A common ground bus is not permitted for both systems.

    C. minimum 2 AWG grounding electrode conductor needed for both.

    D. must bond dc grounding system the ac grounding system.

    Reference: 2017 National Electrical Code – Chapter 6 Special Equipment, Article 690 Solar Photovoltaic (PV) Systems. 692.41 Grounding Electrode System. 694.1(C) Systems with Alternating-Current and Direct-Current Grounding Requirements.

550   **Chapter 6 Special Equipment**

EXAM 10

Chapter 6 Special Equipment

187. The PV system output circuit conductors shall be marked to indicate the _____ where connected to energy storage systems.1.

    A. Maximum overcurrent device protection

    B. Open Circuit voltage

    C. Polarity

    D. Operating voltage

    Reference: 2017 National Electrical Code – Chapter 6 Special Equipment, Article 690 Solar Photovoltaic (PV) Systems. 690.55 Photovoltaic Systems Connected to Energy Storage

188. What information must be indicated on a permanent label applied at the PV dc power source disconnect by the installer?

    A. maximum rated output current of the charge controller (if installed)

    B. maximum system voltage and circuit current

    C. rated maximum power-point current and voltage

    D. A through C

    Reference: 2017 National Electrical Code – Chapter 6 Special Equipment, Article 690 Solar Photovoltaic (PV) Systems. 690.53 Direct-Current Photovoltaic Power Source.

189. The rated ac output current and nominal operating ac voltage and the point of interconnection of the PV system power source to other sources must be marked at an accessible location at the:

    A. array

    B. disconnecting means

    C. module

    D. none of these

    Reference: 2017 National Electrical Code – Chapter 6 Special Equipment, Article 690 Solar Photovoltaic (PV) Systems. 690.54 Interactive System Point of Interconnection.

EXAM 10

Chapter 6 Special Equipment

190. A permanent _____ must be installed on the exterior of any building or structure with a stand-alone PV system indicating that the structure contains a stand-alone power system, and the location of the disconnecting means, at a readily visible location acceptable to the authority having jurisdiction.

   A. plaque

   B. directory

   C. both A and B

   D. either A or B

   Reference: 2017 National Electrical Code – Chapter 6 Special Equipment, Article 690 Solar Photovoltaic (PV) Systems. 690.56 Identification of Power Sources. 690.56(A) Facilities with Stand-Alone Systems.

191. A permanent _____ must be installed in any building or structure containing both utility service and a PV system, located at both the service disconnecting means and the PV disconnecting means if they are not in the same location indicating the location of the other system.

   A. directory

   B. plaque

   C. both A and B

   D. either A or B

   Reference: 2017 National Electrical Code – Chapter 7 Special Conditions, Article 705 Interconnected Electric Power Production Sources. 705.10 Directory.

192. True or False: Interactive systems can only contain inverters and ac PV modules that are identified and listed as interactive.

   A. True

   B. False

   Reference: 2017 National Electrical Code – Chapter 6 Special Equipment, Article 690 Solar Photovoltaic (PV) Systems. 694.60 Identified Interactive Equipment.

EXAM 10

Chapter 6 Special Equipment

193. In an fuel cell system, an ac module or inverter must automatically de-energize its output that is connected to the electrical distribution system, and remain de-energized until the electrical distribution system voltage has been restore, upon a _____ of voltage.

    A. loss

    B. spike

    C. surge

    D. unbalance

Reference: 2017 National Electrical Code – Chapter 6 Special Equipment, Article 690 Solar Photovoltaic (PV) Systems. 690.61 Loss of Interactive System Power.

194. When there is loss of voltage from the local utility company, an ac module or an inverter in an fuel cell system shall:

    A. automatically de-energize its output

    B. be required to be manually reset before re-energized

    C. continue to operate

    D. not operate as a stand-alone system

Reference: 2017 National Electrical Code – Chapter 6 Special Equipment, Article 690 Solar Photovoltaic (PV) Systems. 690.61 Loss of Interactive System Power.

195. under what requirements shall a PV source circuit comply to 706.23

    A. if matched to the voltage rating and charge current requirements of the inter connected battery cells

    B. if the source circuit is connected to the a grounded battery cell

    C. maximum charging current multiplied by 1 hour is less than 3 percent of the rating battery capacity

    D. both A and C

Reference: 2017 National Electrical Code – Chapter 6 Special Equipment, Article 690 Solar Photovoltaic (PV) Systems. 690.72 Self-Regulated PV Charge Control.

EXAM 10

EXAM 10 ANSWERS

196. article 691 covers the installation of large-scale PV electric power production facilities with a generating capacity no less than _____.

    A. 3000 kW

    B. 4000 kW

    C. 5000 kW

    D. 6000 kW

    Reference: *2017 National Electrical Code – Chapter 6 Special Equipment, Article 690 Solar Photovoltaic (PV) Systems. 690.71 Installation. 690.71(C) Current Limiting.*

197. Flexible cables used for battery interconnections on PV systems that are identified as moisture resistant in Article 400 and listed for hard-service use must be at least:

    A. 1/0 AWG

    B. 2/0 AWG

    C. 3/0 AWG

    D. 4/0 AWG

    Reference: *2017 National Electrical Code – Chapter 7 Special Conditions, Article 708 Critical Operations Power Systems (COPS). 706.32 Battery Interconnections.*

198. True or False: When flexible cables are installed for PV systems, they are allowed only between batteries and cells within the battery enclosure, or a nearby junction box and the battery terminals, and must connect to an approved wiring method.

    A. True

    B. False

    Reference: *2017 National Electrical Code – Chapter 7 Special Conditions, Article 708 Critical Operations Power Systems (COPS). 706.32 Battery Interconnections.*

199. When used for battery interconnections for PV systems, flexible, fine-stranded cables are required to terminated in connectors, devices, lugs, or terminals that have been _____ for fine-stranded conductors.

    A. certified

    B. listed

    C. either A or B

    D. both A and B

    Reference: *2017 National Electrical Code – Chapter 1 General, Article 110 Requirements for Electrical Installations. 110.14 Electrical Connections*

EXAM 10

EXAM 10 ANSWERS

1. **Answer C.** both A and B

   Fixed, mobile, or portable electric signs, section signs, outline lighting, photovoltaic (PV) powered signs, and retrofit kits, regardless of voltage, *shall be listed, provided with installation instructions, and installed in conformance with that listing, unless otherwise approved by special permission.*

   Reference: 2017 National Electrical Code – Chapter 6 Special Equipment, Article 600 Electric Signs and Outline Lighting. 600.3 Listing.

   This Code is intended to be suitable for mandatory application by governmental bodies that exercise legal jurisdiction over electrical installations, including signaling and communications systems, and for use by insurance inspectors. The authority having jurisdiction for enforcement of the Code has the responsibility for making interpretations of the rules, for deciding on the approval of equipment and materials, and for granting the special permission contemplated in a number of the rules.

   By special permission, the authority having jurisdiction may waive specific requirements in this Code or permit alternative methods where it is assured that equivalent objectives can be achieved by establishing and maintaining effective safety.

   This Code may require new products, constructions, or materials that may not yet be available at the time the Code is adopted. In such event, the authority having jurisdiction may permit the use of the products, constructions, or materials that comply with the most recent previous edition of this Code adopted by the jurisdiction.

   Reference: 2017 National Electrical Code, Article 90 Introduction. 90.4 Enforcement.

2. **Answer B.** listed

   Field-installed skeleton tubing shall not be required to be listed where installed in conformance with this Code.

   Reference: 2017 National Electrical Code – Chapter 6 Special Equipment, Article 600 Electric Signs and Outline Lighting. 600.3 Listing. 600.3(A) Field-Installed Skeleton Tubing.

3. **Answer B.** False

   Outline lighting shall not be required to be listed as a system when it consists of listed Luminaires wired in accordance with Chapter 3.

   Reference: 2017 National Electrical Code – Chapter 6 Special Equipment, Article 600 Electric Signs and Outline Lighting. 600.3 Listing. 600.3(B) Outline Lighting.

4. **Answer B.** current

   Signs and outline lighting systems shall be listed; marked with the manufacturer's name, trademark, or other means of identification; and input voltage and current rating.

   Reference: 2017 National Electrical Code – Chapter 6 Special Equipment, Article 600 Electric Signs and Outline Lighting. 600.4 Markings. 600.4(A) Signs and Outline Lighting Systems.

5. **Answer D.** A and C

   Signs and outline lighting systems shall be listed; marked with the manufacturer's name, trademark, *or other means of identification; and input voltage and current rating.*

   Reference: 2017 National Electrical Code – Chapter 6 Special Equipment, Article 600 Electric Signs and Outline Lighting. 600.4 Markings. 600.4(A) Signs and Outline Lighting Systems.

6. **Answer B.** 1/4 in.

   Signs and outline lighting systems with lampholders for incandescent lamps shall be marked to indicate the maximum allowable lamp wattage per lampholder. The markings shall be permanently installed, *in letters at least 6 mm (1/4 in.) high, and shall be located where visible during relamping.*

   Reference: 2017 National Electrical Code – Chapter 6 Special Equipment, Article 600 Electric Signs and Outline Lighting. 600.4 Markings. 600.4(C) Signs with Lampholders for Incandescent Lamps.

EXAM 10

EXAM 10 ANSWERS

7. **Answer B.** False

   Each commercial building and each commercial occupancy accessible to pedestrians shall be provided with at least one outlet in an accessible location at each entrance to each tenant space for sign or outline lighting system use. *The outlet(s) shall be supplied by a branch circuit rated at least 20 amperes that supplies no other load. Service hallways or corridors shall not be considered accessible to pedestrians.*

   Reference: 2017 National Electrical Code – Chapter 6 Special Equipment, Article 600 Electric Signs and Outline Lighting. 600.5 Branch Circuits. 600.5(A) Required Branch Circuit.

8. **Answer A.** entrance

   Each commercial building and each commercial occupancy accessible to pedestrians *shall be provided with at least one outlet in an accessible location at each entrance to each tenant space for sign or outline lighting system use.* The outlet(s) shall be supplied by a branch circuit rated at least 20 amperes that supplies no other load. Service hallways or corridors shall not be considered accessible to pedestrians.

   Reference: 2017 National Electrical Code – Chapter 6 Special Equipment, Article 600 Electric Signs and Outline Lighting. 600.5 Branch Circuits. 600.5(A) Required Branch Circuit.

9. **Answer A.** accessible

   Each commercial building and each commercial occupancy accessible to pedestrians shall be provided with at least one outlet in an accessible location at each entrance to each tenant space for sign or outline lighting system use. The outlet(s) shall be supplied by a branch circuit rated at least 20 amperes that supplies no other load. *Service hallways or corridors shall not be considered accessible to pedestrians.*

   Reference: 2017 National Electrical Code – Chapter 6 Special Equipment, Article 600 Electric Signs and Outline Lighting. 600.5 Branch Circuits. 600.5(A) Required Branch Circuit.

10. **Answer B.** 20 amps

    Each commercial building and each commercial occupancy accessible to pedestrians shall be provided with at least one outlet in an accessible location at each entrance to each tenant space for sign or outline lighting system use. *The outlet(s) shall be supplied by a branch circuit rated at least 20 amperes that supplies no other load.* Service hallways or corridors shall not be considered accessible to pedestrians.

    Reference: 2017 National Electrical Code – Chapter 6 Special Equipment, Article 600 Electric Signs and Outline Lighting. 600.5 Branch Circuits. 600.5(A) Required Branch Circuit.

11. **Answer B.** 1200

    Each commercial building and each commercial occupancy accessible to pedestrians shall be provided with at least one outlet in an accessible location at each entrance to each tenant space for sign or outline lighting system use. The outlet(s) shall be supplied by *a branch circuit rated at least 20 amperes* that supplies no other load. Service hallways or corridors shall not be considered accessible to pedestrians.

    Reference: 2017 National Electrical Code – Chapter 6 Special Equipment, Article 600 Electric Signs and Outline Lighting. 600.5 Branch Circuits. 600.5(A) Required Branch Circuit.

    Sign and outline lighting outlets shall be calculated at a minimum of 1200 volt-amperes for each required branch circuit specified in 600.5(A).

    Reference: 2017 National Electrical Code – Chapter 2 Wiring and Protection, Article 220 Branch-Circuit, Feeder, and Service Calculations. 220.14 Other Loads - All Occupancies. 220.14(F) Sign and Outline Lighting.

EXAM 10

EXAM 10 ANSWERS

12. **Answer B.** 125%

    Branch circuits that supply signs shall be rated in accordance with 600.5(B)(1) or (B)(2) and shall be considered to be continuous loads for the purposes of calculations.

    Reference: 2017 National Electrical Code – Chapter 6 Special Equipment, Article 600 Electric Signs and Outline Lighting. 600.5 Branch Circuits. 600.5(B) Rating.

    Branch-circuit conductors shall have an ampacity not less than the maximum load to be served. Conductors shall be sized to carry not less than the larger of 210.19(A)(I)(a) or (b).

    (a) Where a branch circuit supplies continuous loads or any combination of continuous and noncontinuous loads, the minimum *branch-circuit conductor size shall have an allowable ampacity not less than the noncontinuous load plus 125 percent of the continuous load.*

    Reference: 2017 National Electrical Code – Chapter 2 Wiring and Protection, Article 210 Branch Circuits. 210.19 Conductors – Minimum Ampacity and Size. 210.19(A) Branch Circuits not More than 600 Volts. 210.19(A)(1) General.

    A load where the maximum current is expected to continue for 3 hours or more. (CMP-2)

    Reference: 2017 National Electrical Code – Chapter 1 General, Article 100 Definitions. Continuous Load.

13. **Answer C.** 30

    Branch circuits that supply neon tubing installations shall not be rated in excess of 30 amperes.

    Reference: 2017 National Electrical Code – Chapter 6 Special Equipment, Article 600 Electric Signs and Outline Lighting. 600.5 Branch Circuits. 600.5(B) Rating. 600.5(B)(1) Neon Signs.

14. **Answer C.** 30

    Branch circuits that supply neon tubing installations shall not be rated in excess of 30 amperes.

    Reference: 2017 National Electrical Code – Chapter 6 Special Equipment, Article 600 Electric Signs and Outline Lighting. 600.5 Branch Circuits. 600.5(B) Rating. . 600.5(B)(1) Neon Signs.

15. **Answer A.** 20

    Branch circuits that supply all other signs and outline lighting systems shall be rated not to exceed 20 amperes.

    Reference: 2017 National Electrical Code – Chapter 6 Special Equipment, Article 600 Electric Signs and Outline Lighting. 600.5 Branch Circuits. 600.5(B) Rating. 600.5(B)(2) All Other Signs.

16. **Answer A.** True

    The wiring method used to supply signs and outline lighting systems shall terminate within a sign, an outline lighting system enclosure, a suitable box, or a conduit body.

    Reference: 2017 National Electrical Code – Chapter 6 Special Equipment, Article 600 Electric Signs and Outline Lighting. 600.5 Branch Circuits. 600.5(C) Wiring Methods. 600.5(C)(1) Supply.

17. **Answer B.** False

    Signs and transformer enclosures shall be permitted to be used as pull or junction boxes for conductors supplying other **adjacent signs, outline lighting systems, or floodlights that are part of a sign and shall be permitted to contain both branch and secondary circuit conductors.**

    Reference: 2017 National Electrical Code – Chapter 6 Special Equipment, Article 600 Electric Signs and Outline Lighting. 600.5 Branch Circuits. 600.5(C) Wiring Methods. 600.5(C)(2) Enclosures as Pull Boxes.

18. **Answer A.** junction box

    Signs and transformer enclosures shall be permitted to be used as pull or junction boxes for conductors supplying other adjacent signs, outline lighting systems, or floodlights that are part of a sign and shall be permitted to contain both branch and secondary circuit conductors.

    Reference: 2017 National Electrical Code – Chapter 6 Special Equipment, Article 600 Electric Signs and Outline Lighting. 600.5 Branch Circuits. 600.5(C) Wiring Methods. 600.5(C)(2) Enclosures as Pull Boxes.

EXAM 10
EXAM 10 ANSWERS

19. **Answer A.** True

Metal or nonmetallic poles used to support signs shall be permitted to enclose supply conductors, provided the poles and conductors are installed in accordance with 410.30(B).

Reference: 2017 National Electrical Code – Chapter 6 Special Equipment, Article 600 Electric Signs and Outline Lighting. 600.5 Branch Circuits. 600.5(C) Wiring Methods. 600.5(C)(3) Metal or Nonmetallic Poles.

20. **Answer B.** False

Metal or nonmetallic poles used to support signs shall be permitted to enclose supply conductors, provided the poles and conductors are installed in accordance with 410.30(B).

Reference: 2017 National Electrical Code – Chapter 6 Special Equipment, Article 600 Electric Signs and Outline Lighting. 600.5 Branch Circuits. 600.5(C) Wiring Methods. 600.5(C)(3) Metal or Nonmetallic Poles.

(3) A metal pole shall be provided with an equipment grounding terminal as follows:

    a. A pole with a handhole shall have the equipment grounding terminal accessible from the handhole.

    b. A pole with a hinged base shall have the equipment grounding terminal accessible within the base.

Exception to (3): No grounding terminal shall be required in a pole 2.5 m (8ft) or less in height abovegrade where the supply wiring method *continues without splice or pull, and where the interior of the pole and any splices are accessible by removing the luminaire.*

Reference: 2017 National Electrical Code – Chapter 4 Equipment for General Use, Article 410 Luminaires, Lampholders, and Lamps. 410.30 Supports. 410.30(B) Metal or Nonmetallic Poles Supporting Luminaires

21. **Answer C.** grounding

Metal or nonmetallic poles used to support signs shall be permitted to enclose supply conductors, provided the poles and conductors are installed in accordance with 410.30(B).

Reference: 2017 National Electrical Code – Chapter 6 Special Equipment, Article 600 Electric Signs and Outline Lighting. 600.5 Branch Circuits. 600.5(C) Wiring Methods. 600.5(C)(3) Metal or Nonmetallic Poles.

Metal or nonmetallic poles shall be permitted to be used to support luminaires and as a raceway to enclose supply conductors, provided the following conditions are met:

(1) A pole shall have a handhole not less than 50 mm x 100 mm (2 in. x 4 in.) with a cover suitable for use in wet locations to provide access to the supply terminations within the pole or pole base.

Exception No.1: No handhole shall be required in a pole 2.5 m (8 ft.) or less in height abovegrade *where the supply wiring method continues without splice or pull point, and where the interior of the pole and any splices are accessible by removing the luminaire.*

Exception No.2: *No handhole shall be required in a pole 6.0 m (20 ft.) or less in height abovegrade that is provided with a hinged base.*

Reference: 2017 National Electrical Code – Chapter 4 Equipment for General Use, Article 410 Luminaires, Lampholders, and Lamps. 410.30 Supports. 410.30(B) Metal or Nonmetallic Poles Supporting Luminaires

EXAM 10

EXAM 10 ANSWERS

22. **Answer C.** 2 in. x 4 in.

    Metal or nonmetallic poles used to support signs shall be permitted to enclose supply conductors, provided the poles and conductors are installed in accordance with 410.30(B).

    Reference: 2017 National Electrical Code – Chapter 6 Special Equipment, Article 600 Electric Signs and Outline Lighting. 600.5 Branch Circuits. 600.5(C) Wiring Methods. 600.5(C)(3) Metal or Nonmetallic Poles.

    Metal or nonmetallic poles shall be permitted to be used to support luminaires and as a raceway to enclose supply conductors, provided the following conditions are met:

    (1) A pole shall have a handhole not less than 50 mm x 100 mm (2 in. x 4 in.) with a cover suitable for use in wet locations to provide access to the supply terminations within the pole or pole base.

    Exception No.1: No handhole shall be required in a pole 2.5 m (8 ft.) or less in height abovegrade where the supply wiring method continues without splice or pull point, and where the interior of the pole and any splices are accessible by removing the luminaire.

    Exception No.2: No handhole shall be required in a pole 6.0 m (20 ft.) or less in height abovegrade that is provided with a hinged base.

    Reference: 2017 National Electrical Code – Chapter 4 Equipment for General Use, Article 410 Luminaires, Lampholders, and Lamps. 410.30 Supports. 410.30(B) Metal or Nonmetallic Poles Supporting Luminaires

23. **Answer B.** 8

    Metal or nonmetallic poles used to support signs shall be permitted to enclose supply conductors, provided the poles and conductors are installed in accordance with 410.30(B).

    Reference: 2017 National Electrical Code – Chapter 6 Special Equipment, Article 600 Electric Signs and Outline Lighting. 600.5 Branch Circuits. 600.5(C) Wiring Methods. 600.5(C)(3) Metal or Nonmetallic Poles.

    Metal or nonmetallic poles shall be permitted to be used to support luminaires and as a raceway to enclose supply conductors, provided the following conditions are met:

    (1) A pole shall have a handhole not less than 50 mm x 100 mm (2 in. x 4 in.) with a cover suitable for use in wet locations to provide access to the supply terminations within the pole or pole base.

    Exception No.1: No handhole shall be required in a pole 2.5 m (8 ft.) or less in height abovegrade where the supply wiring method continues *without splice or pull point, and where the interior of the pole and any splices are accessible by removing the luminaire.*

    Exception No.2: No handhole shall be required in a pole 6.0 m (20 ft.) or less in height abovegrade that is provided with a hinged base.

    Reference: 2017 National Electrical Code – Chapter 4 Equipment for General Use, Article 410 Luminaires, Lampholders, and Lamps. 410.30 Supports. 410.30(B) Metal or Nonmetallic Poles Supporting Luminaires

24. **Answer B.** False

    Each sign and outline lighting system, feeder conductor(s), or branch circuit(s) supplying a sign, outline lighting system, or skeleton tubing shall be controlled by an externally operable switch or circuit breaker that opens all ungrounded conductors and controls no other load. The switch or circuit breaker shall open all ungrounded conductors simultaneously on multi-wire branch circuits in accordance with 210.4(B). Signs and outline lighting systems located within fountains shall have the disconnect located in accordance with 680.13.

    Exception No. 1: A disconnecting means shall not be required for an exit directional sign located within a building.

    Exception No. 2: A disconnecting means shall not be required for cord connected signs with an attachment plug.

    Informational Note: The location of the disconnect is intended to allow service or maintenance personnel complete and local control of the disconnecting means.

    Reference: 2017 National Electrical Code – Chapter 6 Special Equipment, Article 600 Electric Signs and Outline Lighting. 600.6 Disconnects.

EXAM 10
EXAM 10 ANSWERS

25. **Answer A.** exit

    Each sign and outline lighting system, feeder conductor(s), or branch circuit(s) supplying a sign, outline lighting system, or skeleton tubing shall be controlled by an externally operable switch or circuit breaker that opens all ungrounded conductors and controls no other load. The switch or circuit breaker shall open all ungrounded conductors simultaneously on multi-wire branch circuits in accordance with 210.4(B). Signs and outline lighting systems located within fountains shall have the disconnect located in accordance with 680.13.

    Exception No. 1: A disconnecting means shall not be required for an exit directional sign located within a building.

    Exception No. 2: A disconnecting means shall not be required for cord connected signs with an attachment plug.

    Informational Note: The location of the disconnect is intended to allow service or maintenance personnel complete and local control of the disconnecting means.

    Reference: 2017 National Electrical Code – Chapter 6 Special Equipment, Article 600 Electric Signs and Outline Lighting. 600.6 Disconnects.

26. **Answer C.** within sight

    The disconnecting means shall be within sight of the sign or outline lighting system that it controls. Where the disconnecting means is out of the line of sight from any section that is able to be energized, the disconnecting means shall be lockable in accordance with 110.25. A permanent field-applied marking identifying the location of the disconnecting means shall be applied to the sign in a location visible during servicing. The warning label shall comply with 110.21(B).

    Reference: 2017 National Electrical Code – Chapter 6 Special Equipment, Article 600 Electric Signs and Outline Lighting. 600.6 Disconnects. 600.6(A) Location. 600.6(A)(2)Within Sight of the Sign.

    Where this Code specifies that one equipment shall be "in sight from," "within sight from," or "within sight of," and so forth, another equipment, the specified equipment is to be visible and not more than 15 m (50 ft.) distant from the other. (CMP-1)

    Reference: 2017 National Electrical Code – Chapter 1 General, Article 100 Definitions. In Sight From (Within Sight From, Within Sight).

27. **Answer C.** 50

    The disconnecting means shall be within sight of the sign or outline lighting system that it controls. Where the disconnecting means is out of the line of sight from any section that is able to be energized, the disconnecting means shall be lockable in accordance with 110.25. A permanent field-applied marking identifying the location of the disconnecting means shall be applied to the sign in a location visible during servicing. The warning label shall comply with 110.21(B).

    Reference: 2017 National Electrical Code – Chapter 6 Special Equipment, Article 600 Electric Signs and Outline Lighting. 600.6 Disconnects. 600.6(A) Location. 600.6(A)(2)Within Sight of the Sign.

    Where this Code specifies that one equipment shall be "in sight from," "within sight from," or "within sight of," and so forth, *another equipment, the specified equipment is to be visible and not more than 15 m (50 ft.) distant from the other.* (CMP-1)

    Reference: 2017 National Electrical Code – Chapter 1 General, Article 100 Definitions. In Sight From (Within Sight From, Within Sight).

28. **Answer A.** True

    The following shall apply for signs or outline lighting systems operated by electronic or electromechanical controllers located external to the sign or outline lighting system:

    (1) The disconnecting means shall be located within sight of the controller or in the same enclosure with the controller.

    (2) The disconnecting means shall disconnect the sign or outline lighting system and the controller from all ungrounded supply conductors.

    (3) The disconnecting means shall be designed such that no pole can be operated independently and shall be lockable in accordance with 110.25.

    Exception: Where the disconnecting means is not located within sight of the controller, a permanent field-applied marking identifying the location of the disconnecting means shall be applied to the controller in a location visible during servicing. The warning label shall comply with 110.21(B).

    Reference: 2017 National Electrical Code – Chapter 6 Special Equipment, Article 600 Electric Signs and Outline Lighting. 600.6 Disconnects. 600.6(A) Location. 600.6(A)(3) Within Sight of the Controller.

EXAM 10

EXAM 10 ANSWERS

29. Answer B. ungrounded

The following shall apply for signs or outline lighting systems operated by electronic or electromechanical controllers located external to the sign or outline lighting system:

(1) The disconnecting means shall be located within sight of the controller or in the same enclosure with the controller.

(2) The disconnecting means shall disconnect the sign or outline lighting system and the controller from all ungrounded supply conductors.

(3) The disconnecting means shall be designed such that no pole can be operated independently and shall be lockable in accordance with 110.25.

Exception: Where the disconnecting means is not located within sight of the controller, a permanent field-applied marking identifying the location of the disconnecting means shall be applied to the controller in a location visible during servicing. The warning label shall comply with 110.21(B).

Reference: 2017 National Electrical Code – Chapter 6 Special Equipment, Article 600 Electric Signs and Outline Lighting. 600.6 Disconnects. 600.6(A) Location. 600.6(A)(3) Within Sight of the Controller.

30. Answer B. False

Switches, flashers, and similar devices controlling transformers and electronic power supplies shall be rated for controlling inductive loads or have a current rating not less than twice the current rating of the transformer or the electronic power supply.

Reference: 2017 National Electrical Code – Chapter 6 Special Equipment, Article 600 Electric Signs and Outline Lighting. 600.6 Disconnects. 600.6(B) Control Switch Rating.

31. Answer D. twice

Switches, flashers, and similar devices controlling transformers and electronic power supplies shall be rated for controlling inductive loads or *have a current rating not less than twice the current rating of the transformer or the electronic power supply.*

Reference: 2017 National Electrical Code – Chapter 6 Special Equipment, Article 600 Electric Signs and Outline Lighting. 600.6 Disconnects. 600.6(B) Control Switch Rating.

32. Answer B. False

Metal equipment of signs, outline lighting, and skeleton tubing systems shall be grounded by connection to the equipment grounding conductor of the supply branch circuit(s) or feeder using the types of equipment grounding conductors specified in 250.118.

Reference: 2017 National Electrical Code – Chapter 6 Special Equipment, Article 600 Electric Signs and Outline Lighting. 600.7 Grounding and Bonding. 600.7(A) Grounding. 600.7(A)(1) Equipment Grounding.

33. Answer B. False

Metal parts of a building shall not be permitted as a secondary return conductor or an equipment grounding conductor.

Reference: 2017 National Electrical Code – Chapter 6 Special Equipment, Article 600 Electric Signs and Outline Lighting. 600.7 Grounding and Bonding. 600.7(A) Grounding. 600.7(A)(5) Metal Building Parts.

34. Answer B. 100 ft.

Listed flexible metal conduit or listed liquidtight flexible metal conduit that encloses the secondary circuit conductor from a transformer, *power supply for use with neon tubing shall be permitted as a bonding means if the total accumulative length of the conduit in the secondary circuit does not exceed 30 m (100 ft.).*

Reference: 2017 National Electrical Code – Chapter 6 Special Equipment, Article 600 Electric Signs and Outline Lighting. 600.7 Grounding and Bonding. 600.7(B) Bonding. 600.7(B)(4) Flexible Metal Conduit Length.

35. Answer D. 3/4 in.

Small metal parts not exceeding 50 mm (2 in.) in any dimension, not likely to be energized, and *spaced at least 19 mm (3/4 in.) from neon tubing, shall not require bonding.*

Reference: 2017 National Electrical Code – Chapter 6 Special Equipment, Article 600 Electric Signs and Outline Lighting. 600.7 Grounding and Bonding. 600.7(B) Bonding. 600.7(B)(5) Small Metal Parts.

EXAM 10
EXAM 10 ANSWERS

36. **Answer C.** 1-1/2 in.

    Where listed nonmetallic conduit is used to enclose the secondary circuit conductor from a transformer or power supply and a bonding conductor is required, *the bonding conductor shall be installed separate and remote from the nonmetallic conduit and be spaced at least 38 mm (1-1/2 in.) from the conduit when the circuit is operated at 100 Hz or less* or 45 mm (1-3/4 in.) when the circuit is operated at over 100 Hz.

    Reference: 2017 National Electrical Code – Chapter 6 Special Equipment, Article 600 Electric Signs and Outline Lighting. 600.7 Grounding and Bonding. 600.7(B) Bonding. 600.7(B)(6) Nonmetallic Conduit.

37. **Answer D.** 1-3/4 in.

    Where listed nonmetallic conduit is used to enclose the secondary circuit conductor from a transformer or power supply and a bonding conductor is required, *the bonding conductor shall be installed separate* and remote from the nonmetallic conduit and be spaced at least 38 mm (1-1/2 in.) from the conduit when the circuit is operated at 100 Hz or less or *45 mm (1-3/4 in.) when the circuit is operated at over 100 Hz.*

    Reference: 2017 National Electrical Code – Chapter 6 Special Equipment, Article 600 Electric Signs and Outline Lighting. 600.7 Grounding and Bonding. 600.7(B) Bonding. 600.7(B)(6) Nonmetallic Conduit.

38. **Answer A.** 14 AWG

    Bonding conductors shall comply with (1) and (2).

    (1) Bonding conductors shall be copper and not smaller than 14 AWG.

    (2) Bonding conductors installed externally of a sign or raceway shall be protected from physical damage.

    Reference: 2017 National Electrical Code – Chapter 6 Special Equipment, Article 600 Electric Signs and Outline Lighting. 600.7 Grounding and Bonding. 600.7(B) Bonding. 600.7(B)(7) Bonding Conductors.

39. **Answer B.** False

    Live parts, other than lamps, and neon tubing shall be enclosed. *Transformers and power supplies provided with an integral enclosure, including a primary and secondary circuit splice enclosure, shall not require an additional enclosure.*

    Reference: 2017 National Electrical Code – Chapter 6 Special Equipment, Article 600 Electric Signs and Outline Lighting. 600.8 Enclosures.

40. **Answer A.** enclosed

    Live parts, other than lamps, and neon tubing shall be enclosed. Transformers and power supplies provided with an integral enclosure, including a primary and secondary circuit splice enclosure, shall not require an additional enclosure.

    Reference: 2017 National Electrical Code – Chapter 6 Special Equipment, Article 600 Electric Signs and Outline Lighting. 600.8 Enclosures.

41. **Answer A.** True

    Enclosures shall have ample structural strength and rigidity.

    Reference: 2017 National Electrical Code – Chapter 6 Special Equipment, Article 600 Electric Signs and Outline Lighting. 600.8 Enclosures. 600.8(A) Strength.

42. **Answer A.** corrosion

    Metal parts of equipment shall be protected from corrosion.

    Reference: 2017 National Electrical Code – Chapter 6 Special Equipment, Article 600 Electric Signs and Outline Lighting. 600.8 Enclosures. 600.8 (D) Protection of Metal.

43. **Answer D.** 14 ft.

    Sign or outline lighting system equipment shall be at least 4.3 m (14 ft.) above areas accessible to vehicles unless protected from physical damage.

    Reference: 2017 National Electrical Code – Chapter 6 Special Equipment, Article 600 Electric Signs and Outline Lighting. 600.9 Location. 600.9(A) Vehicles

44. **Answer A.** accessible

    Neon tubing, other than listed, dry-location, portable signs, readily accessible to pedestrians shall be protected from physical damage.

    Informational Note: See 600.41(D) for additional requirements.

    Reference: 2017 National Electrical Code – Chapter 6 Special Equipment, Article 600 Electric Signs and Outline Lighting. 600.9 Location. 600.9(B) Pedestrians.

EXAM 10

EXAM 10 ANSWERS

45. **Answer A.** 90°C

    Signs and outline lighting systems shall be installed so that adjacent combustible materials are not subjected to temperatures in excess of 90°C (194°F).

    The spacing between wood or other combustible materials and an incandescent or HID lamp or lampholder shall not be less than 50 mm (2 in.).

    Reference: 2017 National Electrical Code – Chapter 6 Special Equipment, Article 600 Electric Signs and Outline Lighting. 600.9 Location. 600.9(C) Adjacent to Combustible Materials.

46. **Answer B.** 2 in.

    Signs and outline lighting systems shall be installed so that adjacent combustible materials are not subjected to temperatures in excess of 90°C (194°F).

    The spacing between wood or other combustible materials and an incandescent or HID lamp or lampholder shall not be less than 50 mm (2 in.).

    Reference: 2017 National Electrical Code – Chapter 6 Special Equipment, Article 600 Electric Signs and Outline Lighting. 600.9 Location. 600.9(C) Adjacent to Combustible Materials.

47. **Answer A.** 1/4 in. to 1/2 in.

    Signs and outline lighting system equipment for wet location use, other than listed watertight type, shall be weatherproof and *have drain holes, as necessary, in accordance with the following:*

    (1) Drain holes shall not be larger than 13 mm (1/2 in.) or smaller than 6 mm (1/4 in.).

    (2) Every low point or isolated section of the equipment shall have at least one drain hole.

    (3) Drain holes shall be positioned such that there will be no external obstructions.

    Reference: 2017 National Electrical Code – Chapter 6 Special Equipment, Article 600 Electric Signs and Outline Lighting. 600.9 Location. 600.9(D) Wet Location.

48. **Answer D.** supported

    (A) Support. *Portable or mobile signs shall be adequately supported and readily movable without the use of tools.*

    (B) Attachment Plug. An attachment plug shall be provided for each portable or mobile sign.

    (C) Wet or Damp Location. Portable or mobile signs in wet or damp locations shall comply with 600.10(C)(1) and (C)(2).

    Reference: 2017 National Electrical Code – Chapter 6 Special Equipment, Article 600 Electric Signs and Outline Lighting. 600.10 Portable or Mobile Signs.

49. **Answer A.** True

    Portable or mobile signs shall be adequately supported and readily movable without the use of tools.

    Reference: 2017 National Electrical Code – Chapter 6 Special Equipment, Article 600 Electric Signs and Outline Lighting. 600.10 Portable or Mobile Signs. 600.10(A) Support.

50. **Answer D.** 12 in.

    Portable or mobile signs in wet or damp locations shall comply with 600.10(C)(1) and (C)(2).

    (1) Cords. All cords shall be junior hard-service or hard-service types as designated in Table 400.4 and have an equipment grounding conductor.

    (2) Ground-Fault Circuit Interrupter. The manufacturer of portable or mobile signs shall provide listed ground-fault circuit-interrupter protection for personnel. *The ground-fault circuit interrupter shall be an integral part of the attachment plug or shall be located in the power-supply cord within 300 mm (12 in.) of the attachment plug.*

    Reference: 2017 National Electrical Code – Chapter 6 Special Equipment, Article 600 Electric Signs and Outline Lighting. 600.10 Portable or Mobile Signs. 600.10(C) Wet or Damp Location.

51. **Answer A.** True

    All cords shall be junior hard-service or hard-service types as designated in Table 400.4 and have an equipment grounding conductor.

    Reference: 2017 National Electrical Code – Chapter 6 Special Equipment, Article 600 Electric Signs and Outline Lighting. 600.10 Portable or Mobile Signs. 600.10(C) Wet or Damp Location. 600.10(C)(1) Cords.

EXAM 10

EXAM 10 ANSWERS

52. **Answer A.** ground-fault-circuit-interrupter

    The manufacturer of portable or mobile signs shall provide listed ground-fault circuit-interrupter protection for personnel. The ground-fault circuit interrupter shall be an integral part of the attachment plug or shall be located in the power-supply cord within 300 mm (12 in.) of the attachment plug.

    Reference: 2017 National Electrical Code – Chapter 6 Special Equipment, Article 600 Electric Signs and Outline Lighting. 600.10 Portable or Mobile Signs. 600.10(C) Wet or Damp Location. 600.10(C)(2) Ground-Fault Circuit Interrupter.

53. **Answer C.** 15 ft.

    Portable or mobile signs in dry locations shall meet the following:

    (1) Cords shall be SP-2, SPE-2, SPT-2, or heavier, as designated in Table 400.4.

    (2) The cord shall not exceed 4.5 m (15 ft.) in length.

    Reference: 2017 National Electrical Code – Chapter 6 Special Equipment, Article 600 Electric Signs and Outline Lighting. 600.10 Portable or Mobile Signs. 600.10(D) Dry Location.

54. **Answer D.** near

    Ballasts, transformers, electronic power supplies, and Class 2 power sources shall be installed as *near to the lamps or neon tubing as practicable to keep the secondary conductors as short as possible.*

    Reference: 2017 National Electrical Code – Chapter 6 Special Equipment, Article 600 Electric Signs and Outline Lighting. 600.21 Ballasts, Transformers, Electronic Power Supplies, and Class 2 Power Sources. 600.21(B) Location.

55. **Answer B.** outdoor

    Ballasts, transformers, electronic power supplies, and Class 2 power sources used in wet locations *shall be of the weatherproof type or be of the outdoor type and protected from the weather by placement in a sign body or separate enclosure.*

    Reference: 2017 National Electrical Code – Chapter 6 Special Equipment, Article 600 Electric Signs and Outline Lighting. 600.21 Ballasts, Transformers, Electronic Power Supplies, and Class 2 Power Sources. 600.21(C) Wet Location.

56. **Answer C.** 3 ft. high x 3 ft. wide x 3 ft. deep

    A working space at least 900 mm (3 ft.) high x 900 mm (3 ft.) wide x 900 mm (3 ft.) deep shall be provided at each ballast, transformer, electronic power supply, and Class 2 power source or at its enclosure where not installed in a sign.

    Reference: 2017 National Electrical Code – Chapter 6 Special Equipment, Article 600 Electric Signs and Outline Lighting. 600.21 Ballasts, Transformers, Electronic Power Supplies, and Class 2 Power Sources. 600.21(D) Workings Space.

57. **Answer B.** 36 in. x 22-1/2 in.

    Ballasts, transformers, electronic power supplies, and Class 2 power sources shall be permitted to be located in attics and soffits, provided there is an access door at least 900 mm x 562.5 mm (36 in. x 22-1/2 in.) and a passageway of at least 900 mm (3 ft.) high x 600 mm (2 ft.) wide with a suitable permanent walkway at least 300 mm (12 in.) wide extending from the point of entry to each component. At least one lighting outlet containing a switch or controlled by a wall switch shall be installed in such spaces. At least one point of control shall be at the usual point of entry to these spaces. The lighting outlet shall be provided at or near the equipment requiring servicing.

    Reference: 2017 National Electrical Code – Chapter 6 Special Equipment, Article 600 Electric Signs and Outline Lighting. 600.21 Ballasts, Transformers, Electronic Power Supplies, and Class 2 Power Sources. 600.21(E) Attic and Soffit Locations.

58. **Answer A.** 3 ft. x 2 ft.

    Ballasts, transformers, electronic power supplies, and Class 2 power sources shall be permitted to be located in attics and soffits, provided there is an access door at least 900 mm x 562.5 mm (36 in. x 22-1/2 in.) and *a passageway of at least 900 mm (3 ft.) high x 600 mm (2 ft.) wide with a suitable permanent walkway* at least 300 mm (12 in.) wide extending from the point of entry to each component. At least one lighting outlet containing a switch or controlled by a wall switch shall be installed in such spaces. At least one point of control shall be at the usual point of entry to these spaces. The lighting outlet shall be provided at or near the equipment requiring servicing.

    Reference: 2017 National Electrical Code – Chapter 6 Special Equipment, Article 600 Electric Signs and Outline Lighting. 600.21 Ballasts, Transformers, Electronic Power Supplies, and Class 2 Power Sources. 600.21(E) Attic and Soffit Locations.

EXAM 10

EXAM 10 ANSWERS

59. Answer B. 12 in.

Ballasts, transformers, electronic power supplies, and Class 2 power sources shall be permitted to be located in attics and soffits, provided there is an access door at least 900 mm x 562.5 mm (36 in. x 22-1/2 in.) and a passageway of at least 900 mm (3 ft.) high x 600 mm (2 ft.) wide with *a suitable permanent walkway at least 300 mm (12 in.) wide extending from the point of entry to each component*. At least one lighting outlet containing a switch or controlled by a wall switch shall be installed in such spaces. At least one point of control shall be at the usual point of entry to these spaces. The lighting outlet shall be provided at or near the equipment requiring servicing.

Reference: 2017 National Electrical Code – Chapter 6 Special Equipment, Article 600 Electric Signs and Outline Lighting. 600.21 Ballasts, Transformers, Electronic Power Supplies, and Class 2 Power Sources. 600.21(E) Attic and Soffit Locations.

60. Answer B. False

Ballasts, transformers, electronic power supplies, and Class 2 power sources shall be permitted to be located above suspended ceilings, provided that their enclosures are securely fastened in place and *not dependent on the suspended-ceiling grid* for support. *Ballasts, transformers, and electronic power supplies installed in suspended ceilings shall not be connected to the branch circuit by flexible cord.*

Reference: 2017 National Electrical Code – Chapter 6 Special Equipment, Article 600 Electric Signs and Outline Lighting. 600.21 Ballasts, Transformers, Electronic Power Supplies, and Class 2 Power Sources. 600.21(F) Suspended Ceilings.

61. Answer D. thermally

(A) Type. Ballasts shall be identified for the use and shall be listed.

(B) *Thermal Protection. Ballasts shall be thermally protected*.

Reference: 2017 National Electrical Code – Chapter 6 Special Equipment, Article 600 Electric Signs and Outline Lighting. 600.22 Ballasts.

62. Answer C. 300 mA

Transformers and electronic power supplies shall have a secondary-circuit current rating of not more than 300 mA.

Reference: 2017 National Electrical Code – Chapter 6 Special Equipment, Article 600 Electric Signs and Outline Lighting. 600.23 Transformers and Electronic Power Supplies. 600.23(D) Rating.

63. Answer A. bushing

Bushings shall be used to protect wires passing through an opening in metal

Reference: 2017 National Electrical Code – Chapter 6 Special Equipment, Article 600 Electric Signs and Outline Lighting. 600.31 Neon Secondary-Circuit Wiring, 1000 Volts or Less, Nominal. 600.31(E) Protection of Leads.

64. Answer A. True

Conductors shall be installed in rigid metal conduit, intermediate metal conduit, *liquidtight flexible nonmetallic conduit, flexible metal conduit, liquidtight flexible metal conduit, electrical metallic tubing, metal enclosures; on insulators in metal raceways; or in other equipment listed for use with neon secondary circuits over 1000 volts.*

Reference: 2017 National Electrical Code – Chapter 6 Special Equipment, Article 600 Electric Signs and Outline Lighting. 600.32 Neon Secondary-Circuit Wiring, over 1000 Volts, Nominal. 600.32(A) Wiring Methods. 600.32(A)(1) Installation.

65. Answer D. listed

Conductors shall be insulated, listed as gas tube sign and ignition cable type GTO, rated for 5, 10, or 15 kV, not smaller than 18 AWG, and have a minimum temperature rating of 105°C (221°F).

Reference: 2017 National Electrical Code – Chapter 6 Special Equipment, Article 600 Electric Signs and Outline Lighting. 600.32 Neon Secondary-Circuit Wiring, over 1000 Volts, Nominal. 600.32(B) Insulation and Size.

66. Answer D. 18 AWG

Conductors shall be insulated, listed as gas tube sign and ignition cable type GTO, rated for 5, 10, or 15 kV, *not smaller than 18 AWG,* and have a minimum temperature rating of 105°C (221°F).

Reference: 2017 National Electrical Code – Chapter 6 Special Equipment, Article 600 Electric Signs and Outline Lighting. 600.32 Neon Secondary-Circuit Wiring, over 1000 Volts, Nominal. 600.32(B) Insulation and Size.

EXAM 10

EXAM 10 ANSWERS

67. **Answer D.** 105°C

    Conductors shall be insulated, listed as gas tube sign and ignition cable type GTO, rated for 5, 10, or 15 kV, not smaller than 18 AWG, and **have a minimum temperature rating of 105°C (221°F).**

    Reference: 2017 National Electrical Code – Chapter 6 Special Equipment, Article 600 Electric Signs and Outline Lighting. 600.32 Neon Secondary-Circuit Wiring, over 1000 Volts, Nominal. 600.32(B) Insulation and Size.

68. **Answer C.** 1-1/2 in.

    Secondary conductors shall be separated from each other and from all objects other than insulators or neon tubing by a spacing of not less than 38 mm (1-1/2 in.). GTO cable installed in metal conduit or tubing requires no spacing between the cable insulation and the conduit or tubing.

    Reference: 2017 National Electrical Code – Chapter 6 Special Equipment, Article 600 Electric Signs and Outline Lighting. 600.32 Neon Secondary-Circuit Wiring, over 1000 Volts, Nominal. 600.32(E) Spacing.

69. **Answer B.** False

    Insulators and bushings for conductors shall be listed for use with neon secondary circuits over 1000 volts.

    Reference: 2017 National Electrical Code – Chapter 6 Special Equipment, Article 600 Electric Signs and Outline Lighting. 600.32 Neon Secondary-Circuit Wiring, over 1000 Volts, Nominal. 600.32(F) Insulators and Bushings.

70. **Answer C.** 4 in.

    The insulation on all conductors shall extend not less than 65 mm (2 1/2 in.) beyond the metal conduit or tubing.

    Reference: 2017 National Electrical Code – Chapter 6 Special Equipment, Article 600 Electric Signs and Outline Lighting. 600.32 Neon Secondary-Circuit Wiring, over 1000 Volts, Nominal. 600.32(G) Conductors in Raceways.

71. **Answer C.** midpoint

    Conductors shall be permitted to run between the ends of neon tubing or to the secondary circuit midpoint return of listed transformers or listed electronic power supplies and provided with terminals or leads at the midpoint.

    Reference: 2017 National Electrical Code – Chapter 6 Special Equipment, Article 600 Electric Signs and Outline Lighting. 600.32 Neon Secondary-Circuit Wiring, over 1000 Volts, Nominal. 600.32(H) Between Neon Tubing and Midpoint Return.

72. **Answer A.** True

    Equipment having an open circuit voltage exceeding 1000 volts shall not be installed in or on dwelling occupancies.

    Reference: 2017 National Electrical Code – Chapter 6 Special Equipment, Article 600 Electric Signs and Outline Lighting. 600.32 Neon Secondary-Circuit Wiring, over 1000 Volts, Nominal. 600.32(I) Dwelling Occupancies.

EXAM 10

EXAM 10 ANSWERS

73. **Answer B.** 1000

Equipment having an open circuit voltage exceeding 1000 volts shall not be installed in or on dwelling occupancies.

Reference: 2017 National Electrical Code – Chapter 6 Special Equipment, Article 600 Electric Signs and Outline Lighting. 600.32 Neon Secondary-Circuit Wiring, over 1000 Volts, Nominal. 600.32(I) Dwelling Occupancies.

74. **Answer D.** 50 ft.

The length of secondary circuit conductors from a high-voltage terminal or lead of a transformer or electronic power supply to the first neon tube electrode shall not exceed the following:

(1) 6 m (20 ft.) where installed in metal conduit or tubing

(2) 15 m (50 ft.) where installed in nonmetallic conduit.

Reference: 2017 National Electrical Code – Chapter 6 Special Equipment, Article 600 Electric Signs and Outline Lighting. 600.32 Neon Secondary-Circuit Wiring, over 1000 Volts, Nominal. 600.32(J) Length of Secondary Circuit Conductors. 600.32(J) (1) Secondary Conductor to the First Electrode.

75. **Answer A.** 1/4 in.

A spacing of not less than 6 mm (1/4 in.) shall be maintained between the tubing and the nearest surface, other than its support.

Reference: 2017 National Electrical Code – Chapter 6 Special Equipment, Article 600 Electric Signs and Outline Lighting. 600.41 Neon Tubing. 600.41(C) Spacing.

76. **Answer A.** mechanically

Connections shall be made by use of a connection device, twisting of the wires together, or use of an electrode receptacle. *Connections shall be electrically and mechanically secure and shall be in an enclosure listed for the purpose.*

Reference: 2017 National Electrical Code – Chapter 6 Special Equipment, Article 600 Electric Signs and Outline Lighting. 600.42 Electrode Connections. 600.42(C) Electrode Connections.

77. **Answer D.** 6 in.

Neon secondary conductor(s) shall be supported not more than 150 mm (6 in.) from the electrode connection to the tubing.

Reference: 2017 National Electrical Code – Chapter 6 Special Equipment, Article 600 Electric Signs and Outline Lighting. 600.42 Electrode Connections. 600.42(D) Support.

78. **Answer A.** receptacles

Where electrodes penetrate an enclosure, bushings listed for the purpose shall be used unless receptacles are provided.

Reference: 2017 National Electrical Code – Chapter 6 Special Equipment, Article 600 Electric Signs and Outline Lighting. 600.42 Electrode Connections. 600.42(F) Bushings.

EXAM 10 ANSWERS

EXAM 10

EXAM 10 ANSWERS

Table 310.15(B)(16) see Table 310-15-B-16 in Tables folder on CD-ROM

79. Answer C. 8 AWG

The ampacity of the supply conductors shall be not less than the I *1eff* value on the rating plate. Alternatively, if the I *1eff* is not given, the ampacity of the supply conductors shall not be less than the current value determined by multiplying the rated primary current in amperes given on the welder rating plate by the factor shown in Table 630.11(A) based on the duty cycle of the welder.

Reference: 2017 National Electrical Code – Chapter 6 Special Equipment, Article 630 Electric Welders. 630.11 Ampacity of Supply Conductors. 630.11(A) Individual Welders. Table 630.11(A) Duty Cycle Multiplication Factors for Arc Welders (page 70-577)

Reference: 2017 National Electrical Code – Chapter 3 Wiring Methods and Materials. Table 310.15(B)(16) (formerly Table 310.16) Allowable Ampacities of Insulated Conductors Rated Up to and Including 2000 Volts, 60°C Through 90°C (140°F Through 194°F), Not More Than Three Current-Carrying Conductors in Raceway, Cable, or Earth (Directly Buried), Based on Ambient Temperature of 30°C (86°F)* (page 70-161)

80. Answer C. separated by fire-resistant-rate walls, floors, and ceilings

The room is separated from other occupancies by fire resistant- rated walls, floors, and ceilings with protected openings.

Informational Note: For further information on room construction requirements, see NFPA 75 -2017, Standard for the Fire Protection of Information Technology Equipment, – Chapter 5.

Reference: 2017 National Electrical Code – Chapter 6 Special Equipment, Article 645 Information Technology Equipment. 645.4 Special Requirements for Information Technology Equipment Room. 645.4(5)

81. Answer C. 125

The branch-circuit conductors supplying one or more units of *information technology equipment shall have an ampacity not less than 125 percent of the total connected load*.

Reference: 2017 National Electrical Code – Chapter 6 Special Equipment, Article 645 Information Technology Equipment. 645.5 Supply Circuits and Interconnecting Cables.

EXAM 10

EXAM 10 ANSWERS

82. **Answer C.** 15 feet

Information technology equipment shall be permitted to *be connected to a branch circuit by a power-supply cord.*

(1) Power-supply cords shall not exceed 4.5 m (15 ft.).

(2) Power cords shall be listed and a type permitted for use on listed information technology equipment or shall be constructed of listed flexible cord and listed attachment plugs and cord connectors of a type permitted for information technology equipment.

Informational Note: One method of determining if cords are of a type permitted for the purpose is found in UL 60950-1-2007, Safety of Information Technology Equipment - Safety Part I: General Requirements; or UL 62368-1-2012, Audio/Video, Information and Communication Technology Equipment - Part 1: Safety Requirements.

Reference: 2017 National Electrical Code – Chapter 6 Special Equipment, Article 645 Information Technology Equipment. 645.5 Supply Circuits and Interconnecting Cables. 645.5(B) Power Supply Cords.

83. **Answer B.** 60 volts

This article covers the installation and wiring of separately derived systems operating at 120 volts line-to-line and *60 volts to ground for sensitive electronic equipment.*

Reference: 2017 National Electrical Code – Chapter 6 Special Equipment, Article 647 Sensitive Electronic Equipment. 647.1 Scope.

84. **Answer B.** flexible cord to facilitate disconnection for maintenance

Fixed or stationary equipment, other than underwater luminaires, for **a permanently installed pool** shall be permitted to be connected with **a flexible cord and plug to facilitate the removal or disconnection for maintenance or repair**

Reference: 2017 National Electrical Code – Chapter 6 Special Equipment, Article 680 Swimming Pools, Fountains, and Similar Installations. 680.8 Cord-and-Plug-Connected Equipment.

85. **Answer A.** 3

For other than storable pools, the flexible cord shall not exceed 900 mm (3 ft.) in length.

Reference: 2017 National Electrical Code – Chapter 6 Special Equipment, Article 680 Swimming Pools, Fountains, and Similar Installations. 680.8 Cord-and-Plug-Connected Equipment. . 680.8(A) Length.

EXAM 10

EXAM 10 ANSWERS

Table 680.9(A) Overhead Conductor Clearances

	Clearance Parameters	Insulated Cables, 0–750 Volts to Ground, Supported on and Cabled Together with a Solidly Grounded Bare Messenger or Solidly Grounded Neutral Conductor		All Other Conductors Voltage to Ground			
				0 through 15 kV		Over 15 through 50 kV	
		m	ft	m	ft	m	ft
A.	Clearance in any direction to the water level, edge of water surface, base of diving platform, or permanently anchored raft	6.9	22.5	7.5	25	8.0	27
B.	Clearance in any direction to the observation stand, tower, or diving platform	4.4	14.5	5.2	17	5.5	18
C.	Horizontal limit of clearance measured from inside wall of the pool	This limit shall extend to the outer edge of the structures listed in A and B of this table but not less than 3 m (10 ft).					

86. Answer A. 14.5 feet

With respect to service-drop conductors, overhead service conductors, and open overhead wiring. Swimming pool and similar installations shall comply with the minimum clearances given in Table 680.8(A) and illustrated in Figure 680.8(A). Table 680.8(A) Overhead Conductor Clearances on page 70-607. Figure 680.8(A) on page 70-606.

Reference: 2017 National Electrical Code – Chapter 6 Special Equipment, Article 680 Swimming Pools, Fountains, and Similar Installations. 680.9 Overhead Conductor Clearances. . 680.9(A) Power.

87. Answer C. 48, 60

All electric pool water heaters shall have the heating elements subdivided into loads not exceeding 48 amperes and protected at not over 60 amperes. The ampacity of the branch-circuit conductors and the rating or setting of overcurrent protective devices shall not be less than 125 percent of the total nameplate-rated load.

Reference: 2017 National Electrical Code – Chapter 6 Special Equipment, Article 680 Swimming Pools, Fountains, and Similar Installations. 680.10 Electric Pool Water Heaters.

88. Answer D. any of the above

Underground wiring shall be permitted where installed in rigid metal conduit, intermediate metal conduit, rigid polyvinyl chloride conduit, reinforced thermosetting resin conduit, or Type MC cable, suitable for the conditions subject to that location. Underground wiring shall not be permitted under the pool unless this wiring is necessary to supply pool equipment permitted by this article.

Minimum cover depths shall be as given in Table 300.5. Table 300.5. page (70-137)

Reference: 2017 National Electrical Code – Chapter 6 Special Equipment, Article 680 Swimming Pools, Fountains, and Similar Installations. 680.11 Underground Wiring Location.

89. Answer D. Either A or C

Underground wiring shall be permitted where installed in rigid metal conduit, intermediate metal conduit, rigid polyvinyl chloride conduit, reinforced thermosetting resin conduit, or Type MC cable, suitable for the conditions subject to that location. Underground wiring shall not be permitted under the pool unless this wiring is necessary to supply pool equipment permitted by this article.

Minimum cover depths shall be as given in Table 300.5. Table 300.5. page (70-137)

Reference: 2017 National Electrical Code – Chapter 6 Special Equipment, Article 680 Swimming Pools, Fountains, and Similar Installations. 680.10 Underground Wiring Location.

EXAM 10

EXAM 10 ANSWERS

90. Answer A.   True

Underground wiring shall be permitted where installed in rigid metal conduit, intermediate metal conduit, rigid polyvinyl chloride conduit, reinforced thermosetting resin conduit, or Type MC cable, suitable for the conditions subject to that location. *Underground wiring shall not be permitted under the pool unless this wiring is necessary to supply pool equipment permitted by this article.*

Minimum cover depths shall be as given in Table 300.5. Table 300.5. page (70-137)

Reference: 2017 National Electrical Code – Chapter 6 Special Equipment, Article 680 Swimming Pools, Fountains, and Similar Installations. 680.10 Underground Wiring Location.

91. Answer A.   3 feet

Pool-associated motors shall be permitted to employ cord-and-plug connections. The flexible cord shall not exceed 900 mm (3 ft.) in length. The flexible cord shall include a copper equipment grounding conductor sized in accordance with 250.122 but not smaller than 12 AWG. The cord shall terminate in a grounding-type attachment plug.

Reference: 2017 National Electrical Code – Chapter 6 Special Equipment, Article 680 Swimming Pools, Fountains, and Similar Installations. 680.21 Motors. 680.21(A) Wiring Methods. 680.21(A)(3) Cord-and-Plug Connections.

92. Answer C.   20 feet

Where a permanently installed pool is installed, no fewer than one 125-volt, 15- or 20- ampere receptacle on a general-purpose branch circuit shall be located not less than 1.83 m (6 ft) from, and *not more than 6.0 m (20 ft) from, the inside wall of the pool.* This receptacle shall be located not more than 2.0 m (6 ft 6 in.) above the floor, platform, or grade level serving the pool.

Reference: 2017 National Electrical Code – Chapter 4 Equipment for General Use, Article 680 Swimming Pools, Fountains, and Similar Installations. 680.22 Lighting, Receptacles, and Equipment. 680.22(A) Receptacles. 680.22(A)(1) Required Receptacle, Location.

93. Answer C.   Have GFCI protection

Receptacles that provide power for water-pump motors or for other loads directly related to the circulation and sanitation system shall be located at least 1.83 m (6 ft) from the inside walls of the pool. *These receptacles shall have GFCI protection and be of the grounding type.*

Reference: 2017 National Electrical Code – Chapter 6 Special Equipment, Article 680 Swimming Pools, Fountains, and Similar Installations. 680.22 Lighting, Receptacles, and Equipment. 680.22(A) Receptacles. 680.22(A)(2) Circulation and Sanitation System, Location.

94. Answer B.   6 feet

Receptacles that provide power for water-pump motors or for other loads *directly related to the circulation and sanitation system shall be located at least 1.83 m (6 ft) from the inside walls of the pool.* These receptacles shall have GFCI protection and be of the grounding type.

Reference: 2017 National Electrical Code – Chapter 6 Special Equipment, Article 680 Swimming Pools, Fountains, and Similar Installations. 680.22 Lighting, Receptacles, and Equipment. 680.22(A) Receptacles. 680.22(A)(2) Circulation and Sanitation System, Location.

95. Answer B.   6

Other receptacles shall be not less than 1.83 m (6 ft.) from the inside walls of a pool.

Reference: 2017 National Electrical Code – Chapter 6 Special Equipment, Article 680 Swimming Pools, Fountains, and Similar Installations. 680.22 Lighting, Receptacles, and Equipment. 680.22(A) Receptacles. 680.22(A)(3) Other Receptacles, Location.

96. Answer C.   12 feet

In outdoor pool areas, luminaires, lighting outlets, and ceiling-suspended (paddle) fans installed above the pool or the area extending 1.5 m (5 ft.) horizontally from the inside *walls of the pool shall be installed at a height not less than 3.7 m (12 ft.) above the maximum water level of the pool.*

Reference: 2017 National Electrical Code – Chapter 6 Special Equipment, Article 680 Swimming Pools, Fountains, and Similar Installations. 680.22 Lighting, Receptacles, and Equipment. 680.22(B) Luminaires, Lighting Outlets, and Ceiling-Suspended (Paddle) Fans. 680.22(B)(1) New Outdoor Installation Clearances.

EXAM 10

EXAM 10 ANSWERS

97. Answer A. 5

Switching devices shall be located at least 1.5 m (5 ft.) horizontally from the inside walls of a pool unless separated from the pool by a solid fence, wall, or other permanent barrier. Alternatively, a switch that is listed as being acceptable for use within 1.5 m (5 ft.) shall be permitted.

Reference: 2017 National Electrical Code – Chapter 6 Special Equipment, Article 680 Swimming Pools, Fountains, and Similar Installations. 680.22 Lighting, Receptacles, and Equipment. 680.22(C) Switching Devices.

98. Answer B. dry location

All wet-niche luminaires shall be removable from the water for inspection, relamping, or other maintenance. *The forming shell location and length of cord in the forming shell shall permit personnel to place the removed luminaire on the deck or other dry location for such maintenance. The luminaire maintenance location shall be accessible without entering or going in the pool water.*

Reference: 2017 National Electrical Code – Chapter 6 Special Equipment, Article 680 Swimming Pools, Fountains, and Similar Installations. 680.23 Underwater Luminaires. . 680.23(B) Wet-Niche Luminaires. 680.23(B)(6) Servicing.

99. Answer D. Schedule 40 rigid polyvinyl chloride conduit (PVC)

Conduit shall be installed from the forming shell to a junction box or other enclosure conforming to the requirements in 680.24. Conduit shall be rigid metal, intermediate metal, liquidtight flexible nonmetallic, or rigid nonmetallic.

(a) *Metal Conduit.* Metal conduit shall be approved and shall be of brass or other approved corrosion-resistant metal.

(b) *Nonmetallic Conduit. Where a nonmetallic conduit is used, an 8 AWG insulated solid or stranded copper bonding jumper shall be installed in this conduit unless a listed* low-voltage lighting system not requiring grounding is used. The bonding jumper shall be terminated in the forming shell, junction box or transformer enclosure, or ground-fault circuit-interrupter enclosure. The termination of the 8 AWG bonding jumper in the forming shell shall be covered with, or encapsulated in, a listed potting compound to protect the connection from the possible deteriorating effect of pool water.

Reference: 2017 National Electrical Code – Chapter 6 Special Equipment, Article 680 Swimming Pools, Fountains, and Similar Installations. 680.23 Underwater Luminaires. 680.23(B) Wet-Niche Luminaires. 680.23(B)(2) Wiring Extending Directly to the Forming Shell.

100. Answer B. 8 AWG

The parts specified in 680.26(B)(1) through (B)(7) shall be bonded together using solid copper conductors, insulated covered, or bare, not smaller than 8 AWG or with rigid metal conduit of brass or other identified corrosion-resistant metal. Connections to bonded parts shall be made in accordance with 250.8. An 8 AWG or larger solid copper bonding conductor provided to reduce voltage gradients in the pool area shall not be required to be extended or attached to remote panelboards, service equipment, or electrodes.

Reference: 2017 National Electrical Code – Chapter 6 Special Equipment, Article 680 Swimming Pools, Fountains, and Similar Installations. 680.26 Equipotential Bonding. 680.26(B) Bonded Parts.

(a) *Structural Reinforcing Steel.* Unencapsulated structural reinforcing steel shall be bonded together by steel tie wires or the equivalent. Where structural reinforcing steel is encapsulated in a nonconductive compound, a copper conductor grid shall be installed in accordance with 680.26(B)(1)(b).

Reference: 2017 National Electrical Code – Chapter 6 Special Equipment, Article 680 Swimming Pools, Fountains, and Similar Installations. 680.26 Equipotential Bonding. 680.26(B) Bonded Parts. 680.26(B)(1) Conductive Pool Shells. 680.26(B)(1)(b)(a)

EXAM 10

EXAM 10 ANSWERS

101. **Answer A.** 3 feet

The perimeter surface to be bonded shall be considered to extend for 1 m (3 ft) horizontally beyond the inside walls of the pool and shall include unpaved surfaces and other types of paving. Perimeter surfaces separated from the pool by a permanent wall or building 1.5 m (5 ft) in height or more shall require equipotential bonding only on the pool side of the permanent wall or building. Bonding to perimeter surfaces shall be provided as specified in 680.26(B)(2)(a) or (2)(b) and shall be attached to the pool reinforcing steel or copper conductor grid at a minimum of four (4) points uniformly spaced around the perimeter of the pool. For nonconductive pool shells, bonding at four points shall not be required.

(a) Structural Reinforcing Steel. Structural reinforcing steel shall be bonded in accordance with 680.26(B)(1)(a).

(b) Alternate Means. Where structural reinforcing steel is not available or is encapsulated in a nonconductive compound, a copper conductor(s) shall be utilized where the following requirements are met:

(1) At least one minimum 8 AWG bare solid copper conductor shall be provided.

(2) The conductors shall follow the contour of the perimeter surface.

(3) Only listed splices shall be permitted.

(4) The required conductor shall be 450 mm to 600 mm (18 in. to 24 in.) from the inside walls of the pool.

(5) The required conductor shall be secured within or under the perimeter surface 100 mm to 150 mm (4 in. to 6 in.) below the subgrade.

Reference: 2017 National Electrical Code – Chapter 6 Special Equipment, Article 680 Swimming Pools, Fountains, and Similar Installations. 680.26 Equipotential Bonding. 680.26(B) Bonded Parts. 680.26(B)(2) Perimeter Surfaces.

102. **Answer A.** 5 feet

A clearly labeled emergency shutoff or control switch for the purpose of stopping the motor(s) that provide power to the recirculation system and jet system shall be installed at a point readily accessible to the users and *not less than 1.5 m (5 ft.) away, adjacent to, and within sight of the spa or hot tub. This requirement shall not apply to one-family dwellings.*

Reference: 2017 National Electrical Code – Chapter 6 Special Equipment, Article 680 Swimming Pools, Fountains, and Similar Installations. 680.41 Emergency Switch for Spas and Hot Tubs.

103. **Answer C.** 15 feet

Cord-and-plug connections with a cord not longer than 4.6 m (15 ft.) shall be permitted where protected by a ground-fault circuit interrupter.

Reference: 2017 National Electrical Code – Chapter 6 Special Equipment, Article 680 Swimming Pools, Fountains, and Similar Installations. 680.42 Outdoor Installations. 680.42(A) Flexible Connections. 680.42(A)(2) Cord-and-Plug Connections.

104. **Answer A.** 5 feet

Switches shall be located at least 1.5 m (5 ft.), measured horizontally, from the inside walls of the spa or hot tub.

Reference: 2017 National Electrical Code – Chapter 6 Special Equipment, Article 680 Swimming Pools, Fountains, and Similar Installations. 680.43 Indoor Installations. 680.43(C) Switches.

105. **Answer B.** 8 AWG

All metal parts associated with the spa or hot tub shall *be bonded by any of the following methods:*

(1) The interconnection of threaded metal piping and fittings

(2) Metal-to-metal mounting on a common frame or base

(3) *The provisions of a solid copper bonding jumper, insulated, covered, or bare, not smaller than 8 AWG*

Reference: 2017 National Electrical Code – Chapter 6 Special Equipment, Article 680 Swimming Pools, Fountains, and Similar Installations. 680.43 Indoor Installations. 680.43(E) Methods of Bonding.

EXAM 10

EXAM 10 ANSWERS

106. Answer A. 5 ft.

A fixed or stationary electric sign installed within a fountain shall be not less than 1.5 m (5 ft.) inside the fountain measured from the outside edges of the fountain.

Reference: 2017 National Electrical Code – Chapter 6 Special Equipment, Article 680 Swimming Pools, Fountains, and Similar Installations. 680.57 Signs. 680.57(C) Location. 680.57(C)(1) Fixed or Stationary.

107. Answer C. 6 feet

Hydromassage bathtubs and their associated electrical components shall be on an individual branch circuit(s) and protected by a readily accessible ground-fault circuit interrupter. *All 125-volt, single-phase receptacles not exceeding 30 amperes and located within 1.83 m (6 ft.) measured horizontally of the inside walls of a hydromassage tub shall be protected by a ground-fault circuit interrupter.*

Reference: 2017 National Electrical Code – Chapter 6 Special Equipment, Article 680 Swimming Pools, Fountains, and Similar Installations. 680.71 Protection.

108. Answer B. 5 feet

On land, the service equipment for floating structures and submersible electrical equipment shall be located no closer than 1.5 m (5 ft.) horizontally from the shoreline and live parts shall be elevated a minimum of 300 mm (12 in.) above the electrical datum plane. Service equipment shall disconnect when the water level reaches the height of the established electrical datum plane.

Reference: 2017 National Electrical Code – Chapter 6 Special Equipment, Article 682 Naturally and Artificially Made Bodies of Water. 682.11 Location of Service Equipment.

109. Answer A. 5 feet

On land, the service equipment for floating structures and submersible electrical equipment shall be located no closer than 1.5 m (5 ft.) horizontally from the shoreline and live parts shall be elevated a minimum of 300 mm (12 in.) above the electrical datum plane. Service equipment shall disconnect when the water level reaches the height of the established electrical datum plane.

Reference: 2017 National Electrical Code – Chapter 6 Special Equipment, Article 682 Natural and Artificially Made Bodies of Water. 682.11 Location of Service Equipment.

110. Answer D. solar PV

This article applies to **solar PV systems, other than those covered by Article 691, including the array circuit(s), inverter(s), and controller(s) for such systems. [See Figure 690.1(a) and Figure 690.1(b).] The systems covered by this article** may be interactive with other electrical power production sources or stand-alone or both, and may or may not be connected to energy storage systems such as batteries. These PV systems may have ac or dc output for utilization.

Informational Note: Article 691 covers the installation of largescale PV electric supply stations.

Reference: 2017 National Electrical Code – Chapter 6 Special Equipment, Article 690 Solar Photovoltaic (PV) Systems. 690.1 Scope

111. Answer D. sunlight

A complete, environmentally protected unit consisting of solar cells, optics, inverter, and other components, exclusive of tracker, *designed to generate ac power when exposed to sunlight.*

Reference: 2017 National Electrical Code – Chapter 6 Special Equipment, Article 690 Solar Photovoltaic (PV) Systems. 690.2 Definitions. Alternating-Current (ac) Module (Alternating-Current Photovoltaic Module)

112. Answer A. array

A mechanically integrated assembly of module(s) or panel(s) with a support structure and foundation, tracker, and other components, as required, to form a dc or ac power producing unit.

Reference: 2017 National Electrical Code – Chapter 6 Special Equipment, Article 690 Solar Photovoltaic (PV) Systems. 690.2 Definitions. *Array*

113. Answer B. inverter

Equipment that is used to change voltage level or waveform, or both, of electrical energy. Commonly, an inverter [also known as a power conditioning unit (PCU) or power conversion system (PCS)] is a device that changes dc input to an ac output. Inverters may also *function as battery chargers* that use alternating current from another source and convert it into direct current for charging batteries.

Reference: 2017 National Electrical Code – Chapter 6 Special Equipment, Article 690 Solar Photovoltaic (PV) Systems. 690.2 Definitions. *Inverter*

EXAM 10

EXAM 10 ANSWERS

114. **Answer B.** inverter input circuit

    Conductors connected to the dc input of an inverter. 2017 National Electrical Code – Chapter 6 Special Equipment, Article 690 Solar Photovoltaic (PV) Systems. 690.2 Definitions. *Inverter Input Circuit*

115. **Answer C.** an inverter output circuit

    Conductors connected to the ac output of an inverter.

    Reference: 2017 National Electrical Code – Chapter 6 Special Equipment, Article 690 Solar Photovoltaic (PV) Systems. 690.2 Definitions. *Inverter Output Circuit*

116. **Answer D.** module

    A complete, environmentally protected unit consisting of solar cells, optics, and other components, exclusive of tracker, designed to generate dc power when exposed to sunlight.

    Reference: 2017 National Electrical Code – Chapter 6 Special Equipment, Article 690 Solar Photovoltaic (PV) Systems. 690.2 Definitions. *Module*

117. **Answer D.** photovoltaic output circuit

    Circuit conductors between the PV source circuit(s) and the inverter or dc utilization equipment.

    Reference: 2017 National Electrical Code – Chapter 6 Special Equipment, Article 690 Solar Photovoltaic (PV) Systems. 690.2 Definitions. Photovoltaic Output Circuit

118. **Answer C.** power source

    An array or aggregate of arrays that generates dc power at system voltage and current.

    Reference: 2017 National Electrical Code – Chapter 6 Special Equipment, Article 690 Solar Photovoltaic (PV) Systems. 690.2 Definitions. *Photovoltaic Power Source*

119. **Answer D.** photovoltaic source circuit

    Circuits between modules and from modules to the common connection point(s) of the dc system.

    Reference: 2017 National Electrical Code – Chapter 6 Special Equipment, Article 690 Solar Photovoltaic (PV) Systems. 690.2 Definitions. *Photovoltaic Source Circuit*

120. **Answer A.** True

    The direct current (dc) voltage of any PV source or PV output circuit. For multiwire installations, the PV system voltage is the highest voltage between any two dc conductors.

    Reference: 2017 National Electrical Code – Chapter 6 Special Equipment, Article 690 Solar Photovoltaic (PV) Systems. 690.2 Definitions. *Photovoltaic System Voltage*

121. **Answer C.** solar cell

    The basic PV device that generates electricity when exposed to light.

    Reference: 2017 National Electrical Code – Chapter 6 Special Equipment, Article 690 Solar Photovoltaic (PV) Systems. 690.2 Definitions. Solar Cell

122. **Answer B.** False

    A solar PV system that supplies power independently of an electrical production and distribution network.

    Reference: 2017 National Electrical Code – Chapter 6 Special Equipment, Article 690 Solar Photovoltaic (PV) Systems. 690.2 Definitions. Stand-Alone System

123. **Answer A.** electricity

    Photovoltaic systems shall be permitted to supply a building or other structure in addition to any other electrical supply system(s).

    Reference: 2017 National Electrical Code – Chapter 6 Special Equipment, Article 690 Solar Photovoltaic (PV) Systems. 690.4 General Requirements. 690.4(A) Photovoltaic Systems.

124. **Answer D.** both B and C

    Inverters, motor generators, PV modules, PV panels, ac modules, dc combiners, dc-to-dc converters, and charge controllers intended for use in PV systems *shall be listed or field labeled for the PV application.*

    Reference: 2017 National Electrical Code – Chapter 6 Special Equipment, Article 690 Solar Photovoltaic (PV) Systems. 690.4 General Requirements. 690.4(B) Equipment.

EXAM 10

EXAM 10 ANSWERS

125. **Answer A.** True

Multiple PV systems shall be permitted to be installed in or on a single building or structure. Where the PV systems are remotely located from each other, *a directory in accordance with 705.10 shall be provided at each PV system disconnecting means*.

Reference: 2017 National Electrical Code – Chapter 6 Special Equipment, Article 690 Solar Photovoltaic (PV) Systems. 690.4 General Requirements. 690.4(D) Multiple Inverters.

126. **Answer A.** True

The requirements of Article 690 pertaining to PV source circuits shall not apply to ac modules. The PV source circuit, conductors, and inverters shall be considered as internal wiring of an ac module.

Reference: 2017 National Electrical Code – Chapter 6 Special Equipment, Article 690 Solar Photovoltaic (PV) Systems. 690.6 Alternating-Current (ac) Modules. 690.6(A) Photovoltaic Source Circuits.

127. **Answer A.** inverter

The output of an ac module shall be considered an inverter output circuit.

Reference: 2017 National Electrical Code – Chapter 6 Special Equipment, Article 690 Solar Photovoltaic (PV) Systems. 690.6 Alternating-Current (ac) Modules. 690.6(B) Inverter Output Circuit.

128. **Answer B.** maximum PV system voltage

In a dc PV source circuit or output circuit, the maximum PV system voltage for that circuit shall be calculated in accordance with one of the following methods:

Informational Note: One source for lowest-expected, ambient temperature design data for various locations is the chapter titled Extreme Annual Mean Minimum Design Dry Bulb Temperature found in the ASHRAE Handbook — Fundamentals, 2013. These temperature data can be used to calculate maximum voltage.

(1) Instructions in listing or labeling of the module: The sum of the PV module–rated open-circuit voltage of the series connected modules corrected for the lowest expected ambient temperature using the open-circuit voltage temperature coefficients in accordance with the instructions included in the listing or labeling of the module

(2) Crystalline and multi-crystalline modules: For crystalline and multi-crystalline silicon modules, the sum of the PV module–rated open-circuit voltage of the series connected modules corrected for the lowest expected ambient temperature using the correction factor provided in Table 690.7(A)

(3) PV systems of 100 kW or larger: For PV systems with a generating capacity of 100 kW or greater, a documented and stamped PV system design, using an industry standard method and provided by a licensed professional electrical engineer, shall be permitted.

Informational Note: One industry standard method for calculating maximum voltage of a PV system is published by Sandia National Laboratories, reference SAND 2004-3535, Photovoltaic Array Performance Model. The maximum voltage shall be used to determine the voltage rating of conductors, cables, disconnects, overcurrent devices, and other equipment.

Reference: 2017 National Electrical Code – Chapter 6 Special Equipment, Article 690 Solar Photovoltaic (PV) Systems. 690.7 Maximum Voltage. 690.7(A) Maximum Photovoltaic System Voltage.

EXAM 10

EXAM 10 ANSWERS

129. **Answer A.** True

In a dc PV source circuit or output circuit, the maximum PV system voltage for that circuit shall be calculated in accordance with one of the following methods:

Informational Note: *One source for lowest-expected, ambient temperature design data for various locations is the chapter titled Extreme Annual Mean Minimum Design Dry Bulb Temperature found in the ASHRAE Handbook — Fundamentals, 2013.* These temperature data can be used to calculate maximum voltage.

(1) Instructions in listing or labeling of the module: The sum of the PV module–rated open-circuit voltage of the series connected modules corrected for the lowest expected ambient temperature using the open-circuit voltage temperature coefficients in accordance with the instructions included in the listing or labeling of the module

(2) Crystalline and multi-crystalline modules: For crystalline and multi-crystalline silicon modules, the sum of the PV module–rated open-circuit voltage of the series connected modules corrected for the lowest expected ambient temperature using the correction factor provided in Table 690.7(A)

(3) PV systems of 100 kW or larger: For PV systems with a generating capacity of 100 kW or greater, a documented and stamped PV system design, using an industry standard method and provided by a licensed professional electrical engineer, shall be permitted.

Informational Note: One industry standard method for calculating maximum voltage of a PV system is published by Sandia National Laboratories, reference SAND 2004-3535, Photovoltaic Array Performance Model. The maximum voltage shall be used to determine the voltage rating of conductors, cables, disconnects, overcurrent devices, and other equipment.

Reference: 2017 National Electrical Code – Chapter 6 Special Equipment, Article 690 Solar Photovoltaic (PV) Systems. 690.7 Maximum Voltage. 690.7(A) Maximum Photovoltaic System Voltage.

130. **Answer D.** 600V

The maximum voltage of PV system dc circuits shall be the highest voltage between any two circuit conductors or any conductor and ground. *PV system dc circuits on or in one- and two-family dwellings shall be permitted to have a maximum voltage of 600 volts or less.* PV system dc circuits on or in other types of buildings shall be permitted to have a maximum voltage of 1000 volts or less. Where not located on or in buildings, listed dc PV equipment, rated at a maximum voltage of 1500 volts or less, shall not be required to comply with Parts II and III of Article 490.

Reference: 2017 National Electrical Code – Chapter 6 Special Equipment, Article 690 Solar Photovoltaic (PV) Systems. 690.7 Maximum Voltage.

131. **Answer C.** unqualified person

In one- and two-family dwellings, live parts in PV source circuits and PV output circuits over 150 volts to ground shall not be accessible to other than qualified persons while energized.

Informational Note: See 110.27 for guarding of live parts, and 210.6 for voltage to ground and between conductors.

Reference: 2017 National Electrical Code – Chapter 6 Special Equipment, Article 690 Solar Photovoltaic (PV) Systems. 694.10 Maximum Voltage. 694.10(C) Circuits over 150 Volts to Ground.

EXAM 10

EXAM 10 ANSWERS

132. Answer A. True

The maximum current shall be calculated by one of the following methods:

(1) The sum of parallel-connected PV module-rated short circuit currents multiplied by 125 percent

(2) For PV systems with a generating capacity of 100 kW or greater, a documented and stamped PV system design, using an industry standard method and provided by a licensed professional electrical engineer, shall be permitted. The calculated maximum current value shall be based on the highest 3-hour current average resulting from the simulated local irradiance on the PV array accounting for elevation and orientation. The current value used by this method shall not be less than 70 percent of the value calculated using 690.8(A)(1)(1).

Informational Note: One industry standard method for calculating maximum current of a PV system is available from Sandia National Laboratories, reference SAND 2004-3535, Photovoltaic Array Performance Model. This model is used by the System Advisor Model simulation program provided by the National Renewable Energy Laboratory.

Reference: 2017 National Electrical Code – Chapter 6 Special Equipment, Article 690 Solar Photovoltaic (PV) Systems. 690.8 Circuit Sizing and Current. 690.8(A) Calculation of Maximum Circuit Current. 690.8(A)(1) Photovoltaic Source Circuit Currents.

133. Answer A. 690.8(A)(1)

The maximum current shall be the sum of parallel source circuit maximum currents as calculated in 690.8(A)(1).

Reference: 2017 National Electrical Code – Chapter 6 Special Equipment, Article 690 Solar Photovoltaic (PV) Systems. 690.8 Circuit Sizing and Current. 690.8(A) Calculation of Maximum Circuit Current. 690.8(A)(2) Photovoltaic Output Circuit Currents.

134. Answer B. continuous

The maximum current shall be the inverter continuous output current rating.

Reference: 2017 National Electrical Code – Chapter 6 Special Equipment, Article 690 Solar Photovoltaic (PV) Systems. 690.8 Circuit Sizing and Current. 690.8(A) Calculation of Maximum Circuit Current. 690.8(A)(3) Inverter Output Circuit Current.

135. Answer A. continuous

PV system currents shall be considered to be continuous. Circuit conductors shall be sized to carry not less than the larger of 690.8(B)(1) or (B)(2) or where protected by a listed adjustable electronic overcurrent protective device in accordance 690.9(B)(3), not less than the current in 690.8(B)(3).

Reference: 2017 National Electrical Code – Chapter 6 Special Equipment, Article 690 Solar Photovoltaic (PV) Systems. 690.8 Circuit Sizing and Current. 690.8(B) Conductor Ampacity

136. Answer C. 125%

Overcurrent devices used in PV system dc circuits shall be listed for use in PV systems. Overcurrent devices, where required, shall be rated in accordance with one of the following:

(1) Not less than 125 percent of the maximum currents calculated in 690.8(A).

(2) An assembly, together with its overcurrent device(s), that is listed for continuous operation at 100 percent of its rating shall be permitted to be used at 100 percent of its rating.

(3) Adjustable electronic overcurrent protective devices rated or set in accordance with 240.6.

Informational Note: Some electronic overcurrent protective devices prevent back feed current.

Reference: 2017 National Electrical Code – Chapter 6 Special Equipment, Article 690 Solar Photovoltaic (PV) Systems. 690.9 Overcurrent Protection. 690.9(B) Overcurrent Device Ratings.

EXAM 10

EXAM 10 ANSWERS

137. Answer C. overcurrent

A single overcurrent protective device, where required, shall be permitted to protect the PV modules and conductors of each source circuit or the conductors of each output circuit. Where single overcurrent protection devices are used to protect PV source or output circuits, all overcurrent devices shall be placed in the same polarity for all circuits within a PV system. The overcurrent devices shall be accessible but shall not be required to be readily accessible.

Informational Note: Due to improved ground-fault protection required in PV systems by 690.41(B), a single overcurrent protective device in either the positive or negative conductors of a PV system in combination with this ground-fault protection provides adequate overcurrent protection.

Reference: 2017 National Electrical Code – Chapter 6 Special Equipment, Article 690 Solar Photovoltaic (PV) Systems. 690.9 Overcurrent Protection. 690.9(C) Photovoltaic Source and Output Circuits.

138. Answer B. False

A single overcurrent protective device, where required, shall be permitted to protect the PV modules and conductors of each source circuit or the conductors of each output circuit. Where single overcurrent protection devices are used to protect PV source or output circuits, all overcurrent devices shall be placed in the same polarity for all circuits within a PV system. *The overcurrent devices shall be accessible but shall not be required to be readily accessible.*

Informational Note: Due to improved ground-fault protection required in PV systems by 690.41(B), a single overcurrent protective device in either the positive or negative conductors of a PV system in combination with this ground-fault protection provides adequate overcurrent protection.

Reference: 2017 National Electrical Code – Chapter 6 Special Equipment, Article 690 Solar Photovoltaic (PV) Systems. 690.9 Overcurrent Protection. 690.9(C) Photovoltaic Source and Output Circuits.

139. Answer B. False

A single overcurrent protective device, where required, shall be permitted to protect the PV modules and conductors of each source circuit or the conductors of each output circuit. Where single overcurrent protection devices are used to protect PV source or output circuits, all overcurrent devices shall be placed in the same polarity for all circuits within a PV system. The overcurrent devices shall be accessible but shall not be required to be readily accessible.

Informational Note: Due to improved ground-fault protection required in PV systems by 690.41(B), a single overcurrent protective device in either the positive or negative conductors of a PV system in combination with this ground-fault protection provides adequate overcurrent protection.

Reference: 2017 National Electrical Code – Chapter 6 Special Equipment, Article 690 Solar Photovoltaic (PV) Systems. 690.9 Overcurrent Protection. 690.9(C) Photovoltaic Source and Output Circuits.

140. Answer B. less

Power supply to premises wiring systems shall be permitted to have less capacity than the calculated load. The capacity of the stand-alone supply shall be equal to or greater than the load posed by the largest single utilization equipment connected to the system. Calculated general lighting loads shall not be considered as a single load.

Reference: 2017 National Electrical Code – Chapter 7 Special Conditions, Article 712 Stand-Alone Systems. 710.15 General.

141. Answer B. False

Energy storage or backup power supplies are not required.

Reference: 2017 National Electrical Code – Chapter 7 Special Conditions, Article 712 Stand-Alone Systems. 710.15 General. 710.15(D) Energy Storage or Backup Power System Requirements

142. Answer A. True

Means shall be provided to disconnect the PV system from all wiring systems including power systems, energy storage systems, and utilization equipment and its associated premises wiring.

Reference: 2017 National Electrical Code – Chapter 6 Special Equipment, Article 690 Solar Photovoltaic (PV) Systems. 690.13 Building or Other Structure Supplied by a Photovoltaic System.

EXAM 10

EXAM 10 ANSWERS

143. **Answer D.** either A or B

The PV system disconnecting means shall be installed at a readily accessible location.

Informational Note: PV systems installed in accordance with 690.12 address the concerns related to energized conductors entering a building.

Reference: 2017 National Electrical Code – Chapter 6 Special Equipment, Article 690 Solar Photovoltaic (PV) Systems. 690.13 Building or Other Structure Supplied by a Photovoltaic System. 690.13(A) Location.

144. **Answer A.** True

Each PV system disconnecting means shall plainly indicate whether in the open (off) or closed (on) position and be permanently marked "PV SYSTEM DISCONNECT" or equivalent. Additional markings shall be permitted based upon the specific system configuration. *For PV system disconnecting means where the line and load terminals may be energized in the open position, the device shall be marked with the following words or equivalent:*

WARNING

ELECTRIC SHOCK HAZARD

TERMINALS ON THE LINE AND LOAD

SIDES MAY BE

ENERGIZED IN THE OPEN POSITION

The warning sign(s) or label(s) shall comply with 110.21(B).

Reference: 2017 National Electrical Code – Chapter 6 Special Equipment, Article 690 Solar Photovoltaic (PV) Systems. 690.17 Disconnect Type. 690.17(E) Interrupting Rating.

145. **Answer C.** permanently marked

Each PV system disconnecting means shall plainly indicate whether in the open (off) or closed (on) position and be *permanently marked "PV SYSTEM DISCONNECT"* or equivalent. Additional markings shall be permitted based upon the specific system configuration. For PV system disconnecting means where the line and load terminals may be energized in the open position, the device shall be marked with the following words or equivalent:

WARNING

ELECTRIC SHOCK HAZARD

TERMINALS ON THE LINE AND LOAD

SIDES MAY BE

ENERGIZED IN THE OPEN POSITION

The warning sign(s) or label(s) shall comply with 110.21(B

Reference: 2017 National Electrical Code – Chapter 6 Special Equipment, Article 690 Solar Photovoltaic (PV) Systems. 690.13 Building or Other Structure Supplied by a Photovoltaic System. 690.13(B) Marking.

146. **Answer A.** True

Isolating devices shall be provided to isolate PV modules, ac *PV modules, fuses, dc-to-dc converters inverters, and charge controllers from all conductors that are not solidly grounded. An equipment disconnecting means or a PV system disconnecting means shall be permitted in place of an isolating device. Where the maximum circuit current is greater than 30 amperes for the output circuit of a dc combiner or the input circuit of a charge controller or inverter,* an equipment disconnecting means shall be provided for isolation. Where a charge controller or inverter has multiple input circuits, a single equipment disconnecting means shall be permitted to isolate the equipment from the input circuits.

Informational Note: The purpose of these isolating devices are for the safe and convenient replacement or service of specific PV system equipment without exposure to energized conductors.

Reference: 2017 National Electrical Code – Chapter 6 Special Equipment, Article 690 Solar Photovoltaic (PV) Systems. 690.15 Disconnection of Photovoltaic Equipment

EXAM 10

EXAM 10 ANSWERS

147. Answer A. True

Means shall be provided to disconnect a fuse from all sources of supply where the fuse is energized from both directions and is accessible to other than qualified persons. Switches, pullouts, or similar devices that are rated for the application shall be permitted to serve as a means to disconnect fuses from all sources of supply.

Reference: 2017 National Electrical Code – Chapter 6 Special Equipment, Article 690 Solar Photovoltaic (PV) Systems. 694.26 Fuses. 694.26 Disconnecting Means.

148. Answer B. 6 Switches/6 sets

Each PV system disconnecting means shall consist of not more than six switches or six sets of circuit breakers, or a combination of not more than six switches and sets of circuit breakers, mounted in a single enclosure, or in a group of separate enclosures. A single PV system disconnecting means shall be permitted for the combined ac output of one or more inverters or ac modules in an interactive system.

Informational Note: This requirement does not limit the number of PV systems connected to a service as permitted in 690.4(D). This requirement allows up to six disconnecting means to disconnect a single PV system. For PV systems where all power is converted through interactive inverters, a dedicated circuit breaker, in 705.12(B)(1), is an example of a single PV system disconnecting means.

Reference: 2017 National Electrical Code – Chapter 6 Special Equipment, Article 690 Solar Photovoltaic (PV) Systems. 690.13 Photovoltaic System Disconnecting Means. 690.13(D) Maximum Number of Disconnects.

149. Answer A. True

Devices marked with "line" and "load" shall not be permitted for backfeed or reverse current.

Reference: 2017 National Electrical Code – Chapter 6 Special Equipment, Article 690 Solar Photovoltaic (PV) Systems. 690.13 Fuses. 690.13(F)(2) Devices Marked "Line" and "Load"

150. Answer A. True

The disconnecting means shall not be required to be suitable for use as service equipment. The disconnecting means for ungrounded conductors shall consist of manually operable switches or circuit breakers complying with all of the following requirements:

(1) They shall be located where readily accessible.

(2) They shall be externally operable without exposing the operator to contact with live parts.

(3) They shall plainly indicate whether in the open or closed position.

(4) They shall have an interrupting rating sufficient for the nominal circuit voltage and the current that is available at the line terminals of the equipment.

Where all terminals of the disconnecting means are capable of being energized in the open position, a warning sign shall be mounted on or adjacent to the disconnecting means. The sign shall be clearly legible and shall have the following words or equivalent:

WARNING.

ELECTRIC SHOCK HAZARD.

DO NOT TOUCH TERMINALS.

TERMINALS ON BOTH THE LINE

AND LOAD SIDES MAY BE

ENERGIZED IN THE OPEN POSITION.

The warning sign(s) or label(s) shall comply with 110.21(B).

Reference: 2017 National Electrical Code – Chapter 6 Special Equipment, Article 690 Solar Photovoltaic (PV) Systems. 694.22 Additional Provisions. 694.22(A) Disconnecting Means.

151. Answer B. two PV source circuits

DC PV arrays shall be provided with dc ground-fault protection meeting the requirements of 690.41(B)(1) and (2) to reduce fire hazards.

Exception: PV arrays with not more than two PV source circuits and with all PV system dc circuits not on or in buildings shall be permitted without ground-fault protection where solidly grounded.

Reference: 2017 National Electrical Code – Chapter 6 Special Equipment, Article 690 Solar Photovoltaic (PV) Systems. 690.41 System Grounding. 690.41(B)Ground-Fault Protection

EXAM 10

EXAM 10 ANSWERS

152. Answer D. A and C

An isolating device shall not be required to simultaneously disconnect all current-carrying conductors of a circuit. *The isolating device shall be one of the following:*

(1) A connector meeting the requirements of 690.33 and listed and identified for use with specific equipment

(2) A finger safe fuse holder

(3) An isolating switch that requires a tool to open

(4) An isolating device listed for the intended application

An isolating device shall be rated to open the maximum circuit current under load or be marked "Do Not Disconnect Under Load" or "Not for Current Interrupting."

Reference: 2017 National Electrical Code – Chapter 6 Special Equipment, Article 690 Solar Photovoltaic (PV) Systems. 690.18 Installation and Service of an Array.

153. Answer A. True

All raceway and cable wiring methods included in this Code, other wiring systems and fittings specifically listed for use on PV arrays, and wiring as part of a listed system shall be permitted. Where wiring devices with integral enclosures are used, sufficient length of cable shall be provided to facilitate replacement.

Where PV source and output circuits operating at voltages greater than 30 volts are installed in readily accessible locations, circuit conductors shall be guarded or installed in Type MC cable or in raceway. For ambient temperatures exceeding 30°C (86°F), conductor ampacities shall be corrected in accordance with Table 690.31(A).

Reference: 2017 National Electrical Code – Chapter 6 Special Equipment, Article 690 Solar Photovoltaic (PV) Systems. 690.31 Methods Permitted. 690.31(A) Wiring Systems.

154. Answer C. readily accessible, 30V

All raceway and cable wiring methods included in this Code, other wiring systems and fittings specifically listed for use on PV arrays, and wiring as part of a listed system shall be permitted. Where wiring devices with integral enclosures are used, sufficient length of cable shall be provided to facilitate replacement.

Where PV source and output circuits operating at voltages greater than 30 volts are installed in readily accessible locations, circuit conductors shall be guarded or installed in Type MC cable or in raceway. For ambient temperatures exceeding 30°C (86°F), conductor ampacities shall be corrected in accordance with Table 690.31(A).

Reference: 2017 National Electrical Code – Chapter 6 Special Equipment, Article 690 Solar Photovoltaic (PV) Systems. 690.31 Methods Permitted. 690.31(A) Wiring Systems.

155. Answer A. True

PV source circuits and *PV output circuits shall not be contained in the same raceway, cable tray, cable, outlet box, junction box, or similar fitting as conductors, feeders, branch circuits of other non-PV systems,* or inverter output circuits, unless the conductors of the different systems are separated by a partition. PV system circuit conductors shall be identified and grouped as required by 690.31(B)(1) through (2). The means of identification shall be permitted by separate color coding, marking tape, tagging, or other approved means.

Reference: 2017 National Electrical Code – Chapter 6 Special Equipment, Article 690 Solar Photovoltaic (PV) Systems. 690.31 Methods Permitted. 690.31(B) Identification and Grouping.

156. Answer A. True

PV source circuits and PV output circuits shall not be contained in the same raceway, cable tray, cable, outlet box, junction box, or similar fitting as conductors, feeders, branch circuits of other non-PV systems, or inverter output circuits, unless the conductors of the different systems are separated by a partition. *PV system circuit conductors shall be identified and grouped as required by 690.31(B)(1) through (2). The means of identification shall be permitted by separate color coding, marking tape, tagging, or other approved means.*

Reference: 2017 National Electrical Code – Chapter 6 Special Equipment, Article 690 Solar Photovoltaic (PV) Systems. 690.31 Methods Permitted. 690.31(B) Identification and Grouping.

EXAM 10

EXAM 10 ANSWERS

157. **Answer A.** True

    PV system circuit conductors shall be identified at all accessible points of termination, connection, and splices.

    The means of identification shall be permitted by separate color coding, marking tape, tagging, or other approved means. Only solidly grounded PV system circuit conductors, in accordance with 690.41(A)(5), shall be marked in accordance with 200.6.

    Exception: Where the identification of the conductors is evident by spacing or arrangement, further identification shall not be required.

    Reference: 2017 National Electrical Code – Chapter 6 Special Equipment, Article 690 Solar Photovoltaic (PV) Systems. 690.31 Methods Permitted. 690.31(B) Identification and Grouping. 690.31(B)(1) Identification.

158. **Answer A.** True

    PV system circuit conductors shall be identified at all accessible points of termination, connection, and splices.

    The means of identification shall be permitted by separate color coding, marking tape, tagging, or other approved means. Only solidly grounded PV system circuit conductors, in accordance with 690.41(A)(5), shall be marked in accordance with 200.6.

    Exception: Where the identification of the conductors is evident by spacing or arrangement, further identification shall not be required.

    Reference: 2017 National Electrical Code – Chapter 6 Special Equipment, Article 690 Solar Photovoltaic (PV) Systems. 690.31 Methods Permitted. 690.31(B) Identification and Grouping. 690.31(B)(1) PV Output and Inverter Circuits.

159. **Answer A.** True

    Where the conductors of more than one PV system occupy the same junction box or raceway with a removable cover(s), the ac and dc conductors of each system shall be grouped separately by cable ties or similar means at least once and shall then be grouped at intervals not to exceed 1.8 m (6 ft).

    Exception: The requirement for grouping shall not apply if the circuit enters from a cable or raceway unique to the circuit that makes the grouping obvious.

    Reference: 2017 National Electrical Code – Chapter 6 Special Equipment, Article 690 Solar Photovoltaic (PV) Systems. 690.31 Methods Permitted. 690.31(B) Identification and Grouping. 690.31(B)(2 Grouping.

160. **Answer D.** 6 ft.

    Where the conductors of more than one PV system occupy the same junction box or raceway with a removable cover(s), the ac and dc conductors of each system shall be grouped separately by cable ties or similar *means at least once and shall then be grouped at intervals not to exceed 1.8 m (6 ft).*

    Exception: The requirement for grouping shall not apply if the circuit enters from a cable or raceway unique to the circuit that makes the grouping obvious.

    Reference: 2017 National Electrical Code – Chapter 6 Special Equipment, Article 690 Solar Photovoltaic (PV) Systems. 690.31 Methods Permitted. 690.31(B) Identification and Grouping. 690.31(B)(2) Grouping.

161. **Answer A.** True

    Where the conductors of more than one PV system occupy the same junction box or raceway with a removable cover(s), the ac and dc conductors of each system shall be grouped separately by cable ties or similar means at least once and shall then be grouped at intervals not to exceed 1.8 m (6 ft).

    Exception: The requirement for grouping shall not apply if the circuit enters from a cable or raceway unique to the circuit that makes the grouping obvious.

    Reference: 2017 National Electrical Code – Chapter 6 Special Equipment, Article 690 Solar Photovoltaic (PV) Systems. 690.31 Methods Permitted. 690.31(B) Identification and Grouping. 690.31(B)(2) Grouping.

162. **Answer B.** listed and labeled

    Single-conductor cable Type USE-2 and *single conductor cable listed and identified as photovoltaic* (PV) wire shall be permitted in exposed outdoor locations in PV source circuits within the PV array. PV wire shall be installed in accordance with 338.10(B)(4)(b) and 334.30.

    Reference: 2017 National Electrical Code – Chapter 6 Special Equipment, Article 690 Solar Photovoltaic (PV) Systems. 690.31 Methods Permitted. 690.31(C) Single-Conductor Cable. 690.31(C)(1) General.

EXAM 10
EXAM 10 ANSWERS

163. **Answer A.** True

Single-conductor cable Type USE-2 and single conductor cable listed and identified as photovoltaic (PV) wire shall be permitted in exposed outdoor locations in PV source circuits within the PV array. PV wire shall be installed in accordance with 338.10(B)(4)(b) and 334.30.

Reference: 2017 National Electrical Code – Chapter 6 Special Equipment, Article 690 Solar Photovoltaic (PV) Systems. 690.31 Methods Permitted. 690.31(C) Single-Conductor Cable. 690.31(C)(1) General.

All raceway and cable wiring methods included in this Code, other wiring systems and fittings specifically listed for use on PV arrays, and wiring as part of a listed system shall be permitted. Where wiring devices with integral enclosures are used, sufficient length of cable shall be provided to facilitate replacement.

Where PV source and output circuits operating at voltages greater than 30 volts are installed in readily accessible locations, circuit conductors shall be guarded or installed in Type MC cable or in raceway. For ambient temperatures exceeding 30°C (86°F), conductor ampacities shall be corrected

Reference: 2017 National Electrical Code – Chapter 6 Special Equipment, Article 690 Solar Photovoltaic (PV) Systems. 690.31 Methods Permitted. 690.31(A) Wiring Systems.

164. **Answer D.** any of these

Where PV system dc circuits run inside a building, they shall be contained in metal raceways, Type MC metal-clad cable that complies with 250.118(10), or metal enclosures from the point of penetration of the surface of the building to the first readily accessible disconnecting means. The disconnecting means shall comply with 690.13(B) and (C) and 690.15(A) and (B). The wiring methods shall comply with the additional installation requirements in 690.31(G)(1) through (4).

Reference: 2017 National Electrical Code – Chapter 6 Special Equipment, Article 690 Solar Photovoltaic (PV) Systems. 690.31 Methods Permitted. 690.31(G) Direct-Current Photovoltaic Source and Direct-Current Output Circuits on or Inside a Building.

165. **Answer A.** True

Where circuits are embedded in built-up, laminate, or membrane roofing materials in roof areas not covered by *PV modules and associated equipment, the location of circuits shall be clearly marked using a marking protocol that is approved as being suitable for continuous exposure to sunlight and weather.*

Reference: 2017 National Electrical Code – Chapter 6 Special Equipment, Article 690 Solar Photovoltaic (PV) Systems. 690.31 Methods Permitted. 690.31(G) Direct-Current Photovoltaic Source and Direct-Current Output Circuits on or Inside a Building. 690.31(G)(1) Embedded in Building Surfaces.

166. **Answer B.** 10 ft.

The labels or markings shall be visible after installation. The labels shall be reflective, and all letters shall be capitalized and shall be a minimum height of 9.5 mm (3⁄8 in.) in white on a red background. PV system dc circuit labels shall appear on every section of the wiring system that is separated by enclosures, walls, partitions, ceilings, or floors. *Spacing between labels or markings, or between a label and a marking, shall not be more than 3 m (10 ft).* Labels required by this section shall be suitable for the environment where they are installed.

Reference: 2017 National Electrical Code – Chapter 6 Special Equipment, Article 690 Solar Photovoltaic (PV) Systems. 690.31 Methods Permitted. 690.31(G) Direct-Current Photovoltaic Source and Direct-Current Output Circuits on or Inside a Building. 690.31(G)(4) Marking and Labeling Methods and Locations.

167. **Answer A.** flexible, fine-stranded cables

Flexible, fine-stranded cables shall be terminated only with terminals, lugs, devices, or connectors in accordance with 110.14.

Reference: 2017 National Electrical Code – Chapter 6 Special Equipment, Article 690 Solar Photovoltaic (PV) Systems. 690.31 Methods Permitted. 690.31(H) Flexible, Fine-Stranded Cables.

EXAM 10

EXAM 10 ANSWERS

168. **Answer C.** separated

Where the sum, without consideration of polarity, of the voltages of the two monopole subarrays exceeds the rating of the conductors and connected equipment, monopole subarrays in a bipolar PV system shall be physically separated, and the electrical output circuits from each monopole subarray shall be installed in separate raceways until connected to the inverter. The disconnecting means and overcurrent protective devices for each monopole subarray output shall be in separate enclosures. All conductors from each separate monopole subarray shall be routed in the same raceway. Solidly grounded bipolar PV systems shall be clearly marked with a permanent, legible warning notice indicating that the disconnection of the grounded conductor(s) may result in overvoltage on the equipment.

Exception: Listed switchgear rated for the maximum voltage between circuits and containing a physical barrier separating the disconnecting means for each monopole subarray shall be permitted to be used instead of disconnecting means in separate enclosures.

Reference: 2017 National Electrical Code – Chapter 6 Special Equipment, Article 690 Solar Photovoltaic (PV) Systems. 690.31 Methods Permitted. 690.31(I) Bipolar Photovoltaic Systems.

169. **Answer D.** A and C

Where PV system dc circuits run inside a building, they shall be contained in metal raceways, Type MC metal-clad cable that complies with 250.118(10), or metal enclosures from the point of penetration of the surface of the building to the first readily accessible disconnecting means. The disconnecting means shall comply with 690.13(B) and (C) and 690.15(A) and (B). The wiring methods shall comply with the additional installation requirements in 690.31(G)(1) through (4).

Reference: 2017 National Electrical Code – Chapter 6 Special Equipment, Article 690 Solar Photovoltaic (PV) Systems. 690.31 Methods Permitted. 690.31(G) Module Connection Arrangement.

170. **Answer D.** A through C

Connectors, other than those covered by 690.32, shall comply with 690.33(A) through (E).

(A) Configuration. *The connectors shall be polarized* and shall have a configuration that is non interchangeable with receptacles in other electrical systems on the premises.

(B) Guarding. *The connectors shall be constructed and installed so as to guard against inadvertent contact with live parts by persons.*

(C) Type. The connectors shall be of the latching or locking type. Connectors that are *readily accessible and that are used in circuits operating at over 30 volts dc or 15 volts ac shall require a tool for opening.*

Reference: 2017 National Electrical Code – Chapter 6 Special Equipment, Article 690 Solar Photovoltaic (PV) Systems. 690.33 Connectors.

171. **Answer A.** True

Junction, pull, and outlet boxes located behind modules or panels shall be so installed that the wiring contained in them can be rendered accessible directly or by displacement of a module(s) or panel(s) secured by removable fasteners and connected by a flexible wiring system.

Reference: 2017 National Electrical Code – Chapter 6 Special Equipment, Article 690 Solar Photovoltaic (PV) Systems. 690.34 Access to Boxes.

172. **Answer C.** ground-fault protection

DC PV arrays shall be provided with dc ground-fault protection meeting the requirements of 690.41(B)(1) and (2) to reduce fire hazards.

Reference: 2017 National Electrical Code – Chapter 6 Special Equipment, Article 690 Solar Photovoltaic (PV) Systems. 690.41(b) Ground-Fault Protection.

EXAM 10

EXAM 10 ANSWERS

173. Answer A. 2-wire

One or more of the following system grounding configurations shall be employed:

(1) 2-wire PV arrays with one functional grounded conductor

(2) Bipolar PV arrays according to 690.7(C) with a functional ground reference (center tap)

(3) PV arrays not isolated from the grounded inverter output circuit

(4) Ungrounded PV arrays

(5) Solidly grounded PV arrays as permitted in 690.41(B) Exception

(6) PV systems that use other methods that accomplish equivalent system protection in accordance with 250.4(A) with equipment listed and identified for the use

Reference: 2017 National Electrical Code – Chapter 6 Special Equipment, Article 690 Solar Photovoltaic (PV) Systems. 690.41 System Grounding.

174. Answer A. single

Systems with a ground-fault protective device in accordance with 690.41(B) shall have any current-carrying conductor-to-ground connection made by the ground-fault protective device. For solidly grounded PV systems, *the dc circuit grounding connection shall be made at any single point on the PV output circuit.*

Reference: 2017 National Electrical Code – Chapter 6 Special Equipment, Article 690 Solar Photovoltaic (PV) Systems. 690.42 Point of System Grounding Connection.

175. Answer A. identified

Devices and systems used for mounting PV modules that are also used for bonding module frames shall be listed, labeled, and identified for bonding PV modules. Devices that mount adjacent PV modules shall be permitted to bond adjacent PV modules.

Reference: 2017 National Electrical Code – Chapter 6 Special Equipment, Article 690 Solar Photovoltaic (PV) Systems. 690.43 Equipment Grounding. 690.43(A) Photovoltaic Mounting Systems and Devices.

176. Answer D. All of the above

Devices and systems *used for mounting PV modules that are also used for bonding module frames shall be listed, labeled*, and *identified* for bonding PV modules. *Devices that mount adjacent PV modules shall be permitted to bond adjacent PV modules.*

Reference: 2017 National Electrical Code – Chapter 6 Special Equipment, Article 690 Solar Photovoltaic (PV) Systems. 690.43 Equipment Grounding. 690.43(E) Adjacent Modules.

177. Answer A. equipment grounding conductor

Devices listed, labeled, and identified for bonding and grounding the metal parts of PV systems shall be permitted to bond the equipment to grounded metal supports. Metallic support structures shall have identified bonding jumpers connected between separate metallic sections or shall be identified *for equipment bonding and shall be connected to the equipment grounding conductor.*

Reference: 2017 National Electrical Code – Chapter 6 Special Equipment, Article 690 Solar Photovoltaic (PV) Systems. 690.43 Equipment Grounding. 690.43(B) Equipment Grounding Conductor Required.

178. Answer D. both B and C

Devices listed, labeled, and identified for bonding and grounding the metal parts of PV systems shall be permitted to bond the equipment to grounded metal supports. Metallic support structures shall have identified bonding jumpers connected between separate metallic sections or shall be identified for equipment bonding and shall be connected to the equipment grounding conductor.

Reference: 2017 National Electrical Code – Chapter 6 Special Equipment, Article 690 Solar Photovoltaic (PV) Systems. 690.43 Equipment Grounding. 690.43(C) Structure as Equipment Grounding Conductor.

EXAM 10

EXAM 10 ANSWERS

179. Answer A.   identified, identified

Devices listed, labeled, and identified for bonding and grounding the metal parts of PV systems shall be permitted to bond the equipment to grounded metal supports. *Metallic support structures shall have identified bonding jumpers connected between separate metallic sections or shall be identified for equipment bonding and shall be connected to the equipment grounding conductor.*

Reference: 2017 National Electrical Code – Chapter 6 Special Equipment, Article 690 Solar Photovoltaic (PV) Systems. 690.43 Equipment Grounding. 690.43(C) Structure as Equipment Grounding Conductor.

180. Answer A.   True

Equipment grounding conductors for the PV array and support structure (where installed) *shall be contained within the same raceway, cable, or otherwise run with the PV array circuit conductors when those circuit conductors leave the vicinity of the PV array.*

Reference: 2017 National Electrical Code – Chapter 6 Special Equipment, Article 690 Solar Photovoltaic (PV) Systems. 690.43 Equipment Grounding. 690.43(C) With Circuit Conductors.

181. Answer A.   250.122

Equipment grounding conductors for PV source and PV output circuits shall be sized in accordance with 250.122. Where no overcurrent protective device is used in the circuit, an *assumed overcurrent device rated in accordance with 690.9(B) shall be used when applying Table 250.122.* Increases in equipment grounding conductor size to address voltage drop considerations shall not be required. An equipment grounding conductor shall not be smaller than 14 AWG.

Reference: 2017 National Electrical Code – Chapter 6 Special Equipment, Article 690 Solar Photovoltaic (PV) Systems. 690.45 Size of Equipment Grounding Conductors.

182. Answer C.   Table 250.122

Equipment grounding conductors for PV source and PV output circuits shall be sized in accordance with 250.122. Where no overcurrent protective device is used in the circuit, an assumed overcurrent device rated in accordance with 690.9(B) shall be used when applying Table 250.122. Increases in equipment grounding conductor size to address voltage drop considerations shall not be required. An equipment grounding conductor shall not be smaller than 14 AWG.

Reference: 2017 National Electrical Code – Chapter 6 Special Equipment, Article 690 Solar Photovoltaic (PV) Systems. 690.45 Size of Equipment Grounding Conductors.

183. Answer B.   False

For PV modules, equipment grounding conductors smaller than 6 AWG shall comply with 250.120(C).

Reference: 2017 National Electrical Code – Chapter 6 Special Equipment, Article 690 Solar Photovoltaic (PV) Systems. 690.46 Array Equipment Grounding Conductors. Where not routed with circuit conductors as permitted in 250.130(C) and 250.134(B) Exception No. 2, equipment grounding conductors *smaller than 6 AWG shall be protected from physical damage by an identified raceway or cable armor unless installed within hollow spaces of the framing members of buildings or structures and where not subject to physical damage.*

Reference: 2017 National Electrical Code – Chapter 2 Wiring and Protection, Article 250 Grounding and Bonding. 250.120(C)

184. Answer D.   ground and roof-mounted

Grounding electrodes shall be permitted to be installed in accordance with 250.52 and 250.54 at the location of ground and roof-mounted PV arrays. The electrodes shall be permitted to be connected directly to the array frame(s) or structure. The grounding electrode conductor shall be sized according to 250.66. The structure of a ground-mounted PV array shall be permitted to be considered a grounding electrode if it meets the requirements of 250.52. Roof mounted PV arrays shall be permitted to use the metal frame of a building or structure if the requirements of 250.52(A)(2) are met.

Reference: 2017 National Electrical Code – Chapter 6 Special Equipment, Article 690 Solar Photovoltaic (PV) Systems. 690.47 Grounding Electrode System. 690.47(B) Additional Auxiliary Electrodes for Array Grounding.

EXAM 10
EXAM 10 ANSWERS

185. **Answer B.** operating current

Modules shall be marked with identification of terminals or leads as to polarity, maximum overcurrent device rating for module protection, and with the following ratings:

(1) Open-circuit voltage

(2) Operating voltage

(3) Maximum permissible system voltage

(4) Operating current

(5) Short-circuit current

(6) Maximum power

Reference: 2017 National Electrical Code – Chapter 6 Special Equipment, Article 690 Solar Photovoltaic (PV) Systems. 690.51 Modules.

186. **Answer D.** must bond dc grounding system the ac grounding system.

When fuel cell power systems have both alternating-current (ac) and *direct-current (dc) grounding requirements, the dc grounding system shall be bonded to the ac grounding system*. The bonding conductor shall be sized according to 692.45. A single common grounding electrode and grounding bar may be used for both systems, in which case the common grounding electrode conductor shall be sized to meet the requirements of both 250.66 (ac) and 250.166 (dc).

Reference: 2017 National Electrical Code – Chapter 6 Special Equipment, Article 690 Solar Photovoltaic (PV) Systems. 692.41 Grounding Electrode System. 694.1(C) Systems with Alternating-Current and Direct-Current Grounding Requirements.

187. **Answer C.** Polarity

The PV system output circuit conductors shall be marked to indicate the polarity where connected to energy storage systems.

Reference: 2017 National Electrical Code – Chapter 6 Special Equipment, Article 690 Solar Photovoltaic (PV) Systems. 690.55 Photovoltaic Systems Connected to Energy Storage. Systems.

188. **Answer D.** A through C

A permanent label for the dc PV power source indicating the information specified in (1) through (3) shall be provided by the installer at dc PV system disconnecting means and at each dc equipment disconnecting means required by 690.15. Where a disconnecting means has more than one dc PV power source, the values in 690.53(1) through (3) shall be specified for each source.

(1) Maximum voltage

Informational Note to (1): See 690.7 for voltage.

(2) Maximum circuit current

Informational Note to (2): See 690.8(A) for calculation of maximum circuit current.

(3) *Maximum rated output current of the charge controller or dc-to-dc converter (if installed)*

Reference: 2017 National Electrical Code – Chapter 6 Special Equipment, Article 690 Solar Photovoltaic (PV) Systems. 690.53 Direct-Current Photovoltaic Power Source.

189. **Answer B.** disconnecting means

All interactive system(s) points of interconnection with other sources shall be marked at an accessible location at the *disconnecting means as a power source and with the rated ac output current and the nominal operating ac voltage.*

Reference: 2017 National Electrical Code – Chapter 6 Special Equipment, Article 690 Solar Photovoltaic (PV) Systems. 690.54 Interactive System Point of Interconnection.

190. **Answer D.** either A or B

Any structure or building with a PV power system that is not connected to a utility service source and is *a stand-alone system shall have a permanent plaque or directory installed on the exterior of the building or structure at a readily visible location.* The plaque or directory shall indicate the location of system disconnecting means and that the structure contains a stand-alone electrical power system.

Reference: 2017 National Electrical Code – Chapter 6 Special Equipment, Article 690 Solar Photovoltaic (PV) Systems. 690.56 Identification of Power Sources. 690.56(A) Facilities with Stand-Alone Systems.

EXAM 10

EXAM 10 ANSWERS

191. Answer D. either A or B

Plaques or directories shall be installed in accordance with 705.10.

Reference: 2017 National Electrical Code – Chapter 6 Special Equipment, Article 690 Solar Photovoltaic (PV) Systems. 690.56 Identification of Power Sources. 690.56(B) Facilities with Utility Services and Photovoltaic Systems. *A permanent plaque or directory denoting the location of all electric power source* disconnecting means on or in the premises shall be installed at each service *equipment location and at the location(s) of the system disconnect(s)* for all electric power production sources capable of being interconnected. The marking shall comply with 110.21(B).

Reference: 2017 National Electrical Code – Chapter 7 Special Conditions, Article 705 Interconnected Electric Power Production Sources. 705.10 Directory.

192. Answer A. True

Only inverters that are listed, labeled, and identified as interactive shall be permitted in interactive systems.

Reference: 2017 National Electrical Code – Chapter 6 Special Equipment, Article 690 Solar Photovoltaic (PV) Systems. 694.60 Identified Interactive Equipment.

193. Answer A. loss

The fuel cell system shall be provided with a means of detecting when the electrical production and distribution network has become de-energized and shall not feed the electrical production and distribution network side of the point of common coupling during this condition. The fuel cell system shall remain in that state until the electrical production and distribution network voltage has been restored.

A normally interactive fuel cell system shall be permitted to operate as a stand-alone system to supply loads that have been disconnected from electrical production and distribution network sources.

Reference: 2017 National Electrical Code – Chapter 6 Special Equipment, Article 690 Solar Photovoltaic (PV) Systems. 690.61 **Loss of Interactive System Power.**

194. Answer A. automatically de-energize its output

The fuel cell system shall be provided with a means of detecting when the electrical production and distribution network has *become de-energized and shall not feed the electrical production and distribution network side of the point of common coupling during this condition.* The fuel cell system shall remain in that state until the electrical production and distribution network voltage has been restored.

A normally interactive fuel cell system shall be permitted to operate as a stand-alone system to supply loads that have been disconnected from electrical production and distribution network sources.

Reference: 2017 National Electrical Code – Chapter 6 Special Equipment, Article 690 Solar Photovoltaic (PV) Systems. 690.61 Loss of Interactive System Power.

195. Answer D. both A and C

The PV source circuit shall be considered to comply with the requirements of 706.23 if:

(1) The PV source circuit is matched to the voltage rating and charge current requirements of the interconnected battery cells and,

(2) The maximum charging current multiplied by 1 hour is less than 3 percent of the rated battery capacity expressed in ampere-hours or as recommended by the battery manufacturer

Reference: 2017 National Electrical Code – Chapter 6 Special Equipment, Article 690 Solar Photovoltaic (PV) Systems. 690.72 Self-Regulated PV Charge Control.

EXAM 10
EXAM 10 ANSWERS

196. Answer C. 5000 kW

This article covers the installation of large-scale PV electric power production facilities with a generating capacity of no less than 5000 kW, and not under exclusive utility control.

Informational Note No. 1: Facilities covered by this article have specific design and safety features unique to large-scale PV facilities and are operated for the sole purpose of providing electric supply to a system operated by a regulated utility for the transfer of electric energy.

Informational Note No. 2: Section 90.2(B)(5) includes information about utility-owned properties not covered under this Code. For additional information on electric supply stations, see ANSI/IEEE C2-2012, National Electrical Safety Code.

Reference: 2017 National Electrical Code – Chapter 6 Special Equipment, Article 690 Solar Photovoltaic (PV) Systems. 690.71 Installation. 690.71(C) Current Limiting.

197. Answer B. 2/0 AWG

Flexible cables, as identified in Article 400, in sizes 2/0 AWG and larger shall be permitted within the battery enclosure from battery terminals to a nearby junction box where they shall be connected to an approved wiring method. Flexible battery cables shall also be permitted between batteries and cells within the battery enclosure. Such cables shall be listed for hard-service use and identified as moisture resistant.

Flexible, fine-stranded cables shall be terminated only with terminals, lugs, devices, or connectors in accordance with 110.14.

Reference: 2017 National Electrical Code – Chapter 7 Special Conditions, Article 708 Critical Operations Power Systems (COPS). 706.32 Battery Interconnections.

198. Answer A. True

Flexible cables, as identified in Article 400, in sizes 2/0 AWG and larger shall be permitted within the battery enclosure from battery terminals to a nearby junction box where they shall be connected to an approved wiring method. Flexible battery cables shall also be permitted between batteries and cells within the battery enclosure. Such cables shall be listed for hard-service use and identified as moisture resistant.

Flexible, fine-stranded cables shall be terminated only with terminals, lugs, devices, or connectors in accordance with 110.14.

Reference: 2017 National Electrical Code – Chapter 7 Special Conditions, Article 708 Critical Operations Power Systems (COPS). 706.32 Battery Interconnections.

199. Answer D. both A and B

Flexible cables, as identified in Article 400, in sizes 2/0 AWG and larger shall be permitted within the battery enclosure from battery terminals to a nearby junction box where they shall be connected to an approved wiring method. Flexible battery cables shall also be permitted between batteries and cells within the battery enclosure. Such cables shall be listed for hard-service use and identified as moisture resistant.

Flexible, fine-stranded cables shall be terminated only with terminals, lugs, devices, or connectors in accordance with 110.14.

Reference: 2017 National Electrical Code – Chapter 7 Special Conditions, Article 708 Critical Operations Power Systems (COPS). 706.32 Battery Interconnections. Because of different characteristics of dissimilar metals, devices such as pressure terminal or pressure splicing connectors and soldering lugs shall be identified for the material of the conductor and shall be properly installed and used. Conductors of dissimilar metals shall not be intermixed in a terminal or splicing connector where physical contact occurs between dissimilar conductors (such as copper and aluminum, copper and copper-clad aluminum, or aluminum and copper-clad aluminum), unless the device is identified for the purpose and conditions of use. Materials such as solder, fluxes, inhibitors, and compounds, where employed, shall be suitable for the use and shall be of a type that will not adversely affect the conductors, installation, or equipment.

Connectors and terminals for conductors more finely stranded than Class B and Class C stranding as shown in Chapter 9, Table 10, shall be identified for the specific conductor class or classes.

Reference: 2017 National Electrical Code – Chapter 1 General, Article 110 Requirements for Electrical Installations. 110.14 Electrical Connections

EXAM 11

Chapter 7 Special Conditions

1. Emergency power systems are intended to automatically supply power and/or illumination that is essential for _____ and are legally required and classed as emergency by any governmental agency having jurisdiction.

    A. community activity

    B. police and emergency services exclusively

    C. public recreation

    D. safety to human life

    Reference: 2017 National Electrical Code – Chapter 7 Special Conditions, Article 700 Emergency Systems. 700.2 Definitions

2. The authority having jurisdiction will require periodic maintenance of batteries in auxiliary engines that are used for:

    A. control or ignition

    B. starting

    C. Both A and B

    D. none of these

    Reference: 2017 National Electrical Code – Chapter 7 Special Conditions, Article 700 Emergency Systems. 700.3 Tests and Maintenance. 700.3(C) Maintenance.

3. In an emergency system, how much of the loads should it have the rating and capacity to operate simultaneously?

    A. 80% of the loads

    B. 125% of the load

    C. all loads

    D. none of these

    Reference: 2017 National Electrical Code – Chapter 7 Special Conditions, Article 700 Emergency Systems. 700.4 Capacity. 700.4(A) Capacity and Rating.

4. Which of the following is a requirement of emergency systems transfer equipment, including transfer switches?

    A. approved by the authority having jurisdiction

    B. automatic

    C. identified for emergency use

    D. all of these

    Reference: 2017 National Electrical Code – Chapter 7 Special Conditions, Article 700 Emergency Systems. 700.5 Transfer Equipment. 700.5(A) General.

Chapter 7 Special Conditions

EXAM 11

Chapter 7 Special Conditions

5. Which of the following is an emergency transfer switch for emergency systems required to supply?

   A. computer equipment

   B. emergency loads

   C. UPS equipment

   D. all of these

   Reference: 2017 National Electrical Code – Chapter 7 Special Conditions, Article 700 Emergency Systems. 700.5 Transfer Equipment. 700.5(D) Use.

6. Emergency source distribution overcurrent protection to emergency loads, or emergency source wiring must be kept separate of all other equipment and wiring except when in:

   A. exit or emergency luminaires supplied from two sources

   B. listed load control relays supplying emergency or exit luminaires

   C. transfer equipment enclosures

   D. all of these

   Reference: 2017 National Electrical Code – Chapter 7 Special Conditions, Article 700 Emergency Systems. 700.10 Wiring, Emergency System. 700.10(B) Wiring.

7. Wiring circuits for emergency systems must be located and designed to minimize any hazards that would possibly cause failure due to:

   A. fire

   B. icing

   C. vandalism

   D. all of these

   Reference: 2017 National Electrical Code – Chapter 7 Special Conditions, Article 700 Emergency Systems. 700.10 Wiring, Emergency System. 700.10(C) Wiring Design and Location.

EXAM 11

Chapter 7 Special Conditions

8. Equipment for emergency systems shall be designed and located so as to minimize the hazards that might cause complete failure due to:

   A. fires

   B. flooding

   C. icing, and vandalism

   D. all of these

   Reference: 2017 National Electrical Code – Chapter 7 Special Conditions, Article 700 Emergency Systems. 700.12 General Requirements.

9. What type of batteries are not allowed to be used as a power source in an emergency?

   A. alkali type

   B. automotive

   C. lead acid type

   D. all of these

   Reference: 2017 National Electrical Code – Chapter 7 Special Conditions, Article 700 Emergency Systems. 700.12 General Requirements. 700.12(A) Storage Battery.

10. If the prime mover for an emergency system is an internal-combustion engine, it is required to have on-premises fuel storage that will give at least how many hours of system operation at full-demand?

    A. 2

    B. 3

    C. 4

    D. 5

    Reference: 2017 National Electrical Code – Chapter 7 Special Conditions, Article 700 Emergency Systems. 700.12 General Requirements. 700.12(B)(2) Generator Set. 700.12(B)(2) Internal Combustion Engines as Prime Movers.

Chapter 7 Special Conditions

EXAM 11
Chapter 7 Special Conditions

11. True or False: The disconnecting means for an emergency system power generator that is installed outdoors is not required to be within sight of the structure or building being served if documented safe switching procedures are established and maintained for disconnection, and the conditions of supervision and maintenance ensure that only qualified persons will service and monitor the installation.

    A. True

    B. False

    Reference: 2017 National Electrical Code – Chapter 7 Special Conditions, Article 700 Emergency Systems. 700.12 General Requirements. 700.12(B) Generator Set. 700.12(B)(6) Outdoor Generator Sets.

12. Only lamps and appliances required for emergency use may be supplied in emergency systems by:

    A. emergency circuits

    B. HID-rated circuit breakers

    C. multiwire branch circuits

    D. Both A and B

    Reference: 2017 National Electrical Code – Chapter 7 Special Conditions, Article 700 Emergency Systems. 700.15 Loads on Emergency Branch Circuits.

13. True or False: It is not required for plug-in type backfed circuit breakers for a multimode or stand-alone inverter attached to a stand-alone PV system to be secured in place with additional fasteners that require more than a pull to release the breaker from the panelboard.

    A. True

    B. False

    Reference: 2017 National Electrical Code – Chapter 7 Special Conditions, Article 712 Direct Current Microgrids. 710.15 General. 710.15(E) Back-Fed Circuit Breakers.

14. True or False: It is allowable for circuit breakers on stand-alone PV systems marked "Line" and "Load" to be backfed.

    A. True

    B. False

    Reference: 2017 National Electrical Code – Chapter 7 Special Conditions, Article 712 Direct Current Microgrids. 710.15 General. 710.15(E) Back-Fed Circuit Breakers.

EXAM 11

Chapter 7 Special Conditions

15. In emergency circuits, branch-circuit overcurrent devices are accessible only to:

    A. authorized persons

    B. qualified persons

    C. the authority having jurisdiction

    D. the general public

    Reference: 2017 National Electrical Code – Chapter 7 Special Conditions, Article 700 Emergency Systems. 700.30 Accessibility.

16. All supply-side overcurrent devices _____ overcurrent devices for emergency power systems.

    A. can be selectively coordinated with

    B. shall be a higher amperage than

    C. shall be selectively coordinated with

    D. shall be the same amperage as

    Reference: 2017 National Electrical Code – Chapter 7 Special Conditions, Article 700 Emergency Systems. 700.32 Selective Coordination.

17. A test of the complete legally required standby system when installed must be conducted and witnessed by the:

    A. authority having jurisdiction

    B. electrical engineer

    C. manufacturer's representative

    D. qualified person

    Reference: 2017 National Electrical Code – Chapter 7 Special Conditions, Article 701 Legally Required Standby Systems. 701.3 Tests and Maintenance. 701.3(A) Conduct or Witness Test.

18. The authority having jurisdiction must require periodic maintenance of batteries that are used for _____ of prime movers in legally required standby systems.

    A. control

    B. starting or ignition

    C. Both A and B

    D. none of these

    Reference: 2017 National Electrical Code – Chapter 7 Special Conditions, Article 701 Legally Required Standby Systems. 701.3 Tests and Maintenance. 701.3(C) Maintenance.

Chapter 7 Special Conditions

EXAM 11

Chapter 7 Special Conditions

19. A legally required standby system must have rating and capacity sufficient for how much of the loads expected to operate at the same time on the standby system?

    A. 80% of the loads

    B. 100% of the loads

    C. 125% of the loads

    D. none of these

    Reference: 2017 National Electrical Code – Chapter 7 Special Conditions, Article 701 Legally Required Standby Systems. 701.4 Capacity and Rating.

20. Which of the following requirements is relevant for transfer equipment, including automatic transfer switches, on legally required standby systems?

    A. approved by the authority having jurisdiction

    B. automatic

    C. identified for standby use

    D. all of these

    Reference: 2017 National Electrical Code – Chapter 7 Special Conditions, Article 701 Legally Required Standby Systems. 701.5 Transfer Equipment. 701.5(A) General.

21. For on-site legally required standby power sources, it is required to have a sign at the service equipment showing which of the following?

    A. location

    B. manufacturer

    C. type

    D. Both A and C

    Reference: 2017 National Electrical Code – Chapter 7 Special Conditions, Article 701 Legally Required Standby Systems. 701.7 Signs. 701.7(A) Mandated Standby.

EXAM 11

Chapter 7 Special Conditions

22. Connections ahead of and not within the same vertical switchgear section, vertical switchboard section, enclosure, or cabinet as the service disconnecting means may be allowed for _____ standby service, with the approval of the authority having jurisdiction.

    A. emergency

    B. legally required

    C. optional

    D. all of these

    Reference: 2017 National Electrical Code – Chapter 7 Special Conditions, Article 701 Legally Required Standby Systems. 701.12 General Requirements. 701.12(E) Connection Ahead of Service Disconnecting Means.

23. True or False: Ground-fault-protection of equipment is not required for the alternate source for legally required standby systems.

    A. True

    B. False

    Reference: 2017 National Electrical Code – Chapter 7 Special Conditions, Article 701 Legally Required Standby Systems. 701.26 Ground-Fault Protection of Equipment.

24. Which type of optional standby systems used for backup power in public or private facilities, or property where life safety does not depend on the performance of the system, is covered in Article 702?

    A. permanently installed

    B. portable

    C. both A and B

    D. none of these

    Reference: 2017 National Electrical Code – Chapter 7 Special Conditions, Article 702 Optional Standby Systems. 702.2 Definition.

Chapter 7 Special Conditions   597

EXAM 11

Chapter 7 Special Conditions

25. An optional standby system that uses automatic transfer equipment must have rating and capacity sufficient for the supply of:

    A. all emergency lighting and power loads

    B. the load, as calculated in Article 220

    C. 100% of appliance loads & 50% of lighting loads

    D. 100% of lighting loads & 75% of appliance loads

    Reference: 2017 National Electrical Code – Chapter 7 Special Conditions, Article 702 Optional Standby Systems. 702.4 Capacity and Rating. 702.4(B) System Capacity. 702.4(B) (2) Automatic Transfer Equipment.

26. The temporary connection of a portable generator without transfer equipment may be allowed for optional standby systems, provided that maintenance and supervision make certain that only qualified persons service the installation, and the normal supply is physically isolated by:

    A. a lockable disconnecting means

    B. an extended power outage

    C. the disconnection of the normal supply conductors

    D. either A or C

    Reference: 2017 National Electrical Code – Chapter 7 Special Conditions, Article 702 Optional Standby Systems. 702.5 Transfer Equipment.

27. True or False: The wiring for an optional standby system may be located with other more general wiring in the same boxes, cabinets, cables, and raceways.

    A. True

    B. False

    Reference: 2017 National Electrical Code – Chapter 7 Special Conditions, Article 702 Optional Standby Systems. 702.10 Wiring Optional Standby Systems.

EXAM 11

Chapter 7 Special Conditions

28. Which article covers the installation of electric power production services that operate parallel with a more primary source of electricity?

    A. 700

    B. 701

    C. 702

    D. 705

    Reference: 2017 National Electrical Code – Chapter 7 Special Conditions, Article 705 Interconnected Electric Power Production Sources. 705.1 Scope.

29. What is the correct term for the generating source and all distribution equipment associated with an interconnected electric power production source that generates electricity from a source other than a utility supplied service?

    A. a service drop

    B. power production equipment

    C. the service point

    D. utilization equipment

    Reference: 2017 National Electrical Code – Chapter 7 Special Conditions, Article 705 Interconnected Electric Power Production Sources. 705.2 Definitions.

30. The installation of one or more electric power production sources operating in parallel for interconnected electric power production sources must only be done by:

    A. a utility company

    B. qualified persons

    C. the authority having jurisdiction

    D. Either B or C

    Reference: 2017 National Electrical Code – Chapter 7 Special Conditions, Article 705 Interconnected Electric Power Production Sources. 705.8 System Installation.

Chapter 7 Special Conditions

EXAM 11

Chapter 7 Special Conditions

31. A permanent _____, denoting all electric power sources on or in the premises, shall be installed at each service equipment location and at locations of all electric power production sources capable of being interconnected.

    A. directory

    B. label

    C. plaque

    D. Either A or C

    Reference: 2017 National Electrical Code – Chapter 7 Special Conditions, Article 705 Interconnected Electric Power Production Sources. 705.10 Directory.

32. True or False: An electric power production source is allowed to be connected to the supply side of the service disconnecting means, for interconnected electric power production sources.

    A. True

    B. False

    Reference: 2017 National Electrical Code – Chapter 7 Special Conditions, Article 705 Interconnected Electric Power Production Sources. 705.12 Point of Connection. 705.12(A) Supply Side.

33. True or False: The sum of the ratings of all overcurrent devices for interconnected electric power production sources is allowed to be more than the rating of the service.

    A. True

    B. False

    Reference: 2017 National Electrical Code – Chapter 7 Special Conditions, Article 705 Interconnected Electric Power Production Sources. 705.12 Point of Connection. 705.12(A) Supply Side.

EXAM 11

Chapter 7 Special Conditions

34. True or False: The output of a utility-interactive inverter for an interconnected electric power production source may connect to the load side of the service disconnecting means at any distribution equipment located on the property.

    A. True   B. False

    Reference: A. 2017 National Electrical Code – Chapter 7 Special Conditions, Article 705 Interconnected Electric Power Production Sources. 705.12 Point of Connection. 705.12(B) Load Side.

35. True or False: A dedicated circuit breaker or fusible disconnecting means is where the source interconnection of one or more inverters installed in one system.

    A. True   B. False

    Reference: 2017 National Electrical Code – Chapter 7 Special Conditions, Article 705 Interconnected Electric Power Production Sources. 705.12 Point of Connection. 705.12(B) Load Side. 705.12(B) (1) Dedicated Overcurrent and Disconnect.

36. True or False: Where two sources, one an inverter and the other a utility, are located at either end of a busbar containing loads, according to Article 705, a permanent warning label must be affixed to the panelboard so that other are warned not to relocate the inverter output connection circuit breaker.

    A. True   B. False

    Reference: 2017 National Electrical Code – Chapter 7 Special Conditions, Article 705 Interconnected Electric Power Production Sources. 705.12 Point of Connection. 705.12(B) Load Side. 705.12(B) (2) Bus or Conductor Ampere Rating. 705.12(B)(2)(3)(B)Busbars

37. True or False: Panelboards containing ac inverter circuit breakers for interconnected electric power production sources are required to be field marked to show the presence of more than one ac power source.

    A. True   B. False

    Reference: 2017 National Electrical Code – Chapter 7 Special Conditions, Article 705 Interconnected Electric Power Production Sources. 705.12 Point of Connection. 705.12(B) Load Side. 705.12(B)(3) Marking.

Chapter 7 Special Conditions

EXAM 11
Chapter 7 Special Conditions

38. _____ are suitable for backfeeding unless otherwise marked on interconnected electric power production sources.

    A. Circuit breakers

    B. Fused disconnects

    C. PV system overcurrent devices

    D. Utility-interactive inverters

    Reference: 2017 National Electrical Code – Chapter 7 Special Conditions, Article 705 Interconnected Electric Power Production Sources. 705.12 Point of Connection. 705.12(B) Load Side. 705.12(B)(4) Suitable for Backfeed.

39. True or False: In accordance with 408.36(D), dedicated ac inverter circuit breakers for interconnected electric power production sources that are backfed are required to have an additional fastener securing them in place.

    A. True

    B. False

    Reference: 2017 National Electrical Code – Chapter 7 Special Conditions, Article 705 Interconnected Electric Power Production Sources. 705.12 Point of Connection. 705.12(B) Load Side. 705.12(B)(5) Fastening.

40. True or False: Upon loss of utility source power on an interconnected electric power production source, it must be manually disconnected from all ungrounded conductors and may not be reconnected to the utility source until it has been restored.

    A. True

    B. False

    Reference: 2017 National Electrical Code – Chapter 7 Special Conditions, Article 705 Interconnected Electric Power Production Sources. 705.40 Loss of Primary Source.

41. True or False: If Class 2 and Class 3 cable is not identified for future use and not terminated at equipment it shall be considered abandoned.

    A. True

    B. False

    Reference: 2017 National Electrical Code – Chapter 7 Special Conditions, Article 725 Class 1, Class 2, and Class 3 Remote-Control, Signaling, and Power-Limited Circuits. 725.2 Definitions.

EXAM 11

Chapter 7 Special Conditions

42. Additional _____ are required to give protection against electric shock hazards, since Class 3 control circuits allow higher levels of current and voltage than Class 2 control circuits.

    A. circuits

    B. conditions

    C. requirements

    D. safeguards

    Reference: 2017 National Electrical Code – Chapter 7 Special Conditions, Article 725 Class 1, Class 2, and Class 3 Remote-Control, Signaling, and Power-Limited Circuits. 725.2 Definitions.

43. If a raceway containing power-limited, remote-control, and signaling circuits is where condensation is known to be a problem and is subjected to different temperatures, it is required for the raceway to be filled with a material to prevent the circulation of warm air to a colder section of the raceway, that is approved by the authority having jurisdiction. Explosionproof seals:

    A. are required for this purpose

    B. are the only method of doing this

    C. aren't required for this purpose

    D. have been proven effective for this purpose

    Reference: 2017 National Electrical Code Chapter 3 Wiring Methods and Materials, Article 300 General Requirements for Wiring Methods and Materials. 300.7 Raceways Exposed to Different Temperatures. 300.7(A) Sealing.

44. True or False: an accumulation of power-limited, remote-control or signaling wire and cables that prevent removal of panels, including suspended-ceiling panels must not deny access to electrical equipment.

    A. True

    B. False

    Reference: 2017 National Electrical Code – Chapter 7 Special Conditions, Article 725 Class 1, Class 2, and Class 3 Remote-Control, Signaling, and Power-Limited Circuits. 725.21 Access to Electrical Equipment Behind Panels

Chapter 7 Special Conditions

EXAM 11

Chapter 7 Special Conditions

45. True or False: Hangers, staples, straps, or similar fittings design and installed to not damage the cable is required for support of exposed Class 2 and Class 3 cables.

    A. True

    B. False

    Reference: 2017 National Electrical Code – Chapter 7 Special Conditions, Article 725 Class 1, Class 2, and Class 3 Remote-Control, Signaling, and Power-Limited Circuits. 725.24 Mechanical Execution of Work.

46. A tag of sufficient durability to withstand _____ is required to mark Class 2 cables that have been identified for future use.

    A. humidity

    B. moisture

    C. the environment involved

    D. none of these

    Reference: 2017 National Electrical Code – Chapter 7 Special Conditions, Article 725 Class 1, Class 2, and Class 3 Remote-Control, Signaling, and Power-Limited Circuits. 725.25 Abandoned Cables.

47. When are Class 1 circuit conductor and power-supply conductors are allowed to be in the same cable, enclosure, or raceway?

    A. under no circumstances

    B. when both have functional association with equipment

    C. where the circuits involved are not a mixture of ac and dc

    D. none of these

    Reference: 2017 National Electrical Code – Chapter 7 Special Conditions, Article 725 Class 1, Class 2, and Class 3 Remote-Control, Signaling, and Power-Limited Circuits. 725.48 Conductors of Different Circuits in the Same Cable, Cable Tray, Enclosure, or Raceway. 725.48(B) Class 1 Circuits with Power-Supply Circuits. 725.48(B) (1) In a Cable, Enclosure, or Raceway.

EXAM 11

Chapter 7 Special Conditions

48. The NEC allows Class 1 control-circuit conductors and motor branch-circuits to use the same raceway, as long as the control circuit conductors:

    A. Are functionally associated with the motor system

    B. Carry no more than 24 volts

    C. Have a voltage to ground not to exceed 150 volts

    D. Have a voltage to ground not to exceed 277 volts

    Reference: 2017 National Electrical Code – Chapter 7 Special Conditions, Article 725 Class 1, Class 2, and Class 3 Remote-Control, Signaling, and Power-Limited Circuits. 725.48 Conductors of Different Circuits in the Same Cable, Cable Tray, Enclosure or Raceway. 725.48(B) Class 1 Circuits with Power-Supply Circuits. 725.48(B)(1) In A Cable, Enclosure, or Raceway.

49. What should be indicated by durable markings on equipment supplying Class 2 or Class 3 circuits?

    A. conductor size on each circuit

    B. the VA rating of the circuit

    C. whether the circuit is a Class 2 or Class 3

    D. all of these

    Reference: 2017 National Electrical Code – Chapter 7 Special Conditions, Article 725 Class 1, Class 2, and Class 3 Remote-Control, Signaling, and Power-Limited Circuits. 725.124 Circuit Marking.

Chapter 7 Special Conditions

EXAM 11

Chapter 7 Special Conditions

50. When can conductors of Class 2 and Class 3 circuits be placed in the same cable, enclosure, raceway or similar fitting as electric light or power conductors or conductors of Class 1 circuits?

    A. insulated for the maximum voltage present

    B. separated by a barrier

    C. totally comprised of aluminum conductors

    D. all of these

    Reference: 2017 National Electrical Code – Chapter 7 Special Conditions, Article 725 Class 1, Class 2, and Class 3 Remote-Control, Signaling, and Power-Limited Circuits. 725.136 Separation from Electric Light, Power, Class 1, Non-Power-Limited Fire Alarm Circuit Conductors, and Medium-Power Network-Powered Broadband Communications Cables.

51. True or False: Raceways must not be used to support Class 2 or Class 3 cables.

    A. True

    B. False

    Reference: 2017 National Electrical Code – Chapter 7 Special Conditions, Article 725 Class 1, Class 2, and Class 3 Remote-Control, Signaling, and Power-Limited Circuits. 725.143 Support of Conductors.

52. Class 3 single conductors are required to be Type CL3, and must be a minimum of:

    A. 14 AWG

    B. 16 AWG

    C. 18 AWG

    D. 20 AWG

    Reference: 2017 National Electrical Code – Chapter 7 Special Conditions, Article 725 Class 1, Class 2, and Class 3 Remote-Control, Signaling, and Power-Limited Circuits. 725.179 Listing and Marking of Class 2, Class 3, and Type PLTC Cables; Communications Raceways; and Cable Routing Assemblies. 725.179(H) Class 3 Single Conductors.

53. What is the allowable ampacity of size 22 AWG conductors of instrumentation tray cable?

    A. 3 amperes

    B. 5 amperes

    C. 7 amperes

    D. 10 amperes

    Reference: 2017 National Electrical Code – Chapter 7 Special Conditions, Article 727 Instrumentation Tray Cable: Type ITC. 727.8 Allowable Ampacity.

EXAM 11

Chapter 7 Special Conditions

54. Which of the following is included in a fire alarm system?

    A. fire detection and alarm notification

    B. guard's tour

    C. sprinkler waterflow

    D. all of these

    Reference: 2017 National Electrical Code – Chapter 7 Special Conditions, Article 760 Fire Alarm Systems. 760.1 Scope.

55. If a raceway that is subjected to different temperatures, where condensation is known to be a problem, is used for the installation of fire alarm conductors, it is required for the raceway to be filled with a material to prevent the circulation of warm air to colder sections of the raceway that is approved by the authority having jurisdiction. An explosion proof seal:

    A. has been proven effective for this purpose

    B. is required for this purpose

    C. is the only method of doing this

    D. isn't required for this purpose

    Reference: 2017 National Electrical Code Chapter 3 Wiring Methods and Materials, Article 300 General Requirements for Wiring Methods and Materials. 300.7 Raceways Exposed to Different Temperatures. 300.7(A) Sealing.

56. True or False: A bushing to reduce potential abrasion at the place where the cables enter the raceway, when raceways are used to support or protect cables for fire alarm circuits.

    A. True

    B. False

    Reference: 2017 National Electrical Code Chapter 3 Wiring Methods and Materials, Article 300 General Requirements for Wiring Methods and Materials. 300.15 Boxes, Conduit Bodies, or Fittings - Where Required. 300.15(C) Protection.

EXAM 11

Chapter 7 Special Conditions

57. True or False: If fire alarm cable is abandoned, the accessible portions must be removed.

    A. True   B. False

    Reference: 2017 National Electrical Code – Chapter 7 Special Conditions, Article 760 Fire Alarm Systems. 760.25 Abandoned Cables.

58. Fire alarm circuits must be identified at all junction and terminal locations so that prevention of unintentional signals on the fire alarm system circuits during:

    A. installation of the system   C. testing and servicing of other systems

    B. renovations of any systems   D. all of these

    Reference: 2017 National Electrical Code – Chapter 7 Special Conditions, Article 760 Fire Alarm Systems. 760.30 Fire Alarm Circuit Identification.

59. True or False: Either an arc-fault circuit interrupter or a ground-fault circuit interrupter may be used to supply the power source for a power-limited fire alarm circuit.

    A. True   B. False

    Reference: 2017 National Electrical Code – Chapter 7 Special Conditions, Article 760 Fire Alarm Systems. 760.41 NPLFA Circuit Power Source Requirements. 760.41(B) Branch Circuit.

60. Other than utilization equipment, which of the following may be used to contain cable splices or terminations in power-limited fire alarm systems?

    A. boxes or enclosures   C. fittings

    B. fire alarm devices   D. any of these

    Reference: 2017 National Electrical Code – Chapter 7 Special Conditions, Article 760 Fire Alarm Systems. 760.130 Wiring Methods and Materials on Load Side of the PLFA Power Source. 760.130(B) PLFA Wiring Methods and Materials. 760.130(B) (1) In Raceways, Exposed on Ceilings or Sidewalls, or Fished in Concealed Spaces

608   Chapter 7 Special Conditions

EXAM 11

Chapter 7 Special Conditions

61. True or False: The same cable, cable tray, cable routing assembly, enclosure, or raceway may have the cables and conductors for two or more power-limited fire alarm circuits.

    A. True   B. False

    Reference: 2017 National Electrical Code – Chapter 7 Special Conditions, Article 760 Fire Alarm Systems. 760.139 Installation of Conductors of Different PLFA Circuits, Class 2, Class 3, and Communications Circuits in the Same Cable, Enclosure, Cable Tray, Raceway, or Cable Routing Assembly.

62. True or False: It is permissible to Attach, strap, or tape power-limited fire alarm cables to the exterior of a conduit or raceway.

    A. True   B. False

    Reference: 2017 National Electrical Code – Chapter 7 Special Conditions, Article 760 Fire Alarm Systems. 760.143 Support of Conductors.

63. Power-limited fire alarm cable must have a moisture-impervious metal sheath or be listed for the purpose if they are used in what kind of location?

    A. damp   C. hazardous
    B. dry   D. wet

    Reference: 2017 National Electrical Code – Chapter 7 Special Conditions, Article 760 Fire Alarm Systems. 760.179 Listing and Marking of PLFA Cables and Insulated Continuous Line-Type Fire Detectors.

64. What besides optical fibers do composite optical fiber cables contain?

    A. current-carrying electrical conductors   C. vapor barriers
    B. strength members   D. none of these

    Reference: 2017 National Electrical Code – Chapter 1 General, Article 100 Definitions

EXAM 11

Chapter 7 Special Conditions

65. True or False: Nonconductive optical fiber cable is assembled in a factory of one or more optical fibers, has no materials to conduct electricity, and has an overall covering.

    A. True
    B. False

    Reference: 2017 National Electrical Code – Chapter 1 General , Article 100 Definitions

66. An optical fiber installation's point of entrance is the point at which the optical fiber cable emerges from a concrete floor slab, from an external wall, from intermediate metal conduit, or from rigid metal conduit:

    A. on the building
    B. outside a building
    C. within a building
    D. none of these

    Reference: 2017 National Electrical Code – Chapter 1 General , Article 100 Definitions

67. Optical fiber cables on ceiling and walls surfaces must be supported by the building structure so that the cable will not be damaged by normal use of the building if they are:

    A. concealed
    B. exposed
    C. hidden
    D. both A and B

    Reference: 2017 National Electrical Code – Chapter 7 Special Conditions, Article 770 Optical Fiber Cables and Raceways. 770.24 Mechanical Execution of Work.

EXAM 11

Chapter 7 Special Conditions

68. Which of the following describes accepted industry practices for optical fiber installations?

    A. ANSI/NECA/BICSI 568, Standard for Installing Commercial Building Telecommunications Cabling

    B. ANSI/NECA/FOA 301, Standard for Installing and Testing Fiber Optic Cables

    C. other ANSI-approved installation standards

    D. all of these

    Reference: 2017 National Electrical Code – Chapter 7 Special Conditions, Article 770 Optical Fiber Cables and Raceways. 770.24 Mechanical Execution of Work.

69. What must be done with approved ratings, to maintain the fire-resistance rating, to openings around penetrations of raceways for communications and optical fiber cables through fire-resistant-rated ceilings, floors, partitions, and walls?

    A. closed

    B. opened

    C. draft stopped

    D. firestopped

    Reference: 2017 National Electrical Code – Chapter 7 Special Conditions, Article 770 Optical Fiber Cables and Raceways. 770.26 Spread of Fire or Products of Combustion.

EXAM 11
EXAM 11 ANSWERS

1. **Answer D.** safety to human life

   Those systems legally required and classed as emergency by municipal, state, federal, or other codes, or by any governmental agency having jurisdiction. These systems are intended to automatically supply illumination, power, or both, to designated areas and equipment in the event of failure of the normal supply or in the event of accident to elements of a system intended to supply, distribute, and control power and illumination *essential for safety to human life.* (See Figure 700.2).

   Informational Note: Emergency systems are generally installed in places of assembly where artificial illumination is required for safe exiting and for panic control in buildings subject to occupancy by large numbers of persons, such as hotels, theaters, sports arenas, health care facilities, and similar institutions. Emergency systems may also provide power for such functions as ventilation where essential to maintain life, fire detection and alarm systems, elevators, fire pumps, public safety communications systems, industrial processes where current interruption would produce serious life safety or health hazards, and similar functions.

   Reference: 2017 National Electrical Code – Chapter 7 Special Conditions, Article 700 Emergency Systems. 700.2 Definitions. Emergency Systems

2. **Answer C.** Both A and B

   Emergency system equipment shall be maintained in accordance with manufacturer instructions and industry standards.

   Reference: 2017 National Electrical Code – Chapter 7 Special Conditions, Article 700 Emergency Systems. 700.3 Tests and Maintenance. 700.3(C) Maintenance.

3. **Answer C.** all loads

   An emergency system shall have adequate capacity and rating for all loads to be operated simultaneously. The emergency system equipment shall be suitable for the maximum available fault current at its terminals.

   Reference: 2017 National Electrical Code – Chapter 7 Special Conditions, Article 700 Emergency Systems. 700.4 Capacity. 700.4(A) Capacity and Rating.

4. **Answer D.** all of these

   Transfer equipment, including automatic transfer switches, shall be automatic, identified for emergency use, and approved by the authority having jurisdiction. Transfer equipment shall be designed and installed to prevent the inadvertent interconnection of normal and emergency sources of supply in any operation of the transfer equipment. Transfer equipment and electric power production systems installed to permit operation in parallel with the normal source shall meet the requirements of Article 705.

   Reference: 2017 National Electrical Code – Chapter 7 Special Conditions, Article 700 Emergency Systems. 700.5 Transfer Equipment. 700.5(A) General.

5. **Answer B.** emergency loads

   Transfer equipment shall supply only emergency loads.

   Reference: 2017 National Electrical Code – Chapter 7 Special Conditions, Article 700 Emergency Systems. 700.5 Transfer Equipment. 700.5(D) Use.

EXAM 11

EXAM 11 ANSWERS

6. **Answer D.** all of these

   Wiring of two or more emergency circuits supplied from the same source shall be permitted in the same raceway, cable, box, or cabinet. *Wiring from an emergency source or emergency source distribution overcurrent protection to emergency loads shall be kept entirely independent of all other wiring and equipment, unless otherwise permitted in 700.10(B)(1) through (5):*

   (1) *Wiring from the normal power source located in transfer equipment enclosures*

   (2) *Wiring supplied from two sources in exit or emergency luminaires*

   (3) *Wiring from two sources in a listed load control relay supplying exit or emergency luminaires, or in a common junction box, attached to exit or emergency luminaires*

   (4) Wiring within a common junction box attached to unit equipment, containing only the branch circuit supplying the unit equipment and the emergency circuit supplied by the unit equipment

   Reference: 2017 National Electrical Code – Chapter 7 Special Conditions, Article 700 Emergency Systems. 700.10 Wiring, Emergency System. 700.10(B) Wiring.

7. **Answer D.** all of these

   Emergency wiring circuits shall be designed and located so as to minimize the hazards that might cause failure due to flooding, fire, icing, vandalism, and other adverse conditions.

   Reference: 2017 National Electrical Code – Chapter 7 Special Conditions, Article 700 Emergency Systems. 700.10 Wiring, Emergency System. 700.10(C) Wiring Design and Location.

8. **Answer D.** all of these

   Current supply shall be such that, in the event of failure of the normal supply to, or within, the building or group of buildings concerned, emergency lighting, emergency power, or both shall be available within the time required for the application but not to exceed 10 seconds. The supply system for emergency purposes, in addition to the normal services to the building and meeting the general requirements of this section, shall be one or more of the types of systems described in 700.12(A) through (E). Unit equipment in accordance with 700.12(F) shall satisfy the applicable requirements of this article. In selecting an emergency source of power, consideration shall be given to the occupancy and the type of service to be rendered, whether of minimum duration, as for evacuation of a theater, or longer duration, as for supplying emergency power and lighting due to an indefinite period of current failure from trouble either inside or outside the building. Equipment shall be designed and located so as to minimize the hazards that might cause complete failure due to flooding, fires, icing, and vandalism.

   Equipment for sources of power as described in 700.12(A) through (E) shall be installed either in spaces fully protected by approved automatic fire suppression systems (sprinklers, carbon dioxide systems, and so forth) or in spaces with a 1-hour fire rating where located within the following:

   (1) Assembly occupancies for more than 1000 persons

   (2) Buildings above 23 m (75 ft.) in height with any of the following occupancy classes — assembly, educational, residential, detention and correctional, business, and mercantile

   (3) Health care occupancies where persons are not capable of self-preservation

   (4) Educational occupancies with more than 300 occupants

   Informational Note No. 1: For the definition of Occupancy Classification, see Section 6.1 of NFPA 101-2015, Life Safety Code.

   Informational Note No. 2: For further information, see ANSI/

   IEEE 493-2007, Recommended Practice for the Design of Reliable

   Industrial and Commercial Power Systems.

   Reference: 2017 National Electrical Code – Chapter 7 Special Conditions, Article 700 Emergency Systems. 700.12 General Requirements.

EXAM 11 ANSWERS

EXAM 11

EXAM 11 ANSWERS

9. **Answer B.** automotive

   Storage **batteries shall** be of suitable rating and capacity to supply and maintain the total load for a minimum period of 1½ hours, without the voltage applied to the load falling below 87½ percent of normal. **Automotive-type batteries shall not be used.**

   An automatic battery charging means shall be provided.

   Reference: 2017 National Electrical Code – Chapter 7 Special Conditions, Article 700 Emergency Systems. 700.12 General Requirements. 700.12(A) Storage Battery.

10. **Answer A.** 2

    Where internal combustion engines are used as the prime mover, an on-site fuel supply shall be provided with an on-premises fuel supply sufficient for not less than 2 hours' full-demand operation of the system. Where power is needed for the operation of the fuel transfer pumps to deliver fuel to a generator set day tank, this pump shall be connected to the emergency power system.

    Reference: 2017 National Electrical Code – Chapter 7 Special Conditions, Article 700 Emergency Systems. 700.12 General Requirements. 700.12(B)(2) Generator Set. 700.12(B)(2) Internal Combustion Engines as Prime Movers.

11. **Answer A.** True

    Where an outdoor housed generator set is equipped with a readily accessible disconnecting means in accordance with 445.18, and the disconnecting means is located within sight of the building or structure supplied, an additional disconnecting means shall not be required where ungrounded conductors serve or pass through the building or structure. Where the generator supply conductors terminate at a disconnecting means in or on a building or structure, the disconnecting means shall meet the requirements of 225.36.

    Exception: For installations under single management, where conditions of maintenance and supervision ensure that only qualified persons will monitor and service the installation and where documented safe switching procedures are established and maintained for disconnection, the generator set disconnecting means shall not be required to be located within sight of the building or structure served.

    Reference: 2017 National Electrical Code – Chapter 7 Special Conditions, Article 700 Emergency Systems. 700.12 General Requirements. 700.12(B) Generator Set. 700.12(B)(6) Outdoor Generator Sets.

12. **Answer A.** emergency circuits

    No appliances and no lamps, other than those specified as required for emergency use, shall be supplied by emergency lighting circuits.

    Reference: 2017 National Electrical Code – Chapter 7 Special Conditions, Article 700 Emergency Systems. 700.15 Loads on Emergency Branch Circuits.

13. **Answer B.** False

    Plug-in type back-fed circuit breakers connected to a stand-alone or multimode inverter output in stand-alone systems shall be secured in accordance with 408.36(D). Circuit breakers marked "line" and "load" shall not be back-fed.

    Reference: 2017 National Electrical Code – Chapter 7 Special Conditions , Article 712 Direct Current Microgrids. 710.15 General. 710.15(E) Back-Fed Circuit Breakers.

EXAM 11

EXAM 11 ANSWERS

14. **Answer B.** False

    Plug-in type back-fed circuit breakers connected to a stand-alone or multimode inverter output in stand-alone systems shall be secured in accordance with 408.36(D). *Circuit breakers marked "line" and "load" shall not be back-fed.*

    Reference: 2017 National Electrical Code – Chapter 7 Special Conditions, Article 712 Direct Current Microgrids. 710.15 General. 710.15(E) Back-Fed Circuit Breakers.

15. **Answer A.** authorized persons

    The branch-circuit overcurrent devices in emergency circuits *shall be accessible to authorized persons only*.

    Reference: 2017 National Electrical Code – Chapter 7 Special Conditions, Article 700 Emergency Systems. 700.*30 Accessibility*.

16. **Answer C.** shall be selectively coordinated with

    Emergency system(s) overcurrent devices shall be selectively coordinated with all supply-side overcurrent protective devices.

    *Selective coordination shall be selected by a licensed professional engineer or other qualified persons engaged primarily in the design, installation, or maintenance of electrical system*s. The selection shall be documented and made available to those authorized to design, install, inspect, maintain, and operate the system.

    Exception: Selective coordination shall not be required between two overcurrent devices located in series if no loads are connected in parallel with the downstream device.

    Reference: 2017 National Electrical Code – Chapter 7 Special Conditions, Article 700 Emergency Systems. 700.*32 Selective Coordination*.

17. **Answer A.** authority having jurisdiction

    The authority having jurisdiction shall conduct or witness a test of the complete system upon installation.

    Reference: 2017 National Electrical Code – Chapter 7 Special Conditions, Article 701 Legally Required Standby Systems. 701.3 Tests and Maintenance. 701.3(A) Conduct or Witness Test.

18. **Answer C.** Both A and B

    Legally required standby system equipment shall be maintained in accordance with manufacturer instructions and industry standards.

    Reference: 2017 National Electrical Code – Chapter 7 Special Conditions, Article 701 Legally Required Standby Systems. 701.3 Tests and Maintenance. 701.3(C) Maintenance.

19. **Answer B.** 100% of the loads

    A legally required standby system shall have adequate capacity and rating for the supply of all equipment intended to be operated at one time. Legally required standby system equipment shall be suitable for the maximum available fault current at its terminals. The legally required standby alternate power source shall be permitted to supply both legally required standby and optional standby system loads under either of the following conditions:

    (1) Where the alternate source has adequate capacity to handle all connected loads

    (2) Where automatic selective load pickup and load shedding is provided that will ensure adequate power to the legally required standby circuits

    Reference: 2017 National Electrical Code – Chapter 7 Special Conditions, Article 701 Legally Required Standby Systems. 701.4 Capacity and Rating.

20. **Answer D.** all of these

    Transfer equipment, including automatic transfer switches, *shall be automatic and identified for standby use and approved by the authority having jurisdiction*. Transfer equipment shall be designed and installed to prevent the inadvertent interconnection of normal and alternate sources of supply in any operation of the transfer equipment. Transfer equipment and electric power production systems installed to permit operation in parallel with the normal source shall meet the requirements of Article 705.

    Reference: 2017 National Electrical Code – Chapter 7 Special Conditions, Article 701 Legally Required Standby Systems. 701.5 Transfer Equipment. 701.5(A) General.

EXAM 11

EXAM 11 ANSWERS

21. **Answer D.** Both A and C

    A sign shall be placed at the service entrance indicating type and location of each on-site legally required standby power source.

    Exception: A sign shall not be required for individual unit equipment as specified in 701.12(G).

    Reference: 2017 National Electrical Code – Chapter 7 Special Conditions, Article 701 Legally Required Standby Systems. 701.7 Signs. 701.7(A) Mandated Standby.

22. **Answer B.** legally required

    Where acceptable to the authority having jurisdiction, connections located ahead of and not within the same cabinet, enclosure, vertical switchgear section, or vertical switchboard section as the service disconnecting means shall be permitted. *The legally required standby service shall be sufficiently separated from the normal main service* disconnecting means to minimize simultaneous interruption of supply through an occurrence within the building or groups of buildings served.

    Informational Note: See 230.82 for equipment permitted on the supply side of a service disconnecting means.

    Reference: 2017 National Electrical Code – Chapter 7 Special Conditions, Article 701 Legally Required Standby Systems. 701.12 General Requirements. 701.12(E) Connection Ahead of Service Disconnecting Means.

23. **Answer A.** True

    The alternate source for legally required standby systems shall not be required to provide ground-fault protection of equipment with automatic disconnecting means. *Ground-fault indication at the legally required standby source shall be provided in accordance with 701.6(D) if ground-fault protection of equipment with automatic disconnecting means is not provided.*

    Reference: 2017 National Electrical Code – Chapter 7 Special Conditions, Article 701 Legally Required Standby Systems. 701.26 Ground-Fault Protection of Equipment.

24. **Answer C.** both A and B

    The provisions of this article apply to the installation and operation of optional standby systems.

    The systems covered by this article consist of those that are permanently installed in their entirety, including prime movers, and those that are arranged for a connection to a premises wiring system from a **portable** alternate power supply.

    Reference: 2017 National Electrical Code – Chapter 7 Special Conditions, Article 702 Optional Standby Systems. 702.1 Scope.

    Those systems intended to supply power to public or private facilities or property where life safety does not depend on the performance of the system. These systems are intended to supply on-site generated power to selected loads either automatically or manually.

    Informational Note: Optional standby systems are typically installed to provide an alternate source of electric power for such facilities as industrial and commercial buildings, farms, and residences and to serve loads such as heating and refrigeration systems, data processing and communications systems, and industrial processes that, when stopped during any power outage, could cause discomfort, serious interruption of the process, damage to the product or process, or the like.

    Reference: 2017 National Electrical Code – Chapter 7 Special Conditions, Article 702 Optional Standby Systems. 702.2 Definition. Optional Standby Systems

EXAM 11

EXAM 11 ANSWERS

25. Answer B. the load, as calculated in Article 220

The calculations of load on the standby source shall be made in accordance with Article 220 or by another approved method.

Reference: 2017 National Electrical Code – Chapter 7 Special Conditions, Article 702 Optional Standby Systems. 702.4 Capacity and Rating. 702.4(B) System Capacity.

Where automatic transfer equipment is used, an optional standby system shall comply with (2)(A) or (2)(B).

(A) Full Load. The standby source shall be capable of supplying the full load that is transferred by the automatic transfer equipment.

(B) Load Management. Where a system is employed that will automatically manage the connected load, the standby source shall have a capacity sufficient to supply the maximum load that will be connected by the load management system.

Reference: 2017 National Electrical Code – Chapter 7 Special Conditions, Article 702 Optional Standby Systems. 702.4 Capacity and Rating. 702.4(B) System Capacity. 702.4(B) (2) Automatic Transfer Equipment.

26. Answer D. either A or C

Transfer equipment shall be suitable for the intended use and designed and installed so as to prevent the inadvertent interconnection of normal and alternate sources of supply in any operation of the transfer equipment. Transfer equipment and electric power production systems installed to permit operation in parallel with the normal source shall meet the requirements of Article 705.

Transfer equipment, located on the load side of branch circuit protection, shall be permitted to contain supplemental overcurrent protection having an interrupting rating sufficient for the available fault current that the generator can deliver. The supplementary overcurrent protection devices shall be part of a listed transfer equipment.

Transfer equipment shall be required for all standby systems subject to the provisions of this article and for which an electric utility supply is either the normal or standby source.

Exception: Temporary connection of a portable generator without transfer equipment shall be permitted where conditions of maintenance and supervision ensure that only qualified persons service the installation and where the normal supply is physically isolated by a lockable disconnecting means or by disconnection of the normal supply conductors.

The short-circuit current rating of the transfer equipment, based on the specific overcurrent protective device type and settings protecting the transfer equipment, shall be field marked on the exterior of the transfer equipment.

Reference: 2017 National Electrical Code – Chapter 7 Special Conditions, Article 702 Optional Standby Systems. 702.5 Transfer Equipment.

EXAM 11

EXAM 11 ANSWERS

27. Answer A.   True

The optional standby system wiring shall be permitted to occupy the same raceways, cables, boxes, and cabinets with other general wiring.

Reference: 2017 National Electrical Code – Chapter 7 Special Conditions, Article 702 Optional Standby Systems. 702.10 Wiring Optional Standby Systems.

28. Answer D.   705

This article covers installation of one or more electric power production sources operating in parallel with a primary source(s) of electricity.

Informational Note: Examples of the types of primary sources include a utility supply or an on-site electric power source(s).

Reference: 2017 National Electrical Code – Chapter 7 Special Conditions, Art*icle 705 Interconnected Electric Power Production Sources*. 705.1 Scope.

29. Answer B.   power production equipment

The generating source, and all distribution equipment associated with it, that generates electricity from a source other than a utility supplied service.

Informational Note: Examples of *power production equipment include such items as generators, solar photovoltaic systems, and fuel cell systems.*

Reference: 2017 National Electrical Code – Chapter 7 Special Conditions, Article 705 Interconnected Electric Power Production Sources. 705.2 Definitions. Power Production Equipment

30. Answer B.   qualified persons

Installation of one or more electrical power production sources operating in parallel with *a primary source(s) of electricity shall be performed only by qualified persons.*

Informational Note: See Article 100 for the definition of Qualified

Person.

Reference: 2017 National Electrical Code – Chapter 7 Special Conditions, Article 705 Interconnected Electric Power Production Sources. 705.8 System Installation.

31. Answer D.   Either A or C

A permanent plaque or directory denoting the location of all electric power source disconnecting means on or in the premises shall be installed at each service equipment location and at the location(s) of the system disconnect(s) for all electric power production sources capable of being interconnected. The marking shall comply with 110.21(B).

Exception: Installations with large numbers of power production sources shall be permitted to be designated by groups.

Reference: 2017 National Electrical Code – Chapter 7 Special Conditions, Article 705 Interconnected Electric Power Production Sources. 705.10 Directory.

32. Answer A.   True

An electric power production source shall be permitted to be connected to the supply side of the service disconnecting means as permitted in 230.82(6). The sum of the ratings of all overcurrent devices connected to power production sources shall not exceed the rating of the service.

Reference: 2017 National Electrical Code – Chapter 7 Special Conditions, Article 705 Interconnected Electric Power Production Sources. 705.12 Point of Connection. 705.12(A) Supply Side.

33. Answer B.   False

An electric power production source shall be permitted to be connected to the supply side of the service disconnecting means as permitted in 230.82(6). *The sum of the ratings of all overcurrent devices connected to power production sources shall not exceed the rating of the service.*

Reference: 2017 National Electrical Code – Chapter 7 Special Conditions, Article 705 Interconnected Electric Power Production Sources. 705.12 Point of Connection. 705.12(A) Supply Side.

EXAM 11

EXAM 11 ANSWERS

34. **Answer A.** True

    The output of an interconnected electric power source shall be permitted to be connected to the load side of the service disconnecting means of the other source(s) at any distribution equipment on the premises. Where distribution equipment, including switchgear, switchboards, or panelboards, is fed simultaneously by a primary source(s) of electricity and one or more other power source(s), and where this distribution equipment is capable of supplying multiple branch circuits or feeders, or both, the interconnecting provisions for other power sources shall comply with 705.12(B)(1)through (B)(5).

    (1) Dedicated Overcurrent and Disconnect. Each source interconnection of one or more power sources installed in one system shall be made at a dedicated circuit breaker or fusible disconnecting means.

    (2) Bus or Conductor Ampere Rating. One hundred twentyfive percent of the power source output circuit current shall be used in ampacity calculations for the following:

    (1) Feeders. Where the power source output connection is made to a feeder at a location other than the opposite end of the feeder from the primary source overcurrent device, that portion of the feeder on the load side of the power source output connection shall be protected by one of the following:

    b. An overcurrent device on the load side of the power source connection shall be rated not greater than the ampacity of the feeder.

    (2) Taps. In systems where power source output connections are made at feeders, any taps shall be sized based on the sum of 125 percent of the power source(s) output circuit current and the rating of the overcurrent device protecting the feeder conductors as calculated in 240.21(B).

    (3) Busbars. One of the methods that follows shall be used to determine the ratings of busbars in panelboards.

    (A) The sum of 125 percent of the power source(s) output circuit current and the rating of the overcurrent device protecting the busbar shall not exceed the ampacity of the busbar.

    Informational Note: This general rule assumes no limitation in the number of the loads or sources applied to busbars or their locations.

    (B) Where two sources, one a primary power source and the other another power source, are located at opposite ends of a busbar that contains loads, the sum of 125 percent of the power source(s) output circuit current and the rating of the overcurrent device protecting the busbar shall not exceed 120 percent of the ampacity of the busbar. The busbar shall be sized for the loads connected in accordance with Article 220. A permanent warning label shall be applied to the distribution equipment adjacent to the back-fed breaker from the power source that displays the following or equivalent wording:

    WARNING:

    POWER SOURCE OUTPUT CONNECTION —

    DO NOT RELOCATE THIS OVERCURRENT DEVICE.

    The warning sign(s) or label(s) shall comply with 110.21(B).

    (C) The sum of the ampere ratings of all overcurrent devices on panelboards, both load and supply devices, excluding the rating of the overcurrent device protecting the busbar, shall not exceed the ampacity of the busbar. The rating of the overcurrent device protecting the busbar shall not exceed the rating of the busbar. Permanent warning labels shall be applied to distribution equipment displaying the following or equivalent wording:

    WARNING:

    THIS EQUIPMENT FED BY MULTIPLE SOURCES.

    TOTAL RATING OF ALL OVERCURRENT DEVICES

    EXCLUDING MAIN SUPPLY OVERCURRENT DEVICE

    SHALL NOT EXCEED AMPACITY OF BUSBAR.

EXAM 11

EXAM 11 ANSWERS

The warning sign(s) or label(s) shall comply with 110.21(B).

(D) A connection at either end, but not both ends, of a center-fed panelboard in dwellings shall be permitted where the sum of 125 percent of the power source(s) output circuit current and the rating of the overcurrent device protecting the busbar does not exceed 120 percent of the current rating of the busbar.

(E) Connections shall be permitted on multiple-ampacity busbars where designed under engineering supervision that includes available fault current and busbar load calculations.

(3) Marking. Equipment containing overcurrent devices in circuits supplying power to a busbar or conductor supplied from multiple sources shall be marked to indicate the presence of all sources.

(4) Suitable for Backfeed. Circuit breakers, if backfed, shall be suitable for such operation.

Informational Note: Fused disconnects, unless otherwise marked, are suitable for backfeeding.

(5) Fastening. Listed plug-in-type circuit breakers backfed from electric power sources that are listed and identified as interactive shall be permitted to omit the additional fastener normally required by 408.36(D) for such applications.

Reference: 2017 National Electrical Code – Chapter 7 Special Conditions, Article 705 Interconnected Electric Power Production Sources. 705.12 Point of Connection. 705.12(B) Load Side.

35. **Answer A.** True

Each source interconnection of one or more power sources installed in one system *shall be made at a dedicated circuit breaker or fusible disconnecting means.*

Reference: 2017 National Electrical Code – Chapter 7 Special Conditions, Article 705 Interconnected Electric Power Production Sources. 705.12 Point of Connection. 705.12(B) Load Side. 705.12(B) (1) Dedicated Overcurrent and Disconnect.

36. **Answer A.** True

(B) Where two sources, one a primary power source and the other another power source, are located at opposite ends of a busbar that contains loads, the sum of 125 percent of the power source(s) output circuit current and the rating of the overcurrent device protecting the busbar shall not exceed 120 percent of the ampacity of the busbar. The busbar shall be sized for the loads connected in accordance with Article 220. *A permanent warning label shall be applied to the distribution equipment adjacent to the back-fed breaker from the power source that displays the following or equivalent wording:*

WARNING:

POWER SOURCE OUTPUT CONNECTION —

DO NOT RELOCATE THIS OVERCURRENT DEVICE.

The warning sign(s) or label(s) shall comply with 110.21(B).

(C) The sum of the ampere ratings of all overcurrent devices on panelboards, both load and supply devices, excluding the rating of the overcurrent device protecting the busbar, shall not exceed the ampacity of the busbar. The rating of the overcurrent device protecting the busbar shall not exceed the rating of the busbar. Permanent warning labels shall be applied to distribution equipment displaying the following or equivalent wording:

WARNING:

THIS EQUIPMENT FED BY MULTIPLE SOURCES.

TOTAL RATING OF ALL OVERCURRENT DEVICES

EXCLUDING MAIN SUPPLY OVERCURRENT DEVICE

SHALL NOT EXCEED AMPACITY OF BUSBAR.

EXAM 11

EXAM 11 ANSWERS

The warning sign(s) or label(s) shall comply with 110.21(B).

(D) A connection at either end, but not both ends, of a center-fed panelboard in dwellings shall be permitted where the sum of 125 percent of the power source(s) output circuit current and the rating of the overcurrent device protecting the busbar does not exceed 120 percent of the current rating of the busbar.

(E) Connections shall be permitted on multiple-ampacity busbars where designed under engineering supervision that includes available fault current and busbar load calculations.

Reference: 2017 National Electrical Code – Chapter 7 Special Conditions, Article 705 Interconnected Electric Power Production Sources. 705.12 Point of Connection. 705.12(B) Load Side. 705.12(B) (2) Bus or Conductor Ampere Rating. 705.12(B)(2)(3)(B) Busbars

37. Answer A. True

Equipment containing overcurrent devices in circuits supplying power to a *busbar or conductor supplied from multiple sources shall be marked to indicate the presence of all sources.*

Reference: 2017 National Electrical Code – Chapter 7 Special Conditions, Article 705 Interconnected Electric Power Production Sources. 705.12 Point of Connection. 705.12(B) Load Side. 705.12(B)(3) Marking.

38. Answer B. Fused disconnects

Circuit breakers, if backfed, shall be suitable for such operation.

Informational Note: *Fused disconnects, unless otherwise marked, are suitable for backfeeding.*

Reference: 2017 National Electrical Code – Chapter 7 Special Conditions, Article 705 Interconnected Electric Power Production Sources. 705.12 Point of Connection. 705.12(B) Load Side. 705.12(B)(4) Suitable for Backfeed.

39. Answer B. False

Listed plug-in-type circuit breakers backfed from electric power sources that are listed and identified as interactive shall be permitted to omit the additional fastener normally required by 408.36(D) for such applications.

Reference: 2017 National Electrical Code – Chapter 7 Special Conditions, Article 705 Interconnected Electric Power Production Sources. 705.12 Point of Connection. 705.12(B) Load Side. 705.12(B)(5) Fastening.

40. Answer B. False

Upon loss of primary source, an electric power production source shall be automatically disconnected from all ungrounded conductors of the primary source and shall not be reconnected until the primary source is restored.

Exception: A listed interactive inverter shall be permitted to automatically cease exporting power upon loss of primary source and shall not be required to automatically disconnect all ungrounded conductors from the primary source. A listed interactive inverter shall be permitted to automatically or manually resume exporting power to the utility once the primary source is restored.

Informational Note No. 1: Risks to personnel and equipment associated with the primary source could occur if an utility interactive electric power production source can operate as an intentional island. Special detection methods are required to determine that a primary source supply system outage has occurred and whether there should be automatic disconnection.

When the primary source supply system is restored, special detection methods can be required to limit exposure of power production sources to out-of-phase reconnection.

Informational Note No. 2: Induction-generating equipment on systems with significant capacitance can become self-excited upon loss of the primary source and experience severe overvoltage as a result. An interactive inverter shall be permitted to operate as a stand-alone system to supply loads that have been disconnected from electrical production and distribution network sources.

Reference: 2017 National Electrical Code – Chapter 7 Special Conditions, Article 705 Interconnected Electric Power Production Sources. 705.40 Loss of Primary Source.

41. Answer A. True

Installed Class 2, Class 3, and PLTC cable that is not terminated at equipment and not identified for future use with a tag.

Reference: 2017 National Electrical Code – Chapter 7 Special Conditions, Article 725 Class 1, Class 2, and Class 3 Remote-Control, Signaling, and Power-Limited Circuits. 725.2 Definitions. Abandoned Class 2, Class 3, and PLTC Cable.

EXAM 11

EXAM 11 ANSWERS

42. **Answer D.** safeguards

    The portion of the wiring system between the load side of a Class 3 power source and the connected equipment. Due to its power limitations, a Class 3 circuit considers safety from a fire initiation standpoint. Since higher levels of voltage and current than for Class 2 are permitted, *additional safeguards are specified to provide protection from an electric shock hazard that could be encountered.*

    Reference: 2017 National Electrical Code – Chapter 7 Special Conditions, Article 725 Class 1, Class 2, and Class 3 Remote-Control, Signaling, and Power-Limited Circuits. 725.2 Definitions. Class 3 Circuit.

43. **Answer C.** aren't required for this purpose

    Installations shall comply with 300.7(A).

    Reference: 2017 National Electrical Code – Chapter 7 Special Conditions, Article 725 Class 1, Class 2, and Class 3 Remote-Control, Signaling, and Power-Limited Circuits. 725.3 Other Articles. 725.3(H) Raceways Exposed to Different Temperatures.

    Where portions of a raceway or sleeve are known to be subjected to different temperatures, and where condensation is known to be a problem, as in cold storage areas of buildings or where passing from the interior to the exterior of a building, the raceway or sleeve shall be filled with an approved material to prevent the circulation of warm air to a colder section of the raceway or sleeve. *An explosion proof seal shall not be required for this purpose.*

    Reference: 2017 National Electrical Code Chapter 3 Wiring Methods and Materials, Article 300 General Requirements for Wiring Methods and Materials. 300.7 Raceways Exposed to Different Temperatures. 300.7(A)Sealing.

44. **Answer A.** True

    Access to electrical equipment shall not be denied by an accumulation of wires and cables that prevents removal of panels, including suspended ceiling panels.

    Reference: 2017 National Electrical Code – Chapter 7 Special Conditions, Article 725 Class 1, Class 2, and Class 3 Remote-Control, Signaling, and Power-Limited Circuits. 725.21 Access to Electrical Equipment Behind Panels. Designed to Allow Access.

45. **Answer A.** True

    Class 1, Class 2, and Class 3 circuits shall be installed in a neat and workmanlike manner. Cables and conductors installed exposed on the surface of ceilings and sidewalls shall be supported by the building structure in such a manner that the cable will not be damaged by normal building use. *Such cables shall be supported by straps, staples, hangers, cable ties, or similar fittings designed and installed so as not to damage the cable. The installation shall also comply with 300.4(D).*

    Reference: 2017 National Electrical Code – Chapter 7 Special Conditions, Article 725 Class 1, Class 2, and Class 3 Remote-Control, Signaling, and Power-Limited Circuits. 725.24 Mechanical Execution of Work.

46. **Answer C.** the environment involved

    The accessible portion of abandoned Class 2, Class 3, and PLTC cables shall be removed. Where cables are identified for future use with a tag, *the tag shall be of sufficient durability to withstand the environment involved*.

    Reference: 2017 National Electrical Code – Chapter 7 Special Conditions, Article 725 Class 1, Class 2, and Class 3 Remote-Control, Signaling, and Power-Limited Circuits. 725.25 Abandoned Cables.

EXAM 11

EXAM 11 ANSWERS

47. Answer B. when both have functional association with equipment

Class 1 circuits and power-supply circuits shall be *permitted to occupy the same cable, enclosure, or raceway only where the equipment powered is functionally associated.*

Reference: 2017 National Electrical Code – Chapter 7 Special Conditions, Article 725 Class 1, Class 2, and Class 3 Remote-Control, Signaling, and Power-Limited Circuits. 725.48 Conductors of Different Circuits in the Same Cable, Cable Tray, Enclosure, or Raceway. 725.48(B) Class 1 Circuits with Power-Supply Circuits. 725.48(B) (1) In a Cable, Enclosure, or Raceway.

48. Answer A. Are functionally associated with the motor system

Class 1 circuits and power-supply circuits shall be permitted to occupy the same cable, enclosure, or raceway only where the equipment powered is functionally associated.

Reference: 2017 National Electrical Code – Chapter 7 Special Conditions, Article 725 Class 1, Class 2, and Class 3 Remote-Control, Signaling, and Power-Limited Circuits. 725.48 Conductors of Different Circuits in the Same Cable, Cable Tray, Enclosure or Raceway. 725.48(B) Class 1 Circuits with Power-Supply Circuits. 725.48(B)(1) In A Cable, Enclosure, or Raceway.

49. Answer C. whether the circuit is a Class 2 or Class 3

The equipment supplying the circuits shall be durably marked where plainly visible to indicate each *circuit that is a Class 2 or Class 3 circuit.*

Reference: 2017 National Electrical Code – Chapter 7 Special Conditions, Article 725 Class 1, Class 2, and Class 3 Remote-Control, Signaling, and Power-Limited Circuits. 725.124 Circuit Marking.

50. Answer B. separated by a barrier

(A) General. Cables and conductors of Class 2 and Class 3 circuits shall not be placed in any cable, cable tray, compartment, enclosure, manhole, outlet box, device box, raceway, or similar fitting with conductors of electric light, power, Class 1, non–power-limited fire alarm circuits, and medium-power network-powered broadband communications circuits unless permitted by 725.136(B) through (I).

(B) Separated by Barriers. Class 2 and Class 3 circuits shall be permitted to be installed together with the conductors of electric light, power, Class 1, non–power-limited fire alarm and medium power network-powered broadband communications circuits where they are separated by a barrier.

(C) Raceways Within Enclosures. In enclosures, Class 2 and Class 3 circuits shall be permitted to be installed in a raceway to separate them from Class 1, non–power-limited fire alarm and medium-power network-powered broadband communications circuits.

(D) Associated Systems Within Enclosures. Class 2 and Class 3 circuit conductors in compartments, enclosures, device boxes, outlet boxes, or similar fittings shall be permitted to be installed with electric light, power, Class 1, non–power-limited fire alarm, and medium-power network-powered broadband communications circuits where they are introduced solely to connect the equipment connected to Class 2 and Class 3 circuits, and where (1) or (2) applies:

(1) The electric light, power, Class 1, non–power-limited fire alarm, and medium-power network-powered broadband communications circuit conductors are routed to maintain a minimum of 6 mm (0.25 in). separation from the conductors and cables of Class 2 and Class 3 circuits.

(2) The circuit conductors operate at 150 volts or less to ground and also comply with one of the following: *of 6 mm (0.25 in.). or by a nonconductive sleeve or nonconductive barrier from all other conductors.*

b. The Class 2 and Class 3 circuit conductors are installed as a Class 1 circuit in accordance with 725.41.

Reference: 2017 National Electrical Code – Chapter 7 Special Conditions, Article 725 Class 1, Class 2, and Class 3 Remote-Control, Signaling, and Power-Limited Circuits. 725.136 Separation from Electric Light, Power, Class 1, Non-Power-Limited Fire Alarm Circuit Conductors, and Medium-Power Network-Powered Broadband Communications Cables.

EXAM 11
EXAM 11 ANSWERS

51. Answer A. True

Class 2 or Class 3 circuit conductors shall not be strapped, taped, or attached by any means to the exterior of any conduit or other raceway as a means of support. These conductors shall be permitted to be installed as permitted by 300.11(C)(2).

Reference: 2017 National Electrical Code – Chapter 7 Special Conditions, Article 725 Class 1, Class 2, and Class 3 Remote-Control, Signaling, and Power-Limited Circuits. 725.143 Support of Conductors.

52. Answer C. 18 AWG

Class 3 single conductors used as other wiring within buildings shall not be smaller than 18 AWG and shall be Type CL3. Conductor types described in 725.49(B) that are also listed as Type CL3 shall be permitted.

Informational Note: One method of defining resistant to the spread of fire is that the cables do not spread fire to the top of the tray in the UL flame exposure, vertical tray flame test in ANSI/UL 1685-2010, Standard for Safety for Vertical-Tray Fire-Propagation and Smoke-Release Test for Electrical and Optical-Fiber Cables. The smoke measurements in the test method are not applicable.

Another method of defining resistant to the spread of fire is for the damage (char length. not to exceed 1.5 m (4 ft 11 in.) when performing the CSA vertical tray flame test for cables in cable trays, as described in CSA C22.2 No. 0.3-M-2001, Test Methods for Electrical Wires and Cables).

Reference: 2017 National Electrical Code – Chapter 7 Special Conditions, Article 725 Class 1, Class 2, and Class 3 Remote-Control, Signaling, and Power-Limited Circuits. 725.179 Listing and Marking of Class 2, Class 3, and Type PLTC Cables; Communications Raceways; and Cable Routing Assemblies. 725.179(H) Class 3 Single Conductors.

53. Answer A. 3 amperes

The allowable ampacity of the conductors shall be 5 amperes, *except for 22 AWG conductors, which shall have an allowable ampacity of 3 amperes.*

Reference: 2017 National Electrical Code – Chapter 7 Special Conditions, Article 727 Instrumentation Tray Cable: Type ITC. 727.8 Allowable Ampacity.

54. Answer D. all of these

This article covers the installation of wiring and equipment of fire alarm systems, including all circuits controlled and powered by the fire alarm system.

Informational Note No. 1: *Fire alarm systems include fire detection and alarm notification, guard's tour, sprinkler waterflow, and sprinkler supervisory systems.* Circuits controlled and powered by the fire alarm system include circuits for the control of building systems safety functions, elevator capture, elevator shutdown, door release, smoke doors and damper control, fire doors and damper control and fan shutdown, but only where these circuits are powered by and controlled by the fire alarm system. For further information on the installation and monitoring for integrity requirements for fire alarm systems, refer to the NFPA 72 -2013, National Fire Alarm and Signaling Code.

Reference: 2017 National Electrical Code – Chapter 7 Special Conditions, Article 760 Fire Alarm Systems. 760.1 Scope.

55. Answer D. isn't required for this purpose

Installations shall comply with 300.7(A).

Reference: 2017 National Electrical Code – Chapter 7 Special Conditions, Article 725 Class 1, Class 2, and Class 3 Remote-Control, Signaling, and Power-Limited Circuits. 725.3 Other Articles. 725.3(H) Raceways Exposed to Different Temperatures.

Where portions of a raceway or sleeve are known to be subjected to different temperatures, and where condensation is known to be a problem, as in cold storage areas of buildings or where passing from the interior to the exterior of a building, the raceway or sleeve shall be filled with an approved material to prevent the circulation of warm air to a colder section of the raceway or sleeve. An explosionproof seal shall not be required for this purpose.

Reference: 2017 National Electrical code – Chapter 3 Wiring Methods and Materials , Article 300 General Requirements for Wiring Methods and Materials . 300.7 Raceways Exposed to Different Temperatures. 300.7(A) Sealing

EXAM 11

EXAM 11 ANSWERS

56. Answer A. True

A bushing shall be installed where cables emerge from raceway used for mechanical support or protection in accordance with 300.15(C).

Reference: 2017 National Electrical Code – Chapter 7 Special Conditions, Article 760 Fire Alarm Systems. 760.3 Other Articles. 760.3(K) Bushing.

A box or conduit body shall not be required where cables enter or exit from conduit or tubing that is used to provide cable support or protection against physical damage. A fitting shall be provided on the end(s) of the conduit or tubing to protect the cable from abrasion.

Reference: 2017 National Electrical Code Chapter 3 Wiring Methods and Materials, Article 300 General Requirements for Wiring Methods and Materials. 300.15 Boxes, Conduit Bodies, or Fittings - Where Required. 300.15(C) Protection.

57. Answer A. True

The accessible portion of abandoned fire alarm cables shall be removed. Where cables are identified for future use with a tag, the tag shall be of sufficient durability to withstand the environment involved.

Reference: 2017 National Electrical Code – Chapter 7 Special Conditions, Article 760 Fire Alarm Systems. 760.25 Abandoned Cables.

58. Answer C. testing and servicing of other systems

Fire alarm circuits shall be identified at terminal and junction locations in a manner that *helps to prevent unintentional signals on fire alarm system circuit(s) during testing and servicing of other systems.*

Reference: 2017 National Electrical Code – Chapter 7 Special Conditions, Article 760 Fire Alarm Systems. 760.30 Fire Alarm Circuit Identification.

59. Answer B. False

The branch circuit supplying the fire alarm equipment(s) shall supply no other loads. The location of the branch-circuit overcurrent protective device shall be permanently identified at the fire alarm control unit. *The circuit disconnecting means shall have red identification, shall be accessible only to qualified personnel, and shall be identified as "FIRE ALARM CIRCUIT."* The red identification shall not damage the overcurrent protective devices or obscure the manufacturer's markings. This branch circuit shall not be supplied through ground-fault circuit interrupters or arc-fault circuit-interrupters.

Informational Note: See 210.8(A)(5), Exception, for receptacles in dwelling-unit unfinished basements that supply power for fire alarm systems.

Reference: 2017 National Electrical Code – Chapter 7 Special Conditions, Article 760 Fire Alarm Systems. 760.41 NPLFA Circuit Power Source Requirements. 760.41(B) Branch Circuit.

60. Answer D. any of these

Cable splices or terminations shall be made in listed fittings, boxes, enclosures, fire alarm devices, or utilization equipment. Where installed exposed, cables shall be adequately supported and installed in such a way that maximum protection against physical damage is afforded by building construction such as baseboards, door frames, ledges, and so forth. Where located within 2.1 m (7 ft.) of the floor, cables shall be securely fastened in an approved manner at intervals of not more than 450 mm (18 in.).

Reference: 2017 National Electrical Code – Chapter 7 Special Conditions, Article 760 Fire Alarm Systems. 760.130 Wiring Methods and Materials on Load Side of the PLFA Power Source. 760.130(B) PLFA Wiring Methods and Materials. 760.130(B) (1) In Raceways, Exposed on Ceilings or Sidewalls, or Fished in Concealed Spaces

61. Answer A. True

Cable and conductors of two or more power-limited fire alarm circuits, communications circuits, or Class 3 circuits shall be permitted within the same cable, enclosure, cable tray, raceway, or cable routing assembly.

Reference: 2017 National Electrical Code – Chapter 7 Special Conditions, Article 760 Fire Alarm Systems. 760.139 Installation of Conductors of Different PLFA Circuits, Class 2, Class 3, and Communications Circuits in the Same Cable, Enclosure, Cable Tray, Raceway, or Cable Routing Assembly.

EXAM 11

EXAM 11 ANSWERS

62. **Answer B.** False

    Power-limited fire alarm circuit conductors shall not be strapped, taped, or attached *by any means to the exterior of any conduit or other raceway as a means of support.*

    Reference: 2017 National Electrical Code – Chapter 7 Special Conditions, Article 760 Fire Alarm Systems. 760.143 Support of Conductors.

63. **Answer D.** wet

    PLFA cables installed as wiring within buildings shall be listed as being resistant to the spread of fire and other criteria in accordance with 760.179(A) through (H) and shall be marked in accordance with 760.179(I). Insulated continuous line-type fire detectors shall be listed in accordance with 760.179(J). *Cable used in a wet location shall be listed for use in wet locations or have a moisture-impervious metal sheath.*

    Reference: 2017 National Electrical Code – Chapter 7 Special Conditions, Article 760 Fire Alarm Systems. 760.179 Listing and Marking of PLFA Cables and Insulated Continuous Line-Type Fire Detectors.

64. **Answer A.** current-carrying electrical conductors

    A cable *containing optical fibers and current-carrying* electrical conductors.

    Reference: 2017 National Electrical Code – Chapter 1 General, Article 100 Definitions. Composite Optical Fiber Cable

65. **Answer A.** True

    A factory assembly of *one or more optical fibers having an overall covering and containing no electrically conductive materials.*

    Reference: 2017 National Electrical Code – Chapter 1 General, Article 100 Definitions. Nonconductive Optical Fiber Cable

66. **Answer C.** within a building

    The point *within a building* at which the optical fiber cable emerges from an external wall or from a concrete floor slab

    Reference: 2017 National Electrical Code – Chapter 1 General, Article 100 Definitions. Point of Entrance

67. **Answer B.** exposed

    Optical fiber cables shall be installed in a neat and workmanlike manner. *Cables installed exposed on the surface of ceilings and sidewalls shall be supported by the building structure in such a manner that the cable will not be damaged by normal building use.* Such cables shall be secured by hardware including straps, staples, cable ties, hangers, or similar fittings designed and installed so as not to damage the cable. The installation shall also conform with 300.4(D) through (G) and 300.11. Nonmetallic cable ties and other nonmetallic cable accessories used to secure and support cables in other spaces used for environmental air plenums. shall be listed as having low smoke and heat release properties.

    Informational Note No. 1: Accepted industry practices are described in ANSI/NECA/BICSI 568-2006, Standard for Installing Commercial Building Telecommunications Cabling; ANSI/NECA/FOA 301-2009, Standard for Installing and Testing Fiber Optic Cables; and other ANSI-approved installation standards.

    Informational Note No. 2: See 4.3.11.2.6.5 and 4.3.11.5.5.6 of NFPA 90A-2012, Standard for the Installation of Air-Conditioning and Ventilating Systems, for discrete combustible components installed in accordance with 300.22(C).

    Informational Note No. 3: Paint, plaster, cleaners, abrasives, corrosive residues, or other contaminants may result in an undetermined alteration of optical fiber cable properties.

    Reference: 2017 National Electrical Code – Chapter 7 Special Conditions, Article 770 Optical Fiber Cables and Raceways. 770.24 Mechanical Execution of Work.

EXAM 11

EXAM 11 ANSWERS

68. **Answer D.** all of these

Optical fiber cables shall be installed in a neat and workmanlike manner. Cables installed exposed on the surface of ceilings and sidewalls shall be supported by the building structure in such a manner that the cable will not be damaged by normal building use. Such cables shall be secured by hardware including straps, staples, cable ties, hangers, or similar fittings designed and installed so as not to damage the cable. The installation shall also conform with 300.4(D) through (G) and 300.11. Nonmetallic cable ties and other nonmetallic cable accessories used to secure and support cables in other spaces used for environmental air plenums. shall be listed as having low smoke and heat release properties.

Informational Note No. 1: *Accepted industry practices are described in ANSI/NECA/BICSI 568-2006, Standard for Installing Commercial Building Telecommunications Cabling; ANSI/NECA/FOA 301-2009, Standard for Installing and Testing Fiber Optic Cables; and other ANSI-approved installation standards.*

Informational Note No. 2: See 4.3.11.2.6.5 and 4.3.11.5.5.6 of NFPA 90A-2012, Standard for the Installation of Air-Conditioning and Ventilating Systems, for discrete combustible components installed in accordance with 300.22(C).

Informational Note No. 3: Paint, plaster, cleaners, abrasives, corrosive residues, or other contaminants may result in an undetermined alteration of optical fiber cable properties.

Reference: 2017 National Electrical Code – Chapter 7 Special Conditions, Article 770 Optical Fiber Cables and Raceways. 770.24 Mechanical Execution of Work.

69. **Answer D.** firestopped

Installations of optical fiber cables and communications raceways in hollow spaces, vertical shafts, and ventilation or air-handling ducts shall be made so that the possible spread of fire or products of combustion will not be substantially increased. *Openings around penetrations of optical fiber cables and communications raceways through fire-resistant–rated walls, partitions, floors, or ceilings shall be firestopped using approved methods to maintain the fire resistance rating.*

Informational Note: Directories of electrical construction materials published by qualified testing laboratories contain many listing installation restrictions necessary to maintain the fireresistive rating of assemblies where penetrations or openings are made. Building codes also contain restrictions on membrane penetrations on opposite sides of a fire resistance–rated wall assembly. An example is the 600-mm (24-in.) minimum horizontal separation that usually applies between boxes installed on opposite sides of the wall. Assistance in complying with 770.26 can be found in building codes, fire resistance directories, and product listings.

Reference: 2017 National Electrical Code – Chapter 7 Special Conditions, Article 770 Optical Fiber Cables and Raceways. 770.26 Spread of Fire or Products of Combustion.

EXAM 12

Chapter 8 Communications Systems

1. True or False: Communications cables are considered abandoned if they are not identified for future use or terminated at both ends with a connector or other equipment.

    A. True   B. False

    Reference: 2017 National Electrical Code – Chapter 8 Communications Systems, Article 800 Communications Circuits. 800.2 Definitions.

2. True or False: It is required that equipment intended for permanent electrical connection to a communications network be listed.

    A. True   B. False

    Reference: 2017 National Electrical Code – Chapter 8 Communications Systems, Article 800 Communications Circuits. 800.18 Installation of Equipment.

3. If communications cables are installed on the surface of ceilings or walls, they must be supported by the building structure so that normal building use will not damage the cable, if it is:

    A. concealed   C. hidden

    B. exposed   D. both A and B

    Reference: 2017 National Electrical Code – Chapter 8 Communications Systems, Article 800 Communications Circuits. 800.24 Mechanical Execution of Work.

4. True or False: If communications cable is abandoned, accessible portions must be removed.

    A. True   B. False

    Reference: 2017 National Electrical Code – Chapter 8 Communications Systems, Article 800 Communications Circuits. 800.25 Abandoned Cables.

EXAM 12

Chapter 8 Communications Systems

5. What is the minimum separation for overhead communications wires and cables at any point in the span from supply service-drops of up to 750 volts?

    A. 12 inches

    B. 18 inches

    C. 24 inches

    D. 30 inches

    Reference: 2017 National Electrical Code – Chapter 8 Communications Systems, Article 800 Communications Circuits. 800.44 Overhead Aerial. Communications Wires and Cables. 800.44(A)On Poles and In-Span. 800.44(A)(4) Clearance.

6. What is the minimum clearance for communications wires and cables above all points of roofs above which they pass?

    A. 3 feet

    B. 4 feet

    C. 6 feet

    D. 8 feet

    Reference: 2017 National Electrical Code – Chapter 8 Communications Systems, Article 800 Communications Circuits. 800.44 Overhead Aerial. Communications Wires and Cables. 800.44(B) Above Roofs.

7. If the cable for outside plant communications is no more than _____, and the cable enters the building from the outside and is terminated in an enclosure or on a listed primary protector, it is not required to be listed.

    A. 25 ft.

    B. 30 ft.

    C. 50 ft.

    D. 100 ft.

    Reference: 2017 National Electrical Code – Chapter 8 Communications Systems, Article 800 Communications Circuits. 800.48 Unlisted Cables Entering Buildings.

8. What is the minimum separation that shall be maintained, where practicable, between lightning conductors and communications wires and cables on buildings?

    A. 18 inches

    B. 24 inches

    C. 4 feet

    D. 6 feet

    Reference: 2017 National Electrical Code – Chapter 8 Communications Systems, Article 800 Communications Circuits. 800.53 Lightning Conductors

EXAM 12

Chapter 8 Communications Systems

9. Which of the following is the requirements for the metallic sheath members of communications cable that enters a building, as close as practicable to the point of entrance?

    A. grounded as specified in 800.100

    B. interrupted by an insulating joint or equivalent device

    C. either A or B

    D. both A and B

    Reference: 2017 National Electrical Code – Chapter 8 Communications Systems, Article 800 Communications Circuits. 800.93 Grounding or Interruption of Metallic Sheath Members of Communications Cables. 800.93(A) Entering Buildings.

10. During lightning events, limiting the length of the primary protector grounding conductors for communications circuits assists in reducing voltage between the buildings communications systems and:

    A. fire alarm

    B. lighting

    C. lightning protection

    D. power

    Reference: 2017 National Electrical Code – Chapter 8 Communications Systems, Article 800 Communications Circuits. 800.100 Cable and Primary Protector Bonding and

11. True or False: If communications cables and wires are installed in a Chapter 3 raceway, it must be installed to comply with the requirements of Chapter 3.

    A. True

    B. False

    Reference: 2017 National Electrical Code – Chapter 8 Communications Systems, Article 800 Communications Circuits. 800.110 Raceways and Cable Routing Assemblies for

Chapter 8 Communications Systems

EXAM 12

Chapter 8 Communications Systems

12. Unless otherwise permitted, communications cables and wires must be separated at least 2 in. from which circuit conductors?

    A. power

    B. lighting

    C. Class 1

    D. all of these

    Reference: 2017 National Electrical Code – Chapter 8 Communications Systems, Article 800 Communications Circuits. 800.133 Installation of Communications Wires, Cables, and Equipment. 800.133(A) Separation from Other Conductors. 800.133(A)(2) Other Applications.

13. Which Article has the requirements for the installation of wiring for radio and television receiving equipment, including amateur/citizen band radio equipment antennas and digital satellite receiving equipment for television signals.

    A. 680

    B. 700

    C. 810

    D. 840

    Reference: 2017 National Electrical Code – Chapter 8 Communications Systems, Article 810 Radio and Television Equipment. 810.1 Scope.

14. How far must the separation be between any light, power, or Class 1 conductors or radio and television conductors, and underground antenna conductors for radio and television receiving equipment.

    A. 12 in.

    B. 18 in.

    C. 5 ft.

    D. 6 ft.

    Reference: 2017 National Electrical Code – Chapter 8 Communications Systems, Article 810 Radio and Television Equipment. 810.18 Clearances - Receiving Stations. 810.18(A) Outside of Buildings.

15. True or False: The same enclosure that holds conductors of other wiring systems, when separated by an effective permanently installed barrier, can also hold indoor antenna lead-in conductors for radio and television receiving equipment.

    A. True

    B. False

    Reference: 2017 National Electrical Code – Chapter 8 Communications Systems, Article 810 Radio and Television Equipment. 810.18 Clearances - Receiving Stations. 810.18(C) In Boxes or Other Enclosures.

EXAM 12

Chapter 8 Communications Systems

16. What type of protection is needed for the grounding electrode conductor for an antenna if it is subject to physical damage?

    A. arc-fault

    B. electrical

    C. mechanical

    D. none of these

    Reference: 2017 National Electrical Code – Chapter 8 Communications Systems, Article 820 Community Antenna Television and Radio Distribution Systems. 820.100 Cable Bonding and Grounding. 820.100 (A) Bonding Conductor or Grounding Electrode Conductor. 820.100 (A) (6) Physical Protection.

17. A grounding electrode or bonding conductor for a radio/television antenna system must have protection if it is subject to physical damage. If that protection is installation in a metal raceway then the _____ conductor must have both ends of the raceway bonded to it.

    A. contained

    B. grounded

    C. ungrounded

    D. either B or C

    Reference: 2017 National Electrical Code – Chapter 8 Communications Systems, Article 820 Community Antenna Television and Radio Distribution Systems. 820.100 Cable Bonding and Grounding. 820.100 (A) Bonding Conductor or Grounding Electrode Conductor. 820.100 (A) (6) Physical Protection.

18. True or False: The bonding conductor for an antenna mast must be connected to the intersystem bonding termination if the building has one.

    A. True

    B. False

    Reference: 2017 National Electrical Code – Chapter 8 Communications Systems, Article 820 Community Antenna Television and Radio Distribution Systems. 820.100 Cable Bonding and Grounding. 820.100 (A) Bonding Conductor or Grounding Electrode Conductor. 820.100 (A) (1) In Buildings or Structures with an Intersystem Bonding

EXAM 12

Chapter 8 Communications Systems

19. A bonding jumper no smaller than _____ AWG copper or equivalent must be connected between the radio and television equipment grounding electrode and the power grounding electrode system when they are separate.

    A. 6
    B. 8
    C. 10
    D. 1/0

    Reference: 2017 National Electrical Code – Chapter 8 Communications Systems, Article 820 Community Antenna Television and Radio Distribution Systems. 820.100 Cable Bonding and Grounding. 820.100 (D) Bonding of Electrodes

20. Coaxial cable is a cylindrical assembly, usually covered by an insulating jacket, composed of a conductor centered inside a metallic shield or tube, and separated by what kind of material?

    A. conductive
    B. dielectric
    C. insulating
    D. isolating

    Reference: 2017 National Electrical Code – Chapter 1 General

21. If the current supply is from a transformer or other power-limiting device, CATV coaxial cable can deliver power to directly associated radio frequency distribution system equipment, as long as the voltage does not exceed:

    A. 60V
    B. 120V
    C. 180V
    D. 270V

    Reference: 2017 National Electrical Code – Chapter 8 Communications Systems, Article 820 Community Antenna Television and Radio Distribution Systems. 820.15 Power Limitations.

Chapter 8 Communications Systems   633

EXAM 12

Chapter 8 Communications Systems

22. If CATV coaxial cables are installed on the surface of ceilings and walls, they must be supported by the building structure so that the cables will not be damaged by the normal use of the building, if they are:

    A. concealed

    B. exposed

    C. hidden

    D. both A and B

    Reference: 2017 National Electrical Code – Chapter 8 Communications Systems, Article 820 Community Antenna Television and Radio Distribution Systems. 820.24 Mechanical Execution of Work.

23. True or False: If CATV cable is abandoned and not tagged for future use, accessible portions must be removed.

    A. True

    B. False

    Reference: 2017 National Electrical Code – Chapter 8 Communications Systems, Article 820 Community Antenna Television and Radio Distribution Systems. 820.25 Abandoned Cables.

24. It is not required to list or mark community antenna television and radio system coaxial cables if the cable is not more than _____ from where the cable enters the building from the outside to where it is terminated at a grounding block.

    A. 25 ft.

    B. 30 ft.

    C. 50 ft.

    D. 100 ft.

    Reference: 2017 National Electrical Code – Chapter 8 Communications Systems, Article 820 Community Antenna Television and Radio Distribution Systems. 820.48 Unlisted Cables Entering Buildings.

25. If a conductor is used to ground the outer cover of a CATV coaxial cable, it may be:

    A. 14 AWG minimum

    B. bare

    C. insulated

    D. all of these

    Reference: 2017 National Electrical Code – Chapter 8 Communications Systems, Article 820 Community Antenna Television and Radio Distribution Systems. 820.100 Cable Bonding and Grounding. 820.100(A) Bonding Conductor or Grounding Electrode Conductor.

EXAM 12

Chapter 8 Communications Systems

26. In one- and two-family dwellings, a separate grounding electrode as specified in 250.52(A)(5), (A)(6), or (A)(7) may be used where it is not practicable to attain an overall maximum bonding or equipment grounding conductor length for CATV of:

    A. 5 ft.

    B. 8 ft)

    C. 10 ft.

    D. 20 ft.

    Reference: 2017 National Electrical Code – Chapter 8 Communications Systems, Article 820 Community Antenna Television and Radio Distribution Systems. 820.100 Cable Bonding and Grounding. 820.100(A) Bonding Conductor or Grounding Electrode Conductor. 820.100(A)(4) Length.

27. Where exposed to physical damage, bonding conductors and grounding electrode conductors must be:

    A. electrically

    B. arc-fault

    C. protected

    D. none of these

    Reference: 2017 National Electrical Code – Chapter 8 Communications Systems, Article 820 Community Antenna Television and Radio Distribution Systems. 820.100 Cable Bonding and Grounding. 820.100(A) Bonding Conductor or Grounding Electrode Conductor. 820.100(A)(6) Physical Protection.

28. True or False: The raceway fill limitations detailed in 300.17 will apply to coaxial cables.

    A. True

    B. False

    Reference: 2017 National Electrical Code – Chapter 8 Communications Systems, Article 820 Community Antenna Television and Radio Distribution Systems. 820.110 Raceways and Cable Routing Assemblies for Coaxial Cables. 820.110(B) Raceway Fill for Coaxial Cables.

EXAM 12

EXAM 12 ANSWERS

1. **Answer A.** True

   Installed communications cable that is not terminated at both ends at a connector or other equipment and not identified for future use with a tag.

   Informational Note: See Part I of Article 100 for a definition of Equipment.

   Reference: 2017 National Electrical Code – Chapter 8 Communications Systems, Article 800 Communications Circuits. 800.2 Definitions. Abandoned Communications Cable

2. **Answer A.** True

   Equipment electrically connected to a communications network shall be listed in accordance with 800.170.

   Reference: 2017 National Electrical Code – Chapter 8 Communications Systems, Article 800 Communications Circuits. 800.18 Installation of Equipment.

3. **Answer B.** exposed

   Communications circuits and equipment shall be installed in a neat and workmanlike manner. *Cables installed exposed on the surface of ceilings and sidewalls shall be supported by the building structure* in such a manner that the cable will not be damaged by normal building use. Such cables shall be secured by hardware, including straps, staples, cable ties, hangers, or similar fittings, designed and installed so as not to damage the cable. The installation shall also conform to 300.4(D) and 300.11. Nonmetallic cable ties and other nonmetallic cable accessories used to secure and support cables in other spaces used for environmental air plenums. shall be listed as having low smoke and heat release properties in accordance with 800.170(C).

   Informational Note No. 1: Accepted industry practices are described in ANSI/NECA/BICSI 568-2006, Standard for Installing Commercial Building Telecommunications Cabling; ANSI/TIA-568.1-D-2015, Commercial Building Telecommunications Infrastructure Standard; ANSI/TIA-569-D-2015, Telecommunications Pathways and Spaces; ANSI/TIA-570-C-2012, Residential Telecommunications Infrastructure Standard ; ANSI/TIA-1005-A-2012, Telecommunications Infrastructure Standard for Industrial Premises; ANSI/TIA-1179-2010, Healthcare Facility Telecommunications Infrastructure Standard; ANSI/TIA-4966-2014, Telecommunications Infrastructure Standard for Educational Facilities; and other ANSI-approved installation standards.

   Informational Note No. 2: See 4.3.11.2.6.5 and 4.3.11.5.5.6 of NFPA 90A-2015, Standard for the Installation of Air-Conditioning and Ventilating Systems, for discrete combustible components installed in accordance with 300.22(C).

   Informational Note No. 3: Paint, plaster, cleaners, abrasives, corrosive residues, or other contaminants may result in an undetermined alteration of communications wire and cable properties.

   Reference: 2017 National Electrical Code – Chapter 8 Communications Systems, Article 800 Communications Circuits. 800.24 Mechanical Execution of Work.

4. **Answer A.** True

   The accessible portion of abandoned communications cables shall be removed. Where cables are identified for future use with a tag, the tag shall be of sufficient durability to withstand the environment involved.

   Reference: 2017 National Electrical Code – Chapter 8 Communications Systems, Article 800 Communications Circuits. 800.25 Abandoned Cables.

EXAM 12

EXAM 12 ANSWERS

5. **Answer A.** 12 inches

Supply service drops and sets of overhead service conductors of 0 to 750 volts running above and parallel to communications service drops shall have a *minimum separation of 300 mm (12 in.)* at any point in the span, including the point of and at their attachment to the building, provided that the ungrounded conductors are insulated and that a clearance of not less than 1.0 m (40 in.) is maintained between the two services at the pole.

Reference: 2017 National Electrical Code – Chapter 8 Communications Systems, Article 800 Communications Circuits. 800.44 Overhead Aerial. Communications Wires and Cables. 800.44(A)On Poles and In-Span. 800.44(A)(4) Clearance.

6. **Answer D.** 8 feet

Communications wires and cables shall have a vertical clearance of not less than 2.5 m (8 ft) from all points of roofs above which they pass.

Exception No. 1: Communications wires and cables shall not be required to have a vertical clearance of not less than 2.5 m (8 ft) above auxiliary buildings, such as garages and the like.

Exception No. 2: A reduction in clearance above only the overhanging portion of the roof to not less than 450 mm (18 in.) shall be permitted if (A) not more than 1.2 m (4 ft) of communications service-drop conductors pass above the roof overhang and (B) they are terminated at a through- or above-the-roof raceway or approved support.

Exception No. 3: Where the roof has a slope of not less than 100 mm in 300 mm (4 in. in 12 in.), a reduction in clearance to not less than

900 mm (3 ft) shall be permitted.

Informational Note: For additional information regarding overhead

Aerial. wires and cables, see ANSI/IEEE C2-2012, National

Electrical Safety Code, Part 2, Safety Rules for Overhead Lines.

Reference: 2017 National Electrical Code – Chapter 8 Communications Systems, Article 800 Communications Circuits. 800.44 Overhead Aerial. Communications Wires and Cables. 800.44(B) Above Roofs.

7. **Answer C.** 50 ft.

Unlisted outside plant communications cables shall be permitted to be installed in building spaces other than risers, ducts used for environmental air, plenums used for environmental air, and other spaces used for environmental air, where the length of the cable within the building, measured from its point of entrance, *does not exceed 15 m (50 ft) and the cable enters the building from the outside and is terminated in an enclosure or on a listed primary protector*. The point of entrance shall be permitted to be extended from the penetration of the external wall or floor slab by continuously enclosing the entrance cables in rigid metal conduit (RMC) or intermediate metal conduit (IMC) to the point of emergence.

Informational Note No. 1: Splice cases or terminal boxes, both metallic and plastic types, are typically used as enclosures for splicing or terminating telephone cables.

Informational Note No. 2: This section limits the length of unlisted outside plant cable to 15 m (50 ft), while 800.90(B) requires that the primary protector be located as close as practicable to the point at which the cable enters the building. Therefore, in installations requiring a primary protector, the outside plant cable may not be permitted to extend 15 m (50 ft) into the building if it is practicable to place the primary protector closer than 15 m (50 ft) to the point of entrance.

Reference: 2017 National Electrical Code – Chapter 8 Communications Systems, Article 800 Communications Circuits. 800.48 Unlisted Cables Entering Buildings.

EXAM 12

EXAM 12 ANSWERS

8. **Answer D.** 6 feet

   Where practicable, a separation of **at least 1.8 m (6 ft)** shall be maintained between communications wires and cables on buildings and lightning conductors.

   Informational Note: Specific separation distances may be calculated from the sideflash equation in NFPA 780-2014, Standard for the Installation of Lightning Protection Systems, 4.16.2.

   Reference: 2017 National Electrical Code – Chapter 8 Communications Systems, Article 800 Communications Circuits. 800.53 Lightning Conductors.

9. **Answer C.** either A or B

   In installations where the communications cable enters a building, the metallic sheath members of the **cable shall be either grounded as specified in 800.100 or interrupted by an insulating joint or equivalent device.** The grounding or interruption shall be as close as practicable to the point of entrance.

   Reference: 2017 National Electrical Code – Chapter 8 Communications Systems, Article 800 Communications Circuits. 800.93 Grounding or Interruption of Metallic Sheath Members of Communications Cables. 800.93(A) Entering Buildings.

10. **Answer D.** power

    The primary protector bonding conductor or grounding electrode conductor shall be as short as practicable. In one- and two-family dwellings, the primary protector bonding conductor or grounding electrode conductor shall be as short as practicable, not to exceed 6.0 m (20 ft) in length.

    Informational Note: Similar bonding conductor or grounding electrode conductor length limitations applied at apartment buildings and commercial buildings **help to reduce voltages that may be developed between the building's power and communications systems during lightning events.**

    Exception: In one- and two-family dwellings where it is not practicable to achieve an overall maximum primary protector bonding conductor or grounding electrode conductor length of 6.0 m (20 ft), a separate communications ground rod meeting the minimum dimensional criteria of 800.100(B)(3)(2) shall be driven, the primary protector shall be connected to the communications ground rod in accordance with. 800.100(C), and the communications ground rod shall be connected to the power grounding electrode system in accordance with 800.100(D).

    Reference: 2017 National Electrical Code – Chapter 8 Communications Systems, Article 800 Communications Circuits. 800.100 Cable and Primary Protector Bonding and Grounding. 800.100(A) Bonding Conductor or Grounding Electrode Conductor. 800.100(A) (4) Length.

11. **Answer A.** True

    Communications wires and cables shall be permitted to be installed in any raceway included in Chapter 3. The raceways shall be installed in accordance with the requirements of Chapter 3.

    Reference: 2017 National Electrical Code – Chapter 8 Communications Systems, Article 800 Communications Circuits. 800.110 Raceways and Cable Routing Assemblies for Communications Wires and Cables. 800.110(A) Types of Raceways. 800.110(A) (1) Raceways Recognized in Chapter 3.

EXAM 12

EXAM 12 ANSWERS

12. Answer D. all of these

Communications wires and cables shall be separated at least 50 mm (2 in.) from conductors of any electric light, power, Class 1, non–power-limited fire alarm, or medium-power network-powered broadband communications circuits.

Exception No. 1: Section 800.133(A)(2) shall not apply where either

(1) all of the conductors of the electric light, power, Class 1, non–powerlimited fire alarm, and medium-power network-powered broadband communications circuits are in a raceway or in metal-sheathed, metalclad, nonmetallic-sheathed, Type AC, or Type UF cables, or (2) all of the conductors of communications circuits are encased in raceway.

Exception No. 2: Section 800.133(A)(2) shall not apply where the communications wires and cables are permanently separated from the conductors of electric light, power, Class 1, non–power-limited fire alarm, and medium-power network-powered broadband communications circuits by a continuous and firmly fixed nonconductor, such as porcelain tubes or flexible tubing, in addition to the insulation on the wire.

Reference: 2017 National Electrical Code – Chapter 8 Communications Systems, Article 800 Communications Circuits. 800.133 Installation of Communications Wires, Cables, and Equipment. 800.133(A) Separation from Other Conductors. 800.133(A)(2) Other Applications.

13. Answer C. 810

810.1 Scope. This article covers antenna systems for radio and television receiving equipment, amateur and citizen band radio transmitting and receiving equipment, and certain features of transmitter safety. This article covers antennas such as wire-strung type, multi-element, vertical rod, flat, or parabolic and also covers the wiring and cabling that connect them to equipment. This article does not cover equipment and antennas used for coupling carrier current to power line conductors.

Reference: 2017 National Electrical Code – Chapter 8 Communications Systems, Article 810 Radio and Television Equipment. 810.1 Scope.

14. Answer A. 12 in.

Lead-in conductors attached to buildings shall be installed so that they cannot swing closer than 600 mm (2 ft) to the conductors of circuits of 250 volts or less between conductors, or 3.0 m (10 ft) to the conductors of circuits of over 250 volts between conductors, except that in the case of circuits not over 150 volts between conductors, where all conductors involved are supported so as to ensure permanent separation, the clearance shall be permitted to be reduced but shall not be less than 100 mm (4 in.). The clearance between lead-in conductors and any conductor forming a part of a lightning protection system shall not be less than 1.8 m (6 ft). ***Underground conductors shall be separated at least 300 mm (12 in.)*** *from conductors of any light or power circuits or Class 1 circuits.*

Exception: Where the electric light or power conductors, Class 1 conductors, or lead-in conductors are installed in raceways or metal cable armor.

Informational Note No. 1: See 250.60 for grounding associated with lightning protection components — strike termination devices. For further information, see NFPA 780-2014, Standard for the Installation of Lightning Protection Systems, which contains detailed information on grounding, bonding, and spacing from lightning protection systems, and the calculation of specific separation distances using the sideflash equation in Section 4.6.

Informational Note No. 2: Metal raceways, enclosures, frames, and other non–current-carrying metal parts of electrical equipment installed on a building equipped with a lightning protection system may require bonding or spacing from the lightning protection conductors in accordance with NFPA 780 -2014, Standard for the Installation of Lightning Protection Systems. Separation from lightning protection conductors is typically 1.8 m (6 ft) through air or 900 mm (3 ft) through dense materials such as concrete, brick, or wood.

Reference: 2017 National Electrical Code – Chapter 8 Communications Systems, Article 810 Radio and Television Equipment. 810.18 Clearances - Receiving Stations. 810.18(A) Outside of Buildings.

EXAM 12

EXAM 12 ANSWERS

15. **Answer A.** True

    Indoor antennas and indoor lead-ins shall be permitted to occupy the same box or enclosure with conductors of other wiring systems where separated from such other conductors by an effective permanently installed barrier.

    Reference: 2017 National Electrical Code – Chapter 8 Communications Systems, Article 810 Radio and Television Equipment. 810.18 Clearances - Receiving Stations. 810.18(C) In Boxes or Other Enclosures.

16. **Answer C.** mechanical

    Bonding conductors and grounding electrode conductors shall be protected where exposed to physical damage. Where the bonding conductor or grounding electrode conductor is *installed in a metal raceway, both ends of the raceway shall be bonded to the contained conductor or to the same terminal or electrode to which the bonding conductor* or grounding electrode conductor is connected.

    Reference: 2017 National Electrical Code – Chapter 8 Communications Systems, Article 820 Community Antenna Television and Radio Distribution Systems. 820.100 Cable Bonding and Grounding. 820.100 (A) Bonding Conductor or Grounding Electrode Conductor. 820.100 (A) (6) Physical Protection.

17. **Answer A.** contained

    Bonding conductors and grounding electrode conductors shall be protected where exposed to physical damage. Where the bonding conductor or grounding electrode conductor is installed in a metal raceway, both ends of the raceway shall be *bonded to the contained conductor or to the same terminal or electrode to which the bonding conductor or grounding electrode conductor is connected*.

    Reference: 2017 National Electrical Code – Chapter 8 Communications Systems, Article 820 Community Antenna Television and Radio Distribution Systems. 820.100 Cable Bonding and Grounding. 820.100 (A) Bonding Conductor or Grounding Electrode Conductor. 820.100 (A) (6) Physical Protection.

18. **Answer A.** True

    If the building or structure served has an intersystem bonding termination *as required by 250.94, the bonding conductor shall be connected to the intersystem bonding termination.*

    Informational Note: See Article 100 for the definition of Intersystem Bonding Termination.

    Reference: 2017 National Electrical Code – Chapter 8 Communications Systems, Article 820 Community Antenna Television and Radio Distribution Systems. 820.100 Cable Bonding and Grounding. 820.100 (A) Bonding Conductor or Grounding Electrode Conductor. 820.100 (A) (1) In Buildings or Structures with an Intersystem Bonding. Termination.

19. **Answer A.** 6

    A bonding jumper not smaller than 6 AWG copper or equivalent shall be connected between the community antenna television system's grounding electrode and the power grounding electrode system at the building or structure served where separate electrodes are used.

    Exception: At mobile homes as covered in 820.106. Informational Note No. 1: See 250.60 for connection to a lightning protection system. Informational Note No. 2: Bonding together of all separate electrodes limits potential differences between them and between their associated wiring systems.

    Reference: 2017 National Electrical Code – Chapter 8 Communications Systems, Article 820 Community Antenna Television and Radio Distribution Systems. 820.100 Cable Bonding and Grounding. 820.100 (D) Bonding of Electrodes

EXAM 12

EXAM 12 ANSWERS

20. Answer B. dielectric

A cylindrical assembly composed of a conductor centered *inside a metallic tube or shield, separated by a dielectric material, and usually covered by an insulating jacket.*

Reference: 2017 National Electrical Code – Chapter 1 General. ARTICLE 100 Definitions . Coaxial Cable

21. Answer A. 60V

Coaxial cable shall be permitted to deliver power to equipment that is directly associated with the radio frequency distribution *system if the voltage is not over 60 volts and if the current is supplied by a transformer or other device that has power-limiting characteristics*.

Power shall be blocked from premises devices on the network that are not intended to be powered via the coaxial cable.

Reference: 2017 National Electrical Code – Chapter 8 Communications Systems, Article 820 Community Antenna Television and Radio Distribution Systems. 820.15 Power Limitations.

22. Answer B. exposed

Community television and radio distribution systems shall be installed in a neat and workmanlike manner. *Coaxial cables installed exposed on the surface of ceiling and sidewalls shall be supported by the building structure in such a manner that the cables will not be damaged by normal building use.* Such cables shall be secured by hardware including straps, staples, cable ties, hangers, or similar fittings designed and installed so as not to damage the cable. The installation shall also conform to 300.4(D) and 300.11. Nonmetallic cable ties and other nonmetallic cable accessories used to secure and support cables in other spaces used for environmental air plenums. shall be listed as having low smoke and heat release properties in accordance with 800.170(C).

Informational Note No. 1: Accepted industry practices are described in ANSI/NECA/BICSI 568–2006, Standard for Installing Commercial Building Telecommunications Cabling; ANSI/TIA-568.1-D-2015, Commercial Building Telecommunications Infrastructure Standard; ANSI/TIA-569-D-2015, Telecommunications Pathways and Spaces; ANSI/TIA-570-C-2012, Residential Telecommunications Infrastructure Standard; ANSI/TIA-1005-A-2012, Telecommunications Infrastructure Standard for Industrial Premises; ANSI/TIA-1179-2010, Healthcare Facility Telecommunications Infrastructure Standard; ANSI/TIA-4966-2014, Telecommunications Infrastructure Standard for Educational Facilities; and other ANSI-approved installation standards.

Informational Note No. 2: See 4.3.11.2.6.5 and 4.3.11.5.5.6 of NFPA 90A -2015, Standard for the Installation of Air-Conditioning and Ventilating Systems, for discrete combustible components installed in accordance with 300.22(C).

Informational Note No. 3: Paint, plaster, cleaners, abrasives, corrosive residues, or other contaminants may result in an undetermined alteration of coaxial cable properties.

Reference: 2017 National Electrical Code – Chapter 8 Communications Systems, Article 820 Community Antenna Television and Radio Distribution Systems. 820.24 Mechanical Execution of Work.

EXAM 12

EXAM 12 ANSWERS

23. **Answer A.** True

    The accessible portion of abandoned coaxial cables shall be removed. Where cables are identified for future use with a tag, the tag shall be of sufficient durability to withstand the environment involved.

    Reference: 2017 National Electrical Code – Chapter 8 Communications Systems, Article 820 Community Antenna Television and Radio Distribution Systems. 820.25 Abandoned Cables.

24. **Answer C.** 50 ft.

    Unlisted outside plant coaxial cables shall be permitted to be installed in building spaces other than risers, ducts used for environmental air, plenums used for environmental air, and other spaces used for environmental air, where the length of the cable within the building, measured ***from its point of entrance, does not exceed 15 m (50 ft.)*** and the cable enters the building from the outside and is terminated at a grounding block. The point of entrance shall be permitted to be extended from the penetration of the external wall or floor slab by continuously enclosing the entrance cables in rigid metal conduit (RMC) or intermediate metal conduit (IMC) to the point of emergence.

    Reference: 2017 National Electrical Code – Chapter 8 Communications Systems, Article 820 Community Antenna Television and Radio Distribution Systems. 820.48 Unlisted Cables Entering Buildings.

EXAM 12

EXAM 12 ANSWERS

25. **Answer D.** all of these

    (1) Insulation. The bonding conductor or grounding electrode conductor shall be listed and shall be permitted to be *insulated, covered, or bare.*

    (2) Material. The bonding conductor or grounding electrode conductor shall be copper or other corrosion-resistant conductive material, stranded or solid.

    (3) Size. The bonding conductor or grounding electrode conductor *shall not be smaller than 14 AWG*. It shall have a current-carrying capacity not less than the outer sheath of the coaxial cable. The bonding conductor or grounding electrode conductor shall not be required to exceed 6 AWG.

    (4) Length. The bonding conductor or grounding electrode conductor shall be as short as practicable. In one- and twofamily dwellings, the bonding conductor or grounding electrode conductor shall be as short as practicable, not to exceed 6.0 m (20 ft) in length.

    Informational Note: Similar bonding conductor or grounding electrode conductor length limitations applied at apartment buildings and commercial buildings help to reduce voltages that may be developed between the building's power and communications systems during lightning events.

    Exception: In one- and two-family dwellings where it is not practicable to achieve an overall maximum bonding conductor or grounding electrode conductor length of 6.0 m (20 ft), a separate grounding electrode as specified in 250.52(A)(5), (A)(6), or (A)(7) shall be used, the grounding electrode conductor shall be connected to the separate grounding electrode in accordance with 250.70, and the separate grounding electrode shall be connected to the power grounding electrode system in accordance with 820.100(D).

    (5) Run in Straight Line. The bonding conductor or grounding electrode conductor shall be run in as straight a line as practicable.

    (6) Physical Protection. Bonding conductors and grounding electrode conductors shall be protected where exposed to physical damage. Where the bonding conductor or grounding electrode conductor is installed in a metal raceway, both ends of the raceway shall be bonded to the contained conductor or to the same terminal or electrode to which the bonding conductor or grounding electrode conductor is connected.

    Reference: 2017 National Electrical Code – Chapter 8 Communications Systems, Article 820 Community Antenna Television and Radio Distribution Systems . 820.100 Cable Bonding and Grounding. 820.100(A) Bonding Conductor or Grounding Electrode Conductor.

26. **Answer D.** 20 ft.

    The bonding conductor or grounding electrode conductor shall be as short as practicable. In one- and two family dwellings, the bonding conductor or *grounding electrode conductor shall be as short as practicable, not to exceed 6.0 m (20 ft) in length*.

    Informational Note: Similar bonding conductor or grounding electrode conductor length limitations applied at apartment buildings and commercial buildings help to reduce voltages that may be developed between the building's power and communications systems during lightning events.

    Exception: In one- and two-family dwellings where it is not practicable to achieve an overall maximum bonding conductor or grounding electrode conductor length of 6.0 m (20 ft), a separate grounding electrode as specified in 250.52(A)(5), (A)(6), or (A)(7) shall be used, the grounding electrode conductor shall be connected to the separate grounding electrode in accordance with 250.70, and the separate grounding electrode shall be connected to the power grounding electrode system in accordance with 820.100(D).

    Reference: 2017 National Electrical Code – Chapter 8 Communications Systems, Article 820 Community Antenna Television and Radio Distribution Systems. 820.100 Cable Bonding and Grounding. 820.100(A) Bonding Conductor or Grounding Electrode Conductor. 820.100(A)(4) Length.

27. **Answer C.** protected

    Bonding conductors and grounding electrode conductors shall be protected where exposed to physical damage. Where the bonding conductor or grounding electrode conductor is installed in a metal raceway, both ends of the raceway shall be bonded to the contained conductor or to the same terminal or electrode to which the bonding conductor or grounding electrode conductor is connected.

    Reference: 2017 National Electrical Code – Chapter 8 Communications Systems, Article 820 Community Antenna Television and Radio Distribution Systems. 820.100 Cable Bonding and Grounding. 820.100(A) Bonding Conductor or Grounding Electrode Conductor. 820.100(A)(6) Physical Protection.

EXAM 12

EXAM 12 ANSWERS

28. **Answer B.** False

    The raceway fill requirements of *Chapters 3 and 9 shall not apply to coaxial cables*.

    Reference: 2017 National Electrical Code – Chapter 8 Communications Systems, Article 820 Community Antenna Television and Radio Distribution Systems. 820.110 Raceways and Cable Routing Assemblies for Coaxial Cables. 820.110(B) Raceway Fill for Coaxial Cables.

EXAM 13

Chapter 9 Tables

1. What is the maximum cross-sectional value that conduit nipples under 24 inches long may be filled?

   A. 30%   C. 54%

   B. 40%   D. 60%

   Reference: 2017 National Electrical Code – Chapter 9 Tables

2. In a trade size 1-1/4 in. electrical metallic tubing (EMT) 18 inches long, what is the maximum number of size 4 AWG THHN copper conductors that may be installed?

   A. 10   C. 12

   B. 11   D. 13

   Reference: 2017 National Electrical Code – Chapter 9 Tables

3. The minimum bending radius, in inches, for a 3/4" EMT, using a Full Shoe bender is:

   A. 3.5   C. 5.5

   B. 4.5   D. 7.25

   Reference: 2017 National Electrical Code – Chapter 9 Tables

4. A 2" EMT using a One Shot bender has a minimum bending radius of:

   A. 7   C. 9.5

   B. 8.25   D. 11

   Reference: 2017 National Electrical Code – Chapter 9 Tables

Chapter 9 Tables

EXAM 13

Chapter 9 Tables

5. If more than 2 conductors are used in a tube of EMT conduit, total interior area that can be filled is no more than _____ percent.

    A. 31

    B. 40

    C. 53

    D. 60

    Reference: 2017 National Electrical Code – Chapter 9 Tables

6. What is the minimum allowable trade size intermediate metal conduit (IMC) required to contain a total of ten (10) copper THW conductors in a 20 foot run, five (5) size 1 AWG and five (5) size 3 AWG?

    A. 1-1/2 in.

    B. 2 in.

    C. 2-1/2 in.

    D. 3 in.

    Reference: 2017 National Electrical Code – Chapter 9 Tables

7. What is the approximate diameter, on No. 2 RHW wire in inches?

    A. .125

    B. .275

    C. .375

    D. .472

    Reference: 2017 National Electrical Code – Chapter 9 Tables

8. Given the following information, what is the maximum approximate distance a single-phase, 240-volt, 42 ampere load can be located from a panelboard?

    A. 50 feet

    B. 110 feet

    C. 160 feet

    D. 195 feet

    Reference: 2017 National Electrical Code – Chapter 9 Tables

EXAM 13

Chapter 9 Tables

9. Where K=12.9, what is the approximate voltage-drop on a circuit where an 80-ampere, 240-volt, single-phase load is supplied with size 3 AWG copper conductors with THWN insulation, and placed 200 feet from a panelboard?

    A. 4.0 volts   C. 7.84 volts

    B. 6.0 volts   D. 9.2 volts

Reference: 2017 National Electrical Code – Chapter 9 Tables

EXAM 13

EXAM 13 ANSWERS

CHAPTER 9   TABLES

Table 5 Dimensions of Insulated Conductors and Fixture Wires

Type	Size (AWG or kcmil)	Approximate Area mm²	Approximate Area in.²	Approximate Diameter mm	Approximate Diameter in.
Type: FFH-2, RFH-1, RFH-2, RFHH-2, RHH*, RHW*, RHW-2*, RHH, RHW, RHW-2, SF-1, SF-2, SFF-1, SFF-2, TF, TFF, THHW, THW, THW-2, TW, XF, XFF					
RFH-2, FFH-2, RFHH-2	18	9.355	0.0145	3.454	0.136
	16	11.10	0.0172	3.759	0.148
RHH, RHW, RHW-2	14	18.90	0.0293	4.902	0.193
	12	22.77	0.0353	5.385	0.212
	10	28.19	0.0437	5.994	0.236
	8	53.87	0.0835	8.280	0.326
	6	67.16	0.1041	9.246	0.364
	4	86.00	0.1333	10.46	0.412
	3	98.13	0.1521	11.18	0.440
	2	112.9	0.1750	11.99	0.472
	1	171.6	0.2660	14.78	0.582
	1/0	196.1	0.3039	15.80	0.622
	2/0	226.1	0.3505	16.97	0.668
	3/0	262.7	0.4072	18.29	0.720
	4/0	306.7	0.4754	19.76	0.778
	250	405.9	0.6291	22.73	0.895
	300	457.3	0.7088	24.13	0.950
	350	507.7	0.7870	25.43	1.001

1. **Answer D.** 60%

   Where conduit or tubing nipples having a maximum length not to exceed 600 mm (24 in.) are installed between boxes, cabinets, and similar enclosures, **the nipples shall be permitted to be filled to 60 percent** of their total cross-sectional area, and 310.15(B)(3)(A) adjustment factors need not apply to this condition.

   Reference: 2017 National Electrical Code – Chapter 9 Tables. Notes to Tables (4)

2. **Answer B.** 11

   When calculating the maximum number of conductors or cables permitted in a conduit or tubing, all of the same size (total cross-sectional area including insulation), the next higher whole number shall be used to determine the maximum number of conductors permitted when the calculation results in a decimal greater than or equal to 0.8. When calculating the size for conduit or tubing permitted for a single conductor, one conductor shall be permitted when the calculation results in a decimal greater than or equal to 0.8.

   Reference: 2017 National Electrical Code – Chapter 9 Tables. Note 7 to Chapter 9 Tables

897 sq. in. (conduit) = 10.8 = 11 wires

0824 sq. in. (wire

Reference: 2017 National Electrical Code – Chapter 9 Tables. Table 4 Dimensions and Percent Area of Conduit and Tubing Areas of Conduit or Tubing for the Combinations of Wires Permitted in Table 1, Chapter 9. (page 70-679)

Reference: 2017 National Electrical Code – Chapter 9 Tables. Table 5 Dimensions of Insulated Conductors and Fixture Wires (page 70-684)

3. **Answer B.** 4.5

   For a 3/4" EMT using a Full Shoe bender, **the minimum radius is 4-1/2 inches.**

   Reference: 2017 National Electrical Code – Chapter 9 Tables. Table 2 Radius of Conduit and Tubing Bends (page 70-679)

EXAM 13

EXAM 13 ANSWERS

Table 2 Radius of Conduit and Tubing Bends

Conduit or Tubing Size		One Shot and Full Shoe Benders		Other Bends	
Metric Designator	Trade Size	mm	in.	mm	in.
16	½	101.6	4	101.6	4
21	¾	114.3	4½	127	5
27	1	146.05	5¾	152.4	6
35	1¼	184.15	7¼	203.2	8
41	1½	209.55	8¼	254	10
53	2	241.3	9½	304.8	12
63	2½	266.7	10½	381	15
78	3	330.2	13	457.2	18
91	3½	381	15	533.4	21
103	4	406.4	16	609.6	24
129	5	609.6	24	762	30
155	6	762	30	914.4	36

4. **Answer C.** 9.5

The minimum bending radius for a 2" EMT using a One Shot bender is 9-1/2".

Reference: 2017 National Electrical Code – Chapter 9 Tables. Table 2 Radius of Conduit and Tubing Bends (page 70-679)

5. **Answer B.** 40

The total interior area of a tube of EMT conduit that can be filled *if more than 2 conductors are used is 40 percent*.

Reference: 2017 National Electrical Code – Chapter 9 Tables. Table 4 Dimensions and Percent Area of Conduit and Tubing Areas of Conduit or Tubing for the Combinations of Wires Permitted in Table 1, Chapter 9. (page 70-680)

6. **Answer C.** 2-1/2 in.

Size 1 AWG THW = .1901 sq. in. x 5 = .9505 sq. in.

Size 3 AWG THW = .1134 sq. in. x 5 = .537 sq. in.

Total = 1.5175 sq. in.

*NOTE: A trade size 2-1/2 in. IMC with an allowable 40% fill of 2.054 sq. in. should be selected.

Reference: 2017 National Electrical Code – Chapter 9 Tables. Table 4 Dimensions and Percent Area of Conduit and Tubing Areas of Conduit or Tubing for the Combinations of Wires Permitted in Table 1, Chapter 9. (page 70-681)

Reference: 2017 National Electrical Code – Chapter 9 Tables. Table 5 Dimensions of Insulated Conductors and Fixture Wires (page 70-761)

7. **Answer D.** 472

On No.2 RHW wire, the approximate diameter is *.472* inches.

Reference: 2017 National Electrical Code – Chapter 9 Tables. Table 5 Dimensions of Insulated Conductors and Fixture Wires (page 70-684)

* copper conductors – K = 12.9

* size 8 AWG THWN/THHN conductors are used

* Limit voltage drop to 3%

8. **Answer B.** 110 feet

Reference: 2017 National Electrical Code – Chapter 9 Tables. Table 8 Conductor Properties (page 70-766)

Distance Formula

1st. find allowable VD - 240 volts x 3% = 7.2 volts

D = CM x VDD = 16,510 x 7.2 = 118,872 = 109.7 feet
     2 x K x I   2 x 12.9 x 42   1,083.6

EXAM 13

EXAM 13 ANSWERS

CHAPTER 9   **TABLES**

Table 4 Dimensions and Percent Area of Conduit and Tubing (Areas of Conduit or Tubing for the Combinations of Wires Permitted in Table 1, Chapter 9)

Article 358 — Electrical Metallic Tubing (EMT)

Metric Designator	Trade Size	Over 2 Wires 40%		60%		1 Wire 53%		2 Wires 31%		Nominal Internal Diameter		Total Area 100%	
		mm^2	$in.^2$	mm^2	$in.^2$	mm^2	$in.^2$	mm^2	$in.^2$	mm	in.	mm^2	$in.^2$
16	½	78	0.122	118	0.182	104	0.161	61	0.094	15.8	0.622	196	0.304
21	¾	137	0.213	206	0.320	182	0.283	106	0.165	20.9	0.824	343	0.533
27	1	222	0.346	333	0.519	295	0.458	172	0.268	26.6	1.049	556	0.864
35	1¼	387	0.598	581	0.897	513	0.793	300	0.464	35.1	1.380	968	1.496
41	1½	526	0.814	788	1.221	696	1.079	407	0.631	40.9	1.610	1314	2.036
53	2	866	1.342	1299	2.013	1147	1.778	671	1.040	52.5	2.067	2165	3.356
63	2½	1513	2.343	2270	3.515	2005	3.105	1173	1.816	69.4	2.731	3783	5.858
78	3	2280	3.538	3421	5.307	3022	4.688	1767	2.742	85.2	3.356	5701	8.846
91	3½	2980	4.618	4471	6.927	3949	6.119	2310	3.579	97.4	3.834	7451	11.545
103	4	3808	5.901	5712	8.852	5046	7.819	2951	4.573	110.1	4.334	9521	14.753

Article 362 — Electrical Nonmetallic Tubing (ENT)

Metric Designator	Trade Size	Over 2 Wires 40%		60%		1 Wire 53%		2 Wires 31%		Nominal Internal Diameter		Total Area 100%	
		mm^2	$in.^2$	mm^2	$in.^2$	mm^2	$in.^2$	mm^2	$in.^2$	mm	in.	mm^2	$in.^2$
16	½	73	0.114	110	0.171	97	0.151	57	0.088	15.3	0.602	184	0.285
21	¾	131	0.203	197	0.305	174	0.269	102	0.157	20.4	0.804	328	0.508
27	1	215	0.333	322	0.499	284	0.441	166	0.258	26.1	1.029	537	0.832
35	1¼	375	0.581	562	0.872	497	0.770	291	0.450	34.5	1.36	937	1.453
41	1½	512	0.794	769	1.191	679	1.052	397	0.616	40.4	1.59	1281	1.986
53	2	849	1.316	1274	1.975	1125	1.744	658	1.020	52	2.047	2123	3.291
63	2½	—	—	—	—	—	—	—	—	—	—	—	—
78	3	—	—	—	—	—	—	—	—	—	—	—	—
91	3½	—	—	—	—	—	—	—	—	—	—	—	—

Article 348 — Flexible Metal Conduit (FMC)

Metric Designator	Trade Size	Over 2 Wires 40%		60%		1 Wire 53%		2 Wires 31%		Nominal Internal Diameter		Total Area 100%	
		mm^2	$in.^2$	mm^2	$in.^2$	mm^2	$in.^2$	mm^2	$in.^2$	mm	in.	mm^2	$in.^2$
12	⅜	30	0.046	44	0.069	39	0.061	23	0.036	9.7	0.384	74	0.116
16	½	81	0.127	122	0.190	108	0.168	63	0.098	16.1	0.635	204	0.317
21	¾	137	0.213	206	0.320	182	0.283	106	0.165	20.9	0.824	343	0.533
27	1	211	0.327	316	0.490	279	0.433	163	0.253	25.9	1.020	527	0.817
35	1¼	330	0.511	495	0.766	437	0.677	256	0.396	32.4	1.275	824	1.277
41	1½	480	0.743	720	1.115	636	0.985	372	0.576	39.1	1.538	1201	1.858
53	2	843	1.307	1264	1.961	1117	1.732	653	1.013	51.8	2.040	2107	3.269
63	2½	1267	1.963	1900	2.945	1678	2.602	982	1.522	63.5	2.500	3167	4.909
78	3	1824	2.827	2736	4.241	2417	3.746	1414	2.191	76.2	3.000	4560	7.069
91	3½	2483	3.848	3724	5.773	3290	5.099	1924	2.983	88.9	3.500	6207	9.621
103	4	3243	5.027	4864	7.540	4297	6.660	2513	3.896	101.6	4.000	8107	12.566

Article 342 — Intermediate Metal Conduit (IMC)

Metric Designator	Trade Size	Over 2 Wires 40%		60%		1 Wire 53%		2 Wires 31%		Nominal Internal Diameter		Total Area 100%	
		mm^2	$in.^2$	mm^2	$in.^2$	mm^2	$in.^2$	mm^2	$in.^2$	mm	in.	mm^2	$in.^2$
12	⅜	—	—	—	—	—	—	—	—	—	—	—	—
16	½	89	0.137	133	0.205	117	0.181	69	0.106	16.8	0.660	222	0.342
21	¾	151	0.235	226	0.352	200	0.311	117	0.182	21.9	0.864	377	0.586

(continues)

EXAM 13

EXAM 13 ANSWERS

Table 8 Conductor Properties

Size (AWG or kcmil)	Area		Conductors						Direct-Current Resistance at 75°C (167°F)					
			Stranding		Overall				Copper				Aluminum	
				Diameter		Diameter		Area	Uncoated		Coated			
	mm²	Circular mils	Quantity	mm	in.	mm	in.	mm²	in.²	ohm/km	ohm/kFT	ohm/km	ohm/kFT	ohm/km	ohm/kFT
18	0.823	1620	1	—	—	1.02	0.040	0.823	0.001	25.5	7.77	26.5	8.08	42.0	12.8
18	0.823	1620	7	0.39	0.015	1.16	0.046	1.06	0.002	26.1	7.95	27.7	8.45	42.8	13.1
16	1.31	2580	1	—	—	1.29	0.051	1.31	0.002	16.0	4.89	16.7	5.08	26.4	8.05
16	1.31	2580	7	0.49	0.019	1.46	0.058	1.68	0.003	16.4	4.99	17.3	5.29	26.9	8.21
14	2.08	4110	1	—	—	1.63	0.064	2.08	0.003	10.1	3.07	10.4	3.19	16.6	5.06
14	2.08	4110	7	0.62	0.024	1.85	0.073	2.68	0.004	10.3	3.14	10.7	3.26	16.9	5.17
12	3.31	6530	1	—	—	2.05	0.081	3.31	0.005	6.34	1.93	6.57	2.01	10.45	3.18
12	3.31	6530	7	0.78	0.030	2.32	0.092	4.25	0.006	6.50	1.98	6.73	2.05	10.69	3.25
10	5.261	10380	1	—	—	2.588	0.102	5.26	0.008	3.984	1.21	4.148	1.26	6.561	2.00
10	5.261	10380	7	0.98	0.038	2.95	0.116	6.76	0.011	4.070	1.24	4.226	1.29	6.679	2.04
8	8.367	16510	1	—	—	3.264	0.128	8.37	0.013	2.506	0.764	2.579	0.786	4.125	1.26
8	8.367	16510	7	1.23	0.049	3.71	0.146	10.76	0.017	2.551	0.778	2.653	0.809	4.204	1.28
6	13.30	26240	7	1.56	0.061	4.67	0.184	17.09	0.027	1.608	0.491	1.671	0.510	2.652	0.808
4	21.15	41740	7	1.96	0.077	5.89	0.232	27.19	0.042	1.010	0.308	1.053	0.321	1.666	0.508
3	26.67	52620	7	2.20	0.087	6.60	0.260	34.28	0.053	0.802	0.245	0.833	0.254	1.320	0.403
2	33.62	66360	7	2.47	0.097	7.42	0.292	43.23	0.067	0.634	0.194	0.661	0.201	1.045	0.319
1	42.41	83690	19	1.69	0.066	8.43	0.332	55.80	0.087	0.505	0.154	0.524	0.160	0.829	0.253
1/0	53.49	105600	19	1.89	0.074	9.45	0.372	70.41	0.109	0.399	0.122	0.415	0.127	0.660	0.201
2/0	67.43	133100	19	2.13	0.084	10.62	0.418	88.74	0.137	0.3170	0.0967	0.329	0.101	0.523	0.159
3/0	85.01	167800	19	2.39	0.094	11.94	0.470	111.9	0.173	0.2512	0.0766	0.2610	0.0797	0.413	0.126
4/0	107.2	211600	19	2.68	0.106	13.41	0.528	141.1	0.219	0.1996	0.0608	0.2050	0.0626	0.328	0.100
250	127	—	37	2.09	0.082	14.61	0.575	168	0.260	0.1687	0.0515	0.1753	0.0535	0.2778	0.0847
300	152	—	37	2.29	0.090	16.00	0.630	201	0.312	0.1409	0.0429	0.1463	0.0446	0.2318	0.0707
350	177	—	37	2.47	0.097	17.30	0.681	235	0.364	0.1205	0.0367	0.1252	0.0382	0.1984	0.0605

9. Answer C.   7.84 volts

Voltage-drop formula

VD = 2KID   VD = 2 x 12.9 x 80 amps x 200 ft. = 7.84 volts

CM52.620 CM

Reference: 2017 National Electrical Code – Chapter 9 Tables. Table 8 Conductor Properties (page 70-766)

EXAM 14

Annexes

1. The ampacity rating of No. 1 (AWG) copper-clad aluminum conductors at 90°C in multiconductor cables with up to three insulated conductors, rated 0 through 2000 volts, with an ambient temperature of 40°C, in free air, for type MC cables is:

    A. 84
    B. 108
    C. 120
    D. 126

    Reference: 2017 National Electrical Code – Annex B. , Table B.310.15(B)(2)(3) Ampacities of Multiconductor Cables with Not More Than Three Insulated Conductors, Rated 0 Through 2000 Volts, in Free Air Based on Ambient Air Temperature of 40°C (104°F) (for Types Te, MC, MI, UF, and USE Cables) on page 70-701 of the code.

2. No. 4 (AWG) copper conductors at 75°C. in multiconductor UF cables, with up to three insulated conductors, rated 0 through 2000 Volts, in free air, with an ambient air temperature of 40°C has an ampacity rating of _____ for type UF and USE cables.

    A. 69
    B. 89
    C. 100
    D. 104

    Reference: 2017 National Electrical Code – Annex B: , Table B.310.15(B)(2)(3) Ampacities of Multiconductor Cables with Not More Than Three Insulated Conductors. Rated 0 Through 2000 Volts, in Free Air Based on Ambient Air Temperature of 40°C (104°F) (for Types TC, MC, MI, UF, and USE Cables) on page 70-701 of the code.

3. For electrical metallic tubing for No.3 Type TW conductors, in trade size 63 tubing, there can be up to _____ conductors or fixture wires.

    A. 8
    B. 10
    C. 15
    D. 20

    Reference: 2017 National Electrical Code – Annex C, Table C.1 Maximum Number of Conductors and Fixture Wires in Electrical Metallic Tubing (EMT) (page 70-713).

EXAM 14

Annexes

4. How many size 10 AWG conductors with THWN insulation are permitted in 3/4 in. diameter EMT (electrical metallic tubing) over 24 inches in length?

   A. 6   C. 10

   B. 8   D. 14

   Reference: 2017 National Electrical Code – Annex C, Table C.1 Maximum Number of Conductors and Fixture Wires in Electrical Metallic Tubing (EMT) (page 70-791)

5. For electrical metallic tubing for No. 14 Type THHN conductors in trade size 27 tubing, the maximum number of conductors or fixture wires is:

   A. 22   C. 61

   B. 35   D. 84

   Reference: 2017 National Electrical Code – Annex C, Table C.1 Maximum Number of Conductors or Fixture Wires in Electrical Metallic Tubing (EMT) (Based on Table 1, Chapter 9) on page 713 of the code.

6. When electrical metallic tubing (EMT) is installed in a 50 foot conduit run, what is the minimum trade size required for enclosing eight (8) size 6 AWG copper conductors with THHW insulation?

   A. 1 in.   C. 1-1/2 In.

   B. 1-1/4 in.   D. 2 in.

   Reference: 2017 National Electrical Code – Annex C, Table C.1 Maximum Number of Conductors and Fixture Wires in Electrical Metallic Tubing (EMT) (page 70-713)

7. The maximum number of No. 12 Type THHW conductors that can be used in trade size 27 electrical metallic tubing is:

   A. 6   C. 19

   B. 10   D. 28

   Reference: 2017 National Electrical Code – Annex C, Table C.10 Maximum Number of Conductors or Fixture Wires in Rigid PVC Conduit, Schedule 40 and HDPE Conduit (page 70-767)

Annexes   653

EXAM 14

Annexes

8. For a trade size 3 in. rigid Schedule 40 PVC conduit over 24 inches long, what is the maximum number of size 1/0 AWG XHHW compact conductors allowed?

   A. 14

   B. 18

   C. 19

   D. 21

   Reference: 2017 National Electrical Code – Annex C, Table C.10 Maximum Number of Conductors or Fixture Wires in Rigid PVC Conduit, Schedule 40 and HDPE Conduit (page 70-767)

9. When a dwelling has a 1500 sq. ft. floor area, an unfinished attic, an unfinished cellar not adaptable for future use, and open porches. It has a 12-kW range and a 5.5 kW, 240-V dryer for appliances. Assume kW ratings for both are equivalent to kVA ratings in accordance with Article 220.54 and 220.55. The net calculated total load in VA units for the dwelling is:

   A. 15,600

   B. 18,600

   C. 22,600

   D. 30,500

   Reference: 2017 National Electrical Code – Annex D.

10. When a dwelling has a 1500 sq. ft. floor area, an unfinished attic, an unfinished cellar not adaptable for future use, and open porches. It has a 12-kW range and a 5.5 kW, 240-V dryer for appliances. Assume kW ratings for both are equivalent to kVA ratings in accordance with Article 220.54 and 220.55. The VA units for the general lighting load is:

    A. 2700 VA

    B. 3800 VA

    C. 4500 VA

    D. 6000 VA

    Reference: 2017 National Electrical Code – Annex D.

EXAM 14

EXAM 14 ANSWERS

11. When a dwelling has a 1500 sq. ft. floor area, an unfinished attic, an unfinished cellar not adaptable for future use, and open porches. It has a 12-kW range and a 5.5 kW, 240-V dryer for appliances. Assume kW ratings for both are equivalent to kVA ratings in accordance with Article 220.54 and 220.55. The number of branch general light circuits is at least:

    A. Two 15-A, 2-wire and two 20-A, 2-wire circuits

    B. Three 15-A, 2-wire or two 20-A, 2-wire circuits

    C. Four 15-A, 2-wire or three 20-A, 2-wire circuits

    D. Five 15-A, 2-wire or three 20-A, 2-wire circuits

    Reference: 2017 National Electrical Code – Annex D.

12. When a dwelling has a 1500 sq. ft. floor area, an unfinished attic, an unfinished cellar not adaptable for future use, and open porches. It has a 12-kW range and a 5.5 kW, 240-V dryer for appliances. Assume kW ratings for both are equivalent to kVA ratings in accordance with Article 220.54 and 220.55. What is the minimum required service size in amperes, assuming the swelling is fed by a 120/240-V 3-wire, single-phase service?

    A. 60

    B. 100

    C. 150

    D. 200

    Reference: 2017 National Electrical Code – Annex D.

EXAM 14

EXAM 14 ANSWERS

13. When a dwelling has 1500 sq. ft. of floor area, excluding an unfinished attic, unfinished cellar not adaptable for future use, and open porches; six 7-A, 230-V room air-conditioning units, two 4-kW wall-mounted ovens, two 20-A small appliance circuits, one 5.1-kW counter-mounted cooking unit, one 5-kW combination clothes washer and dryer, one 4.5-kW water heater, one 1.5-kW, 230 V permanently installed bathroom space heater, one 1.2-kW dishwasher, and one 20-A laundry circuit, and we assume wall-mounted ovens, counter-mounted cooking unit, water heater, dishwasher, and combination clothes washer and dryer kW ratings equivalent to kVA. If we assume the dwelling is fed by a 120/240-V, 3-wire, single-phase service, what is the minimum required service rating and the total calculated load in VA required?

   A. 100 A, 19,200 VA

   B. 110 A , 25,700 VA

   C. 122 A, 29,200 VA

   D. 175 A, 39,200 VA

   Reference: 2017 National Electrical Code – Annex D. Example D2(b) One-Family Dwelling on page 793 of the code.

EXAM 14

EXAM 14 ANSWERS

14. A dwelling has: 1500 sq. ft. of floor space, not considering an unfinished attic, unfinished cellar not adaptable for future use and open porches; six 7-A, 230-V room air-conditioning units, two 4-kW wall-mounted ovens, two 20-A small appliance circuits, one 5.1-kW combination clothes washer and dryer, a 1.5-kW, 230V permanently installed bathroom space heater, and one 20-A laundry circuit. Assume: combination clothes washer and dryer, counter-mounted cooking unit, dishwasher, wall-mounted ovens, and water heater kW ratings equivalent to kVA. Assume: the 5.1-kVA counter-mounted cooking unit is supplied by one branch circuit, and the two 4-kVA wall-mounted ovens are supplied by a separate circuit. What is the total required minimum service rating and the total calculated load for the service in VA?

    A. Minimum Service Rating 60A, Calculated Service load 5,200 VA

    B. Minimum Service Rating 100A, Calculated Service load 15,200 VA

    C. Minimum Service Rating 122A, Calculated Service load 29,200 VA

    D. Minimum Service Rating 150A, Calculated Service load 39,200 VA

    Reference: 2017 National Electrical Code – Annex D. Example D2(b) One-Family Dwelling on page 793 of the code.

15. A dwelling has floor area of 1500 sq. ft., excluding an unfinished attic, unfinished cellar not adaptable for future use, and open porches. There are six 7-A, 230-V room air-conditioning units, two 4-kW wall-mounted ovens, two 20-A small appliance circuits, one 5.1-kW counter-mounted cooking unit, a 5-kW combination clothes washer and dryer, a 4.5-kW water heater, a 1.5-kW permanently installed bathroom space heater, a 1.2-kW dishwasher, and one 20-A laundry circuit. If we assume a counter-mounted cooking unit, wall-mounted ovens, dishwasher, combination clothes washer and dryer, and water heater kW ratings equivalent to kVA, what is the total amperes of the air conditioner load?

    A. 18

    B. 36

    C. 42

    D. 50

    Reference: 2017 National Electrical Code – Annex D Examples Example D2(b) Optional Calculation for One-Family Dwelling, Air Conditioning Larger Than Heating [see 220.82(A) and 220.82(C)] on page 792 of the code.

EXAM 14

EXAM 14 ANSWERS

16. If a dwelling has a 2000 sq. ft. floor area, not counting an unfinished attic, unfinished cellar not adaptable for future use, and open porches, a 12-kW range, a 5-kW clothes dryer, a 4.5-kW water heater, a 2-1/2 ton (24-A) heat pump with 15 kW of backup heat, and a 1.2-kW dishwasher, what are the VA units for the total heating and supplementary heat?

    A. 5,760

    B. 15,000

    C. 15,510

    D. 20,760

    Reference: 2017 National Electrical Code – Annex D. Example D2(c) Optional Calculation for One-Family Dwelling with Heat Pump (Single-Phase, 240/120-Volt Service) on page 793 of the code.

17. For a 3000 sq. ft. store with 30 ft. of show window, with a total of 80 duplex receptacles, what is the total calculated general lighting load in VA if the service is 120/240 V, single-phase wire service, and the actual connected lighting load is 8500 VA?

    A. 6,000

    B. 9,000

    C. 12,000

    D. 16,200

    Reference: 2017 National Electrical Code – Annex D. Example D3 Store Building on page 793 of the code.

18. If a 3000 sq. ft. store has 30 ft. of show window, a total of 80 duplex receptacles, service of 120/240 V, single phase 3-wire, and actual connected lighting load of 8500 VA, what is the total calculated lighting load for the show windows in VA?

    A. 5000

    B. 6000

    C. 7000

    D. 9000

    Reference: 2017 National Electrical Code – Annex D Examples Example D3 Store Building on page 793 of the code.

EXAM 14

EXAM 14 ANSWERS

19. A 3000 sq. ft. store has 80 duplex receptacles and 30 ft. of show windows. Service is single phase 3-wire, 120/240 V, and actual connected lighting load is 8500 VA. The total calculated receptacle load in VA is:

    A. 2,200

    B. 10,000

    C. 12,200

    D. 14,400

    Reference: 2017 National Electrical Code – Annex D Examples Example D3 Store Buildings, on page 793 of the code.

20. For a 40 unit multi-family dwelling unit, with meters in two banks of 20 each and individual meters to each dwelling unit, could you use 2 15A circuits to handle the general lighting load? Half (20) of the dwelling units have electric ranges up to 12 kW each. Assume range kW rating the same as kVA rating in accordance with Article 220.55. Each dwelling unit has 840 sq. ft. of space. Laundry facilities are on premises and available to all tenants. The other half of the ranges are gas.

    A. Yes

    B. No

    Reference: 2017 National Electrical Code – Annex D. Example D4(a) Multifamily Dwelling on page 796 of the code.

21. For a 40 unit multi-family dwelling unit, with meters in two banks of 20 each and individual meters to each dwelling unit. Half (20) of the dwelling units have electric ranges up to 12 kW each. Assume range kW rating the same as kVA rating in accordance with Article 220.55. Each dwelling unit has 840 sq. ft. of space. Laundry facilities are on premises and available to all tenants. The other half of the ranges are gas. The general lighting load for each unit, in VA is:

    A. 1520

    B. 2050

    C. 2520

    D. 3630

    Reference: 2017 National Electrical Code – Annex D Examples Example D4(a) Multifamily Dwelling, on page 796 of the code.

EXAM 14

EXAM 14 ANSWERS

1. **Answer D.** 126

   For No. 1 (AWG) copper-clad aluminum conductors at 90°C in multiconductor cables with up to three insulated conductors, rated 0 through 2000 volts, with an ambient temperature of 40°C, in free air, the ampacity rating for type MC cables is 126.

   Reference: 2017 National Electrical Code – Informative Annex B. Table B.310.15(B)(2)(3) Ampacities of Multiconductor Cables with Not More Than Three Insulated Cond2uctors, Rated 0 Through 2000 Volts, in Free Air Based on Ambient Air Temperature of 40°C (104°F) (for Types Te, MC, MI, UF, and USE Cables) on page 70-701 of the code.

2. **Answer B.** 89

   The ampacity rating of No. 4 (AWG) copper conductors at 75°C in multiconductor UF cables, with up to three insulated conductors, rated 0 through 2000 volts, in free air, with an ambient air temperature of 40°C is 89 for type UF and USE cables.

   Reference: 2017 National Electrical Code – Informative Annex B: Table B.310.15(B)(2)(3) Ampacities of Multiconductor Cables with Not More Than Three Insulated Conductors. Rated 0 Through 2000 Volts, in Free Air Based on Ambient Air Temperature of 40°C (104°F) (for Types TC, MC, MI, UF, and USE Cables) on page 70-701 of the code.

3. **Answer D.** 20

   There can be up to 20 conductors or fixture wires for electrical metallic tubing for No. 3 Type TW conductors, in trade size 63 tubing.

   Reference: 2017 National Electrical Code – Informative Annex C Table C.1 Maximum Number of Conductors and Fixture Wires in Electrical Metallic Tubing (EMT) (page 70-713).

4. **Answer C.** 10

   Reference: 2017 National Electrical Code – Informative Annex C Table C.1 Maximum Number of Conductors and Fixture Wires in Electrical Metallic Tubing (EMT) (page 70-791)

5. **Answer B.** 35

   The maximum number of conductors or fixture wires for electrical metallic tubing for No. 14 Type THHN conductors in trade size 27. Conductors is 35.

   Reference: 2017 National Electrical Code – Informative Annex C Table C.1 Maximum Number of Conductors or Fixture Wires in Electrical Metallic Tubing (EMT) (Based on Table 1, Chapter 9) on page 713 of the code.

6. **Answer B.** 1-1/4 in.

   Reference: 2017 National Electrical Code – Informative Annex C Table C.1 Maximum Number of Conductors and Fixture Wires in Electrical Metallic Tubing (EMT) (page 70-713)

7. **Answer C.** 19

   There can be a maximum of 27 No. 12 Type THHW conductors used in trade size 27 electrical metallic tubing.

   Reference: 2017 National Electrical Code – Informative Annex C Table C.10 Maximum Number of Conductors or Fixture Wires in Rigid PVC Conduit, Schedule 40 and HDPE Conduit (page 70-767)

8. **Answer C.** 19

   Reference: 2017 National Electrical Code – Informative Annex C Table C.10 Maximum Number of Conductors or Fixture Wires in Rigid PVC Conduit, Schedule 40 and HDPE Conduit (page 70-767)

EXAM 14

EXAM 14 ANSWERS

Type	Conductor Size (AWG/kcmil)	⅜ (12)	½ (16)	¾ (21)	1 (27)	1¼ (35)	1½ (41)	2 (53)	2½ (63)	3 (78)	3½ (91)	4 (103)	5 (129)	6 (155)
	800	—	0	0	0	0	1	1	1	3	3	5	—	—
	900	—	0	0	0	0	0	1	1	2	3	4	—	—
	1000	—	0	0	0	0	0	1	1	2	3	4	—	—
	1250	—	0	0	0	0	0	1	1	1	2	3	—	—
	1500	—	0	0	0	0	0	1	1	1	1	2	—	—
	1750	—	0	0	0	0	0	0	1	1	1	2	—	—
	2000	—	0	0	0	0	0	0	1	1	1	1	—	—
THHN, THWN, THWN-2	14	—	12	22	35	61	84	138	241	364	476	608	—	—
	12	—	9	16	26	45	61	101	176	266	347	443	—	—
	10	—	5	10	16	28	38	63	111	167	219	279	—	—
	8	—	3	6	9	16	22	36	64	96	126	161	—	—
	6	—	2	4	7	12	16	26	46	69	91	116	—	—
	4	—	1	2	4	7	10	16	28	42	56	71	—	—
	3	—	1	1	3	6	8	13	24	36	47	60	—	—
	2	—	1	1	3	5	7	11	20	30	40	51	—	—
	1	—	1	1	1	4	5	8	15	22	29	37	—	—
	1/0	—	1	1	1	3	4	7	12	19	25	32	—	—
	2/0	—	0	1	1	2	3	6	10	16	20	26	—	—
	3/0	—	0	1	1	1	3	5	8	13	17	22	—	—
	4/0	—	0	1	1	1	2	4	7	11	14	18	—	—
	250	—	0	0	1	1	1	3	6	9	11	15	—	—
	300	—	0	0	1	1	1	3	5	7	10	13	—	—
	350	—	0	0	1	1	1	2	4	6	9	11	—	—
	400	—	0	0	0	1	1	1	4	6	8	10	—	—
	500	—	0	0	0	1	1	1	3	5	6	8	—	—
	600	—	0	0	0	1	1	1	2	4	5	7	—	—
	700	—	0	0	0	1	1	1	2	3	4	6	—	—
	750	—	0	0	0	0	1	1	1	3	4	5	—	—
	800	—	0	0	0	0	1	1	1	3	4	5	—	—
	900	—	0	0	0	0	1	1	1	3	3	4	—	—
	1000	—	0	0	0	0	1	1	1	2	3	4	—	—
FEP, FEPB, PFA, PFAH, TFE	14	—	12	21	34	60	81	134	234	354	462	590	—	—
	12	—	9	15	25	43	59	98	171	258	337	430	—	—
	10	—	6	11	18	31	42	70	122	185	241	309	—	—
	8	—	3	6	10	18	24	40	70	106	138	177	—	—
	6	—	2	4	7	12	17	28	50	75	98	126	—	—
	4	—	1	3	5	9	12	20	35	53	69	88	—	—
	3	—	1	2	4	7	10	16	29	44	57	73	—	—
	2	—	1	1	3	6	8	13	24	36	47	60	—	—
PFA, PFAH, TFE	1	—	1	1	2	4	6	9	16	25	33	42	—	—
PFA, PFAH, TFE, Z	1/0	—	1	1	1	3	5	8	14	21	27	35	—	—
	2/0	—	0	1	1	3	4	6	11	17	22	29	—	—
	3/0	—	0	1	1	2	3	5	9	14	18	24	—	—
	4/0	—	0	1	1	1	2	4	8	11	15	19	—	—
Z	14	—	14	25	41	72	98	161	282	426	556	711	—	—
	12	—	10	18	29	51	69	114	200	302	394	504	—	—
	10	—	6	11	18	31	42	70	122	185	241	309	—	—
	8	—	4	7	11	20	27	44	77	117	153	195	—	—
	6	—	3	5	8	14	19	31	54	82	107	137	—	—
	4	—	1	3	5	9	13	21	37	56	74	94	—	—
	3	—	1	2	4	7	9	15	27	41	54	69	—	—
	2	—	1	1	3	6	8	13	22	34	45	57	—	—
	1	—	1	1	2	4	6	10	18	28	36	46	—	—

Table C.1 Maximum Number of Conductors or Fixture Wires in Electrical Metallic Tubing (EMT) page 70-714 of the Code

EXAM 14

EXAM 14 ANSWERS

Table C.1 Maximum Number of Conductors or Fixture Wires in Electrical Metallic Tubing (EMT)
(Based on Chapter 9: Table 1, Table 4, and Table 5)

Type	Conductor Size (AWG/kcmil)	Trade Size (Metric Designator)												
		⅜ (12)	½ (16)	¾ (21)	1 (27)	1¼ (35)	1½ (41)	2 (53)	2½ (63)	3 (78)	3½ (91)	4 (103)	5 (129)	6 (155)
					CONDUCTORS									
RHH, RHW, RHW-2	14	—	4	7	11	20	27	46	80	120	157	201	—	—
	12	—	3	6	9	17	23	38	66	100	131	167	—	—
	10	—	2	5	8	13	18	30	53	81	105	135	—	—
	8	—	1	2	4	7	9	16	28	42	55	70	—	—
	6	—	1	1	3	5	8	13	22	34	44	56	—	—
	4	—	1	1	2	4	6	10	17	26	34	44	—	—
	3	—	1	1	1	4	5	9	15	23	30	38	—	—
	2	—	1	1	1	3	4	7	13	20	26	33	—	—
	1	—	0	1	1	1	3	5	9	13	17	22	—	—
	1/0	—	0	1	1	1	2	4	7	11	15	19	—	—
	2/0	—	0	1	1	1	2	4	6	10	13	17	—	—
	3/0	—	0	0	1	1	1	3	5	8	11	14	—	—
	4/0	—	0	0	1	1	1	3	5	7	9	12	—	—
	250	—	0	0	0	1	1	1	3	5	7	9	—	—
	300	—	0	0	0	1	1	1	3	5	6	8	—	—
	350	—	0	0	0	1	1	1	3	4	6	7	—	—
	400	—	0	0	0	1	1	1	2	4	5	7	—	—
	500	—	0	0	0	0	1	1	2	3	4	6	—	—
	600	—	0	0	0	0	1	1	1	3	4	5	—	—
	700	—	0	0	0	0	0	1	1	2	3	4	—	—
	750	—	0	0	0	0	0	1	1	2	3	4	—	—
	800	—	0	0	0	0	0	1	1	2	3	4	—	—
	900	—	0	0	0	0	0	1	1	1	3	3	—	—
	1000	—	0	0	0	0	0	1	1	1	2	3	—	—
	1250	—	0	0	0	0	0	1	1	1	1	2	—	—
	1500	—	0	0	0	0	0	1	1	1	1	1	—	—
	1750	—	0	0	0	0	0	1	1	1	1	1	—	—
	2000	—	0	0	0	0	0	1	1	1	1	1	—	—
TW, THHW, THW, THW-2	14	—	8	15	25	43	58	96	168	254	332	424	—	—
	12	—	6	11	19	33	45	74	129	195	255	326	—	—
	10	—	5	8	14	24	33	55	96	145	190	243	—	—
	8	—	2	5	8	13	18	30	53	81	105	135	—	—
RHH*, RHW*, RHW-2*	14	—	6	10	16	28	39	64	112	169	221	282	—	—
	12	—	4	8	13	23	31	51	90	136	177	227	—	—
	10	—	3	6	10	18	24	40	70	106	138	177	—	—
	8	—	1	4	6	10	14	24	42	63	83	106	—	—
TW, THW, THHW, THW-2, RHH*, RHW*, RHW-2*	6	—	1	3	4	8	11	18	32	48	63	81	—	—
	4	—	1	1	3	6	8	13	24	36	47	60	—	—
	3	—	1	1	3	5	7	12	20	31	40	52	—	—
	2	—	1	1	2	4	6	10	17	26	34	44	—	—
	1	—	1	1	1	3	4	7	12	18	24	31	—	—
	1/0	—	0	1	1	2	3	6	10	16	20	26	—	—
	2/0	—	0	1	1	1	3	5	9	13	17	22	—	—
	3/0	—	0	1	1	1	2	4	7	11	15	19	—	—
	4/0	—	0	0	1	1	1	3	6	9	12	16	—	—
	250	—	0	0	1	1	1	3	5	7	10	13	—	—
	300	—	0	0	1	1	1	2	4	6	8	11	—	—
	350	—	0	0	0	1	1	1	4	6	7	10	—	—
	400	—	0	0	0	1	1	1	3	5	7	9	—	—
	500	—	0	0	0	1	1	1	3	4	6	7	—	—
	600	—	0	0	0	1	1	1	2	3	4	6	—	—
	700	—	0	0	0	0	1	1	1	3	4	5	—	—
	750	—	0	0	0	0	1	1	1	3	4	5	—	—

(continues)

EXAM 14

EXAM 14 ANSWERS

Type	Conductor Size (AWG/kcmil)	⅜ (12)	½ (16)	¾ (21)	1 (27)	1¼ (35)	1½ (41)	2 (53)	2½ (63)	3 (78)	3½ (91)	4 (103)	5 (129)	6 (155)
XHHW, ZW, XHHW-2, XHH	14	—	8	15	25	43	58	96	168	254	332	424	—	—
	12	—	6	11	19	33	45	74	129	195	255	326	—	—
	10	—	5	8	14	24	33	55	96	145	190	243	—	—
	8	—	2	5	8	13	18	30	53	81	105	135	—	—
	6	—	1	3	6	10	14	22	39	60	78	100	—	—
	4	—	1	2	4	7	10	16	28	43	56	72	—	—
	3	—	1	1	3	6	8	14	24	36	48	61	—	—
	2	—	1	1	3	5	7	11	20	31	40	51	—	—
XHHW, XHHW-2, XHH	1	—	1	1	1	4	5	8	15	23	30	38	—	—
	1/0	—	1	1	1	3	4	7	13	19	25	32	—	—
	2/0	—	0	1	1	2	3	6	10	16	21	27	—	—
	3/0	—	0	1	1	1	3	5	9	13	17	22	—	—
	4/0	—	0	1	1	1	2	4	7	11	14	18	—	—
	250	—	0	0	1	1	1	3	6	9	12	15	—	—
	300	—	0	0	1	1	1	3	5	8	10	13	—	—
	350	—	0	0	1	1	1	2	4	7	9	11	—	—
	400	—	0	0	0	1	1	1	4	6	8	10	—	—
	500	—	0	0	0	1	1	1	3	5	6	8	—	—
	600	—	0	0	0	1	1	1	2	4	5	6	—	—
	700	—	0	0	0	0	1	1	2	3	4	6	—	—
	750	—	0	0	0	0	1	1	1	3	4	5	—	—
	800	—	0	0	0	0	1	1	1	3	4	5	—	—
	900	—	0	0	0	0	1	1	1	3	3	4	—	—
	1000	—	0	0	0	0	0	1	1	2	3	4	—	—
	1250	—	0	0	0	0	0	1	1	1	2	3	—	—
	1500	—	0	0	0	0	0	1	1	1	1	3	—	—
	1750	—	0	0	0	0	0	0	1	1	1	2	—	—
	2000	—	0	0	0	0	0	0	1	1	1	1	—	—
FIXTURE WIRES														
RFH-2, FFH-2, RFHH-2	18	—	8	14	24	41	56	92	161	244	318	407	—	—
	16	—	7	12	20	34	47	78	136	205	268	343	—	—
SF-2, SFF-2	18	—	10	18	30	52	71	116	203	307	401	513	—	—
	16	—	8	15	25	43	58	96	168	254	332	424	—	—
	14	—	7	12	20	34	47	78	136	205	268	343	—	—
SF-1, SFF-1	18	—	18	33	53	92	125	206	360	544	710	908	—	—
RFH-1, TF, TFF, XF, XFF	18	—	14	24	39	68	92	152	266	402	524	670	—	—
	16	—	11	19	31	55	74	123	215	324	423	541	—	—
XF, XFF	14	—	8	15	25	43	58	96	168	254	332	424	—	—
TFN, TFFN	18	—	22	38	63	109	148	244	426	643	839	1073	—	—
	16	—	17	29	48	83	113	186	325	491	641	819	—	—
PF, PFF, PGF, PGFF, PAF, PTF, PTFF, PAFF	18	—	21	36	59	103	140	231	404	610	796	1017	—	—
	16	—	16	28	46	79	108	179	312	471	615	787	—	—
	14	—	12	21	34	60	81	134	234	354	462	590	—	—
ZF, ZFF, ZHF	18	—	27	47	77	133	181	298	520	786	1026	1311	—	—
	16	—	20	35	56	98	133	220	384	580	757	967	—	—
	14	—	14	25	41	72	98	161	282	426	556	711	—	—
KF-2, KFF-2	18	—	40	71	115	199	271	447	781	1179	1539	1967	—	—
	16	—	28	49	80	139	189	312	545	823	1074	1372	—	—
	14	—	19	33	54	93	127	209	366	553	721	922	—	—
	12	—	13	23	37	65	88	146	254	384	502	641	—	—
	10	—	8	15	25	43	58	96	168	254	332	424	—	—

Table C.1 Maximum Number of Conductors or Fixture Wires in Electrical Metallic Tubing (EMT) page 70-715 of the Code

EXAM 14

EXAM 14 ANSWERS

General Lighting		4,500 VA
Small Appliance		3,000 VA
Laundry		1,500 VA
	Total	9,000 VA
3000 VA at 100%		3,000 VA
9000 VA – 3000 VA = 6000 VA at 35%		2,100 VA
	Net Load	5,100 VA
Range (see Table 220.55)		8,000 VA
Dryer Load (see Table 220.54)		5,500 VA
Net Calculated Load		18,600 VA

See 70-791 in Tables folder on CD-ROM

9. **Answer B.** 18,600

The net calculated total load in VA units is 18,600.

Reference: 2017 National Electrical Code – Informative Annex D. Example D1(a) One-Family Dwelling on page 791 of the code.

10. **Answer C.** 4500 VA

The VA units for the general lighting load is 4500 VA.

Reference: 2017 National Electrical Code – Informative Annex D. Example D1(a) One-Family Dwelling on page 791 of the code.

Minimum Size Feeder Required [see 220.40]

General Lighting   4,500 VA

11. **Answer B.** Three 15-A, 2-wire or two 20-A, 2-wire circuits

The minimum number of branch general light circuits is three 15-A, 2-wire or two 20-A, 2 wire circuits.

Reference: 2017 National Electrical Code – Informative Annex D. Example D1(a) One-Family Dwelling on page 791 of the code.

12. **Answer B.** 100

The minimum required service size is 100 amperes.

Reference: 2017 National Electrical Code – Informative Annex D. Example D1(a) One-Family Dwelling on page 791 of the code.

13. **Answer C.** 122 A, 29,200 VA

The total calculated load in VA is 29,200 VA, and the minimum required service rating is 122 A.

Reference: 2017 National Electrical Code – Informative Annex D. Example D2(b) One-Family Dwelling on page 793 of the code.

14. **Answer C.** Minimum Service Rating 122A, Calculated Service load 29,200 VA

The total calculated load in VA is 29,200 VA, and the minimum required service rating is 122 A.

Reference: 2017 National Electrical Code – Informative Annex D. Example D2(b) One-Family Dwelling on page 793 of the code.

15. **Answer C.** 42

The total of the air conditioner load is 42 amperes. Air Conditioning kVA Calculation Total amperes = 6 units × 7 A = 42 A

Reference: 2017 National Electrical Code – Informative Annex D Examples Example D2(b) Optional Calculation for One-Family Dwelling, Air Conditioning Larger Than Heating see [220.82(A) and 220.82(C)] on page 792 of the code.

16. **Answer C.** 15,510

The total heating and supplementary heat is 15,510 VA units.

Reference: 2017 National Electrical Code – Informative Annex D. Example D2(c) Optional Calculation for One-Family Dwelling with Heat Pump (Single-Phase, 240/120-Volt Service) on page 793 of the code.

EXAM 14

EXAM 14 ANSWERS

1500 ft^2 at 3 VA		4,500 VA
Two 20-A small-appliance circuits at 1500 VA each		3,000 VA
Laundry circuit		1,500 VA
Two ovens		8,000 VA
One cooking unit		5,100 VA
Water heater		4,500 VA
Dishwasher		1,200 VA
Washer/dryer		5,000 VA
	Total general load	32,800 VA
First 10 kVA at 100%		10,000 VA
Remainder at 40% (22.8 kVA × 0.4 × 1000)		9,120 VA
	Subtotal general load	19,120 VA
Air conditioning		10,080 VA
	Total	29,200 VA

See 70-792 in Tables folder on CD-ROM

17. Answer B. 9,000

The total calculated general lighting load is 9000 VA.

Reference: 2017 National Electrical Code – Informative Annex D. Example D3 Store Building on page 793 of the code.

18. Answer B. 6000

The total calculated lighting load for the show windows is 6000 VA.

Reference: 2017 National Electrical Code – Informative Annex D Examples Example D3 Store Building on page 793 of the code.

19. Answer C. 12,200

The total calculated receptacle load is 12,200 VA.

Reference: 2017 National Electrical Code – Informative Annex D Examples Example D3 Store Buildings, on page 793 of the code.

20. Answer A. Yes

You could use 2 15A circuits to handle the general lighting load.

Reference: 2017 National Electrical Code – Informative Annex D. Example D4(a) Multifamily Dwelling on page 796 of the code.

21. Answer C. 2520

The general lighting load for each unit is 2520 VA.

Reference: 2017 National Electrical Code – Informative Annex D Examples Example D4(a) Multifamily Dwelling, on page 796 of the code.

EXAM 15

Blueprint Reading

1. A detailed plan of a building that is orthographically drawn with a conventional representation of lines, and includes symbols and abbreviations is a:

    A. drawing

    B. map

    C. print

    D. none of these

    Reference: Builder's Comprehensive Dictionary

2. What kind of line is always drawn as a series of equal length dashes?

    A. above ground

    B. hidden

    C. underground

    D. none of these

    Reference: Builder's Comprehensive Dictionary, 3rd Ed. Hidden Lines

3. A fixed point that all measurements showing a building lot are made is a:

    A. beginning point

    B. center point

    C. perspective point

    D. reference point

4. What kind of planes does an orthographic drawing called an elevation show?

    A. diagonal

    B. horizontal

    C. inverse

    D. vertical

    Reference: Builder's Comprehensive Dictionary, 3rd Ed. Orthographic Drawing

5. A section view of a building is most commonly taken through the:

    A. exterior door

    B. inside partition

    C. outside wall

    D. window

    Reference: Builder's Comprehensive Dictionary

EXAM 15

Blueprint Reading

6. Where are cutting planes for section view shown?

   A. floor plan

   B. plot plan

   C. both A and B

   D. neither A nor B

   Reference: Builder's Comprehensive Dictionary, 3rd Ed. Floor Plan

7. What are the standard procedures from the Construction Specifications Institute helpful for writing?

   A. codes

   B. plans

   C. specifications

   D. none of these

   Reference: Builder's Comprehensive Dictionary, 3rd Ed. Construction Specifications Institute (C.S.I.)

8. A shortened form of a word or phrase is an:

   A. abbreviation

   B. initial

   C. symbol

   D. none of these

   Reference: Builder's Comprehensive Dictionary, 3rd Ed.

9. True or False: The NEC® is a design specification.

   A. True

   B. False

   Reference: 2017 National Electrical Code – Article 90 - Introduction 90.1 Purpose. (A) Practical Safeguarding.

10. What kind of projection is each part of a building represented in a print of a set of working drawings?

    A. auxiliary

    B. isometric

    C. oblique

    D. orthographic

    Reference: Builder's Comprehensive Dictionary, 3rd Ed. Orthographic Drawing

Blueprint Reading

EXAM 15

Blueprint Reading

11. Which division of the CSI MasterFormat is for electrical work?

    A. 16   C. 26

    B. 21   D. 36

    Reference: Builder's Comprehensive Dictionary

12. A graphic representation of an object is a:

    A. abbreviation   C. symbol

    B. initial   D. none of these

    Reference: Builder's Comprehensive Dictionary, 3rd Ed. Symbol

13. Which of the following, when drawn at a larger scale, is referred to as a detail?

    A. elevation   C. section

    B. plan   D. all of the above

    Reference: Builder's Comprehensive Dictionary, 3rd Ed.

14. Which plans show the location and dimensions of all interior partitions and exterior walls?

    A. building   C. floor

    B. construction   D. none of these

    Reference: Builder's Comprehensive Dictionary, 3rd Ed. Floor Plan

15. True or False: the plot plan shows the location of all electrical, gas, sewer, and water utilities.

    A. True   B. False

    Reference: Builder's Comprehensive Dictionary, 3rd Ed. Plot Plan

EXAM 15

Blueprint Reading

16. What kind of section is lengthwise view through a building?

    A. cross

    B. latitudinal

    C. longitudinal

    D. none of these

    Reference: Builder's Comprehensive Dictionary, 3rd Ed. Longitudinal Section

17. True or False: All prints must be drawn to 1/4" = 1'-0" scale.

    A. True

    B. False

    Reference: Builder's Comprehensive Dictionary, 3rd Ed.

18. What is the abbreviation for volt?

    A. V

    B. VT

    C. either A or B

    D. neither A nor B

    Reference: Builder's Comprehensive Dictionary, 3rd Ed. Volt (V)

19. Cross-reference numbers, line numbers, terminal numbers, and as much other information as needed must always be included in what diagrams of larger or complex electrical systems?

    A. Blueprints

    B. Ladder diagrams

    C. Layout and location drawings

    D. Wiring diagrams

    Reference: Builder's Comprehensive Dictionary, 3rd Ed.

20. Which of the following is the abbreviation for specification?

    A. SP

    B. SPEC

    C. SPF

    D. none of these

    Reference: Builder's Comprehensive Dictionary, 3rd Ed.

EXAM 15

Blueprint Reading

21. What is the abbreviation for circuit breaker?

    A. C

    B. CB

    C. either A or B

    D. neither A nor B

    Reference: Builder's Comprehensive Dictionary, 3rd Ed.

22. Which of the following is the abbreviation for current?

    A. C

    B. CR

    C. I

    D. none of these

    Reference: Builder's Comprehensive Dictionary, 3rd Ed.

23. What is the abbreviation for dryer?

    A. D

    B. DR

    C. DY

    D. none of these

    Reference: Builder's Comprehensive Dictionary, 3rd Ed.

24. True or False: For small sets of prints, electrical information is directly shown on the floor plans.

    A. True

    B. False

    Reference: Builder's Comprehensive Dictionary, 3rd Ed.

25. Which takes precedence in the event of a discrepancy between prints and specifications?

    A. prints

    B. specifications

    C. either A or B

    D. neither A nor B

    Reference: Builder's Comprehensive Dictionary, 3rd Ed.

EXAM 15

Blueprint Reading

26. Because symbols can be understood no matter what language is spoken, this makes them:

    A. graphical

    B. literal

    C. universal

    D. none of these

    Reference: Builder's Comprehensive Dictionary, 3rd Ed.

27. What is the abbreviation for overload?

    A. O

    B. OD

    C. OL

    D. OV

    Reference: Builder's Comprehensive Dictionary, 3rd Ed.

28. True or False: Computer software programs such as Cad are commonly used to produce drawings these days.

    A. True

    B. False

    Reference: Builder's Comprehensive Dictionary, 3rd Ed. CAD

29. What is a plot plan?

    A. an orthographic drawing

    B. drawing that shows the contour of the land

    C. drawing that shows the location of the structure

    D. all of these

    Reference: Builder's Comprehensive Dictionary, 3rd Ed. Plot Plan

30. What kind of section is taken crosswise?

    A. latitudinal

    B. obverse

    C. transverse

    D. none of these

    Reference: Builder's Comprehensive Dictionary, 3rd Ed. Transverse Section

EXAM 15

Blueprint Reading

31. Objects on a floor plan are shown with _____ lines when they are _____ an elevation.

    A. hidden; above
    B. object; below
    C. either A or B
    D. neither A nor B

    Reference: Builder's Comprehensive Dictionary, 3rd Ed.

32. What is the abbreviation for benchmark?

    A. B
    B. BC
    C. BK
    D. BM

    Reference: Builder's Comprehensive Dictionary, 3rd Ed. Benchmark (BM)

33. Which of the following is the abbreviation for basement?

    A. BASE
    B. BMT
    C. BSMT
    D. BT

    Reference: Builder's Comprehensive Dictionary, 3rd Ed.

34. True or False: The abbreviation for amps, anode, and area is A.

    A. True
    B. False

    Reference: Builder's Comprehensive Dictionary, 3rd Ed.

35. Which of the following is the abbreviation for dining room and door?

    A. D
    B. DR
    C. either A or B
    D. neither A nor B

    Reference: Builder's Comprehensive Dictionary, 3rd Ed.

EXAM 15

Blueprint Reading

36. What is the abbreviation for ground-fault circuit interrupter?

    A. GCI

    B. GFCI

    C. either A or B

    D. neither A nor B

    Reference: Builder's Comprehensive Dictionary, 3rd Ed. Ground-Fault Circuit Interrupter (GFCI)

37. Which of the following is the abbreviation for horsepower?

    A. H

    B. HP

    C. HRS

    D. HW

    Reference: Builder's Comprehensive Dictionary, 3rd Ed. Horsepower

38. What is the abbreviation for single-pole circuit breaker?

    A. PCB

    B. SCB

    C. SPCB

    D. none of these

    Reference: Builder's Comprehensive Dictionary, 3rd Ed.

39. Which of the following is the abbreviation for outside diameter?

    A. DO

    B. OD

    C. OUD

    D. OUT

    Reference: Builder's Comprehensive Dictionary, 3rd Ed. Outside Diameter (OD)

40. True or False: S1S is the abbreviation for surface one side.

    A. True

    B. False

    Reference: Builder's Comprehensive Dictionary, 3rd Ed.

Blueprint Reading

EXAM 15

Blueprint Reading

41. True or False: Three abbreviations are correct for transformer: T, TRANS, and XFMR.

    A. True   B. False

    Reference: Builder's Comprehensive Dictionary, 3rd Ed.

42. The abbreviation for watts or west is:

    A. W   C. either A or B

    B. WT   D. neither A nor B

    Reference: Builder's Comprehensive Dictionary, 3rd Ed.

43. What is the abbreviation for three-wire?

    A. 3W   C. either A or B

    B. W3   D. neither A nor B

    Reference: Builder's Comprehensive Dictionary, 3rd Ed.

44. Which of the following is the abbreviation for number?

    A. #   C. NUM.

    B. NO.   D. none of these

    Reference: Builder's Comprehensive Dictionary, 3rd Ed.

45. What is the abbreviation for overcurrent protection device?

    A. DOP   C. OPD

    B. OCPD   D. PD

    Reference: Builder's Comprehensive Dictionary, 3rd Ed.

EXAM 15

Blueprint Reading

46. Which of the following is the abbreviation for point of beginning?

    A. BP

    B. PB

    C. POB

    D. none of these

    Reference: Builder's Comprehensive Dictionary, 3rd Ed. Point of Beginning (POB)

47. True or False: Print sets can include: details, elevations, floor plans, schedules, sectional views, site plans, and wiring diagrams.

    A. True

    B. False

    Reference: Builder's Comprehensive Dictionary, 3rd Ed.

48. True or False: Print divisions are basically divided into break, center, cutting-plane, dimension, extension, hidden, leader, object, and section types.

    A. True

    B. False

    Reference: Builder's Comprehensive Dictionary, 3rd Ed.

49. True or False: Electrical schedule types include branch circuit panels, feeders, fixtures, main switchboards, and transformers.

    A. True

    B. False

    Reference: Builder's Comprehensive Dictionary, 3rd Ed.

50. True or False: The revision information is one of the most important parts of the title block.

    A. True

    B. False

    Reference: Builder's Comprehensive Dictionary, 3rd Ed. Revision Block

EXAM 15

Blueprint Reading

51. True or False: A circle divided in half by a horizontal line and a cutting-plane line drawn through the selected item is the symbol for a detail drawing.

    A. True B. False

    Reference: Builder's Comprehensive Dictionary, 3rd Ed.

52. True or False: Dimension information identifying columns and a point of reference are all provided by a schedule.

    A. True B. False

    Reference: Builder's Comprehensive Dictionary, 3rd Ed.

53. True or False: Measuring the size of a drawn object by using a specific scale is done with an architectural or architect's scale.

    A. True B. False

    Reference: Builder's Comprehensive Dictionary, 3rd Ed. Architectural Scale

54. True or False: The codes, company policies and ordinances complied with during a project are listed in a general note.

    A. True B. False

    Reference: Builder's Comprehensive Dictionary, 3rd Ed.

55. True or False: The CSI MasterFormat™ is a master list of titles and numbers that is used to organize construction activities, projects, and requirements are organized into a standard sequence.

    A. True B. False

    Reference: Builder's Comprehensive Dictionary, 3rd Ed. Construction Specifications Institute (C.S.I.)

EXAM 15

Blueprint Reading

56. True or False: The line that indicates the path where an object will be cut so internal features can be seen is called a cutting-plane line.

    A. True B. False

    Reference: Builder's Comprehensive Dictionary, 3rd Ed. Cutting Plane

57. What is the area of a print the holds the important information regarding the contents of the print?

    A. revision record C. title block

    B. sheet note D. none of these

    Reference: Builder's Comprehensive Dictionary, 3rd Ed. Title Block

58. A note that applies to a specific item and accompanies it in the drawing is a:

    A. revision record C. title block

    B. sheet note D. none of these

    Reference: Builder's Comprehensive Dictionary, 3rd Ed.

59. An agreed-upon method of displaying information on prints is a:

    A. graphic convention C. print convention

    B. graphic standard D. print standard

    Reference: Builder's Comprehensive Dictionary, 3rd Ed.

Blueprint Reading

EXAM 15

Blueprint Reading

60. A letter or group of letters representing a phrase or term is an:

    A. abbreviation	C. either A or B

    B. initials	D. neither A nor B

    Reference: Builder's Comprehensive Dictionary, 3rd Ed. Leader

61. What do the print numbering for a set of electrical prints or a subdivision of electrical prints start with?

    A. E1	C. ES1

    B. EA	D. ESA

    Reference: Builder's Comprehensive Dictionary, 3rd Ed. Leader

62. What kind of line connects a specific feature of a drawn object with a written description such as a dimension, note, or specification?

    A. break	C. dimension

    B. cutting-plane	D. leader

    Reference: Builder's Comprehensive Dictionary, 3rd Ed. Leader

63. What chart displays information in an organized and concise format and conserves space?

    A. flow chart	C. schedule

    B. pie graph	D. title block

    Reference: Builder's Comprehensive Dictionary, 3rd Ed. Schedule

EXAM 15

Blueprint Reading

64. Which organization develops standardized specifications for construction?

    A. American Institute of Architects (AIA)

    B. Associated General Contractors of America (AGC)

    C. Associated Specialty Contractors (ASC)

    D. Construction Specifications Institute (CSI)

    Reference: Builder's Comprehensive Dictionary, 3rd Ed. Construction Specifications Institute (C.S.I.)

65. What item on a drawing or print is identified by a symbol with a number or letter inside a circle, square, or triangle?

    A. elevation

    B. dimension

    C. revision

    D. schedule

    Reference: Builder's Comprehensive Dictionary, 3rd Ed. Revision Block

66. If drawing information does not fit inside the space of the drawing, often a sentence or two providing the information is in the form of a:

    A. legend

    B. note

    C. schedule

    D. specification

    Reference: Builder's Comprehensive Dictionary, 3rd Ed. Note

67. True or False: The way devices and components are connected together in a circuit is represented through the use of symbols.

    A. True

    B. False

    Reference: Builder's Comprehensive Dictionary, 3rd Ed. Leader

EXAM 15

Blueprint Reading

68. True or False: Government departments, national, international, and private organizations, as well as technical societies and trade associations are all examples of standards organizations.

    A. True   B. False

    Reference: Builder's Comprehensive Dictionary, 3rd Ed.

69. True or False: ANSI, the American National Standards Institute, develops standards for worldwide use and is an international standards developing organization.

    A. True   B. False

    Reference: Builder's Comprehensive Dictionary, 3rd Ed. American national Standards Institute (ANSI)

70. True or False: Asterisks, flags, and notes can be used if a symbol has multiple meanings, to clarify intent.

    A. True   B. False

    Reference: Builder's Comprehensive Dictionary, 3rd Ed.

71. True or False: Terminal symbols are designed so that the connection points on one symbol line up with the connection points of the next, and are drawn to a relative size.

    A. True   B. False

    Reference: Builder's Comprehensive Dictionary, 3rd Ed.

72. True or False: On both residential and commercial prints, lighting symbols show the type of lamp and style of fixture, as well as the location.

    A. True   B. False

    Reference: Builder's Comprehensive Dictionary, 3rd Ed.

EXAM 15

Blueprint Reading

73. True or False: Whether the wiring for a system is hidden in ceilings or walls, or exposed is indicated on electrical prints with various lines.

    A. True   B. False

    Reference: Builder's Comprehensive Dictionary, 3rd Ed.

74. True or False: All site plans must show a point of beginning for surveying and show proper orientation, by having a North arrow.

    A. True   B. False

    Reference: Builder's Comprehensive Dictionary, 3rd Ed.

75. True or False: Location, types of objects, and electrical devices located around a building are shown by numbers on site plans.

    A. True   B. False

    Reference: Builder's Comprehensive Dictionary, 3rd Ed.

76. National and international organizations that work with governmental standards groups are called:

    A. Standards organizations   C. Trade associations

    B. Technical societies   D. Trade societies

    Reference: Builder's Comprehensive Dictionary, 3rd Ed.

77. By which of the following means is electrical power distributed to a building?

    A. aboveground   C. underground

    B. combination of aboveground   D. all of the above
       and underground

    Reference: Builder's Comprehensive Dictionary, 3rd Ed.

Blueprint Reading

EXAM 15

Blueprint Reading

78. True or False: 'Prints' is a generic term often used for diagrams, drawings, and plans.

      A. True   B. False

Reference: Builder's Comprehensive Dictionary, 3rd Ed.

79. True or False: The actual layout and position of all components and devices used in an electrical circuit is shown on a site plan.

      A. True   B. False

Reference: Builder's Comprehensive Dictionary, 3rd Ed.

80. True or False: Orthographic projection is used to draw an object as a two-dimensional drawing.

      A. True   B. False

Reference: Builder's Comprehensive Dictionary, 3rd Ed. Orthographic Projection

81. True or False: A drawing that shows the way individual components or parts are placed together to produce a finished piece of equipment or result as closely as possible is called an assembly drawing.

      A. True   B. False

Reference: Builder's Comprehensive Dictionary, 3rd Ed. Assembly Drawing

82. True or False: A drawing to define architectural style, features, and structural materials of a building or structure is called a location drawing.

      A. True   B. False

Reference: Builder's Comprehensive Dictionary, 3rd Ed.

EXAM 15

Blueprint Reading

83. True or False: Both pictorial or orthographic views may be used for views of sectional drawings.

    A. True   B. False

    Reference: Builder's Comprehensive Dictionary, 3rd Ed.

84. True or False: Surveyors use detail drawings to find the precise location of a building on a property and be certain that all boundaries and easements are met.

    A. True   B. False

    Reference: Builder's Comprehensive Dictionary, 3rd Ed. Detail

85. True or False: Building materials such as concrete, masonry, steel or wood needed to build the main support of a structure are established with structural plans.

    A. True   B. False

    Reference: Builder's Comprehensive Dictionary, 3rd Ed. Structural Drawings

86. True or False: The drawing that shows the intended path and location of communication cables and electrical, gas, sewage and water utilities is called a utility plan.

    A. True   B. False

    Reference: Builder's Comprehensive Dictionary, 3rd Ed.

87. True or False: The internal features of an object are indicated on a sectional drawing.

    A. True   B. False

    Reference: Builder's Comprehensive Dictionary, 3rd Ed.

Blueprint Reading

EXAM 15

Blueprint Reading

88. What type of drawing shows the use of a particular product in an application or piece of equipment?

    A. application
    B. orthographic
    C. usage
    D. working

    Reference: Builder's Comprehensive Dictionary, 3rd Ed.

89. What type of drawings are normally shown on service bulletins and typically used during the assembly and/or construction of components and devices?

    A. Application
    B. Construction
    C. Detail
    D. Working

    Reference: Builder's Comprehensive Dictionary, 3rd Ed. Detail

90. What type of plan is a drawing of land contours with structural building information so that landscaping can be designed and created?

    A. elevation
    B. landscape
    C. surveying
    D. topographic

    Reference: Builder's Comprehensive Dictionary, Ed. Landscape Plan

91. What is a drawing of an object from above called?

    A. overhead
    B. plan
    C. print
    D. none of these

    Reference: Builder's Comprehensive Dictionary, 3rd Ed. Plan

EXAM 15

Blueprint Reading

92. A drawing that shows all exterior walls, cabinetry, doors, fireplaces, room partitions, stairs, windows, and any appliances or fixtures is a:

    A. architectural graphic
    B. floor plan
    C. overhead
    D. none of these

    Reference: Builder's Comprehensive Dictionary, 3rd Ed. Floor Plan

93. What type of drawings are frequently used in operational and installation manuals to show where to position indicating lamps, displays and switches, and to connect external wires?

    A. Detail
    B. Location
    C. Survey
    D. none of these

    Reference: Builder's Comprehensive Dictionary, 3rd Ed.

94. What type of drawing is intended to show how to perform a task using the safest and/or simplest technique?

    A. assembly
    B. elevation
    C. instructional
    D. sectional

    Reference: Builder's Comprehensive Dictionary, 3rd Ed.

95. What type of drawing is created by a surveyor or civil engineer licensed for the task, that accurately shows topographic dimensions, information, and other essential data about the features of a property and the properties adjacent to it?

    A. floor plan
    B. site plan
    C. survey plan
    D. all of the above

    Reference: Builder's Comprehensive Dictionary, 3rd Ed.

EXAM 15

Blueprint Reading

96. What type of plans specify construction, drainage, excavating, and waterproofing information for foundation construction, as well as other design information?

    A. Elevation

    B. Excavated

    C. Foundation

    D. Instructional

    Reference: Builder's Comprehensive Dictionary, 3rd Ed. Foundation Plan

97. Which of the following types of drawings provides all the details required to clearly understand the size and type of a component, device, or object?

    A. detail

    B. elevation

    C. sectional

    D. all of the above

    Reference: Builder's Comprehensive Dictionary, 3rd Ed.

98. True or False: Voltages being fed into a building and main transformers being used to distribute specific voltages are normally shown on one-line diagrams.

    A. True

    B. False

    Reference: Builder's Comprehensive Dictionary, 3rd Ed.

99. True or False: On ladder diagrams, the lines between symbols never cross and are never vertical, but always diagonal or horizontal.

    A. True

    B. False

    Reference: Builder's Comprehensive Dictionary, 3rd Ed.

100. True or False: An operational diagram is a type of ladder diagram downloaded to a programmable logic controller (PLC) after being created on a computer.

    A. True

    B. False

    Reference: Builder's Comprehensive Dictionary, 3rd Ed.

EXAM 15

Blueprint Reading

101. True or False: Wiring diagrams indicate the actual device and component layout with all connections and are used in troubleshooting.

    A. True   B. False

    Reference: Builder's Comprehensive Dictionary, 3rd Ed. Wiring Diagram

102. True or False: Schematic diagrams are used for troubleshooting electronic circuits as well as designing them.

    A. True   B. False

    Reference: Builder's Comprehensive Dictionary, 3rd Ed. Schematic

103. True or False: Operational diagrams must stay as simple as possible, with wires or cables crossing one another kept at a minimum.

    A. True   B. False

    Reference: Builder's Comprehensive Dictionary, 3rd Ed.

104. True or False: Input signals and resulting output signals are shown on operational diagrams and/or data sheets for photoelectric sensors.

    A. True   B. False

    Reference: Builder's Comprehensive Dictionary, 3rd Ed.

105. True or False: Proprietary information such as precise component or device information that a manufacturer might not want released is protected by wiring diagrams.

    A. True   B. False

    Reference: Builder's Comprehensive Dictionary, 3rd Ed. Wiring Diagram

Blueprint Reading

EXAM 15

Blueprint Reading

106. True or False: An alternative method for programming a programmable logic control or relay is a function-block diagram.

    A. True   B. False

    Reference: Builder's Comprehensive Dictionary, 3rd Ed.

107. True or False: to find a problem in an electrical circuit, block troubleshooting diagrams can be set up for 'yes' or 'no' questions.

    A. True   B. False

    Reference: Builder's Comprehensive Dictionary, 3rd Ed.

108. What kind of diagram is used to design the power distribution system for a building, and show the major distribution equipment, power panels, required voltages, and types of transformers?

    A. All-line   C. One-line

    B. Electrical-line   D. Straight-line

    Reference: Builder's Comprehensive Dictionary, 3rd Ed.

109. What kind of diagrams show how input devices (limit switches, pushbuttons, temperature switches, etc.), output components (lamps, motor starters, solenoids, etc.) and other circuit control equipment (timers, counters, etc.) are interconnected?

    A. Ladder   C. Wiring

    B. Line   D. none of these

    Reference: Builder's Comprehensive Dictionary, 3rd Ed.

EXAM 15

Blueprint Reading

110. What diagrams show how all components and devices of a circuit or system are wired together or how an individual component or device is wired?

    A. Ladder

    B. Line

    C. Wiring

    D. none of these

    Reference: Builder's Comprehensive Dictionary, 3rd Ed. Wiring Diagram

111. Which diagram is a kind of electrical drawing showing external connections between all system components and devices?

    A. interconnecting

    B. line

    C. wiring

    D. none of these

    Reference: Builder's Comprehensive Dictionary, 3rd Ed.

112. What kind of diagram shows the contents of a circuit, component, or device?

    A. block

    B. interconnecting

    C. line

    D. wiring

    Reference: Builder's Comprehensive Dictionary, 3rd Ed.

113. Which type of diagram is an electrical drawing using basic symbols and a single line to show the circuit disconnect, current path, overcurrent protection devices, panels, transformers, and voltage values for a circuit or system?

    A. ladder (line)

    B. one-line

    C. PLC programming

    D. wiring

    Reference: Builder's Comprehensive Dictionary, 3rd Ed.

Blueprint Reading

EXAM 15

Blueprint Reading

114. What diagram provides a fast and easy way to understand how individual objects connect to one another in a system, making them the most important types of electrical drawings?

    A. Interconnecting

    B. Ladder

    C. Pictorial

    D. Schematic

    Reference: Builder's Comprehensive Dictionary, 3rd Ed.

115. What kind of diagrams trace a circuit's operating without any regard to the actual location, shape, or size of the components and devices?

    A. Block

    B. Informational

    C. Schematic

    D. all of these

    Reference: Builder's Comprehensive Dictionary, 3rd Ed. Schematic

116. Which diagram is an electrical drawing showing the operation of individual components and devices used in a circuit?

    A. function-block

    B. one-line diagram

    C. operational diagram

    D. pictorial drawing

    Reference: Builder's Comprehensive Dictionary, 3rd Ed.

117. What kind of diagrams include counters, logic blocks, and timers?

    A. Function-block

    B. Ladder

    C. Operational

    D. none of these

    Reference: Builder's Comprehensive Dictionary, 3rd Ed.

EXAM 15

Blueprint Reading

118. True or False: The two power prints most commonly used by electricians are power floor plans and single-line diagrams.

    A. True   B. False

    Reference: Builder's Comprehensive Dictionary, 3rd Ed.

119. True or False: The mounting height of outlets is provided by power floor plans and specifications.

    A. True   B. False

    Reference: Builder's Comprehensive Dictionary, 3rd Ed.

120. True or False: Each floor of a commercial building has a power floor plan.

    A. True   B. False

    Reference: Builder's Comprehensive Dictionary, 3rd Ed.

121. True or False: Single-line diagrams normally include the equipment designations and general location of electrical equipment.

    A. True   B. False

    Reference: Builder's Comprehensive Dictionary, 3rd Ed.

122. True or False: Residential or commercial lighting floor plans do not show the locations of switchers.

    A. True   B. False

    Reference: Builder's Comprehensive Dictionary, 3rd Ed.

123. True or False: In addition to the location of light fixtures and switches, circuit numbers and panel designations are shown on commercial power diagrams.

    A. True   B. False

    Reference: Builder's Comprehensive Dictionary, 3rd Ed.

EXAM 15

Blueprint Reading

124. True or False: Emergency lighting fixtures, exterior lighting fixtures, illuminated exit signs and interior lighting fixtures are included in light fixture schedules.

    A. True   B. False

Reference: Builder's Comprehensive Dictionary, 3rd Ed.

125. True or False: Circuit breaker information for electrical equipment, dimension information, location of lugs for incoming power, and mounting information are shown on electrical elevation drawings.

    A. True   B. False

Reference: Builder's Comprehensive Dictionary, 3rd Ed.

126. True or False: Ladder diagrams are used by electricians for information on conduit and wire size for power distribution panel feeders, motor loads, and primary and secondary transformer feeders.

    A. True   B. False

Reference: Builder's Comprehensive Dictionary, 3rd Ed.

127. True or False: Whether a circuit returns to a motor control panel or a service panel is indicated by the type of hash marks used on a line.

    A. True   B. False

Reference: Builder's Comprehensive Dictionary, 3rd Ed.

128. What drawing shows the doors, elevator shafts, equipment locations, plumbing fixtures, rooms, stairways, walls and windows on a floor?

    A. architectural graphic   C. orthographic drawing

    B. floor plan   D. site plan

Reference: Builder's Comprehensive Dictionary, 3rd Ed. Floor Plan

EXAM 15

Blueprint Reading

129. Which of the following plans do NOT show light fixtures or switches?

      A. commercial power floor   C. residential power floor

      B. floor   D. wiring

Reference: Builder's Comprehensive Dictionary, 3rd Ed.

130. What kind of print shows exit lights, lighting fixtures, panels, switches, and transformers?

      A. architectural graphic   C. power floor plan

      B. lighting floor plan   D. wiring diagram

Reference: Builder's Comprehensive Dictionary, 3rd Ed.

131. What term might light fixture schedules use instead of fixture?

      A. luminaire   C. switch

      B. outlet   D. none of these

Reference: Builder's Comprehensive Dictionary, 3rd Ed.

132. What kind of plan shows the complete building site including all electrical items to be installed below ground and the layout of the planned buildings?

      A. lighting floor   C. site

      B. power floor   D. none of these

Reference: Builder's Comprehensive Dictionary, 3rd Ed. Plot Plan

133. What kind of plan shows all of the power circuits for a specific floor of a building?

      A. building   C. reflected ceiling

      B. power floor   D. residential

Reference: Builder's Comprehensive Dictionary, 3rd Ed.

EXAM 15

Blueprint Reading

134. What kind of drawing provides in-depth information that cannot be shown on a lighting print, power print, or site plan?

    A. electrical detail

    B. lighting view

    C. riser

    D. single-line

    Reference: Builder's Comprehensive Dictionary, 3rd Ed.

135. Which of the following gives detailed information such as the name of the fixture manufacturer, number of lamps, type of fixture, and voltage rating for the various fixtures to be installed?

    A. Fixture diagrams

    B. Fixture schedules

    C. Lighting floor plans

    D. Reflected ceiling plans

    Reference: Builder's Comprehensive Dictionary, 3rd Ed.

136. What kind of drawings have information like

    Reference: _____ contain information such as kVA rating, primary and secondary coil voltages and side feeder sizes, and transformer mounting types?

    A. Prints

    B. Single-line diagrams

    C. Transformer floor plans

    D. Transformer schedules

    Reference: Builder's Comprehensive Dictionary, 3rd Ed.

137. True or False: An item located in a VDV (voice, data, and video) system legend has a number or letter associated with it that is on the print where the information is needed.

    A. True

    B. False

    Reference: Builder's Comprehensive Dictionary, 3rd Ed.

EXAM 15

Blueprint Reading

138. True or False: the size of conduit or raceway for backbone cables, and the exact route of the cables are always shown on VDV (voice, data, and video) riser diagrams.

    A. True B. False

    Reference: Builder's Comprehensive Dictionary, 3rd Ed.

139. True or False: Much of the same information is contained in VDV (voice, data, and video) floor plans for commercial and residential projects.

    A. True B. False

    Reference: Builder's Comprehensive Dictionary, 3rd Ed.

140. True or False: The location of all residential VDV (voice, data, and video) outlets are indicated on the print, and most are mounted at the same height.

    A. True B. False

    Reference: Builder's Comprehensive Dictionary, 3rd Ed.

141. True or False: Riser details for VDV (voice, data, and video) give the general information for every type of related outlet.

    A. True B. False

    Reference: Builder's Comprehensive Dictionary, 3rd Ed.

142. True or False: Typically, a basic VDV (voice, data, and video) system is shown with lighting and power information on a residential floor plan.

    A. True B. False

    Reference: Builder's Comprehensive Dictionary, 3rd Ed.

EXAM 15

Blueprint Reading

143. True or False: Abbreviations for VDV (voice, data, and video) are those specific to cable TV, telecommunications, and wiring systems.

    A. True   B. False

    Reference: Builder's Comprehensive Dictionary, 3rd Ed.

144. True or False: VDV (voice, data, and video) abbreviations are always included as sheet notes, but sometimes on a separate print.

    A. True   B. False

    Reference: Builder's Comprehensive Dictionary, 3rd Ed.

145. True or False: Residential VDV (voice, data, and video) floor plans are drawn for banks, office buildings, retail stores, schools, and other such buildings.

    A. True   B. False

    Reference: Builder's Comprehensive Dictionary, 3rd Ed.

146. True or False: For VDV (voice, data, and video) outlet details, additional information includes exact details on the size and type of label used for a VDV outlet faceplate, along with the font and size of font.

    A. True   B. False

    Reference: Builder's Comprehensive Dictionary, 3rd Ed.

147. A list of abbreviations and symbols, and a legend that is used throughout the set of prints is included for a set of:

    A. floor plans   C. voice, data, and video (VDV) prints

    B. site plans   D. wiring diagrams

    Reference: Builder's Comprehensive Dictionary, 3rd Ed.

EXAM 15

Blueprint Reading

148. What kind of VDV (voice, data, and video) installation commonly has two coaxial cables and two UTP cables run to a single outlet in each room from a distribution cabinet?

    A. commercial   C. residential

    B. industrial   D. temporary

Reference: *Builder's Comprehensive Dictionary, 3rd Ed.*

149. Which kind of drawings show the necessary details on locations and mounting methods for all VDV (voice, data, and video) equipment?

    A. Communication   C. Wiring

    B. Equipment room   D. none of these

Reference: *Builder's Comprehensive Dictionary, 3rd Ed.*

150. What is used along with elevations to show location of cable ladders, connector blocks, equipment racks, raceways, and termination backboards?

    A. Longitudinal drawings   C. Plan views

    B. Orthographic projections   D. none of these

Reference: *Builder's Comprehensive Dictionary, 3rd Ed.*

151. What part of a VDV (voice, data, and video) system can be single or double gang, floor or wall mounted, or mounted on modular furniture?

    A. outlets   C. sockets

    B. receptacles   D. none of these

Reference: *Builder's Comprehensive Dictionary, 3rd Ed.*

Blueprint Reading

EXAM 15

Blueprint Reading

152. What is a unique system of numbers and/or letters that is used to identify the cables and termination locations for VDV (voice, data, and video) systems?

    A. abbreviation   C. site plan

    B. outlet address   D. VDV tag

Reference: Builder's Comprehensive Dictionary, 3rd Ed.

153. What provides an overview of the backbone cabling for a VDV (voice, data, and video) system in a building?

    A. electrical diagrams   C. power floor plans

    B. elevation plans   D. riser diagrams

Reference: Builder's Comprehensive Dictionary, 3rd Ed.

154. Which papers give information for VDV (voice, data, and video) component installation and outlet addressing?

    A. Floor plans   C. Sheet notes

    B. Path panels   D. all of these

Reference: Builder's Comprehensive Dictionary, 3rd Ed.

155. Additional information that cannot be shown on VDV (voice, data, and video) riser diagrams or floor plans are supplied with a high degree of precision by:

    A. detail drawings   C. single-line diagrams

    B. section view drawings   D. site plans

Reference: Builder's Comprehensive Dictionary, 3rd Ed.

EXAM 15

Blueprint Reading

156. What factor in the construction project determines the number and type of VDV (voice, data, and video) detail drawings?

    A. cost

    B. location

    C. size

    D. none of these

    Reference: Builder's Comprehensive Dictionary, 3rd Ed.

157. True or False: Detail drawings, floor plans, and riser diagrams and included in fire alarm system prints.

    A. True

    B. False

    Reference: Builder's Comprehensive Dictionary, 3rd Ed. Detail

158. True or False: Fire alarm system devices are depicted with a specific set of symbols.

    A. True

    B. False

    Reference: Builder's Comprehensive Dictionary, 3rd Ed.

159. True or False: The riser diagrams for fire alarms in multistory buildings are always drawn to scale.

    A. True

    B. False

    Reference: Builder's Comprehensive Dictionary, 3rd Ed.

160. True or False: There are normally separate floor plans for each floor of a building with a small commercial fire alarm system.

    A. True

    B. False

    Reference: Builder's Comprehensive Dictionary, 3rd Ed.

Blueprint Reading

EXAM 15

Blueprint Reading

161. True or False: General locations for initiating devices and notification components are provided on most fire alarm system floor plans.

    A. True   B. False

    Reference: Builder's Comprehensive Dictionary, 3rd Ed.

162. True or False: A reflected ceiling plan will not show lines depicting the conduit/conductors that connect the fire alarm equipment together.

    A. True   B. False

    Reference: Builder's Comprehensive Dictionary, 3rd Ed.

163. True or False: Splicing details are included on detail drawings for common types of fire alarm systems.

    A. True   B. False

    Reference: Builder's Comprehensive Dictionary, 3rd Ed.

164. True or False: Most fire alarm system components and devices have mounted detail drawings provided.

    A. True   B. False

    Reference: Builder's Comprehensive Dictionary, 3rd Ed.

165. True or False: Some security system designers and manufacturers prefer to use their own symbols even though standards for security system symbols exist.

    A. True   B. False

    Reference: Builder's Comprehensive Dictionary, 3rd Ed.

166. True or False: Whether or not a separate security floor plan is needed is determined by the cost and location of a security system.

    A. True   B. False

    Reference: Builder's Comprehensive Dictionary, 3rd Ed.

EXAM 15

Blueprint Reading

167. Fire alarm system installations in multistory buildings typically have what kind of diagrams provided?

    A. Construction   C. Wiring

    B. Riser   D. none of these

Reference: Builder's Comprehensive Dictionary, 3rd Ed.

168. Which components have to be in a location where they can be heard and seen by everyone occupying the floor of a building?

    A. Alarm   C. Notification

    B. Electrical   D. none of these

Reference: Builder's Comprehensive Dictionary, 3rd Ed.

169. Information on how cables and conductors are spliced and how cables and conductors are terminated at specific components and devices is provided in which details?

    A. Communications   C. Wiring

    B. Fixture   D. none of these

Reference: Builder's Comprehensive Dictionary, 3rd Ed.

170. Which of the following systems is more likely to be shown on a fire alarm and life safety floor plan than a power floor plan, due to similarities in the nature of the two systems?

    A. security   C. both A and B

    B. sprinkler   D. neither A nor B

Reference: Builder's Comprehensive Dictionary, 3rd Ed.

Blueprint Reading

EXAM 15

Blueprint Reading

171. Which drawings show how security devices like door contacts and electric door strikes, are interfaced with the components of a building?

    A. Electrical

    B. Elevation

    C. Riser

    D. Topographic

Reference: Builder's Comprehensive Dictionary, 3rd Ed.

172. A riser diagram normally shows one device with an abbreviation of _____ next to the device when there is more than one device of the same type, and print space is limited.

    A. AFF

    B. CSI

    C. TS or FS

    D. TYP

Reference: Builder's Comprehensive Dictionary, 3rd Ed.

173. Which of the following would require sheet notes with additional information for specific installation requirements?

    A. connection of the FACP to the monitoring company or agency

    B. panel designations and circuit numbers

    C. power source for the fire alarm control panel (FACP)

    D. all of these

Reference: Builder's Comprehensive Dictionary, 3rd Ed.

174. What is used by some fire alarm prints to show where components and devices on a specific floor are located?

    A. detail

    B. lighting fixture

    C. reflected ceiling

    D. riser

Reference: Builder's Comprehensive Dictionary, 3rd Ed.

EXAM 15

Blueprint Reading

175. Due to their multiple applications and locations, what is likely to have the largest number of detail drawings?

    A. Fire extinguishers

    B. Smoke detectors

    C. Sprinkler systems

    D. none of these

    Reference: Builder's Comprehensive Dictionary, 3rd Ed.

176. What provides additional information for a security system that security system floor plans cannot show?

    A. abbreviations

    B. detail drawings

    C. electrical plans

    D. riser plans

    Reference: Builder's Comprehensive Dictionary, 3rd Ed. Detail

177. True or False: More than one type of HVAC control system print may be on a single sheet, for a small project.

    A. True

    B. False

    Reference: Builder's Comprehensive Dictionary, 3rd Ed.

178. True or False: Depending on the application, there can be more than one meaning for some HVAC control system abbreviations.

    A. True

    B. False

    Reference: Builder's Comprehensive Dictionary, 3rd Ed.

179. True or False: Mechanical elements of a HVAC system, such as sheet metal ducts and filters, are not depicted by HVAC symbols.

    A. True

    B. False

    Reference: Builder's Comprehensive Dictionary, 3rd Ed.

Blueprint Reading 703

EXAM 15

Blueprint Reading

180. True or False: Each subsystem of an HVAC system in a building is provided with separate HVAC system prints.

    A. True   B. False

    Reference: *Builder's Comprehensive Dictionary, 3rd Ed.*

181. True or False: An HVAC system print will contain a condensed view of a mechanical piping system.

    A. True   B. False

    Reference: *Builder's Comprehensive Dictionary, 3rd Ed.*

182. True or False: HVAC system prints include the addresses of actuators and sensors that are part of a networked HVAC control system.

    A. True   B. False

    Reference: *Builder's Comprehensive Dictionary, 3rd Ed.*

183. True or False: Exact location, mounting, or routing information for electrical equipment will always be provided on HVAC system drawings.

    A. True   B. False

    Reference: *Builder's Comprehensive Dictionary, 3rd Ed.*

184. True or False: An overall view of the components mounted inside a control panel is provided by a panel mounting detail.

    A. True   B. False

    Reference: *Builder's Comprehensive Dictionary, 3rd Ed.*

185. True or False: HVAC wiring diagrams provide voltage information and related equipment for the HVAC control system.

    A. True   B. False

    Reference: *Builder's Comprehensive Dictionary, 3rd Ed.*

EXAM 15

Blueprint Reading

186. True or False: Every actuator and sensor had wiring details provided for it.

    A. True
    B. False

    Reference: Builder's Comprehensive Dictionary, 3rd Ed.

187. Where besides the legend are HVAC control system definitions and symbols found for a set of prints?

    A. abbreviation sheets
    B. revision record
    C. title block
    D. none of these

    Reference: Builder's Comprehensive Dictionary, 3rd Ed.

188. Which HVAC diagrams are created to show plainly how components and devices for HVAC control panels and mechanical equipment panels are wired together, along with the terminal strips for the internal components?

    A. duct
    B. floor
    C. panel wiring
    D. none of these

    Reference: Builder's Comprehensive Dictionary, 3rd Ed.

189. Which drawings include enclosure, mounting, and panel layout details?

    A. Fixture
    B. Floor plan
    C. Panel detail
    D. Wiring

    Reference: Builder's Comprehensive Dictionary, 3rd Ed.

190. Which kind of detail drawing provides information on terminating conductors at specific actuators or sensors?

    A. fixture
    B. floor plan
    C. panel
    D. wiring

    Reference: Builder's Comprehensive Dictionary, 3rd Ed.

Blueprint Reading 705

EXAM 15

Blueprint Reading

191. What provides a troubleshooter with a guide for an HVAC control system?

    A. manufacturer's instruction

    B. panel diagram

    C. sequence of operation

    D. wiring diagram

    Reference: Builder's Comprehensive Dictionary, 3rd Ed.

192. Sometimes these show an entire HVAC control panel, and other times they only show the control panel's terminal strip.

    A. electrical prints

    B. panel detail drawings

    C. system sheet notes

    D. wiring diagrams

    Reference: Builder's Comprehensive Dictionary, 3rd Ed. Wiring Diagram

193. To determine which components and devices must be wired together when installing an HVAC control system, both HVAC wiring diagrams and these must be used.

    A. detail drawings

    B. plot plans

    C. sheet notes

    D. system prints

    Reference: Builder's Comprehensive Dictionary, 3rd Ed.

194. When print space does not allow information to be shown on HVAC system prints or HVAC wiring diagrams, then the information is provided on HVAC:

    A. detail drawings

    B. layout diagrams

    C. system prints

    D. none of these

    Reference: Builder's Comprehensive Dictionary, 3rd Ed. Detail

EXAM 15

Blueprint Reading

195. Which type of detail drawing gives an elevation view of both the front and side of an HVAC control system panel?

    A. enclosure   C. terminal

    B. mounting   D. wiring

Reference: Builder's Comprehensive Dictionary, 3rd Ed.

196. What is the term for the list of the major items that make up a control panel, as well as the actuators and sensors that are field mounted?

    A. bill of materials   C. HVAC system diagram

    B. blueprint   D. panel mounting detail

Reference: Builder's Comprehensive Dictionary, 3rd Ed. Bill of Materials

197. True or False: Since most PLC software uses the ladder diagram format for designing its circuits, an understanding of line diagrams is important.

    A. True   B. False

Reference: Builder's Comprehensive Dictionary, 3rd Ed.

198. True or False: When more than one load is connected to the same control section of a ladder diagram, loads cannot be connected in parallel.

    A. True   B. False

Reference: Builder's Comprehensive Dictionary, 3rd Ed.

199. True or False: Examples of loads that are connected directly to L2 in a line diagram are alarms, control relay coils, pilot lights and solenoids.

    A. True   B. False

Reference: Builder's Comprehensive Dictionary, 3rd Ed.

EXAM 15

Blueprint Reading

200. True or False: For faster identification of the location of components and devices in smaller individual circuits, each line in a control circuit is numbered.

    A. True   B. False

    Reference: *Builder's Comprehensive Dictionary, 3rd Ed.*

201. True or False: A standard ladder diagram format is not always used for the control circuit part of a manufacturer's schematic diagram, but the rules for ladder diagrams will always be followed.

    A. True   B. False

    Reference: *Builder's Comprehensive Dictionary, 3rd Ed.*

202. True or False: Each wire in a control circuit when a terminal strip is used is assigned a reference point on the ladder diagram, and a reference number is assigned to each reference point.

    A. True   B. False

    Reference: *Builder's Comprehensive Dictionary, 3rd Ed.*

203. To make them easier to modify, program and/or understand using software, what are drawn in ladder diagram format?

    A. Electrical control circuits   C. Lighting circuits

    B. Overload Circuits   D. Video circuits

    Reference: *Builder's Comprehensive Dictionary, 3rd Ed.*

204. A method of identifying various mechanically connected contacts of a device that are on different lines of a complex ladder diagram by line numbers is:

    A. fusion block   C. either A or B

    B. numerical cross-reference   D. neither A nor b

    Reference: *Builder's Comprehensive Dictionary, 3rd Ed.*

EXAM 15

Blueprint Reading

205. Any electrical component in a line diagram and takes electrical power form L1 is a:

    A. circuit
    B. device
    C. load
    D. terminal

    Reference: Builder's Comprehensive Dictionary, 3rd Ed.

206. Which of the following are connected on a ladder diagram between the load and L1?

    A. Limit switches
    B. Pressure switches
    C. Pushbuttons
    D. all of these

    Reference: Builder's Comprehensive Dictionary, 3rd Ed.

207. To trace the action of a circuit in complex line diagrams, what type of system is necessary?

    A. Dashed line
    B. Numerical cross-reference
    C. Terminal number
    D. Wire reference number

    Reference: Builder's Comprehensive Dictionary, 3rd Ed.

208. True or False: Symbols to show components and devices and their interconnections are used in electrical prints such as line and wiring diagrams.

    A. True
    B. False

    Reference: Builder's Comprehensive Dictionary, 3rd Ed.

EXAM 15

Blueprint Reading

209. Each component and device is directly wired to the next component or device specified in the line diagram when performing:

    A. direct hardwiring   C. line wiring

    B. diagram wiring   D. none of these

Reference: Builder's Comprehensive Dictionary, 3rd Ed.

210. What type of drawing helps locate components and devices for testing during system modification and troubleshooting?

    A. layout and location drawing   C. wiring drawing

    B. schematic drawing   D. none of these

Reference: Builder's Comprehensive Dictionary, 3rd Ed.

211. What may or may not be included between components even when layout and location drawings are provided?

    A. relative locations   C. terminal strips

    B. required space   D. wiring

Reference: Builder's Comprehensive Dictionary, 3rd Ed.

EXAM 15

EXAM 15 ANSWERS

1. Answer C print

2. Answer B hidden

   In drafting, lines that are not seen directly in a view but are behind the surface of any view. Hidden lines are normally not shown in architectural blueprints unless essential to an understanding of the structure. Foundations are shown in elevation with hidden lines.

   Reference: Builder's Comprehensive Dictionary, 3rd Ed. Hidden Lines

3. Answer A beginning point

4. Answer D vertical

   In drafting, a view made looking straight at the building, as a plain view or an elevation.

   Reference: Builder's Comprehensive Dictionary, 3rd Ed. Orthographic Drawing

5. Answer C outside wall

6. Answer A floor plan

   Plan view (orthographic view looking straight down) of a floor. An imaginary cut is made across the building 2 or 3 feet off the floor to expose the floor. Walls, partitions, doors, windows, fixtures, stairs, and dimensions are shown. Floor plans are identified by their location in a structure: a first floor plan, second floor plan, basement plan, foundation plan.

   Reference: Builder's Comprehensive Dictionary, 3rd Ed. Floor Plan

7. Answer C specifications

   An organization that has developed standardized construction specifications. There are four major groupings: Bidding Requirements, Contract forms, General Conditions, and Specifications (Technical). There are 17 permanent divisions under the specifications format. These are used to write standard technical specs.

   Reference: Builder's Comprehensive Dictionary, 3rd Ed. Construction Specifications Institute (C.S.I.)

8. Answer A abbreviation

9. Answer B False

   The purpose of this Code is the practical safeguarding of persons and property from hazards arising from the use of electricity. This Code is not intended as a design specification or an instruction manual for untrained persons.

   Reference: 2014 National Electrical Code – Article 90 - Introduction, 90.1 Purpose. (A) Practical Safeguarding.

10. Answer D orthographic

    In drafting, a view made looking straight at the building, as a plain view or an elevation.

    Reference: Builder's Comprehensive Dictionary, 3rd Ed. Orthographic Drawing

11. Answer C 26

12. Answer C symbol

    A pictorial view or sign that represents something; for example, a circle is an electrical symbol for a lighting outlet.

    Reference: Builder's Comprehensive Dictionary, 3rd Ed. Symbol

13. Answer D all of the above

14. Answer C floor

    Plan view (orthographic view looking straight down) of a floor. An imaginary cut is made across the building 2 or 3 feet off the floor to expose the floor. Walls, partitions, doors, windows, fixtures, stairs, and dimensions are shown. Floor plans are identified by their location in a structure: a first floor plan, second floor plan, basement plan, foundation plan.

    Reference: Builder's Comprehensive Dictionary, 3rd Ed. Floor Plan

15. Answer A True

    Plan view of a building site with existing features shown and the proposed structure located on the lot. Basic lot and building dimensions are noted; north arrow is located. Existing and finish contour lines are shown; elevation of key points is given.

    Reference: Builder's Comprehensive Dictionary, 3rd Ed. Plot Plan

EXAM 15

EXAM 15 ANSWERS

16. Answer C   longitudinal

    Cross-cut view of a structure made end to end.

    Reference: Builder's Comprehensive Dictionary, 3rd Ed. Longitudinal Section

17. Answer B   False

18. Answer A   V

    Electromotive force that causes current to flow in a circuit. This force can be thought of as similar to water pressure in a plumbing system. In an electrical system a power supply provides the force or voltage. Two voltages are normally used in the home; 110 volts for convenience outlets and 220 volts for equipment and heavy appliances. Industry uses 440 volts.

    volts = amperes X ohms

    volts = watts ÷ amperes

    Reference: Builder's Comprehensive Dictionary, 3rd Ed. Volt (V)

19. Answer B   Ladder diagrams
20. Answer B   SPEC
21. Answer B   CB
22. Answer C   I
23. Answer A   D
24. Answer A   True
25. Answer B   specifications
26. Answer C   universal
27. Answer C   OL
28. Answer A   True

    Computer-assisted drafting.

    Reference: Builder's Comprehensive Dictionary, 3rd Ed. CAD

29. Answer D   all of these

    Plan view of a building site with existing features shown and the proposed structure located on the lot. Basic lot and building dimensions are noted; north arrow is located. Existing and finish contour lines are shown; elevation of key points is given.

    Reference: Builder's Comprehensive Dictionary, 3rd Ed. Plot Plan

30. Answer C   transverse

    Cross-cut view of a structure made from side to side.

    Reference: Builder's Comprehensive Dictionary, 3rd Ed. Transverse Section

31. Answer C   either A or B
32. Answer D   BM

    A permanent survey marker giving accurate elevation above sea level as determined by the U.S. Geological Survey. Often used to determine local datum point.

    Reference: Builder's Comprehensive Dictionary, 3rd Ed. Benchmark (BM)

33. Answer C   BSMT
34. Answer A   True
35. Answer B   DR
36. Answer B   GFCI

    Special device to interrupt electrical circuit where a weak electrical loss or ground occurs. Required on receptacles in bathrooms, garages, and swimming pool areas. The GFCI provides protection against accidental grounding in the circuit that is not sufficient to trip the circuit breaker. The GFCI senses the unbalanced current and opens the circuit to prevent a possible shock to someone using the circuit. GFCI's are also required on temporary receptacle outlets on construction sites.

    Reference: Builder's Comprehensive Dictionary, 3rd Ed. Ground-Fault Circuit Interrupter (GFCI)

37. Answer B   HP

    Work unit of 33,000 foot-pounds per minute. A 3-horsepower (hp) motor can do 99,000 foot-pounds of work per minute.

    Reference: Builder's Comprehensive Dictionary, 3rd Ed. Horsepower

EXAM 15

EXAM 15 ANSWERS

38. Answer C   SPCB

39. Answer B   OD

Diameter of something measured from the outside surface, as the outside diameter of a pipe. Outside diameter does not take into consideration the pipe wall thickness. Opposed to inside diameter.

Reference: Builder's Comprehensive Dictionary, 3rd Ed. Outside Diameter (OD)

40. Answer A   True
41. Answer A   True
42. Answer A   W
43. Answer A   3W
44. Answer B   NO.
45. Answer B   OCPD
46. Answer C   POB

In surveying, the beginning of a metes-and-bounds survey. The plot-plan corner that is surveyed directly to the datum point. Also called place of beginning.

Reference: Builder's Comprehensive Dictionary, 3rd Ed. Point of Beginning (POB)

47. Answer A   True
48. Answer B   False
49. Answer A   True
50. Answer A   True

Area near title block on drawing to describe any change or revision made to the drawing. Number of the change, date, and initials of approving authority are given.

Reference: Builder's Comprehensive Dictionary, 3rd Ed. Revision Block

51. Answer B   False
52. Answer B   False
53. Answer A   True

Scale with drawing reductions built into the separate sides. The triangular scale has 15 separate scales built in. For example, the 1/4" = 1'-0" scale has divisions representing measurements figured at that reduction.

Reference: Builder's Comprehensive Dictionary, 3rd Ed. Architectural Scale

54. Answer B   False
55. Answer A   True

An organization that has developed standardized construction specifications. There are four major groupings: Bidding Requirements, Contract forms, General Conditions, and Specifications (Technical). There are 17 permanent divisions under the specifications format. These are used to write standard technical specs.

Reference: Builder's Comprehensive Dictionary, 3rd Ed. Construction Specifications Institute (C.S.I.)

56. Answer A   True

Imaginary plane for cutting building to produce floor-plan views and sections.

Reference: Builder's Comprehensive Dictionary, 3rd Ed. Cutting Plane

57. Answer C   title block

On a blueprint, the blocked-off area where the drawing is identified, usually the lower right-hand corner or right side.

Reference: Builder's Comprehensive Dictionary, 3rd Ed. Title Block

58. Answer B   sheet note
59. Answer C   print convention
60. Answer A   abbreviation
61. Answer A   E1
62. Answer D   leader

In drafting, an arrow on a blueprint that points to something.

Reference: Builder's Comprehensive Dictionary, 3rd Ed. Leader

EXAM 15

EXAM 15 ANSWERS

63. Answer C   schedule

Tables used on blueprints giving number, size, type, manufacturer and location of building parts or finish. Schedules are made for: windows, doors, room finish, beams, columns, reinforcement, and bending (or reinforcement).

Reference: Builder's Comprehensive Dictionary, 3rd Ed. Schedule

64. Answer D   Construction Specifications Institute (CSI)

An organization that has developed standardized construction specifications. There are four major groupings: Bidding Requirements, Contract forms, General Conditions, and Specifications (Technical). There are 17 permanent divisions under the specifications format. These are used to write standard technical specs.

Reference: Builder's Comprehensive Dictionary, 3rd Ed. Construction Specifications Institute (C.S.I.)

65. Answer C   revision

Area near title block on drawing to describe any change or revision made to the drawing. Number of the change, date, and initials of approving authority are given.

Reference: Builder's Comprehensive Dictionary, 3rd Ed. Revision Block

66. Answer B   note

Information printed on a blueprint.

Reference: Builder's Comprehensive Dictionary, 3rd Ed. Note

67. Answer A   True
68. Answer A   True
69. Answer B   False

An association that publishes standards in various areas of building construction, including safety and drafting.

Reference: Builder's Comprehensive Dictionary, 3rd Ed. American national Standards Institute (ANSI)

70. Answer A   True
71. Answer B   False
72. Answer B   False
73. Answer A   True
74. Answer A   True
75. Answer B   False
76. Answer A   Standards organizations
77. Answer D   all of the above
78. Answer A   True
79. Answer B   False
80. Answer A   True

In drafting, drawing the object looking straight at it, as if imaginary lines were projected out to a viewing plane.

Reference: Builder's Comprehensive Dictionary, 3rd Ed. Orthographic Projection

81. Answer A   True

Drawing that shows how the parts of an assemblage, structure, or machine go together.

Reference: Builder's Comprehensive Dictionary, 3rd Ed. Assembly Drawing

82. Answer B   False
83. Answer A   True
84. Answer B   False

In drafting, a large-scale drawing of a small part of a structure. Details are drawn in isometric or orthographic views. Sometimes an interior elevation is called a detail.

Reference: Builder's Comprehensive Dictionary, 3rd Ed. Detail

85. Answer A   True

Blueprints that show structural detail, the support of a building as the location of steel beams and columns. Identified by an S in the title box.

Reference: Builder's Comprehensive Dictionary, 3rd Ed. Structural Drawings

EXAM 15

EXAM 15 ANSWERS

86. Answer A   True
87. Answer A   True
88. Answer A   application
89. Answer C   Detail

In drafting, a large-scale drawing of a small part of a structure. Details are drawn in isometric or orthographic views. Sometimes an interior elevation is called a detail.

Reference: Builder's Comprehensive Dictionary, 3rd Ed. Detail

90. Answer B   landscape

The total development of an area or site; land-use plan, includes traditional site planning and environmental planning for the total site area. Not to be confused with the landscaping plan.

Reference: Builder's Comprehensive Dictionary, Ed. Landscape Plan

91. Answer B   plan

In drafting, a drawing made looking straight down (orthographic view) on a structure. A floor plan is a plan view of the floor after the top part has been cut away (in imagination) and removed. A plan view is identified by what is shown: site plan, plot plan, first floor plan, second floor plan, basement plan, foundation plan. Also, when used in the plural, plans, a general reference to the complete set of blueprints.

Reference: Builder's Comprehensive Dictionary, 3rd Ed. Plan

92. Answer B   floor plan

Plan view (orthographic view looking straight down) of a floor. An imaginary cut is made across the building 2 or 3 feet off the floor to expose the floor. Walls, partitions, doors, windows, fixtures, stairs, and dimensions are shown. Floor plans are identified by their location in a structure: a first floor plan, second floor plan, basement plan, foundation plan.

Reference: Builder's Comprehensive Dictionary, 3rd Ed. Floor Plan

93. Answer B   Location
94. Answer C   instructional
95. Answer C   survey plan
96. Answer C   Foundation

Plan view that shows the footings and foundation wall.

Reference: Builder's Comprehensive Dictionary, 3rd Ed. Foundation Plan

97. Answer D   all of the above
98. Answer A   True
99. Answer B   False
100. Answer B   False
101. Answer B   False

Schematic showing the wiring layout and connections

Reference: Builder's Comprehensive Dictionary, 3rd Ed. Wiring Diagram

102. Answer A   True

A structural or procedural diagram, especially of an electrical or mechanical system.

Reference: Builder's Comprehensive Dictionary, 3rd Ed. Schematic

103. Answer B   False
104. Answer A   True
105. Answer B   False

Schematic showing the wiring layout and connections

Reference: Builder's Comprehensive Dictionary, 3rd Ed. Wiring Diagram

106. Answer A   True
107. Answer A   True
108. Answer C   One-line
109. Answer A   Ladder
110. Answer C   Wiring

Schematic showing the wiring layout and connections

Reference: Builder's Comprehensive Dictionary, 3rd Ed. Wiring Diagram

EXAM 15

EXAM 15 ANSWERS

111. Answer A   interconnecting

112. Answer A   block

113. Answer B   one-line

114. Answer B   Ladder

115. Answer C   Schematic

   A structural or procedural diagram, especially of an electrical or mechanical system.

   Reference: Builder's Comprehensive Dictionary, 3rd Ed. Schematic

116. Answer C   operational diagram

117. Answer A   Function-block

118. Answer A   True

119. Answer B   False

120. Answer A   True

121. Answer A   True

122. Answer B   False

123. Answer B   False

124. Answer A   True

125. Answer A   True

126. Answer B   False

127. Answer B   False

128. Answer B   floor plan

   Plan view (orthographic view looking straight down) of a floor. An imaginary cut is made across the building 2 or 3 feet off the floor to expose the floor. Walls, partitions, doors, windows, fixtures, stairs, and dimensions are shown. Floor plans are identified by their location in a structure: a first floor plan, second floor plan, basement plan, foundation plan.

   Reference: Builder's Comprehensive Dictionary, 3rd Ed. Floor Plan

129. Answer A   commercial power floor

130. Answer B   lighting floor plan

131. Answer A   luminaire

132. Answer C   site

   A plot plan.

   Reference: Builder's Comprehensive Dictionary, 3rd Ed. Site Plan

   Plan view of a building site with existing features shown and the proposed structure located on the lot. Basic lot and building dimensions are noted; north arrow is located. Existing and finish contour lines are shown; elevation of key points is given.

   Reference: Builder's Comprehensive Dictionary, 3rd Ed. Plot Plan

EXAM 15

EXAM 15 ANSWERS

133. Answer B   power floor
134. Answer A   electrical detail
135. Answer B   Fixture schedules
136. Answer D   Transformer schedules
137. Answer A   True
138. Answer B   False
139. Answer A   True
140. Answer A   True
141. Answer B   False
142. Answer A   True
143. Answer A   True
144. Answer B   False
145. Answer B   False
146. Answer A   True
147. Answer C   voice, data, and video (VDV) prints
148. Answer C   residential
149. Answer B   Equipment room
150. Answer C   Plan views
151. Answer A   outlets
152. Answer B   outlet address
153. Answer D   riser diagrams
154. Answer C   Sheet notes
155. Answer A   detail drawings
156. Answer C   size
157. Answer A   True

In drafting, a large-scale drawing of a small part of a structure. Details are drawn in isometric or orthographic views. Sometimes an interior elevation is called a detail.

Reference: Builder's Comprehensive Dictionary, 3rd Ed. Detail

158. Answer A   True
159. Answer B   False
160. Answer B   False
161. Answer A   True
162. Answer A   True
163. Answer A   True
164. Answer A   True
165. Answer A   True
166. Answer B   False
167. Answer B   Riser
168. Answer C   Notification
169. Answer C   Wiring
170. Answer A   security
171. Answer B   Elevation
172. Answer D   TYP
173. Answer D   all of these
174. Answer C   reflected ceiling
175. Answer B   Smoke detectors
176. Answer B   detail drawings

In drafting, a large-scale drawing of a small part of a structure. Details are drawn in isometric or orthographic views. Sometimes an interior elevation is called a detail.

Reference: Builder's Comprehensive Dictionary, 3rd Ed. Detail

EXAM 15 ANSWERS

EXAM 15

EXAM 15 ANSWERS

177. Answer A True

178. Answer A True

179. Answer B False

180. Answer A True

181. Answer A True

182. Answer A True

183. Answer B False

184. Answer B False

185. Answer A True

186. Answer B False

187. Answer A abbreviation sheets

188. Answer C panel wiring

189. Answer C Panel detail

190. Answer D wiring

191. Answer C sequence of operation

192. Answer D wiring diagrams

   Schematic showing the wiring layout and connections.

   Reference: Builder's Comprehensive Dictionary, 3rd Ed. Wiring Diagram

193. Answer D system prints

194. Answer A detail drawings

   In drafting, a large-scale drawing of a small part of a structure. Details are drawn in isometric or orthographic views. Sometimes an interior elevation is called a detail.

   Reference: Builder's Comprehensive Dictionary, 3rd Ed. Detail

195. Answer A enclosure

196. Answer A bill of materials

   List of materials or parts needed for a specific project or to construct something.

   Reference: Builder's Comprehensive Dictionary, 3rd Ed. Bill of Materials

197. Answer A True

198. Answer B False

199. Answer A True

200. Answer A True

201. Answer A True

202. Answer A True

203. Answer A Electrical control circuits

204. Answer B numerical cross-reference

205. Answer C load

206. Answer D all of these

207. Answer B Numerical cross-reference

208. Answer A True

209. Answer A direct hardwiring

210. Answer A layout and location drawing

211. Answer D wiring

AC/DC FORMULAS

AC/DC FORMULAS

To Find	Direct Current	Alternating Current		
		1Ø, 115 or 120 V	1Ø, 208, 230 or 240 V	3Ø - All Voltages
Amperes When Horsepower Is Known	$\dfrac{HP \times 746}{E \times E_{FF}}$	$\dfrac{HP \times 746}{E \times E_{FF} \times PF}$	$\dfrac{HP \times 746}{E \times E_{FF} \times PF}$	$\dfrac{HP \times 746}{1.73 \times E \times E_{FF} \times PF}$
Amperes When Kilowatts Is Known	$\dfrac{kW \times 1000}{E}$	$\dfrac{kW \times 1000}{E \times PF}$	$\dfrac{kW \times 1000}{E \times PF}$	$\dfrac{kW \times 1000}{1.73 \times E \times PF}$
Amperes When kVA Is Known		$\dfrac{kVA \times 1000}{E}$	$\dfrac{kVA \times 1000}{E}$	$\dfrac{kVA \times 1000}{1.73 \times E}$
Kilowatts	$\dfrac{I \times E}{1000}$	$\dfrac{I \times E \times PF}{1000}$	$\dfrac{I \times E \times PF}{1000}$	$\dfrac{I \times E \times 1.73 \times PF}{1000}$
Kilovolt-amps		$\dfrac{I \times E}{1000}$	$\dfrac{I \times E}{1000}$	$\dfrac{I \times E \times 1.73}{1000}$
Horsepower (output)	$\dfrac{I \times E \times E_{FF}}{746}$	$\dfrac{I \times E \times E_{FF} \times PF}{746}$	$\dfrac{I \times E \times E_{FF} \times PF}{746}$	$\dfrac{I \times E \times 1.73 \times E_{FF} \times PF}{746}$

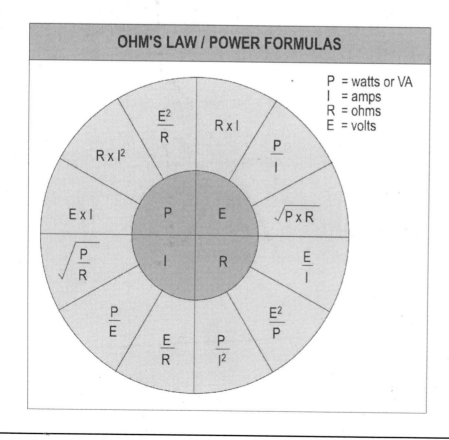

OHM'S LAW / POWER FORMULAS

P = watts or VA
I = amps
R = ohms
E = volts

THREE-PHASE VALUES WITHOUT USING FULL SQUARE ROOT OF THREE

for 208 volts x 1.732, use 360
for 230 volts x 1.732, use 398
for 240 volts x 1.732, use 416
for 440 volts x 1.732, use 762
for 460 volts x 1.732, use 797
for 480 volts x 1.732, use 831

THREE-PHASE VALUES USING FULL SQUARE ROOT OF THREE

for 208 volts x 1.732, use 360.256
for 230 volts x 1.732, use 398.36
for 240 volts x 1.732, use 415.68
for 440 volts x 1.732, use 762.08
for 460 volts x 1.732, use 796.72
for 480 volts x 1.732, use 831.36